T0181383

Communications in Computer and Information Science 849

Commenced Publication in 2007
Founding and Former Series Editors:
Alfredo Cuzzocrea, Xiaoyong Du, Orhun Kara, Ting Liu, Dominik Ślęzak,
and Xiaokang Yang

Editorial Board

More information about this series at http://www.springer.com/series/7899

Hanning Yuan · Jing Geng
Chuanlu Liu · Fuling Bian
Tisinee Surapunt (Eds.)

Geo-Spatial Knowledge and Intelligence

5th International Conference, GSKI 2017
Chiang Mai, Thailand, December 8–10, 2017
Revised Selected Papers, Part II

 Springer

Editors
Hanning Yuan
Beijing Institute of Technology
Beijing
China

Jing Geng
Beijing Institute of Technology
Beijing
China

Chuanlu Liu
Beijing Institute of Technology
Beijing
China

Fuling Bian
Wuhan University
Wuhan
China

Tisinee Surapunt
Beijing Institute of Technology
Beijing
China

ISSN 1865-0929   ISSN 1865-0937 (electronic)
Communications in Computer and Information Science
ISBN 978-981-13-0895-6   ISBN 978-981-13-0896-3   (eBook)
https://doi.org/10.1007/978-981-13-0896-3

Library of Congress Control Number: 2018944420

Printed on acid-free paper

This Springer imprint is published by the registered company Springer Nature Singapore Pte Ltd.
part of Springer Nature
The registered company address is: 152 Beach Road, #21-01/04 Gateway East, Singapore 189721, Singapore

Preface of GSKI 2017

The 5th 2017 International Conference on Geo-Spatial Knowledge and Intelligence (GSKI 2017) was held in Chiang Mai, Thailand, during December 8–10, 2017. The conference aims to bring together researchers, engineers, and students working in the areas of geo-spatial knowledge and intelligence. GSKI 2017 featured a unique mix of topics including smart city, spatial data acquisition, processing and management, modeling and analysis, and recent applications in the context of building a healthier ecology and resource management. The conference provided a forum for sharing experiences and original research contributions on these topics. Researchers and practitioners alike were invited to submit their contributions to GSKI 2017.

We received 579 submissions from various parts of the world. The International Program Committee worked very hard to have all papers peer-peer reviewed before the review deadline. The final program consisted of 142 papers. There were five keynote speeches. All the keynote speakers are internationally recognized leading experts in their research fields, who have demonstrated outstanding proficiency and have achieved distinction in their profession. The proceedings were published as two volumes in Springer's *Communications in Computer and Information Science* (CCIS) series. Some excellent papers were selected and recommended to the special issue of *Journal of Environmental Science and Pollution*, a Science Citation Index Expanded journal. We would like to mention that, owing to the limitation of the conference venue capacity, we were not able to include many fine papers in the program. Our apology goes to these authors.

We would like to express our sincere gratitude to all the members of international Program Committee and organizers for their enthusiasm, time, and expertise. Our thanks also go to many volunteers and staff for the long hours and hard work they generously contributed to GSKI 2017. We are very grateful to Professor Thomas Blaschke and Professor Shihong Du for their support in making GSKI 2017 possible. The generous support from Beijing Institute of Technology is greatly appreciated. Finally, we would like to thank all the authors, speakers, and participants of this conference for their contributions to GSKI 2017.

May 2018

Hanning Yuan
Jing Geng
Chuanlu Liu
Fuling Bian
Tisinee Surapunt

5th Annual 2017 International Conference on Geo-Spatial Knowledge and Intelligence [GSKI 2017]

http://www.GSKI2017.org/
December 8–10, 2017, Chiang Mai, Thailand

Publisher

 Springer

5th Annual 2017 International Conference on Geo-Spatial
Knowledge and Intelligence (GSKI 2017)

https://www.GSKI2017.org
December 8–10, 2017, Chiang Mai, Thailand

Publisher

Organization

Keynote Speakers

Thomas Blaschke	University of Salzburg, Austria
Nopasit Chakpitak	Chiang Mai University, Thailand
Shihong Du	Peking University, China
Wang Shuliang	Beijing Institute of Technology, China
F. Benjamin Zhan	Texas State University, USA

Honorary Chairs

Zeeshan Ahmad	Nanjing University of Science and Technology, China
Fuling Bian	Wuhan University, Wuhan, China
Erin M. Hodgess	University of Houston, USA
Phongsak Phakamach	North Eastern University, Thailand

General Chair

Wang Shuliang	Beijing Institute of Technology, Beijing, China

Co-chairs

İsmail Rakıp Karaş	Karabuk University, Turkey
Zongyao Sha	Wuhan University, Wuhan, China

International Program Committee

Arun Agarwal	Siksha 'O' Anusandhan University, India
Ramesh K. Agarwal	Washington University, USA
Naveed Ahmed	Yonsei University, South Korea
Zeeshan Ahmad	Nanjing University of Science and Technology, China
Ulas Akkucuk	Bogazici University, Turkey
Mohammed A. Akour	Yarmouk University, Jordan
Iyad Al Khatib	Politecnico di Milano, Italy
Mohamad Al Ladan	Haigazian University, Lebanon
Shadi G. Alawneh	Oakland University, USA
Alberta Albertella	Technische Universität München, Germany
Mehdi Ammi	University of Paris-Sud, France
Jose Anand	KCG College of Technology, India
Tomasz Andrysiak	UTP University of Science and Technology, Poland
Ho Pham Huy Anh	Ho Chi Minh City University of Technology (HUT), Vietnam

Rkia Aouinatou	LRIT Laboratory, Rabat, Morocco
Kamran Arshad	Ajman University of Science and Technology, UAE
M. Arunachalam	K.L.N College of Information Technology, India
Bahareh Asadi	Islamic Azad University of Tabriz, Iran
Anjali Awasthi	Concordia University, Canada
Tchangani Ayeley	University Toulouse III, France
Nur Sukinah Aziz	TATI University College, Malaysia
Megat Farez Azril	Universiti Kuala Lumpur, Malaysia
Jianjun Bai	Shaanxi Normal University, China
Sen Bai	Chongqing Communication Institute, China
Yuqi Bai	Tsinghua University, China
K. Balakrishnan	Karpaga Vinayaga College of Engineering and Technology, India
Mirko Barbuto	Roma Tre University, Italy
Abul Bashar	Prince Mohammad Bin Fahd University, Saudi Arabia
Sabine Baumann	Technische Universität München, Germany
Muhammed Enes Bayrakdar	Duzce University, Turkey
Emna Ben Slimane	National Engineering School of Tunis, Tunisia
Marija Boban	University of Split, Croatia
Leszek Borzemski	Wroclaw University of Technology, Poland
Alexandra Bousia	University of Thessaly, Greece
Peter Brída	University of Zilina, Slovakia
Nor Amani Filzah Bt. Mohd Kamil	University Tun Husseion Onn Malaysia, Malaysia
Manfred F. Buchroithner	Technische Universität Dresden, Germany
Changsheng Cai	Central South University, China
Alberto Cano	Virginia Commonwealth University, USA
Fali Cao	Xi'an Jiaotong University, China
Hongjun Cao	Ocean University of China, China
Yanan Cao	Institute of Information Engineering, China
Yuan-Long Cao	Jiangxi Normal University, China
Yue Cao	University of Surrey, UK
Gina Cavan	Manchester Metropolitan University, UK
Saman Shojae Chaeikar	K. N. Toosi University of Technology, Iran
Chee-Ming Chan	Universiti Tun Hussein Onn Malaysia, Malaysia
Meng-Chou Chang	National Changhua University of Education, Taiwan, China
Ray-I Chang	National Taiwan University, China
Wong Man Sing Charles	The Hong Kong Polytechnic University, SAR China
Chin-Ling Chen	Chaoyang University of Technology, Taiwan, China
Deng Chen	Wuhan Institute of Technology, China
Duanduan Chen	Beijing Institute of Technology, China
Hongli Chen	ZheJiang Sci-Tech University, China
Hsing-Chung Chen	Asia University, Taiwan, China
Jianjiao Chen	Georgia Institute of Technology, USA
Jianping Chen	China University of Geosciences, China

Jyh-Cheng Chen	National Yang-Ming University, Taiwan, China
Ken Chen	Chengdu University of Technology, China
Siwei Chen	National University of Defense Technology, China
Tao Chen	Tsinghua University, Beijing, China
Wei Chen	China University of Mining and Technology, China
Yanying Chen	Meteorological Science Institute of Chongqing, China
Bo Cheng	Beijing University of Posts and Telecommunications, China
Bo Cheng	Earth Observation and Digital Earth Chinese Academy of Sciences, China
James Cheng	Manchester Metropolitan University, UK
Qiang (Shawn) Cheng	University of Kentucky, USA
Cheng-Yuan	Huafan University, Taiwan, China
Yee-Jin Cheon	University of Science and Technology, South Korea
Simon K. S. Cheung	The Open University of Hong Kong, SAR China
Hung-Chun Chien	Jinwen University of Science and Technology, Taiwan, China
Gihwan Cho	Chonbuk National University, South Korea
Chi-Wai Chow	National Chiao Tung University, Taiwan, China
Edwin Chow	Texas State University, USA
Rajdeep Chowdhury	JIS College of Engineering, India
George Christakos	San Diego State University, USA
Basile Christaras	Aristotle University of Thessaloniki, Greece
Ying-Chun Chuang	Kun Shan University, Taiwan, China
Arie Croitoru	George Mason University, USA
Shengcheng Cui	Chinese Academy of Sciences, China
Yaodong Cui	Guangxi University, China
Agnieszka Cydzik-Kwiatkowska	University of Warmia and Mazury in Olsztyn, Poland
D. M. D'Addona	University of Naples Federico II, Italy
Arianna D'Ulizia	University of Rome La Sapienza, Italy
Rocío Pérez de Prado	University of Jaén, Spain
Jan Dempewolf	University of Maryland, USA
Weihua Dong	Beijing Normal University, China
Zhenjiang Dong	Nanjing University of Science and Technology, China
Chunjiang Duanmu	Zhejiang Normal University, China
Rahul Dutta	Oracle India Pvt. Ltd., India
Ahmed Moustafa Elmahalawy	Menoufia University, Egypt
Ahmet H. Ertas	Karabuk University, Turkey
Ismail Erturk	Kocaeli University, Turkey
Oscar Esparza	Universitat Politècnica de Catalunya, Spain
Kong Fah	University of Greenwich, UK
Ahmad Fakharian	Islamic Azad University, Iran
Hong Fan	Institute of Remote Sensing and Digital Earth Chinese Academy of Sciences, China

Ping Fang	Tongji University, China
Kuishuang Feng	University of Maryland, USA
David Forrest	University of Glasgow, UK
Ximing Fu	Tsinghua University, China
Gurjot Singh Gaba	Lovely Professional University, Jalandhar, India
Chenfei Gao	AT&T Labs, USA
Jinzhu Gao	University of the Pacific, USA
Lianru Gao	Chinese Academy of Sciences, China
Qiang Gao	Beihang University, Beijing, China
Zhenguo Gao	Harbin Engineering University, China
Krzysztof Gdawiec	University of Silesia, Poland
Jing Geng	Beijing Institute of Technology, China
Rozaida Ghazali	Universiti Tun Husssein Onn Malaysia, Malaysia
Grigoras Gheorghe	Gheorghe Asachi Technical University of Iasi, Romania
Apostolos Gkamas	University Ecclesiastical Academy of Vella, Greece
Andrzej Glowacz	AGH University of Science and Technology, Poland
Adam Glowacz	AGH University of Science and Technology, Poland
Luis Gomez Deniz	University of Las Palmas de Gran Canaria, Spain
Prosanta Gope	Singapore University of Technology and Design, Singapore
Aldy Gunawan	Singapore Management University, Singapore
Jeonghwan Gwak	Gwangju Institute of Science and Technology, South Korea
Malka N. Halgamuge	The University of Melbourne, Australia
Maria Hallo	Notre Dame University of Belgium, Belgium
Saouli Hamza	University Khider Mohamed, Biskra, Algeria
Shuqing Hao	China University of Mining and Technology, China
Maguid H. M. Hassan	The British University in Egypt, Egypt
Anhua He	China Earthquake Administration, China
Anqi He	Queen Mary University of London, UK
Qian He	Guilin University of Electronic Technology, China
Trong-Minh Hoang	Posts and Telecommunication Institute of Technology, Vietnam
Gassan Hodaifa Meri	Pablo de Olavide University, Spain
Erin M. Hodgess	University of Houston, USA
Soon Hyung Hong	Korea Advanced Institute of Science and Technology, South Korea
Fangyong Hou	National University of Defense Technology, China
Yi-You Hou	Southern Taiwan University of Science and Technology, Taiwan, China
Hui-Mi Hsu	National Ilan University, Taiwan, China
Wenchen Hu	University of North Dakota, USA
Yu-Chen Hu	Providence University, Taiwan, China
Yupeng Hu	Hunan University, China
Fangjun Huang	Sun Yat-sen University, China

Fei Huang	Ocean University of China, China
Gordon Huang	University of Regina, Canada
Jen-Fa Huang	National Cheng Kung University, Taiwan, China
Qinghui Huang	Tongji University, China
Shian-Chang Huang	National Changhua University of Education, Taiwan, China
Shuqiang Huang	Jinan University, China
Wanchen Huang	Wu Feng University, Taiwan, China
I-Shyan Hwang	Yuan Ze University, Taiwan, China
Lain-Chyr Hwang	I-Shou University, Taiwan, China
Min-Shiang Hwang	Asia University, Taiwan, China
Mahmood K. Ibrahem Al Ubaidy	Al-Nahrain University, Iraq
Hamidah Ibrahim	Universiti Putra Malaysia, Kuala Lumpur, Malaysia
Mohd Haziman Wan Ibriahim	Universiti Tun Hussein Onn Malaysia, Malaysia
Choi Jaeho	Chonbuk National University, South Korea
Yogendra Kumar Jain	Samrat Ashok Technological Institute, India
Sadaqat Jan	University of Engineering and Technology, Pakistan
Jin Su Jeong	Technical University of Madrid, Spain
Fuucheng Jiang	Tunghai University, Taiwan, China
Liangxiao Jiang	China University of Geosciences, China
Zhiyu Jiang	University of Chinese Academy of Sciences, China
Fusheng Jin	Beijing Institute of Technology, China
Behshad Jodeiri Shokri	Hamedan University of Technology, Iran
Hanmin Jung	Korea Institute of Science and Technology Information, South Korea
Yasin Kabalci	Nigde University, Turkey
Amjad Kallel	Ecole Nationale d'Ingénieurs de Sfax, Tunisia
Massila Kamalrudin	Universiti Teknikal Malaysia Melaka, Malaysia
Chi-Wai Kan	Hong Kong Polytechnic University, SAR China
Dimitris Kanellopoulos	University of Patras, Greece
Ismail Rakip Karas	Karabuk University, Turkey
Ali Karrech	University of Western Australia, Australia
Sedat Keleş	Çankırı Karatekin University, Turkey
Elsayed Esam M. Khaled	Assiut University, Egypt
Syed Abdul Rehman Khan	Iqra University and Brasi School of Supply Chain Management, Pakistan
Najeeb Ullah Khan	CECOS University, Pakistan
Manoj Khandelwal	Federation University, Australia
Ittipong Khemapech	University of the Thai Chamber of Commerce, Thailand
Hyunsung Kim	Kyungil University, South Korea
Chan King-ming	Hong Kong, SAR China
Janusz Klink	Wroclaw University of Technology, Poland
Marcin Kowalczyk	Warsaw University of Technology, Poland

Artur Krawczyk	AGH University of Science and Technology, Poland
Piotr Kulczycki	Polish Academy of Sciences, Poland
Ashok Kumar Kulkarni	Malla Reddy Institute of Medical Sciences, Thailand
Andrew Kusiak	The University of Iowa, USA
Guoming Lai	Guangdong Polytechnic of Science and Technology, China
Wen Cheng Lai	National Taiwan University of Science and Technology, Taiwan, China
Alain Lambert	University of Paris-Sud, France
Huey-Ming Lee	Chinese Culture University, Taiwan, China
Jiann-Shu Lee	National University of Tainan, China
Tzong-Yi Lee	Yuan Ze University, Taiwan, China
Bai Li	Zhejiang University, China
Chaokui Li	Hunan University of Science and Technology, China
Guoqing Li	Institute of Soil and Water Conservation, CAS & MWR, China
Hongjun Li	Beijing Forestry University, China
Hongyi Li	Jiangxi University of Finance and Economics, China
Mengxue Li	University of Maryland, USA
Ming-Jian Li	University of Wisconsin Madison, USA
Tianhong Li	Peking University, China
Wenwen Li	Arizona State University, USA
Xiaolei Li	Wuhan University, China
Ying Li	Dalian Maritime University, China
Zengxiang Li	Institute of High Performance Computing, Singapore
Zhaoyang Li	Jilin University, China
Zhenhong Li	University of Glasgow, UK
Chiangchi Liao	National Kaohsiung First University of Science and Technology, Taiwan, China
Guo-Shiang Lin	Da-Yeh University, Taiwan, China
Lily Lin	China University of Technology, Taiwan, China
Yi-Kuei Lin	National Taiwan University of Science and Technology, Taiwan, China
Yo-Sheng Lin	National Chi Nan University, Nantou, Taiwan, China
Yun Lin	Harbin Engineering University, China
Zhiting Lin	Anhui University, China
Bin Liu	Dalian University of Technology, China
Binyi Liu	Tongji University, China
Chang-Yu Liu	South China Agricultural University, China
Chengyu Liu	Shandong University, China
Jiangwei Liu	National Institute for Materials Science, Japan
Lei Liu	Beijing University of Technology, China
Lin Liu	University of Cincinnati, USA
Quanyi Liu	Tsinghua University, China
Shuai Liu	Inner Mongolia University, China

Shuo Liu	Institute of Remote Sensing and Digital Earth Chinese Academy of Sciences, China
Weimo Liu	George Washington University, Washington, USA
Yan Liu	The University of Queensland, Australia
Yu Liu	Peking University, China
Roberto Llorente	Universitat Politècnica de València, Spain
Elena Simona Lohan	Tampere University of Technology, Finland
Yongmei Lu	Texas State University, USA
Arnulfo Luévanos Rojas	Autonomous University of Coahuila, México
Edwin Lughofer	Johannes Kepler University Linz, Austria
Dandan Ma	University of Chinese Academy of Sciences, China
Qianli Ma	University of California, USA
Xiuyan Ma	Dalian University of Technology, China
José Manuel Machado	University of Minho, Portugal
Dionisio Machado Leite	Federal University of Mato Grosso do Sul, Brazil
Elżbieta Macioszek	Silesian University of Technology, Poland
Mojtaba Maghrebi	University of New South Wales, Australia
Basel Ali Mahafzah	The University of Jordan, Jordan
Abdallah Makhoul	University of Bourgogne Franche-Comté, France
Bappaditya Mandal	Institute for Infocomm Research, Singapore
Parvaneh Mansouri	Azad University, Iran
Guojun Mao	Central University of Finance and Economics, China
Amin Riad Maouche	M'Hamed Bougara Univerity of Boumerdes, Algeria
Stephan Mäs	Technische Universität Dresden, Germany
Samaneh Mashhadi	Iran University of Science and Technology, Iran
Imran Memon	Zhejiang University, China
Lei Meng	Nanyang Technological University, Singapore
Aleksandra Mileva	Goce Delchev University, Macedonia
Jolanta Mizera-Pietraszko	Institute of Mathematics and Computer Science, Opole University, Poland
Helmi Zulhaidi Mohd Shafri	Universiti Putra Malaysia, Malaysia
Nursabillilah Binti Mohd Ali	Universiti Teknikal Malaysia Melaka, Malaysia
Sheikh Ahmad Izaddin Sheikh Mohd Ghazali	Applied Sciences, Malaysia
Rosmayati Binti Mohemad	Universiti Malaysia Terengganu, Malaysia
Sathaporn Monprapussorn	Srinakharinwirot University, Thailand
Abderrahmen Mtibaa	Texas A&M University, Qatar
Alan Murray	Arizona State University, USA
Faizal Mustapha	Universiti Putra Malaysia, Malaysia
Houda Mzoughi	National Engineering School of Sfax, Tunisia
Barbara Namyslowska-Wilczynska	Wroclaw University of Science and Technology, Poland
Andrea Nanetti	Nanyang Technological University, Singapore
Roberto Nardone	University of Naples Federico II, Italy

Zulkifli Mohd Rosli	Universiti Teknikal Malaysia Melaka, Malaysia
Huada Daniel Ruan	Beijing Normal University, Hong Kong Baptist University United International College (UIC), China
Xiukai Ruan	Wenzhou University, China
Rukhsana Ruby	Shenzhen University, China
Paul Loh Ruen Chze	Nanyang Polytechnic, Singapore
Zuraidi Saad	Universiti of Teknologi MARA, Malaysia
Maytham Safar	Kuwait University, Kuwait
Youssef Said	National Engineering School of Tunis, Tunisia
Amirhossein Sajadi	Case Western Reserve University, USA
Furkan Hassan Saleh Rabee	University of Kufa, Iraq
Carlos Humberto Salgado	Universidad Nacional de San Luis, Argentina
Jaime Santos Reyes	Systems Engineering Department, Mexico
Arun K. Saraf	India
Biju T. Sayed Mohammed	Dhofar University, Oman
Hassene Seddik	ENSIT Tunisia, Tunisia
Indranil SenGupta	North Dakota State University, USA
Delia B. Senor	Mapua Institute of Technology Manila, Philippines
Zongyao Sha	Wuhan University, China
Imran Shafique Ansari	Texas A&M University at Qatar, Qatar
B. Shanmugapriya	Sri Ramakrishna College of Arts and Science for Women, India
Chun Shi	Hainan Normal University, China
Khor Shing Fhan	Universiti Malaysia Perlis, Malaysia
Muh-Tian Shiue	National Central University, China
Andy Shui-Yu Lai	Technological and Higher Education Institute of Hong Kong, SAR China
André Skupin	San Diego State University, USA
Sarmad Sohaib	University of Engineering and Technology, Pakistan
Ivo Stachiv	National Taiwan University, China
Anthony Stefanidis	George Mason University, USA
Ching-Liang Su	Da Yeh University, Taiwan, China
K. M. Suceendran	Tata Consultancy Services, India
Jianguo Sun	Harbin Engineering University, China
Le Sun	Victoria University, Australia
Rui Sun	Beijing Normal University, China
Wen-Tsai Sung	National Chin-Yi University of Technology, Taiwan, China
Fengqi Tan	University of Chinese Academy of Sciences, China
Xicheng Tan	Wuhan University, China
Cheng-Yuan Tang	Huafan University, New Taipei, Taiwan, China
Qian Tang	Xidian University, China
Zhu Tang	National University of Defense Technology, China
Kai Tao	Nanyang Technological University, Singapore
Daniel Thalmann	Nanyang Technological University, Singapore

Ming Ming Wong	Sarawak Campus, Malaysia
Mike Worboys	The University of Maine, USA
Ben Wu	Princeton University, USA
Qunyong Wu	Fuzhou University, China
Wei-Chiang Wu	Da-Yeh University, Taiwan, China
Yong Xia	Northwestern Polytechnical University, Xian, China
Meng Xianyong	Zhuhai College of Jilin University, China
Wanan Xiong	University of Electronic Science and Technology of China, China
Chuanfei Xu	Concordia University, Canada
Qing-zheng Xu	Xi'an Communications Institute, China
Tianhua Xu	University College London, UK
Xin Yan	Wuhan University of Technology, China
Chaowei Yang	George Mason University, USA
Hui Yang	Beijing University of Posts and Telecommunications, Beijing, China
Huijun Yang	Northwest A&F University, China
Jingyu Yang	Shenyang Aerospace University, Shenyang, China
Liang Yang	Guangdong University of Technology, China
Liping Yang	Huazhong Agricultural University, China
Ting Yang	Tianjin University, China
Nicole Yang Lai Fong	Taylor's University Malaysia, Malaysia
Xiaojun Yang	Florida State University, USA
Jun Ye	Sichuan University of Science and Engineering, China
Qiang Ye	Nanjing Institute of Physical Education and Sports, China
Chien-Hung Yeh	Feng Chia University, Taiwan, China
Shih-Chuan Yeh	De Lin Institute of Technology, Taiwan, China
Ben-Shun Yi	Wuhan University, Wuhan, China
Peng-Yeng Yin	National Chi Nan University, Taiwan, China
Lee Beng Yong	Universiti Teknologi MARA Sarawak, Malaysia
Huan Yu	Chengdu University of Technology, Chengdu, China
Weiyu Yu	South China University of Technology, China
Xianchuan Yu	Beijing Normal University, China
Cheng Yuan	Huafan University, Taiwan, China
Hanning Yuan	Beijing Institute of Technology, China
Yang Yue	Juniper Networks, USA
Chau Yuen	Singapore University of Technology and Design (SUTD), Singapore
Noor Zaman	King Faisal University, Saudi Arabia
Muhammad Zeeshan	National University of Sciences and Technology, Pakistan
F. Benjamin Zhan	Texas State University, USA
Xianglin Zhan	Civil Aviation University of China, China
Di Zhang	Waseda University, Japan
Jianxun Zhang	Chongqing University of Technology, China

Keynote Speakers of GSKI 2017

Geospatial Data Science and Knowledge Discovery in Environmental Health Research

F. Benjamin Zhan
Texas State University, USA

Prof. F. Benjamin Zhan is Professor of Geographic Information Science in the Department of Geography at Texas State University. He was the founding director of the Texas Center for Geographic Information Science, and served as director of the center from 2003 to 2015. Among other honors, Professor Zhan was recipient of the Presidential Award for Excellence in Scholarly/Creative Activities at Texas State University, and held a Chang Jiang Scholar Guest Chair Professorship at Wuhan University in China from 2008 to 2011.

Abstract. There are over 80, 000 chemicals lurking in the environment and in everyday items. How some of these chemicals affect human health, particularly human reproductive health, remains unknown. The availability of geographically referenced environmental monitoring data and health outcome data makes it possible to examine the associations between maternal exposure to some of these chemicals and health issues in offspring. This presentation reports a data-driven approach for investigating these associations. The presentation first outlines the components of geospatial data science to support environmental health research. It then reports the datasets, analysis procedures, and results of two case studies based on large geographically referenced datasets. The first case study examines the association of maternal residential proximity to industrial facilities with toxic air emissions and birth defects in offspring. The second case study investigates the association of maternal residential exposure to some chemicals in the environment and low birth weights in offspring. Results from the two case studies demonstrate the power and potential of using geospatial data science to support environmental health research.

Spatial Data Mining: Theory and Application

Shuliang Wang

Beijing Institute of Technology, China

Shuliang Wang, PhD, a scientist in data science and software engineering, is a professor at the Beijing Institute of Technology in China. His research interests include spatial data mining and software engineering. For his innovatory study of spatial data mining, he was awarded the Fifth Annual InfoSci-Journals Excellence in Research Awards of IGI Global, IEEE Outstanding Contribution Award for Granular Computing, and one of China's National Excellent Doctoral Thesis Prizes.

URL: http://www.springer.com/gp/book/9783662485361#aboutAuthors

He is Guest Editor of:

(1) *International Journal of Systems Science*
(2) *International Journal of Data Warehousing and Mining*
(3) *Lecture Notes in Artificial Intelligence*

Abstract. The talk offers a systematic and practical overview of spatial data mining, which combines computer science and geo-spatial information science, allowing each field to profit from the knowledge and techniques of the other. To address the spatiotemporal specialties of spatial data, the authors introduce the key concepts and algorithms of the data field, cloud model, mining view, and Deren Li methods. The data field method captures the interactions between spatial objects by diffusing the data contribution from a universe of samples to a universe of population, thereby bridging the gap between the data model and the recognition model. The cloud model is a qualitative method that utilizes quantitative numerical characters to bridge the gap between pure data and linguistic concepts. The mining view method discriminates between the different requirements by using scale, hierarchy, and granularity in order to uncover the anisotropy of spatial data mining. The Deren Li method performs data preprocessing to prepare it for further knowledge discovery by selecting a weight for iteration in order to clean the observed spatial data as much as possible. In addition to the essential algorithms and techniques, the contribution provides application examples of spatial data mining in geographic information science and remote sensing. The practical projects include spatiotemporal video data mining for protecting public security, serial image mining on nighttime lights for assessing the severity of the Syrian crisis, and the applications in the government project "The Belt and Road Initiatives."

The Development of Geomatics Systems Based on Government Policy for Driving Thailand 4.0

Nopasit Chakpitak
Chiang Mai University, Thailand

Chakpitak Nopasit is Dean of the International College Chiang Mai University, Thailand. He was Dean of the College of Arts, Media and Technology, Chiang Mai University between 2004 and 2011. He was then promoted to be an assistant to the president, academic and international affairs, Chiang Mai University during 2011–2014. Before working at Chiang Mai University, he was responsible for many projects related to electronic engineering. His research interests lie in knowledge engineering and AI application in the power industry. Moreover, he collaborates and organizes conferences that linked to European and Asian countries.

Abstract. Thailand is an agricultural country which provides a huge amount of cultivation information. However, there is no system to properly organize and analyze this information. With the rapid growth of technology, geomatics systems are playing an important role in helping the Ministry of Agriculture and Cooperatives with decision-making. The Thai government's policy is to improve the economy, termed "Thailand 4.0." Tourism part is the most important factor to drive the Thai economy. The government has launched the 12th National Development Plan for the period 2017–2021, which involves the wealth of the nation and focuses on agriculture, light industry, heavy industry, and industry for the future. In the past, Thailand has had a middle-income trap, an inequality trap, and an imbalance trap. Thus, the government's policy encompasses the best practices that can be improved by three engines: the productive growth engine, the inclusive growth engine, and the green growth engine. Therefore, the national development plan can help Thailand to accomplish the goal of prosperity, security, and sustainability.

Smart Knowledge-Based Remote Sensing Analysis

Thomas Blaschke
University of Salzburg, Austria

Professor Blaschke's research interests include methodological issues of the integration of GIS, remote sensing, and image processing including aspects of participation and human–environment interaction. He has held several lecturer, senior lecturer, and professor positions in Germany, Austria, and the UK as well as temporary affiliations as guest professor and visiting scientist in Germany and the USA, including about 115 journal publications. He is author, co-author, or editor of 17 books, has received several academic prizes and awards including the Christian Doppler Prize in 1995 and was elected as a corresponding member of the Austrian Academy of Sciences in 2015. He has been project leader in various international and national research projects and serves on various editing boards of international journals, conference committees, and a dozen national research councils.

Publications: https://scholar.google.at/citations?user=kMroJzUAAAAJ&hl=de

Abstract. In response to the ever-increasing amount of spaceborne imaging sensors, a research group at the University of Salzburg developed a methodology for "smart" (knowledgeable), effective, and efficient Earth observation (EO) image-content extraction. It utilizes content-based image retrieval systems. The methodology is based on a priori 4D spatiotemporal scene domain knowledge to be mapped onto the image domain in terms of 2D image features and spatial constraints. This 4D to 2D mapping capability holds the solution to the vision problems, where the semantic gap from sensory data to high-level information products must be filled in. Another pivotal component is the concept of (geographic) object-based image analysis – GEOBIA or OBIA in short. OBIA aims for the generation of geographic information (in GIS-ready format) from which new spatial knowledge can be obtained. I will outline how OBIA methods and methodologies can structure the complexity of our environment and, likewise, the complexity of measurements into scaled representations for further analysis and monitoring tasks.

Segmentation Scale Selection in Geographic Object-Based Image Analysis (GEOBIA)

Shihong Du
Peking University, China

Shihong Du is currently Associate Professor of GIScience in the School of Earth and Space Sciences at Peking University and the vice director of the Institute of Remote Sensing and GIS. His research interests include spatial knowledge representation and reasoning, as well as intelligent mining and understanding of geospatial data including GIS and remote sensing data. He authored/co-authored over 80 journal articles and two books, and was awarded the New Century Excellent Talents in University and Second Place Award of National Science and Technology Progress in Surveying and Mapping.

Abstract. Geographic object-based image analysis (GEOBIA) with very-high-resolution (VHR) images plays an important role in geographical investigations, but its uncertainty in segmentation scale significantly affects the accuracy and reliability of GEOBIA results, e.g., object segmentations and classifications. Therefore, a scale-selection method is needed to determine the optimal scale for GEOBIA, which, however, can be influenced by three factors, i.e., categories, surrounding contrasts, and internal heterogeneities of objects. Thus, if we want to select the optimal scale, the three factors should be totally considered. The existing scale selections including supervised and unsupervised methods partly considered these three factors, but could not resolve all of them, thus, this issue is still open and needs further study. This report reviews five kinds of scale-selection methods, compares their advantages and disadvantages, and discusses the future direction of scale selections.

Segmentation Scale Selection in Geographic Object-Based Image Analysis (GEOBIA)

Shihong Du

Contents – Part II

**Applications of Geo-Informatics in Resource Management
and Sustainable Ecosystem**

Contents – Part I

Spatial Data Acquisition Through RS and GIS in Resource Management and Sustainable Ecosystem

Ecological and Environmental Data Processing and Management

Advanced Geospatial Model and Analysis for Understanding Ecological and Environmental Process

Feature Point Detection and Target Tracking Based on SIFT and KLT

Huajing Zheng[(⊠)] and Changchang Chen

School of Optoelectronic Information, University of Electronic Science
and Technology, Chengdu 610054, China
zhjl2@163.com

Abstract. The Scale Invariant Feature Transform, SIFT, has good ability to detect very stable feature points. But at present, there are very little researches on SIFT in our country, and most of them are concentrated in the areas of Image Registration and Image Stitching. In this paper, SIFT and KLT will be combined for feature points detection and tracking. First, SIFT algorithms is used to detect stable feature points, and then the KLT method is used to track the feature points. The experimental results show that the new method provides a good method in the field of feature points detection and tracking.

Keywords: Feature points detection · Tracking · SIFT · KLT

1 Introduction

Moving target tracking in video sequence has been an important research topic in the field of computer vision, digital video and image processing and pattern recognition. It has a wide range of application value and good application prospects in the fields of robot navigation, intelligent visual monitoring system, medical image analysis, industrial inspection and military security.

Feature points are points set with singularity on multiple directions, which is the most commonly used image feature, including object edge points, corner points, and line intersection points. The storage of the whole image can be greatly reduced by extracting the feature points and identifying the objects in the image with the feature points. The KLT feature point detection and tracking method was originally proposed by LucaseKanade [1] and was improved by Tomasi and Kanade [2]. Shi and Tomasi [3] extended this algorithm for more complex changes considering the Radial Transformation Model. They proposed techniques to monitor the quality of the feature points being tracked. In order to find more stable feature points, feature points that are insensitive to changes in scale, rotation, illumination changes and 3D viewpoint changes, DG Low proposed a feature-point-based detection method [4] with constant scale in 1999. Crowley, Riff and Piater put forward the improvement based on this [5]. In 2004, DG Lowe proposed a more complete scale-invariant feature point detection [6] called SIFT (the Scale Invariant Feature Transform).

In this paper, two methods of SIFT and KLT are synthesized. First, the feature points are detected by the SIFT method, and then the KLT method is used to track the

© Springer Nature Singapore Pte Ltd. 2018
H. Yuan et al. (Eds.): GSKI 2017, CCIS 849, pp. 3–12, 2018.
https://doi.org/10.1007/978-981-13-0896-3_1

feature points. And the SIFT method has been improved at some extent. Finally, experiments show that our method has achieved good results.

2 The Method of SIFT

The use of SIFT (Scale Invariance Feature Transform) feature points extracted from the image can be used for reliable matching of an object or scene from different angles of view, the extracted feature points of image rotation and scale remain unchanged which is also robust to illumination changes, affine transformation, noise.

The feature points of SIFT filtering process is probably in Pyramid by stratified Gauss differential extremum obtained candidate feature points by filtering out the characteristics of low contrast and located at the edges, and finally get the stable feature points, as shown in Fig. 1, stable feature points are given.

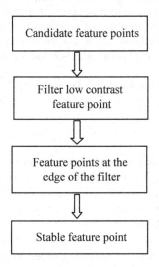

Fig. 1. The process of filtering feature point

2.1 Generating Gaussian Differential Pyramid

First, the input image is filtered and sampled by Gauss kernel function of different scales, forming the Gauss Pyramid image. Then the DOG (Difference of Gaussian) operator is calculated. The DOG operator is defined as the difference in the Gauss kernel of two different scales and the convolution of the image. The calculation formula is as follows:

$$\begin{aligned} D(x,y,\sigma) &= (G(x,y,k\sigma) - G(x,y,\sigma)) \otimes I(x,y) \\ &= L(x,y,k\sigma) - L(x,y,\sigma) \end{aligned} \tag{1}$$

In the formula, $G(x, y, \sigma)$ is the Gauss function, and k is a constant. The process of DOG generation is shown in Fig. 2.

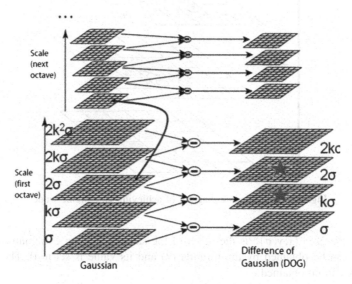

Fig. 2. The schematic diagram of generating DOG.

2.2 Extreme Value Detection in DOG

To obtain the extreme points in the Gaussian difference image, the sample pixels need to be compared with the adjacent 8 pixels in the same scale and each 9 pixels in the upper and lower adjacent layers. As shown in Fig. 3, the fork is the pixel point to be compared. If the sample point is the extreme value point (maximum or minimum value) of these points, we should extract this point as a candidate feature point, otherwise we will continue to compare other pixel points according to this rule. In Fig. 2, the right Gaussian differential Pyramid hierarchical structure has only second or 3 level images in each group, which satisfy the above comparison conditions, and can extract candidate feature points

After getting the candidate feature points, it is necessary to filter down the low contrast (the noise sensitive) or the point at the edge.

2.3 The Filtration of Low Contrast Feature Points

The scale space function Taylor can be expanded, and the maximum to 2 term approximation can be written:

$$D(X) = D + \frac{\partial D^T}{\partial X}X + \frac{1}{2}X^T\frac{\partial^2 D}{\partial X^2}X \tag{2}$$

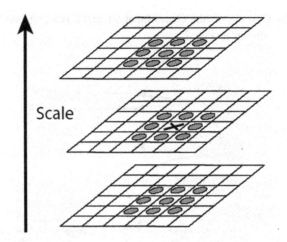

Fig. 3. The schematic diagram of achieving an extreme value

Where the $X = (x, y, \sigma)^T$ is the offset of the sample. For the extremum of X, the derivative can be obtained by the formula (2) and its value is set to 0. The extreme value of X can be obtained:

$$\hat{X} = -\frac{\partial^2 D^{-1}}{\partial X^2}\frac{\partial D}{\partial X} \tag{3}$$

If the value $\hat{X}$ in either direction is greater than 0.5, it means that the maximum offset with the addition of the sample points are very close, so the sample points will be changed, then use interpolation instead of sample points, the offset is added to the sample point to get the interpolation in the extreme position estimate:

$$D\left(\hat{X}\right) = D + \frac{1}{2}\frac{\partial D^T}{\partial X}\hat{X} \tag{4}$$

2.4   The Filtration of Edge Feature Points

A feature point at the edge of the image has a larger principal curvature at the peak of the Gaussian difference function and crosses the edge, but the curvature value in the vertical direction is small. We can use this property to filter out the low contrast feature points at the edge.

We know that the Hessian matrix of 2×2 is:

$$H = \begin{bmatrix} D_{xx} & D_{xy} \\ D_{xy} & D_{yy} \end{bmatrix} \tag{5}$$

Assuming that the larger eigenvalue of the Hessian matrix is a smaller eigenvalue, we can calculate the ratio of the sum to the sum by the following formula.

$$Tr(H) = D_{xx} + D_{yy} = \alpha + \beta \tag{6-1}$$

$$Det(H) = D_{xx}D_{yy} - (D_{xy})^2 = \alpha\beta \tag{6-2}$$

Make $\alpha = r\beta$, then:

$$ratio = \frac{Tr(H)^2}{Det(H)} = \frac{(\alpha+\beta)^2}{\alpha\beta} = \frac{(r\beta+\beta)^2}{r\beta^2} = \frac{(r+1)^2}{r} \tag{7}$$

SIFT is often taken $r = 10$, if $ratio > (r+1)^2/r$, it is believed that the point is located on the edge and is filtered out.

3 The Algorithm of KTL

KLT algorithm [7, 8] is a tracking algorithm based on Sum of Squared Intensity Differences (SSD) to track windows in video frames.

For grayscale images, the KLT algorithm assumes a feature window containing the feature texture information, which is satisfied at the time frame and the position in the frame of the time image.

$$I(x, y, t+\tau) = I(x - \xi, y - \eta, t) \tag{8}$$

That is, each pixel in $I(x, y, t+\tau)$ can be obtained by the pixel point displacement $\vec{d} = (\xi, \eta)$ of the corresponding window in the $I(x, y, t)$. The purpose of the KLT algorithm is to find them $\vec{d}$.

Assuming that the feature window at the $t+\tau$ time is $J(\vec{X}) = I(x, y, t+\tau)$, and the feature window of the t time is $I(\vec{X} - \vec{d}) = I(x - \xi, y - \eta, t)$.

Considering the general situation, there are

$$J(\vec{X}) = I(\vec{X} - \vec{d}) + n(\vec{X}) \tag{9}$$

$n(\vec{X})$ is the noise generated by the change of light conditions in time τ.

By integrating $n(\vec{X})$ square and integrating the whole window, we get the SSD of the window image.

$$\varepsilon = \int_W \left[I(\vec{X} - \vec{d}) - J(\vec{X}) \right]^2 w d\vec{X} \tag{10}$$

w is a weighted function, and it can take 1 in a simple case. If you want to emphasize the central area of the feature matching window, you can use the Gauss function.

At this time, as long as the minimum of ε is minimized, the feature points of each feature matching window can be guaranteed to be tracked more reliably. To minimize the ε, when the $\vec{d}$ is smaller, $I\left(\vec{X} - \vec{d}\right)$ Taylor is expanded to get rid of the high order.

$$I\left(\vec{x} - \vec{d}\right) = I(\vec{x}) - \vec{g} \cdot \vec{d} \tag{11}$$

Substituting (13) in formula (12)

$$\varepsilon = \int_W \left[I(\vec{X}) - \vec{g} \cdot \vec{d} - J(\vec{X})\right]^2 w d\vec{X} = \int_W \left(h - \vec{g} \cdot \vec{d}\right)^2 w d\vec{X} \tag{12}$$

Among them, $h = I(\vec{X}) - J(\vec{X})$. When the two sides of the opposite type (14) are guided to the $\vec{d}$, take 0, and make the arrangement, we can get the following equation:

$$G \cdot \vec{d} = \vec{e} \tag{13}$$

$$G = \int_W ZwdA = \int_W ZdA, \; Z = gg^T = \begin{bmatrix} g_x^2 & g_xg_y \\ g_xg_y & g_y^2 \end{bmatrix}, \; e = \int_W h\vec{g}wd\vec{A},$$

$$d\vec{A} = d\vec{X}d\vec{d}.$$

For each frame, the solution Eq. (16) can be used to find the displacement $\vec{d} = (\xi, \eta)$ of the feature window. The Newton iterative method is generally calculated until a certain precision is satisfied, thus the tracking of the image feature points can be achieved. In the KLT tracking algorithm, when the matrix Z two eigenvalues λ_1, λ_2, to meet the conditions for the advance $\min(\lambda_1, \lambda_2) > \lambda$, λ is the threshold value, then we will select this feature windows tracking.

4 Feature Point Detection and Tracking Method Based on SIFT and KLT

The idea of this method is to use the improved SIFT method to detect the feature points in the image, and then use the KLT method to track it.

Step 1. In order to extract more stable feature points, the image is pre-processed to eliminate image blur. We use the Gaussian function of the image convolution operation, in order to achieve the purpose of preprocessing.

Step 2. Using different sampling distances for the image to form a pyramid image hierarchy, sampled every 0.5-pixel distance on the first sample, which means that the original image is doubled, the first sample Image as the image of the first group, and then sampling the images by multiple sampling distances of 1.5, 3, 4.5, and 6 pixels respectively to generate the second, third, fourth and fifth groups of images. This creates a pyramid-shaped image hierarchy.

Step 3. Gauss kernel function is used to filter and form the hierarchical structure of Gauss Pyramid image. Different Gauss filtering factors are used for each layer of image's Gauss filtering. In Fig. 2, the filter factor of the Gauss filter function is identified in the Gauss Pyramid layers on the left side. The SIFT feature point detection method is improved in this paper. Only one Gauss difference image is calculated in each level, then the extreme value is compared between the level and the level as the candidate feature point, which can greatly reduce the computation.

Step 4. After screening the low contrast of candidate feature points and the feature points at the edge, the stable feature points are finally extracted. In the selection process, if we compare the 26 points to determine the extreme value, then we will compare it in a larger radius to determine whether it is still the extreme value. If so, we record it as the key point, otherwise we will discard this point. In this way, the amount of computation can be reduced and the number of feature points extracted is reduced.

In this paper, some improvements have been made in SIFT to reduce the amount of computation and reduce the number of feature points extracted. While tracking the KLT algorithm, the KLT is combined with the hierarchical method, that is, the hierarchical KLT tracking, so that the tracking effect is improved.

5 Test and Conclusion

The same video sequence is tracked with the traditional KLT method and the method in this paper, and the comparison is made.

The first experiment uses this method to track the sequence of aircraft in a real and complicated environment. The sequence has 100 frames, and the result is shown in Fig. 4. In the process of tracking, no new feature points are found, and the location of the first frame is not removed from the lost point. Figure 4 (a) is the result of SIFT's feature point detection for the first frame, and Fig. 4 (b) is the selection of 19 points in the first frame for tracking. It can be seen that the detected feature points are very stable and have good tracking effect.

For the same 100 frame sequence above, the KLT method is used to detect tracking, as shown in Fig. 5. In the process of tracking, no new feature points are found, but the points that are lost will no longer be displayed. Figure 5 (a) uses KLT to detect the feature point of the first frame, and chooses the best 20 points to be tracked.

Among the 20 points, the method of KLT keeps up with 6 points, and the method of this article keeps up with 8 points, indicating that the method in this paper can improve the stability of tracking. However, the SIFT method is slower than the KLT detection method, although this article improves SIFT detection and improves detection speed, it is still slightly slower than KLT. So, for the simple background map, using the KLT test is good, but for the complex background, the advantage of this method is highlighted.

The second experiment was to track a car with a shade in a static background. In this sequence, an algorithm is added to the complement point, that is, when the remaining feature points in the picture are reduced, the detection points are automatically detected. The best 100 feature points are detected. Because the feature point is

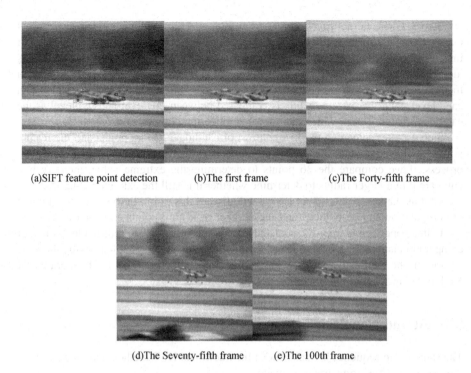

(a)SIFT feature point detection   (b)The first frame   (c)The Forty-fifth frame

(d)The Seventy-fifth frame   (e)The 100th frame

Fig. 4. The results of this approach to the tracking test of a 100 frame plane sequence

very stable and there is a patch algorithm, the feature points can still not be lost after the car passes through the column, and keep stable tracking (Fig. 6).

The third experiment is the sudden change of the brightness of the image, because when working outside, it may cause sudden change of light, that is, the sudden change of brightness. In Fig. 7, the two adjacent frames are adjacent, but the brightness of the images in the two frames has changed considerably. Figure 7 (a), Fig. 7 (b) is used to detect and track the feature points with KLT. 150 feature points are selected, but only one frame interval is only a small change, but only 29 feature points are detected. Figure 7 (c), Fig. 7 (d), using this method, detects 41 feature points. It can be seen that the method in this paper is robust to the change of brightness.

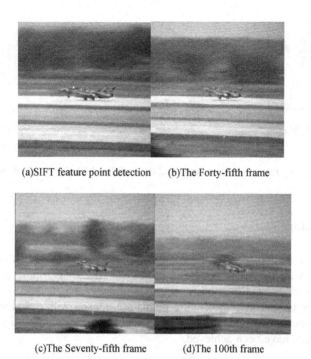

(a)SIFT feature point detection   (b)The Forty-fifth frame

(c)The Seventy-fifth frame   (d)The 100th frame

Fig. 5. the results of traditional approach to the tracking test of a 100 frame plane sequence

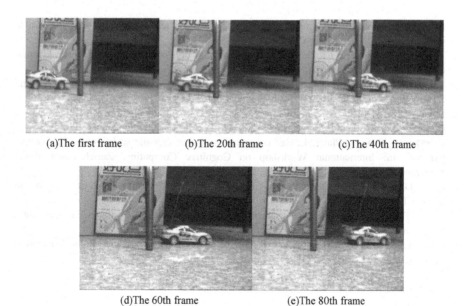

(a)The first frame   (b)The 20th frame   (c)The 40th frame

(d)The 60th frame   (e)The 80th frame

Fig. 6. The results of traditional approach to the tracking test of an80-tracked car frame sequence

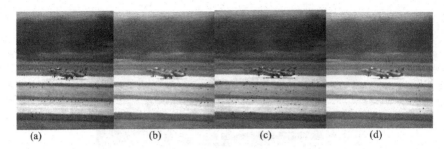

(a)   (b)   (c)   (d)

Fig. 7. The tracking results of this method and the traditional KLT method when the brightness changes

6 Conclusion

In this paper, a method of detecting and tracking the feature points by combining the SIFT method with the KLT method is proposed. The SIFT feature point detection method is carried out and improved, and the improved SIFT method is used to detect the feature points, and then the feature points are tracked with the hierarchical KLT method. This method is used to test the real scene of different complexity respectively, and good results have been achieved.

References

1. Lucas, B.D., Kanade, T.: An Iterative image registration technique with an application to stereo vision. In: IJCA181, pp. 121–130 (1981)
2. Tomasi, C., Kanade, T.: Detection and Tracking of Point Features, Technical report CMU-CS-91-132, April 1991
3. Shi, J., Tomasi, C.: Good feature to track. In: IEEE Conference on Computer Vision and Pattern Recognition (CVPR94), Seattle, June 1994
4. Lowe, D.G.: Object recognition from local scale-invariant features. In: International Conference on Computer Vision, pp. 1150–1157, Corfu, Greece, September 1999
5. Crowley, J., Riff, O., Piater, J.: Fast computation of characteristic scale using a half octave pyramid. In: International Workshop on Cognitive Computing, Zurich, Switzerland, September 2002
6. Lowe, D.G.: Distinctive image features from scale-invariant keypoints. Int. J. Comput. Vision 2(60), 91–110 (2004)
7. Shi, J., Tomasi, C.: Good features to track. In: Proceedings of IEEE Conference on Computer Vision and Pattern Recognition, Seattle, pp. 593–600 (1994)
8. Carlo, T., Kanada, T.: Detection and tracking of point features. Carnegie Mellon University, Pittsburgh, CMUCS-91-132 (1991)

Research on the Handwriting Character Recognition Technology Based on the Image Statistical Characteristics

Yongfeng Sun[✉], Zhonghua Guo, and Weijiang Qiu

China Electric Power Research Institute,
No. 15, Xiaoying East Road, Haidian District, Beijing, China
{YongfengSun, ZhonghuaGuo,
WeijiangQiu-sunyongfeng}@epri.sgcc.com.cn

Abstract. The research on the image pattern recognition has always been a hot topic. In this paper, the automatic identification technology of image is studied, the research contents include image preprocessing, image feature extraction and image content identification. BP neural network is used for the research on the image content identification. The processing methods in this article include the following steps, first, the pre-processing of the image. Including image de-noising and feature extraction; second, training the BP neural network with the processed handwriting character image; third, the recognition test of the unknown handwritten character. 95% recognition accuracy is realized, and the research has some practical application value.

Keywords: Handwriting character recognition · Image recognition
Back propagation neural network

1 Introduction

Pattern recognition technology is used to simulate people's various recognition abilities which mainly simulates human visual and auditory abilities. It is the main content of computer pattern recognition that the ultimate goal of digital image processing is to use computers instead of people to recognize images and to find objects in an image that people are interested in. Image pattern recognition is a technique to solve the problem of direct communication between computer and external environment by means of processing and identifying information such as text, image and scenery.

It has great theoretical significance and practical value of the recognition technology of image pattern in the fields that need to automatically identify and process information. There are so many applications for image recognition technique in the field of recognition of vehicle license [1], postal code [2], handwritten document [3], printed document [4], web page verification code [5].

Artificial neural network [6] aroused in the 1980s, has a good fault tolerance, adaptability, associative memory function and highly nonlinear processing ability, which has achieved success in the field of pattern recognition that many traditional methods are difficult to. Image recognition technology based on the artificial neural

H. Yuan et al. (Eds.): GSKI 2017, CCIS 849, pp. 13–20, 2018.
https://doi.org/10.1007/978-981-13-0896-3_2

network is a traditional method of image recognition on the basis of artificial neural network,which has been developed with the development of modern computer technology, image processing, artificial intelligence and pattern recognition theory.

2 Image Preprocessing

Image preprocessing includes image feature extraction, image keyword processing and feature value normalization.

2.1 Image Feature Extraction

The grid feature extraction algorithm [7] is adopted. First identify the pixel values in each unit, set value is one when the pixel is black, set value is one when the pixel is black at the same time value is zero when white. The image resolution adopted in this paper is 28 by 28, the total number of pixels is 784. Second divide the original image into n by n grids, count the number of black pixels in each grid, the obtained value is defined as the grid feature, all the grid feature values are written into the value file. Each line in the value file is written by one image's feature value and separated by space.

2.2 Image Keyword Processing

To handwritten digital image file, the keyword is defined as the corresponding number; To handwritten Chinese character image file, the keyword is defined as the decimal number converted from the binary number of the character. The keyword for the image is appended on the last column for each line. The mapping of the keyword and the character is also generated at the same time.

2.3 Image Feature Value Normalization

The purpose for normalization is to make input variables with different physical meanings and dimensional standards to be used equally. The excitation function used in the artificial neural network is the sigmoid function, one of reason for normalization is to prevent that the absolute value of the input value is so large as to cause output neurons excessive saturation. The third reason is to keep the small output value not to be ignored. The last reason is to accelerate the convergence.

Using linear function transformation, the expression is as follows:

$$y = (x - \text{Min Value})/(\text{Max Value} - \text{Min Value}) \tag{1}$$

X and y are the values before and after the normalization, Max Value and Min Value are the maximum and minimum values of the feature value.

3 Image Recognition

The image recognition includes the following steps, neural network training and handwriting character recognition.

3.1 Neural Network Training

The neural network training includes the following steps, initializing neural network, calculating the output of hidden layer and output layer, calculating the error of output to target, updating the Weights and bias. When the minimum value of error reaches the target, the calculation ends, otherwise the calculation is carried out from step of calculating the output.

3.2 Initializing Neural Network

Suppose the number of nodes in the input layer is n, the number of nodes of the hidden layer is l, and the number of nodes of the output layer is m, the weight of the input layer to the hidden layer is ω_{ij}, the weight of the hidden layer to the output layer is ω_{jk}, the bias of Input layer to implicit layer is a_j, the bias of hidden layer to output layer is b_k, the learning rate is η. The excitation function is $g(x)$, taken the sigmoid function as the expression. It is in the form of

$$g(x) = \frac{1}{1 + e^{-x}} \tag{2}$$

Calculating the Output of Hidden Layer and Output Layer
The output of hidden layer is H_j. It is in the form of

$$H_j = g\left(\sum_{i=1}^{n} \omega_{ij} x_i + a_j\right) \tag{3}$$

The output of output layer is O_k. It is in the form of

$$O_k = \sum_{j=1}^{l} H_j \omega_{jk} + b_k \tag{4}$$

Calculating Error
The expression of error is E. It is in the form of

$$E = \frac{1}{2} \sum_{k=1}^{m} (Y_k - O_k)^2 \tag{5}$$

In the above formula, the value of i is to take the integer from 1 to n, j is 1 to l, k is 1 to m.

Y_k is the desired output. It is denoted that $Y_k - O_k$ as e_k, and E can be expressed as

$$E = \frac{1}{2}\sum_{k=1}^{m} e_k^2. \tag{6}$$

Updating the Weights and the Bias

The formula to the renewal of the weights is as follows

$$\begin{cases} \omega_{ij} = \omega_{ij} + \eta H_j \left(1 - H_j\right) x_i \sum_{k=1}^{m} \omega_{jk} e_k \\ \omega_{jk} = \omega_{jk} + \eta H_j e_k \end{cases} \tag{7}$$

In the process of error back propagation, the goal is to achieve the minimum error value of the error function, using minE as the error formula, using the gradient descent method to update the weights.

The renewal formula of the weights of hidden layer to output layer is expressed as follows:

$$\frac{\partial E}{\partial \omega_{jk}} = \sum_{k=1}^{m} (Y_k - O_k)\left(-\frac{\partial O_k}{\partial \omega_{jk}}\right) = (Y_k - O_k)(-H_j) = -e_k H_j \tag{8}$$

The renewal formula of the weight function is

$$\omega_{jk} = \omega_{jk} + \eta H_j e_k \tag{9}$$

The renewal formula of the weights of input layer to hidden layer is expressed as follows:

$$\frac{\partial E}{\partial \omega_{ij}} = \frac{\partial E}{\partial H_j} \cdot \frac{\partial H_j}{\partial \omega_{ij}} \tag{10}$$

$$\begin{aligned} \frac{\partial E}{\partial H_j} &= (Y_1 - O_1)\left(-\frac{\partial O_1}{\partial H_j}\right) + \cdots + (Y_m - O_m)\left(-\frac{\partial O_m}{\partial H_j}\right) \\ &= -(Y_1 - O_1)\omega_{j1} - \cdots - (Y_m - O_m)\omega_{jm} \\ &= -\sum_{k=1}^{m} (Y_k - O_k)\omega_{jk} = -\sum_{k=1}^{m} \omega_{jk} e_k \\ \frac{\partial H_j}{\partial \omega_{ij}} &= \frac{\partial g\left(\sum_{i=1}^{n} \omega_{ij} x_i + a_j\right)}{\partial \omega_{ij}} \\ &= g\left(\sum_{i=1}^{n} \omega_{ij} x_i + a_j\right) \cdot \left[1 - g\left(\sum_{i=1}^{n} \omega_{ij} x_i + a_j\right)\right] \\ &\quad \cdot \frac{\partial \sum_{i=1}^{n} \omega_{ij} x_i + a_j}{\partial \omega_{ij}} = H_j\left(1 - H_j\right) x_i \end{aligned}$$

The renewal formula of the weight function is expressed as follows:

$$\omega_{ij} = \omega_{ij} + \eta H_j \left(1 - H_j\right) x_i \sum_{k=1}^{m} \omega_{jk} e_k \tag{11}$$

The renewal formula of the bias is as follows:

$$\begin{cases} a_j = a_j + \eta H_j(1 - H_j)\sum_{k=1}^{m} \omega_{jk}e_k \\ b_k = b_k + \eta e_k \end{cases} \tag{12}$$

The renewal formula of the bias from hidden layer to output layer is as follows:

$$\frac{\partial E}{\partial b_k} = (Y_k - O_k)\left(-\frac{\partial O_k}{\partial b_k}\right) = -e_k \tag{13}$$

$$b_k = b_k + \eta e_k \tag{14}$$

the renewal formula of the bias from input layer to hidden layer is expressed as follows:

$$\frac{\partial E}{\partial a_j} = \frac{\partial E}{\partial H_j} \cdot \frac{\partial H_j}{\partial a_j} \tag{15}$$

$$\frac{\partial H_j}{\partial a_j} = \frac{\partial g\left(\sum_{i=1}^{n} \omega_{ij}x_i + a_j\right)}{\partial a_j}$$

$$= g\left(\sum_{i=1}^{n} \omega_{ij}x_i + a_j\right) \cdot \left[1 - g\left(\sum_{i=1}^{n} \omega_{ij}x_i + a_j\right)\right] \cdot \frac{\partial \sum_{i=1}^{n} \omega_{ij}x_i + a_j}{\partial a_j} = H_j(1 - H_j)$$

$$\frac{\partial E}{\partial H_j} = (Y_1 - O_1)\left(-\frac{\partial O_1}{\partial H_j}\right) + \cdots + (Y_m - O_m)\left(-\frac{\partial O_m}{\partial H_j}\right)$$
$$= -(Y_1 - O_1)\omega_{j1} - \cdots - (Y_m - O_m)\omega_{jm}$$
$$= -\sum_{k=1}^{m}(Y_k - O_k)\omega_{jk} = -\sum_{k=1}^{m}\omega_{jk}e_k$$

The formula of the bias of Input layer to implicit layer is as follows:

$$a_k = a_k + \eta H_j(1 - H_j)\sum_{k=1}^{m} \omega_{jk}e_k \tag{16}$$

4 Tested Character Recognition

In the experimental part, extensive tests have been carried out in different samples. In the first experiment, we used the images of numbers from 0 to 9 for testing. Handwritten digital characters are from the reference [8]. There are 500 images in the format of JPG for each number, the size of each image is 28 by 28. When extracting image feature, we divide image into four grids with the size of 14 by 14, count the number of pixes in each grid, get four feature values, till now the pixel feature data is transformed from 784 units data to four grids data. The screenshot of test data is shown as follows (Figs. 1, 2, 3, 4, 5, 6, 7, 8, 9 and 10).

In the second experiment, we used the images of Chinese characters as test data which is 啊, 躲, 角, 墨, 薯 and 蜓. Handwritten CASIA Chinese characters are from reference [9]. The files of the HWDB1.1trn_gnt packet are used as training data, and

Fig. 1. The image of number 0 written with different styles

Fig. 2. The image of number 1 written with different styles

Fig. 3. The image of number 2 written with different styles

Fig. 4. The image of number 3 written with different styles

Fig. 5. The image of number 4 written with different styles

Fig. 6. The image of number 5 written with different styles

Fig. 7. The image of number 6 written with different styles

Fig. 8. The image of number 7 written with different styles

Fig. 9. The image of number 8 written with different styles

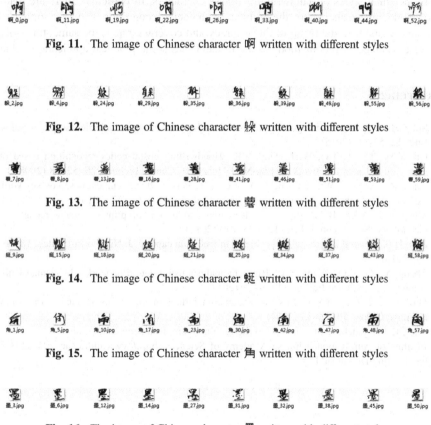

Fig. 10. The image of number 9 written with different styles

HWDB1.1tst_gnt as test data. There are 40 images for each Chinese character in the training data packet with the format of JPG, 10 in the test data packet, the size of each image is 28 by 28. When extracting image feature, we divide image into 49 grids with the size of 4 by 4, count the number of pixes in each grid, get 49 feature values, till now the pixel feature data is transformed from 784 units data to 49 grids data. The screenshot of test data is shown as follows (Figs. 11, 12, 13, 14, 15 and 16):

Fig. 11. The image of Chinese character 啊 written with different styles

Fig. 12. The image of Chinese character 躲 written with different styles

Fig. 13. The image of Chinese character 薯 written with different styles

Fig. 14. The image of Chinese character 蜒 written with different styles

Fig. 15. The image of Chinese character 角 written with different styles

Fig. 16. The image of Chinese character 墨 written with different styles

The statistical results are show in Table 1.

Two numbers are not correctly identified in the first test, one is zero, another is seven. Three Chinese character in the second test, one is 躲, another is 角, the third is 薯.

Table 1. Statistical results for each test data packet

No.	Training time (s)	Test time (ms)	Rate of accuracy	Rate of coverage
1	128	1.21	95%	100%
2	13	23.8	95%	100%

5 Conclusions

In the proposed method, not only is there no reduction in the feature information, but also the amount of information data is reduced .95% recognition accuracy is realized, 100% rate of coverage is realized. especially in the second test, although there are too many personal styles of handwritten Chinese characters, In particular, there are many strokes of Chinese characters, the problem of character recognition is more complicated than in the first test, the result of the accuracy and coverage rate is the same, this is the major advantage of this method, so the research has some practical application value.

References

1. Su, S.H.: Research on image recognition technology based on vehicle license plate. Softw. Eng. **12**, 57–58 (2015)
2. Gu, Y.W., Li, P., Tao, W.H., Tian, S.K.: Handwriting postal codes recognition based on improved BP neural network. J. LiaoNing Univ. Pet. Chem. Technol. **28**, 52–58 (2008)
3. Chen, R., Tang, Y.: Writer verification for Chinese handwritten document based on keywords extraction. J. Sichuan Univ. (Natural Science Edition) **50**, 719–727 (2013)
4. Meng, L.J., Wen, B., Zhang, X.C.: Research and design of print document recognition technology. Sci. Technol. Eng. **15**, 185–190 (2015)
5. Zhu, H.P.: Several key technical problems in web data capture. J. Ningbo Inst. Educ. **18**, 66–69 (2016)
6. Zhang, Y., Guo, Q., Wang, J.Y.: Big data analysis using neural networks. J. Sichuan Univ. (Engineering Science Edition) **49**, 9–18 (2017)
7. Qiu, Y.Q.: Large capacity lossless information hiding in images using integer transform. J. Image Graph. **19**, 28–35 (2014)
8. The MNIST database of handwritten digits. http://yann.lecun.com/exdb/mnist/
9. Institute of Automation, Chinese Academy of Sciences. http://www.nlpr.ia.ac.cn/databases/handwriting/Download.html

A Listwise Approach for Learning to Rank Based on Query Normalization Network

Chongchong Zhu, Fusheng Jin[✉], Yan Li, and Tu Peng

Beijing Institute of Technology, Beijing 100081, China
{2120151097, jfs21cn, pengtu}@bit.edu.cn,
liy_007@126.com

Abstract. Learning to rank is one of the hotspots in the intersection between information retrieval and machine learning. In the traditional listwise approach for learning to rank based on the neural network, the model predicts the score of each document independently, which cannot reflect the link between those documents associated with the same query. To solve the problem, this paper proposes a new ranking neural network model called Query Normalization Network (QNN). In QNN, normalization is added as a part of the original neural network model to perform the normalization operation for each query sample collection. Through this operation, the prediction scores of documents returned by the same query are also associated with each other. Then, this paper proposes a listwise approach called Optimizing Normalized Discounted Cumulative Gain (NDCG) Query Normalization Network (OptNDCGQNN) which based on QNN and directly optimize the evaluation measure NDCG. OptNDCGQNN use QNN as model and Stochastic Gradient Descent (SGD) as optimization algorithm to optimize an upper bound function of the original loss function, which directly defined according to the evaluation measure NDCG. Experimental results show that OptNDCGQNN has better ranking performance than other traditional ranking algorithms. It also show that when the amount of training data is large enough, OptNDCGQNN can enhance the ranking performance by training deep neural network.

Keywords: Learning to rank · Neural network · Query Normalization Network
Directly optimizing evaluation measure

1 Introduction

As a supporting technology of information retrieval, collaborative filtering and other applications whose major issues are ranking, learning to rank has gain more and more attention recently. According to the definition of loss function, learning to rank algorithms can be divided into three categories: pointwise approach, pairwise approach and listwise approach. The pointwise approach and pairwise approach cast the ranking problem as a classification or regression problem of single document or ordinal pairs of documents. The listwise approach takes individual lists as instances to train the ranking model, which is more in line with the nature of the ranking problem. Previous studies [1, 2] also show that listwise approach performs better in general than other approach.

© Springer Nature Singapore Pte Ltd. 2018
H. Yuan et al. (Eds.): GSKI 2017, CCIS 849, pp. 21–30, 2018.
https://doi.org/10.1007/978-981-13-0896-3_3

It is obvious that all the documents returned by the same query are associated with each other and have a sequential relationship, therefore the prediction scores of them should also be associated with each other. However, the previous listwise ranking methods [1, 2, 3] based on the neural network only take lists of objects to calculate the back propagation gradient, in the process of forward propagation to get the prediction scores still use separate document. Those algorithms ignore the link between documents associated with the same query in the process of forward propagation to get documents scores. In 2015, Google's paper [4] proposed a method to speed up the deep network training called Batch Normalization which normalizing the inputs of each node with mini batch of samples. It inspires us associating all the documents returned by the same query through normalizing the inputs of each node with lists of objects.

This paper first propose a novel ranking neural network model called Query Normalization Network (QNN). In QNN, a normalization operation is added to the inputs of each node on the non-input layer with each query sample collection. The normalization includes two steps: (1) Neuron calculates the z-score of all the input data in a query samples instead of the original input. (2) Add a linear transformation to the transformed data, and then activate the output with the activation function.

Through the two steps, the neurons in the network are transformed into neurons with normalization function, so that the scores predicted by the model of all the documents associated with same query are concatenated. Based on QNN, a listwise ranking algorithm is put forward which directly optimize the evaluation measure NDCG and we call it OptNDCGQNN. To solve the problem that the loss function defined by NDCG is not continuous and differentiable, an upper bound function of original loss function is defined as a surrogate loss function, then use QNN as model and SGD as method to optimize the surrogate function. Experiments show that OptNDCGQNN has better ranking effect than traditional learning to rank algorithms. We also conducted an experiment to verify that OptNDCGQNN can directly train deep network model to obtain better ranking performance when the training data is large.

2   Related Work

Listwise approach solves the ranking problem in a straightforward fashion and experimental results show that the listwise approach usually outperforms the pointwise and pairwise approaches. Existing listwise approach falls into two categories.

For the first sub-category, the loss function indicates the difference be-tween the predicted list and the ground truth list. Cao et al. [1] proposed the first listwise approach called ListNet. In ListNet, the loss function is defined as cross entropy between the probability distributions of predicted list permutation and the probability distributions of ground truth list permutations. Xia et al. [2] conducted theoretical analysis of the properties of different loss functions, including consistency, soundness, continuity, differentiability, convexity, and efficiency. Then they introduced a novel listwise method called ListMLE whose loss functions is likelihood loss.

For the second sub-category, the loss function is explicitly related to evaluation measures. Taliror et al. [5] proposed the SoftRank algorithm which introduces randomness to the ranking process by regarding the real score of a document as a random variable, whose mean is the score given by the scoring function, so that a document can have different probabilities to be ranked at any position. Qin et al. [3] pointed that the reason why the evaluation measures function is discontinuous is that the position function of the document is discontinuous, and proposed a method which using the continuous and differentiable approximation function to replace the non-derivative evaluation function. Xu and Li [6] pointed out that the evaluation measures can be directly embedded in the Boosting framework to optimize, without the need for their own continuity, and based on this they put forward the AdaRank algorithm. Valizadegan propose a probabilistic framework [7] to direct optimization of NDCG measures by optimizing the expectation of NDCG over all the possible permutations of documents, which has similar aim to our work.

3 The Query Normalization Network Model

Before introducing the technology, we take a brief description of the notation in learning to rank. Assume that we have a training sample collection of N queries, denoted by $Q = \{q^1, q^2, \ldots, q^N\}$. For each query q^k, it has a collection of m_k documents, denoted by $D_k = \{d_i^k, i = 1, 2, \ldots, m_k\}$, it also has a label collection of m_k document labels, denoted by $R_k = \{r_i^k, i = 1, 2, \ldots, m_k\}$. For query q^k, all query-document pair (d, q) generate a collection of query-document pair feature vectors $\{X_1, X_2, \ldots, X_{m_k}\}$. Then those vectors are used to get the prediction scores.

In the traditional listwise approach based on neural network, the query-document pair feature vector is used as the input of the neural network, forward propagate to output the score, then calculate the gradient at the output layer, finally use the BP algorithm to update the model parameters [1, 2]. Documents are independently used to calculating the scores. This approach ignores the link of all documents associated with the same query during forward propagation.

In order to solve the problem, this paper proposes a novel ranking neural network model called QNN. In QNN, we improve the neuron nodes on the non-input layers, giving them the ability of normalization to the sample inputs coming from the same query. Figure 1(a) shows how the node in traditional neural network handle multiple inputs coming from the upper layer and Fig. 1(b) shows how the node in QNN do. Suppose that query q has a contains n query-document pair feature vectors that need input to the network to calculate the scores, for a given node on the non-input layer in the network, the n inputs $\{x_1, x_2, \ldots, x_n\}$ from the previous layer are accepted, where each input is the weighted sum of all outputs on the previous layer. For the traditional neural network, the neuron processes each input independently, which activates by the activation function and output the result to the next layer. It can be seen that the final score for each query-document pair vector depends only on its own values and model parameters, and is not associated with other documents associated with the same query. However, the function of the neuron becomes more complicated in QNN. Figure 1(b) shows that the neuron adds a normalization operation to the data before passing the n inputs from the upper layer to the activation function and then add a linear transformation, the following we detail the two operations.

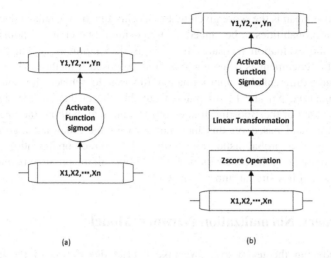

Fig. 1. (a) The node in traditional neural network; (b) The node in QNN

For n feature vectors associated with a certain query, there will be n inputs from the upper layer for each node of the non-input layer, assuming they are $\{x_1, x_2, \ldots, x_n\}$. The neuron will normalize the initial n inputs by calculating the z-score which mapping them to a set with an average of 0 and a variance of 1. The specific mapping formula is as follows:

$$\hat{x}_k = \frac{x_k - \mu_x}{\sqrt{\sigma_x^2}} \tag{1}$$

Where μ_x and σ_x^2 are the mean and variance of the input data of the neuron, respectively, and can be calculated by the following formula:

$$\mu_x = \frac{1}{n}\sum_{i=1}^{n} x_i \tag{2}$$

$$\sigma_x^2 = \frac{1}{n}\sum_{i=1}^{n} (x_i - \mu_x)^2 \tag{3}$$

The inputs of the neuron are mapped from $\{x_1, x_2, \ldots, x_n\}$ to $\{\hat{x}_1, \hat{x}_2, \ldots, \hat{x}_n\}$ by the above operation. This normalization operation on the node inputs reflects the link between all the documents associated with the same query and can accelerates the model convergence because the inputs of neuron become more normative. However, the normalization operation maps the input data to a set of data with 0 mean and unit variance, but the activation function in the neural network is generally the sigmoid function, if we directly input the normalized data into the activation function, we can only use the linear part of the activation function, which obviously reduces the expression ability of the model. Therefore, after doing the normalization with inputs, we adds a linear transformation operation before activating. The conversion formula is as follows:

$$y_k = \gamma \hat{x}_k + \beta \tag{4}$$

where the two parameters, γ and β, are two variable parameters in the neuron, which can be obtained by learning with the training data. It can be seen that the original input can be reproduced when the two parameters γ and β are μ_x and σ_x respectively. The prediction score of each document by the QNN is no longer independent of the input vector and model parameters, but is associated with other documents associated with the same query.

After determining the network structure, the following gives how to train the model. Since QNN is an improved network model for listwise ranking methods, we can use a variety of listwise loss functions that can be trained by the neural network. So in this section we only discuss how to update the model parameters and we discuss how to calculate the output layer gradient in the next section. Since the normalization operation and the linear transformation operation are all still basic function transforming, the parameters in the network are still differentiable, so we can use the chain derivation rule to calculate the gradient of the loss function to each parameter in the model, and then update the network parameters with their gradients. Assuming that the loss function is defined as l and the stochastic query training sample has n feature vectors, for each neuron, we can back propagate the gradient of loss l as follow:

$$\frac{\partial l}{\partial \hat{x}_i} = \frac{\partial l}{\partial y_i} \cdot \gamma \tag{5}$$

$$\frac{\partial l}{\partial \sigma_x^2} = \sum_{i=1}^{n} \frac{\partial l}{\partial \hat{x}_i} \cdot (x_i - \mu_x) \cdot \frac{-1}{2} \cdot \left(\sigma_x^2 + \epsilon\right)^{-3/2} \tag{6}$$

$$\frac{\partial l}{\partial \mu_x} = \left(\sum_{i=1}^{n} \frac{\partial l}{\partial \hat{x}_i} \cdot \frac{-1}{\sqrt{\sigma_x^2 + \epsilon}}\right) + \frac{\partial l}{\partial \sigma_x^2} \cdot \frac{\sum_{i=1}^{n} -2(x_i - \mu_x)}{n} \tag{7}$$

$$\frac{\partial l}{\partial x_i} = \frac{\partial l}{\partial \hat{x}_i} \cdot \frac{1}{\sqrt{\sigma_x^2 + \epsilon}} + \frac{\partial l}{\partial \sigma_x^2} \cdot \frac{2(x_i - \mu_x)}{n} + \frac{1}{n} \frac{\partial l}{\partial \mu_x} \tag{8}$$

$$\frac{\partial l}{\partial \gamma} = \sum_{i=1}^{n} \frac{\partial l}{\partial y_i} \cdot \hat{x}_i \tag{9}$$

$$\frac{\partial l}{\partial \beta} = \sum_{i=1}^{n} \frac{\partial l}{\partial y_i} \tag{10}$$

For the neuron in the output layer, $\partial l / \partial y_i$ is solved directly by the loss function and the prediction scores. For the gradient of parameters in the hidden layers in the network, we use the BP algorithm to back propagate the gradient.

For model prediction, it is only necessary to input all the document vectors associated with the same query into the trained ranking network and get the prediction scores for each document, then rank the document according to the prediction score of each document.

4 A Listwise Approach of Directly Optimizing Measure NDCG

NDCG is the most popular evaluation measure in the learning to rank study. The NDCG value of the previous k position is defined as follows:

$$NDCG@k = N_K^{-1} \sum\nolimits_{j=1}^{k} \frac{2^{r_j} - 1}{log_2(1+j)} \tag{11}$$

where r_j is the labeled level of the jth document in the ranked list, N_K^{-1} is the normalization factor, which represents the DCG value of ideal ranked list, so that NDCG@k is always a number between 0 and 1. If we consider all the documents associated with a query, assuming there are n documents in that query, we can get the NDCG by

$$NDCG = NDCG@n = N_n^{-1} \sum\nolimits_{j=1}^{n} \frac{2^{r_j} - 1}{log_2(1+j)} \tag{12}$$

In order to associate the NDCG and the final prediction score for each document, we can write the NDCG formula as follows:

$$NDCD = N_n^{-1} \sum_{x \in X} \frac{2^{r_x} - 1}{log_2(1 + \pi(x))} \tag{13}$$

where X is the set of documents in the query, and the position function $\pi(x)$ represents the position of the document x given by the model, defined as follows:

$$\pi(x) = 1 + \sum_{y \in X, y \neq x} 1\{s_x - s_y < 0\} \tag{14}$$

In formula (14), s_x and s_y represent the prediction scores for document x and document y by the ranking model, respectively. $1\{A\}$ is a discriminant function, output 1 when A is true, and 0 when A is false. When document x has the highest score, $\pi(x) = 1$; When document x has the lowest time score, $\pi(x) = n$; Thus, formula (13) and formula (14) are equivalent.

We can define the loss function directly related to NDCG measures on query q_i as follows:

$$L(q_i) = 1 - N_n^{-1} \sum_{x \in X} \frac{2^{r_x} - 1}{log_2(1 + \pi(x))} \tag{15}$$

It is possible to achieve the purpose of maximizing the evaluation measures NDCG by minimizing $L(q_i)$. However, the position function $\pi(x)$ is a discontinuous function, so the loss function $L(q_i)$ is also a discontinuous function. We cannot directly use the QNN to optimize it. For the discontinuous function, it can be optimized by optimizing its approximate function or boundary function. Qin [3] proposed a method which using the sigmoid function to approximate the 0–1 recognition function. Wang [8] proposed a method which optimize the bound function of NDCG to aggregate multiple rank sub model. In this paper, we minimize the $L(q_i)$ function by finding a surrogate function which is an upper bound function of the original function and is optimizable by neural network.

For an arbitrary x, the inequality $e^{-x} > 1\{x < 0\}$ is always established. So we can find an upper bound function $\bar{\pi}(x)$ of the position function $\pi(x)$ according to the inequality mentioned above.

$$\bar{\pi}(x) = 1 + \sum_{y \in X, y \neq x} e^{s_y - s_x} \tag{16}$$

It is obvious that $\bar{\pi}(x)$ is always greater than $\pi(x)$. Replacing $\pi(x)$ in $L(q_i)$ with $\bar{\pi}(x)$, we can get an upper bound function of $L(q_i)$ function, denoted $\bar{L}(q_i)$, in the form of:

$$\bar{L}(q_i) = 1 - N_n^{-1} \sum_{x \in X} \frac{2^{r_x} - 1}{log_2(1 + \bar{\pi}(x))} = 1 - N_n^{-1} \sum_{x \in X} \frac{2^{r_x} - 1}{log_2\left(2 + \sum_{y \in X, y \neq x} e^{s_y - s_x}\right)} \tag{17}$$

$\bar{L}(q_i)$ is a continuously differentiable function, and we can achieve the purpose of optimizing the original function $L(q_i)$ by minimizing the value of it.

After completing the definition of the objective function, we use the QNN as model and SGD as algorithm to minimize the surrogate loss function $\bar{L}(q_i)$. We call this ranking algorithm OptNDCGQNN. For the node in the output layer, we can get the gradient of y_i by formula (18).

$$\frac{\partial \bar{L}}{\partial y_i} = N_n^{-1} \sum_{x \in X} \frac{\partial \frac{2^{r_x} - 1}{log_2(1 + \bar{\pi}(x))}}{\partial \bar{\pi}(x)} \cdot \frac{\partial \bar{\pi}(x)}{\partial s_i} \cdot \frac{\partial s_i}{\partial y_i} \tag{18}$$

where

$$\frac{\partial \bar{\pi}(x)}{\partial s_i} = \sum_{y \in X, y \neq x} -e^{-s_{xy}} \cdot \frac{\partial s_{xy}}{\partial s_i} \tag{19}$$

For the neurons in the hidden layers, the gradient of y_i can be calculated by accumulating the back propagation error of all nodes in the upper layer. It is similar to the BP algorithm but only the process of the derivation in each node is different. This paper has explained how to derive in each node in the third section.

5 Experimental Results and Analysis

5.1 Experimental Design

We selected two benchmark datasets from the LETOR [9] to conduct experiments. One is OHSUMED which includes 63 queries, and the other is MSLR-WEB10K which includes 10000 queries. We conduct experiment on OHSUMED to verify the OptNDCGQNN algorithm has the better ranking performance than other traditional ranking methods. In the large dataset MSLR-WEB10K, we will verify that the OptNDCGQNN algorithm can train deep network model without other auxiliary algorithm and achieve better ranking effect.

For each experiment, we used the data split provided in LETOR to conduct five-fold cross validation experiments. The model with the highest NDCG@10 on validate set is taken as the final model to test on the test set.

In the first experiment, the network has 4 hidden layers and the nodes of each layer are 45, 50, 60, 50, 40, 1. The initial learning rate is set to 0.01, when the error on the validation set increases, we lower the learning rate to a multiple of 0.8, and control the minimum learning rate of 0.00001. The max number of iterations is set to 200 times and we set the dropout rate 0.5. We choose Mean Average Precision (MAP), NDCG@1, NDCG@5, NDCG@10, Precision(P)@1, P@5, P@10 as the evaluation measures.

In the second experiment, the network models with hidden layers 0, 2, 4 are selected, and the number of nodes per layer is as follows: {136, 1}, {136, 100, 50, 1}, {136, 100, 100, 60, 20, 1}. In the experiment, the learning rate is initially set to 0.01, and if the error on validate set on this iteration is greater than the last iteration, lower the learning rate to a multiple of 0.8 and keep the lowest learning rate is 0.00001. The default number of iterations is 500. We also use the two parameters dropout rates and L2 regularization in the model to prevent over-fitting.

5.2 Analysis of Experimental Results

The first experimental results are shown in Table 1. The ranking performance of the different ranking algorithms on OHSUMED are given in the table. We choose 10 kinds of classical ranking algorithms as the benchmark algorithms, which covers the three categories of ranking algorithms. Among them, RankAgg.NDCG is a ranking aggregation algorithm proposed by Wang et al. [8].

We marked the best result in each evaluation measure with bold in Table 1. According to the experimental result in the table, it can be concluded that the OptNDCGQNN has excellent ranking performance in all measures, which also reflects the significance of this algorithm proposed in this paper.

In the experiment to verify the expansibility of OptNDCGQNN in the depth of the network, we experiment with different depth network structure on MSLR-WEB10K

Table 1. The ranking performance comparison on OHSUMED

Algorithms	MAP	N@1	N@5	N@10	P@1	P@5	P@10
BM25	0.4263	0.4088	0.3984	0.3985	0.5283	0.5208	0.4755
Regression	0.4220	0.4456	0.4278	0.4110	0.5965	0.5337	0.4666
RankSVM	0.4334	0.4958	0.4164	0.4140	0.5974	0.5319	0.4864
RankBoost	0.4411	0.4632	0.4494	0.4302	0.5576	0.5447	0.4966
Frank	0.4439	0.5300	0.4588	0.4433	0.6429	0.5638	0.5016
ListNet	0.4457	0.5326	0.4432	0.4410	0.6524	0.5502	0.4975
AdaRank-MAP	0.4487	0.5388	0.4613	0.4429	0.6338	0.5674	0.4967
AdaRank-NDCG	0.4498	0.5330	0.4673	0.4496	0.6719	0.5767	0.5087
SVMMAP	0.4453	0.5229	0.4516	0.4319	0.6433	0.5523	0.4910
RankAgg-NDCG	0.4498	0.5867	0.4826	0.4606	0.6883	0.5759	0.5152
OptNDCGQNN	**0.4607**	**0.5936**	**0.5105**	**0.4723**	**0.7333**	**0.6286**	**0.5419**

dataset and the experimental result is shown Fig. 2. According to the trend of the folding lines in Fig. 2, it can be seen that OptNDCGQNN can continue the training of the model when the depth of the network model increases without any other auxiliary algorithms and can get better ranking performance with the increasing of the number of hidden layers. In theory, we can increase the number of hidden layers to improve the ranking effect, but with the depth of the model increases, it is easy to encounter the over-fitting problem if the training data is small. Thus a complicated model is better suited for large data, it is why we conducted this experiment with a large-scale dataset.

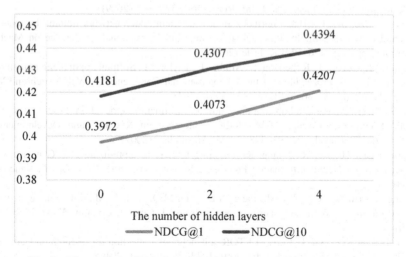

Fig. 2. The ranking effect of OptNDCGQNN with different hidden layers

6 Conclusion

This paper proposes a ranking neural network for learning to rank called Query Normalization Network (QNN). Then, based on this network model, this paper proposes a listwise approach called OptNDCGQNN which directly optimizes the measure NDCG. In OptNDCGQNN, an upper bound function of the original loss function defined according to NDCG is used as surrogate loss function, then use the QNN as model and SGD as algorithm to minimize the surrogate function to achieve the purpose of maximizing the evaluation measure NDCG. The experiments on OHSUMED show OptNDCGQNN has the better performance than the other algorithms. Finally, we verified that the OptNDCGQNN algorithm can train the depth network to achieve better ranking effect on dataset MSLR-WEB10K. The QNN can also be used for other listwise approaches whose loss functions are defined by ranking list, and more application attempts can be made in the future.

References

1. Cao, Z., Qin, T., Liu, T.Y., Tsai, M.F., Li, H.: Learning to rank: from pairwise approach to listwise approach. In: Proceedings of the 24th International Conference on Machine Learning, pp. 129–136. ACM, Corvallis (2007)
2. Xia, F., Liu, T.Y., Wang, J., Zhang, W., Li, H.: Listwise approach to learning to rank-theorem and algorithm. In: Proceedings of the 25th International Conference on Machine Learning, pp. 1192–1199. DBLP, Helsinki (2008)
3. Qin, T., Liu, T.Y., Li, H.: A general approximation framework for direct optimization of information retrieval measures. J. Inf. Retr. **13**(4), 375–397 (2009)
4. Ioffe, S., Szegedy, C.: Batch normalization: accelerating deep network training by reducing internal covariate shift. In: Proceedings of the 32nd International Conference on Machine Learning, pp. 448–456. PMLR, Lille (2015)
5. Taylor, M., Guiver, J., Robertson, S., Minka, T., Taylor, M.: Softrank: optimising non-smooth rank metrics. In: Proceedings of the 1st International Conference on Web Search and Web Data Mining, pp. 77–86. WSDM, New York (2008)
6. Xu, J., Li, H.: Adarank: a boosting algorithm for information retrieval. In: Proceedings of the 30th Annual International ACM SIGIR Conference on Research and Development in Information Retrieval, pp. 391–398. ACM, Amsterdam (2007)
7. Valizadegan, H., Jin, R., Zhang, R.: Learning to rank by optimizing NDCG measure. In: Conference on Neural Information Processing Systems, pp. 1883–1891. DBLP, Vancouver (2009)
8. Wang, Y., Huang, Y.L., Lu, M., Pang, X.D., Xie, M.Q., Liu, J.: Multiple rank aggregation based on directly optimizing performance measure. J. Chin. J. Comput. **37**(8), 1658–1668 (2014)
9. Qin, T., Liu, T.Y., Xu, J., Li, H.: LETOR: a benchmark collection for research on learning to rank for information retrieval. J. Inf. Retr. J. **13**(4), 346–374 (2010)

Soft Frequency Reuse Scheme with Maximum Energy Efficiency in Power Telecommunication Networks

Lina Cao[1(✉)], Daosheng Li[2], Fei Xia[3], Xiaobo Huang[3], Siwen Zhao[4], and Shuang Liu[2]

[1] State Grid Liaoning Electric Power Company Limited,
Shenyang 110006, China
merry_99@sina.com
[2] Liaoning Planning and Designing Institute of Post and Telecommunication
Company Limited, Shenyang 110011, China
[3] State Grid Liaoyang Electric Power Supply Company,
Liaoyang 111000, China
[4] China Resources Power Investment Co., Ltd.,
Northeast Branch, Shenyang 110043, China

Abstract. This paper, we investigates the energy efficiency optimization problem in SFR-based cellular networks. To the end, we uses divide-and-conquer method to improve network energy efficiency. We build an optimization model with an objective function denoting energy efficiency of networks, which is a fractional program and very hard to be solved directly. To solve the model, we transform the objective function into another form. Then we utilize the Lagrange function and dual function to obtain the optimal energy efficiency with the gradient method updating the transmitting power allocation. Finally, we make a numerical simulation to validate the algorithm proposed. The simulation results show that the performance of our method is feasible.

Keywords: Soft frequency reuse · Inter-cell interference · Energy efficiency
Lagrange dual function · Optimization

1 Introduction

With fast development of mobile communication technologies, network traffic shows many new features [1–3]. However, the wireless spectrum is very limited. The frequency reuse factor (FRF) is used to reflect the frequency reuse efficiency, when reuse factor is 1, it means that the frequency efficiency is 1; when the reuse factor is 3, it means the frequency efficiency is 1/3. In order to increase the frequency efficiency, we try to make the reuse factor to 1, but there will cause more inter-cell interference (ICI) from adjacent cells on the same frequency especially for cell-edge users and increase the energy consumption. Fractional frequency reuse (FFR) and soft frequency reuse (SFR) are two kinds of inter-cell interference coordinate method which could improve spectrum efficiency and decrease energy consumption by setting different

© Springer Nature Singapore Pte Ltd. 2018
H. Yuan et al. (Eds.): GSKI 2017, CCIS 849, pp. 31–42, 2018.
https://doi.org/10.1007/978-981-13-0896-3_4

transmitting power levels [4–7]. Energy efficiency has been another more important problem. The energy-efficient SFR have become a hot topic [8–10].

Jiang et al. [4] used the sleeping scheme to obtain green cooperative multicast networking. Mahmud et al. [5] evaluated the energy efficiency in bits/J and energy efficiency per channel per cell in bits/J/Hz/cell for both the static FFR and SFR systems. Zappone et al. [6] researched the energy efficiency optimization with a fractional program method. Xie et al. [7] jointly analyzed the area spectral efficiency and area energy efficiency in a wireless heterogeneous network with inter-tier FFR. Jiang et al. [8, 10] studied channel allocation and energy-efficient multicasting in wireless networks. They also studied energy-efficient multi-constraint routing method to smart city applications [11]. Han et al. [12] used Game theory to obtain the energy-efficient optimization in cognitive radio networks. Lahoud et al. [13] studied the energy-efficient joint scheduling and power control problem in cell networks.

This paper investigates the energy efficiency optimization in SFR-based cellular network with divide-and-conquer method. Firstly, we talk about the assumption of the SFR-based cellular network scenarios. Secondly, we formulate an objective function with the energy efficiency optimization, but the objective function is a fractional program which is very hard to be solved directly. Thirdly, we transform the objective function into another form, and utilize the Lagrange function and dual function to obtain the optimal energy efficiency, then with the gradient method to update transmitting power allocation until reached the optimal energy efficiency in single-cell. For the multi-cell scenarios, we extend the single-cell EE optimization method, and make it suitable for multi-cell scenario. At last, we make a numerical simulation to validate the algorithm proposed. The simulation results suggest that the performance of our method is better than the greedy energy efficiency maximum method. This indicates that our approach is effective and feasible.

2 Problem Statement

Soft frequency reuse is an effective scheme to coordinate the inter-cell interference. In wireless network, the frequency, time, space are the physical resource block (PRB). The power control is the core for each BS which affects energy efficiency and inter-cell interference, then we will talk about the transmitting power allocation and PRB allocation scheme for coordinating interference and optimizing energy efficiency.

2.1 Basic Assumptions

The frequency allocation and cell division for SFR scheme is shown in Fig. 1.

(1) *Cells and Users*: We use term i donates the BS, there are total I regular hexagon cells which wrapped each other in the cellular network, and each cell is divided into two parts with the inner radius, e.g. cell edge and cell center, as Fig. 1(a) shows. We use term m donates the user, and there are M users which are uniformly randomly distributed in each cell. All the users in each cell is parted into two

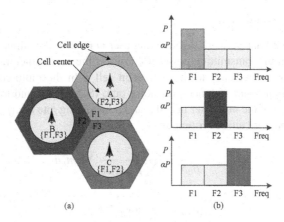

Fig. 1. Frequency allocation for SFR.

categories by the inner radius, e.g. cell-edge users (Ue) who at the cell-edge region and cell-central users (Uc) who at the cell-center region.

(2) *Bandwidth and Sub-carriers*: The bandwidth is B MHz and is divided into N sub-channels. For the SFR scheme, the carriers are assigned as two categories by the transmission power levels, e.g. the major and minor sub-carriers;

(3) *Channel assignment rule*: the major sub-carriers are mainly used to serve cell-edge users and the minor sub-carriers mainly used by the cell-central users. A cell-edge user may be blocked or denied access if there are no more available major sub-carriers in the current cells; and a cell-central users may be blocked when there aren't other major or minor sub-carriers to be allocated. A PRB can be only allocated to one user, and other users cannot share the PRB which have been allocated.

(4) *Transmitting powers allocation rule*: the SFR scheme is proposed to coordinate inter-cell interference through control the transmitting power on the same carriers. To reuse the same set of PRBs and achieve a frequency reuse factor close to one, the SFR scheme assigns different carriers as the major carriers between adjacent cells, and specifies that major and minor carriers use different transmitting power, as Fig. 1 shows. Carrier F1 in cell A is major carriers, but that in its adjacent cells B and C is minor carriers; carriers in other cells are similar. For major carriers, they are mainly used to serve cell-edge users, so those available transmitting power range is higher than the minor carriers, but no more than P, and the minor carriers available transmitting power range is no more than αP, where $0 \leq \alpha \leq 1$, as Fig. 1 (b) shows.

(5) *Channel gain*: The channel gain are mainly used to describe the power received by users from BS. Users can receive transmitting power from its associated BS or the neighboring BSs on the same frequency. We use term g_{imn} donate the channel gain of user m received power from BS i on sub-channel n, it's the channel gain of useful signal; the term g_{jmn} donate the channel gain of user m received power from neighboring BS j on sub-channel n, it's the channel gain of interference signal.

2.2 Problem Formulation

In the downlink cellular network, assume that user m receive downlink data from cell i on channel n with the transmitting power p_{imn}. p_{jmn} is the co-channel transmit power of the BS j who has interference to the user m in cell i. In the multi-cell network, the instantaneous signal-to-interference-plus-noise ratio (SINR) γ_{imn} and total transmitting rate $R_{im}(a_{imn}, p_{imn})$ of the m-th user in cell i, and transmitting rate $r_{imn}(p_{imn})$ for the m-th user on sub-channel n can be written as

$$\gamma_{imn} = \frac{p_{imn}g_{imn}}{B_0 N_0 + \sum_{j \neq i} p_{jmn}g_{jmn}}, \forall i, m, n \tag{1}$$

$$r_{imn}(p_{imn}) = B_0 \log_2(1 + \gamma_{imn}) \tag{2}$$

$$R_{im}(a_{imn}, p_{imn}) = \sum_{n=1}^{N} a_{imn} r_{imn}(p_{imn}) \tag{3}$$

where B_0 is the sub-channel bandwidth and N_0 is the power spectral density of the additive Gaussian white noise with zero mean and unit variation; a_{imn} is the sub-channel allocation indicator and can only be 1 which means allocate to user m or 0 is.

The total power consumption of BS i and its Energy-Efficiency (EE) are

$$P_i(a_{imn}, p_{imn}) = \sum_{m=1}^{M} \sum_{n=1}^{N} a_{imn} p_{imn} + Pc_i \tag{4}$$

$$\eta_i = \frac{R_i(a, p)}{P_i(a, p)} \tag{5}$$

where Pc_i is the circuit power consumption of BS i; EE η_i is defined as ratio of the summary transmitting rate to the total power consumption of BS i.

The below optimization model for EE is obtained:

$$\max \eta_i \tag{6}$$

$$\text{s.t.} \sum_{n=1}^{N} a_{imn} \leq 1, a_{imn} \in \{0, 1\}, \forall i, m, n \tag{6a}$$

$$\sum_{n=1}^{N} a_{imn} R_{imn} \geq R_{\min}, \forall m, i \tag{6b}$$

$$\sum_{m=1}^{M} \sum_{n=1}^{N} a_{imn} p_{imn} \leq P_{\max}, \forall i \tag{6c}$$

$$p_{imnc} \leq \alpha P, \forall i, m \in \{Uc_i\}, 0 \leq \alpha \leq 1 \tag{6d}$$

$$p_{imne} \leq P, \forall i, m \in \{Ue_i\} \tag{6e}$$

$$p_{imn} \geq 0, \forall i, m, n \tag{6f}$$

The process of solving the objective function in (6) is to find the optimal resource allocation scheme.

3   Sub-channel and Power Allocation Algorithm

Because the objectives function in (6) is a non-linear fractional program. Based on the non-linear fractional programming theory, we transform it as a difference program.

Theorem 1. We assume that η_i^* is the optimal energy efficiency, then it is the feasible solution of the objective function in (6) and satisfies the constraints in (6a), (6b), (6c), (6d), (6e) and (6f), so the equation $R_i(a_i^*, p_i^*) - \eta_i^* P(a_i^*, p_i^*) = 0$ is true, where a_i^* and p_i^* is the optimal PRB and transmitting power allocation scheme.

The optimal energy efficiency η_i^* is difficult to be obtained directly. We can use the heuristic algorithm to obtain the optimal solution. Based on the optimal energy efficiency in Theorem 1, we reformulate the objective function in (6) as

$$\max_{\{a_i, p_i\}} F(a_i, p_i) = R_i(a_i, p_i) - \eta_i P(a_i, p_i) \tag{7}$$

which is subject to constrains in (6a), (6b), (6c), (6d), (6e) and (6f).

For the objective in (7), when the variable η_i is fixed, it is a convex function and with constraints. Then we transform it as a Lagrange function.

$$L(a_i, p_i, \beta, \mu, \lambda) = R_i(a_i, p_i) - \eta_i P(a_i, p_i) + \sum_{m=1}^{M} \beta_i (\sum_{n=1}^{N} a_{imn} R_{imn}(a_i, p_i) - R_{min})$$

$$+ \mu(P_{max} - \sum_{m=1}^{M} \sum_{n=1}^{N} a_{imn} p_{imn}) + \sum_{n=1}^{N} (\lambda_{ie}(P - p_{imne}) + \lambda_{ic}(\alpha P - p_{imnc})) \tag{8}$$

where β, μ and λ are both the Lagrange-multiplier vector associated with the constraints and satisfy $\beta \geq 0$, $\mu \geq 0$ and $\lambda \geq 0$. For the Lagrange function in (8), its dual function can be expressed as

$$\min_{\{\beta, \mu, \lambda\}} g(\beta, \mu, \lambda) = \min \max_{\{a_i, p_i\}} L(a_i, p_i, \beta, \mu, \lambda) \tag{9}$$

The Lagrange function is a linear convex function, while its dual function is a convex function. Then we use the dual decomposition method to solve this dual problem, because of the primal Lagrange function is convex, the gap between the primal function and its dual function is zero, so the solution of the dual problem is also the solution of the primal problem. For the integer variable a_{imn}, we can use the Hungarian algorithm or Table matching algorithm to allocate PRB for each user. The variable can be regarded as $a_{imn} = 1$ and the Lagrange dual function can be written as

$$\min_{\{\beta,\mu,\lambda\}} g(\beta,\mu,\lambda) = \min \max_{\{p_i\}} L(p_i,\beta,\mu,\lambda) \tag{10}$$

Then the KKT conditions for the Lagrange dual function can be written as

$$\frac{\partial L(p_i)}{p_i} = 0 \tag{11}$$

$$\beta_i \left(\sum_{n=1}^{N} R_{imn} - R_{\min} \right) = 0 \tag{12}$$

$$\mu \left(P_{\max} - \sum_{m=1}^{M} \sum_{n=1}^{N} p_{imn} \right) = 0 \tag{13}$$

$$\lambda_{ie}(P - p_{imne}) = 0 \tag{14}$$

$$\lambda_{ic}(\alpha P - p_{imnc}) = 0 \tag{15}$$

According to (11), the optimal power allocation can be formulated as

$$p_{imne} = \left[\frac{(1+\beta_i)}{(\eta_i + \mu + \lambda_{ie})} - \frac{\sigma^2 + I}{g_{imne}} \right]^+ \tag{16}$$

$$p_{imnc} = \left[\frac{(1+\beta_i)}{(\eta_i + \mu + \lambda_{ic})} - \frac{\sigma^2 + I}{g_{imnc}} \right]^+ \tag{17}$$

where $[x]^+ = \max(0,x)$, p_{imne} and p_{imnc} are the optimal power allocation for edge users and central users respectively. Then, the gradient method can be utilized to solve the dual problem, and the changing gradient can be written as

$$\nabla \beta_i = \sum_{n=1}^{N} R_{imn} - R_{\min}, \forall i,m \tag{18}$$

$$\nabla \mu = P_{\max} - \sum_{m=1}^{M} \sum_{n=1}^{N} p_{imn}, \forall i \tag{19}$$

$$\nabla \lambda_{ie} = P - p_{imne}, \forall i, m \in \{Ue_i\} \tag{20}$$

$$\nabla \lambda_{ic} = \alpha P - p_{imnc} \forall i, m \in \{Uc_i\} \tag{21}$$

In order to optimal the energy efficiency in the cellular network with adaptive SFR algorithm, we can utilize the divide-and-conquer method to find the optimal energy efficiency for each SFR-cell. We describe the optimal PRB and transmitting power allocation for a single cell, and apply this algorithm into the multi-cell scenarios.

3.1 Single Cell Scenario

(1) Initialization: In the SFR-cell, we first need to classify the users with the inner-radius or the channel gain, and assign subcarriers for each user; we also need to allocate the transmitting power for each user.

(2) Adjustment: Based the current sub-carriers assignment and transmitting power allocation, adjust the sub-carriers for users, using gradient method to update the transmitting powert. The algorithm for the single-cell as the Table 1.

Table 1. The EE optimization algorithm in single-cell scenario

Algorithm 1. Single cell EE optimization algorithm	
1	Initialize the maximum tolerance ε, and the maximum number of iterations N, the energy efficiency $\eta = 0$.
2	Initialize the users' type based on inner radius or channel gain and the channel assignment.
3	for $i = 1 : N$
4	Solve the transmitting power allocation using (16)-(17) and the gradient elements (18)-(21), then adjust the channel assignment with table matching method.
5	Obtain a_i, p_i and $R_i(a_i, p_i)$, $P(a_i, p_i)$
6	if $\left\| \dfrac{R_i(a_i, p_i)}{P(a_i, p_i)} - \eta \right\| < \varepsilon$
7	break;
8	else
9	$\eta = \dfrac{R_i(a_i, p_i)}{P(a_i, p_i)}$
10	end if
11	end for

3.2 Multi Cell Scenario

In the multi-cell scenario, there are many SFR-cells in the network, then we can divide the multi-cell resource allocation problem into several single-cell resource allocation problems, for each cell, it obtains the inter-cell interference from its adjacent cells, so its optimal energy efficiency affects by the resource allocation of its adjacent cells, we can utilize the iterative method for all the cells, after some iterations, the approximate optimization points for each cell could be found.

In the process of energy efficiency optimization, we should allocate carriers for each cells, the major carriers which allocated for cell edge users in the adjacent cells is orthogonal. Then, we use the single-cell algorithm for each SFR-based cell. Then the multi-cell scenario algorithm is shown in Table 2.

Table 2. The EE optimization algorithm in multi cells scenario

	Algorithm 2. multi-cell EE optimization algorithm
1	Initialize the maximum tolerance ε, and the maximum number of iterations N, the energy efficiency for each cell $\eta_i = 0$, the number of cells C.
2	Allocate the major and minor carriers for each cell;
3	Initialize the users' type based on inner radius or channel gain and the channel assignment.
4	for $t = 1:N$
5	for i=1:C
6	Obtain the transmitting power allocation using (16)- (17) and the channel assignment (The detailed procedure is similar with Algorithm 1)
7	Obtain a_i, p_i and $R_i(a_i, p_i)$, $P(a_i, p_i)$
8	end for
9	if $\left\| \dfrac{R_i(a_i,p_i)}{P_i(a_i,p_i)} - \eta_i^{t-1} \right\| \le \varepsilon$
10	break;
11	else
12	$\eta_i^t = \dfrac{R_i(a_i,p_i)}{P(a_i,p_i)}$
13	end if
14	end for

4   Simulation Result and Analysis

To validate the EE optimization algorithm, we make a numerical simulation. We consider a cellular network based on SFR with 19 wrap-around cells. The system bandwidth is 10 MHz and each sub-channel bandwidth is 180 kHz. In each cells, there are 20 users which uniformly randomly distributed. The minimum data transmitting rate of each edge and central user is 500 Kbps which is referred to 3GPP standard [16]. The simulation environment parameters is shown in Table 3.

Figure 2 shows the energy efficiency for cell1 to cell 7, we note that after 13 iterations, the energy efficiency for each cell is convergence, the other cells have the same trend. The energy efficiency fluctuation at the front iteration process, it mainly caused by the initial state and the energy efficiency adjustment with the divide-and-conquer method. Figure 3 shows the energy power consumption in the process of energy efficiency adjustment, with the energy efficiency increasing, the total power for each cell decreased. At the same process, each cell adjust its inter-cell interference to enhance the energy efficiency for each cell.

Table 3. Simulation environment parameters

Parameters	Value	Parameters	Value
Maximum transmit power	40 W	Thermal noise power	−174 dBm/Hz
Circuit power consumption	20 W	Coverage radius	1 km
Sub-channel bandwidth	180 kHz	Inner radius	0.7 km
System bandwidth	10 MHz	Path loss model	$148.53 + 38 * \log_{10}(d)$ [17]

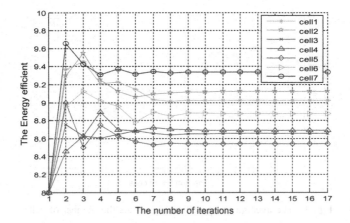

Fig. 2. The energy efficiency for each cell versus the number of iterations.

Figure 4 shows the average energy efficiency and the number of cells. When the number of cells increasing, there are more interference in the network, so the energy efficiency is decreasing. And we also make the comparison with the Single-cell energy efficiency optimization algorithm (ScEEO), the Fig. 4 shows that the divide-and-conquer method (DCM) has a better performance than the SoEEO algorithm about the energy efficiency. We believe that in process of transmitting power allocation of DCM, the each cell changes its transmitting power with the channel state and make a coordinate with its neighboring cells. Figure 5 shows the average transmitting power consumption of DCM and ScEEO. We note that average transmitting power consumption both of DCM and ScEEO algorithm are convergence, and DCM consume less energy than the ScEEO algorithm.

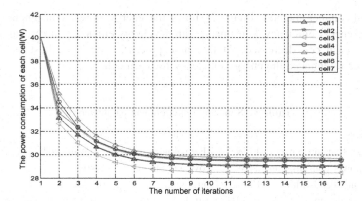

Fig. 3. The power consumption of each cell versus the number of iterations.

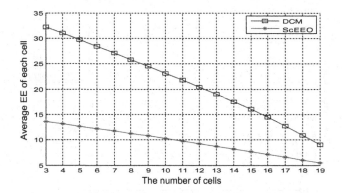

Fig. 4. The average energy efficiency versus the number of cells

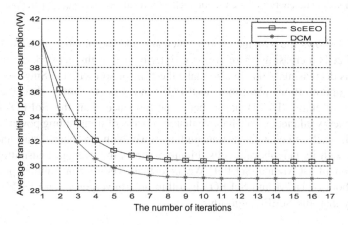

Fig. 5. The average transmitting power consumption versus number of iterations

5 Conclusions

Inter-cell Interference coordinate and energy efficiency optimization are very important for the wireless network. For the SFR scheme, it can coordinate the inter-cell interference effectively, then we have studied the energy efficiency optimization performance for the SFR scheme with the divide-and-conquer method for the distributed cellular network. We formulate an objective with the energy efficiency optimization, then with the Lagrange function and dual function to obtain the optimal energy efficiency, and we also use the gradient method to update transmitting power allocation until reached the optimal energy efficiency in single-cell. For the multi-cell scenario, we extend the single-cell EE optimization method, and make it suitable for multi-cell scenario. At last, we make a numerical simulation to validate the algorithm proposed. The results show that its performance is better than the greedy energy efficiency maximum method.

References

1. Jiang, D., Xu, Z., Chen, Z., et al.: Joint time-frequency sparse estimation of large-scale network traffic. Comput. Netw. **55**(10), 3533–3547 (2011)
2. Jiang, D., Xu, Z., Xu, H.: A novel hybrid prediction algorithm to network traffic. Ann. Telecommun. **70**(9), 427–439 (2015)
3. Novlan, T., Andrews, J.G., Sohn, I., Ganti, R.K.: Comparison of fractional frequency reuse approaches in the OFDMA cellular downlink. In: Global Telecommunications Conference, pp. 1–5. IEEE (2010)
4. Jiang, D., Li, W., Lv, H.: An energy-efficient cooperative multicast routing in multi-hop wireless networks for smart medical applications. Neurocomputing **220**, 160–169 (2017)
5. Mahmud, A., Lin, Z., Hamdi, K.A.: On the energy efficiency of fractional frequency reuse techniques. In: Wireless Communications and Networking Conference, pp. 2348–2353. IEEE (2014)
6. Zappone, A., Jorswieck, E.A.: Energy-efficient resource allocation in future wireless networks by sequential fractional programming. Digit. Signal Process. **60**, 324–337 (2017)
7. Xie, B., Zhang, Z., Hu, R., Wu, G., Papathanassiou, A.: Joint spectral efficiency and energy efficiency in FFR based wireless heterogeneous networks. IEEE Trans. Veh. Technol., 1 (2017)
8. Jiang, D., Wang, Y., Han, Y., et al.: Maximum connectivity-based channel allocation algorithm in cognitive wireless networks for medical applications. Neurocomputing **220**, 41–51 (2017)
9. Yassin, M., Lahoud, S., Khawam, K., Ibrahim, M., Mezher, D., Cousin, B.: Centralized versus decentralized multi-cell resource and power allocation for multiuser OFDMA networks. In: IFIP Networking Conference, pp. 112–124. IEEE (2016)
10. Jiang, D., Xu, Z., Li, W., et al.: An energy-efficient multicast algorithm with maximum network throughput in multi-hop wireless networks. J. Commun. Netw. **18**(5), 713–724 (2016)
11. Jiang, D., Zhang, P., Lv, Z., et al.: Energy-efficient multi-constraint routing algorithm with load balancing for smart city applications. IEEE Internet Things J. **3**(6), 1437–1447 (2016)

12. Han, S., Lu, Y., Yang, S., Mu, X., Wang, N.: Game theory-based energy efficiency optimization for multi-user cognitive radio over MIMO interference channels. In: Vehicular Technology Conference, pp. 1–5. IEEE (2017)
13. Lahoud, S., Khawam, K., Martin, S., Feng, G., Liang, Z., Nasreddine, J.: Energy efficient joint scheduling and power control in multi-cell wireless networks. IEEE J. Sel. Areas Commun., 1 (2016)

Mining High Utility Co-location Patterns Based on Importance of Spatial Region

Jiasong Zhao[1,2], Lizhen Wang[1(✉)], Peizhong Yang[1],
and Hongmei Chen[1]

[1] Department of Computer Science and Engineering, Yunnan University,
Kunming, China
zhaojs75@163.com, lzhwang@ynu.edu.cn
[2] Department of Electronic and Information Engineering,
Yunnan Agricultural University, Kunming, China

Abstract. Co-location pattern mining aims at finding the subsets of spatial features whose instances are frequently located together in geographic space. Most studies mainly focus on whether spatial feature instances are frequently located together. However, the utilities of spatial instances in different space regions are different. Based on the importance of spatial a region, the utility value of the region is determined, and then a utility participation index of co-location patterns as a new interestingness measure is defined. We present a basic high utility co-location pattern mining algorithm. To reduce the computational cost, an improved mining algorithm with pruning strategy is developed by cutting down the search space. The experiments on synthetic and real world datasets show that the proposed methods are effective and efficient.

Keywords: Spatial data mining · Co-location pattern · High utility
Spatial region

1 Introduction

Owing to the rapid generation of spatial data and wide use of spatial databases, it's essential to discover spatial knowledge automatically from spatial datasets. Spatial co-location mining is to discover a set of spatial features of which instances frequently appear in a spatial neighborhood of each other. Mining spatial co-location patterns is an important spatial data mining task with broad applications [1, 2].

The participation index is used to measure the prevalence (or frequency) of a co-location pattern in the traditional approaches of co-location pattern mining. It mainly focused on whether spatial feature instances are frequently located together. However, the utility of the feature instances in different spatial regions is different. For example, in the study of plant symbiosis, the symbiotic plants that grow in the poor ecological environment (soil, humidity, altitude, etc.) are more general than those that grow in the good ecological environment. Another example, in the research field of public safety, social effect of criminal cases occurring in the downtown is absolutely different from ones occurring in the school. Therefore, it is necessary to establish the importance of spatial region in mining spatial co-location patterns. After setting of

© Springer Nature Singapore Pte Ltd. 2018
H. Yuan et al. (Eds.): GSKI 2017, CCIS 849, pp. 43–55, 2018.
https://doi.org/10.1007/978-981-13-0896-3_5

region utility values based on regional importance, the utility value of the instance is the utility value of the region where the instance is located. By the way of mining high utility co-location patterns similar to the literature [3], the method of discovery high utility co-location patterns can not only detect some low-frequency but high-utility (interesting) patterns, but also remove some common-sense patterns (high-frequency but low-utility).

Here, we use a specific example to illustrate this problem. Figure 1 shows a sample spatial dataset consisting of four features, A, B, C, and D. A.2 represents the second instance of spatial feature A. Two instances are connected by edges (shown as solid lines) if they have a spatial neighbor relationship, and the whole space is divided into four equal regions. Suppose the utility values of these four regions are 8, 5, 2, and 1 respectively. According to the traditional co-location pattern mining method, the participation index of co-location {C, D} is 1/3. If the prevalence threshold is not less than 0.6, {C, D} would be regarded as a non-prevalent co-location. However, two row instances of {C, D}, {C.5, D.5} and {C.6, D.6}, all appear in Region 1 which shows the highest utility value. So the utility of each feature in {C, D} accounts for a large proportion of its total utility. {C, D} may be interesting to users. As to the pattern {B, C}, in contrast, the participation index of {B, C} is 2/3, the utility participation index of {B, C} is lower. So {B, C} may be non-interesting to users.

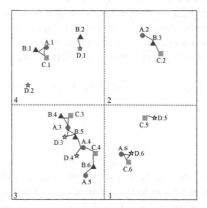

Fig. 1. A sample spatial dataset

Therefore, the real interesting co-location patterns cannot be found by traditional approach because the importance of different regions is ignored. In the paper, we focus on high utility co-location mining based on importance of spatial regions.

1.1   Related Work

Morimoto et al. [4] first defined the problem of finding frequent neighboring co-locations in spatial databases. Huang et al. [5] proposed a general approach for mining co-location patterns, the join-based approach, which defined the participation index to measure the prevalence of a co-location. After that, different algorithms were proposed to improve the efficiency of the mining process, such as join-less algorithm [6] proposed by Yoo et al., and density based algorithm [2] proposed by Xiao et al. Wang et al. also presented a new join-less algorithm based on the CPI-tree [7] and an approach based on order-clique for discovering maximal co-locations [8]. Previous approaches focus on discovering global co-locations in a spatial dataset. The results of these approaches are usually not able to capture or represent the characteristics of different zones. Celik et al. [9] defined the problem of zonal co-location mining. He proposed an index structure based on the Quad-tree to support dynamic parameters for zonal co-location mining. Dai et al. [10] developed a new index structure and algorithm to mine zonal co-locations more efficiently. Sengstock et al. [11] introduced a new general class of interestingness measures that are based on the spatial distribution of co-location patterns. A new measurement using an evenness coefficient of the feature distribution was introduced, and a novel algorithm for discovering prevalent and evenly distributional co-location patterns was proposed in [12].

Much works on high utility pattern mining have presented different approaches in the transactional data sets [13]. A two-phase algorithm to efficiently prune down the number of candidates, through transaction-weighted downward closure property was presented in [14]. UP-Growth proposed in [15] enhances the mining performance in utility mining through maintaining the information of high utility itemsets by UP-tree. There are just a very limited number of studies on high utility co-location pattern mining. A framework for mining high utility co-locations was proposed in [16]. Wang et al. [17] discussed a problem of incremental mining high utility co-locations on spatial databases which are constantly changed with added and disappeared data. Recently Wang et al. [3] presented a method of mining high utility co-locations from spatial data sets with instance-specific utilities.

1.2   Contribution

The main contributions of this paper are as follows.

First, based on the importance of spatial regions, we propose a new measure called the utility participation index for high utility co-location pattern mining.

Second, we present a basic algorithm to discover high utility co-locations. In order to reduce the computational cost, an improved algorithm is given.

Finally, we evaluate our algorithms with experiments on both synthetic and real world data sets.

The remainder of this paper is organized as follows. Section 2 introduces basic concepts and definitions of high utility co-location pattern mining based on the importance of spatial regions. A basic algorithm and an improved algorithm with a pruning strategy are presented in Sect. 3. Experimental results are shown in Sect. 4. The last section is conclusions.

2 Basic Concepts and Problem Definition

2.1 Basic Concepts

A set of spatial features represents a collection of different kinds of items in space, as $F = \{f_1, f_2, \cdots, f_k\}$. An object with a specific spatial position is called a spatial instance, and a set of instances, as $S = S_1 \cup S_1 \cup \ldots S_k$, in which $S_i (1 \le i \le k)$ is an instance collection that corresponds to spatial feature. Each instance denoted by the feature type and a numeric id value e.g. B.1. If the Euclidean distance of two instances is not greater than the given threshold d, which means the two instances meet neighbor relationship R. A co-location pattern c is a set of spatial features, in which $c \subseteq F$. The instance set I is a row instance of co-location pattern c, if (1) I contains all features of c, and no proper subset of I does so; (2) any two instances, i_i and i_j, $i_i, i_j \in I$, $R(i_i, i_j)$, that is, i_i and i_j are neighbors. The set of all row instances of c is the table instance of c, denoted as $T(c)$.

When the participation index of a co-location pattern is not less than the given threshold, it is referred as a prevalent co-location pattern. The participation index of co-location pattern c is expressed as $PI (c)$, which is the minimum of participation ratios among all spatial features of c, defining as follows:

$$PI(c) = \min_{f_i \in c} \{Pr(c, f_i)\} \tag{1}$$

The participation ratio of spatial feature f_i in co-location pattern c is expressed as $Pr (c, f_i)$, defined as:

$$Pr(c, f_i) = \frac{\text{Number of distinct instance of } f_i \text{ in any row instance of } c}{\text{Number of instance of } f_i} \tag{2}$$

2.2 Problem Definition

In practical applications, the effect of feature instances in different space regions is different. Therefore, we will set spatial region utility values based on the importance of each region, and then the region utilities will be transformed into the instances. In this section, some related definitions about mining high utility co-location patterns based on the region importance will be given.

Definition 1 (spatial region utility). *The spatial region utility is used to describe the importance of different spatial regions. We denote the spatial region utility of Region i as u_i.*

Definition 2 (spatial instance utility). *Let spatial instance $f_i.j$ be the j-th instance of feature f_i. We denote the utility of spatial instance $f_i.j$ as $u(f_i.j)$, which is the utility of region where $f_i.j$ is located in it.*

For example, in Fig. 1, A.2 is located in Region 2. $u(A.2) = u_2 = 5$.

Definition 3 (total utility of feature). *The total utility of a feature f_i is the sum of utilities of its instances, denoted as $u(f_i) = \sum_{f_i.j \in S_i} u(f_i.j)$, where S_i is the a set of instances belonging to f_i.*

For example, the total utility of feature A in Fig. 1 is $u(A) = u(A.1) + u(A.2) + u(A.3) + u(A.4) + u(A.5) + u(A.6) = 1 + 5 + 2 \times 3 + 8 = 20$.

Definition 4 (utility of feature in co-location). *Given a size-k co-location pattern $c = \{f_1, f_2, ..., f_k\}$, the utility of f_i in c is defined as the sum of utilities of instances belonging to feature $f_i \in c$ in table instance $T(c)$. It is denoted as $u(c, f_i) = \sum_{f_i.j \in \pi_{f_i}(T(c))} u(f_i.j)$, where π is the relational projection operation with duplication elimination.*

For example, in Fig. 1, considering the size-2 co-location pattern $c = \{C, D\}$, T$(c) = \{\{C.5, D.5\}, \{C.6, D.6\}\}$. The utility of D in c is $u(c, D) = u(D.5) + u(D.6) = 8 + 8 = 16$.

Definition 5 (Utility Participation Ratio, UPR). *The utility participation ratio of feature f_i in co-location pattern c is defined as the proportion of f_i's utility in c to its total utility. The utility participation ratio can be computed as:*

$$UPR(c, f_i) = \frac{u(c, f_i)}{u(f_i)} \tag{3}$$

For example, in Fig. 1, for pattern $c = \{C, D\}$, the utility participation ratio of each feature in c is computed as

$$UPR(c, C) = \frac{u(C.5) + u(C.6)}{u(C)} = \frac{16}{26}, UPR(c, D) = \frac{u(D.5) + u(D.6)}{u(D)} = \frac{16}{22}.$$

Definition 6 (Utility Participation Index, UPI). *The utility participation index UPI(c) of a co-location pattern $c = \{f_1, f_2, ..., f_k\}$ is the minimum in all UPR(c, f_i) of co-location c:*

$$UPI(c) = \min_{i=1}^{k} \{UPR(c, f_i)\} \tag{4}$$

Definition 7 (high utility co-location pattern, UCP). *Given a minimum UPI threshold θ, a co-location pattern c is a high utility co-location pattern if UPI(c) $\geq \theta$ holds.*

The prevalent patterns may not be high utility patterns and the high utility patterns may not be prevalent as well. For example, for patterns {B, C} and {C, D} in Fig. 1, PI ({B, C}) = 0.67 and UPI({B, C}) = 0.38, while PI({C, D}) = 0.33 and UPI({C, D}) = 0.62. If both of minimum PI threshold and minimum UPI threshold are 0.6, we can identify {B, C} is prevalent easily, but {C, D} is not. At the same time, {C, D} is a high utility co-location pattern, but {B, C} is not.

Lemma 1. *The utility participation ratio and the utility participation index are anti-monotone (monotonically non-increasing) as the size of the co-location increases.*

Proof: The utility participation ratio is antimonotonic because a spatial feature instance that participates in a row instance of a co-location c also participates in a row instance of a co-location c', where $c' \subseteq c$. Because the utility participation index is the minimum in all $UPR(c, f_i)$ of co-location c, when the size of the co-location increases, the utility participation index is decreases, so it is also monotonically non-increasing.

Theorem 1. *If a size-k co-location pattern $c_k = \{f_1, f_2, \ldots f_k\}$ is the high utility co-location pattern, each size-(k-1) co-location pattern $c_{k-1} \subset c_k$ must be the high utility co-location.*

Proof: According to lemma 1, it is easy to be proved.

3   UCP Mining

3.1   Basic Algorithm

The basic UCP mining algorithm uses the generate-and-test methods, that is, generate candidates, and test each candidate to identify whether it is a high utility co-location pattern. Algorithm 1 shows the pseudocode of the basic UPC mining.

Algorithm 1. Basic UCP Mining
Input: F: a set of spatial features, S: a set of spatial instances, d: a distance threshold, θ: a utility participation index threshold.
Output: A set of high utility co-locations.
Variables: k: co-location size, C_k: a set of size-k candidates, T_k: a set of table instances of C_k, U_k: a set of size-k high utility co-location patterns
Methods:
1. the data space is divided into m regions;
2. set the utility value for the region, respectively, $u_1, u_2, \ldots, u_m$;
3. $U_1 = F$; $T_1 = S$;
4. for ($k = 2$; $U_{k-1} \neq \varphi$; $k{+}{+}$) do
5. C_k = gen_candidate_colocations(k, U_{k-1});
6. T_k = gen_table_instances(C_k, T_{k-1}, d);
7.   Calculate_UPI(C_k, T_k) ;
8. U_k = select_high_utility_colocations(C_k, T_k, θ);
9. end for
10. Return $\cup(U_2, U_3, \ldots, U_k)$

Initialization (Step 1–3): First of all, according to the importance of the regions, the data space is divided into m regions, and the utility value for these regions is set, respectively, $u_1, u_2,..., u_m$. And then size-1 high utility co-location patterns sets and size-1 table instance sets are initialized.

Generating Candidate Co-locations (Step 4–6): Given a spatial data set and a distance threshold, all neighboring instance pairs can be found by using a geometric method such as plane sweep. Meanwhile, the set of size-2 candidates and the set of table instances of C_2 can be generated from the neighbor instance pairs. For $k > 2$, size-k candidate co-locations and table instances of them are generated from size-$(k-1)$ high utility co-location patterns. Here, we use the antimonotone of utility participation index to prune the set of generated candidate patterns.

Discovering High Utility Co-locations (Step 7–8): First, we calculate the UPI of each candidate co-location according to the Definition 6. Then, we identify high utility co-location patterns by the UPIs of candidate co-locations and the given UPI threshold θ.

Steps 4–9 are repeated with the increment of size k. Note that the row instances which lie across two regions are ignored in Algorithm 1.

3.2 Improved Algorithm

The basic UCP mining algorithm can efficiently discover utility co-location patterns due to the antimonotone property of UPI. In this section, we present an improved UCP mining algorithm for reducing the computational cost.

As shown in Fig. 1, the instances of feature B and C in pattern {B, C} exist in a high utility region, but there is no row instance of {B, C}. Therefore, the utility participation index of {B, C} is low. Through this observation, we get the improvement of basic algorithm: m regions are sorted from high to low according to the utility values, and the regional number is 1, 2,..., m in turn. And then we mine high utility co-location pattern with the strategy of generate-and-test based on the sorting regions.

Definition 7 (utility of feature within a region). *Within region l, suppose S_i^l is a set of instances belonging to a feature f_i. The utility of f_i within region l is denoted as $u_l(f_i) = \sum_{f_i.j \in S_i^l} u(f_i.j)$.*

For example, in Fig. 1, the utility of feature A within Region 1 is $u_1(A) = u(A.6) = 8$.

Definition 8 (utility of feature in co-location within a region). *Within region l, given a size-k co-location pattern $c = \{f_1, f_2, ..., f_k\}$, the utility of f_i in c is defined as the sum of utilities of instances belonging to feature $f_i \in c$ in $R^l(c)$, where $R^l(c)$ is the set of row instance of c within region l. It is denoted as $u_l(c, f_i) = \sum_{f_i.j \in \pi_{f_i}(R^l(c))} u(f_i.j)$, where π is the relational projection operation with duplication elimination.*

For example, in Fig. 1, within Region 1, considering the size-2 co-location pattern $c = \{A, C\}$, $R^1(c) = \{A.6, C.6\}$. The utility of A in c within Region 1 is $u_1(c, A) = u(A.6) = 8$.

Lemma 2. *Let m regions are sorted from high to low according to the utility value, and the regional number is from 1, 2, ..., m in turn. After the related utility values of the first l regions are calculated, the maximum utility participation ratio of feature f_i is $UPR (c, f_i)_{maxl}$.*

$$UPR(c, f_i)_{maxl} = \frac{u(f_i) - \sum_{r=1}^{l} u_r(f_i) + \sum_{r=1}^{l} u_r(c, f_i)}{u(f_i)} \tag{5}$$

Proof:

$$UPR(c, f_i) = \frac{\sum_{r=1}^{l} u_r(c, f_i) + \sum_{r=l+1}^{m} u_r(c, f_i)}{u(f_i)} \leq \frac{\sum_{r=1}^{l} u_r(c, f_i) + \sum_{r=l+1}^{m} u_r(f_i)}{u(f_i)}$$

$$UPR(c, f_i) \leq \frac{\sum_{r=1}^{l} u_r(c, f_i) + u(f_i) - \sum_{r=1}^{l} u_r(f_i)}{u(f_i)}$$

Theorem 2. *Given a size-k co-location pattern $c = \{f_1, f_2, ..., f_k\}$, if $UPR (c, f_i)_{maxl} < \theta$ holds, then c must be a non-high utility co-location pattern, i.e., pattern c can be pruned.*

Proof: According to Definition 6 and Lemma 2, we have $UPI (c) \leq UPR (c, f_i)$ $UPR (c, f_i)_{maxl}$. So, when $UPR (c, f_i)_{maxl} < \theta$ holds, pattern c can be pruned.

For example, in Fig. 1, for pattern $c = \{B, C\}$, we have

$$UPR(c, B)_{max1} = \frac{u(B) - u_1(B) + u_1(c, B)}{u(B)} = \frac{13 - 0 + 0}{13} = 1$$

$$UPR(c, C)_{max1} = \frac{u(C) - u_1(C) + u_1(c, C)}{u(C)} = \frac{26 - 16 + 0}{26} \approx 0.38$$

If minimum UPI threshold θ is 0.6, pattern {B, C} can be pruned by Theorem 2.

Algorithm 2. Improved UCP Mining

Input: F: a set of spatial features, S: a set of spatial instances, d: a distance threshold, θ: a utility participation index threshold.
Output: A set of high utility co-locations.
Variables:
k: co-location size
C_k: a set of size-k candidates
T_k^l : a set of table instances of C_k within region l
U_k: a set of size-k high utility co-location patterns
Methods:
1. The data space is divided into m regions;
2. sort regions and make the utility values of region 1, 2, ..., m meet $u_1 > u_2 > ... > u_m$;
3. $U_1 = F$; $T_1 = S$;
4. for ($k = 2$; $U_{k-1} \neq \varphi$; k++) do
5. C_k = gen_candidate_colocations(k, U_{k-1});
6.   for each c in C_k
7.   for l = 1 to m do
8. t_c=gen_table_instances(c, T_{k-1}^l, d);
9.   Calculate_UPR_{maxl} (c, t_c);
10.   if $UPR(c, f_i)_{maxl} < \theta$ then
11.   remove c from C_k; break;
12.   end if
13.   append t_c to T_k^l ;
14.   end for
15.   end for
16. $U_k \leftarrow C_k$;
17. end for
18. Return $\cup (U_2, U_3, ..., U_k)$

According to Theorem 2, the basic mining algorithm can be optimized. Instead of scanning the entire dataset, candidate patterns and their table instances can be generated and UPI can be calculated. In particular, the initialization is similar to the basic algorithm, but the m regions should be sorted from high to low (step 2) according to their utility values. Then, we use size-$(k-1)$ high utility co-location patterns to generate size-k candidate co-locations (step 5). And then, the table instance t_c is generated according to the regional order, one by one. Finally, the UPR $(c, f_i)_{maxl}$ is calculated. The unpruned candidate pattern C_k is the high utility pattern U_k (step 6–17). In the process of generating the table instance t_c of each pattern c, the time consumption for the improved algorithm will be reduced as a result of reducing the scanning scope of the dataset. Algorithm 2 shows the pseudocode of the improved UPC mining.

4 Experimental Evaluation

In this section, we perform a series of experiments to verify the effect and the efficiency of the basic UCP (BUCP) algorithm and the improved UCP (IUCP) algorithm on synthetic and real datasets.

The algorithms are implemented in JAVA and are memory-based algorithms. All the experiments were performed on an Intel core i7-6700 3.4 GHz PC with 8G MB main memory, running on Microsoft Windows10.

4.1 Datasets

For the synthetic dataset, we generate instances and randomly distribute them into a 1000×1000 space, and the utilities of regions are assigned randomly between 1 and 10. For the real dataset, we use a plant dataset of the "Three Parallel Rivers of Yunnan Protected Areas", we set the utilities of regions by an expert judge method.

4.2 Quality of Mining Results

The criterion $Q(c) = \sum_{f \in c} u(c,f) \big/ \sum_{f \in c} u(f)$ is used to evaluate the quality of a mined co-location pattern c, and the bigger $Q(c)$ is, c has the higher utilities [3]. We compare the quality of mining results identified by the traditional participation index (PI) and the UPI proposed in our paper.

Mining results on the synthetic dataset. The number of spatial features we take is 20; the total number of instances n is 15 K; the distance threshold d is 25; and the number of regions m is 9. Figure 2(a) shows the sum of quality of top-k interesting co-location patterns identified by the measure PI and UPI respectively. The results show that UPI measure can discover higher quality co-location patterns.

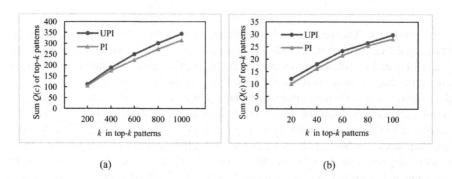

(a)   (b)

Fig. 2. The quality of mining results (a) on the synthetic dataset, (b) on the real dataset

Mining results on the real dataset. In Fig. 2(b), we use a real-world plant distribution dataset which the number of plant species (spatial features) is 25 and the number of instances is 13348 in a 90 km $\times$ 90 km area. According to the soil properties, this space is divided into 7 regions. With the same results of the synthetic dataset, the quality of mining results by UPI measure is still better than the quality of mining results by PI measure.

4.3 UCP Mining Performance Evaluation

In this subsection, we compare running time of BUCP algorithm and IUCP algorithm on synthetic datasets.

Effect of the number of instances n. The number of spatial features we set is 20; the distance threshold d is 10; the number of regions m is 25; and the utility participation index threshold θ is 0.3, the running time of two algorithms by increasing the number of instances n is shown in Fig. 3(a). We can see that with the increase of n, the running time of the two algorithms is increased. This is because that the increase of n will produce more clique instances, leading to more time consumption. When $n > 70$ K, the algorithm IUCP is obviously superior to that of BUCP, because the IUCP algorithm can prune non-high utility candidate patterns through scanning parts of data space.

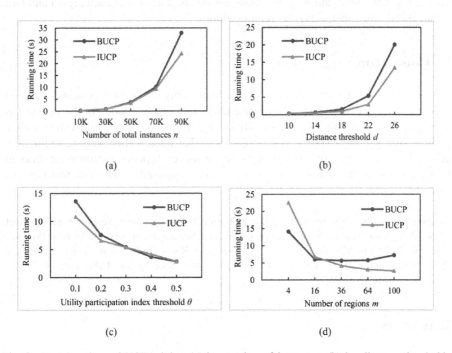

Fig. 3. Running time of UCP mining (a) by number of instances, (b) by distance threshold, (c) by utility participation index threshold, (d) by number of regions

Effect of the distance threshold d. In Fig. 3(b), the number of spatial features is 20, $n = 20$ K, $m = 25$, $\theta = 0.3$. Similarly, the running time is increased with the increase of d, because a larger value of d means more instances which could form cliques to bring more join operations. The performance of IUCP algorithm is still better than BUCP algorithm, as there is a pruning strategy in IUCP algorithm.

Effect of the utility participation index threshold θ. In Fig. 3(c), the number of spatial features is 20, $n = 60$ K, $m = 25$, $d = 10$. As θ becomes higher, more patterns dissatisfy the condition of the high utility patterns, naturally, the performance of two algorithms meliorate. When $\theta < 0.3$, the running time of IUCP algorithm is less than BUCP. When $\theta > 0.3$, the running time of the two algorithms is almost equal. This is because that when θ value is larger, BUCP algorithm has greatly reduced the running time by using antimonotone property of UPI.

Effect of number of regions m. In Fig. 3(d), the number of spatial features is 20, $n = 60$ K, $d = 10$, $\theta = 0.3$. When $m > 25$, the running time of IUCP algorithm is less than that of BUCP algorithm. Besides, with the increase of m, the pruning utility of IUCP algorithm is better and its running time is less, while the UPI calculation amount of the algorithm BUCP is increased and its running time is slightly increased. When $m < 25$, with the increase of m, the running time of the two algorithms is reduced. However, the running time of IUCP algorithm is more than BUCP, because the pruning strategy of IUCP algorithm is invalid and it scans the entire datasets when identifying high utility patterns. In this way, the table instance is generated in each region and UPI is calculated, thus, increasing the running time.

5   Conclusions

In this paper, we present a method to find high utility co-location patterns based on importance of spatial regions. We use the utility participation index of the patterns as interestingness measure and present BUCP algorithm and IUCP algorithm with a pruning strategy. The experimental results show that we can effectively mine the high utility co-location patterns. IUCP algorithm achieves superior performance than to BUCP algorithm. In the future, we plan to validate our method with different types of datasets.

Acknowledgments. This work is supported by the National Natural Science Foundation of China (61472346, 61662086, 61762090), the Natural Science Foundation of Yunnan Province (2015FB114,2016FA026), the Project of Innovative Research Team of Yunnan Province (XT412011), and the Spectrum Sensing and Borderlands Security Key Laboratory of Universities in Yunnan (C6165903).

References

1. Shekhar, S., Huang, Y.: Discovering spatial co-location patterns: a summary of results. In: Proceedings of 7th International Symposium on Advances in Spatial and Temporal Databases (SSTD), pp. 236–256 (2001)
2. Xiao, X., Xie, X., Luo, Q., Ma, W.: Density based co-location pattern discovery. In: Proceedings of 16th ACM SIGSPATIAL International Conference on Advances in Geographic Information Systems, pp. 1–10 (2008)

 3. Wang, L., Jiang, W., Chen, H., Fang, Y.: Efficiently mining high utility co-location patterns from spatial data sets with instance-specific utilities. In: Proceedings of 22nd International Conference on Database Systems for Advanced Applications, pp. 458–474 (2017)
 4. Morimoto, Y.: Mining frequent neighboring class sets in spatial databases. In: Proceedings of 7th ACM SIGKDD International Conference on Knowledge Discovery and Data Mining, pp. 353–358 (2001)
 5. Huang, Y., Shekhar, S., Xiong, H.: Discovering colocation patterns from spatial data sets: a general approach. IEEE Trans. Knowl. Data Eng. **16**(12), 1472–1485 (2004)
 6. Yoo, J.S., Shekhar, S.: A joinless approach for mining spatial colocation patterns. IEEE Trans. Knowl. Data Eng. **18**(10), 1323–1337 (2006)
 7. Wang, L., Bao, Y., Lu, J., Yip, J.: A new join-less approach for co-location pattern mining. In: Proceedings of 8th IEEE International Conference on Computer and Information Technology (CIT2008), pp. 197–202 (2008)
 8. Wang, L., Zhou, L., Lu, J., Yip, J.: An order-clique-based approach for mining maximal co-locations. Inf. Sci. **179**(19), 3370–3382 (2009)
 9. Celik, M., Kang, J.M., Shekhar, S.: Zonal co-location pattern discovery with dynamic parameters. In: Proceedings of 7th IEEE International Conference on Data Mining, pp. 433–438 (2007)
10. Dai, B.R., Lin, M.Y.: Efficiently mining dynamic zonal co-location patterns based on maximal co-locations. In: Proceedings of 11th IEEE International Conference on Data Mining Workshops, pp. 861–868 (2011)
11. Sengstock, C., Gertz, M., Canh, T.V.: Spatial interestingness measures for co-location pattern mining. In: Proceedings of 12th IEEE International Conference on Data Mining Workshops, pp. 821–826 (2012)
12. Zhao, J., Wang, L., Bao, X., Tan, Y.: Mining co-location patterns with spatial distribution characteristics. In: International Conference on Computer, Information and Telecommunication Systems, pp. 26–30 (2016)
13. Yao, H., Hamilton, H.J., Butz, C.J.: A foundational approach to mining itemset utilities from databases. In: Proceedings of 4th SIAM International Conference on Data Mining, pp. 482–486 (2004)
14. Liu, Y., Liao, W., Choudhary, A.: A two-phase algorithm for fast discovery of high utility itemsets. In: Pacific-Asia Conference on Advances in Knowledge Discovery and Data Mining, pp. 689–695 (2005)
15. Tseng, V.S., Wu, C.W., Shie, B.E., Yu, P.S.: UP-Growth: an efficient algorithm for high utility itemset mining. In: Proceedings of 16th ACM SIGKDD International Conference on Knowledge Discovery and Data Mining, pp. 253–262 (2010)
16. Yang, S., Wang, L., Bao, X., Lu, J.: A framework for mining spatial high utility co-location patterns. In: Proceedings 12th International Conference on Fuzzy Systems and Knowledge Discovery, pp. 595–601 (2015)
17. Wang, X., Wang, L.: Incremental mining of high utility co-locations from spatial database. In: IEEE International Conference on Big Data and Smart Computing, pp. 215–222 (2017)

Analyzing Community Structure Based on Topology Potential over Complex Network System

Kanokwan Malang$^{(\boxtimes)}$, Shuliang Wang, and Tianru Dai

School of Software Engineering, Beijing Institute of Technology,
No. 5, South Zhong Guan Cun Street, Beijing 100081
People's Republic of China
kanokwan.malang@yahoo.com, slwang2011@bit.edu.cn

Abstract. Community structure is one of complex network properties which reveals the main organizing proposition in most real-world complex networks. The special interests are groups of vertices within the intense edges or connections that are not only overlapping, but also change over-time. In this paper, we present the overview of structured complex network properties that affect the process of discovering community structure. Topology potential of nodes in complex network is also described. Topology potential is a measurement method to investigate the interaction among community members. From the recent literatures, the community structure discovered by topology potential needs to be improved in term of performance and accuracy in order to obtain more meaningful results.

Keywords: Topology potential · Community structure · Complex network

1 Introduction

Over the past decade, complex network has gained wide interest in the scientific research field. Non-trivial topological features such as small-world, scale-free, and community structure are adopted in most complex networks [1, 2]. It is widely assumed that one of the specific features of complex network which can effectively describe the relationship among network members is "community structure" [3]. The community structure is defined as a group of nodes that have a high number of edges within the same group. This characteristic is shared by all real-world complex network in different domain e.g. sociology, biology, technology and information etc. Discovering community structure over complex network can improve the accuracy of search engine [4, 5] web service composition [6, 7] and forecasting the information among users in social network [8, 9].

With the increased availability of large-scale complex network in the era of big data, the community structures are often overlapping and the interaction among its member are more complicated. However, the most all existed community detection algorithms navigate network to classify community based on the absence information of global properties. If we want to explain the mechanism and growth of network that vary overtime, these global properties sometimes are not able to provide the sufficient

© Springer Nature Singapore Pte Ltd. 2018
H. Yuan et al. (Eds.): GSKI 2017, CCIS 849, pp. 56–68, 2018.
https://doi.org/10.1007/978-981-13-0896-3_6

information [10]. Therefore, the community structure of a complex network requires to optimize procedure based on local information from network topology. The definition of topology potential was introduced by Han et al. (2009) [10]. The topology potential is an effective tool to provide the local information which naturally explains how well a node is connected to each other. The tool is used for measuring the interaction among community members.

This paper aims to investigate the strength and weakness of topology potential in order to improve the accuracy of community detection algorithm. An overview of topology potential and other related works are described. The rest of this paper is organized as follows: Sect. 2 provides background knowledge including the basic information of complex network, community structure, and topology potential. This basic information points out how topology potential is important for analyzing the structural properties in complex network. Section 3 presents some related works which illustrates how topology potential are applied in various perspectives. The strengths and weakness of topology potential implemented in the network are also discovered. Finally, Sect. 4 is the conclusion of this paper.

2   Background Knowledge

This section, we point out the importance of topology potential for analyzing the structural properties in complex network. There are 3 main concepts to describe, including complex network, community structure, and topology potential.

2.1   Complex Network

Complex networks typically exhibit many interesting emerging patterns and share some common network structures that contribute to deeper understanding of complex network behavior [11]. It is the considerable effort that has been made to understand numerous real-world complex systems in terms of random graphs, consisting of vertices and edges. The characterization and modelling of complex network results some structured properties as follows: Firstly, the degree distribution follows a power-law, $P(k) \sim k^{-\gamma}$; where the degree is the number of edges or links connecting to a given vertex [12].

Secondly, complex network reflects the small-world property, i.e. most of nodes are not neighbors of one another, but they can be reached from every other by a small number of links [8].

Thirdly, many real-world networks are highly inhomogeneous with a few highly connected nodes and a large majority of nodes with low degree have "scale-free" property, simply say the property of having the same functional form at all scales.

The model of network growth is also introduced by Barabási–Albert (BA) and called as the preferential attachment rule [3, 13]. With this rule, a node is newly added and connects to m existing nodes by following the probability linearly proportional to the degree of target node. This result can be explained by "rich-get-richer" principle, in which the node with higher degrees always acquire new links at higher rates than low-degree nodes.

Finally, the community structure is noted as the most attractive area to investigate the potential characteristic of such complex network. Communities can be defined as groups of nodes such that there is a higher density of edges within groups than between them. For example, the tightly connected groups of nodes in a Wikipedia network represent individuals belonging to area of articles, topics, and contents as communities [14, 15]. Finding the communities within a network is a powerful tool for understanding the function of network, as well as for identifying an interactive relationship within a complex architecture. The more details about network community structure are described in the next section.

All complex network properties that mentioned above can explain the characteristics and behavior of real-world complex network in different perspectives. The complex network can be characterized into two structures; the structure in global scale and local scale. The structure in global scale describes network by focusing on the overall architecture, rather than merely a neighborhood of a certain node. In contrast with the local structure, the nodes which are the most relevant for network organization and function are taken into account. This characterizing of complex network properties brings us to understand the important of local constraints that may affect to community structure discovering in both theoretical and practical terms. As the interaction between two neighbors nodes in network are always correlated with the distance and inherit abilities among them. So, examining the network community patterns and its interactive relationship based on local structures are assumed to give more meaningful results. This reason brings our research on discovering community structure into the fundamental of local structured-based concept.

2.2 Community Structure

Community structure is an important property of complex networks as described before. Community structure can be defined as the presence of fairly independent groups of nodes with a high density of links between nodes of the same group, and a comparatively low density of links between nodes of different groups [3, 16].

Given a graph $G(V, E)$, a community is a sub graph $G(V', E')$ whose nodes are tightly connected, i.e. cohesive. Since the structural cohesion of the nodes of G' can be quantified in several different ways by using the definitions of community structures. Such as community structure that considers every distinct pairs of community members are adjacent and connected with each other called clique. Another different class of definition, the community structure is defined based on the frequency of links. Hence, G' is a community when the sum of all degrees within G' is larger than the sum of all degrees toward the rest of the graph. As is shown in Fig. 1, So-called communities are defined as groups of nodes who has a high density of links within a group, whereas links between other cohesive group have a comparative lower density [3, 17, 18].

Based on the study of [7] The community structure can be classified into 3 types, and each of them has different community topology properties, including global property, local property and semantic property [13].

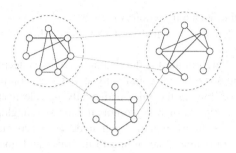

Fig. 1. Community structure in complex network [9]

Firstly, global properties which represent property of community structure whose requires consideration of the entire network in a sense of network space, distance, curve or surface. The community structure which is characterized by global property is closely related to modularity, community size distribution, average shortest path length, and clustering coefficient [10, 19].

Whilst, the second community structure is based on local properties that show how well a node is connected to the community. Local properties are related to the communities themselves and contain community size, scaled density, distance, hub dominance, and topology potential. Topology potential is introduced as a new paradigm to discover community structure and knowledge pattern with potential value. It is classified into the concepts of local structure that always exist in the real-world complex network [20]. Topology potential is motivated by the concept that the diversity of large complex network is characterized by the interaction of nodes. One node will affect the others and it can also be affected by its neighbors. Topology potential distribution has the same characteristic with community structure. When the nodes close to community centers, they connect densely and have higher topology potential value; nodes near the borders connect loosely with smaller topology potential value. Hence, the community structure and its member could be discovered on the basis of topology potential distribution [20]. We will give more explanation in topology potential in the next section.

Thirdly, the community structure can be represented by semantic property. For example, the operation inside the community that provides the information on how a network is partitioned into communities and how structural properties of each community is.

In order to understand the theoretical point of view and evolution of community structure, this research examines the existing research on community structure in two aspects; the overview of discovering community structure based on the different methods or techniques, and the overview of discovering community structure which have been applied in other application domains.

Based on the first perspective, many community detection methods have been proposed. The first modern age of community detection algorithm in graph is based on spectral partitioning. In which partitioning properties employ adjacency matrix and the eigen values of an appropriate input matrix [21, 22].Although, the recent spectral bisection method gives better global solution than the traditional methods, it requires some prior information to process e.g. size and number of expected communities.

Moreover, the algorithm generally requires the computational complexity at $O(N^2)$ to calculate the eigenvector of $N \times N$ matrix. This brings difficulty to deal with the large scale complex networks.

For the hierarchical algorithm, it is divided into 2 divisive techniques. The divisive technique integrates all nodes as one community at first, then continuously delete edges in the community according to the rules and finally get the result. Another type of hierarchical-based technique which is commonly used is agglomerative technique. Agglomerative technique firstly regards each node as a separate community, then continuously merges communities according to the rules and finally get the result of community detection [3, 23]. Although, the hierarchical algorithm not requires any prior knowledge to investigate the community structure, they do not achieve the best division of network. Furthermore, the results of community classification leave out some relevant node from a major group.

During that decade, some researches focused on the dynamic random walks in graph which follow the fundamental rule that nodes with short random walks tend to form communities [24–26]. Consequently, one typical method extended by the divisive hierarchical method has been proposed by Given and Newman (GN algorithm). They examine node betweenness centralities which express the number of shortest paths between pair of nodes that pass through the links [1, 2]. The method uses edge betweenness centralities to measure the importance of edges and continuously removes the edges whose betweenness are largest until network break up into the components. After that, the Fast GN method is also introduced [27]. The Fast GN adopts modularity as objective function and obtains optimal outcome when the value of modularity Q is the largest. GN algorithm produced a good result in various complex networks. However, it runs in $O(K^2N)$ time, and requires a high computation demand which inhibit the computation in very large scale complex networks.

At the second aspect, the existing researches on community structure can be described in term of its applied applications. Over the past decade, there exists many researches that focus on the problem of overlapping community structure. The concept of discovering community structure are applied in many fields such as biology, sociology, technology and information. In biological field, Xiao et al. [20] presents a new community detection algorithm based on topology potential value. The algorithm is applied with the A. thaliana protied metabolic network that can express the effective results in biological area. Their analysis not only demonstrates the objective assessment of the algorithms quality, but also aims to improve the accuracy and performance of discovering community structures in the underlying complex network.

In addition, discovering community structure over complex network can improve the performance of search engine. Community detection algorithm is applied in the citation network in order to improve the performance of scholar search engine [4]. Bracamonte et al. [5] research the application of community detection algorithm to the tags graph induce from the multimedia search results. Each resulting cluster represents a topic computed online for that particular search. Their proposed technique was measured in terms of quantitative number and size of the clusters produced.

Some research employed community detection into web service composition [6, 7]. From their work, the complex networks topological features e.g. shortest path length and node degree, are combined into the heuristic search functions. Based on their work, web service composition algorithm takes advantage of two salient complex network properties; community structure and centrality distribution.

In social network, community structure stands for the investigation of interactive relationship among users. It can be used for predicting the information exchange among user, as well as their behaviors e.g. Face book network, and a game in a multi-agent environment [8, 9].

From the study, community detection algorithms that has been proposed in the recent years mostly relies on the objective assessment of the algorithms quality. However, it appears that employing algorithm in the artificial data to the real-world network is difficult and insufficient to extrapolate the algorithm behavior. Some algorithms have been criticized for its inefficiency when dealing with large scale data sets. Some algorithm cannot guarantee to reach the best partitions of community network, especially when apply on the time-dependent and overlapping network. This brings us to the effort of complexity-handling and improving algorithm performance by focusing on a measured-topology potential.

2.3 Topology Potential

During the recent years, topology potential is paid more attention in most research areas on discovering community structure and community members classification. Topology potential is the way to derive the characteristics of all elements in the significant network, either describes the interaction and association among community members. The Topology Potential is defined as the prospective of any nodes in the network are influenced by the topology structure of its neighbors. Simply say that topology potential reveals how important the nodes is, as well as investigate the underlying characteristics of underlying importance distribution with its surroundings [1, 10].

Topology potential is based on the assumption that the diversified characteristic in large complex network are often influenced by a local constraint on node interconnectivity.

Given the network $G = (V, E)$, V is the set of nodes, E is the set of edges and $|E| = m$. So, topology potential can be represented as the differential position of each node in the network, that is to say, the potential of node in its position [10]. Each node's influence will quickly decay as distance increases. In term of mathematic definitions, topology potential of any node v_i is defined in a form of Gaussian function and can be computed as follow;

$$\varphi(v_i) = \sum_{j \in N}(m_j * exp - \left(\frac{d_{ij}}{\sigma}\right)^2) \tag{1}$$

Where $\varphi(v_i)$ is the topology potential of node v_i, for $v_i \in V$, d_{ij} is the distance between node v_i to node v_j; parameter σ is used to control the influence factor of each node in the process of community detection; $m_i \geq 0$ is the mass of node $v_i(i = 1, 2, .., n)$.

For d_{ij} that represent the distance between node v_i to node v_j, can be estimated with the topological distance of shunt-wound circuit [20]. When the network has only one reachable path between v_i and v_j, the topological distance is equal to the length of the reachable path. When there are k reachable paths between v_i and v_j, with different length $N_1, N_2, \ldots, N_k$. Then, d_{ij} satisfies $0 < N < min\ (N_1, N_2, \ldots, N_k)$.

As the modularity structure of real-world network implies that the interaction among nodes has local characteristic. Therefore, the topological potential score of each node can reflect nodes importance in the topology by optimizing influence factor. Our paper looks further to take advantage of one significant research on structured property in complex network from [1]. Their research presents the novel of topology potential that can be regarded as the influence region. The potential entropy H is introduced in order to measure the uncertainty of the topological space. Therefore, a minimum-entropy method can be used for the optimal choice of σ.

According to the Eq. 1, let the potential score of each node $v_1, v_2, \ldots, v_n$ be $\varphi(v_1), \varphi(v_2), \ldots, \varphi(v_n)$ respectively. Potential entropy H can be introduced as follow;

$$H = -\sum_{i=1}^{n} \frac{\varnothing(v_i)}{Z} log \frac{\varnothing(v_i)}{Z} \qquad (2)$$

where Z is the normalization factor, for any $\sigma \in (0, +\infty)$, H satisfy $0 \leq H \leq log\ (n)$ and reach maximum value $log\ (n)$ if and only if $\varphi(v_1), \varphi(v_2), \ldots, \varphi(v_n)$.

Node mass $m_i \geq 0$ is the mass of node $v_j (i = 1, 2, \ldots, n)$. Based on data field, the mass value represents the strength of the data field from v_j and meets the normalization condition $\sum_{i \in n} m_i = 1$. For measuring topology potential, each node is supposed to be equal in mass, indicating the same influence over network space. Then, the simplified potential function is taken from [21], and can be derived from Eq. (3);

$$\varphi(x) = \frac{1}{n} + \sum_{i=1}^{n} K\left(\frac{\|x - x_i\|}{\sigma}\right) \qquad (3)$$

Essentially, the topology potential can provide a strong description framework for measuring the characterization of community structure in complex network system. The minimum entropy value for each node makes a result of community structure analysis more reasonable. Because it can be used to determine the largest differences between node positions in the topology. In addition, some researchers consider the mass of node which is mapped by node's ability. The ability of node corresponds to different physical variables in different real-world network. The mass is a monotone and odd function when the network contains one or more physical variable on node mass. However, the difference between node mass is ignored in the most researches. In order to get the most appropriate algorithm, their influence parameter need to be estimated carefully.

3   Related Works

As mentioned before, the interests of community identification over the past decade are plenty driven by the concept of topology potential. In this section, we investigate all related works to see how they apply the concept of topology potential for analyzing community structure. Moreover, the strength and weakness of some related works are also discovered.

The notion of topology potential was introduced according to the field of physics. In which the topology potential is a function of differential position of each node that influence proportional to distance and directly proportional to magnitude of particle's mass and charge [10]. Consequently, the optimal influence factor is also considered by regarding the interaction ability of node and the influence region of topology. This method leads the research on topology potential to produce more effective results for complex network analysis.

Topology potential are firstly applied to the problem of community detection that expected to identify clear community structure in complex network. Jianpei et al. [28] presented soft-partition method based on topology potential which is the extension of hard method. While, hard method describes a network in terms of short-range field, in which communities in network can be reached by follow the local maxima node, called a representative. Soft-partition method considers the boundary node whose are attracted by multi-representatives. It is assumed to retain some useful information and bring more accurate results for the overlapping complex network community than the hard method. Soft-partition method is not only able to partition network into communities, but the clear community structures are also quantified by the boundary nodes community-identity algorithm.

Furthermore, the topology potential is brought to evaluate the importance of node within the network according to their role playing and distance from the community representatives [29]. Wang et al. [30] proposed the local maximum potential point search algorithm for the effective results of searching influenced nodes within the complex network. The proposed LMPS algorithm chooses the node with higher potential value than all its neighbor nodes. Then, adding the nodes which has the local maximum potential into the queue. This for preventing one weakness of Hill-climbing algorithm that always leaves out some important nodes from the searching space. However, the algorithm operated by scanning the whole network caused much computational time consuming.

In order to interpret the significant characteristic of network communities, the study of topology potential whereupon fall into the idea for identifying community structure and clarifying the roles, status and characteristics of community members. Han et al. [1] proposed CMITP (Community Members Identification based on Topology Potential) algorithm which can divide network into different communities by followed the nodes that has higher influence on others. The applied topology potential algorithm is defined in a form of Gaussian function that belongs to the nuclear force short-range field. With this function, the iterative force calculation can be omitted whenever the distance between two nodes is greater than the influence field. Hence, computational complexity is reduced. By adjusting the range of influence factor that can reflect the local influence of nodes in network, the clear community structure can be obtained. In order to measure the accuracy and performance of algorithm, their experiment was done by judging the community number and modularity distribution. The results show that different roles of community member are successfully identified. However, the obtained community number in some experiment data set is not resulted in accordance with the actual network.

Besides, the different application domains that exist in the real-world complex networks are benefitted from topology potential. For example, when applied topology potential in biological field [20], and social network compression [29].

Xiao et al. [20] applied topology potential as a new index to describe node connection dense in such network. The NTP algorithm reveals the interaction among nodes which is tightly related with the distance, ability of nodes (m node mass) and nodes' topology location (σ influence factor). Based on data field theory, node topology potential can be represented as a visual NTP field in a network. The nodes around the local maximum NTPs gather round local center due to the attraction. This statement confirmed that community membership can be detected on the basis of NTPs distribution. Results show that the A. thaliana proteid network can obviously represent some relative concepts of community memberships e.g. topology center, latent topology center, single and multi-centers communities. The complexity of topology distance over network is also reduced by applying the simplify NTP model. By comparing NTP with GN algorithm, NPT algorithm can generate same granularity results but more effective in term of less computational demands.

In social network, the community structure identification based on topology potential is facing with many difficulties. The reason of this phenomenon is because of it relies heavily on the increasing size of social network. Moreover, the information of social networks is not only overlapping but also changes overtime. In order to simplify analyzing community structure and make use of its interactive relationship among members, the size of such social network need to be reduced. Xuhui [29] applied the topology potential with the network lossless compression method. Two approaches based on topology potential in which judging the importance of nodes by its roles and distance has been proposed. The algorithm not only retains the basic community structure in the network during the network compression, but also remains the relationship from all among communities in complex network.

In order to improve the prediction accuracy of the collaborative filtering recommendation algorithm in user social network, the community algorithm based on topology potential has been integrated [31]. Topology potential is considered in term the inherit peak-valley structure in order to determine the community attachment of nodes based on its position in topology potential field. Combining between these two algorithms, users in social network who has similar interests are put into the same community. Hence, the algorithm searches the nearest neighbor from the same community and targets to the specific communities instead of whole network.

Recently, a novel of topology potential is combined with other techniques in order to solve some research problems e.g. reduce additional process, improve accuracy of algorithm and its performance. There exists the research that aims to uncovering the community structure of a network, relies on the combination of topology potential and spectral clustering technique [32]. The algorithm they proposed constructs the normalize Laplacian matrix with the node topology potential. This is used fulfilling some of weakness of matrix method whose lack ability to get the proper community number from the ladder distribution of eigenvector elements. Their experiments were done in both artificial networks and real-world networks. By Comparing with other methods in the artificial network, their algorithm achieves better results. The community number found by algorithms closest when comparing with the real community number. However, when apply the algorithm with the real-world network Zachary karate club, the distribution of topology potential σfurther increases. This results shows that one node can be connected with almost all other nodes. Thus, the algorithm cannot truly reflect the structure characteristic.

According to Table 1. After investigating all related works, we can summarize the applications of topology potential for analyzing community structure into 4 main scopes. Firstly, the scope of research indentifying explicit community structure in network. The obvious structure of community is one of the index to measure the accuracy of the topology potential function. In most research, the quantitative number of discovered communities are taken as the parameter to measure the accuracy of the algorithm [1, 20, 28, 29, 32]. Secondly, the scope of research in identifying the different status of community member [1, 20, 31]. Thirdly, some researches analyze border nodes of community network [20, 28]. This is one of the research scope to improve the accuracy of identifying community structure. Border node is the topology potential node whose attracted by more than one topological center. The process of ensuring which community a border node belong to, can reveals the clear community structure in the overlapping complex network. Finally, the research scope that fall into examining three parameters of topology potential function. The distance between a pair of nodes can be defined by the reachable path length [1, 20, 28, 30–32] and hop steps [29]. While the minimum entropy stands for the optimal influence factor. We found that although the distance and influence factor of the topology algorithm are well defined, the mass of node which assumed to be equal over the network falls into the problem of unclear parameter. Most research ignored the different of mass. Thus, the inaccuracy of the algorithm may be resulted. Moreover, when applying the algorithm in most research, the number of community discovered by algorithm is not resulted in accordance with the actual network.

Table 1. Summarize of research scope on topology potential-based community identification

Research scope	[28]	[1]	[20]	[29]	[32]	[30]	[31]
Identify explicit community structure	✓	✓	✓	✓	✓	–	–
Identify different status of members	–	✓	✓	–	–	–	✓
Identify boundary nodes	✓	–	✓	–	–	–	–
Examining topology potential function:							
Distance	✓	✓	✓	✓	✓	✓	✓
Minimum entropy	✓	✓	✓	✓	✓	✓	✓
Node mass	–	✓	✓	–	✓	✓	✓

4 Conclusion

In this paper, the overview concepts and literature reviews on community structure and discovering communities based on topology potential are described. Topology potential is a new paradigm of community detection algorithm that explains importance of a nodes defined by its neighbors. Based on local properties in complex network, the communities are investigated according to the interactive relationship among nodes, rather than examine the whole network structure. Two main problems have been found when applying topology potential. Firstly, the algorithm provides inaccuracy results when apply topology potential in the large-scale and real-world network. Secondly, the hypothesis on node mass parameter is controversial. The mass of node reflects ability of node are assumed to be equal over the whole network. This assumption may reflect the community structured which contains less meaningful and inaccurate results.

In order to improve the accuracy of discovering community structure, we plan to develop topology potential-based community detection algorithm by extending the consideration on node mass parameter in the next coming step. The hypothesis on different node mass that reflects the accuracy of algorithm need to be examined. For the further outcome, topology potential will be chosen to the process of community network analysis when working with the overlapping and dynamically real-world network. At a final result, we will use topology potential algorithm to forecast the behavior and evolution trend of encyclopedic Wikipedia network which is noted as the most complicated complex in the recent year [33].

Acknowledgments. This work was supported by National Key Research and Development Plan of China (2016YFB0502604, 2016YFC0803000), National Natural Science Fund of China (61472039), and Frontier and Interdisciplinary Innovation Program of Beijing Institute of Technology (2016CX11006), International Scientific and Technological Cooperation and Academic Exchange Program of Beijing Institute of Technology (GZ2016085103).

References

1. Han, Y., Li, D., Wang, T.: Identifying different community members in complex networks based on topology potential. Front. Comput. Sci. China **5**(1), 87–99 (2011)
2. Maslov, S., Sneppen, K., Zaliznyak, A.: Complex network: detection of topological patterns in complex networks: correlation pro le of the internet. Phys. A **333**, 529–540 (2004)
3. Boccaletti, S., Latora, V., Moreno, Y., Chavez, M., Hwang, D.-U.: Complex networks: structure and dynamic. Phys. Rep. **424**(4), 175–308 (2006). Bracamonte, T.s
4. Zhong, M., Zhong, C.: TopSeer: a novel scholar search engine based on community detection in citation network. In: Proceedings of 11th Joint International Conference on Information Sciences, Atlantis Press (2008)
5. Hogan, A., Poblete, B.: Applying community detection methods to cluster tags in multimedia search results. In: 2016 IEEE International Symposium Multimedia (ISM), pp. 467–474. IEEE Press, New York (2016)

6. Chhun, S., Malang, K., Cherifi, C., Moalla, N., Ouzrout, Y.: A web service composition framework based on centrality and community structure. In: Proceedings of 11th International Conference Signal-Image Technology & Internet-Based Systems (SITIS), pp. 489–496. IEEE Press, New York (2015)

7. Cherifi, C., Santucci, J.F.: Community structure in interaction web service networks. Int. J. Web Based Commun. **9**(3), 392–410 (2013)

8. Hajibagheri, A., Alvari, H., Hamzeh, A., Hashemi, S.: Community detection in social networks using information diffusion. In: Proceedings of the 2012 International Conference on Advances in Social Networks Analysis and Mining (ASONAM 2012), pp. 702–703. IEEE Computer Society (2012)

9. Varamesh, A., Akbari, M.K., Fereiduni, M., Sharifian, S., Bagheri, A.: Distributed clique percolation based community detection on social networks using MapReduce. In: 2013 5th Conference Information and Knowledge Technology (IKT), pp. 478–483. IEEE Press, New York (2013)

10. Han, Y., Hu, J., Li, D., Zhang, S.: A novel measurement of structure properties in complex networks. In: Zhou, J. (ed.) Complex 2009. LNICST, vol. 5, pp. 1292–1297. Springer, Heidelberg (2009). https://doi.org/10.1007/978-3-642-02469-6_10

11. Wiedermann, M., Donges, J.F., Kurths, J., Donner, R.V.: Spatial network surrogates for disentangling complex system structure from spatial embedding of nodes. Phys. Rev. E **93** (4), 042308 (2016)

12. Kim, D.H., Rodgers, G.J., Kahng, B., Kim, D.: Modelling hierarchical and modular complex networks: division and independence. Phys. A **351**(2), 671–679 (2005)

13. Capocci, A., Servedio, V.D.P., Colaiori, F., Buriol, L.S., Donato, D., Leonardi, S., Caldarelli, G.: Preferential attachment in the growth of social networks: the internet encyclopedia wikipedia. Am. Phys. Soc. **74**(3), 036116 (2006)

14. Masucci, A.P., Kalampokis, A., Eguíluz, V.M., Hernández-García, E.: Wikipedia information flow analysis reveals the scale-free architecture of the semantic space. PLoS ONE **6**(2), e17333 (2011)

15. Schönhofen, P.: Identifying document topics using the wikipedia category network. Web Intell. Agent Syst. Int. J. **7**(2), 195–207 (2009)

16. Chopade, P., Zhan, J.: Structural and functional analytics for community detection in large-scale complex networks. J. Big Data **2**(1), 11 (2015)

17. Fortunato, S., Lancichinetti, A.: Community detection algorithms: a comparative analysis: invited presentation, extended abstract. In: Proceedings of the Fourth International ICST Conference on Performance Evaluation Methodologies and Tools, p. 27 (2009)

18. Newman, M.E.: Detecting community structure in networks. Eur. Phys. J. B-Condens Matter Complex Syst. **38**(2), 321—330 (2004)

19. Estrada, E., Higham, D.J., Hatano, N.: Communicability betweenness in complex networks. Phys. A **388**(5), 764–774 (2009)

20. Xiao, L., Wang, S., Li, J.: Discovering community membership in biological networks with node topology potential. In: 2012 IEEE International Conference Granular Computing (GrC), pp. 541–546. IEEE Press, New York (2012)

21. Li, D., Wang, S., Li, D.: Spatial Data Mining: Theory and Application. Springer, Heidelberg (2016). https://doi.org/10.1007/978-3-662-48538-5

22. Seary, A.J., Richards, W.D.: Spectral methods for analyzing and visualizing networks: an introduction. pp. 209–228 (2003)

23. Ma, X., Gao, L.: Non-traditional spectral clustering algorithms for the detection of community structure in complex networks: a comparative analysis. J. Statis. Mech. Theor. Exp. **2011**(05), P05012 (2011)

24. Rahman, M.S., Ngom, A.: A fast agglomerative community detection method for protein complex discovery in protein interaction networks. In: Ngom, A., Formenti, E., Hao, J.-K., Zhao, X.-M., van Laarhoven, T. (eds.) PRIB 2013. LNCS, vol. 7986, pp. 1–12. Springer, Heidelberg (2013). https://doi.org/10.1007/978-3-642-39159-0_1
25. Pons, P., Latapy, M.: Computing communities in large networks using random walks. In: Yolum, p., Güngör, T., Gürgen, F., Özturan, C. (eds.) ISCIS 2005. LNCS, vol. 3733, pp. 284–293. Springer, Heidelberg (2005). https://doi.org/10.1007/11569596_31
26. Rosvall, M., Bergstrom, C.T.: Maps of random walks on complex networks reveal community structure. Proc. Natl. Acad. Sci. **105**(4), 1118–1123 (2008)
27. Newman, M.E.: Fast algorithm for detecting community structure in networks. Phys. Rev. E **69**(6), 066133 (2004)
28. Jianpei, Z., Hongbo, L., Jing, Y., Jinbo, B., Yan, C.: Network soft partition based on topological potential. In: 2011 6th International ICST Conference Communications and Networking in China (CHINACOM), pp. 725–729. IEEE Press, New York (2011)
29. Xuhui, W.: Lossless network compression based on topology potential community discovery. J. Theor. Appl. Inf. Technol. **50**, 7 (2005)
30. Wang, Z., Chen, Z., Zhao, Y., Nui, Q.: Topology potential: a novel local maximum potential point search algorithm for topology potential field. Int. J. Hybrid Inf. Technol. **7**(2), 1–8 (2014)
31. Ding, X., Chen, Z.W.S., Huang, Y.: Community-based collaborative filtering recommendation algorithm. Int. J. Hybrid Inf. Technol. **8**(2), 149–158 (2015)
32. Wang, Z., Chen, Z., Zhao, Y., Chen, S.: A community detection algorithm based on topology potential and spectral clustering. Sci. World J. **2014**, 1–9 (2014)
33. Nielsen, F.Å.: Wikipedia research and tools: Review and comments (2012)

Static Detection Method for C/C++ Memory Defects Based on Triad Memory Model

Yuxia Wang[1], Fusheng Jin[1(✉)], Xiangyu Han[2], and Runan Wang[1]

[1] Beijing Institute of Technology, No. 5, ZhongGuanCun South Street, Haidian District, Beijing 100081, China
jfs2lcn@bit.edu.cn
[2] Aerospace Automatic Control Institute, Beijing, China

Abstract. The improper use of pointers in C/C++ programming language brings about a lot of memory-related issues. In this paper, causes of four kinds of memory defects are analyzed and summarized. Besides, a novel triad memory model has been proposed. Based on the model and the variable life cycle methodology, an approach for inner-procedure and inter-procedure detection has been presented too. Eventually, the prototype CAnalyzer is implemented on the basis of Clang static analyzer. Experiment results show that CAnalyzer can effectively detect the four types of memory defects.

Keywords: Memory defects · Memory model · Life cycle
Inner and Inter-procedure detection

1 Introduction

The dynamic memory management mechanism and the application of pointers in C/C++ programming language significantly enhance the flexibility of programs, but which also gives rise to memory-related issues under improper operations by developers, like memory leaks, null pointer references. These memory defects are severely dangerous and difficult to detect, which might lead to performance degradation and even failure of system. Especially when such an illegal program has been running on a large server for a long time, the consequence will be catastrophic. Besides, in the Common Weakness Enumeration Top25 Most Dangerous Software Errors (2010), both 3rd defect and the 18th one are associated with memory. Therefore, it is completely necessary to analyze and detect the defects before they are released.

In order to detect memory defects, a large amount of research has been done in recent years. Compared with dynamic analysis techniques, static analysis techniques can cover all the branch paths of the code, detect defects at the early stage of development and has low cost, high efficiency, simple deployment as well as fast execution speed, therefore, static analysis method has been commonly used in field of defect detection, such as path-sensitive method (Xu et al. 2015; Zhang et al. 2015; Jung and Yi 2008), non-path-sensitive method (Sui et al. 2012; Cherem et al. 2007). Among the path-sensitive methods, all the systems operate based on the output of compiler's lexical analysis, grammatical analysis, semantic analysis and other intermediate representations. For example, cppCheck_IP (2015) uses token stream generated from

H. Yuan et al. (Eds.): GSKI 2017, CCIS 849, pp. 69–78, 2018.
https://doi.org/10.1007/978-981-13-0896-3_7

lexical analysis, Melton (2015), SPARROW (2008) work on the basis of the abstract syntax tree (AST) built up from the semantic analysis. Path-sensitive methods are applied widely for its higher accuracy compared with non-sensitive ones. Most of the detection tools tend to sum up the error modes based on the analysis of the causes for various types of memory defects (Wang et al. 2017). For example, (Li et al. 2017) classifies the data set of null pointer dereference defect via ID3 classification algorithm based on Rough Set Theory. Afterwards, variables related to error modes are extracted from sources or intermediate files as the foundation of detection. Validation is necessary after the detection (Li et al. 2017). But these prevailing problems are challenging as follows:

1. Most prototypes and tools detecting memory defects generally solve just one problem, some focus on memory leak, others concern about array cross-border, or null pointer reference. As for memory defects, there is not a unified memory model. At the same time, most function summary generation and detection algorithms have a certain degree of pertinence, lacking of expansibility in the detection capabilities.
2. In static analysis methods and tools, the problem of variable scope and life cycle is seldom considered.
3. The rate of false negatives and false positives is high, which cannot be accurately positioned to the most initial position causing errors, and the format of the errors is out of order and unclear.

To alleviate these shortcomings, this paper introduces CAnalyzer, a memory defects detection system for C/C++ programs. CAnalyzer uses path-sensitive static analysis techniques and focuses on memory models that are not significantly impacted by obfuscations. Experiments indicate that CAnalyzer can detect four types of memory defects effectively.

The contributions of this paper are as follows:

1. Causes of four kinds of defects including memory leaks, buffer overflows, null pointer references, and suspected pointer references are analyzed and formulated.
2. A novel triad memory model has been proposed based on region memory model.
3. Based on the memory model and the variable life cycle methodology, an inter-procedures detection approach has been presented. In addition, the prototype CAnalyzer is implemented based on Clang front-end.

The remainder of this paper is structured as follows. Section 2 presents triad memory model. Section 3 introduces our approach for detecting defects inner & inter procedures. Section 4 presents the experiment results. Section 5 concludes and discusses the future work.

2 Memory Model

The memory model is the basis of simulating dynamic loading and running in static detection, which is an abstract representation of machine instructions. There are two traditional memory models: Name-binding model and Array Simulation model.

Name Binding Model is a series of key-value pairs <name, value>. The key problem is that the Name-binding model does not have the concept of memory, but memory abstraction is indispensable for C/C++ languages with pointer types.

Array Simulation model considers the memory as a long array, element indexes of an array are seen as memory locations of variables. Storage of values is achieved by modifying the values of the corresponding units in an array. This model solves alias problems, but variable-length arrays and heap objects of unknown size cannot be represented through this model. Moreover, hierarchical relationships among memory objects cannot be exhibited too. Xu and Ted proposed a region-based triad model (Alam et al. 2017). The model introduces two mapping relations, namely:

$$Env : Variable \rightarrow Location$$
$$Store : Location \rightarrow value$$

Location is represented by Region instead of array index in Array Simulation Model.

This paper extended the region memory model and presented a new triad memory model.

2.1 Triad Memory Model

In order to simplify the hierarchical relationships in region memory model, this paper defines three layer region – (Meta Region, Construct Region, Top Region). Meta Region is the memory area storing basic type, pointer type and void type; Construct Region is the memory area storing construction type; The top memory area is the real storage area, which will be classified into three sections including Static Data Region, Stack Region, Heap Region due to the differences of their life cycle and the application-release mechanism. On the data structure mentioned above, triad memory model is represented as <memory state, pointer state, memory behavior>. The detailed statement is as follows.

1. *Memory State*

The contents of the static data area exist throughout the life of the program, and their memory space is allocated by the compiler at compile time. Contents on the stack exist only within the scope of the function, and when the function is ended, the contents are automatically removed. For both static data area and stack area, the system automatically allocates and releases memory, so memory state here is mainly for heap memory state. The heap is dynamically allocated by the malloc() series functions or 'new' operator. The life cycle is determined by free() or delete. They will exist until being released or the end of the program. Here we define the following three states:

(1) Allocated: Unavailable
(2) Freed: Available
(3) Leaked: Error

2. *Pointer State*

The pointer stores the memory address and points to the value stored in this address. Therefore, pointers are actually the bridge between variables and values. In the life cycle of the pointer, the pointer states are divided into the following five categories:

(1) illegal state($S_{illegal}$): 1. After the pointer is defined, before the initialization or assignment, the internal storage content is invalid, pointing to the illegal memory area; 2. After the memory space is released without setting to NULL, the value stored in this space has not changed, so it cannot be cited;

(2) NULL state(S_{null}): 1. After the pointer is initialized or assigned to NULL; 2. After dynamic memory is allocated unsuccessfully with a return value NULL

(3) Heap state(S_{heap}): The pointer points to a dynamic allocated heap memory space, and the memory state is allocated;

(4) Stack state(S_{stack}): The pointer points to stack area;

(5) Static and Global state(S_{static}): The pointer points to static data area;

3. *Memory Behavior*

Memory behavior is the motivation of memory state changes, and the memory behavior is abstracted into the following eight categories:

(1) Malloc(p): Dynamically allocate memory space for pointer p. Memory allocation operations include malloc()/calloc()/realloc() and new.

(2) Free(p): Release the memory space pointed by pointer p. Release operations include free() and delete.

(3) Move(p): Pointer p changes in the memory area.

(4) Location(Var): Take the address value of the variable, that is, the left value.

(5) Store(p): Take the value stored in the memory space pointed by pointer p. That is the right value of the variable.

(6) Access(p): access p

(7) Remove(p, M): The pointer p is removed from the memory space M, that is, p refers to the other memory address rather than the scale of M.

(8) Add(p, M): Pointer p points to an address in memory space M.

2.2 Defect Classification and Representation

The classification of memory defects is exhibited in Table 1. These defects are represented using triad memory model as follows. Among them, V represents a set of all pointers to memory block M, $p \in V$; Status(M) means to get memory status; Status(p) is to get the status of p; Init represents the first address returned when the memory M is allocated successfully; size(M) means to get the size of M.

Table 1. Description and classification of defect types

Defect type	Detailed classification	Brief description
Memory leak	Non-release operation	Memory space is requested on a reachable path, but there is no release operation on that path
	Can't be released	Lose control of all/only references to dynamically allocated memory
	Incomplete release	When released, the pointer does not point to the initial address
	Improper release	Releases memory containing the only reference to another block of memory
	Repeat release	Double Free
	Unmatched apply-release	malloc/delete new/free
	Uninitialized struct pointer member	The member pointer of a struct does not point to legal memory
Buffer overflow	Heap overflow	Inappropriate use of C/C++ string and file read, write, copy and other related library functions
	Stack overflow	
	Static area overflow	Array, dynamic memory index crossed
Null pointer Reference –		NULL pointer dereference
Suspected pointer Reference –		Dereference of the released dynamic memory pointer

(1) F_{NF}: Allocated memory is not released (Non-Free)

$$\forall p \in V, (Status(M) == M_{Allocated}) \wedge (Status(p)$$
$$== S_{heap}) \wedge (\neg \exists Free(p)) \longrightarrow F_{NF}$$

(2) F_{NP}: There is no pointer pointing to an allocated memory, which is a special case of F_{NF} and will lead a memory space not to be released (Non-Point)

$$\forall p \in V, (Status(M) == M_{Allocated}) \wedge (Status(p)$$
$$== S_{heap}) \wedge remove(p, M) \longrightarrow F_{NP}$$

(3) F_{FF}: When memory is released, the pointer does not point to the initial address of the memory space (Non-First-address Free)

$$\forall p \in V, (Status(M) == M_{Allocated}) \wedge (Status(p) == S_{heap} \wedge (p!$$
$$= init)) \wedge Free(p) \longrightarrow F_{FF}$$

(4) F_{IF}: Releases the memory containing the only reference to other blocks of memory (Inappropriate Free)

$$\forall p_{M1} \in V_{M1}, (Store(M_1) == Location(M_2)) \wedge (Status(M_{1\&2})$$
$$== M_{Allocated}) \wedge Free(p_{M1}) \longrightarrow F_{IF}$$

(5) F_{DF}: Repeat release operation (Double Free)

$$\forall p \in V, (Status(M) == M_{Freed}) \wedge (Status(p) == S_{illegal}) \wedge Free(p) \longrightarrow F_{DF}$$

(6) F_{UF}: The allocation and release operations do not match (Unmatched Free)

(7) F_{IM}: Struct member pointer is not initialized (illegal Memory)

$$\forall p \in V, (Status(p) == S_{illegal}) \wedge Store(p) \longrightarrow F_{IM}$$

(8) F_{BO}: Buffer overflow includes stack overflow, heap overflow and static data area overflow. When move() is executed to pointer p, the value of pointer p may crosses the interval [init, init + size(M)-1] (Buffer Overflow)

$$\forall p \in V, (Status(M) == M_{Allocated}) \wedge (Status(p) == S_{heap}) \wedge (Move(p, M) \vee Access(p)) \longrightarrow F_{BO}$$
$$\forall p \in V, (Status(p) == S_{stack}) \wedge (Move(p, M) \vee Access(p)) \longrightarrow F_{BO}$$
$$\forall p \in V, (Status(p) == S_{static}) \wedge (Move(p, M) \vee Access(p)) \longrightarrow F_{BO}$$

(9) F_{ND}: NULL pointer is referred (Null Dereference)

$$\forall p \in V, (Status(p) == S_{null}) \wedge Access(p) \longrightarrow F_{ND}$$

(10) F_{SD}: suspected pointer is referred (Suspected pointer Dereference);

$$\forall p \in V, (Status(M) == M_{Freed}) \wedge (Status(p) == S_{heap}) \wedge Access(p) \longrightarrow F_{SD}$$

3 Detection Method

3.1 Inner-Procedure Detection

In the inner-procedure detection, program states are stored, meanwhile memory behavior of each defect in Table 2 will be checked when traversing each statement. After the judgement, reachable marks will be gained and recorded.

Program states mentioned above includes memory status, pointer status and point.

Memory Status = {allocated, released, le aked} = {1, 0, −1}
Memory Pointer Status = {illegal, null, heap, stack, static} = {−1, 0, 1, 2, 3}
Point = Pointer address - first address of allocated memory, it indicates the length between the first address of the memory block and this pointer, and the normal range of point is [0,size-1]

Table 2. Detection rules

Defect type	Alias	Status(M)	Status(p)	Point	Behavior	Mark
1. Non-Free	F_{NF}	1	1	N/A	Non Free	1
2. Non-Point	F_{NP}	1	1	N/A	remove()	1
3. Non-First-address Free	F_{FF}	1	1	!= 0	Free()	1
4. Inappropriate Free	F_{IF}	1	1	N/A	Free()	0/1
5. Double Free	F_{DF}	0	−1	N/A	Free()	1
6. Unmatched Free	F_{UF}	1	1	N/A	Free()	0/1
7. Illegal Memory	F_{IM}	N/A	−1	N/A	Store()	1
8. Buffer Overflow	F_{BO}	1	1/2/3	![0,size-1]	Move()	1
9. NULL Dereference	F_{ND}	N/A	0	N/A	Access()	1
10. Suspected Dereference	F_{SD}	0	−1	N/A	Access()	1

Reachable mark: 0/1, 0 indicates unreachable; 1 means reachable

During the process of inner-procedure detection, the memory status, pointer status, point value and reachable mark value will be stored as a program state. At the same time, defects will be judged whether they are reachable or not according to Table 2. If they are reachable, they are marked as 1 and their context information is recorded; otherwise, marked as 0. Particularly, in order to detect *memory leak* more accurately, we propose *the assumption* combined with the life cycle and scope of variables: In a function, when the scope of the variable ends, the temporary memory space allocated in the stack for variables should be destroyed. If the dynamic memory M is not released before the end of the scope, the pointer pointing to the dynamic memory M is neither static nor global, simultaneously it isn't passed to any static or global variables either, thus the program loses the control of the dynamic memory M when the scope ends, so the memory has been leaked.

3.2 Inter-Procedure Detection

In the inter-Procedure Detection, defects are detected in each reachable path by using function call diagrams, function summaries and context information including program states and reachable mark values generated from Sect. 3.1.

Inter-Procedure Detection Method:

Input: Function call diagrams, abstract syntax trees, and sub functions' summaries

Explanation: In order to avoid repeated analysis of the same function, function summary is generated from the AST. The function call graph is sorted by topology to get the order of function summaries' generation.

Process: GenFunction Summary()

1: Depth first traversal of abstract syntax trees

When encountering the generation or use of the memory pointer node, extract the relevant information, then go to step 2;
When encountering function call nodes, perform step 3;
Otherwise, go to step 4.

2: At the node of the memory pointer generation or use, get pointer identification information;

To filter the pointer variable and judge whether it's the parameters, class members or global variables, if the answer is yes, there may be some memory defects between functions, this pointer needs to be added to the function summary, and perform step 5;
Otherwise, do not set up any summaries and go to step 4.

3: In the function call node, judge whether the function has function summary

If it has, then connect the function summary to current part.
At the same time, judge whether it is the parameters, class members or global variables, to determine if the function needs to be spread up continuously.
If it needs, go to step 5, otherwise go to step 4.

4: Judge whether the current node is the last node of AST.

If it is, end the function summary calculation;
Otherwise, go to the next node, go to step 1 and execute iteratively.

5: Establish an entity class that holds the function summary information and records the information that needs to be detected, including the pointer identifier, the heap memory information pointed to by the pointer, the memory behavior of the pointer and the specific constraint information of the behavior, the function information of the pointer, and so on. After adding to the function summary, proceed to step 4.

Output: function summary

4 Experiment Results and Analysis

The detection algorithm is implemented in CAnalyzer, the following three experiments will show its detection capability on memory defects.

Experiment 1 takes 40 customized C/C++ programs as test cases including inappropriate uses of standard library functions, pointers, strings, files and other usual mistakes in practice. The Table 3 shows the result of the comparison experiment between Clang static analyzer and CAnalyzer in these customized test cases.

The test files in Experiment 2 are from a test case set for C/C++ defects–Common Weakness Enumeration (CWE), including CWE121 (Stack Based Buffer Overflow), CWE122 (Heap Based Buffer Overflow), CWE401 (Memory Leak). The results are compared with Cppcheck1.7.2 and Klocwork9 showing in Table 4. CAnalyzer has improved detection accuracy significantly in memory defect detection.

Experiment 3 tests four open-source projects, the results present that in these four open source projects, CAnalyzer explores 35 memory defects, among which 13 defects have been confirmed and repaired during the version upgrade of these four open source projects showing in Table 5.

Table 3. The comparison between clang static analyzer and CAnalyzer

Defect type	Alias	Test cases	Clang	CAnalyzer
Non-release operation	F_{NF}	7	2	7
Cannot be released	F_{NP}	6	6	6
Incomplete release	F_{FF}	4	4	4
Improper release	F_{IF}	1	0	1
Repeat release	F_{DF}	1	1	1
Unmatched apply-release	F_{UF}	4	4	4
Uninitializedstruct pointer member	F_{IM}	3	0	3
Heap overflow	F_{BO}	10	2	10
Stack overflow	F_{BO}	10	2	10
Static area overflow	F_{BO}	9	2	9
NULL Dereference	F_{ND}	6	2	6
Suspected Dereference	F_{SD}	5	5	5

Table 4. CAnalyzer/CppCheck/K9 CWE comparison experiment.

File name	File number	Defects sum	Cppcheck	Klocwork9	CAnalyzer
CWE121	8264	8264	263	631	3976
CWE122	10160	10160	734	80	5342
CWE401	2824	2824	398	463	2019

Table 5. Results of Experiment 3

Project	Report defects	Confirmed defects number
libxslt-1.1.20	11	2
openssh3.5p1	7	3
lhttpd0.1	6	5
bftpd1.0.24	12	3

The memory defects identified in this experiment illustrate that this method can be applied to practical engineering, and can find memory defects in the actual project, which has practical value.

5 Conclusion and Future Work

In this paper, the detection method of memory defects is implemented in CAnalyzer. Based on the proposed novel triad memory model, and the reachable rules of each memory defect are put forward. Experimental results demonstrates that compared with other static detection tools, CAnalyzer has significantly improved in the detection accuracy. In future work, we will make CAnalyzer classify, recognize and define the error mode automatically based on machine learning or deep learning algorithms instead of the rules defined by experts artificially.

References

Xu, Z., Zhang, J., Xu, Z.: Melton: a practical and precise memory leak detection tool for C programs. Front. Comput. Sci. **9**(1), 34–54 (2015)

Zhang, S., Shang, Z.: Software defect pattern analysis and location based on Cppcheck. Comput. Eng. Appl. **51**(3), 69–73 (2015). (in Chinese)

Jung, Y., Yi, K.: Practical memory leak detector based on parameterized procedural summaries. In: Proceedings of the 7th International Symposium on Memory Management, pp. 131–140. ACM (2008)

Cherem, S., Princehouse, L., Rugina, R.: Practical memory leak detection using guarded value-flow analysis. In: Proceedings of PLDI, pp. 480–491 (2007)

Sui, Y., Ye, D., Xue, J.: Static memory leak detection using full-sparse value-flow analysis. In: Proceedings of International Symposium on Software Testing and Analysis. pp. 254–264 (2012)

Li, Q., Pan, M., Li, X.: Memory leak detection tools and evaluation methods. Comput. Sci. Explor. **3**(1), 29–35 (2010). (in Chinese)

Wang, S., Quan, Y., Sun, J.: False positive recognition method for hull pointer reference defect based on classification. J. Comput. Appl. **10**(2968), 2972–3005 (2017). (in Chinese)

Li, X., Zhou, Y., Li, M.C., Chen, Y.J., Xu, G.Q., Wang, L.Z., Li, X.D.: Automatically validating static memory leak warnings for C/C++ programs. Ruan Jian Xue Bao/J. Softw. **28**(4), 827–844 (2017). (in Chinese)

Xu, Z., Kremenek, T., Zhang, J.: A memory model for static analysis of C programs. In: Margaria, T., Steffen, B. (eds.) ISoLA 2010. LNCS, vol. 6415, pp. 535–548. Springer, Heidelberg (2010). https://doi.org/10.1007/978-3-642-16558-0_44

Alam, S., Qu, Z., Riley, R., et al.: DroidNative: automating and optimizing detection of android native code malware variants. Comput. Secur. **65**, 230–246 (2017)

Xie, Y., Aiken, A.: Context-and path-sensitive memory leak detection. In: ACM SIGSOFT Software Engineering Notes, vol. 30(5), pp. 115–125. ACM (2005)

An Immune Neural Network Model for Aeroengine Performance Monitoring

Wei Wang$^{(\boxtimes)}$, Shengli Hou, and Jing Guo

Department of Aviation Material Management, Air Force Logistics College,
No. 85 Xige Street, Xuzhou 221000, Jiangsu, China
wwleilei@126.com

Abstract. In this paper, an aeroengine performance monitoring and fault detection model, based on immune neural network, is put forward. By combining artificial immune system recognition mechanism with artificial neural network, the deviation degree of aeroengine performance (abnormal degree) can be determined, and the monitoring of performance trend can be achieved. With this method, the overall performance change of aeroengine can be reflected sensitively and accurately, the abnormity recognition rate of aeroengine performance can be enhanced, and potential early engine fault can be detected to prevent further development. This method is proved effective through the monitoring of a certain type of turbofan aeroengine.

Keywords: Aerospace propulsion system · Aeroengine
Performance monitoring · Artificial immune system · Immune neural network

1 Introduction

Nowadays, a variety of methods for aeroengine performance monitoring and fault diagnosis have been developed home and abroad, such as statistical analysis, neural network and synthetic exponent method. Generally, these methods require sufficient fault samples to achieve satisfying monitoring and detection effect. For example, through the integration of different performance parameters of the aeroengine, a synthetic exponent is obtained with the synthetic exponent method. This parameter quantitatively reflects the overall performance index, and thus can be used to monitor the overall performance of the aeroengine. However, when synthetic exponent is calculated with weighted method, the impact of each parameter on the overall performance of the aeroengine, namely the weight of each parameter, needs to be determined. Whichever method to be used in determining the weight [1, 2], a sufficient number of aeroengine abnormity or fault data are required as training samples, or the promotional value of the weight is poor, which will lead to the insensitivity of the synthetic exponent to other types of faults.

In recent years, inspiration was obtained from the operating mechanism of biological immune system, and an application-oriented immune system calculation model called Artificial Immune System (AIS) was developed to solve practical engineering problems. Immune system is a complex learning system of distributed information processing. Practice shows that the development of the immune system to establish AIS

© Springer Nature Singapore Pte Ltd. 2018
H. Yuan et al. (Eds.): GSKI 2017, CCIS 849, pp. 79–87, 2018.
https://doi.org/10.1007/978-981-13-0896-3_8

is a new way to deal with engineering problems [3, 4]. Many rich ideological mechanisms included in the immune system provide new opportunities for solving engineering problems. Current research focuses on the use of immune mechanism in improving other algorithms to form new algorithms, such as the immune-neural network [5]. The birth of new ideas and new methods in this cross-cutting integration process has extended the ability of AIS to deal with increasingly complex problems. Therefore, this paper attempts to use a neural network model based on immune mechanism for aeroengine performance monitoring and fault detection.

2   Immune Vector Detector

2.1   Immune Recognition

Immune recognition is not only the main function of the immune system, but also the core of AIS. The nature of immune recognition is to distinguish between "self" and "non-self". The "self—non-self" recognition mechanism of immune system can be simply described as follows: there is a kind of immune T-Lymphocytes in the immune system. In the production process, detectors (antibodies) come into being on the T cell surface through a pseudo-random genetic recombination process. Then T cells enter the thymus. Those react with body's own protein are destroyed. Only those who do not destroy their own tissue survive. The whole process is called negative selection. By matching with non-self substance (antigen), these mature T cells recognize non-self substance (antigen), perform immune function, and protect the body against antigens. Through its own learning, the immune system can generate memory for non-self substance, and with a limited number of detectors, it can accurately identify and kill an unlimited number of non-self. Just like the nervous system, the immune system learns new information, recalls previously learned information, depending not on a central controller, but on decentralized testing to respond to foreign invasion. It reflects the immune system's unique intelligent mechanism and extremely robust way to deal with problems [6].

To make discussion easier, the following definitions are provided:

Definition 1. System State Space. Eigenvector X denotes system state. After standardized processing, $X = (x_1, x_2, \cdots, x_n) \in [0, 1]^n$. System state space is denoted by set $G \subseteq [0, 1]^n$, including all the possible state of the system.

Definition 2. Self Space/Normal Space and Non-self Space/Abnormal Space. Self space consists of eigenvectors in normal system state, and is denoted by set $S \subseteq G$. Non-self space consists of eigenvectors in abnormal system state, and is denoted by set NS. NS is the complementary set of S.

Establish the mapping relationship of organism to the system state space. The mapping of organism itself is the self space, while the mapping of non-self substance (antigen) inside and outside the organism is the non-self space. The mapping of antibody on the surface of T cell is the detector. In this way, the mapping of antigen recognition to the system state space is the matching of detector with the non-self space. Detector is then the typical sample in the non-self space.

2.2 Detector

To monitor the performance of the aeroengine, its state space should first be defined by the following steps:

(1) Record all the 9 monitored parameters of aeroengine, respectively, corrected rotation speed of high pressure rotor n_{hcor}, corrected rotation speed of low pressure rotor n_{lcor}, angle of low pressure guide vane $alpha_1$, angle of high pressure guide vane $alpha_2$, vibration value B, lubrication oil consumption ph, temperature of turbine exhaust T_4, slip ratio S, and final nozzle indicating value le.

(2) Standardize each aeroengine operating parameter according to its ideal value, i.e., an efficacy function $\hat{x_i}(t)$ is obtained. The value of this efficacy function $\hat{x_i}(t)$ reflects the performance of the aeroenging, and $0 \leq \hat{x_i}(t) \leq 1$. When the aeroengine is in its top operating condition, $\hat{x_i}(t) = 1$; when it's in fault state, $\hat{x_i}(t) = 0$.

(3) Efficacy functions constitute the eigenvector $X(t) = (\hat{x_1}(t), \hat{x_2}(t), \cdots, \hat{x_n}(t))$, which reflect the operating condition of the aeroengine. It is a function of time, and then can form the aeroengine state space G.

As a result, the detector is in the form of vector, and is called a vector detector. It has the same number of dimensions as normal mode vectors, but is distributed in the non-self space. The vector detector d satisfies the following inequality:

$$E(d, v) > r$$

Wherein, $E(\cdot)$ represents the Euclidean distance, v represents an arbitrary normal mode vector in the self space, and r is the threshold. Vector detectors generated by the above rules are distributed in the non-self space. Immune recognition algorithm shown in Fig. 1 is used in the generation of detectors.

The randomly generated detectors are redistributed to the non-self space through the following learning process.

(1) Specify learning step p;
(2) For each detector d, find its nearest k normal mode vector set Nc;
(3) Calculate the learning step length Δ,

$$\Delta = \frac{\sum_{c \in N_c} (d - c)}{k} \tag{1}$$

(4) Learn with the following formula, where η is the learning rate,

$$d = d + \eta \cdot \Delta \tag{2}$$

(5) Each time after finishing step 2 to 4, check whether d meets the requirements. If it meets the matching rule, d is an effective detector, and should be added into the effective detector set D. After finishing specified learning step p, if the detector still cannot meet the requirements, it should be removed.

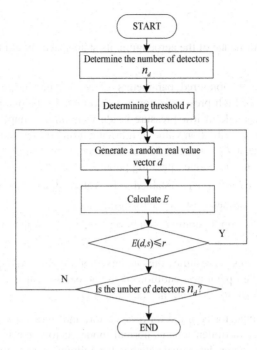

Fig. 1. Flow chart of immune recognition

In the case of a limited number of detectors, the more evenly they are distributed in the non-self space, the better representation they perform. Therefore, in the detector generation process, distribution is conducted by the following method to effectively cover the whole abnormal space, as shown in Fig. 2.

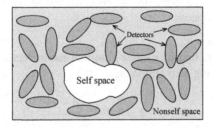

Fig. 2. Distribution of vector detectors

First define the matching function of any two detectors as follows:

$$\mu_{\boldsymbol{d}}(\boldsymbol{d}') = e^{\frac{|d-d'|^2}{2r^2}} \tag{3}$$

For a newly generated detector, in addition to ensuring not matching with the self space, distribution should be regulated by the following equation,

$$\Delta_d = \frac{\sum \mu_d(d')(d - d')}{\sum_{d' \in D} \mu_d(d')} \tag{4}$$

$$d = d + \eta \cdot \Delta_d \tag{5}$$

Where d' is an existing valid detector.

Through the above process, an effective detector set D that covers the non-self space is generated. The number of detectors can be determined according to the need of practical problems. The more the detectors, the better the monitoring effect. But too many detectors will increase the training time of future neural networks.

3 Immune Neural Network Model

Building a reasonable model of the changes in the aeroengine operating state parameters to reflect the trend of overall performance is the key to know exactly the health status of the aeroengine, and to perform further fault prediction and alarm alerting [8]. Typically, there is no clear dividing line between normal and fault conditions of the aeroengine. "Abnormal" itself is a vague concept. So the aeroengine state space G can be mapped to interval [0,1] by the neural network, i.e. $[0, 1]^n \rightarrow [0, 1]$. In this case, the corresponding value indicates the normal level of the aeroengine: 1 indicates normal, 0 indicates fault, and values between 0 and 1 represent the abnormal degree. The smaller the value is, the greater the degree of abnormity.

Immune Neural Network (INN) model is composed of three parts. First, standardizational pretreatment of the actual aeroengine operating parameters is to be conducted with efficacy function. Then generate a vector detector d using the immune recognition algorithm provided in the previous section. Finally, the mapping between input and output is built with neural network. As a three-layer feedforward neural network has the ability to map any function, an adaptable three-layer BP network is used whose structure parameters are as follows: input layer nodes $M = 9$, hidden layer nodes $L = 18$, and output layer nodes $N = 1$.

Among them, the hidden layer and output layer activation function are $h(x) = \frac{1}{1+e^{-x}}$, the hidden layer weight and the output layer value v_j satisfy $0 < w_{i,j}, v_j < 1$.

Immune vector detector D is a representative sample in the non-self space, i.e., the fault sample in the aeroengine state space. In the learning process, let the output of normal sample be 1 and the output of fault sample be zero. The output of the neural network reflects the degree of overall aeroengine performance abnormity. The smaller the output value is, the more overall performance deviates from normal value. Figure 3 shows the learning and monitoring process of the INN model.

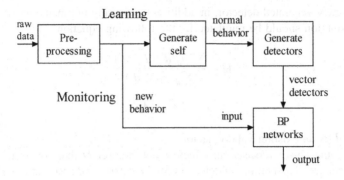

Fig. 3. Learning and monitoring process in immune-neural networks

To clearly express the output of the neural network in the form of curves, the following formula is used to smooth it.

$$\widehat{O}_t = \frac{\sum\limits_{i=1}^{s} O_{t-i}}{s} \tag{6}$$

Where s is the smooth window width; $\widehat{O}_t$ is the average output, or the result of smoothing.

Therefore, the output value of the INN can be used to obtain the aeroengine performance abnormity degree. It serves as a parameter that quantitatively reflects the overall aeroengine performance to monitor the performance trend.

4   Examples of Performance Monitoring

During engine operation, abnormal component performance is often a precursor to aeroengine fault. Although it may still work, the parameters involved will deviate from normal values. As a result, deviation degree/abnormal degree of the aeroengine performance can be determined according to changes in the operating state parameters for early fault detection and judgment.

Based on the above ideas and methods, analysis is carried out of the performance trend of a turbofan aeroengine. Through performance trend calculation program, efficacy function values of the 9 parameters in the 200 normal operating conditions can be achieved to form a self space. Then detectors/fault samples are generated by negative selection method. The number of detectors can be determined experimentally. When it's greater than 200, a better result can be obtained. Use the existing 200 normal samples and the generated 200 detector samples to conduct neural network learning. This neural network can be used to monitor the aeroengine performance trend. It should be noted that this paper aims at detecting abnormal operation through aeroengine performance monitoring, finding out early fault for troubleshooting and potential fault alerting, instead of isolating and recognizing the faults.

Experiment I: Monitor a certain aeroengine that operates 109 times, altogether 122 h, and record the parameter values.

First the efficacy function value corresponded with each parameter is calculated as the input of neural network. Smooth the output with smoothing window width $s = 6$ for the abnormal degree curve that reflects the performance of the aeroengine. Meanwhile, an integrated parametric curve reflecting the performance is obtained with

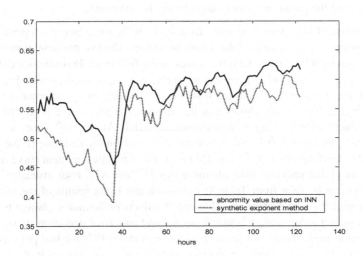

(a) Experiment I

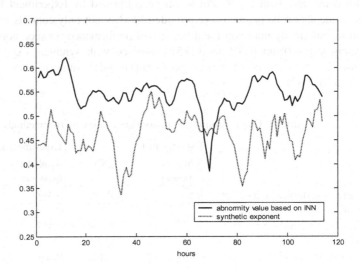

(b) Experiment II

Fig. 4. Curve of Aeroengine performance by abnormity value and synthetic exponent

comprehensive parametric method as comparison. The performance trend determined by the two methods is shown in Fig. 4(a): there have been sharp declines in both parameters, indicating significant deterioration of the performance. The case is the engine electronic controller (EEC) goes wrong and is replaced at the 36th hour. The sharp decline in Fig. 4(a) is caused by the parameter drift before the EEC fault, which indicates abnormal operating state of EEC, leading to the deviation of corresponding aeroengine parameters. With parameter continues to drift, EEC goes wrong at the 36th hour, and the parameter value drops to the lowest point.

Experiment II: Monitor another aeroengine of the same type that operates 102 times, altogether 114 h, and record the parameter values. The low pressure guide vane ($alpha_1$) goes wrong when the aeroengine works to the 69th hour. Performance change curve is drawn with abnormal degree and synthetic exponent, as shown in Fig. 4(b), where synthetic exponent is calculated with the same weight as in Experiment I.

Figure 4(b) clearly shows that the abnormal degree curve produced by INN can accurately reflect changes in performance trend. At the 65th hour, a sharp decline appears, indicating abnormal operating state, and finally resulting in the low pressure guide vane fault at the 69th hour. However, the synthetic exponent curve does not show this trend, but provides false alarms at the 33rd and 82nd hour instead.

As can be seen from Table 1, in Experiment I, the results of the two methods fit well with the actual situation. Although it reflects performance change more distinctly with greater value change between normal and abnormal operating states, the synthetic exponent method may not be more effective than the INN method put forward here. In the calculation of synthetic exponent, normal and fault samples in the parameters are used to optimize the calculation [1, 2]. As a result, it is sensitive only to fault types used in the learning process. For other types or new faults, it may work poorly, or even cannot detect any fault at all, which can be confirmed by Experiment II. In Experiment II, the abnormal degree curve provided by INN not only consists with the actual situation, but greatly improves the difference of performance between normal and fault operating states (from 0.001 to 0.185) compared with synthetic exponent method. Meanwhile, the variance of normal performance index value is also reduced (from 0.0063 to 0.0037).

Table 1. Comparison of the performance index by two methods

	Experiment I		Experiment II	
	Synthetic exponent	INN	Synthetic exponent	INN
Average of performance index at normal	0.563	0.592	0.458	0.564
Value of performance index in fault	0.382	0.451	0.457	0.379
Distance between normal and fault	0.181	0.141	0.001	0.185
Variance of performance index at normal	0.0042	0.0035	0.0063	0.0037

5 Conclusion

Based on the characteristics of aeroengine performance monitoring and fault diagnosis, combining immune mechanism with artificial neural network, this paper puts forward an aeroengine performance monitoring and fault detection model on the basis of INN. The monitoring results of a certain type of turbofan aeroengine show that: this model generates detectors/abnormal samples with normal data, depending less on aeroengine fault data; abnormity of INN output directly reflects the state of the aeroengine performance, reflecting the performance change trend more accurately and sensitively; by setting the alarm threshold, it can not only measure the performance change, but predict and give alarm when or before a engine fault, guiding troubleshooting and preventing major accidents.

Aeroengine fault/abnormity can be detected from the sharp decline of INN output, but concrete causes cannot be reflected in the performance change. So the next step is to establish a mathematical model for performance abnormity analysis. When performance deterioration appears, the model can determine abnormal parameters simultaneously, which is quite beneficial for rapid fault location and isolation.

References

1. Hu, J., Xie, S.: Performance monitoring and fault diagnosis of engines based genetic algorithm. J. Propul. Technol. **24**(3), 198–200 (2003)
2. Hou, S., Hu, J., Li, Y.: Aeroengine performance monitoring and fault diagnosis based on chaos variable. J. Aerospace Power **20**(2), 314–317 (2005)
3. Hou, S., Wang, W., Qiao, L.: Feature extraction and multi-sensor fault diagnosis based on clonal clustering. J. Electron. Optics Control **17**(6), 69–72 (2010)
4. Hou, S., Wang, W., Hu, J.: Neural network-based immune recognition model for aero-engine surge detection. J. Vibr. Shock **29**(1), 170–172 (2010)
5. Gonzalez, F., Dasgupta, D., Kozma, R.: Combining negative selection and classification techniques for anomaly detection. In: Proceedings of the Congress on Evolutionary Computation, pp. 705–710. Hawaii (2012)
6. Esponda, F., Forrest, S., Helman, P.: A formal framework for positive and negative detection schemes. J. IEEE Trans. Syst. Man Cybern. B, Cybern **34**(1), 357–373 (2014)
7. Wei, X., Feng, Y., Liu, F.: Development strategy and key prognostics health management technologies for military aero-engine in China. J. Aerospace Power **26**(9), 2107–2115 (2011)
8. Roemer, M.J., Nwadiogbu, E.O.: Development of diagnostic and prognostic technologies for aerospace health management applications. J. Paper 2001-GT-30, ASME and IGTI Turbo Expo 2012, Munich, Germany (2012)
9. Chiang, L.H., Russell, E.L., Braatz, R.D.: Fault Detection and Diagnosis in Industrial Systems. Springer, London (2001). https://doi.org/10.1007/978-1-4471-0347-9

Based on AHP and Minimum Spanning Tree of Fuzzy Clustering Analysis of Spatial Sequence Arrangement of Old Dismantling Area

Juanmin Cui[1], Wenguang Ji[1,2(✉)], and Yang Jae Lee[2]

[1] Department of Management Engineering,
Hebei Normal University Nationalities, Chengde 067000, Hebei, China
zhxyjwg@163.com
[2] Wonkwang University Municipal Engineering Department, Iksan, Korea

Abstract. This paper discusses the application of AHP, minimum spanning tree and fuzzy cluster analysis in the spatial arrangement of the old dismantling area. A fuzzy clustering analysis method based on minimum spanning tree for spatial sequence arrangement of old dismantling area is proposed. An accurate method is provided for spatial arrangement of old districts. Take lion town in Chengde city of Hebei Province as an example. Establishing suitability evaluation index system of old dismantles area. The weight of each evaluation index is established by using AHP. In view of the characteristics of the spatial sequence of the old dismantling area, the old dismantling project area was established. The minimum spanning tree is used to do the fuzzy clustering to arrange the space of different old demolition projects. The reliability analysis shows that the fuzzy clustering analysis based on minimum spanning tree is a reliable method for the spatial arrangement of the old dismantling area.

Keywords: AHP · Minimum spanning tree · Old dismantling area
Spatial temporal sequence · Fuzzy clustering

1 Introduction

The old dismantling area refers to the construction of rural land for land consolidation and land reclamation into farmland in accordance with the increase or decrease of construction land. Including the abandoned brick kilns, rural industrial land, rural residential land, rural residential land is the key. Land ownership is mainly collective owned. At present, the timing arrangement of the old dismantling area is often realized only by building the suitability evaluation index system of dismantling old and calculating the evaluation score, lacking of reliability.

The minimum spanning tree is given an undirected connected graph G = (V, E) (V represents vertices, E represents edges), where V = {V1, V2, v3,...... Vn}, E = {E1, E2, e3...... En} gives weight W (EI) > 0 for every edge e E in G, and generates spanning tree T = (V, H), H E, making all spanning edges of the spanning tree minimum, and the spanning tree is called minimum spanning tree. The minimum spanning

© Springer Nature Singapore Pte Ltd. 2018
H. Yuan et al. (Eds.): GSKI 2017, CCIS 849, pp. 88–97, 2018.
https://doi.org/10.1007/978-981-13-0896-3_9

tree Kruskal algorithm is: first construct a sub graph, which contains n vertices and the edge set is empty. Each vertex is taken as the root node of each tree in the spanning tree to form a tree network. Then the smallest edge is selected, and the smallest edge is selected at the edge of the net. If the two vertices of this edge above belong to different trees, then the edges join sub graph, on the other hand, if the two vertices of the edge of the falls on the same tree, then this edge is not desirable, need to take a minimum weight edge and try again. According to the analogy mentioned above, there is only one tree in the tree network (that is, there is a n-1 edge in the sub graph). Because of the dismantling of the old area in the spatial timing arrangement, the division between different periods, different regions is not obvious, and the order is not clear, that is, the boundaries are not clear. Therefore, it is necessary to introduce the fuzzy clustering analysis into the spatial temporal study of the old dismantling area, so as to increase the reliability of the measurement results. At present, there is little research on the method of combining minimum spanning tree with fuzzy cluster analysis to the spatial temporal arrangement of the old dismantling area.

2 Establish the Analysis Model of the Spatial Sequence Arrangement of the Old Dismantling Area

2.1 Evaluation Index and Weight Determination

Study on the demolition of the old suitability evaluation system, according to the demolition of the old district, surrounding geographical conditions economic conditions and cultural conditions of three evaluation factors for a total of fifteen level two indexes were analyzed by using the analytic hierarchy process (AHP) to determine the index weight.

2.2 Constructing Fuzzy Clustering Matrix

Select the appropriate statistics X_{ij}, will be classified object set to $X = \{x_1, x_2,\ldots\ldots X_n\}$, because each sample X_i contains M characteristic index, dimension its characteristic index matrix is:

$$X = \begin{Bmatrix} x_{11} & x_{12} & \cdots & x_{1m} \\ x_{21} & x_{22} & \cdots & x_{2m} \\ \vdots & \vdots & \vdots & \vdots \\ x_{n1} & x_{n2} & \cdots & x_{nm} \end{Bmatrix}$$

2.3 Initialization of Data Processing

By using the range normalization, the M characteristic indexes of the original data are processed by dimensionless method, and then the index data is normalized to [0, 1] interval. For the data of polarity (+) data (the bigger the better), the formula is:

$$S_i = \frac{(X_i - X_{min})}{(X_{max} - X_{min})}$$

For the data of polarity (-) data (the smaller the better data), the formula is:

$$S_i = \frac{(X_{max} - X_i)}{(X_{max} - X_{min})}$$

2.4 Constructing Similar Matrices

Using reciprocal of absolute value the similar matrix R of n row n column is constructed, and the formula is as follows:

$$r_{ij} = \begin{cases} 1 & i = j \\ \dfrac{c}{\sum\limits_{k=1}^{m} |S_{ik} - S_{jk}|} & i \neq j \end{cases}$$

Among them, R_{ij} (i = 1,... N; j = 1,..., n) elements for the similar matrix R line I J, C is positive and specific, to ensure that $R_{ij} = 0 \sim 1$. By all the similarity coefficients R_{ij}, the fuzzy similarity matrix R_{mm} between the elements is obtained:

$$R = \begin{Bmatrix} r_{11} & r_{12} & \cdots & r_{1m} \\ r_{21} & r_{22} & \cdots & r_{2m} \\ \vdots & \vdots & \vdots & \vdots \\ r_{m1} & r_{m2} & \cdots & r_{mm} \end{Bmatrix}$$

2.5 Fuzzy Clustering Based on Minimum Spanning Tree

Firstly, the maximal Rij and the meta rij* are extracted from the similar matrix R, and the minimal tree is obtained by analogy. Until there is only one tree in the tree network (ending with n-1 edges). The weight of the graph is less than the edge of the measured lambda, and the connected elements are classified into a class of.

3 Spatial Temporal Arrangement Analysis of Old Demolition Area of Lion Town in Chengde City of Hebei Province

3.1 Index System Establishment and Weight

In this paper, lion town in Hebei city of Chengde province is selected as the research object. The study is based on the results of the revision of the overall land use planning of lion town. Based on data from the 2016 national economic statistics yearbook lion Town, the town of second national land survey results, the quality of cultivated land to supplement and improve the results, the lion town land records, the lion town residents questionnaire and field survey statistics. The index system for suitability of old demolition is established as shown in Table 1.

Table 1. Series research evaluation index system of old area

Evaluation target	Evaluation factor	Weight	Evaluation index	Weight	Combined effect (+, -)
Suitability of old demolition	Geographical conditions A1	0.20	Soil texture A11	0.38	+
			Comprehensive productivity index of agricultural land A12	0.31	+
			Soil structure A13	0.17	+
			Land use efficiency % A14	0.14	+
	Economic condition A2	0.36	Average output value A21	0.13	+
			Agricultural output value/non agricultural output value A22	0.16	+
			Per capita net income in rural areas A23	0.37	+
			Increase and decrease hook potential of demolishing old districts A24	0.13	+
			Level of Agricultural Mechanization A25	0.11	+
	Humanistic conditions A3	0.44	Housing vacancy rate (including damage) % A31	0.09	+
			Ecological environment capacity A32	0.10	−
			Age composition of rural population A33	0.20	+
			Education level A34	0.20	+
			Proportion of people in two or three industry A35	0.23	+
			Proportion of medical insurance and social insurance A36	0.28	

3.2 Data Processing

This study is based on the increasing capacity of urban land use and the demolition of rural residential areas. There are 5 communities and 5 administrative villages in Chengde, Hebei province.

(1) Calculate the average distance between the patches of each residential spot

Using the spatial overlay function in the spatial analysis module of MapGIS7.0, the distance between the settlements of each residential spot was determined by the distance measuring ruler. (as shown in Table 2)

(2) Determination of old demolition project area

Taking the measured mean value as radius, the coverage area of different old villages was cut off, and the village combination was carried out on the basis of residential area. The combination of villages should ensure that the geographical conditions are as uniform as possible, to determine the demolition of the old project area 92.

(3) Adjustment of old dismantling project area

According to the requirements of the village spatial layout planning, and the folk custom, folk customs and related departments' opinions, the village adjustment in the project area will eventually form 88 old demolition projects.

Table 2. The distribution of adjacent distance and the project area of the patch of the residents in the Lion Ditch

Village name	Average distance (m)	Project areas number	Village name	Average distance (m)	Project areas number
Lion creek community	254.34	10	Lion creek village	226.41	7
Trees garden community	222.04	8	Luohangtang village	343.20	6
Lama temple community	225.84	9	Shuxiang temple village	331.91	5
Luohangtang community	254.13	11	Upper two rivers village	201.61	7
Puning temple community	287.34	4	Lama temple village	213.76	15

3.3   Constructing Fuzzy Clustering Matrix

The AHP method is used to determine the appropriate capacity weight of each project area. Because of the large amount of data involved, it is more complicated to determine the appropriate capacity of each project area. Based on the calculation of the appropriate capacity weight of each project area, there is a big difference between different village areas. After normalization of the data listed in the weights and the establishment of fuzzy equivalent matrix, the matrix R is obtained.

$$
\begin{pmatrix}
1 \\
0.50 & 1 \\
0.48 & 0.68 & 1 \\
0.55 & 0.61 & 0.60 & 1 \\
0.72 & 0.61 & 0.61 & 0.53 & 1 \\
0.47 & 0.57 & 0.58 & 0.47 & 0.37 & 1 \\
0.49 & 0.49 & 0.46 & 0.58 & 0.50 & 0.58 & 1 \\
M & M & M & M & M & M & M & M \\
0.56 & 0.56 & 0.49 & 0.45 & 0.43 & 0.50 & 0.45 & L & 1 \\
0.74 & 0.56 & 0.42 & 0.32 & 0.69 & 0.56 & 0.36 & L & 0.57 & 1 \\
0.68 & 0.61 & 0.63 & 0.64 & 0.49 & 0.46 & 0.59 & L & 0.36 & 0.37 & 1 \\
0.49 & 0.64 & 0.63 & 0.59 & 0.55 & 0.48 & 0.41 & L & 0.58 & 0.52 & 0.67 & 1 \\
0.58 & 0.54 & 0.61 & 0.57 & 0.58 & 0.59 & 0.58 & L & 0.40 & 0.59 & 0.45 & 0.63 & 1 \\
0.57 & 0.59 & 0.59 & 0.51 & 0.37 & 0.57 & 0.55 & L & 0.55 & 0.51 & 0.49 & 0.53 & 0.49 & 1 \\
0.49 & 0.59 & 0.59 & 0.55 & 0.44 & 0.47 & 0.59 & L & 0.48 & 0.56 & 0.57 & 0.58 & 0.58 & 0.56 & 1
\end{pmatrix}
$$

3.4   Fuzzy Clustering Based on Minimum Spanning Tree

(1)   Select the most significant element

According to the minimum spanning tree graph, the maximum element is $r6/19 = r17/29 = 0.85$.

(2)   Select sub dayuan:

According to the minimum spanning tree graph, we get $r77/17 = 0.81$.

(3)   Element classification

Search repeatedly for lower level elements to get the smallest tree. The edges whose weights are less than lambda are excluded, and then the connected elements are classified into one class.

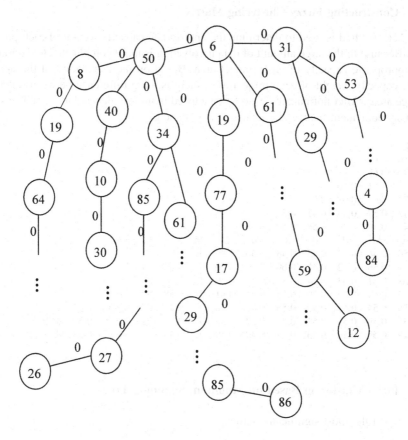

3.5 Analysis Results

Land use planning based on the lion town (2010–2020 years) measured near the long-term demand for urban construction land and fuzzy clustering distribution of general cognitive level selection belongs to the range of {0.8, +∞}; {0.8, 0.7}, {–∞, 0.7}, I am looking for a problem. Then, the connection lines of the project area are truncated and clustered respectively. Finally, three different old dismantling stages were obtained in the 88 project areas. Both preferred the demolition of the old [λ∈{0.8, +∞}]; Middle District Demolition of the old district of [λ∈{0.8, 0.7}]; conditions for the demolition of the old district [λ∈{–∞, 0.7}].

(1) Priority demolition of old areas

13 project areas, including the lion Creek community. The village collective economy is strong in the region, the villagers mainly engaged in the second, third industry, the idea update fast, and all kinds of information access way is more, the desire for urbanization is extremely strong. The region has mature infrastructure and location conditions, and the suitability of dismantling old projects is stronger. At the same time,

most of the project areas in this area are close to the town of lion Town, the future development of economic growth and the construction of regional coordinated development center, foreign investment enthusiastically. Urbanization is the first priority for the construction of new rural areas, the project areas as priority demolition of old areas, but also conducive to the construction of urban and rural construction land new indicators of priority protection.

(2) Interim demolition of the old area

Including the 21 project areas in Shizigou luohangtang community, community, community, Lama Temple Punning temple community. The regional economic development is slow, and the per capita output value is low. Encourages the government, village collective, individual and social funds; built roads, water, electricity, communications and other infrastructure, financing should be in line with the "who invests, benefits" principle, and gradually improve the existing village, the village to prevent blind expansion caused by the hollow village.

(3) Conditional dismantling of old districts

The 54 project areas including the Lion Ditch community, two river village, community garden trees, luohangtang village, lion village. The number of rural residents in this region is large. Have a certain scale of land use, because of their large number and great potential, but because of economic backwardness, the bottleneck of the development of many individual villages in water and soil resources shortage, economic conditions, traffic inconvenience, asymmetric information lag. The old demolition work should be carried out and the rational planning should be carried out to promote the overall development of the old dismantling area through the economic development of the whole town.

4 Reliability Analysis

This paper combines the old demolition project of lion town in Hebei city of Chengde province to do empirical research. The introduction of fuzzy clustering to the demolition of the old time study, reduce the interference of subjective factors, get the lion ditch town of Chengde City, the demolition of the old district projects a total of 88 projects, and in the time series is divided into three time zones, the spatial distribution showed a significant reduction of the structure around the circle pass city center and business district level key. It basically meets the demand and spatial distribution of construction land in different periods of land use planning (2010–2020 years), which meets the requirements of town spatial development planning. The reliability and practicability of three time regions on time series are fully proved. The research method is applied to the scientific nature of time and space arrangement, which will provide reference for the development of old demolition work, the optimal arrangement of projects and the rational utilization of resources in the future.

5 Conclusion

In geographic information elements, temporal information and spatial information are uncertain. In fact, in the demolition of the old district space scheduling, because the demolition of the old district in the space scheduling, between different periods and different regions division is not obvious and the order is not clear, that is to say, the boundaries are not clear. For example, give priority to the demolition of the old district, two adjacent communities or villages affected by geographical location, economic level, natural factors, boundaries between each range distinction is not very obvious, the relationship is fuzzy relation, the quantitative method using common traditional implementation phase of difficult, cannot determine the timing to the specific time. In order to avoid the randomness of the subjective and the interference of the analysis, the reliability of the calculation results is affected. Therefore, the fuzzy clustering analysis is introduced into the timing study of the old dismantling area, which greatly increases the reliability of the measurement results.

References

1. Smith, T.F., Waterman, M.S.: Identification of common molecular subsequences. J. Mol. Biol. **147**, 195–197 (1981)
2. Yimin, C.N., et al.: Land consolidation and its ecological environment effect. Anhui Agric. Sci. Rural Constr. Under Connecting Policy **37**(7), 3166–3168 (2009)
3. Xu, W., Wang, Z.: Land consolidation potential and key areas of Shandong land resources, rural construction linked policy in Shandong Province Based on I, 32–35 (2009)
4. Zhang, X., Zhu, D.: Urban and rural construction land linked to the policy of the rural residential area consolidation mode evaluation. J. Agric. Eng. **1**, 244–249 (2012)
5. Zhang, Y., Minghao, E.: What to hook the increase of urban construction land and the decrease of rural construction land on the hook policy. Chin. Land **3**, 23–24 (2006)
6. Analysis of Xiao Sen Mai land economy and urban construction in Shapingba District of Chongqing city as an example. Southwestern University master thesis, pp. 45–50 (2008)
7. Dai, Y.: Comparative analysis of farmers' resettlement mode in "increase and decrease linked". SEZ Econ. **8**, 170–171 (2011)
8. Sail, H.: Study on the operation mode of urban construction land increase and decrease linking. Xi'an: Chang'an University (2011)
9. Zhang, X., Zhu, D.: Evaluation of patch arrangement model of rural settlements under the policy of linking up and down of urban and rural construction land. J. Agric. Eng. **1**, 244–249 (2012)
10. Zhu, L.: Study on the linking policy of urban and rural construction land increase and decrease of Southwestern University (2010)
11. Xu, X.: Monday star, the city geography sensitive. Higher Education Press, Beijing, July 1997
12. Zhang, H.: Study on rural residential land consolidation in Xinjiang. Urumqi: Xinjiang Agricultural University (2005)
13. Chen, M., Wu, C.: On rural city and rural residential land consolidation. Econ. Geogr., 97–100 (1996)

14. Zhang, W.: Study on comprehensive evaluation of urban sustainable development in Beijing. master's degree thesis. Beijing University of Technology, Beijing, pp. 2–3 (2002)
15. Liu, Y., Hebei, Q.: County land planning revision of urban and rural construction land increase and decrease linkage research China University of Geosciences, May 2011
16. Zhang, W., Wu, X., Zhang, G., et al.: Concise and practical course of China's new rural planning and construction. China Construction Industry Press (2008)

An Improved Method on the Wave Height of Ocean Surface Based on X-Band Radars

Yi Wang[1(✉)], Mingyuan He[1], Haiyang Zhang[2], and Jingjing Ge[3]

[1] Institute of Meteorology and Oceanography, University of Defence Technology, Nanjing 211101, Jiangsu, People's Republic of China
wangyi_rsc@126.com
[2] Army Engineering University of PLA, Zhengzhou, China
[3] 31110 PLA Troops, Nanjing, China

Abstract. It contains plenty of ocean wave and sea surface current information in the sea clutter images formed by X-band marine radar's echo. Applying the method to calculate the significant wave height from the SAR imagery, which supposes the significant wave height in linear relation with the square of the signal-to-noise ratio of radar images, the significant wave height has been obtained from estimating the images of X-band radar. The experimental data were analyzed in the Small Mai-island sea area. Firstly comparing the effect of filtering direct current versus estimating result, deriving the significant wave height estimated by counting the signal-to-noise ratio after filtering direct current which is match better; then according to wave height measured by wave buoy, analyzing low and high wave height to do linear fit and gain calibration coefficient separately, the significant wave height evaluated is all the more precise.

Keywords: X-band radar · Significant wave height · Filtering direct current
Linear fit

1 Introduction

Waves is a with the human relations is the most direct and most closely ocean phenomenon, the wave height, wave direction on defense, shipping, ports, and the safety of offshore oil platform has very important significance. Marine navigation of x-band radar echo of the sea clutter image contains abundant waves, sea surface layer information. Using x-band radar imaging mechanism, by studying the relationship between image spectrum and wave spectrum, can make use of the radar echo intensity inversion of wave spectrum and sea state parameters.

However, compared with the in-situ observation instruments such as the wave buoy, in the direction of the waves from radar image spectrum inversion, can only get the direction of wave spectrum energy relative not get its absolute value. In 1982, Alpers and Hasselmann [1] proposed from synthetic aperture radar (SAR) image to obtain the effective method of wave height, the basic idea of this method is to assume

Supported by Natural Science Founded of Jiangsu Province (BK2016127).

that the significant wave height and from the square root of the signal-to-noise ratio of radar image into a linear relationship, calculated by the signal-to-noise ratio of radar image, significant wave height. In 1994, Ziemer and Gunther [2] for the first time the application of the method of significant wave height is obtained from SAR on the radar, and by using this method by navigation radar image got significant wave height. In 1998, Nieto et al. [3] and others also use this method by the navigation radar image obtained the significant wave height. Especially the method has been successfully used in deep water.

We developed on the basis of x-band radar 'sea Wave flow Information extraction System (Wave and Current Information Extracting System)' abbreviated as 'WCIES', mainly including the x-band radar, signal acquisition and preprocessing System and the surface Wave flow Information extraction software of three parts. We mainly wheat island shore-based experiment was carried out in Qingdao, WCIES will get significant wave height and significant wave height were compared from the wave buoy. The first part of the article mainly introduces the radar image theory of inversion algorithm steps; The second part gives the calculation method of effective wave height; The third part will be the improved method is applied to the experiment data processing, from two cases respectively for wheat island analysis of experimental data in detail; The fourth part gives the experiment results analysis and summary of this article.

2   The Inversion Algorithm of Radar Image

FAs the waves and currents from radar image time series information, select a rectangular area on radar image, corresponding area of the sea. Radar antenna per rotation week, form a picture of a radar image, the area 64 consecutive radar image, modulus conversion of analog signals, will receive the digital signal is stored as a radar image of time series, then the following processing [4].

(1)   Image coordinate transformation: due to radar image extracted by polar coordinates are the coordinates of the corresponding time series, and Fourier transform, the radar image corresponding to the polar coordinates conversion become rectangular coordinates, extraction of pending rectangle radar image grey value with the distribution of space time $g(x, y, t)$.

(2)   Discrete Fourier transform, using the discrete Fourier transform [4] will be 64 consecutive radar image into a 3d image spectrum, $I^{(3)}(k_x, k_y, \omega)$.

(3)   The determination of surface flow: to compare the image spectrum energy location and determined based on the dispersion relation of spectral energy position, with the least square method to determine the surface flow [5].

(4)   Three-dimensional image spectrum filter: use gravity waves meet the dispersion relation of the image spectrum band pass filter, wave energy separated from background noise [4].

(5)   Determination of two-dimensional wave spectrum: the 3d image spectrum in frequency range is integral, obtaining two-dimensional image spectrum $I^{(2)}(k_x, k_y)$, then reusing the modulation transfer function [2, 6], and getting the wave spectrum $F^{(2)}(k_x, k_y)$.

(6) The calculation of wave direction spectrum: The two-dimensional wave spectrum from wave number space transformation to the frequency domain space, get the direction of wave spectrum.

3 Significant Wave Height Inversion

M Due to the nonlinear wave imaging mechanism [4], the waves of significant wave height can not directly from radar image. In 1994, Ziemer and Gunther [2] for the first time Alpers and Hasselmann [1] and others get significant wave height from SAR image method is applied to Marine radar. This method assumes that the significant wave height and the square root of the signal-to-noise ratio of the radar image into a linear relationship, namely

$$H_s = A + B\sqrt{SNR} \tag{1}$$

where A, B are undetermined constants, determined by the radar system, the Hs is the significant wave height of ocean waves, SNR is the signal-to-noise ratio of the radar image. Signal-to-noise ratio SNR is defined as

$$SNR = \frac{SIG}{BGN}, \tag{2}$$

where SIG is the energy of the wave spectrum.

$$SIG = \sum_{i=1}^{N} F^{(2)}(k_{xi}, k_{yi})\Delta k_x \Delta k_y, \tag{3}$$

where BGN is the energy of the background noise.

$$BGN = \sum_{i=1}^{N_x}\sum_{j=1}^{N_y}\sum_{l=1}^{N_t} I^{(3)}(k_{xi}, k_{yj}, \omega_l)\Delta k_x \Delta k_y \Delta \omega - \sum_{i=1}^{N} I^{(2)}(k_{xm}, k_{ym})\Delta k_x \Delta k_y \tag{4}$$

where $F^{(2)}(k_x, k_y)$ is the inversion of wave spectrum, $I^{(3)}(k_x, k_y, \omega)$ is three-dimensional images after the three dimensional Fourier transform spectrum, $I^{(2)}(k_x, k_y)$ is the two-dimensional image spectrum. N is the coordinates of image spectrum meeting the dispersion relation, N_x, N_y, N_t are coordinates of wave number after Fourier transform, the frequency component respectively. $\Delta k_x, \Delta k_y$ are wavenumber resolution, and $\Delta \omega$ is angular frequency resolution.

4 The Experiment and Data Processing

Wheat Island is located in the southeast of Qingdao, in north latitude 36°03′ , east longitude 120°25′, its waters vision, convenient for observation, is an exploration into the island sea area of about 1 km². In February 2007 on March 17, 7 solstice radar YingHai villa roof frame with wheat island platform shore-based tests have been carried out. Radar antenna about 20 m, from sea level in waters of radar detection, with the state oceanic administration of wheat island hydrometric station cloth wave buoy, obtained by radar image can be achieved with the waves than the measurement information. During the experiment period, navigation radar and signal acquisition system was operating, on the sea, and the observed data were recording and storing. Test of the project group's people on duty. General requirements of timing acquisition data, the data acquisition time depending on the sea state, if the sea state is higher, the waves is bigger, will increase the sampling density, such as collect data once every 10 min.

In data processing, we choose several groups of radar image data, (2)–(4) is used to calculate SNR, then On the SNR data and effective wave height wave buoy measured data, using the least squares linear fitting to determine the parameters of A and B.

4.1 The Dc Filter

On radar image gray value varies with space time distribution of the three dimensional Fourier transform, that is, before considering the dc signal component influence on the result, the direct Fourier transform and Fourier transform of the reentry after dc filter, which divided into dc filter and NO dc filter. Dc filter calculation method is as follows.

$$g(x, y, t) = g(x, y, t) - \bar{g}(x, y, t) \qquad (5)$$

Where $\bar{g}(x, y, t)$ is for the average of $g(x, y, t)$. Calculate SNR before, not for dc filter, namely the direct Fourier transform. Chosen wheat island shore-based experimental part of the data of linear fitting results are shown in Fig. 1.

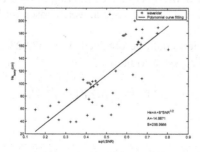

Fig. 1. Least-square fit to obtain the calibration parameters, A and B

From Fig. 1 the relation could be obtained A = −14.9871, B = 256.9955. Therefore, for the selected radar system (Fig. 2),

$$H_s = -14.9871 + 256.9955\sqrt{SNR}\,(\text{cm}) \tag{6}$$

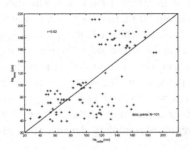

Fig. 2. Scatter plot of the significant wave height (Hs) obtained by the radar and buoy. The correlation coefficient is r = 0.62.

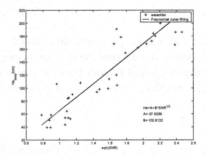

Fig. 3. Least-square fit to obtain the calibration parameters, A and B

Before calculating the SNR, first of all, dc filtering of Fourier transforms. Part of the data of wheat island shore-based experimental were chosen for linear fitting, the results as shown in Fig. 3.

From Fig. 3 the relation could be obtained A = −37.8239, B = 102.8132. Therefore, for the selected radar system (Fig. 4),

$$H_s = -37.8239 + 102.8132\sqrt{SNR}\,(\text{cm}) \tag{7}$$

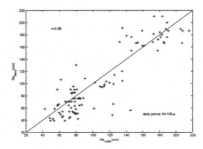

Fig. 4. Scatter plot of the significant wave height (Hs) obtained by the radar and buoy. The correlation coefficient is r = 0.86.

4.2   Takanami High and Low Wave

To make more accurate measurement results, according to the wave buoy is the significant wave height of size, it can be divided into two segments, wave height and wave height lower part of the higher the takanami high and low wave height to processing respectively. By (1), the signal-to-noise ratio of the size of the corresponding to the size of the significant wave height, the experimental results show that the size can be according to the calculated signal-to-noise ratio to block, experiments in SNR = 2.8269 is bounded. The following to calculate SNR before $g(x, y, t)$ dc filter after the data analysis. The high takanami part linear fitting the data was shown in Fig. 5. From Fig. 5 the relation could be obtained A = 109.9281, B = 32.5748. Therefore, for the selected radar system,

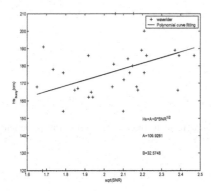

Fig. 5. Least-square fit to obtain the calibration parameters, A and B

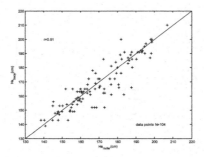

Fig. 6. Scatter plot of the significant wave height (Hs) obtained by the radar and buoy. The correlation coefficient is r = 0.91.

$$H_s = 109.9281 + 32.5748\sqrt{SNR}\,(\text{cm}) \qquad (8)$$

The low wave high part of the linear fitting the data was shown in Fig. 7. From Fig. 7 the relation could be obtained A = −9.0127, B = 69.3173. Therefore, for the selected radar system (Figs. 6 and 8),

$$H_s = -9.0127 + 69.3173\sqrt{SNR}\,(\text{cm}) \qquad (9)$$

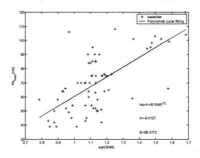

Fig. 7. Least-square fit to obtain the calibration parameters, A and B

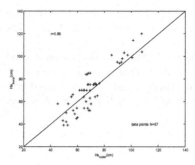

Fig. 8. Scatter plot of the significant wave height (Hs) obtained by the radar and buoy. The correlation coefficient is r = 0.88.

5 Conclusion

Use we developed on the basis of x-band radar waves flow information extraction system, through the analysis of the radar echo intensity, can get sea state parameters of Marine dynamic environment, but the surface of the significant wave height can directly by the radar image sequences to get time. Using Alpers and Hasselmann [1] and others get effective method of wave height from SAR image, can get the waves from the radar image of significant wave height.

From the analysis of experimental data, the dc data after filtering, linear fitting by least square, and which are obtained by inversion, the wave buoy measured significant wave height in accordance with good, and the correlation coefficient is higher; According to the wave buoy wave height will be divided into high reflection of high and low wave to deal with, from the point of the results, their correlation coefficients are higher than when you don't separate, and conform to the better. In practice, can according to the size of the SNR of separate high and low wave height, in this experiment we take SNR is equal to 2.8269. According to the result of calculation shows that the radar image grey value of dc filter and wave height can be divided into two wave height can be considered as a better processing method to analysis, fitting coefficient can be used in practical radar system. Need to point out that our rich data quantity is not enough, if there is enough data, the result will be better.

References

1. Alpers, W., Hasselmann, K.: Spectral signal to clutter and thermal noise properties of ocean wave imaging synthetic aperture radars. Int. J. Remote Sens. **3**, 423–446 (1982)
2. Ziemer, F., Gunther, H.: A system to monitor ocean wave fields. In: Proceedings of the Second International Conference on Air-Sea Interaction and Meteorology and Oceanography of the Coastal Zone, Lisbon, Portugal (1994)
3. Nieto, J.C., Reichert, K., Dittmer, J., et al.: WaMoS II: a wave and current monitoring system. In: Proceedings of the COST 714 Conference on Directional Wave Spectra, Paris (1998)

4. Nieto, J.C., Hessner, K., Reichert, K.: Estimation of the significant wave height with X-band nautical radars. In: Proceedings of OMAE 1999 St. John's, Newfoundland, pp. 11–16, July 1999
5. Senet, C., Seemann, J., Ziemer, J.: The near-surface current velocity determined from images sequences of the sea surface. IEEE Trans. Geosci. Remote Sens. **39**, 492–505 (2001)
6. Ziemer, F., Rosenthal, F.W.: On the transfer function of a shipborne radar for imaging ocean waves. In: Proceedings of IGARSS 1987 Symposium, Ann Arbor, Michigan, May 1987

Short-Term Operation Optimization of Cascade Hydropower Reservoirs with Linear Functional Analysis

Yanke Zhang[1(✉)], Jinjun You[2], Changming Ji[1], and Jiajie Wu[1]

[1] School of Renewable Energy, North China Electric Power University,
Beijing 102206, China
ykzhang2008@163.com, cmji@ncepu.edu.cn,
1014640449@qq.com
[2] China Institute of Water Resources and Hydropower Research,
Beijing 100044, China
youjj@iwhr.com

Abstract. In the operation optimization of cascade hydropower reservoirs, upstream reservoir outflow is usually taken as downstream reservoir inflow, which influences generation scheme accuracy when flow time-lag cannot be neglected. In this study, based on linear space mapping and bounded linear functional theory, the relationship between upstream reservoir outflow and downstream reservoir inflow is quantized. Their corresponding map functions and functional operators are proposed considering river channel storage capacity. Additionally, a short-term generation optimization model of cascade hydropower reservoirs considering flow time-lag is established, with no impact on the objective function and water balance. Furthermore, to verify the feasibility and effectiveness of the model, it is applied to the short-term generation optimization of Jinping-Guandi cascade hydropower reservoirs in Yalong River. Results tally more with the actual operation process compared with the original scheme. This work can increase generation scheduling accuracy and provide reference for short-term operation of cascade hydropower reservoirs.

Keywords: Flow time-lag · Cascade hydropower reservoirs · Short-term
optimization model · Linear functional analysis

1 Introduction

In the process of short-term operation optimization of cascade hydropower reservoirs (CHR), flow time-lag refers to the travel time of outflow from one upstream reservoir to the next downstream reservoir. Influenced by the magnitude of upstream reservoir outflow and river-channel storage between upstream and downstream reservoir, flow time-lag constantly changes in a dynamic way. For example, after a period of τ, we assume that upstream reservoir outflow Q_1 arrives at downstream reservoir and the corresponding inflow is Q_1'. Q_1' does not necessarily equate to Q_1, and τ also changes with different outflow processes [1, 2]. This brings difficulty to short-term operation optimization of CHR. The literature [3] considers the benefit of delayed water, and

© Springer Nature Singapore Pte Ltd. 2018
H. Yuan et al. (Eds.): GSKI 2017, CCIS 849, pp. 107–116, 2018.
https://doi.org/10.1007/978-981-13-0896-3_11

establishes a daily optimal operation model which aims to maximize the sum of CHR power generation benefit and delayed water benefit, taking the Three Gorges-Gezhou Dam CHR as an example for analysis and verification. In the scheduling process of CHR, the literature [4] mainly considers the condition that the flow time-lag is shorter than the scheduling cycle. With such measures as constant output trial simulation and adjusting generation schedules under overrun warning, it presents a method of modifying the generation schemes of CHR.

According to existing research results, the approaches to dealing with flow time-lag can be roughly classified into two types. One is to calculate downstream reservoir inflow based on the river-channel routing calculation method, which can clearly reflect the physical mechanism of flow time lag and obtain a relatively accurate calculation result. But due to cumbersome computation process and difficulty in data acquisition, this type of method has limited applicability. The other is to modify the objective function for CHR operation. It simply makes the upstream reservoir outflow goes a certain period backwards and regards it as the downstream reservoir inflow, which not only ignores the influence of stream attenuation but also involves benefit conversion between different scheduling cycles [5–7]. It is not conducive to working out a generation schedule. So this paper proposes to apply linear space mapping and bounded linear functional theory to the relation analysis of upstream outflow and downstream inflow. In the same scheduling cycle, if the upstream reservoir outflow is known, the downstream reservoir inflow can be obtained simultaneously. In this way, the influence of flow time-lag on water balance and the objective function of CHR can be avoided, enhancing the efficiency and precision in making generation schemes.

2   Solving the Flow Time-Lag Problem Based on Linear Space Mapping and Bounded Linear Functional Theory

This paper only discusses the circumstance in which the CHR comprises two reservoirs and flow time-lag is shorter than the scheduling cycle, without considering local inflow. For CHR with more than two reservoirs, the relationship between each reservoir can be dealt with in a similar way. It is assumed that the upstream reservoir inflow in the scheduling cycle $[1, T]$ is $Q_{1,1}, Q_{1,2}, \cdots, Q_{1,T}$, and there exists a mapping relationship $F = (f_1, f_2, \cdots, f_T)$ between upstream reservoir outflow $q_{1,1}, q_{1,2}, \cdots, q_{1,T}$ and downstream reservoir inflow $Q_{2,1}, Q_{2,2}, \cdots, Q_{2,T}$, where $f_i (i = 1, 2, \cdots, T)$ represents the functional relationship between $Q_{2,i}$ and the upstream reservoir outflow in the ith moment $q_{1,i}$ as well as in the previous τ period $q_{1,i-\tau}, q_{1,i-\tau+1}, \cdots, q_{1,i-1}$. At the same time, $Q_{2,i}$ is influenced by the river-channel storage volume between upstream and downstream reservoir in the $(i$-$\tau)$ th moment, as shown in Fig. 1.

Assuming that both the $\tau + T$-dimensional space $X = (q_{1,1-\tau}, q_{1,2-\tau}, \cdots, q_{1,T})'$ constituted by upstream reservoir outflow and the T-dimensional space $Y = (Q_{2,1}, Q_{2,2}, \cdots, Q_{2,T})'$ constituted by downstream reservoir inflow are linear space, then the problem of flow time-lag from upstream to downstream reservoir can be regarded as a one-to-one mapping from X to Y: $F : X \to Y$, namely:

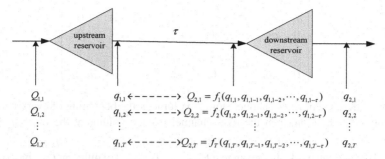

Fig. 1. The relationship between upstream reservoir outflow and downstream reservoir inflow.

$$Y = F(X) \Leftrightarrow \begin{pmatrix} Q_{2,1} \\ Q_{2,2} \\ \vdots \\ Q_{2,T} \end{pmatrix} = \begin{pmatrix} f_1 \\ f_2 \\ \vdots \\ f_T \end{pmatrix} = \begin{bmatrix} a_{1,1}, a_{1,2}, \cdots, a_{1,\tau+T} \\ a_{2,1}, a_{2,2}, \cdots, a_{2,\tau+T} \\ \vdots \\ a_{T,1}, a_{T,2}, \cdots, a_{T,\tau+T} \end{bmatrix} \begin{pmatrix} q_{1,1-\tau} \\ q_{1,2-\tau} \\ \vdots \\ q_{1,T} \end{pmatrix} \quad (1)$$

Where $a_{i,j}(i = 1, 2, \cdots, T; j = 1, 2, \cdots, \tau + T)$ is the j th coefficient in f_i.

To work out F when X, Y is known, as expression (1) is an equation set which contains $T \times (\tau + 1)$ variables, F can be uniquely determined only when there are at least $T \times (\tau + 1)$ linearly independent equations. Because a scheduling cycle has only T periods and $T < T \times (\tau + 1)$, it is hard to obtain a definite F by solving this equation set. Regarding the short-term generation scheduling of CHR as a cyclic process of n cycles, the downstream reservoir inflow act as a function of upstream reservoir outflow. Each cycle is considered as no difference from other cycles in principle. Then we have:

$$\lim_{n \to \infty} (f_1, f_2, \cdots, f_T) = (f, f, \cdots, f), \quad (2)$$

Where f represents the mapping from $X_{t_0} = (q_{1,t_0}, q_{1,t_0-1}, \cdots, q_{1,t_0-1-\tau}, q_{1,t_0-\tau})'$ to Q_{2,t_0} at the moment t_0. If the flow time-lag is longer than the scheduling cycle when $\tau + 1 > T$, the hydraulic connection between upstream and downstream reservoir is relatively weak, meaning that they can be regarded as two single independent reservoirs to be operated separately. Therefore, we only consider the situation when $\tau + 1 \leq T$. It is known from the properties of solutions to linear equations that: when $\tau + 1 \leq T$, if there exist $\tau + 1$ linearly independent X_t, then we can get the unique solution $(a_1, a_2, \cdots, a_{\tau+1})$. In this way, we can obtain the mapping relation between upstream outflow space X and inflow space Y, as follows:

$$F = \begin{bmatrix} a_1 & a_2 & \cdots & a_{\tau+1} & 0 & \cdots & 0 & 0 \\ 0 & a_1 & a_2 & \cdots & a_{\tau+1} & 0 & \cdots & 0 \\ \vdots & \vdots & \vdots & \vdots & \vdots & \vdots & \vdots & \vdots \\ 0 & 0 & \cdots & 0 & a_1 & a_2 & \cdots & a_{\tau+1} \end{bmatrix}. \tag{3}$$

If the difference of river-channel storage volume at the beginning of every period is taken into consideration, then the river-channel storage volume at the moment $k(k = 1, 2, \cdots, T)$ corresponds to the mapping f_k from $X_{t_k} = (q_{1,t_k}, q_{1,t_k-1}, \cdots, q_{1,t_k+1-\tau}, q_{1,t_k-\tau})'$ to Q_{2,t_k}. Then we can work out the range $[Q_{2,t_k\_min}, Q_{2,t_k\_max}]$ of different Q_{2,t_k} based on F_1 and F_2 separately. This can provide some reference for making generation schedules of the downstream reservoir and real-time operation decision.

3 Short-Term Operation Optimization Model of CHR Considering Flow Time-Lag

According to the comprehensive utilization mission of each reservoir and the request of power grid and electrical power system, short-term operation optimization of CHR is actually to get the appropriate outflow of each reservoir through regulating each reservoir inflow using optimization methods. To meet the demand of generating more electrical energy, in this paper, we choose maximizing the total energy output of CHR as the optimum criterion for model construction based DPSA [8–12].

3.1 Objective Function

Taking the amount of energy output as the measurement of generation benefit of CHR, the objective is to maximize the system's total power generation in the scheduling period, with the given reservoir inflow and under the condition that all constraints are satisfied. The corresponding objective function is as follows.

$$\max E = \sum_{i=1}^{n} \sum_{t=1}^{T} N_{i,t} \Delta t = \sum_{i=1}^{n} \sum_{t=1}^{T} K_i q_{i,t} H_{i,t} \Delta t, \tag{4}$$

where E stands for the optimal daily generated energy of CHR; $N_{i,t}$ is the output of hydropower reservoir i in the t th period; Δt is the length of computing period; T is the number of computing periods (for example, in one day when Δt is 15 min, then $T = 96$); n is the number of hydropower reservoir; K_i is the output coefficient of the i th hydropower reservoir; $q_{i,t}$ is the generation outflow and $H_{i,t}$ is the average generating head of hydropower reservoir i in the t th period, respectively.

3.2   Constraints

(a)   The constraint of reservoir water balance.

$$V_{i,t+1} = V_{i,t} + (Q_{i,t} - q_{i,t} - qd_{i,t} - qloss_{i,t})\Delta t \quad (t = 1, 2, \cdots, T; i = 1, 2, \cdots, n),$$
(5)

where $V_{i,t}$ and $V_{i,t+1}$ stand for the water storage of reservoir i in the initial and final stage of the t th period respectively; $Q_{i,t}$ and $q_{i,t}$ are the inflow and outflow of hydropower reservoir i in the t th period respectively; $qd_{i,t}$ and $qloss_{i,t}$ are the abandoned flow and the lost flow of hydropower reservoir i in the t th period respectively.

(b)   Capacity constraint.

$$V_i^{\min} \leq V_{i,t} \leq V_i^{\max} \quad (t = 1, 2, \cdots, T; i = 1, 2, \cdots, n),$$
(6)

Where $V_i^{\min}$ represents the dead storage capacity of the i th hydropower reservoir; $V_i^{\max}$ is the sum of dead storage capacity and utilizable storage capacity of hydropower reservoir i in non-flood season (i.e., the storage capacity corresponding to normal water level), and during flood season it is the storage capacity corresponding to flood limit level.

(c)   Output constraint.

$$N_i^{\min} \leq N_{i,t} \leq N_{i,forc} \quad (t = 1, 2, \cdots, T; i = 1, 2, \cdots, n),$$
(7)

where $N_i^{\min}$, $N_{i,t}$ and N_{forc} denote the minimum output limit, the current actual output and the expected output of the i th hydropower reservoir in the t th period, respectively.

(d)   Discharged flow constraint.

$$\begin{cases} S_{i,t}^{\min} \leq S_{i,t} \leq S_{i,t}^{\max} \\ S_{i,t} = q_{i,t} + qd_{i,t} \end{cases} (t = 1, 2, \cdots, T; i = 1, 2, \cdots, n),$$
(8)

where $S_{i,t}$, $S_{i,t}^{\min}$ and $S_{i,t}^{\max}$ stand for the discharged flow, the allowed minimum discharged flow and the allowed maximum discharged flow of the i th hydropower reservoir in the t th period, respectively.

(e)   Water balance relationship between upstream reservoir and downstream reservoir.

$$Q_{i+1,t} = f_i(S_{i,t-\tau}, S_{i,t-\tau+1}, \cdots, S_{i,t-1}, S_{i,t}) + Q_{i+1,t}^{in},$$
(9)

where $Q_{i+1,t}$ represents the inflow of the lower hydropower reservoir in the t th period $(t = 1, 2, \cdots, T; i = 1, 2, \cdots n - 1)$; $S_{i,t-\tau}$, $S_{i,t-\tau+1}$, $S_{i,t-1}$ and $S_{i,t}$ represent the discharged flow of the upper hydropower reservoir in the $(t - \tau)$ th, $(t - \tau + 1)$ th, $(t - 1)$

th and t th period respectively; $Q_{i+1,t}^{in}$ represents the local inflow of the lower hydropower reservoir in the t th period (not considering the flow time-lag of local inflow in this paper); τ represents the flow time lag from the i th hydropower reservoir to the $i + 1$ th hydropower reservoir.

4   Case Study

4.1   Overview of the Research Object

The Jinping-Guandi cascade hydropower reservoirs consists of Jinping-I, Jinping-II and Guandi hydropower reservoirs. It is directly operated by the national center for electric power operation and control. Jinping-I is an annual-regulation hydropower reservoir and also the control power station of the Jinping-Guandi cascade hydropower reservoirs, while Jinping-II and Guandi are daily-regulation hydropower reservoirs. Figure 2 is a sketch map of the Jinping-Guandi cascade hydropower reservoirs.

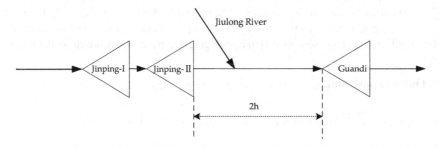

Fig. 2. Sketch map of the Jinping-Guandi cascade hydropower reservoirs.

For the Jinping-Guandi cascade hydropower reservoirs, the influence of flow time-lag is mainly embodied in the outflow travel time from Jinping-II to Guandi. If the scheduling period is 15 min ($\Delta t = 15$ min) and the scheduling cycle is one day ($T = 96\Delta t$), since the time-lag of the generation flow from Jinping-II to Guandi is 2 h, then there are totally 8 periods ($\tau = 8$).

4.2   Results and Discussion

4.2.1   Calculation of the Flow Time-Lag Relation

This paper uses the 2014 daily runoff data for calculation and obtains F. If the influence of river-channel storage volume is considered, the downstream water level of the upstream reservoir at the beginning of the $(t_0 - \tau)$ th period (Z_{t_0}) can be used to represent the initial river-channel storage volume. After calculation we obtain the results of F_1 and F_2.

When Jinping-II outflow is known, on the basis of F, F_1 and F_2, we can work out the corresponding Guandi inflow process, which is denoted as Guandi inflow F, Guandi inflow F_1 and Guandi inflow F_2 respectively, as shown in Fig. 3.

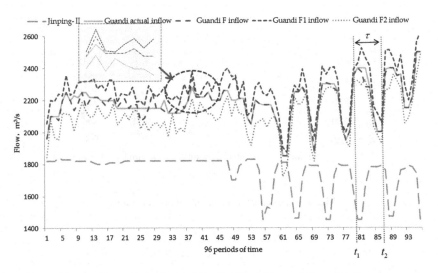

Fig. 3. Comparison chart of Jinping-II outflow and Guandi inflow.

In Fig. 3, on the one hand, the overall variation trend of Guandi inflow F, Guandi inflow F_1 and Guandi inflow F_2 are identical with Guandi actual inflow process, yet with random fluctuation. It is because while the majority of Guandi inflow is from Jinping-II outflow, as can be confirmed by Jinping-2161 generation schedules, a minor portion of Guandi inflow is from the Jiulong River tributary, which changes randomly. On the other hand, compared with the Jinping-II outflow process, the general trend of the obtained Guandi inflow process presents hysteresis to some extent. It can be seen that after 2 h the variation pattern of Jinping-II outflow would appear in Guandi inflow. From $t_1 = 79$ to $t_2 = 87$, it has experienced 8 periods altogether, which further verifies the effectiveness of the method proposed in this paper.

4.2.2 Discussion

Under the five circumstances of using the actual inflow, not considering flow time-lag, considering flow time-lag F, F_1 and F_2, the optimal operation of Jinping-Guandi cascade hydropower reservoirs is conducted using the method introduced above. This CHR gross generation is denoted by Esum0, Esum1, Esum2, Esum3 and Esum4 respectively. The DPSA algorithm is employed, with the result shown in Fig. 4. This CHR gross output is denoted by N_0, N_1, N_2, N_3 and N_4 respectively, and the calculation result is shown in Fig. 5. The output of Guandi hydropower reservoir is denoted by N_GD0, N_GD1, N_GD2, N_GD3 and N_GD4 respectively, and the calculation result is shown in Fig. 6.

It can be observed from Fig. 6 that when flow time-lag is not considered, this CHR gross generated energy is 248.13 million kW·h which is less than the value of 250.71 million kW·h in actual operation, while this CHR gross generated energy is 250.74 million kW·h when flow time lag F is considered, which is close to the actual value. The upper and lower limit of this CHR gross generated energy is 251.36 million kW·h and 249.50 million kW·h respectively when operation is conducted based on F_1 and F_2,

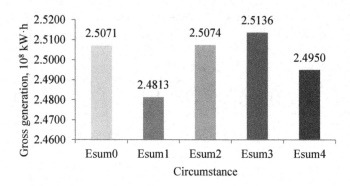

Fig. 4. Area chart of the CHR gross generation.

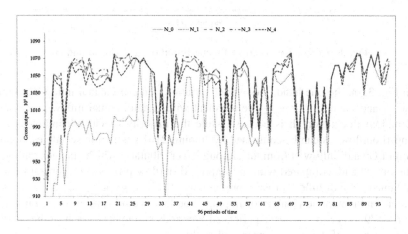

Fig. 5. Comparison chart of the CHR gross output process.

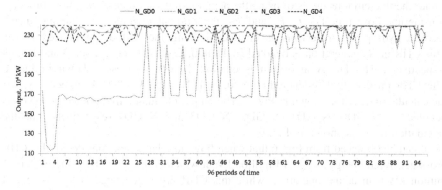

Fig. 6. Comparison chart of Guandi hydropower reservoir output process.

which includes the two situations above. Consequently on the condition that reservoir inflow is definite and flow time-lag is not considered, the formulated generation schedule would deviate from the actual scheduling result by 2.58 million kW·h, whereas using the method introduced in this paper can narrow the error to the range of [0.65,1.21] million kW·h, thus improving the precision of generation schedules, increasing generation benefit and providing more detailed reference for practical operation. For Guandi inflow is considered equal to Jinping-II outflow that would actually arrive at Guandi reservoir about 2 h later, that is why this CHR gross energy and output deviate when flow time lag is not taken into consideration. In Fig. 6, except the situation of considering flow time-lag(N_GD2), the output process of Guandi hydropower reservoir differs from the actual output process in the other three circumstances(N_GD1, N_GD3 and N_GD4). The reason is that at the beginning of the scheduling cycle the river-channel storage volume between Jinping-II and Guandi directly affects Guandi inflow. So when calculating Guandi inflow during the operation process of Jinping-Guandi cascade hydropower reservoirs, we should consider not only the differences in Jinping-II reservoir flow process within the time lag, but also the initial influence of river-channel storage volume on subsequent calculation.

5 Conclusions

This paper puts forward an analytical method of flow time-lag using linear space mapping theory, and establishes the short-term optimal scheduling model of cascade hydropower reservoirs based on flow time-lag. The model is applied to the Jinping-Guandi cascade hydropower reservoirs operation and the analysis shows that whether to consider flow time-lag or not would directly affect the formulation of CHR generation schedules. Neglecting flow time-lag would lead to deviation in generation scheduling and bring unnecessary loss and risk. Considering flow time-lag, however, can calculate CHR generation benefit in the same scheduling cycle and avoid the impact of flow time-lag on CHR water balance and the objective function, because it involves the transformation relationship among the upstream reservoir outflow space, river-channel storage volume and the downstream reservoir inflow space, which actually needs a functional operator space to quantify. Despite a little deviation in the calculation result, a useful attempt is made in this research field to provide more detailed referential information for operation decision makers and reduce unnecessary loss of operation.

Acknowledgments. This study was financially supported by the 13th Five-Year National Key Program of China (2016YFC0402208, 2016YFC0402200), the Open Research Fund of State Key Laboratory of Simulation and Regulation of Water Cycle in River Basin(China Institute of Water Resources and Hydropower Research) (IWHR-SKL-201420, 2016TS04), the National Science Foundation(51709105, 51279062), the Major Consulting Strategic Project of Engineering Institute (2016-ZD-08-05), the National Key R&D Program of China(2017YFC 0405906) and the Fundamental Research Funds for the Central Universities (2016MS51, JB2015169, 2014XS51). The authors are grateful to the anonymous reviewers for their comments and valuable suggestions.

References

1. Zhang, W., et al.: Optimal operation of multi-reservoir systems considering time-lags of flood routing. Water Resour. Manag. **30**, 523–540 (2015)
2. Xu, B., Zhong, P.A., Zhang, M., Zhang, J.: Short term optimization of cascade reservoirs operation considering flow routing. In: Asia-Pacific Power and Energy Engineering Conference, APPEEC (2012)
3. Zhong, P., Zhang, J., Xu, B., Zhang, M.: Daily optimal operation model of cascade reservoirs considering delay of flow propagation. Shuili Fadian Xuebao/J. Hydroelectr. Eng. **31**, 34–38 (2012). (in Chinese)
4. Mou, C., Yu, Q., Hu, Y., Xu, H.: Research on short-term and provisional on-line hydropower dispatching based on neighboring cascade hydropower stations. Hongshui River **33**, 29–35 (2014). (in Chinese)
5. Zhang, X.M., Wang, L.-P., Li, J.W., Zhang, Y.K.: Self-optimization simulation model of short-term cascaded hydroelectric system dispatching based on the daily load curve. Water Resour. Manag. **27**, 5045–5067 (2013)
6. Ma, C., Lian, J., Wang, J.: Short-term optimal operation of three-gorge and Gezhouba cascade hydropower stations in non-flood season with operation rules from data mining. Energy Convers. Manag. **65**, 616–627 (2013)
7. Wang, L., Wang, B., Zhang, P., Liu, M., Li, C.: Study on optimization of the short-term operation of cascade hydropower stations by considering output error. J. Hydrol. **549**, 326–339 (2017)
8. Feng, M., et al.: Identifying changing patterns of reservoir operating rules under various inflow alteration scenarios. Adv. Water Resour. **104**, 23–36 (2017)
9. Feng, Z.K., Niu, W.J., Cheng, C.T., Wu, X.Y.: Optimization of hydropower system operation by uniform dynamic programming for dimensionality reduction. Energy **134**, 718–730 (2017)
10. Li, C., Zhou, J., Ouyang, S., Ding, X., Chen, L.: Improved decomposition-coordination and discrete differential dynamic programming for optimization of large-scale hydropower system. Energy Convers. Manag. **84**, 363–373 (2014)
11. Bai, T., et al.: Synergistic gains from the multi-objective optimal operation of cascade reservoirs in the Upper Yellow River basin. J. Hydrol. **523**, 758–767 (2015)
12. Jiang, Z., Ji, C., Sun, P., Wang, L., Zhang, Y.: Total output operation chart optimization of cascade reservoirs and its application. Energy Convers. Manag. **88**, 296–306 (2014)

Digging More in Neural World: An Efficient Approach for Hyperspectral Image Classification Using Convolutional Neural Network

Adnan Iltaf[1], Matee Ullah[1], Junling Shen[1], Zebin Wu[1], Chuancai Liu[1(✉)], and Zeeshan Ahmad[2]

[1] School of Computer Science and Engineering, Nanjing University of Science and Technology, Nanjing 210094, Jiangsu, China
khsaani@qq.com, {mateeullahkhan,wuzb, chuancailiu}@njust.edu.cn, sjl102468@163.com
[2] School of Electronic and Optical Engineering, Nanjing University of Science and Technology, Nanjing 210094, Jiangsu, China
engr.zeeshan@hotmail.com

Abstract. Classification of hyperspectral images (HSI) can benefit from deep learning models with deep architecture in remote sensing. In this letter, a novel method based on Convolutional Neural Network (CNN) is proposed for the classification of hyperspectral images. Due to using more spatio-spectral features for the classification of hyperspectral images, the proposed method outperforms the existing state-of-the-art classification techniques. Our proposed method first reduces the dimension of hyperspectral images using Principle component analysis (PCA). The spatial and spectral features are then exploited by a fixed size convolutional filter to generate the combine spatio-spectral feature maps. Finally, these feature maps are fed into a Multi-Layer Perceptron (MLP) classifier that predicts the class of the pixel vector. To validate the effectiveness of our proposed method, computer simulations are conducted using three datasets namely Indian Pines, Salinas and Pavia University and comparisons with existing techniques are made.

Keywords: CNN · Hyperspectral classification · PCA
Multi-Layer Perceptron (MLP) · Remote sensing

1 Introduction

Hyperspectral image classification is an important research topic in remote sensing. In the presence of commercial hyperspectral sensors e.g. Airborne Visible/Infrared Imaging Spectrometer (AVIRIS), HSI data is easily available to researchers. AVIRIS which is operated by the NASA Jet Propulsion Laboratory covers 224 continuous spectral bands across the electromagnetic spectrum with a spatial resolution of 3.7 m. The information collected by AVRIS is used to classify the objects on earth surface. Supervised or unsupervised classification algorithms have the ability to quickly obtain categorical information from remote-sensing images and classify the objects present in the image.

© Springer Nature Singapore Pte Ltd. 2018
H. Yuan et al. (Eds.): GSKI 2017, CCIS 849, pp. 117–126, 2018.
https://doi.org/10.1007/978-981-13-0896-3_12

Consequently, such algorithms play an important role in remote-sensing image applications.

The basic purpose of image classification is to classify the labels for each pixel in HSI image, which is a challenging task. The performance of classification techniques is closely affected by high dimensionality of the data, limited labeled samples and spatial variability of spectral information. To overcome such issues, various techniques, such as independent component analysis (ICA) [1], neighborhood preserving embedding [2], linear discriminant analysis (LDA) [3] and wavelet analysis [4], have been proposed for the classification of hyperspectral images. Investigations show that the afore-mentioned techniques did not bring significant improvement in classification accuracy. However, support vector machine(SVM) based methods and Neural networks(NN) present a more attractive solution to image classification in terms of computational cost and classification accuracy [5]. Due to the high diversity of HSI data, it is difficult to determine which feature is more relevant for the classification task.

Moreover, recently introduced deep learning (DL) models automatically learn high-level features from data in a hierarchical manner. Typical deep learning models includes Deep Belief Networks [6], Deep Boltzmann Machines [7], Stacked Denoising Autoencoders [8] and Convolutional Neural network (CNN) [9]. More specifically Autoencoders (AE) [10] has been an efficiently used for the classification of HSI images, basically the input of Autoencoders (AE) is high dimensional vector i.e. flatten the high dimensional image into a vector then feed it to the model later classify it by using logistic regression classifier. A recent state-of-the-art technique proposed by Lee et al. [11], called a contextual deep CNN, consist of nine layers in total, jointly obtained the spatio-spectral features maps and classified by Softmax activation function.

In a similar fashion inspired by [11], in this paper we try to assess the effectiveness of a DL technique namely, Convolutional Neural network (CNN). The basic motivations for us to consider Convolutional approach have two main reasons: the effectiveness of this approach recently proved in numerous remote sensing applications; main characteristics of this technique, which makes it a potential candidate to classify hyperspectral data. In this context, we proposed a Conventional Multi-Layer Perceptron (MLP) network for the classification of remote sensing hyperspectral data. Our proposed structure basically combines the spectral-spatial attributes in initial stage resulting in a high-level spectral-spatial features construction and then implement MLP classifier for probabilistic multiclass HSI classification.

The rest of the paper is organized as follows: In Sect. 2, we provide details of the proposed network. The description of datasets and performance comparison are given in Sect. 3. Finally, Sect. 4 summarizes the process and some probable future work is pointed out.

2   Proposed Architecture

In this section architecture of the proposed system is briefly described. In the first stage the reduction of dimensionality is presented and then the deep structure of CNN and MLP is described.

2.1   Dimensionality Reduction

Usually, HSI data consist of several band/channels along the spectral dimension. Thus, it always has tens of thousands of dimensions resulting in a large amount of redundant information. In most of the cases, the first few band/channels have significant variance and they contain almost 99.9% of information [12]. So in the first layer of our proposed network we introduced PCA, to reduce the dimension to an acceptable scale while reserving the useful spatial information in the meantime. As our main concern is to incorporate the spatial information, so we use PCA along-with the spectral dimension only and retain first several principal components. During our experimentation process on state-of-the-art hyperspectral datasets, we used only 10 to 30 principal components respectively for each dataset.

2.2   Classification Framework

For CNN, Image input data is expressed as a 3-dimensional matrix of width * height * channels (h * w * c). In order to input an HSI image, we have to decompose HSI into patches, each one of which contains spectral and spatial information for a specific pixel. Our proposed network contains 12 convolutional layers. First convolutional layer in network contains 32 features with a filter whose dimension is 3 * 3. The batch size of 30 samples is used and the block size is set to 11. In first convolutional layer, we use a filter of dimension 3 * 3 and get feature maps in subsequent layers as shown in Fig. 1. In a similar manner for further layers filter size remains same but the number of feature maps is increased. For preserving local spatio-spectral correlation we do not increase the filter size. The first convolutional layer is followed by further hidden layers in the network.

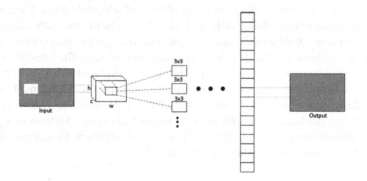

Fig. 1. Filter size and feature map representation.

During the training, network parameters keep changing repeatedly which cause a change in activations, this refers to as "internal covariate shift". To resolve this problem we adopt Batch normalization (BN) [13] which allows us to use much higher learning rate.

Algorithm:

Input: Values of x over a mini-batch: $\beta = \{x_1 \ldots x_m\}$

Parameters to be learned: γ, β

Output : $\{y_i = BN_{\gamma, \beta}(x_i)\}$

$$\mu_\beta \leftarrow \frac{1}{m} \sum_{i=0}^{m} x_i \qquad\qquad (1) \qquad // \quad mini-batch\,mean$$

$$\sigma_\beta^2 \leftarrow \frac{1}{m} \sum_{i=0}^{m} \left(x_i - \mu_\beta\right)^2 \qquad (2) \qquad // \quad mini-batch\,variance$$

$$\hat{x}_i \leftarrow \frac{x_i - \mu_\beta}{\sqrt{\sigma_\beta^2 + \in}} \qquad\qquad (3) \qquad // \quad normalizaiton$$

$$y_i \leftarrow \gamma \hat{x}_i + \beta \equiv BN_{\gamma, \beta}(x_i) \qquad (4) \qquad // \quad Scale\,and\,Shift$$

The algorithm given above presents Batch normalization (BN) transforms where $\beta = \{x_1 \ldots x_m\}$ are the values over mini-batch. Equation (3) implements normalization operation while Eq. (4) implements scaling and shifting learned by γ and β parameters to get the final result y_i. The main characteristic of BN is that it is based on simple differentiable operations, which can be inserted anywhere in CNN network to normalize improper network initialization. BN boost up the performance as well.

After convolving the image fed the neurons to max-pooling layer, the purpose is to take the maximum values from the input and shorten the size of selected features. The pool size is 2 * 2. Next, pooling layer is followed by the Flatten layer which converts the 2D matrix to a vector called Flatten. It allows the output to be processed by standard fully connected layers. ReLU (Rectified linear unit) and dropout are also employed here. The threshold value for dropout is 0.3. The purpose of using ReLU is that it is much faster than other nonlinear functions and Dropout is used to prevent overfitting and complex co-adoptions phenomena.

For classification purpose Softmax activation [14] function issued to output probability-like predications according to the number of classes. Softmax is a generalization of logistic function, and its output can be used to represent the categorical distribution, which is basically a gradient-log-normalizer:

$$p\left(y = j | z^{(i)}\right) = \phi_{soft\,max}\left(z^{(i)}\right) = \frac{e^{z^{(i)}}}{\sum_{j=0}^{k} e^{z_k^{(i)}}} \qquad (5)$$

where z is the net input can be defined as

$$z = w_0 x_0 + w_1 x_1 + \ldots + w_m x_m = \sum_{l=0}^{m} w_l x_l = \mathbf{w}^T \mathbf{x} \qquad (6)$$

where w is the weight vector, w_0 is for bias and x is the feature vector. $z^{(i)}$ is basically a classification function of $j - th$ class which takes "x" as an input and compute probability "y" for each class label. Therefore, Softmax is adopted here because it is a potential candidate for probabilistic multiclass HSI classification problem.

Stochastic gradient descent (SGD) is a classical approach for training deep learning architecture is employed here. SGD algorithm is used to calculate the error and propagate it back to adjust the MLP weights and filters. The architecture of our proposed approach is presented in Fig. 2.

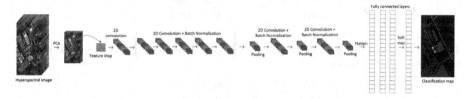

Fig. 2. Graphical representation of proposed network for HIS classification.

3   Experimental Results and Comparative Analysis

3.1   Datasets

AVIRIS and ROSIS sensor datasets are the classical datasets [15]. Particularly, in our experiment the Indian Pines, Salinas and Pavia university datasets are used. Indian Pines dataset depicts a test site in North-western Indiana and consists of 145 * 145 pixels with 224 spectral reflectance bands in the wavelength range from 0.4 to 2.5 µm while spatial resolution is 20 m. Basically, it contains 16 classes but we only use 8 classes because they have a large number of samples among others.

The University of Pavia dataset depicts the scenes acquired by the ROSIS sensor during a flight campaign over Pavia, northern Italy whose number of spectral bands are 102 contains 610 * 340 pixels. It contains 9 classes.

The number of spectral bands and spatial resolutions are 103 and 1.3 m respectively. While the spectral reflectance range from 0.4 to 0.8 µm.

Third dataset "Salinas" is also acquired by AVIRIS sensor over Salina Valley, California. It consists 224-bands with 512 * 217pixels with high spatial resolution 3.7 m. Number of classes of this data set are 16. For both datasets (University of Pavia, Salinas) we use all the classes for training and testing because they have a relatively large number of samples. For all datasets, selected classes and samples are listed in Tables 1, 2 and 3.

Table 1. Number of training and testing samples along with selected classes used from the Indian Pines DataSet.

ID	Class	Train	Test
1	Corn-notill	200	1234
2	Corn-mintill	200	634
3	Grass-pasture	200	297
4	Hay-windrowed	200	289
5	Soybean-notill	200	768
6	Soybean-mintill	200	2268
7	Soybean-clean	200	414
8	Woods	200	1094
Total		**1600**	**6998**

Table 2. Number of training and testing samples along with selected classes used from the University of Pavia DataSet.

ID	Class	Train	Test
1	Asphalt	200	6431
2	Meadows	200	18449
3	Gravel	200	1899
4	Trees	200	2864
5	Sheets	200	1145
6	Bare soil	200	4829
7	Bitumen	200	1130
8	Bricks	200	3482
9	Shadows	200	747
Total		**1800**	**40976**

Table 3. Number of training and testing samples along with selected classes used from salinas dataset.

ID	Class	Train	Test
1	Broccoli greenweeds 1	200	1809
2	Broccoli-greenweeds 2	200	3526
3	Fallow	200	1776
4	Fallow rough plow	200	1194
5	Fallow smooth	200	2478
6	Stubble	200	3759
7	Celery	200	3379
8	Grapes untrained	200	11071
9	Soil vineyard develop	200	6003
10	Corn-green weeds	200	3078
11	Lettuce romaine, 4wk	200	868
12	Lettuce romaine, 5wk	200	1727
13	Lettuce romaine, 6wk	200	716
14	Lettuce romaine, 7wk	200	870
15	Vineyard untrained	200	7068
16	Vineyard vertical trellis	200	1607
Total		**3200**	**50929**

3.2   Comparative Analysis

For comparison, we randomly select 200 samples per class for training and all remaining samples for testing. The basic purpose of selecting 200 samples per class is to evaluate our proposed method with the state of the art approaches reported in [11]. To successfully accomplish all the experiments the CNN Tensor flow framework [16] is used on GPU GTX1060.

Table 4 provides a comparative analysis of classification among the proposed method and the one reported in [11]. The contextual deep CNN used in [11] has 9 convolutional layers while our proposed network has twelve layers, we can say that our network is much deeper than contextual deep CNN [11]. It is obvious that our network has much better performance as compare to contextual deep CNN on all datasets. To further evaluate our network we compare our performance with state-of-the-art RBF kernel-based SVM method [17], which consist two convolutional and two fully connected layer much shallower than our technique. In recent research [18], for a diversified Deep Belief Networks(D-DBN) has much better performance as compared to [17], we also use (D-DBN) as a baseline to in our comparative analysis. For all the datasets, we also use other types of methods which are evaluated in [11]: two-layer NN, three-layer NN, shallower CNN and LeNet-5.

Our proposed network out-performs the baseline approaches on all the datasets. More specifically as compared to [11] for Indian Pines dataset the proposed network gained more than 2% accuracy while in the cases of University of Pavia and Salinas datasets, it gained 1.3% and 2.04% classification accuracy respectively. The significant performance of proposed architecture is just because of its deeper nature which proves, that digging more in the convolutional network leads to high classification accuracy. Figure 3 shows the classification maps of each data set corresponding to their ground truth images.

3.3   Impact of Epochs

During network training weights are updated due to back propagation phenomena, One round of updating the network or the entire training dataset is called an epoch [19]. Figure 4 shows validation loss and classification accuracy on the bases of epoch size. From validation loss plotted in Fig. 4a we observe the performance of the proposed network i.e. the number of lost samples decreased when the number of epochs increased meanwhile the classification accuracy is improved significantly as can be seen in Fig. 4b.

For all the data sets these observations proved that deepness of our network greatly improves overall accuracy meanwhile preserving lower validation loss.

Table 4. Classification accuracy comparison among proposed networks and the base lines on three datasets(%). The best performances among all methods are indicated in bold

Data sets	Two-Layer NN [11]	RBF-SVM [11]	Three-layer NN [11]	LeNet-5 [11]	Shallower CNN [11]	D-DBN [18]	DCNN [11]	Proposed Network
Indian Pines	86.49	87.60	87.93	88.27	90.16	91.03	93.61	**96.13**
University of Pavia	–	90.52	–	–	92.56	93.11	95.97	**97.32**
Salinas	–	91.66	–	–	92.60	–	95.07	**97.11**

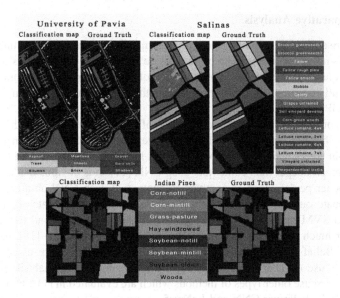

Fig. 3. RGB compositions of resulted classification map by proposed network along with ground truth are shown for University of Pavia, Salinas and Indian Pines datasets.

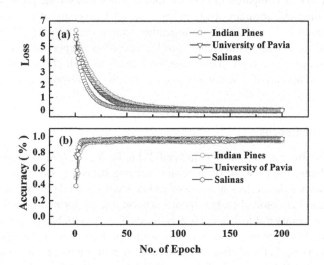

Fig. 4. Classification performance under different set of parameters for all experimental data sets. (a)Validation loss vs. Number of epochs, (b) Classification accuracy over the course of epochs.

4   Conclusion

In this letter, we propose a CNN-based classification method for remote sensing data. The proposed method is much deeper, faster and utilizes more spatio-spectral features for the classification of hyperspectral images. The proposed method and existing state-of-art techniques are compared using three data sets. It is shown that our method achieves better classification accuracy. Simulation results demonstrate the superiority of the proposed method. The future research prospects include to combine the proposed network with a shallower convolutional based network for more enhanced classification performance.

Acknowledgments. This work is sponsored by the National Natural Science Foundation of China under Grant No. 61373063 and 61373062; the project of Ministry of Industry and Information Technology of China (Grant No. E0310/1112/02-1).

References

1. Falco, N., Bruzzone, L., Benediktsson, J.A.: A comparative study of different ICA algorithms for hyperspectral image analysis. In: 2013 5th Workshop on Hyperspectral Image and Signal Processing: Evolution in Remote Sensing (WHISPERS), pp. 1–4 (2013)
2. Zhao, L.Y., Zou, D., Gao, G.: Subsampling based neighborhood preserving embedding for image classification. In: Proceedings - 2013 9th International Conference on Intelligent Information Hiding and Multimedia Signal Processing, IIH-MSP 2013, pp. 358–360 (2013)
3. Yuan, H., Tang, Y.Y., Lu, Y., Yang, L., Luo, H.: Spectral-spatial classification of hyperspectral image based on discriminant analysis. IEEE J. Sel. Top. Appl. Earth Obs. Remote Sens. **7**, 2035–2043 (2014)
4. Gangodagamage, C., Foufoula-Georgiou, E., Brumby, S.P., Chartrand, R., Koltunov, A., Liu, D., Cai, M., Ustin, S.L.: Wavelet-compressed representation of landscapes for hydrologic and geomorphologic applications. IEEE Geosci. Remote Sens. Lett. **13**, 480–484 (2016)
5. Yu, H., Gao, L., Liao, W., Zhang, B., Pizurica, A., Philips, W.: Multiscale superpixel-level subspace-based support vector machines for hyperspectral image classification. IEEE Geosci. Remote Sens. Lett. **14**, 2142–2146 (2017)
6. Chen, Y., Zhao, X., Jia, X.: Spectral-Spatial classification of hyperspectral data based on deep belief network. IEEE J. Sel. Top. Appl. Earth Obs. Remote Sens. **8**, 2381–2392 (2015)
7. Salakhutdinov, R., Hinton, G.: Deep boltzmann machines. In: AISTATS, pp. 448–455 (2009)
8. Vincent, P., Larochelle, H.: Stacked denoising autoencoders: learning useful representations in a deep network with a local denoising criterion Pierre-Antoine manzagol. J. Mach. Learn. Res. **11**, 3371–3408 (2010)
9. Yu, S., Jia, S., Xu, C.: Convolutional neural networks for hyperspectral image classification. Neurocomputing **219**, 88–98 (2017)
10. Lin, Z., Chen, Y., Zhao, X., Wang, G.: Spectral-spatial classification of hyperspectral image using autoencoders. In: 2013 9th International Conference Information, Communication Signal Process, pp. 1–5 (2013)
11. Lee, H., Kwon, H.: Going deeper with contextual CNN for hyperspectral image classification. IEEE Trans. Image Process. **26**, 4843–4855 (2017)
12. Jablonski, J.A.: Reconstruction error and principal component based anomaly detection in hyperspectral imagery. Master thesis, Air Force Institute of Technology, USA (2014)
13. Ioffe, S., Szegedy, C.: Batch normalization: accelerating deep network training by reducing internal covariate shift. In: International Conference on International Conference on Machine Learning, pp. 448–456 (2015)

14. Raschka, S.: Michigan State Uni., USA. https://www.kdnuggets.com/2016/07/softmax-regression-related-logistic-regression.html
15. Hyperspectral remote sensing scenes. http://www.ehu.eus/ccwintco/index.php?title=Hyperspectral_Remote_Sensing_Scenes
16. Abadi, M., Barham, P., Chen, J., Chen, Z., Davis, A., Dean, J., Devin, M., Ghemawat, S., Irving, G., Isard, M., Kudlur, M., Levenberg, J., Monga, R., Moore, S., Murray, D.G., Steiner, B., Tucker, P., Vasudevan, V., Warden, P., Wicke, M., Yu, Y., Zheng, X., Brain, G.: TensorFlow: a system for large-scale machine learning. In: 12th USENIX Symposium on Operating Systems Design and Implementation (OSDI 2016), pp. 265–284 (2016)
17. Hu, W., Huang, Y., Wei, L., Zhang, F., Li, H.: Deep convolutional neural networks for hyperspectral image classification. J. Sens. **2015**, 1–12 (2015)
18. Zhong, P., Gong, Z., Li, S., Schonlieb, C.-B.: Learning to diversify deep belief networks for hyperspectral image classification. IEEE Trans. Geosci. Remote Sens. **55**, 3516–3530 (2017)
19. Brownlee J.: Deep Learning with Python: Develop Deep Learning Models on Theano and TensorFlow Using Keras, 1.7th edn. Machine Learning Mastery, Melbourne (2016)

An Intelligent Cartographic Generalization Algorithm Selecting Mode Used in Multi-scale Spatial Data Updating Process

Junkui Xu[1,2(✉)], Dong Li[1], Longfei Cui[1,2], and Xing Zhang[1,2]

[1] Luoyang Electronic Equipment Test Center of China, Luoyang, China
xjk_uuu@163.com, ascii001@163.com, xmaj2008@163.com
[2] Zhengzhou Institute of Surveying and Mapping, Zhengzhou, China

Abstract. In multi-scale spatial data updating process, cartographic features vary dramatically with the scales evolution. So, it is the critical step to select suitable cartographic generalization algorithm which can perfectly fulfill the scale-transformation task. This problem is also a main obstacle in the way of automatic spatial data updating. Through deeply studying the flows of multi-scale spatial data updating process, an intelligent cartographic generalization algorithm selecting mode is proposed. Firstly cartographic generalization algorithm base, knowledge base and case base is built in this mode. Secondly, based on the step of resolving the cartographic generalization process into segments, a self-adaption cartographic generalization algorithm selecting architecture is constructed. Thirdly, an intelligent cartographic generalization algorithm selecting and using flow is established and put into effect. Overall, this mode provides a new idea to solve the automatic problem of multi-scale spatial data updating.

Keywords: Spatial data · Updating · Cartographic generalization
Intelligent selecting · Multi-scale map

1 Introduction

Multi-scale spatial data updating process involves scale-transformation of spatial objects in every scale. Due to the variety of settlement shape and updating scenes, the scale-transformation algorithms will change according with the updating area and map usage. The same algorithm, such as settlement simplification, will change its contents coping with buildings and blocks. So, it is the kernel steps to develop generalization algorithms for certain scale in spatial data updating. To multi-scale spatial data incremental propagating updating method, how to design scale-transformation algorithm selecting mode is the vital problem.

To realization self-selecting of generalization algorithms, firstly, the basic information of generalization algorithm, such as function, objects, strong and weak points, parameters, etc., should be clarified. And these information should be expressed in language which can be understand by computer. This process will involve the construction of algorithms base. Secondly, computer should be taught something about how to select right algorithm according to generalization scene, which need the ability

© Springer Nature Singapore Pte Ltd. 2018
H. Yuan et al. (Eds.): GSKI 2017, CCIS 849, pp. 127–134, 2018.
https://doi.org/10.1007/978-981-13-0896-3_13

of induction on the basis of generalization knowledge. Thus, generalization knowledge lab should be built to support algorithm selection. Meanwhile, successful generalization process could be store in database as a generalization case, which can be used when updating scene is fitting. On the whole, the self-adapting generalization algorithm selection mode is built on the basis of algorithm base and knowledge lab, and fulfilling algorithm selection with the help of case base.

2   The Construction of Auxiliary Labs of Spatial Data Updating

2.1   The Construction of Generalization Algorithm Base

Through hard work of domestic and abroad researchers, a lot of generalization algorithms are developed. Let's take the point cluster selection algorithms for an example. Deng Hongyan put forward a model of point cluster selection based on genetic algorithms [1]; Qian put forward a point cluster selection algorithm based on CIRCLE character transformation techniques [2]; Cai put forward points group generalization algorithm based on konhonen net [3]; Ai put forward a method of point cluster simplification with spatial distribution properties preserved [4]; Yan put forward a generic algorithm for point cluster generalization based on voronoi diagrams [5]. These algorithms mostly aim to special data type and generalization environment. So, the metadata of these algorithms, such as working environment, function and parameter, should be abstracted and listed [6].

(1)   Abstraction algorithm metadata
   The abstraction of generalization algorithm metadata mainly depends on algorithm using area, function, parameters, evaluation etc. which described in Table 1.

Table 1.   Main algorithm metadata and its description.

Algorithm metadata	Description
Adapting range of algorithm	Map type, scale, district character, etc.
Function of algorithm	The function type of algorithm, such as selecting, simplify, merge, move, etc. operating object of algorithm like point, line and area
Parameter of algorithm	Data should be set and used in generalization algorithm
Basic information of algorithm	Information like development department, member, time, object, contact details

(2)   The construction of generalization algorithm base
   Generalization algorithm base is based on the relational database. According with map scale, map type and map character, the generalization algorithm metadata stored in data tables, and the algorithm itself is stored as binary code in the form of dynamic linking base. The structure of algorithms base is shown in Fig. 1.

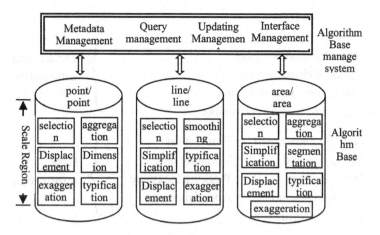

Fig. 1. Structure of generalization algorithm base.

2.2   The Construction of Knowledge Base

(1) The concept of generalization knowledge

If algorithms base is compared to tool-box of generalization operation, knowledge base can be taken as the brain of using these tools. The algorithm base depends on the direction of knowledge lab. Knowledge of generalization mainly comes from the specifications in mapping.

(2) The abstraction of generalization knowledge metadata

It is a difficult work to build generalization knowledge lab. Through abstraction of generalization knowledge metadata, we can fulfill the management of generalization knowledge. The knowledge metadata is data which describing how to use and manage generalization knowledge. It can associate actual algorithm with tools to solve complicate problems. With the analyses of generalization knowledge, the generalization knowledge metadata structure is designed as Fig. 2.

Following the expression of metadata in Fig. 2, the generalization rules like street blocks whose area less than 12 mm^2 should be deleted in 1:250000 maps, and settlement block which doesn't located far from 0.3 mm, can be margined with nearest street block, could be extracted the metadata as Table 2.

(3) The construction of generalization knowledge lab

The generalization knowledge labs are composed with many kinds of knowledge which contain every aspects and factors in generalization process. Meanwhile, there are much information such as threshold, using scope, operator of generation algorithm. The structure of knowledge labs will affect the operation efficiency of all the system. So, on the angle of performance and compatibility, it is suitable to use algorithm base structure to organize the generalization knowledge. Its main structure is shown as Fig. 3 Firstly, knowledge is classed by scale, map type, regional characteristic. Secondly, it is divided by generalization algorithm. And finally, the factor and threshold is decided by actual generalization scenes and algorithm characteristic.

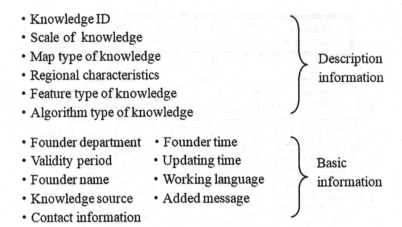

- Knowledge ID
- Scale of knowledge
- Map type of knowledge   } Description
- Regional characteristics   information
- Feature type of knowledge
- Algorithm type of knowledge

- Founder department · Founder time
- Validity period   · Updating time   } Basic
- Founder name   · Working language   information
- Knowledge source   · Added message
- Contact information

Fig. 2. Metadata types of generalization knowledge.

Table 2. The example of knowledge extraction.

Scale	1:25000	1:250000
Maptype	Topographic map	Topographic map
Area character	All	All
Feature type	130204	130204
Algorithm type	Select	Merge
Factor type	Area	Distance
Factor threshold	12 mm^2	0.3 mm
Quantization demand	<	<
Generalization action	Delete	Merge

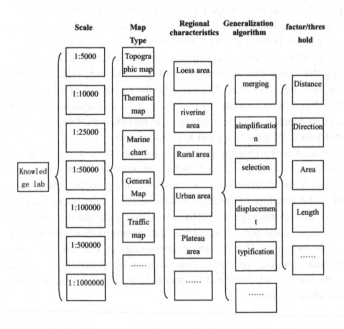

Fig. 3. The structure of generalization knowledge lab

2.3   The Construction of Case Base

(1) The concept of case-based reasoning
CBR (case-based reasoning) is one of the most important ability of human beings' intelligent, which solves problems by the way of similar successful cases. These cases can probably come from knowledge acquisition project from professional people, or comes from searching existing cases. For example, medical training not only depends on the theory model of anatomy and psychology, but also depends on the experience on similar cases [7]. So, CBR can also be used in improving the level of intelligent and automation in generalization field. If we record how the specialist solving generalization problem, the knowledge acquisition process will be probably shorten.

(2) Organization and construction of case base
Generalization scenes and spatial data structures which used in case reasoning vary dramatically. So, the framework skeleton of cases has much relation with the searching and appliance efficiency. In common place, a case is recorded as a relation-group, that is, some of the data list the characteristic of case, and others described steps of problem solving. Otherwise, cases can be expressed in more complicated mode, like proof-tree. In this paper, cases will be organized in relation-group, which is shown in Fig. 4. And case information is divided into three parts, which is Environmental information, functional information and basic information.

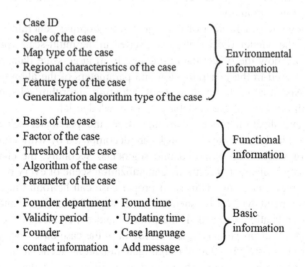

Fig. 4. Metadata of the case

3 Generalization Algorithm Self-adopting Selecting Method

In upwards text, the concept and structure of generalization algorithm base, knowledge lab and case base have been presented. On the basis of these supporting labs, we will propose an intelligent self-adopting generalization algorithm selecting method. In the process of generalization, algorithm base provide tools, and how to use these tool depend on the direction of knowledge labs. Algorithm selecting system based on rules has many merits. Firstly, it can provide experience directly from cartographic experts. Secondly, the knowledge and control separating skeleton will help in circulate knowledge gaining and using.

If only using knowledge-based algorithm selecting method, there are many limitations. Firstly, it is difficult for knowledge-based algorithm selecting method to properly deal with incomplete information and unexpected data. Secondly, in the edge of knowledge, the efficiency of system will decay badly. While case-based algorithm selecting method can easily gain successful case from case base and it will relax the problem of knowledge getting. But case-based algorithm selecting method also has its shortages. First of all, the case can't contain more knowledge. And secondly, it is a hard work to index and choose proper case form hundred and thousands of cases.

Based on these analyses, a new compounding algorithm selecting method, which combines the merits of above tow method, is proposed. In this method, you can firstly search case base, if can't find related cases, knowledge-based algorithm will be used to reason and analysis. Meanwhile, the correctness of system-prompted case can be verified by content in knowledge lab. Moreover, the case which comes from knowledge lab reasoning could be put in the case base too. By this way, the intelligence of the system will improve gradually.

Figure 5 shows the main idea of intelligent self-adopting generalization selecting method. Firstly, the 'GenerAlgList' item is inserted in the multi-scale spatial data link structure to record how the object data produced from large scale data. Secondly, the algorithm which used in the generalization and parameters of the algorithm are put in the case base. And finally, the intelligent self-adopting algorithm selecting method is constructed with the help of the case base and knowledge lab.

In actual generalization process, the algorithm and parameter selecting steps is shown in Fig. 6. Firstly, generalization tasks are decomposed by work control produce. The long line of work is decomposed into segments. Secondly, the characteristic of generalization step is abstracted from the generalization scene of every part, which will be used in case base searching. Thirdly, if proper case can be found in case base, the generalization segment will be finished with the step of found case and parameters. Fourthly, if generalization succeeded, the priority and experience of the case will be increased, and if fail or proper case can't be found in the case base, then the rules will be searched from knowledge lab through generalization scene and updating surroundings. If usable rules is found, then use it to fulfill the last generalization steps, if generalization succeeded, put the generalization scene and algorithm into case lab, if fail or nothing be found in knowledge lab, it is the last way to deal with the work by helping of experts.

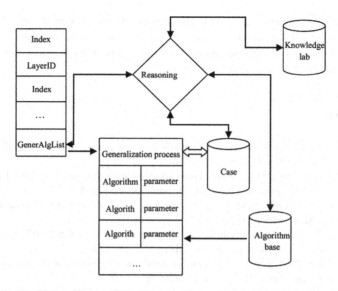

Fig. 5. The Skelton figure of intelligent self-adopting algorithm selecting method

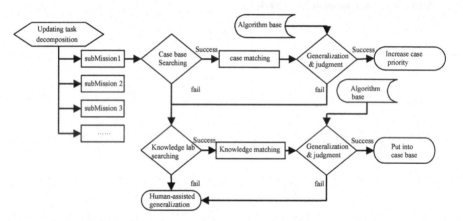

Fig. 6. The flow diagram of intelligent self-adopting algorithm selecting method

4   Conclusions

Multi-scale spatial data updating process involves scale-transformation of spatial objects. Due to the variety of settlement shape, the scale-transformation algorithms will vary with the updating area and map usage. Through deeply studying the flows of multi-scale spatial data updating process, an intelligent cartographic generalization algorithm selecting mode is proposed. Firstly cartographic generalization algorithm base, knowledge base and case base is built in this mode. Secondly, based on the step of resolving the cartographic generalization process into segments, a self-adaption cartographic generalization algorithm selecting architecture is constructed. Thirdly, an intelligent cartographic generalization algorithm selecting and using flow is established and put into effect. Overall, this mode provides a new idea to solve the automatic problem of multi-scale spatial data updating.

References

1. Deng, H., Wu, F., Qian, H., et al.: A model of point cluster selection based on genetic algorithms. J. Image Graph. **8**, 970–974 (2003)
2. Qian, Q., Wu, F., Deng, H.: A point cluster selection algorithm based on CIRCLE character transformation techniques. Sci. Surv. Mapp. **30**(3), 83–85 (2005)
3. Cai, Y., Guo, Q.: Points group generalization based on konhonen net. Geomatics Inf. Sci. Wuhan Univ. **32**(7), 626–629 (2007)
4. Ai, T., Liu, Y.: A method of point cluster simplification with spatial distribution properties preserved. Acta Geodaetica Cartogr. Sin. **31**(2), 175–181 (2002)
5. Yan, H., Wang, J.: A generic algorithm for point cluster generalization based on Voronoi diagrams. J. Image Graph. **10**(5), 633–636 (2005)
6. Qian, H.: Study on Automated Cartographic Generalization and Intelligentized Generalization Process Control. Zhengzhou Institute of Surveying and Mapping, Zhengzhou (2006)
7. Luger, G.F.: Artificial Intelligence: Structures and Strategies for Complex Problem Solving, 6th edn. Pearson Education Inc. (2009)

A Cross-National Analysis of the Correlated Network Structure of Marine Transportation in the Indian Ocean Rim Association

Shuguang Liu[(✉)], Xiaoxin Yang, and Han Zhang

College of Economics, Ocean University of China, No.238, Songling Road,
Qingdao 266100, Shandong, China
Dawnliu9631@126.com,
{carolyangxiaoxin, zhanghan198837}@163.com

Abstract. Taking the countries within Indian Ocean Rim Association as the research objects, this paper analyzes the network pattern of shipping alliance consisting of 21 member countries from 2006 to 2016 through the Circos Graphical Model. The results indicate that the countries with strong position in the shipping field spread out dense network, especially playing a boosting role to lead those with relative low position. The association of maritime transportation in the alliance is transformed from marine correlation between close range and small scope group to the regional broad trading association. The gap of maritime transportation between different countries has gradually narrowed, and the marine transport network with uniform and dense coverage has gradually formed. All these suggest that the countries of the vulnerable group in IOR-ARC are supposed to transform the old preference of internal shipping in close and small group into long-distance association. In the contemporary days, it is necessary for low-level nations to improve the construction level of port facilities while high-level countries should make full usage of the "Network Sprawl" opportunities to strengthen the tightness of connectivity.

Keywords: IOR-ARC · Maritime transportation connectivity
Spatial evolution · Circos analysis · Policy implications

1 Introduction

The Indian Ocean Rim Association for Regional Cooperation (IOR-ARC) refers to the 21 nations around the Indian Ocean Region (South Africa, India, Australia, Kenya, Mauritius, Oman, Singapore, Sri Lanka, Tanzania, Madagascar, Indonesia, Malaysia, Yemen, Mozambique, Seychelles, United Arab Emirates, Iran, Bangladesh, Thailand and Comorin). Having formed a cooperative organization with specific arrangements under free investment and frequent trades, the entire association can be divided into several sub-regions, such as Australasia, Southeast Asia, South Asia, West Asia and South-East Africa, and each sub-region has its independent local scale cooperative bodies, including ASEAN, SAARC, GCC, SADC, etc. Covering Asia, Africa and Oceania geographically, IOR-ARC enjoys wide spatial sphere, abundant natural resources, rich human power resources as well as great market potentials.

© Springer Nature Singapore Pte Ltd. 2018
H. Yuan et al. (Eds.): GSKI 2017, CCIS 849, pp. 135–142, 2018.
https://doi.org/10.1007/978-981-13-0896-3_14

IOR-ARC serves as an organization for economic cooperation around the Indian Ocean and the marine economy constitutes a vital part of national economic development in the association. Widely considered as the loose regional community knitted by the maritime routes of trade, Indian Ocean has occupied nearly half of freight volumes of containers, one third of transportation volumes of dry bulks and two thirds of crude oil transportation in the world, making it lifeline for international trade and transportation [1].

With the rapid progress of China's One Belt One Road initiative (OBOR) since 2013, the economic demands between China and the Indian Ocean Rim Association members are also increasing. Thereby, it is of great importance to study the characters of ocean transportation and evolutionary trend in IOR-ARC. This paper tries to analyze the spatial framework and evolution trend of the marine transportation industry of IOR-ARC nations as well as the related network structure with the Circos visualization method.

2 Method and Data

2.1 Introduction of Analytical Method

When it comes to constructing the related network, Circos is adopted to deal with the bilateral relations of the ocean transportation of the IOR-ARC nations. Circos, developed by a Canadian bioinformatician Martin Krzywinski, is a visual software based on the genomic data of the Perl language. In accordance with the Circos diagram, the position of the genomic sequence with complex arrangement is organized. Besides, the chromosome mapping is painted and genotyping is identified. The Circos diagram has many means of expression, including dot, line, bar, hot point, and circle, among which the cyclized expression of correlations can portray the relations between the objects of the connection link which has some specific attribution, including zero position, size and direction. While analyzing the influence of cell factor released by the immune system on individual behavior, Anthony J visualizes the correlation of the response signals of different cell factors, such as the state of brain activity, interleukin and interferon with Circos, clearly describes the effects of different cell factors on behavior as well as studies the synergistic reaction among various types of cell factor [2]. During the process of rearranging chromosomes, Zhang shows the inter-chromosomal and extra-chromosomal influences as well as the individual and regional changes incurred by the behavior with Circos, and visualizes the sequence of scrambled data in the early studies on T cell [3]. At present, the processing of data visualization based on Circos has formed mature theoretical method and practice in the field of biological genetics. Nonetheless, it is seldom utilized in the academic application of other subjects.

By referring to the application method in the field of biology, the Circos diagram can be used to express complex economic issues, particularly to depict the economic correlation degree among several objects. Besides the Circos diagram, the connectivity map produced by the geo-information system can also express the similar association between different objects. Nevertheless, it not only has a different focus, but also has some limitations in expression. The relation diagram of the geo-information system can intuitively express the space attributes of objects, including the positional relation and spatial distance between different objects. However, it has certain limitations that it can only express these attributes generally, and the visualization effect on expressing the direction and tightness of the relation between different objects decreases rapidly with the increase of the number of objects and the complication of relations. Hence, spatial information materialization has become an obstacle and constraint. While compared with the expression means of the geo-information system, Circos only describes the relationship and quantity of objects without considering their spatial attributes, as well as expresses the quantity with the graduation mode of homogeneous graphics, which can manifest the relation more delicately. Besides, the Circos diagram can diversify the data processing according to the demands, such as screening and ranking, as well as can satisfy a variety of visualization demands with different expression means.

2.2 Research Data

The Liner Shipping Connectivity Index (LSCI), as one of the bases for judging the degree of national integration in the global market, is utilized to analyze the correlation pattern related to maritime industry and shipping, and to examine the links in national networks [4]. All the data are collected from the Database of United Nation http://unctadstat.unctad.org.

3 Empirical Analysis

3.1 Maritime Transportation Network

3.1.1 The Overall Evolution of Maritime Transportation Correlation Networks

As presented in Fig. 1, all the countries in IOR-ARC are put on the annular border of the Circos graphic from 12 o'clock by the total value of LSCI in a descending order, and the length of arc segment is also a direct expression of the value. Singapore, Malaysia, the United Arab Emirates, India, Sri Lanka, Oman, and South Africa are the top eight countries with the most densely associated relationship with other countries in the IOR-ARC area. Nations like Singapore, Malaysia and Sri Lanka own the dominant position and have the closest links with other nations mainly due to the advantages of geographic location as transit choke. On the other side, the United Arab Emirates, India, and South Africa mainly rely on its large economy and huge market, establishing stable marine trade with other countries. Meanwhile, some countries have their specific trading and shipping partners, such as Oman, Mauritius and Mozambique which usually play the role of an importer or exporter in the IOR-ARC shipping network. For clarity of expression, the countries are further divided into high-level countries, medium-level countries and low-level countries according to the ranking of index ranking.

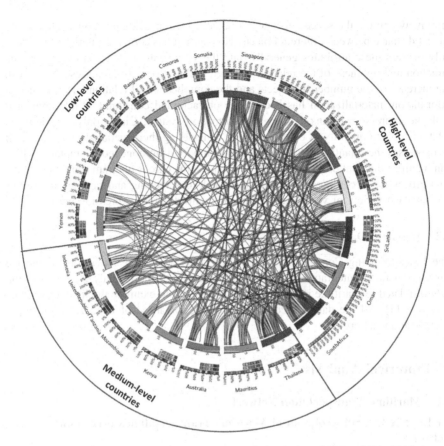

Fig. 1. Bilateral maritime transportation correlation index of IOR-ARC in 2016

3.1.2   The Overall Evolution of Maritime Transportation Correlation Networks

Secondly, to describe the evolution trend of IOR-ARC maritime transportation association network, the whole correlation index value is divided by interquartile range into four levels represented by purple, blue, green and orange respectively in a descending order in 2006, 2011 and 2016. The visualization result is presented in Fig. 2.

The changes of countries' order at the outer arc of Circos graph suggest the variation (shown in Table 1). From 2006 to 2011, the countries with rising correlation were the United Arab Emirates, Oman, Iran, Yemen, Tanzania, Mozambique, Comoros and Bangladesh, among which Iran achieved the maximum increase, improving from the twelfth up to eighth on the ranking. On the contrary, the declining countries are India, Indonesia, Mauritius, Madagascar and Seychelles, among which Indonesia experienced the most drastic reduction from the seventh down to the twelfth. From 2011 to 2016, the overall performance of African countries was outstanding, such as Madagascar, Mozambique, Mauritius and Seychelles, in which Mauritius increased most, from the sixteenth up to the ninth. Analogously, after 2011, the island countries in southeast also

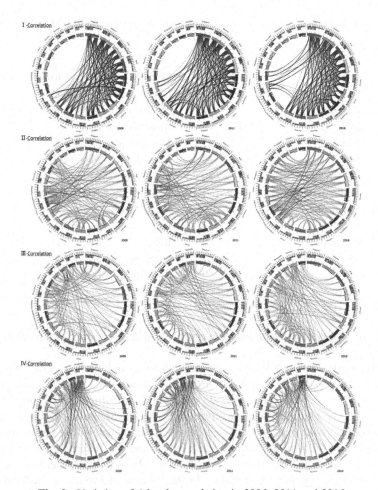

Fig. 2. Variation of 4 levels correlation in 2006, 2011 and 2016

had a strong growing trend. The country with the most dramatic drop was Iran, from the eighth down to the seventeenth. It can be seen that during the periods of 2006–2011 and 2011–2016, Oman and Mozambique went up one position every five years, whereas Indonesia had a significant decline in the two periods.

3.1.3   The Evolution Trend of Maritime Transportation Correlation Network at All Levels

As shown in Fig. 2, in 2006, the I-correlation network mainly existed in high-level and medium-level countries in the graph on the right side. The network between high-level countries was uniform and stable and the links between the medium-level countries transferred from the specific relationship between few countries to full-sided contacts with a great number of countries. In 2016, the short arc links emerged in medium-level countries and the links changed from thick to thin. During the period of 2011–2016, the

Table 1. The order change of maritime transportation correlation index in IOR-ARC from 2006 to 2016.

2006–2011			2011–2016		
Country	Order	Change	Country	Order	Change
United Arab Emirates	4	+1	Oman	7	+1
Oman	8	+1	Thailand	9	+1
Iran	12	+4	Australia	11	+1
Tanzania	14	+1	Mozambique	14	+2
Mozambique	16	+2	Mauritius	16	+7
Yemen	17	+2	Madagascar	18	+2
Comoros	18	+1	Seychelles	21	+3
Bangladesh	21	+2	South Africa	6	−1
India	3	−1	Iran	8	−9
Indonesia	7	−5	Kenya	10	−1
Mauritius	13	−3	Indonesia	12	−2
Madagascar	15	−3	Comoros	17	−3
Seychelles	19	−2	Somalia	20	−1

coverage of I-correlation network constantly expanded to cover the medium-level nations.

The II-correlation network covers the most countries in IOR-ARC. Over the period of 2006–2016, there was obvious structural change. At the early stage, the II-correlation network was built in both low-level and medium-level countries. Particularly in the neighboring countries, the links between Mauritius, Tanzania, Madagascar and Mozambique were dense and complex. Subsequently, the ties increased in the number with uniform and orderly distribution and the II-correlation, in general, tended to be more comprehensive, transforming the specific correlation between African countries to general correlation. In the process of evolution, the high-value national association network played a dominant role in breaking the limitation of geographical distance by the advantage of maritime transportation, in order to develop the uniform maritime transport correlation network.

The overall structure of the III-correlation network changed little. With more network building, there existed close correlation between medium-level countries instead of low-level countries, so that the gap between countries reduced. In 2016, the comprehensive network between both low-level countries and medium-level countries was constructed.

The IV-correlation network developed smoothly from 2006 to 2016. In 2006, it mainly existed among Seychelles, Somalia, and Bangladesh, the lowest three countries and their specific trading partners. In 2016, IV-correlation networks began to develop evenly in the low-level countries and the tail ones of medium-level countries. There was almost no high-level country for all the links with high-level countries going into the higher level. As seen from the Circos graph, short ties between low-level countries increased a lot. Besides, the uniform cross also gradually grew among the countries whose maritime transportation were relatively weak before.

Table 2. Evolution of IOR-ARC maritime transportation correlation network at all levels

Type	Country	I-correlation	II-correlation	III-correlation	IV-correlation
High	Singapore, Malaysia, United Arab Emirates, India, Sri Lanka, Oman, South Africa	High-level countries maintains stability; median-level countries transformed from particular correlation to a wide correlation; The coverage of primary correlation between low-level countries expands	The correlation between high and low countries tends to be extensive; The African countries have developed into a uniform and extensive relationship from specific relations, and then tend to connect with high-level countries	The high-density correlation transfers from the low-level countries to the medium-level countries; There are more countries to build new connect	By focusing on the lowest value of the four countries and the distribution of the low value region, the gap in the four-level correlation is narrowing
Media	Thailand, Mauritius, Australia, Kenya, Mozambique, Tanzania, Indonesia, Yemen				
Low	Madagascar, Iran, Seychelles, Bangladesh, Comoros, Somalia				

3.2   The Overall Evolution of Maritime Transportation Correlation in IOR-ARC

The comparison between Circos graphs in 2006, 2011 and 2016, shows that the association in each level appears in the process of turning the homogeneous, specific bilateral shipping and trading relationships made by the colonial history; the endowment of resources in the early stage is reshaped by maritime transportation network in the whole area. All the countries are assigned with more division of work and specialization of labor along with the constantly expanding network of sea transportation.

Secondly, the II-association with the most significant variation indicates that the association between the neighboring country and local organizations, such as the Common Market for Eastern and Southern Africa (COMESA) and the Southern African Development Community (SADC) is replaced by the association with countries with strong shipping power. Herein, Mauritius, Kenya, Tanzania, Madagascar, and Mozambique are the best examples. With the rapid development of the shipbuilding and Marine technology, distance is no more an essential factor for the shipping transportation. Furthermore, the increase of trade demand and the desire to participate in economic globalization make the weak shipping nations search for more opportunities in a larger scale. The benefit condition is that there is no complex sea route in the whole area, with the advantage of transshipment hub type and the large economic volume is more appealing in boosting the driving ability.

4 Conclusion

The low-level countries ought to fully utilize the advantages of the Indian Ocean, further improve the harbor construction, promote the development of the close maritime relations with the nations in the association, as well as provide solid platform for the further development of marine economy. Meanwhile, African countries should further break through the restrain of the close distance and small range in the future, enhance the cooperation in the field of infrastructure, connectivity, maritime economy, and tourism with the nations on the platform of IOR-ARC, promote the integration of capacity as well as assist industrialization. As the regions with big market and economic growth potential, African landscape will provide various opportunities for all other countries in IOR-ARC.

While the high-level countries in the correlation network should constantly improve the intensive relationship, and increase connection., the intensive and wide marine associated network is the basis of the highly-correlated "commercial network", actively promoting the establishment and improvement of the maritime correlation of the nations in the association. This can not only increase the economic linkage, but also intensify the guarantee of stability, to help the nations benefit from the joint prosperity of the association through peaceful means, to reduce the unnecessary conflicts and friction as well as to prevent the economic losses incurred by regional instability. Meanwhile, enhancing the density and complexity of the correlated network helps the countries to satisfy the sea transportation requirements more flexibly, and prevent the risk brought by the change of sea transportation pattern, such as developing new routes and establishing new trading passages. Thus, the high-level countries are supposed to play a more crucial role in building up an intensive network which will bring prosperity to the entire area.

With the rapid development of the internal economy of IOR-ARC and the enhancement of foreign trade relations, the function of IOR-ARC is perfect and the interlaced maritime transport network has taken shape. In the context of "OBOR" initiated by China, IOR-ARC is currently confronted with the vital strategic opportunity of jointly building the "Maritime Silk Road", and the countries in the association should find the right direction and work together so as to promote the prosperity, development, mutual benefit and win-win situation of the region.

References

1. Kaplan, R.D.: Center stage for the twenty-first century: power plays in the Indian Ocean. Foreign Aff. **88**(2), 16–32 (2009)
2. Filiano, A.J., Xu, Y., Tustison, N.J., et al.: Unexpected role of interferon-γ in regulating neuronal connectivity and social behaviour. Nature **535**(7612), 425–429 (2016)
3. Zhang, J., Ding, L., Holmfeldt, L., et al.: The genetic basis of early T-cell precursor acute lymphoblastic leukaemia. Nature **481**(7380), 157–163 (2012)
4. Fugazza, M., Hoffmann, J.: Liner shipping connectivity as determinant of trade. J. Shipping Trade **2**(1), 1 (2017)

A Software Reliability Combination Model Based on Genetic Optimization BP Neural Network

Runan Wang[1], Fusheng Jin[1(✉)], Li Yang[1], and Xiangyu Han[2]

[1] School of Software, Beijing Institute of Technology, Beijing, China
jfs2lcn@bit.edu.cn
[2] Beijing Aerospace Automatic Control Institute, Beijing, China

Abstract. The software reliability model is the basis for the quantitative analysis and prediction of software reliability. In recent years, neural networks due to its generalization and learning ability have been widely applied in the field of software reliability modeling. However, the slow convergence and local minimum of neural networks may cause unsuccessful prediction. Therefore, this paper presents a software reliability combination model based on genetic optimization BP neural network. This model uses three classical software reliability models as the input of BP neural network, and then uses the genetic algorithm optimization to automatically configure and optimize the weight and the thresholds. The results of experiments show that the model proposed has better fitting effect and prediction ability than other similar models.

Keywords: Software reliability model · Combination model
BP neural network · Genetic algorithm

1 Introduction

Software reliability modeling revolves around the work of pioneers from 1970s. It is an important tool for software reliability prediction, analysis and evaluation. The basic idea is to obtain the predictive value through the mathematical modeling method based on the failure data collected in the software testing.

From the first software reliability model "J-M model" published by Jelinski and Moranda in 1971 [1], hundreds of software reliability models have been proposed. These classical single models have been used to measure software quality, but during the practical applications, there are still some limitations constricting its accuracy of prediction [2].

Regarding to the issues above, the study of Lyu shows that the combination model may have better software reliability prediction results than the single model, and the combination model has stronger anti-data "noise" ability and generalization ability [3]. Lyu and Nikora proposed a hybrid approach selecting and combining the existing software reliability models aiming at finding the empirical patterns of comparison criteria derived from the models [3]. Lyu and Nikora applied some linear combinations of software reliability models, choosing G-O Model, M-O Model and L-V Model as the

© Springer Nature Singapore Pte Ltd. 2018
H. Yuan et al. (Eds.): GSKI 2017, CCIS 849, pp. 143–151, 2018.
https://doi.org/10.1007/978-981-13-0896-3_15

three component models [4]. After that, Park and Baik improved software reliability prediction through a strategy based on dymatic model selection and combination [5]. Recent years, there are still some software researchers devoting to study software reliability models [6–9].

In order to reduce training time and investigate the generalization properties of learned neural networks, this paper proposes a Genetic Algorithm Back Propagation software reliability growth model (GABP-SRGM). GABP-SRGM uses three classical models G-O model, S-shaped model and K-stage model as the input of BP neural network, and in the process, uses genetic algorithm [10–14] to obtain the optimal weights and thresholds of BP neural network.

The structure of this paper is as follows. In Sect. 2, we elaborate the method of GABP-SRGM, including BP neural network to build the combination model and the genetic algorithm optimization. Section 3 discusses the experimental results of our model. Finally, we make a conclusion of this paper in Sect. 4.

2 Method of GABP-SRGM

Section 2 is separated into two parts. In the first part, we explain the structure and modeling process of GABP-SRGM. And the second part describes the method of genetic algorithm and how we applied it into our neural network.

2.1 BP Neural Network for Software Reliability Modeling

In the process of modeling, we choose a three-layer network including an input layer, a hidden layer and an output layer to build our combination model. The first layer with 3 neurons is the basic models as the input of BP neural network, and the hidden layer contains 6 neurons which is decided by Trial method. As for the third layer, there is one neuron of the output.

Through the above-mentioned determination of BP neural network structure, the network structure of GABP-SRGM model proposed in this paper is shown in Fig. 1.

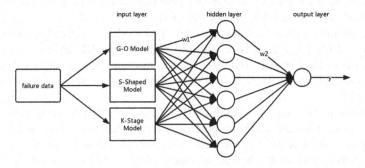

Fig. 1. The combined model of BP neural network structure

GABP-SRGM is based on the classical software reliability model. The choice of the base model determines the fitting and predictive performance of the combination model to the failure data. Therefore, the model chooses three classical software reliability models with expected results. The mean functions of the three models are as follows [4, 16, 17]:

G-O model:

$$m(t) = a(1 - \exp(-bt)) \tag{1}$$

S-shaped model:

$$m(t) = a(1 - (1 + bt)\exp(-bt)) \tag{2}$$

K-stage model:

$$m(t) = a\left(1 - \left(1 + bt + \frac{(bt)^2}{2}\right)e^{-bt}\right) \tag{3}$$

In the mean functions of the above base models, the parameter 'a' represents the mean number of failures found in the software, and the parameter 'b' represents the fault detection rate of the software, which is the probability that an error is detected at a fixed time during the software test.

From the mean function of the base models we can get the following combination model mean function:

$$\begin{aligned} m(t) = {} & w_{11}(1 - \exp(-w_{21}t)) + w_{12}(1 - (1 + w_{22}t)\exp(-w_{22}t)) \\ & + w_{13}\left(1 - \left(1 + w_{23}t + \frac{(bt)^2}{2}\right)e^{-w_{23}t}\right) \end{aligned} \tag{4}$$

w_{ij} denotes the weight of the three base models in the combined model. In this paper, the automatic choosing value and the optimization of the w_{ij} value are realized by the nonlinear fitting ability of the BP neural network method.

2.2 Genetic Algorithm Optimization BP Neural Network

Genetic algorithm optimization BP neural network mainly uses genetic algorithm to optimize the weight and threshold of BP neural network. Genetic algorithm optimization BP neural network consists of the following three parts: BP neural network structure, genetic algorithm optimization BP neural network and BP neural network prediction [15].

The elements of genetic algorithm optimization BP neural network include population initialization, fitness function, selection operation, cross operation and mutation operation. The specific flow chart shown in Fig. 2.

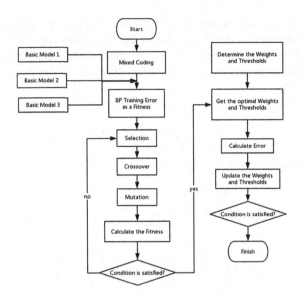

Fig. 2. Genetic algorithm optimization BP neural network flow chart

The weights and thresholds of BP neural network model are obtained by real number genetic algorithm [18]. The details of the weights and offsets for optimizing the BP neural network by genetic algorithms are as follows:

(1) Individual coding and population initialization

The individuals of the genetic algorithm include the weights and thresholds of the BP neural network. In this paper, the coding method of the individual is coded in real numbers. The coding length is:

$$S = 3 \times 6 + 6 \times 1 + 6 + 1 = 31 \tag{5}$$

Usually, the population size is between 100 and 200, and the population used in this paper is 100.

(2) The determination of the fitness function

The weights and thresholds optimized by the genetic algorithm can minimize the sum of the squares of errors between the actual output and the expected output of the BP neural network. So this is a problem of minimum [19]. And the fitness function of this paper is the reciprocal of the square sum of the neural network errors:

$$f = \frac{1}{SE} \tag{6}$$

$$SE = \frac{1}{2} \sum_{i=1}^{n} (y_i - Y_i)^2 \tag{7}$$

SE is the square sum of the predicted output and the actual output in the BP neural network, n is the number of output nodes. From the formula we can know that the smaller the error is, the greater the fitness is, the better the adaptability is.

(3) Selection

The selection method used in this paper is the proportional selection method, the formula is as follows:

$$P_i = \frac{f_i}{\sum\limits_{j=1}^{n} f_j} \tag{8}$$

(4) Crossover

Crossover operation is the main method of generating new individuals in genetic algorithm. The crossover probability is 0.9.

(5) Mutation

The probability of mutation is 0.01.

We use real coding to encode weights and thresholds of BP neural networks, also use them as chromosomes. The chromosomes are assumed to be $[w_1, w_2, w_3, w_4, w_5, w_6]$ and $[w'_1, w'_2, w'_3, w'_4, w'_5, w'_6]$. The parameters in the hidden layer activation function, which are the weights and offsets in the BP neural network calculated by genetic algorithms.

In this model, the optimal weights and offsets of the neural network are obtained through the selection of genetic algorithm, such as crossover and mutation, so that the training neural network has better performance.

3   Experiment

Our dataset for the experiments is a classical datasets. DataSet1 (DS1) is collected by Musa from a real-time command and control system that includes 21,700 target instruction codes, which costs 92 days to collect a total of 136 failure data [20].

Before the experiment, we first normalized the software failure data, making the data range between [0,1]. Second, we divided the dataset into two subsets.

To verify the performance of experimental models, the standard model fitting metric function is usually used to evaluate the analysis results. Commonly the evaluation functions are the mean square error (MSE), regression curve equation correlation index (R-square), error square sum (SSE) and so on. Among them, MSE is a more common measure of real value and predictive value, and more suitable for the evaluation of model long-term forecast, so this paper uses MSE as the evaluation index of model prediction performance, the specific formula is as follows.

$$MSE = \sum_{i=1}^{k} \frac{(y_i - m(t_i))^2}{k} \tag{9}$$

Experiments on the DS1 dataset with 136 sets of failed data. First of all, DS1 data is normalized, followed by the data set is divided into training data and test data. Therefore, the first 75% of the training data is 128, the test data is 8. For the training process, we use the above combination model approach. The parameters of the base model are estimated by the least squares method and the MSE values are used to compare the results.

To compare GABP-SRGM to other software reliability models, we used three classical models and two existing research models. We select the classical model we used to build our BP neural network as the comparison. And one of the research models is Cascade Software Reliability Model, with which four classical models are combined with a feedback neural network to form a new model by Yin [21]. And another model is Cascade Software Reliability Model based on Neural Network. It used 4 classical software reliability models to build the combination model [22].

Table 1 is the result of Dataset 1. We have reported the training MSE and the testing MSE of each models. From the third column we can learn that the prediction performance of GABP-SRGM is exponential improved compared with other 5 models.

Each model's fitting chart of the failure data is shown in Fig. 3.

Table 1. DS1 dataset experiment results.

Model	Training MSE	Testing MSE
G-O model	0.0013	0.0128
S-shaped model	0.0053	0.0346
K-stage model	0.0084	0.0448
Cascade Software Reliability Model	4.14126e−04	6.72693e−04
Cascade Software Reliability Model Based on Neural Network	5.14126e−04	7.73693e−04
GABP-SRGM	6.0815e−05	6.1312e−04

Four figures above show the fitting curve of three single models and GABP-SRGM. With time increasing, the predictive value of first three graphs deviated from the actual failure data. Compared with the former 3 basic models, GABP-SRGM's fitting curve is close to the actual curve, from which GABP-SRGM shows its precise fitting performance.

Therefore, from the experimental results, we can see that GABP-SRGM has better fitting performance than the 3 single models. Contrast to another research combination models, we improved the prediction accuracy on failure data to some degree.

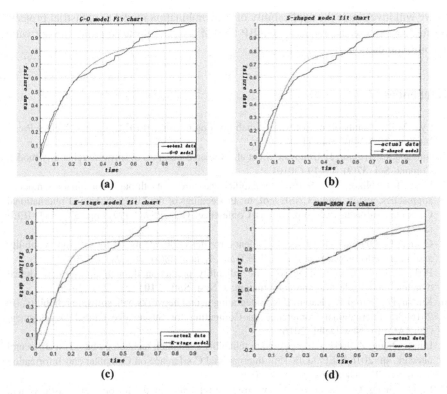

Fig. 3. The fitting curve of (a) G-O Model, (b) S-Shaped Model, (c) K-stage Model and (d) GABP-SRGM

4 Conclusion

In this paper, we have proposed a software reliability combination model based on neural network. We selected three single models with good prediction ability as the input of the neural network. This method configures the weights and thresholds of each model automatically. And in order to overcome the limitation of slow convergence and local minimum, we use genetic optimization algorithm to further improve the neural network, then realize an optimal combination model with good generalization and prediction ability. After that, we compared our combination model with three classical models and two cascade models, and selected MSE as the evaluation index. From the results we can see that the combination model showed its good prediction performance than others through two test datasets.

In the future, we will be committed to finding and learning more neural network optimization methods, such as the strategy to select appropriate learning rate and ways to reduce the training time, to further optimize the neural network prediction capabilities and constantly improve the reliability model. In this paper's experimental part, we only used two data sets to compare and evaluate the capabilities of the model. We are expecting more datasets to prove the better prediction performance of GABP-SRGM.

So, we will investigate the applicability of the combination model to industrial projects and further explore in practice if GABP-SRGM would help to improve the software reliability prediction.

References

1. Lyu, M.R.: Handbook of Software Reliability Engineering. IEEE Computer Society Press, McGraw Hill, New York (1996)
2. Jungang, L., Jianhui, J., Chunyan, S., et al.: Research progress of software reliability model. Comput. Sci. 37(9), 13–19 (2010)
3. Lyu, M.R., Nikora, A.: Software reliability measurements through combination models: approaches, results, and a CASE tool. In: Proceedings of the Fifteenth Annual International Computer Software and Applications Conference, COMPSAC 1991, pp. 577–584. IEEE (1991)
4. Goel, A.L., Okumoto, K.: Time-dependent error-detection rate model for software reliability and other performance measures. IEEE Trans. Reliab. 28(3), 206–211 (1979)
5. Park, J., Baik, J.: Improving software reliability prediction through multi-criteria based dynamic model selection and combination. J. Syst. Softw. 101, 236–244 (2015)
6. Kumar, D., Kansal, Y., Kapur, P.K.: Integrating neural networks with software reliability. In: 2016 3rd International Conference on Computing for Sustainable Global Development (INDIACom), New Delhi (2016)
7. Liu, L., Jiang, Z.: Research on software reliability evaluation technology based on BP neural network. In: 2016 IEEE/ACIS 15th International Conference on Computer and Information Science (ICIS), Okayama, pp. 1–4 (2016)
8. Li, Q., Zhang, C., Zhang, H.: A new software reliability model for open stochastic system based on NHPP. In: 2017 IEEE International Conference on Software Quality, Reliability and Security Companion (QRS-C), Prague, pp. 624–625 (2017)
9. Barraza, N.R.: A mixed poisson process and empirical bayes estimation based software reliability growth model and simulation. In: 2017 IEEE International Conference on Software Quality, Reliability and Security Companion (QRS-C), Prague, pp. 612–613 (2017)
10. Karunanithi, N., Whitley, D., Malaiya, Y.K.: Prediction of software reliability using connectionist models. IEEE Trans. Software Eng. 18(7), 563–574 (1992)
11. Lijun, Y., Kerong, B.: Realization and analysis of software reliability based on neural networks. Comput. Technol. Autom. 21(3), 40–42 (2002)
12. Xuesong, Z., Ping, G.: Research on software reliability prediction based on combinatorial neural network. J. Beijing Normal Univ. 41(6), 559–603 (2005). (Natural Science Edition)
13. Guo, P., Lyu, M.R.: A pseudoinverse learning algorithm for feedforward neural networks with stacked generalization applications to software reliability growth data. Neurocomputing 56, 101–121 (2004)
14. Rajeswari, K., Neduncheliyan, S.: Genetic algorithm based fault tolerant clustering in wireless sensor network. IET Commun. 11(12), 1927–1932 (2017)
15. Li, C.: A prediction on stocks index and futures prices based on BP neural network. Qingdao University (2012)
16. Yamada, S., Ohba, M., Osaki, S.: S-shaped software reliability growth models and their applications. IEEE Trans. Reliab. 33(4), 289–292 (1984)
17. Liu, W.: A k-stage sequential sampling procedure for estimation of normal mean. J. Stat. Plann. Infer. 65, 109–127 (1997)

18. Rajasekaran, S., Pai, G.A.V.: Neural networks, fuzzy logic and genetic algorithm: synthesis and applications (with cd). PHI Learning Pvt. Ltd. (2003)
19. Zhang, X.: Based on genetic algorithm optimization BP neural network stock price forecast. Qingdao University of Science and Technology (2014)
20. Musa, J.D.: DACS Software Reliability Dataset, Data & Analysis Center for Software, January 1980
21. Yin, Q., Li, J., Bom, K.H., et al.: A new cascade software reliability model. In: Third International Conference on Natural Computation, ICNC 2007, vol. 3, pp. 241–245. IEEE (2007)
22. He, Z.Y., Yin, Q.: Cascade software reliability model based on neural network. Comput. Eng. Des. **14**, 036 (2009)

Practical Experience of the Use of RGB Camera Images in UAV for the Generation of 3D Images in the Accurate Detection Distance of Vegetation Risk in Right-of-Way Transmission Line

Mauricio G. M. Jardini[1,2(✉)], Augustinho José Menin Simões[1,2],
José Antonio Jardini[1,2], Jose Mauricio Scovino de Souza[1,2],
and Ferdinando Crispino[1,2]

[1] Department of Engineering and Maintenance, FDTE, São Paulo, Brazil
mjardini@fdte.org.br
[2] CELEOREDES, Rio de Janeiro, Brazil
augustinho.simoes@celeoredes.com

Abstract. The Brazilian National Interconnected System has an extensive power transmission grid, where the lines are mostly located far from the urban centers and in difficult access areas. This makes inspection and maintenance more expensive and complex. In this sense, it is important to monitor and apply technological innovations in terms of equipment (sensors, cameras), telecommunication systems and vehicles, which aim at reducing costs, reducing environmental impacts and increasing reliability. This work will investigate the use of 3D modeling of a training transmission line stretch using RGB images captured using sensor coupled in unmanned aerial vehicle. It is a first investigative step for the specific purpose of detecting, with high accuracy, the vegetation along the right-of-way. Exemplifications and conclusions are presented at the end of the paper.

Keywords: 3D modeling · Camera imaging · Drone
Idenfitifcação de vegetação · Right-of-way · Transmission lines
Unmanned aerial vehicle

1 Introduction

In Brazil, aerial inspection of a transmission line is usually performed by a team composed of at least two technicians flying over the transmission line visually looking for incidents such as broken insulation, broken cables, displaced or broken air signaling spheres, performing thermal analysis, looking for hot spots, rust, etc. This solution implies the cost of renting the aircraft and the embedded measuring device, in addition

This work was supported by: CELEOREDES (Celeo Redes Brasil S.A) and ANEEL (Agência Nacional de Energia Elétrica) P&D (Pesquisa e Desenvolvimento) in Brazil.

to the cost of the team, still conditioned to adequate meteorological conditions, and it is not possible to discard the risks of personal accidents.

In addition to electrical inspection, environmental monitoring is also required, which requires constant monitoring of vegetation growth in the right-of-way, for which subjective criteria are sometimes used to estimate tree height.

To reduce these costs, increase reliability of the measurements and continuous monitoring, some companies are systematically analyzing the application of robots traveling in the surge arresters or conductors.

There are also unmanned aerial vehicles, which at international level stands out the success obtained in applications related to agriculture, forest monitoring and mining. In Brazil, these devices can certainly contribute to the preservation of assets, surveillance and monitoring of assets (for example, transmission lines), and others.

The analyzes are then based on the application of UAV, RGB photographic sensor and post-processing of images in specific computational application. Several tests were carried out in the field and under controlled conditions. The solution analyzed below has advantages and disadvantages over existing solutions associated with geotechnologies; the following stand out:

A. *Satellite imagery*
   This presents high cost mainly for high definition images; frequency of passes over the same point of interest and favorable climatic conditions, both of which must be concomitant.
B. *Flight by airplanes and helicopters*
   It has a high cost; dependence on favorable climatic conditions, low availability outside large urban centers. In this case, specific airplanes and homologated by ANAC - Brazil's National Civil Aviation Agency are usually used, with fuselage cutouts to fix the sensors (photography, video, LiDAR, etc.); therefore, without many offers in the market, even more expensive if it is thought that such aircraft are located in a few large commercial centers (such as Rio de Janeiro, São Paulo, Campinas and Curitiba city) and that when hired to perform tasks in places far there is a significant increase in prices.

2 Test Areas

Basically, there were two pilot areas: the first one, built for training purposes, which can be described as two 500 kV de-energized transmission line spans, built with real-scale equipment in the company yard in the city of Uberlândia/Brazil (Fig. 1); and the second, conducted in the field, in an energized line of 500 kV (Figs. 2 and 3).

Fig. 1. Foto aérea de linha de transmissão em pátio - desenergizada.

Fig. 2. Foto aérea de linha de transmissão em campo - energizada.

Fig. 3. Foto aérea de linha de transmissão em campo – energizada. Detalhe de vegetação sob os cabos condutores na faixa de passagem.

3 Equipmentes

To generate 3D images it is necessary to have a data file containing a point cloud, that is, a file containing coordinate data and the altitude quota of each point. This file, in the geoprocessing area is called ".LAS".

This file can be obtained in some ways. One is through photographic images where a computer application makes use of images and, associated with other information collected in the flight, and applying algorithms can generate 3D image. This is an inexpensive alternative and presents measurements with precisions that must be analyzed for the purpose to be applied.

Another way is to use LiDAR (Light Detection And Ranging) sensor equipment whose ".LAS" file is obtained directly as a measurement product. It is an expensive alternative, however, it has precise measurements. This technology will also be under investigation, but nothing is presented here at this time.

The following are briefly described all the equipment used for the field tests. As already mentioned, the application of UAV in Brazil for commercial purposes is still recent - only now in this year of 2017, ANAC has created a regulatory framework imposing rules and creating classes of aircraft according to their size and weight. The equipment used here was acquired after a technical analysis and attendance to the premises as: cost, ease of handling, among others.

A. *UAV - unmanned aerial vehicle*

The aircraft acquired is the DJI PHANTON 4PRO (Fig. 4). This is a non-professional, yet cost-effective aircraft with factory-implemented, operator-friendly and affordable.

Fig. 4. Imagem de UAV modelo DJI Phanton 4 Pro.

B. *Camera*

Along with this aircraft came a RGB (red, blue, green) camera with 1 "CMOS sensor and 20 M pixels and a 35 mm equivalent lens.

C. *Desktop for post-processing*

The desktop used has the technical specification: Intel Core i3 processor, 4 GB RAM and 64-bit operating system.

D. *Post-processing software*

The photographic images collected in the field are then taken to the office and in a specific computational application are treated to generate 3D images.

It is in this computational application, the Pixel 4D, that it was intended to calculate or measure the distance from the possible risky vegetation to the cable of the transmission line or even to the structure of the tower. In summary, it is a desktop software that allows the visualization of areas or even features through high-capacity ortho-mosaic, DSMs (Digital Surface Model) and clouds of points that generate the desired 3D image. For this, a trial version of 15 days provided by the manufacturer/supplier was used.

4 Filed Tests

For testing and research purposes, several tests have been performed. Only a few will be cited here for purposes of understanding and exemplification.

A. *Test 1*

The flight section was made on the constructions. The flight was pre-programmed for a specific route and 122 images were obtained using the RGB camera. The flight altitude was about 40 meters in relation to the ground. Figure 5 shows the route taken with the UAV and the locations from which the photos were taken (small points identified in the route).

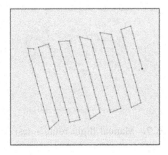

Fig. 5. Pre-programmed flight route – test 1.

Despite the expressive number of photographs collected, even making use of the computational application, it was not possible to generate the point cloud and consequently it was not possible to generate the 3D image.

B. *Test 2*

The image collection was performed on an energized transmission line. A total of 166 photographic images were collected. The flight altitude was about 60 m in relation to the ground. Figure 6 shows the route taken with the UAV and the locations from which the photos were taken.

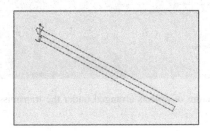

Fig. 6. Pre-programmed flight route – test 2.

Despite the expressive number of photographs collected, it was not possible to generate the point cloud and consequently it was not possible to generate the 3D image either.

C. *Test 3*

In this trial, the planned and mapped flight was practiced, but now, by inserting objects and features in the field so that the quality of information collected with the RGB sensor camera can be measured (Fig. 7). In practice two trees were placed under the span of the transmission line (Figs. 8 and 9).

To understand that in the previous tests it was not possible to generate 3D image due to lack of photographic details, some photos were then made at a 45° angle (beyond 90°) in relation to the ground to proceed with the 3D drawing not only of the line as well as objects, thus obtaining the ".LAS" file.

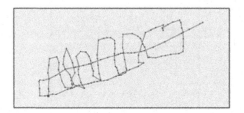

Fig. 7. Manual flight route – test 3.

Fig. 8. Picture of objects arranged under the transmission line.

Fig. 9. Measures taken for calibration purposes.

Fig. 10. Orthomosaic image.

Fig. 11. The corresponding sparse Digital Surface Model (DSM)

Fig. 12. Cloud point 3D picture.

This file is necessary for the final development of the computational application to identify the possible point of interference and vegetation pruning. A total of 120 photographic images were collected at a variable altitude between 10 and 50 m.

With the collected data it was possible to generate orthomosaic image, digital surface model (DSM) and the corresponding sparse DSM (Figs. 10, 11 and 12)

As for the quality of the images, when analyzed with naked eyes in presentation in computer and monitor, it can be affirmed that these have high quality (resolution) as it was expected since the sensor equipment, the camera RGB, has definition of 20 M pixel.

To process the images, it was necessary, for each test, for this computer, about 2 days. It is clear that such post-processing in a more powerful computer is necessary.

5 Conclusions

As previously mentioned, the equipment used is easy to handle, and at an appropriate price, and for this reason it was decided to investigate this alternative of using RGB camera before directing the project to the use of LiDAR sensor. For the specific purpose of the project where it is desired to obtain measurements with high precision, it can be stated that the equipment and sensor used in these tests were not adequate. It is suggested to acquire UAVs with a more precise GPS system where the results will certainly be better.

The same impression applies to the RGB camera, which, although very good and offering images with optimal resolution, still carry possible errors. As explained, these images are the basic information in order to generate the ".LAS" file and consequently the 3D image. With this said it is stated that a higher resolution photographic sensor would be of better use.

In a way, the Pixel 4D software offers processing ensuring image correction, but this has not yet been ascertained by comparing the field measurements with those that we could possibly obtain from the 3D image. Therefore, the more precise the cloud point (".LAS") file, the more assertive the application will be to indicate the specific point for ascertaining and pruning the risky vegetation.

The research and application project continues and in this phase is being acquired more sophisticated LiDAR sensor and UAV.

An Exploratory Study and Application of Data Mining: Railway Alarm Data

Yichuan Yang[1], Hanning Yuan[1(✉)], Dapeng Li[1], Tianyun Shi[2], and Wen Cheng[3]

[1] International School of Software, Beijing Institute of Technology, Beijing 100081, China
{yycsxz,yhn6,dapengli}@bit.edu.cn
[2] Institute of Computing Technologies, China Academy of Railway Sciences, Beijing 100081, China
shitianyun@sina.com
[3] School of Aerospace Engineering, Beijing Institute of Technology, Beijing 100081, China
572705622@qq.com

Abstract. The railway industry generates large data but there are few researches on railway data analysis. The paper presented an exploratory study and application of data mining from railway alarm data. The railway alarm data is analyzed to find the correlation between alarm items and between railway bureaus when alarm occurred and predict the alarm occurring. The paper proposed an alternative measurement mode with three values: support, Kulc and balance to mine the correlation from alarm data analysis, and the results finally indicated the very possibility of associated railway bureaus.

Keywords: Data mining · Association rules · Railway alarm data

1 Introduction

An exploratory study was proposed in this paper from railway alarm data about railway security with a measurement mode of correlation in mining association rules.

In the mining of association rules, there are mainly 7 measurement modes of correlation among which the all_conf, consin, max_conf and Kulc has zero invariant pattern in dealing with large data [1, 2].

The alarm data is analyzed by association rule mining to find the correlations between alarm items and between railway bureaus. And we use the support, Kulc and balance measurement mode [3] in bureaus analysis, with which we got the expected results. We also proposed an alternative measurement value of balance between two confidences and the result indicates the measurement is simple and very useful in mining of association rules [4–6].

In the following sections, Sect. 2 substantially introduces the background of railway data and Sects. 3 and 4 specifically describe the analyzing methods in the correlation between alarm items and between bureaus when alarms occurred. Section 5 we predict the alarm occurring quantity in different time periods. In Sect. 6, several

© Springer Nature Singapore Pte Ltd. 2018
H. Yuan et al. (Eds.): GSKI 2017, CCIS 849, pp. 161–169, 2018.
https://doi.org/10.1007/978-981-13-0896-3_17

insights are discussed based on the analyzing results. And the last section draws the conclusion.

2   Background

In recent years, with the rapid development of Internet, cloud computing and Internet of things, the modern society has entered an information time and growth data has become common in many industries. The data implies chaotic nature of some of the laws [7], and these laws will be the industry's decision-making or decision-making scientific inferences to provide a theoretical basis. The railway industry, as a special industry, a matter of national economy and people's lives, produces data related with railway all the time like production operation information, security information, passenger information and so on. With the continuous improvement of information construction of railway industry [8, 9], the railway industry data could be well preserved. But there are few literatures to study on railway data. So, the problem is how to take advantage of the data and find the potential laws by analyzing approaches such as causal analysis, association rules and trend prediction to provide supplementary reference for decision-making in all aspects of railway.

The railway alarm data includes the alarm information of all kinds of alarm items from different railway bureaus during 2013.11–2016.6. The data was screened first and then analyzed with association rule method. There are nearly 27000 alarms (Table 1) after screening and pre-processing, and each of them includes occurring time, alarm item type and alarm occurring railway bureau. Each alarm bureau has an id represented the bureau (named by the location (city) of bureau) and each alarm item has an id represented the item info (Tables 2 and 3).

Table 1. Railway alarm information

Alarm id	Alarm time	Alarm item	Alarm bureau
1	2013/11/1	S001	N
2	2013/11/2	S002	N
...	...	...	...
26888	2016/6/15	D002	H

Table 2. Railway Bureau Information

Bureau id	Bureau (City)
A	Administration
B	Harbin
...	...
Z	Nanning

Table 3. Alarm item information

Alarm id	Alarm info
S001	MQ transform state
S002	Info synchronization
...	...
D004	Checking report

3 Alarm Item Analysis

There are 27 alarm items including D001, D002, S002... (Fig. 1) and 20 items occurred actually. And the distribution of alarm items is so uneven that S001, S002 is the most part of alarms, and others just occurred not more than 1000 times. And this situation makes it hard to analyze the correlation for the lack of data. So first the alarm occurring time were resampled by day to increase the data density.

Then the correlation matrix was computed according to *support, confidence, lift* measurement mode. Without the prior reference in the selection of the railway alarm data correlation threshold, we try to find the proper threshold by computing the product of support and confidence, support_x_confidence. Figure 2 shows the sorted results.

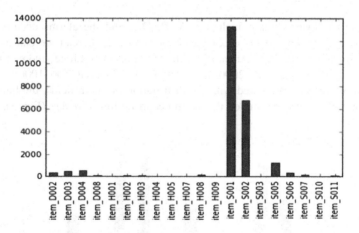

Fig. 1. Alarm item distribution

According to the sort, the support_x_confidence > 0.2 is supposed to be selected as the threshold and three most possible correlations are listed. Table 4 shows all of the correlations have high confidence but the lift almost equaling 1. Because lift << 3, it is not sufficient to say that each of the three has a correlation.

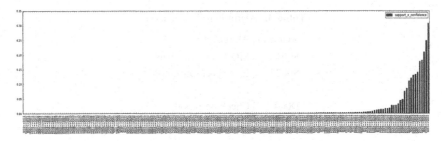

Fig. 2. Sorted support_x_confidence

Table 4. Correlation of alarm items

	Support	Confidence	Support_x_confidence	Lift
D004 => S001	0.291986	0.852564	0.248937	1.016604
S002 => S005	0.355653	0.591241	0.210277	1.579532
S001 => S002	0.508233	0.606021	0.308000	1.007454

4 Bureau Analysis

There are 19 railway bureaus including A, B, D... and the alarms occurred in 18 bureaus. And according to the occurring times from each bureau we can divide the bureaus into 4 parts: H, P, Q bureaus with the most occurring times more than 3000; next G, N, T, W among 1500–2000 times; and G, T, W among 500–1000; others not more than 500 times. Compared with the distribution of alarm items, the bureaus are more even and we also resampled the alarm occurring times by day (Fig. 3).

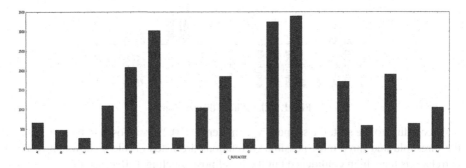

Fig. 3. Alarm of Bureaus distribution

In the analysis of railway bureau correlation, we change to choose the support, Kulc, balance measurement mode. BR (balance ratio) is the ratio of two confidences which represents the balance of the correlation between two items A and B. Similar with the IR (imbalance ratio), the measurement is independent of zero item, and also independent of the total number of items, which is simpler than IR. And BR is supposed to be zero when one of the two confidences is zero.

$$balance\ ratio = \frac{P(A|B)}{P(B|A)} \tag{1}$$

Considering there is no prior reference to determine the threshold's values of support, Kulc and balance, it is necessary to get rid of threshold mode or at least reduce the numbers of thresholds, trying to find a unified representation of the three. To do this, BR was first transformed to balance to make it has the same positive correlation with support and Kulc. Figure 4 shows that the bigger balance value represents the more balance of two items and the biggest value is 1 indicating the perfect situation.

$$balance = \frac{1}{(ln\,BR)^2 + 1} \tag{2}$$

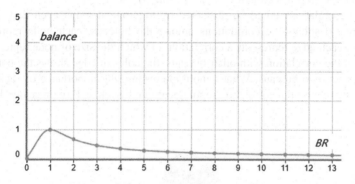

Fig. 4. Balance curve

Figure 5 shows the distribution of support, Kulc and balance. The points located on the upper right has a relatively high value of support and Kulc, combined with

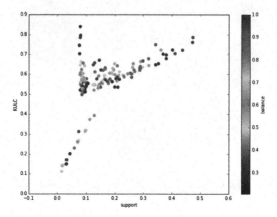

Fig. 5. Distribution of support, Kulc and balance

consideration of balance with red color. Finally, the product of the three values (because all of them are positive correlation) could simply be used to represent correlation.

$$correlation = Kulc \cdot support \cdot balance \qquad (3)$$

Table 5. Correlation of Bureaus

	Support	Kulc	BR	Balance	Correlation
N => P	0.402854	0.722239	0.948275	0.997187	0.290138
G => Q	0.411635	0.703918	1.327623	0.925660	0.268217
H => Q	0.437980	0.720774	1.240000	0.955773	0.301723
N => Q	0.473106	0.760415	1.187739	0.971249	0.349414
P => Q	0.474204	0.784750	1.252525	0.951748	0.354176

With the sorted correlation values, the most possible correlations are easy to find out. We selected top 5 correlation values (Table 5).

All the correlations could be presented by topological graph even they are very weak. Figure 6 shows the correlations among the bureaus, each node represents a bureau, and each edge represents a correlation, in which the size of node represents the summary of the correlation with other bureaus, the color of edge shows the correlation values between two bureaus. What's more interesting, the importance of each bureau could also be seen in the correlation topological graph such as P (represented Beijing),

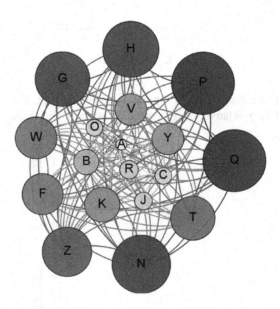

Fig. 6. Bureau correlation topological graph

Q (represented Guangzhou), N (represented Wuhan), H (represented Shanghai) and G (represented Nanchang) bureaus.

5   Alarm Occurring Prediction

The predication of alarm occurring is also one of the good points of penetration. The dataset was divided into two parts, with 2/3 of the data as training set and 1/3 as testing

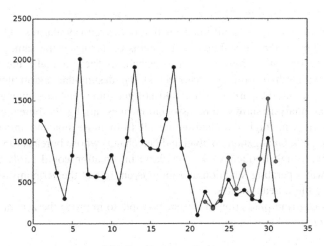

Fig. 7. Alarm prediction

set and the predicating method is xgboost algorithm based on time series to predict the trend of alarm occurring. Figure 7 shows the predicting result and testing set. The result matches the most of the testing set in trends with 87.5% accuracy rate, which shows that alarm occurring has a close contact with time passing.

6   Discussion

In the Sects. 3 and 4, the correlations of alarm items and railway bureaus when alarm occurred were analyzed with association rule mining methods. In the analysis of alarm items, the traditional association rule mining did not get the expected results due to the lack of data and the rare distribution. And in the analysis of railway bureaus, the distribution is even and we changed to use support, Kulc and balance measurement mode and got some association rules in bureaus. Figure 8 shows the high correlation between G (represented Nanchang) and Q (represented Guangzhou) and has proved the result is reliable from the side aspect. In the procedure of bureau analysis, an alternative measurement of correlation balance was proposed and applied to the bureau analysis, with which we found the importance of each bureau in correlations, which is out of expect.

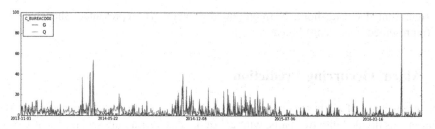

Fig. 8. Correlation between G and Q

The alarm item analysis result indicates that in the railway alarm system, there are no clear correlations among different alarm items occurring at the same time, which means that the design of railway alarm mechanism tries to make the alarm item independent with others or there is defect in the design that alarm items are not sufficient to cover all the parts for we could not get some relations among them.

The bureau analysis shows some association rules among the bureaus. We found that the bureaus with high correlations are all from those hot and important cities (Beijing, Shanghai, Guangzhou, Wuhan and Nanchang) whose bureaus run the railway transactions with high frequency. So, the alarm information could partly reflect each bureau's railway operating situation and more even, reflect the economy situations of the city where the bureau locates.

In alarm occurring prediction, it is very possible to improve the accuracy rate with professional railway knowledge.

7 Conclusion

The paper proposed an exploratory study and application of data mining in railway alarm data from knowledge insights and analyzed the correlations between alarm items and between bureaus when alarm occurred at the same time, and bureau analysis achieves the expected result (strong correlations) with a new measurement we called "correlation", from which we could get some potential information about railway alarm system as the last section discussed. But in the alarm item analysis we did not get the expect result (no strong correlations) for the lack of data. And we are supposed to try more measurement modes in alarm item analysis.

In the future work, we will apply more proper data mining methods to railway alarm data and try to analyze more data from railway industries not just the alarm data but also other data closely related with railway.

Acknowledgments. This work was supported by National Key Research and Development Plan of China (2016YFB0502604, 2016YFC0803000), International Scientific and Technological Cooperation and Academic Exchange Program of Beijing Institute of Technology (GZ2016085103), Frontier and interdisciplinary innovation program of Beijing Institute of Technology (2016CX11006).

References

1. Wang, S., Yuan, H.: Spatial data mining: a perspective of big data. J. Int. J. Data Warehous. Min. **10**, 50–70 (2014)
2. Li, D., Wang, S., Yuan, H.: Software and applications of spatial data mining. Wiley Interdisc. Rev. Data Min. Knowl. Disc. **06**, 84–144 (2016)
3. Wu, X., Zhu, X., Gongqing, W., Ding, W.: Data mining with big data. IEEE Trans. Knowl. Data Eng. **26**, 97–107 (2014)
4. Adedoyin-Olowe, M., Gaber, M.M., Dancausa, C.M., Stahl, F., Gomes, J.B.: A rule dynamics approach to event detection in twitter with its application to sports and politics. Expert Syst. Appl. **55**, 351–360 (2016)
5. Khader, N., Lashier, A., Yoon, S.W.: Pharmacy robotic dispensing and planogram analysis using association rule mining with prescription data. Expert Syst. Appl. **57**, 296–310 (2016)
6. Kim, J., Han, M., Lee, Y., Park, Y.: Futuristic data-driven scenario building: Incorporating text mining and fuzzy association rule mining into fuzzy cognitive map. Expert Systems with Applications **57**, 31–324 (2016)
7. Li, L., Lu, R., Choo, K.-K.R., Datta, A., Shao, J.: Privacy-preserving-outsourced association rule mining on vertically partitioned databases. IEEE Trans. Inf. Forensics Secur. **11**, 1847–1861 (2016)
8. Martin, D., Alcala-Fdez, J., Rosete, A., Herrera, F.: NICGAR: a niching genetic algorithm to mine a diverse set of interesting quantitative association rules. Inf. Sci. **355**, 208–228 (2016)
9. Parkinson, S., Somaraki, V., Ward, R.: Auditing file system permissions using association rule mining. Expert Syst. Appl. **55**, 27–283 (2016)

Research on Smooth Switching Technology of UAV Complex Flight Control Laws

Xianwei Hao[⊠], Aiqun Xiao, Duo Li, and Ying Wang

Beijing Institute of Astronautical Systems Engineering, Beijing 100076, China
haoxw_1220@163.com

Abstract. In order to solve the switching problem between multiple complex control laws during the autonomous flight of Unmanned Aerial Vehicle (UAV), a smooth switching method through series recurrence is proposed to obtain the integrator initial value. Firstly, all links of complex control laws are transformed formally and split into the basic units consisted of the proportion and integral. Secondly, all integrator initial values of complex control laws are deduced in turn to realize the aim of surface smooth switching, which realizes the smooth switching between the different control laws. Simulation verifies that the smooth switching method of multiple complex flight control laws is effective.

Keywords: Unmanned Aerial Vehicle · Autonomous flight
Integrator initial value · Control laws switching

1 Introduction

The UAV autonomous flight process includes flight phases such as takeoff, climbing, high, descending, descending, leveling, landing, and so on. Each flight phase has different control objectives [1]. In order to ensure that UAV has better control performance in each flight phase, according to the UAV characteristic and the control objective of each flight phase, the corresponding flight control law is designed. Different flight phase used different control laws, which inevitably face the problem of switching between multiple sets of complex control laws. The switching between different control laws may cause the momentary jump of the rudder, resulting in a large torque, dramatic changes in attitude, may make the UAV uncontrollable. How to realize the smooth switching of multiple sets of complex control laws, and avoid the steering gear transient, is the key technology of UAV autonomous control.

For the multi-modal control law switching problem, a multi-model switching control law set satisfying the output tracking performance and gradually stabilizing the closed-loop subsystem in the multi-model system is designed based on the parametric feature configuration results and the model tracking method in the literature [2]. Because of the need to coordinate the selection of the parameters in each sub-system control law to suppress the output transition at the switching time, the method is too theoretical to lead to poor project implementation. In [3], the control law logic switching condition between six flight modes is given based on Stateflow, but the control law smoothing switching between different flight modes is not studied. At present, the commonly used control law smoothing method has two-mode synchronous

H. Yuan et al. (Eds.): GSKI 2017, CCIS 849, pp. 170–177, 2018.
https://doi.org/10.1007/978-981-13-0896-3_18

operation transient suppression method and single-mode operation transient suppression method [4]. Although the two-mode synchronous operation transient suppression method has a good transient suppression effect, but need to operate the two modes of flight control laws, take up too much time and memory, and the stability margin of the system is difficult to determine during the switching process. Single-mode operation transient suppression method is improved on the basis of two-mode synchronous operation transient suppression method. Although it is only necessary to calculate the flight control law of the current modal mode, the shortcomings of the two sets of control laws need to be overcome simultaneously, the stability margin of the system is difficult to determine during the switching process too, and it is necessary to adjust the fade time parameter according to the experience to achieve a better switching effect.

Aiming at the problem of smooth switching between multiple sets of complex control laws for UAV, this paper presents a control law smoothing method based on the initial value of series recursive integrator. Firstly, all the links of complex control law are transformed into the basic unit structure composed of proportional and integral. Secondly, aiming at the smooth switching of the rudder surface, the initial values of all the integrators in the complex control law are presented in turn (from the rudder command to the given direction), to realize the smooth switching between different control laws. The validity of the smooth switching method between different control laws is verified by the example simulation.

2 Problem Description

In order to increase the lift of UAV in the process of landing, the flaps will be biased to a specified position. As the flying pressure decreases, the landing gear will be released slowly when the landing gear release conditions are met. The flap deflection and the landing gear release process are called configuration changes. The change in configuration leads to great changes in the aerodynamic characteristics of UAV [5]. In order to ensure the control performance of the landing control system after the change of configuration, it is necessary to design multiple sets of complex control laws, which inevitably faces the switching problem between multiple sets of complex control laws. Because of UAV flight height gradually reduced during the approach landing process, with a strongly flight constraint, it is necessary to take measures to suppress the smooth switching between the complex control law of the rudder surface transient, to improve the tracking accuracy of UAV on the expected landing trajectory, to improve the landing stability and safety of UAV.

The diagram of smooth switching between complex control laws is shown in Fig. 1.

In Fig. 1, flight mode 1 corresponds to control law A, and flight mode 2 corresponds to control law B. Control law A and B are composed of PID controller and integrated correction. Before the control law is switched, UAV is in flight mode 1 and the rudder command $\delta_c = \delta_{c1}$ is obtained by calculating the control law A. When the UAV is in flight mode 2, the task management and control rule scheduling module issues instructions from the control law A to the control law B applicable to the flight mode 2, and the rudder angle command $\delta_c = \delta_{c2}$ is obtained by calculating the control

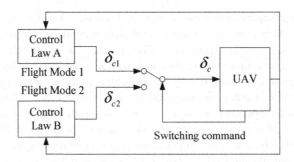

Fig. 1. Switching diagram between two sets of control laws

law B. It can be seen how to ensure that δ_{c2} calculated by the control law B in the first operation cycle is equal to δ_{c1} calculated by the control law A in the previous operation cycle, which is a key study to achieve smooth switching between the two sets of control laws.

3   Smoothing Method of Flight Control Law

Flight control law for UAV is generally conventional PID control including PID controller and integrated correction link. The operation mode of the digital integrator shows that the integrator output value is its initial value during the first operation cycle after the control law switching. In the subsequent operation cycle, the integrator output value is the result of the initial value of the integrator plus the integrator input value [6]. Firstly, according to the characteristics of the integrator all the links of complex control law are transformed into the basic unit structure composed of proportional and integral in the first operation cycle after the two sets of control law smoothing switches. Secondly, aiming at the smooth switching of the rudder surface, the initial values of all the integrators in the complex control law are presented in turn (from the rudder command to the given direction), to realize the smooth switching between different control laws. Finally, all the integrators in the complex control law are assigned the initial value, so that the rudder partial command obtained by the new control law is equal to the rudder partial command obtained by the last operation cycle before the pre-control law switching, to achieve a smooth transition between the two sets of control law.

According to the above description, the comprehensive correction link $G_{jz}(s) = (cs + d)/(as + b)$ is first transformed into a basic unit consisting of proportional and integral, where a, b, c, d are coefficients of the correction link.

$$G_{jz}(s) = \frac{c}{a} + \left(\frac{d}{b} - \frac{c}{a}\right) \cdot \frac{\frac{b}{a} \cdot \frac{1}{s}}{1 + \frac{b}{a} \cdot \frac{1}{s}} \tag{1}$$

The structure diagram of the corrected link $G_{jz}(s)$ is shown in Fig. 2.

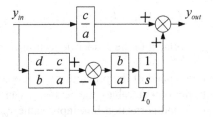

Fig. 2. Structure diagram of the correction link after splitted

Figure 2 contains the integrator link. Let y_{in} be the input of the correction, y_{out} be the output of the correction, and I_0 be the initial value of the integrator.

The following equations hold when the control laws are switched.

$$\begin{cases} y_{in}\frac{c}{a} + I_0 = y_{out} \\ y_{in}\left(\frac{d}{b} - \frac{c}{a}\right) - I_0 = 0 \end{cases} \tag{2}$$

The integrator initial value I_0 and the correction link input value y_{in} can be obtained.

$$\begin{cases} I_0 = \frac{ad - bc}{ad}y_{out} \\ y_{in} = \frac{b}{d}y_{out} \end{cases} \tag{3}$$

The output value y_{out} is related to the rudder deflection command of the previous run cycle in Eq. (3).

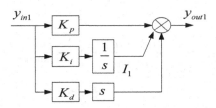

Fig. 3. PID controller structure diagram

The PID controller structure diagram is shown in Fig. 3.

Equation (4) is established when the control law is switched for the following form of PID controller.

$$K_p y_{in1} + I_1 + K_d \dot{y}_{in1} = y_{out1} \tag{4}$$

The expression of the integrator initial value I_1 can be deduced.

$$I_1 = y_{out1} - K_p y_{in1} - K_d \dot{y}_{in1} \qquad (5)$$

The output value y_{out1} is related to the rudder deflection command of the previous run cycle in Eq. (5).

The rudder deflection command of the previous run cycle is known at the time of the control law switching, the output values y_{out} and y_{out1} can be obtained, and then integrator initial values I_0, I_1 and correction link input value y_{in} can also be obtained.

The initial value of the resulting integrator is written into the corresponding integrator of the new control law. The rudder deflection command calculated by the new control law in the first operation cycle after the control law switching is equal to the rudder deflection command of the previous operation cycle, and the smooth switching between different control laws is realized.

4 Examples

Taking the approach landing of a UAV as an example, the switching between the different control laws of the two flight modes of the elevator channel is analyzed.

In order to increase the lift of UAV in the process of landing, the flaps will be biased to a specified position. The landing gear will be released slowly when the landing gear release conditions are met. In order to ensure the control performance of the landing control system after the change of configuration, it is necessary to design two sets of control laws, which inevitably faces the switching problem between two sets of control laws. Switching between two sets of control laws may cause sudden changes in the elevator rudder surface, resulting in a large pitch moment, resulting in dramatic changes in the attitude of the aircraft, so suppressive measures should be taken to avoid sudden changes in the elevator rudder surface. Figure 4 shows the control structure of the elevator channel after configuration change.

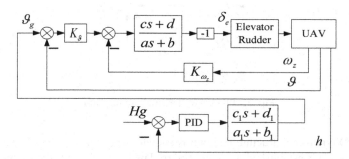

Fig. 4. Control structure of the elevator channel after the configuration change

In Fig. 4, the control law parameter values in the control law are as follows.

$$K_p = 1.5, K_i = 0.32, K_d = 0.9, K_\vartheta = 2.3, K_{\omega_z} = 1.2, a = 1, b = 3.11, c = 2.16,$$
$$d = 2.31, a_1 = 1, b_1 = 4.84, c_1 = 0.77, d_1 = 2.57$$

According to the control law smoothing method based on the initial value of series recursive integrator proposed in Sect. 2, it is necessary to write the initial value to three integrators in two corrections and PID link. The initial value of the integrator in the inner loop correction link is denoted by I_{h0}, and the initial value of the integrator in the outer loop correction section is denoted by I_{h1}, and the initial value of the integrator in the loop of the outer loop is denoted by I_{h2}, the rudder angle skew command δ_{e1} of the previous run cycle is known for the control law switching time, then the expressions of I_{h0}, I_{h1}, I_{h2} are shown below.

$$I_{h0} = -\frac{ad - bc}{ad}\delta_{e1}$$
$$I_{h1} = \frac{a_1 d_1 - b_1 c_1}{a_1 d_1}\vartheta_g$$
$$I_{h2} = \frac{b_1}{d_1}\vartheta_g - K_p(H_g - h) - K_d(\dot{H}_g - \dot{h})$$

where $\vartheta_g = \frac{1}{K_\vartheta}\left(-\frac{b}{d}\delta_{e1} + K_{\omega_z}\omega_z\right) + \vartheta$.

In order to test the rationality and validity of the control law smoothing method proposed in this paper, we will use the two-mode synchronous operation transient suppression method, single-mode transient suppression method and the paper's method to simulate the nonlinear simulation, and simulation results are compared. Record and draw the response curves of flight height H, height tracking error DH (positive height tracking error indicates that the desired height is greater than the actual flight altitude), elevator command δ_e, normal overload n_y and pitch angle ϑ, as shown in Fig. 5. In Fig. 5, x_d is the horizontal distance of UAV to the ideal ground point.

It can be seen from Fig. 5, UAV uses dual mode or single mode switching method to track the expected landing trajectory with poor tracking accuracy and large ground dispersion, where the max high tracking error is 9 m, the vertical deviation of the actual ground point from the ideal ground point is 98 m. However, UAV adopts the smoothing switching method of flight control law based on series recursive integrator initial value proposed in this paper to have the highest tracking accuracy for the expected landing trajectory, where the max high tracking error is 1.3 m, the vertical deviation of the actual ground point from the ideal ground point is only −16.3 m, the max normal overload is only 1.18. It can be seen that the control law smoothing method proposed in this paper is effective, which improves the landing stability and safety of UAV.

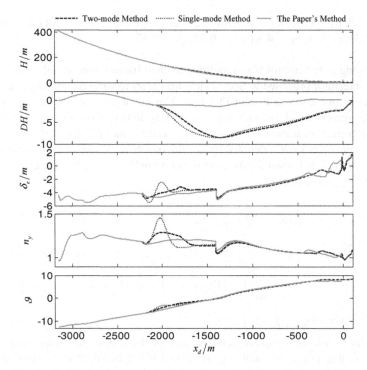

Fig. 5. Simulation comparison of complex control law smooth switching

5 Conclusion

Aiming at the problem of rudder surface transients occurring during the switching between complex control laws in UAV autonomous flight, this paper presents a control law smoothing method based on the initial value of series recursive integrator. This method realizes the smooth switching between complex control law and improves the flight stability and safety of UAV. The control law smoothing method proposed in this paper is not only applicable to UAV flight control system, but also to the control system of missile, robot, automobile, ship and so on, and has wide application significance.

References

1. Xu, X., Feng, Y.: Aircraft Flight Control System. Beijing University of Aeronautics and Astronautics Press, Beijing (1989)
2. Duan, G., Wang, H., Zhang, H.: Parameter design of smooth switching controller and application for bank-to-turn missiles. Aerosp. Control **23**, 41–46 (2005)
3. Wang, Y., Duan, Z., Gao, J., Song, R.: Multimode simulation of UAV flight control law based on simulink/stateflow. Comput. Measur. Control **23**, 1944–1946 (2015)

4. Yidong, Y., Peiyi, N., Hao, J.: The study of transient suppression techniques for multimode flight control system. Acta Aeronautica et Astronautica Sinica **11**, A88–A92 (1990)
5. Hao, X., Wang, Y., Yang, Y., Guo, T.: Optimization design of approach and landing trajectory for variable configuration RLV with multi-control surfaces. J. Beijing Univ. Aeronaut. Astronaut. **41**, 2232–2239 (2015)
6. Liu, C., Hu, N.: Computer Control Technology. Mechanical Industry Press, Beijing (2013)

Study on the Spatial and Temporal Pattern of Qinghai Lake Area in the Past 50 Years

Baokang Liu[1,2(✉)], Yu'e Du[3,4], Weiguo He[5], Shuiqiang Duan[6], and Tiangang Liang[4]

[1] Qinghai Institute of Meteorological Sciences, Xining 810001, China
1542606865@qq.com
[2] Key Laboratory of Disaster Prevention and Mitigation in Qinghai Province,
Xining 810001, China
[3] Natural Energy Research Institute, Gansu Academy of Sciences, .
Lanzhou 730000, China
2437356094@qq.com
[4] College of Pastoral Agriculture Science and Technology, Lanzhou University,
Lanzhou 730000, China
tgliang@lzu.edu.cn
[5] Information Science School, Guangdong University of Finance and
Economics, Guangzhou 510320, China
jarbei@qq.com, 562364821@qq.com
[6] Hydrology and Water Resource Bureau of Qinghai Province,
Xining 810001, China
704868459@qq.com

Abstract. Lakes are not only the essential water resources for life, but also the sensitive indicators of climate change. The change of Lake area has a direct impact on the regulation of ecological environment. The area changes of shoreline were analyzed by using Multi-source Satellite Data and water identification model of Qinghai Lake in the past 50 years, the main conclusions are as follows: (1) The monitoring accuracy of Qinghai Lake area can significantly be improved by using multi-source high satellite data; (2) The experience threshold model based on the combination multi band with single band has a higher recognition accuracy of water when monitoring the area of the Qinghai Lake; (3) In recent 50 years, although the Qinghai Lake area of the stage showed an decreasing trend, since the beginning of twenty-first Century, the Qinghai Lake area increased, especially significantly in 2010, the Qinghai Lake area has been close to in 1995. But overall, still showed a decreasing trend; The analysis of area change in dry and wet season showed that the Qinghai Lake area were increased (R2 = 0.805 and 0.861, P < 0.01) in April and September from 2001 to 2015, since 2005, increasing trend is more obvious; What it is clear changes by the use of environmental mitigation satellite data in Qinghai Tibet Plateau the changes can be used to fine the monitoring area of Qinghai Lake monthly and seasonal occasion. (4) In the past 50 years, Qinghai Lake shoreline change has a large difference between North and south. Qinghai Lake on the west coast of Shi Nai Hai - Heather skin, Quanji river north of Hukou near the east coast of Salix River into the lake and the island Haiyan Bay, lake shoreline retreat is most obvious.

© Springer Nature Singapore Pte Ltd. 2018
H. Yuan et al. (Eds.): GSKI 2017, CCIS 849, pp. 178–191, 2018.
https://doi.org/10.1007/978-981-13-0896-3_19

Keywords: Multi source satellite data · Qinghai lake area · Spatial and temporal pattern

1 Introduction

Lakes are not only the essential water resources for life, but also the sensitive indicators of climate change. The change of Lake area has a direct impact on the regulation of ecological environment [1]. Lakes are the connecting points of the atmosphere, biosphere, lithosphere and terrestrial hydrosphere, and their formation and disappearance, expansion and contraction are the result of the interaction of the surrounding environmental factors. At the same time, the increase and decrease of the lake area can also be achieved by changing Cushion conditions to have an impact on climate change [2]. Qinghai Lake is located in the northeast of the Qinghai-Tibet Plateau, located between 99° 36′–100°16′ east longitude and 36°32′–37°15′ north latitude. Which is Located in the transition zone of the three regions: the western arid zone, the eastern monsoon zone and the Tibetan Plateau region. As the largest inland lagoon in China, Qinghai Lake is an important water body that maintains the ecological security of the Qinghai-Tibet Plateau and is a natural barrier to stop the "eastward move" of desertification in the west [3, 4]. Therefore, it is very important to study the spatial-temporal variations of Qinghai Lake area over the past 50 years in order to study the climate change in the Qinghai-Tibet Plateau.

In recent years, as climate change and human activities intensified, grassland degradation and desertification around Qinghai Lake area have been seriously reduced. Water inflow into rivers and lakes has been reduced. Evaporation has also increased. The area of Qinghai Lake has been shrinking for many years. The ecological environment of Qinghai Lake Basin has aroused the concern of the whole society. The local government in Qinghai Province took the management of ecological environment as the key task of government departments. Many times, experts from national and local scientific research institutes have been organized to provide the Qinghai Lake Basin Ecosystem governance advice. Through the unremitting efforts of all parties over the past 10 years, the ecological environment in Qinghai Lake and the surrounding areas have been further improved, showing a trend of sustained virtuous circle [5].

Traditional lakes inspection and fixed-point observation experiment are greatly influenced by human and financial resources and the research scope is limited. However, Satellite remote sensing has the characteristics of wide coverage, large amount of information, short repetition period [6]. The rapid development of satellite remote sensing technology and the multi-source of satellite data not only save a lot of manpower and material resources, but also grasp the characteristics of changes in lakes so as to provide new measures for the monitoring of lake flooding in the Qinghai-Tibet Plateau [7, 8]. Many scholars at home and abroad study water pattern recognition by using multi-source satellite image data and a variety of methods. Serwan et al. used Landsat TM remote sensing data to extract and classify the ecological information of lake waters and lakes [9]; Birket used the multi-temporal radar and NOAA/AVHRR remote sensing data from 1992 to 1998 to predict and forecast water changes and flood changes of the annual seasonal and intercontinental surface in the basin [10]. Having selected the Landsat-5 TM satellite imagery data of the United States from 1986 to 2005, Feng et al. used the supervised classification method to conduct follow-up monitoring of the Qinghai Lake region up to 20 years [11]; Cao et al. used TM images based on the RNDWI method to monitor dynamically area changes of Miyun reservoir In the recent 20 years [12]; Li et al. used ETM+ images as data sources and two kinds of normalized water indices to quantitatively extract the water area from the remote sensing data, having compared the results of extraction and supervised classification extraction (Jin et al. 2002). Both of them used the decision tree method to extract the water area information from the SPOT remote sensing images [3]; Zhao Shu et al., Tian Huiyun et al. identified lake with MODIS images and they researched respectively area dynamic of Aibi lake and Qinghai lake [4, 5]. Han Fang et al. identified the water body of Lake Dalinuoer and estimated the trend of lake water area from April to September in 2000–2005 by using NOAA/AVHRR data to [6]. Ma et al. monitored the dynamic characteristics of the lake group by using high-resolution remote sensing data of Landsat MSS, TM, ETM+ and China-Brazil satellite from 1973 to 2006 and MODIS data of 250 m resolution [7]. Most of the above studies have used the satellite data of MSS, TM and ETM+ to analyze the changes of lake area and water level in the Qinghai-Tibet Plateau. These satellite data have long transit times, low spatial resolution and small width, It is not only difficult to reflect the monthly and seasonal variation of lake area and water level, but also accurately reflect the occurrence and development of the lake and reservoir in the short term and the impact on the surrounding environment. Domestic domestically produced satellites such as HJ-A/B and high-scores series of satellites have wider width, shorter transit time and more clear sky data than the same satellite data with the same spatial resolution in foreign countries. At present, it is rarely seen by using multi-source satellite data to study on the spatial and temporal difference between the monthly and inter seasonal of Qinghai Lake.

1.1 Source of Information

In this paper, the used data of Qinghai Lake area and the satellite images of the historical during 1957–2010 are from the Hydrological Bureau of Qinghai province; The 250 m MODIS image data in dry season (late) and wet season (late September) of Qinghai Lake 2001–2015 was from the Meteorological Bureau of Qinghai province; The environmental mitigation satellite data from September 2008 to November 2011 was from satellite application sharing service website of environmental satellite data products Chinese Resource Center (http://www.secmep.cn). During the period from September 2008 to November 2011, this paper selected the sky CCD data during 4–11 months after Qinghai Lake thawing to frozen (Table 1).

Table 1. Data characteristic parameters of the environmental disaster reduction satellite CCD

Band number	Spectrum (um)	Spatial resolution (m)	Width (m)	Sway ability	Revisit time (day)
1	0.43–0.52	30	360 (Single),	±30°	4
2	0.52–0.60	30	700 (double)		
3	0.63–0.69	30			
4	0.76–0.90	30			

Qinghai Lake area monitoring season division: 4–5 months after opening the lake, the average area of Qinghai Lake is the spring area. The average value of 6–8 months is summer area. The average value of 9–10 months is the autumn area. The Qinghai Lake area in November is the winter area.

1.2 Treatment Method

Loading environment satellite CCD image data in ENVI5.2 software, according to the spectral characteristics of different objects in different bands of environmental miti-gation satellite, respectively 3, 4 and 2 give the channel for the red, green and blue 3 colors for false color synthesis, we can clearly distinguish between water and land boundary, roughly distinguish table, water and cloud area. The TM image of geometric correction is used in the same area to do the geometric rectification of the CCD image of the environmental disaster reduction satellite. The correction accuracy (RMSE) is less than 0.5 pixels. Then the Flash module of ENVI software is used for atmospheric correction to get the true surface reflectance of the image (Fig. 1).

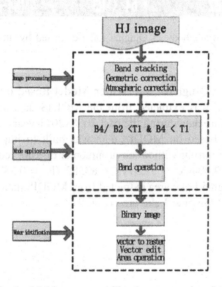

Fig. 1. Multi-source satellite data processing flow

2 Results Analysis

2.1 Comparison of Kinds of Water Body Recognition Models

2.1.1 Accuracy Verification of Different Water Monitoring Models

This paper used the three different water monitoring models which wsa respectively combined multi band and single band method and vegetation index method to extract the area of Qinghai Lake. The results showed that the experience model of multi band and single band combination method (b4/b2 < R1 & b4 < R2) from the area of

Qinghai Lake is better than single band model (b4 < R3) and vegetation index model ((b4 − b3)/(b4 + b3) < R4, B2, B3 and B4 were 2, 3, said the 4 channel reflectivity environmental mitigation satellite, R1, R2, R3, R4, constant) single band extraction is better than vegetation index model (Fig. 2).

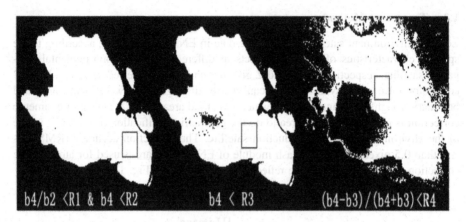

Fig. 2. The area of the water body of Qinghai Lake extracted by different water monitoring models

2.1.2   Revision of the Qinghai Lake Water Model Based on MODIS

The Qinghai Lake area was extracted from the MODIS data and the environmental disaster reduction satellite data during the past 2008–2011 years, and the Qinghai Lake area correction model based on MODIS data was built to improve the accuracy of Qinghai Lake area monitoring without environmental disaster reduction satellites. The revised model is $y = 0.0044x^2 - 37.311x + 83582$ ($R^2 = 0.5878$, P < 0.01). In the formula, X shows Qinghai Lake area extracted from MODIS data on the same day, and Y indicates the revised Qinghai Lake area (Fig. 3).

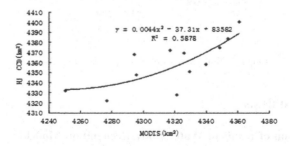

Fig. 3. Revision model of Qinghai Lake area based on MODIS data

2.2 Features of the Changes in the Area of Qinghai Lake in the Past 50 Years

2.2.1 Annual Changes in the Area of Qinghai Lake in the Last 50 Years

The area of Qinghai Lake has changed greatly in the past 50 years (Table 2). The area of 4577.0 km^2 in 1957, and it closed to the low water level in 2003, the lake area was 4216.7 km^2, shrinking 360.3 km^2 from 1957 to 2003 Qinghai Lake area contraction rate was 7.83 km^2/a; The lake area expanded to 4451.45 km^2 in 2010, compared to 2003 234.75 km^2, during 2003 to 2016, area increased 16.77 km^2/a, it was bigger than that of 1976. But it is still less 125.55 km^2 than in 1957. In the past 50 years, the area of Qinghai Lake has been decreasing gradually. However since 21 Century, Qinghai Lake area has been increasing significantly. Compared with 1957, 1976, 1995, 2000 and 2003, there was a significant declined trend. However, the area of Qinghai Lake increased significantly in 2016, which is in good agreement with the increase of precipitation in Qinghai Lake basin since 21 Century.

Table 2. The lake area of Qinghai Lake (including Haiyan Bay, Island Lake) in different periods (km^2)

Name	1957	1976	1995	2000	2003	2016
QinghaiLake (including Haiyan Bay, Island Lake)	4577.0	4400.3	4294.3	4255.4	4203.9	4423.67
Island Lake	Unseparated	Unseparated	23.1	16.8	12.8	27.78
Corresponding water level (m)	3196.66	3195.16	3193.59	3193.35	3192.88	3194.82

2.2.2 Inter Annual Variation of Dry and Wet Periods of Qinghai Lake in the Past 15 Years

The MODIS satellite data from April in dry period and September in wet period were used to monitor the lake area (5). The monitoring data of EOS/MODIS satellite in 2015 showed that the area of Qinghai Lake increased from April to September 2001 (R^2 is 0.805 and 0.861 respectively, $P < 0.01$). In April, the area of Qinghai Lake in dry period increased by 13.95 km^2/a, which the growth rate was 18.90 km^2/a since 2005, showing a significant increase. In September, the area of Qinghai Lake increased by 12.55 km^2/a, among them, the growth rate since 2005 is 16.63 km^2/a, showing a significant increase trend, but the growth rate is less than the dry period. The comparative analysis of water level and area of Qinghai Lake during the same period showed that there was a significant correlation between the water level and the area of Qinghai Lake in April and September, and the trend of both increasing and decreasing was in good agreement. Therefore, we can't get the area of Qinghai Lake when there are continuous rainy days, only to use the water level data of Qinghai lake hydrological observation station to estimate the area and the change of Qinghai Lake in real time (Fig. 4).

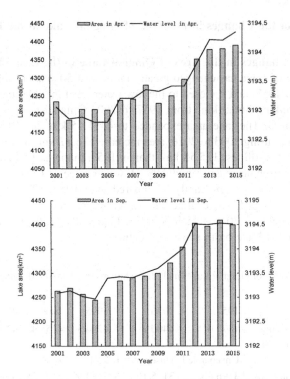

Fig. 4. Change of Qinghai Lake area and water level from April 2001 to September 2015

2.2.3   Seasonal and Monthly Variation of Qinghai Lake Area Based on High Scores of Satellites

Environmental disaster reduction satellites contain optical, thermal infrared, hyperspectral and three sensors. Among them, the optical CCD imagery has a spatial resolution of 30 meters, an image width of 700 km and a transit time of two days, and the temporal resolution is higher than that of TM, SPOT, QUICKBIRD and other foreign high-resolution satellite images. Studies have shown that clear sky information in the area from environmental disaster reduction satellites in the Tibetan Plateau is much higher than other satellite data that are currently common. Seasonal variability of the Qinghai Lake area and its inter annual variability were based on satellite data of disaster reduction environment.

During the period from 2009 to 2011, the area of Qinghai Lake increased and decreased slightly from spring to summer, while the area increased greatly from summer to autumn. What the area decreased from autumn to winter was more significant than that from spring but less than the change from summer to autumn. Mainly due to a substantial reduction in precipitation in winter lake basin, evaporation increased, Qinghai Lake area gradually reduced. In addition, since 2009, the area of Qinghai Lake has shown an increasing trend in all seasons. Among them, the area of Qinghai Lake each season in 2011 was higher than the same period of the previous three years and the autumn area in 2011 increased by 13.44 km², 44.2 km² and

38.52 km^2 compared with that in 2008, 2009 and 2010. The area in winter decreased by 13.44 km^2, 44.2 km^2 and 38.52 km^2 compared with that in 2008, 2009 and 2009. The difference between the largest and the minimum of Qinghai Lake area from 2009 to 2009 was 30.23 km^2, 17.03 km^2 and 34.12 km^2 (Fig. 5).

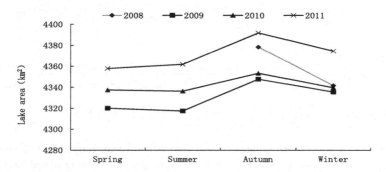

Fig. 5. Seasonal change of Qinghai Lake area based on environmental disaster reduction satellite

According to the monthly data of Qinghai Lake area from 2008 to 2011 (Fig. 6), since September 2008, Qinghai Lake has a regular fluctuation in area from April to November. Among them, from 2008 to 2010, the area of Qinghai Lake decreased gradually from September to before freezing. From 2009 to 2010, the area of Qinghai Lake reached the maximum in September. From 2009 to 2011, Qinghai Lake had the largest monthly area and the minimum difference between them is 46.87 km^2, 53.5 km^2 and 52.43 km^2, respectively. However, compared with the previous three years in 2011, the area of Qinghai Lake was substantially larger than that of the same period of 2010 except July was the same,According to the complete data in September, October and November, the area of Qinghai Lake showed a trend of decreasing first and then increasing from September 2008 to November 2011. The Qinghai Lake area in September was the smallest. The area of Qinghai Lake in October 2011 and November was larger than that of the first three years, and the Qinghai Lake area in October reached the maximum of nearly 4 years, which was 4400.1 km^2.

2.3 Lake Shoreline Changes

2.3.1 The Changes of Shoreline in Qinghai Lake in Recent 50 Years

Through 50 years of topographic maps, remote sensing images were compared and found that due to topographic differences, Qinghai Lake shoreline varies greatly from north to south. In the northwest of Qinghai Lake, Shinaihe-Heather skin, Quanjihe-Shaliuhe estuary and Shadao Lake-Haiyan Bay have the most obvious lake water retreat. In 1957, there was a distance of 4 km away from the coast of Bird Island. The images of 1976 showed, that Bird Island and Heather skin have been linked with the lake shore. From 1957 to 2003, the coastline of Heatherbelt advanced 3–6.5 km; the area of Shek Naihai-Buha estuary advanced by 2.5–3.0 km; the Salix estuary promoted by 1.6–4.3 km; the change of lake east was more prominent, and the original

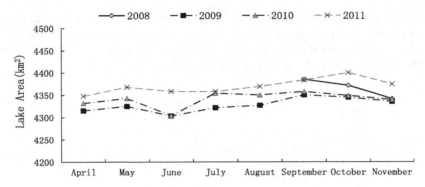

Fig. 6. Monthly change in area of Lake Qinghai

Large bodies of water were separated into Sand Island Lake, Haiyan Bay. Compared with the north and east coasts, the south bank of Qinghai Lake retreated only 0.1–0.2 km (Fig. 7).

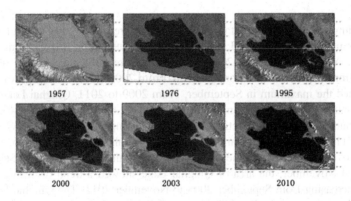

Fig. 7. The difference of lakeshore line for Qinghai Lake from 1957 to 2010 (line is in 1957)

(1) **West Bank Stone is Haihe - Heather Leather Belt**
   Stone Haihei - Heather skin is the largest river in Qinghai Lake - Buha River into the mouth, The lake shore changes during 50 years was very dramatic. From 1957 to 1976, the retreat distance of lake shore was more than 2 km, and Hassipi reached 6 km. The maximum retreat reached 2.2 km from 1976 to 2003. The lake bank expanded outward by about 0.2–1.2 km from 2003 to 2010. The reason for the large change in the northern tip of Hesse may be due to the slower flow rate and faster accumulation of water in the area (Fig. 8(a)).

(2) **Shaliu River in the North Shore and the Surrounding area**
   Shaliu River is located in the northeast corner of Qinghai Lake, Which is the second largest into the Qinghai Lake. Into the eastern lake lakeshore has dramatic changes. From 1957 to 1976, the lakeshore shrank by about 3 km. From 1976 to

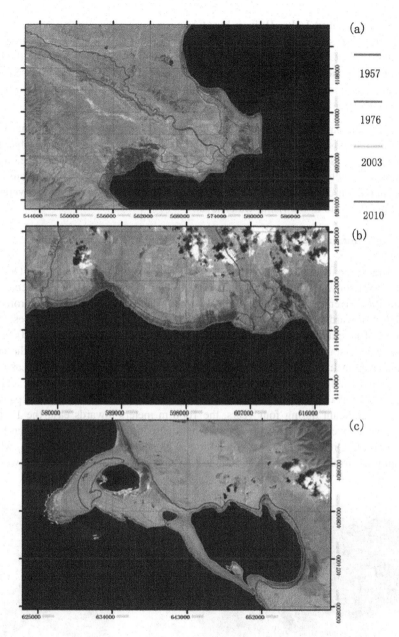

Fig. 8. Changes in the shoreline of the West Bank of Qinghai Lake (a), the North Bank (b) and the East Bank (c)

2003, lakeshore shrank by 0.8–1.5 km. From 2003 to 2010, lakeshore shrank by about 0.2–0.3 km (Fig. 8(b)).

188   B. Liu et al.

(3) **East Lake Sand Lake, Haiyan bay Changes**

In 1957, The sand beam that now excavated Shadao Lake exposed only part of the water surface. In 1976, the northern side of Shaliang was connected with the land and the southern connecting waterway was only 1.5 km wide. In 1995, Shadao Lake was completely separated. After that, It was shrinking from 23.1 km^2 in 1976 to 10.3 km^2 in 2010 (Fig. 8(c)).

In 1957, the sand beam between Haiyan Bay and the main lake of Qinghai Lake had not been exposed yet. In 1976, the length of the sand beam was 12 km, while that of Haiyan Bay was only 0.5 km. In 2003, Haiyan Bay was covered by sand beam and main lake completely cut off. According to the monthly satellite images of environmental mitigation during 2008.9–2011.11, the width of Haiyan Bay Port recovered to 0.5 km in 2010 due to the rising water level.

2.3.2   Interannual Variation of Shoreline of Qinghai Lake from 2008 to 2011

A comparative analysis of satellite imagery of environmental mitigation in the October of 2008–2011 showed that there was the obvious changes on the east and west coasts of Qinghai Lake over the four years (Fig. 9). Among them, the eastern coast promoted 130–630 m towards east, the western coast promoted 100–600 m towards west, The east coast of lake and Qinghai Lake Island was seasonally connected, since 2009, the satellite image data monitoring of Lake Milton Lake period showed that when the rainy season arrived in June and July, the water level of Qinghai Lake and Qinghai Lake had begun to rise through the river together, the water level dropped in November, and the Qinghai Lake off the area for 4 years increased 11.71 km^2, lakeshore line expansion was very significant during four years, the 1600 m meters towards east, the 1700 m meters towards west. The main reason was that the rising water level in Qinghai Lake had caused the Qinghai Lake area continuing to expand during the four years, which eventually led to the lakeside line continuously advancing to the east and the west.

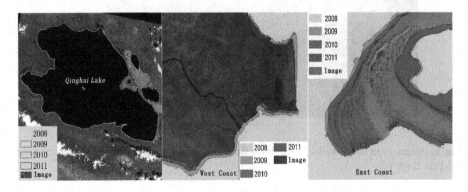

Fig. 9. Qinghai Lake from 2008 to 2011 and its spatial dynamics on the east and west coasts

3   Conclusion and Discussion

3.1   Conclusion

The multi-source satellite data and water body identification model are used to analyze the spatial and temporal variations of Qinghai Lake area and lakeshore line in the past 50 years. The main conclusions are as follows:

(1) The use of multi-source high-resolution satellite data can significantly improve the monitoring accuracy of Qinghai Lake area. Constructing a revised model of Qinghai Lake area based on MODIS with low spatial resolution and high temporal resolution and high-resolution satellite data of the same period is favorable for improving the monitoring accuracy of Qinghai Lake area.

(2) Analysis of the comparative water recognition model with the different types showed that water had a higher recognition accuracy threshold empirical model multi-band operation and a single-band-based method than a single band and fingering vegetation (NDVI).

(3) In the past 50 years, although the Qinghai Lake area of the stage showed increasing trend, especially since the beginning of 21st Century, the Qinghai Lake area increased significantly in 2010 compared to 2000 and 2003 respectively, the Qinghai Lake area increased by 26.9 km^2 and 82.4 km^2, which had been close to the Qinghai Lake area in 1995. But overall, it showed a decreasing trend; The analysis of area change of Qinghai Lake in dry and wet season showed that the area of Qinghai Lake in the April and the September of 2001–2015 increased (R2 = 0.805 and 0.861, P < 0.01),and since 2005, increasing trend was more obvious; The environmental mitigation satellite can be used to finely monitor the inter monthly and inter seasonal variations of the area of Qinghai Lake with the characteristics of the clear sky data of the Qinghai Tibet Plateau.

(4) Remote sensing monitoring of lakeshore using TM and environmental disaster reduction satellite showed that there were great differences between the north and the south of the coastline of Qinghai Lake in past 50 years. Shinaihai-Heather skin on the west bank of Qinghai Lake, Qujing River on the north bank - Shaliu River into the lake mouth, and Shadao Lake-Haiyan Bay on the east coast, the shoreline retreat was the most obvious.

3.2   Discussion

Environmental mitigation satellite in Qinghai Lake water body remote sensing monitoring, with short transit times, clear sky data, free data, easy access, etc., to fine-tune the seasonal and monthly changes in Qinghai Lake,which makes environmental mitigation satellite in the monitoring of water area and flood disaster have more advantages than the majority of foreign satellites with similar to spatial resolution. However, the environment disaster reduction satellite is greatly affected by factors such as turbidity, season, weather and surrounding environment, and long wavelength band of the CCD sensor channel. It is necessary to set the threshold of water recognition model according to the above factors; There is a threshold mutation in the area with large density of algae and algae in the satellite image of environmental disaster reduction. Therefore, We should select the best method and water recognition threshold based on differences in the type of underlying surface and further improve the recognition accuracy of the water area.

In addition, with the rapid development of high-score satellite technology in our country, In recent years, it has launched successively domestic high-score series of satellites, such as China's high score series satellites, China-Pakistan 04 and Resource 3 satellites, The resolution is better than the environmental disaster reduction satellite. Therefore, it is possible to conduct a lake water area identification and monitoring model based on Multi-source Satellite data. It is also possible to monitor the area of Qinghai Lake and the lakeshore line with comprehensive application of Multi-source Satellite data. At the same time, the data assimilation technology is used to construct the historical sequence of Qinghai Lake area in order to better analyze the spatial and temporal pattern of Qinghai Lake and its response to the climate change.

References

1. Ke, C.: Research progress of lake remote sensing. Mar. Lakes Bull. **23**(4), 81–86 (2004)
2. Pu, P., Wang, S.: Research advances in lake science. Chin. J. Lake Sci. **1**(1), 1–11 (1989)
3. Hui, J.: Retrieval and analysis of Poyang Lake water quality parameters based on multi-source remote sensing. Nanchang University (2011)
4. Wang, S., Li, J.: Late Cenozoic Lacustrine sediments and their environmental profile in China. Lake Sci. **5**(1), 1–8 (1993)
5. Zhang, Y.: Progress and prospects of lake optical research. Chin. J. Lake Sci. **04**, 483–497 (2011)
6. Banan, S.M.J.: Use of remote sensing and geographical information systems in developing lake management strategies. Hydrobiology **395-396**(7), 211–226 (1999)
7. Birkett, C.M.: Environ. **72**(2), 218–236 (2000)
8. Medina, C.E., Gomez-Enri, J., Alonso, J.J., et al.: Water level fluctuations derived from ENVISAT Radar Altimeter (RA-2) and in situ measurements in a subtropical waterbody: Lake Izabal (Guatemala). Remote Sens. Environ. **112**(9), 3604–3617 (2008)
9. Amatya, P.M.: Water level fluctuations of Namco Lake in Tibetan Plateau observed from radar and laser altermrty. Master Thesis. University of Twente, Enschede, the Netherlands (2011)
10. Lu, A., Wang, L., Yao, T.: Study on remote sensing of modern changes of lake in Qinghai-Tibet plateau. Remote Sensing Technology and Application **21**(3), 174–177 (2006)
11. Shao, Z., Zhu, D., Meng, X., et al.: Characteristics of major lake changes over Qinghai-Tibet Plateau over the past 25 years. Geological Bulletin **26**(12), 1633–1645 (2007). Ma, M., Song, Y., Wang, X.: Remote sensing dynamic monitoring of Ruqiang Lake Group. Glacier Permafrost, **30**(2), 189–195 (2008)
12. Li, J., Sheng, Y., Luo, J., et al.: Remote mapping of inland lakes on the Tibetan Plateau. Lake Sci. **23**(3), 311–320 (2011)
13. Zhang, G., Xie, H., Yao, T., et al.: Estimation of water balance of ten lakes in China based on ICESat and landsat. Chin. Sci. Bull. **21**(3), 2664–2678 (2013)
14. Liu, B., Wei, X., Feng, S., et al.: Dynamic study on the area of Qinghai Lake based on environmental disaster reduction satellite. Physia Sci. **30**(2), 95–96 (2013)

15. Yao, X., Liu, S., Sun, M., et al.: Analysis of area dynamics and lake spillover of Kusai Lake in Hoh Xil area. Acta Geogr. Sin. **67**(5), 689–698 (2012)
16. Liu, B., Du, Y., Li, L.: Outburst flooding of the moraine-dammed Zhuonai Lake on Tibetan Plateau: causes and impacts. IEEE Geosci. Remote Sens. Lett. **23**(4), 570–574 (2016)
17. Sun, Y., Li, X.: Climate change and its hydrological effects in the Qinghai Lake Basin. Resour. Sci. **30**(3), 354–362 (2008)

An Algebraic Multigrid Preconditioner Based on Aggregation from Top to Bottom

Jianping Wu$^{(\boxtimes)}$, Fukang Yin$^{(\boxtimes)}$, Jun Peng$^{(\boxtimes)}$, and Jinhui Yang$^{(\boxtimes)}$

Academy of Ocean Science and Engineering, National University of Defense Technology, Changsha, China
{wjp,yinfukang,pengjun,yangjinhui}@nudt.edu.cn

Abstract. In aggregation based algebraic multigrids, the current schemes are to construct the grid hierarchy from bottom to top, where several nodes on the finer level are clustered into a node on the coarser level step by step. Therefore this kind of scheme is mainly based on local information. In this paper, we present a new aggregation scheme, where the grid hierarchy is formed from top to bottom in a natural way. The adjacent graph of the original coefficient matrix is partitioned first, and then each part is recursively partitioned until some limitations are met for a certain level. Then the grid hierarchy is formed based on the global information, which is completely different from the classical ones. When partitioning graphs, any kind of method can be used, including those based on coordinate information and those based on the element of the matrix only, such as the methods provided in the software package METIS. Finally, the new scheme is validated from the solution of some discrete two-dimensional systems with preconditioned conjugate gradient iterations.

Keywords: Sparse linear system · Aggregation based algebraic multigrid
Preconditioner · Preconditioned conjugate gradient iteration · Graph partitioning

1 Introduction

Sparse linear algebraic system is widely used in scientific and engineering applications and its solution often occupies much of the total execution time. To solve such sparse linear systems, Krylov subspace methods are often used for their relatively rapid convergence. But the convergence rate is determined by the eigenvalue distribution of the coefficient matrix. To improve this kind of distribution, preconditioning techniques can be used on the condition that the application of the preconditioner to a vector is economic compared to the matrix-vector operation.

In general, any approximate solution method can be used to construct a preconditioner. Multigrid methods can solve sparse linear systems with potential optimal convergence rate. Therefore it can be used as the preconditioner. The efficiency of multigrid methods is determined by the complement of two processes, that is, smoothing and correction, which are used to reduce the error components with relatively higher and lower frequencies respectively. In aggregation based algebraic multigrid [1], when the classical simple grid transfer operators are used, the correction

H. Yuan et al. (Eds.): GSKI 2017, CCIS 849, pp. 192–204, 2018.
https://doi.org/10.1007/978-981-13-0896-3_20

is determined by the grid hierarchy. So when the smoothing is given, its efficiency is determined by the aggregation scheme only.

Up to now, several aggregation algorithms have been presented, which can be classified into two types.

The first type is based merely on the adjacent graph. The most famous is the scheme based on strong connection [2], where two points at most are aggregated. To reduce the number of levels, it can be repeatedly applied to determine the aggregations [3, 4]. Motivated by maintaining of element structures, a method based on coarsening the grid points by a factor of three is provided in [5]. Another scheme based on strong coupling is presented in [6], where each isolated point is added to an adjacent aggregation as soon as possible.

Graph partitioning can be used to construct aggregations too, but up to now, it is only used in two-level methods. Kumar provided such a method [7], where ILU(0) is used as the smoothing process and ILUT as the coarser-grid solution. The experiments show that it is more robust than those based on strength of connections. In [8], Wu et al. provided a two level grid correction for parallel incomplete factorization, to solve sparse linear systems from meso-scale simulation of concrete samples, where the adjacent graph is partitioned, and each part is aggregated into a coarse grid point.

Recently, Chen et al. compared various aggregations and found that those aligned with the anisotropy are the best [9]. Based on this consideration, they aggregate points according to the eigenvectors corresponding to small eigenvalues or a quantity related to the spectral radius of the iterative matrix.

The other type is based on both the adjacent graph and some available geometry information. Braess presented two algorithms for aggregation [10]. The first is to select points to aggregate based on seven prior known structures, and the second is based on two criterions, the edge weights and the number of edges, where the nodes are grouped into subsets with the first criterion, and every two subsets are aggregated based on the second.

The aggregation occupies much of the setup time and with the increase of the problem size, the time required is increased significantly in general. To accelerate this process, Deng et al. analyzed the common pattern for nine-point finite difference method, and provided economic aggregations for different kinds of grids [11].

In reference [12], for model problems, several two-point aggregations are compared and the results show that when Jacobi iteration is used as smoothing, it is difficult to determine the best strategy to aggregate. But if Gauss-Seidel iteration is used as smoothing, the optimal is always among those with matching priority for edges with heave weights.

In this paper, a new aggregation is provided, where the grid hierarchy is constructed from top to bottom and based on graph partitioning. In Sect. 2, preconditioned conjugate gradient iteration with aggregation based algebraic multigrid as the preconditioner is given, and in Sect. 3, the new aggregation will be described. Some numerical results for sparse linear systems from two-dimensional model partial differential equations will be given in Sect. 4 to verify the efficiency and the robustness. And finally some conclusions are drawn in Sect. 5.

2 Preconditioned Conjugate Gradient with Aggregation Based Multigrid as the Preconditioner

Consider a sparse linear system

$$Ax = b, \tag{1}$$

where A is a given symmetric positive definite matrix of order n, b is a known vector, and x is the unknown solution. To solve this kind of sparse linear system, we can adopt the conjugate gradient (CG) method. But the convergence rate of CG relies on the eigenvalue distribution of coefficient matrix A. The relatively narrower region the eigenvalues are located in, the faster the convergence rate will be. To improve the convergence rate, preconditioning techniques can be used, where the linear system is transferred to

$$MAx = Mb. \tag{2}$$

In (2), M is called a preconditioner. Then the CG method can be used to solve (2) with the original Euclid norm replaced by the energy norm $(.,.)_M$, which is defined by $(x, y)_M = (x, My)$. The derived iteration is called the preconditioned conjugate gradient (PCG) iteration. The details can be referred to the Algorithm 9.1 in [13].

In fact, any approximate solution method for (1) can be adapted to a preconditioner, only if M is symmetric positive definite. But the effectiveness is determined by two factors. One is the extent of the eigenvalues of MA approaching to 1, that is, the accuracy of M approaching to A-1. The higher the accuracy is, the more rapidly the PCG iteration will converge. The other is the related computation to the preconditioner. The operation of M to a vector should be economic enough compared to the matrix-vector operation Ax. Otherwise, even if little number of iterations is required, the iteration will be very expensive too, for it is time consuming for each of the iterations.

It is known that the aggregation based algebraic multigrid method can be used to solve the system (1). Therefore it can be adapted as the preconditioner M in (2). The description of the algorithm has no difference from the general multigrid and the details can be referred to Algorithm 2.3.2 in [14]. In this algorithm, the 0-th level is the coarsest grid and the l-the level is the coarser grid of the (l + 1)-th. For description convenience, we reverse the level number. Therefore the 0-th level is the finest and is corresponding to the original linear system. We adopt the V-cycle version and different operators for pre- and post-smoothing. Then they can be denoted as SlR and SlL respectively. It is assumed that the restrictor from level l to level l + 1 is Rl + 1,l, and the prolong operator from level l + 1 to l is Pl,l + 1. The algorithm is invoked recursively, to restrict the error vector to a coarser grid, find the solution with the algorithm again, and interpolate it back to the finer grid to correct the solution. If the number of levels attains a prior given threshold, or the linear system is small enough, the process is stopped. The solution on the coarsest level can be performed with any kind of method.

In the algorithm described as above, the smoother SlR is corresponding to the following iteration

$$x^{(l)} := (I - S_l^R A_l)x^{(l)} + S_l^R b_l,$$

and S_l^L is corresponding to a similar iteration. For the two-level case where the l-th level is the finer level and the $(l+1)$-th level is the coarser, the algorithm is equivalent to the following iteration

$$e^{(l)} := B_l e^{(l)}, \tag{3}$$

where

$$B_l = \left(I - S_l^L A_l\right)\{I - P_{l,l+1}\left(R_{l+1,l}A_l P_{l,l+1}\right)^{-1} R_{l+1,l}A_l\}(I - S_l^R A_l),$$

and $e^{(l)} = x^{(l)} - x$ is the error vector.

When we construct the preconditioner Ml based on the iteration (3), we have the relation Bl = I-MlAl, thus

$$M_l = (S_l^L + S_l^R) + O_l - S_l^L A_l S_l^R + S_l^L A_l O_l A_l S_l^R - (S_l^L A_l O_l + O_l A_l S_l^R),$$

where

$$O_l = P_{l,l+1}\left(R_{l+1,l}A_l P_{l,l+1}\right)^{-1} R_{l+1,l}.$$

Obviously, to ensure that the multigrid algorithm can be used as a preconditioner of PCG, Ml should be symmetric. If we select Rl+1,l = Pl,l+1T and SlL = (SlR)T, since Al is symmetric, we can deduce that Ol and then the preconditioner Ml are symmetric too.

In aggregation based multigrid methods, the coarser grids are formed from aggregation of the grid points on the finer level. In this paper, a new aggregation algorithm from top to bottom will be presented in Sect. 3. For prolong operators, only the classical simplest version is considered here. If there are nl points on the l-th level, the prolong operator Pl,l+1 is an nl by nl+1 matrix. For level l, if the j-th aggregation contains a point i, then the element of Pl,l+1 on the i-th row and the j-th column is 1. All elements not equal to 1 are zeros.

For the smoothing process, any iteration can be used. If the Jacobi iteration is selected, for system (1) with matrix A replaced by Al, b by bl, and x by xl, we have

$$x_l^{(k+1)} := (I - D_l^{-1}A_l)x_l^{(k)} + D_l^{-1}b_l,$$

where D_l is the diagonal part of A_l. Therefore, we can select

$$S_l^R = D_l^{-1}.$$

For Gauss-Seidel iteration, we have

$$x_l^{(k+1)} := (I - (D_l - L_l)^{-1}A_l)x_l^{(k)} + (D_l - L_l)^{-1}b_l,$$

where L_l is the strictly lower triangular part of A_l. Thus, we can select

$$S_l^R = (D_l - L_l)^{-1}.$$

When multigrid is used as the preconditioner of PCG, many information, including the grid hierarchy, the matrices Al, Pl,l+1, and SIR will all be unchanged with the iteration. Thus, they can be derived beforehand and put into the setup process and be used directly in latter iterations as needed.

3   A New Aggregation from Top to Bottom

The most frequently used aggregation methods are the schemes based on strong connection [2–4], which aggregates points with heavy edge weights into subsets, and then applies the process recursively to get the grid hierarchy. The method based on a factor of three [5] follows this order to construct grid levels. The scheme based on strong coupling [6], the Braess algorithms [10], and the algorithm in [11] are also all based on this order. These methods have been proven to be efficient for many problems and this order can capture local information accurately in general, but the ability to exploit global information is very limited.

To exploit global information to control the quality of grid construction and then to improve the efficiency of the derived multigrid methods, the graph partitioning method can be used. In fact this scheme has been used in the two-level grid methods. In [7], Kumar provided such a method and the numerical experiments have validated its robustness and efficiency. In [8], Wu et al. also provided a two level grid correction for parallel incomplete factorization based on graph partitioning. The correction from the coarse grid is added to the approximate solution derived with incomplete factorization, to define the parallel preconditioning process. But these methods are limited to the two-level grid and did not consider the multigrid cases.

In this paper, we present a new scheme based on graph partitioning, which construct the grid hierarchy starting from the coarsest level to the finest level. Consider linear system (1), denoting the adjacent graph of A with G. For the matrix A considered is symmetric, G is an undirected graph. Now we can partition G into m_0 sub-graphs $G_i^{(1)}$, i = 1,2,...,m_0, where m_0 can be given beforehand. Now the vertexes in each $G_i^{(1)}$ can be aggregated into a point in level 1 and there are m_0 nodes in this level. At this time, we have

$$\cup \{G_i^{(1)} : i = 1, 2, \ldots, m_0\} = G,$$

and

$$G_i^{(1)} \cap G_j^{(1)} = \varnothing, i, j = 1, 2, \ldots, m_0.$$

For each $G_i^{(1)}$, it can be partitioned again into p sub-graphs. Since there are m_0 parts in level 1, there will derive pm_0 sub-graphs in all, with each related to a point in level 2. The partitioning process can be continued recursively until some sub-graph in a certain level l is small enough. Each sub-graph on the l-th level is an aggregation of the related nodes in the original graph. The construction details can be illustrated in Fig. 1, where

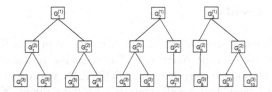

Fig. 1. Illustration of the aggregation method from top to bottom.

p = 2, m_0 = 3 and l = 3.

Denote the vertex set of $G_i^{(j)}$ with $V_i^{(j)}$, we have

$$V_{i+(k-1)p}^{(j+1)} \subset V_k^{(j)}, i = 1, 2, \ldots, p,$$

which means that a grid hierarchy is generated naturally. There are m_0 nodes in level 1, and for level $j(2 \leq j \leq l-1)$, there are $m_0 p^{j-1}$ nodes, where each relates to p nodes on the $(j+1)$-the level. And for level l, each $G_i^{(l)}$ contains $\left|G_i^{(l)}\right|$ nodes. Each $G_i^{(l)}$ contains part of the points of G.

When each graph is partitioned into sub-graphs, we can require that the total number of edges between sub-graphs is minimized on the condition that the number of nodes in each sub-graph is as identical as possible. In this way, the number of levels may be small when the parameter m_0 and p is given. On the other hand, the number of edges between sub-graphs can measure the connectivity. The minimization means that the connectivity between sub-graphs is minimized and the strong connections are moved into the interior of sub-graphs, which is similar to the concept of strong connection in the classical aggregation schemes. But it should be noted that it is not based on the connectivity between nodes, which is local information, but based on the global information, that is, the connections between sub-graphs.

When partitioning, another issue is the selection of the partitioning method. It is clear that any kind of methods can be used. If the physical discrete grid of linear system

(1) is known, the coordinate information can be derived. Thus the partitioning can be based on this information. It is clear that this kind of partitioning is very cheap and will be helpful in reducing the setup time. In addition, it has superiority in shape preserving. Each node contains in a sub-graph will is in a relatively small physical region, which is beneficial to the equality of recursively partitioning.

In many cases, the coordinate information behind the system (1) is not known or does not exist at all. At this time, we can exploit graph-partitioning software packages such as METIS [15]. But it should be mentioned that each sub-graph is corresponding to an aggregation, and thus each sub-graph should be connected, or the quality of the derived multigrid method will degrade. For this purpose, when METIS is used to partition a graph into more than three parts, the interface metis_PartGraphRecursive is recommended, which is based on partitioning recursively.

4 Numerical Results

In this section, all the results are derived on a processor of Intel(R) Xeon(R) CPU E5-2670 0 @ 2.60 GHz (cache 20480 KB). The operating system is Red Hat Linux 2.6.32-279-aftms-TH and the compiler is Intel FORTRAN Version 11.1. For the sparse linear systems encountered here are all symmetric positive definite, PCG is used for all cases. The initial guess is zero and the PCG iteration is stopped when the Euclid norm of the residual vector is reduced by a ratio of 1E-10. In the aggregation based multigrid method, the sparse linear system on the coarsest level is solved with PCG again, preconditioned by incomplete LU factorization without fill, and the stop criterion is the same as that in the outer iteration.

Experiments are performed for six sparse linear systems, including Lin51, Lin52, Lin53, Lin54, Lin91 and Lin92. All the linear systems are derived with finite difference method from a two-dimensional PDE with Dirichlet boundaries

$$-a_1 \partial(\rho \partial u / \partial x) / \partial x - a_2 \partial(\rho \partial u / \partial y) / \partial y + \delta u = f,$$

The definition region is $(0, c) \times (0, c)$. The function f and the boundary values are given from a true solution $u = 1$. There are $n + 2$ points in each dimension and the value $u(x_i, y_j)$ is defined as $u_{i,j}$ for any continuous function u, where x_i and y_j are uniformly distributed in x and y directions respectively.

For system Lin51, $a_1 = a_2 = \rho = 1$, $\delta = 0$ and the following discrete form is used:

$$-u_{i,j-1} - u_{i-1,j} + 4u_{i,j} - u_{i+1,j} - u_{i,j+1} = h^2 f_{i,j}.$$

For system Lin52, $a_1 = a_2 = 1$ and the discrete form used is

$$-\rho_{i,j-1/2} u_{i,j-1} - \rho_{i-1/2,j} u_{i-1,j} + \lambda_{i,j} u_{i,j} - \rho_{i+1/2,j} u_{i+1,j} - \rho_{i,j+1/2} u_{i,j+1} = h^2 f_{i,j}.$$

where

$$\lambda_{i,j} = h^2 \delta_{i,j} + \rho_{i,j-1/2} + \rho_{i-1/2,j} + \rho_{i+1/2,j} + \rho_{i,j+1/2},$$

$\rho = \rho_k$ and $\delta = \delta_k$ when (x, y) is in R_k for $k = 1$, 2 and 3, and

$$R_1 = \{(2, 2.1] \times (1, 2.1]\} \cup \{(2, 2.1] \times (1, 2.1]\}, R_2 = (1, 2) \times (1, 2),$$

$$R_3 = \{[0, 2.1] \times [0, 1)\} \cup \{[0, 1) \times [0, 2.1]\},$$

and

$$\rho_1 = 1, \rho_1 = 2 \times 10^3, \rho_1 = 3 \times 10^5, \delta_1 = 0.02, \delta_2 = 3, \delta_3 = 500.$$

For system Lin53, the discrete form used is the same as that for Lin52, but $\rho = x\rho_k$ and $\delta = x\delta_k$ when (x, y) is in R_k for $k = 1$, 2 and 3.

For linear system Lin54, $\rho = 1$, $\delta = 0$, $a_1 = 1$, $a_2 = 100$, and the discrete form is

$$-100u_{i,j-1} - u_{i-1,j} + 202u_{i,j} - u_{i+1,j} - 100u_{i,j+1} = h^2 f_{i,j}.$$

For sparse linear system Lin91 and Lin92, $a_1 = a_2 = \rho = 1$, $\delta = 0$ and the discrete forms used are

$$-u_{i-1,j-1} - u_{i,j-1} - u_{i+1,j-1} - u_{i-1,j} + 8u_{i,j} - u_{i+1,j}$$
$$-u_{i-1,j+1} - u_{i,j+1} - u_{i+1,j+1} = h^2 f_{i,j},$$

and

$$-u_{i-1,j-1} - 4u_{i,j-1} - u_{i+1,j-1} - 4u_{i-1,j} + 20u_{i,j} - 4u_{i+1,j}$$
$$-u_{i-1,j+1} - 4u_{i,j+1} - u_{i+1,j+1} = h^2 f_{i,j},$$

respectively.

The experiment results with n equal to 1024 are given in Tables 1, 2, 3, 4, 5, 6, 7 and 8. In all the tables, strg denotes the scheme based on the strongest connection, and the suffix denotes the number of points aggregated each time. The symbol coor denotes the new method based on coordinate information. And mtis denotes the new method based on the METIS interface metis_PartGraphRecursive. For the new algorithm, when the number of nodes of some sub-graph on a certain level is less than p, the process to construct the grid hierarchy is stopped. The parameter p is appended as a suffix in both coor and mtis methods to denote the number of parts used when the partitioning is proceeded.

In Table 1, the complexity of the grids, which is denoted as cgrd, is given for different methods and different systems. It is defined as the ratio of the total number of grid points on each level to that on the finest level. It is clear that when p = 2, this parameter is smaller with the new algorithm than that with the strg methods. And when p is larger than 2, the conclusion is reversed. Therefore, the influence of the new algorithm to this parameter is neutral.

Table 1. Cgrd for different methods

	Lin51	Lin52	Lin53	Lin54	Lin91	Lin92
coor2	1.781	1.781	1.781	1.781	1.781	1.781
mtis2	1.781	1.781	1.781	1.781	1.781	1.781
strg2	2.000	2.000	2.000	2.000	2.000	2.000
coor4	1.521	1.521	1.521	1.521	1.521	1.521
mtis4	1.521	1.521	1.521	1.521	1.521	1.521
strg4	1.333	1.333	1.333	1.333	1.333	1.333
coor8	1.446	1.446	1.446	1.446	1.446	1.446
mtis8	1.446	1.446	1.446	1.446	1.446	1.446
strg8	1.143	1.143	1.143	1.143	1.143	1.143

Table 2. Cops for different methods

	Lin51	Lin52	Lin53	Lin54	Lin91	Lin92
coor2	1.821	1.821	1.821	1.821	1.756	1.756
mtis2	2.053	2.053	2.053	2.053	1.696	1.696
strg2	1.999	2.027	2.027	1.999	1.998	1.998
coor4	1.520	1.520	1.520	1.520	1.520	1.520
mtis4	1.691	1.691	1.691	1.691	1.482	1.482
strg4	1.333	1.342	1.342	1.333	1.333	1.333
coor8	1.451	1.451	1.451	1.451	1.443	1.443
mtis8	1.580	1.580	1.580	1.580	1.418	1.418
strg8	1.143	1.158	1.158	1.143	1.142	1.142

Table 3. Number of iterations with jacobi smoothing

	Lin51	Lin52	Lin53	Lin54	Lin91	Lin92
coor2	92	90	90	243	91	91
mtis2	110	106	100	234	96	102
strg2	578	463	461	578	86	86
coor4	94	94	94	234	92	92
mtis4	121	115	114	283	106	112
strg4	655	794	795	655	91	91
coor8	103	106	105	258	100	101
mtis8	130	128	128	329	114	121
strg8	658	772	796	658	116	116

In Table 2, the complexity of the operators, which is denoted as cops, is given. It is defined as the ratio of the total number of non-zeros in the coefficient matrices on each level to that on the finest. We can deduce a similar conclusion as for cgrd, that is, the influence of the new algorithm to this parameter is neutral too. In addition, for linear systems from five point differential schemes, it is better to partition based on coordinate

Table 4. Iteration time in seconds with jacobi smoothing

	Lin51	Lin52	Lin53	Lin54	Lin91	Lin92
coor2	25.23	24.63	24.59	66.41	38.76	38.79
mtis2	36.81	35.57	33.42	78.24	43.06	46.37
strg2	173.4	140.6	139.8	138.8	41.48	41.54
coor4	22.34	22.34	22.19	55.32	34.30	34.29
mtis4	34.33	32.70	32.23	79.97	41.59	43.82
strg4	141.3	170.0	171.0	112.7	31.05	31.10
coor8	23.45	24.26	23.85	58.68	35.61	35.92
mtis8	34.21	33.66	33.40	86.74	42.78	45.33
strg8	127.7	151.3	155.9	102.3	35.05	35.14

Table 5. Total time in seconds with jacobi smoothing

	Lin51	Lin52	Lin53	Lin54	Lin91	Lin92
coor2	32.11	31.51	31.46	73.27	47.24	47.29
mtis2	55.11	53.87	51.76	96.56	66.58	70.18
strg2	175.4	142.6	141.9	140.4	44.88	44.94
coor4	27.48	27.49	27.34	60.47	40.68	40.66
mtis4	50.39	48.87	48.43	96.02	62.49	64.87
strg4	143.3	172.0	173.0	114.3	34.22	34.28
coor8	28.11	28.92	28.50	63.33	41.35	41.64
mtis8	50.22	49.68	49.41	102.6	63.75	66.51
strg8	129.6	153.2	157.8	103.8	38.07	38.16

Table 6. Number of iterations with gauss-seidel smoothing

	Lin51	Lin52	Lin53	Lin54	Lin91	Lin92
coor2	83	79	79	179	81	82
mtis2	96	91	90	191	86	91
strg2	85	92	93	85	84	84
coor4	86	83	82	171	86	86
mtis4	109	102	101	235	98	104
strg4	92	117	110	92	91	91
coor8	94	95	95	187	92	93
mtis8	118	112	112	271	105	112
strg8	110	137	131	110	108	109

information than based on METIS. And for those from nine point schemes, it is better to partition based on METIS.

The arguments cgrd and cops are not the decisive ones for investigating the performance of the related multigrid and can only provide a reference. Table 3 gives a more vital argument, the number of PCG iterations used with Jacobi smoothing. From

Table 7. Iteration time in seconds with gauss-seidel smoothing

	Lin51	Lin52	Lin53	Lin54	Lin91	Lin92
coor2	28.13	26.84	25.77	60.87	43.01	43.62
mtis2	39.39	37.26	38.88	77.87	47.18	52.58
strg2	31.93	34.87	33.61	25.49	50.47	47.71
coor4	24.96	24.15	22.92	49.51	39.75	39.76
mtis4	37.21	34.87	36.34	79.94	46.38	51.92
strg4	23.27	29.52	29.12	18.59	36.23	38.32
coor8	26.26	26.60	25.52	52.15	40.64	41.08
mtis8	37.32	35.49	37.37	85.62	47.36	53.39
strg8	26.11	32.82	29.92	20.81	39.99	38.24

Table 8. Total time in seconds with gauss-seidel smoothing

	Lin51	Lin52	Lin53	Lin54	Lin91	Lin92
coor2	35.01	33.71	32.64	67.74	51.50	52.12
mtis2	57.69	55.56	57.22	96.19	70.70	76.38
strg2	33.93	36.90	35.64	27.09	53.87	51.11
coor4	30.11	29.30	28.07	54.66	46.13	46.13
mtis4	53.27	51.04	52.54	95.99	67.27	72.97
strg4	25.23	31.49	31.09	20.15	39.41	41.50
coor8	30.91	31.27	30.17	56.80	46.38	46.80
mtis8	53.33	51.51	53.38	101.45	68.33	74.56
strg8	28.00	34.71	31.82	22.30	43.01	41.25

the results, we can see that for sparse liner systems derived with nine-point-differential scheme, the coor methods are better than the mtis ones, and are comparable to the strg methods. For those derived with five-point schemes, the coor methods are better than the mtis ones too, and they are both better than the strg methods.

In Table 4, the time used for multigrid preconditioned PCG iterations in seconds for Jacobi smoothing is given. It can be seen that systems from five point discrete schemes, the new methods are by far the better, especially the coor methods. For those from nine point schemes, the coor methods are comparable to the strg ones, and they are better than the mtis methods.

Table 5 presents the total execution time to solve each linear system with Jacobi smoothing, which is the sum of the time used for iteration and setup. The results are similar to those to the iteration time. But since the setup time for the new scheme is much larger, for linear systems from nine point schemes, the coor methods are slightly worse than the strg methods.

Table 6 gives the number of PCG iterations used with Gauss-Seidel smoothing. We can see that for systems except Lin54 which is derived from a PDE with anisotropy along different axes, the coor methods are the best, and then the strg ones. The mtis methods are the worst in general.

The iteration time results with Gauss-Seidel smoothing given in Table 7 show that for isotropic systems, when five point schemes used, the coor methods are slightly better, and when nine point schemes used, the strg methods are slightly better. For anisotropic systems, the strg methods are much better. As for the total execution time with this smoothing, the results are given in Table 8, it is clear that, for isotropic systems, when five point schemes used, the coor methods are comparable to the strg ones, and they are better than the mtis methods. When nine point schemes are used or anisotropic systems are considered, the strg methods are better than the new methods in general.

5 Conclusions

In this paper, we provide a new aggregation method based on graph partitioning, and the grid hierarchy is formed from the coarsest level to the finest level, which is beneficial to exploit global information to improve the robustness. The results from the solution of some two-dimensional model partial differential equations show that the new algorithm has better performance and is more robust than the algorithms based on strong connections in most cases, especially for approximately isotropic problems. For anisotropic cases, the partitioning does not exploit the strength of connections yet in this paper, leading to the performance degradation, which should be considered in future. In addition, the partitioning based on coordinate information leads to better performance than that based on METIS. But the coordinate information behind the linear system is unknown in general, thus how to improve the methods based on general graph partitioning is another direction for future research.

Acknowledgment. This work is funded by NSFC(61379022).

References

1. Notay, Y.: Aggregation-based algebraic multilevel preconditioning. SIAM J. Matrix Anal. Appl. **27**(4), 998–1018 (2006)
2. Kim, H., Xu, J., Zikatanov, L.: A multigrid method based on graph matching for convection-diffusion equations. Numer. Linear Algebra Appl. **10**, 181–195 (2003)
3. Notay, Y.: Aggregation-based algebraic multigrid for convection-diffusion equations. SIAM J. Sci. Comput. **34**(4), A2288–A2316 (2012)
4. D'Ambra, P., Buttari, A., di Serafino, D., Filippone, S., Gentile, S., Ucar, B.: A novel aggregation method based on graph matching for algebraic multigrid preconditioning of sparse linear systems. In: International Conference on Preconditioning Techniques for Scientific & Industrial Applications, May 2011, Bordeaux, France (2011)
5. Dendy Jr., J.E., Moulton, J.D.: Black Box Multigrid with coarsening by a factor of three. Numer. Linear Algebra Appl. **17**(2–3), 577–598 (2010)
6. Vanek, P., Mandel, J., Brezina, M.: Algebraic multigrid by smoothed aggregation for second order and fourth order elliptic problems. Computing **56**, 179–196 (1996)
7. Kumar, P.: Aggregation based on graph matching and inexact coarse grid solve for algebraic two grid. Int. J. Comput. Math. **91**(5), 1061–1081 (2014)

8. Wu, J.P., Song, J.Q., Zhang, W.M., Ma, H.F.: Coarse grid correction to domain decomposition based preconditioners for meso-scale simulation of concrete. Appl. Mech. Mater. **204–208**, 4683–4687 (2012)
9. Chen, M.H., Greenbaum, A.: Analysis of an aggregation-based algebraic two-grid method for a rotated anisotropic diffusion problem. Numer. Linear Algebra Appl. **22**(4), 681–701 (2015)
10. Braess, D.: Towards algebraic multigrid for elliptic problems of second order. Computing **55**, 379–393 (1995)
11. Deng, L.J., Huang, T.Z., Zhao, X.L., Zhao, L., Wang, S.: An economical aggregation algorithm for algebraic multigrid. (AMG). J. Comput. Anal. Appl. **16**(1), 181–198 (2014)
12. Wu, J.P., Yin, F.K., Peng, J., Yang, J.H.: Research on two-point aggregated algebraic multigrid preconditioning methods. In: International Conference on Computer Engineering and Information System [CEIS 2016], Shanghai, China (2016)
13. Saad, Y.: Iterative methods for Sparse Linear Systems. PWS Pub. Co., Boston (1996)
14. Wagner, C.: Introduction to algebraic multigrid, Course Notes, University of Heidelberg (1998/1999). http://www.iwr.uni-heidelberg.de/~Christian.Wagner/
15. Karypis, G., Kumar, G.: MeTiS – a software package for partitioning unstructured graphs, partitioning meshes, and computing fill-reducing orderings of sparse matrices – Version 4.0, Technical report, University of Minnesota, September 1998

COKES: Continuous Top-*k* Keyword Search in Relational Databases

Yanwei Xu[✉] and Yicheng Yang

Shanghai Engineering Research Center for Broadband Technologies and Applications,
150 Honggu Road, Shanghai 200336, China
ywxu@bnc.org.cn

Abstract. Keyword search in relational databases has been widely studied in recent years. Most of existing methods focus on answering snapshot keyword queries in static databases. However, in practice, relational databases are always being updated continually. Reevaluating a keyword query using existing methods after the database is updated is prohibitively expensive. In this paper we describe the COKES system, which keeps the set of answers whose upper bounds of future relevance scores are larger than a threshold for top-*k* answers maintenance. Experimental results show that the proposed method is efficient in answering continuous top-*k* keyword queries in relational databases.

Keywords: Keyword search · Continuous queries · Answers maintenance
Relational databases

1 Introduction

With the proliferation of text data in relational databases, simple ways to exploring such information are of increasing importance. Keyword search is the most popular information retrieval method because users do not need to know either the query language or the underlying structure of the data. Thus, it is desirable to exploit the paradigm of keyword search to query relational databases. Keyword search in relational databases has attracted substantial research efforts in recent years [1–10]. In contrast to traditional keyword search on documents, results of keyword search in relational databases have to be *constructed* by joining multiple tuples.

Example 1. Consider the publication database shown in Fig. 1. To express conveniently, we use the initials of relation names as shorthand, the database schema is $R = \{P, A, W\}$. The *Write* relation specifies the many-to-many relationships between the tuples of *Papers* and *Authors*. *Papers* and *Authors* both have one text column (*Title* and *AuthorName*, respectively) that can be queried by users. For the keyword query "James P2P", there are six tuples that contain at least one keyword in the database: p_1, p_2, p_5, a_1, a_3 and a_5, each of which can be regarded as an answer. However, tuples p_2 and p_5 can be joined with tuples a_1 and a_5 through tuples w_2 and w_5, respectively, according to the foreign key references, to form two more meaningful answers: $p_2 \leftarrow w_2 \rightarrow a_1$ and $p_5 \leftarrow w_5 \rightarrow a_5$.

© Springer Nature Singapore Pte Ltd. 2018
H. Yuan et al. (Eds.): GSKI 2017, CCIS 849, pp. 205–217, 2018.
https://doi.org/10.1007/978-981-13-0896-3_21

Papers			Authors			Write		
Pld	*Title*		*Ald*	*AuthorName*		*Id*	*Pld*	*Ald*
p_1	Exploring VoD in P2P Swarming Systems.		a_1	James S. K. Newell		w_1	p_1	a_2
p_2	The P2P MultiRouter: a black box approach to run-time adaptivity for P2P DHTs.		a_2	Saikat Guha		w_2	p_2	a_1
p_3	A System for Predicting Subcellular Localization of Yeast Genome Using Neural Network.		a_3	James Bailey		w_3	p_3	a_4
			a_4	Sabu M. Thampi		w_4	p_4	a_3
p_4	Logical queries over views: Decidability and expressiveness.		a_5	James Walkerdine		w_5	p_5	a_5
p_5	A framework for P2P application development.		...	...		...	...	...
...	...							

Fig. 1. A publication database (the query is "James P2P", all partial matches are underlined).

Most of the existing keyword search systems assume that the databases are static and focus on answering the *snapshot* keyword queries. However, in practice, databases are often being updated continually. In this paper, we present the COKES (COKES is an acronym of Continuous Keyword Searching.) system to address the problem of *Continuous* top-k keyword search in relational databases. Once a query is issued, COKES first partially evaluates each keyword query to find the set of Joint-Tuple-Trees (JTTs) whose upper bounds of future relevance scores are larger than a threshold θ. The set of found JTTs are then maintained by adding new JTTs whose upper bounds of relevance scores are larger than θ and deleting these JTTs containing the deleted tuples. At any time, the k JTTs with the highest scores that are larger than θ are outputted as the top-k answers. To deal with the deletion of tuples and changes of relevance scores of answers without fully re-computing the top-k answers, COKES finds the top-K answers (instead of top-k) upon query registration, and performs query reevaluations whenever the number of found JTTs whose relevance scores are larger than θ falls below k.

The rest of this paper is organized as follows. Section 2 introduces the basic concepts and highlights the main challenges. Section 3 describes the query processing framework, the technical details are given in Sects. 4, 5 and 6, respectively. The experimental results are presented in Sect. 7. Section 8 surveys the related work. Finally, the paper is concluded in Sect. 9.

2 Preliminaries

The task of keyword search in a relational database is to find *structural information* among the tuples using an l-keyword query, Q, which is a set of l keywords, denoted as $Q = \{w_1, w_2, ..., w_l\}$ [11]. A relational database is viewed as a data graph $G_D(V, E)$, where V represents the set of tuples, and E represents the foreign key reference relationships among the tuples. The structural information to be returned for a keyword query is a set of connected tree of tuples. A connected tree T represents how the *matched* (or related) tuples, which contain the required keywords, are interconnected in a data graph G_D. Such a connected tree is called a *Joint-Tuple-Tree (JTT)*. A JTT is an answer to a keyword query if its each leaf tuple contains at least one keyword. In Example 1, $p_2 \leftarrow w_2 \rightarrow a_1$ is a valid answer since p_2 and a_1 both are matched tuples. The number of matched tuples in T is called the size of T, which is denoted as $sizeof(T)$.

Each JTT corresponds to an output of a relational algebra expression, which is termed as a *Candidate Network (CN)* [8]. We use $CN(T)$ to denote the CN corresponds to T. For example, the CNs of the top-2 answers p_2 and $p_2 \leftarrow w_2 \rightarrow a_1$ in Example 1 are P^Q and $P^Q \leftarrow W \rightarrow A^Q$. The relations with the notation ^{Q} in CNs are called *Tuple Sets*, which are the sets of matched tuples in the relations. For instance, the two tuple sets of Example 1 are $P^Q = \{p_1, p_2, p_5\}$ and $A^Q = \{a_1, a_3, a_5\}$. The number of tuple sets in a CN C is called the size of C, denoted as *sizeof*(C).

We adopt the IR-style answer ranking strategy of [8]. A function *score*(T, Q) is used to score a JTT T for query Q, which uses the following formulas based on the TF-IDF weighting.

$$score(T, Q) = \frac{\sum_{t \in T} tscore(t, Q)}{sizeof(T)}$$

$$tscore(t, Q) = \sum_{w \in Q} \frac{1 + \ln\left(1 + \ln\left(tf_{t,w}\right)\right)}{1 - s + s \cdot \dfrac{dl_t}{avdl}} \qquad (1)$$
$$\cdot \ln\left(\frac{N+1}{df_w}\right)$$

Here, $tf_{t,w}$ is the frequency of keyword w in tuple t, df_w is the number of $R(t)$ tuples that contains w ($R(t)$ means the relation that includes t), dl_t is the size (i.e., number of words) of t, $avdl$ is the average tuple size, N is the total number of tuples in $R(t)$, and s is a constant. $tscore(t, Q)$ is referred as the *tuple score* of the tuple t to query Q.

Table 1 shows the tuple scores of the six matched tuples in Example 1. Hence, the top-2 answers are p_2 (score = 5.38) and $p_2 \leftarrow w_2 \rightarrow a_1$ (score = 4.54). Now assume 60 unmatched tuples are inserted into *Authors*, which only changes the value of N of A^Q to 240; then *tscore*s of a_1, a_3 and a_5 are changed to 3.96, 4.60 and 4.60, respectively. Thus, the top-2 answers are changed to p_2 and a_3 (or a_5).

Table 1. Tuple scores of the matched tuples of P^Q and A^Q computed on $s = 0.2$

Tuple set	P^Q			A^Q		
Statistics	$N = 150$	$df_{P2P} = 3$	$avdl = 9$	$N = 180$	$df_{James} = 3$	$avdl = 2.6$
Tuple	p_1	p_2	p_5	a_1	a_3	a_5
dl	6	14	6	4	2	2
tf	1	2	1	1	1	1
$tscore$	4.20	5.38	4.20	3.70	4.30	4.30

3   The Query Processing Framework

We proposed a new continuous keyword search system COKES as shown in Fig. 2. Each keyword query is registered in company with a parameter η, which indicates the expected interval between two times of query reevaluation. First, COKES generate a set of CNs, whose basic idea is to expand each existing CN by adding a R or R^Q at each step (R is adjacent to one relation in the CN in the database schema graph), beginning from the set of all the non-empty tuple sets and ending when all the CNs of size smaller than a predetermined parameter *MAXN* are generated. COKES uses the CN generation algorithm in [12] as it can avoid isomorphism testing. In Example 1, three CNs are generated if *MAXN* = 3: P^Q, A^Q, and $P^Q{\leftarrow}W{\rightarrow}A^Q$, which are referred as CN_1, CN_2 and CN_3, respectively, in the following discussion.

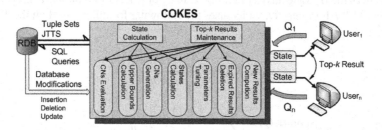

Fig. 2. The framework of COKES

Then the generated CNs are partially evaluated to find the set of answers whose upper bounds of future relevance scores, denoted as $score^{max}$, are larger than the threshold θ, whose value is determined on the fly. After database modifications, the relevance scores of the stored answers are recomputed, the new JTTs of $score^{max} > \theta$ are added to the state, and the expired JTTs are deleted from the state. Keyword queries need to be reevaluated when the upper bounds are out of date, or when the number of found JTTs of $score > \theta$ falls below k.

4   Computing Upper Bound of Relevance Scores

Compared to the method of [13], COKES only needs to compute an upper bound for the future relevance score of each query answer. Specifically, by assuming *avdl* as a constant and an upper bound of the future value of each $\ln\left(\dfrac{N+1}{df_w}\right)$, denoted as $\ln^{max}\left(\dfrac{N+1}{df_w}\right)$, the upper bound of the future relevance score of each JTT T is computed as:

$$T.score^{max} = \frac{\sum_{t \in T} t.tscore^{max}(t, Q)}{sizeof(T)}$$

$$t.tscore^{max} = \sum_{w \in t \cap Q} \frac{1 + \ln(1 + \ln(tf_{t,w}))}{1 - s + s \cdot \dfrac{dl_t}{avdl}} \qquad (2)$$

$$\cdot \ln^{max}\left(\frac{N+1}{df_w}\right)$$

where $t.tscore^{max}$ is the upper bound of the future tuple score of tuple t.

For example, Table 2 shows the $tscore^{max}$ values of the six matched tuples in Example 1 if $\Delta N = \dfrac{N}{10}$ and $\Delta df_w = \dfrac{df_w}{3}$ for all the Ns and df_ws.

Table 2. Upper bounds of tuple scores computed by Eq. (2)

Tuple	a_1	a_3	a_5	p_1	p_2	p_5
$tscore^{max}$	4.15	4.82	4.82	4.73	6.07	4.73

5   State Calculation

COKES uses Algorithm 1 to evaluate the set of generated CNs, which is based on the method of [8] and similar as the well-known Threshold Algorithm [14]. Figure 3 shows the main data structure before evaluating the three CNs of Example 1. Tuples in each tuple set are sorted in descending $tscore^{max}$ order (the $tscore^{max}$ values are shown in Table 2. At any time, the retrieved prefix of all the tuple sets in each CN have been joined to find valid JTTs; hence they are referred as the *joined tuples*. In the initialization (line 3), for each CN, only the first tuple of all the tuple sets (except any one) are marked as joined tuples. The function $getNext(R_i^Q)$ retrieves the first un-joined tuple of R_i^Q.

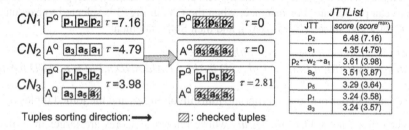

Tuples sorting direction: ⟶   ▨ : checked tuples

Fig. 3. Data structure before CN evaluation

Algorithm 1: CNEvaluation

---

input : *CNSet*: a set of CNs; k: an integer; K: $K = 2k$ (default value);

1 **Define** *Results*: a priority queue for storing found JTTs ordered in their relevance scores;
2 Sort tuples of each tuple set in descending order of $tscore^{max}$;
3 For each CN C, mark the first tuples of $(sizeof(C) - 1)$ tuple sets as *joined* ;
4 **repeat**
5     $C \leftarrow$ the CN with the highest $\tau(CN)$;
6   **begin**   /* Evaluation of C */
7        $R_i^Q \leftarrow$ the tuple set of C with the highest $\tau(TS)$; $t \leftarrow$ getNext(TS_i);
8   Join t with the joined tuples in the other tuple sets except R_i^Q of C and add all the valid JTTs to *Results* ;
9   Mark t as a joined tuple;
10 **until** (The number of JTTs in*Results* whose relevance scores are larger than all the $\tau(CN)$s is larger than K) ;
11 $\theta \longleftarrow$ the highest $\tau(CN)$;
12 Delete the JTTs in *Results* of $score^{max} < \theta$ and then **return** the top-k JTTs in *Results* ;

Algorithm 1 employs the *priority preemptive, round robin* protocol [15], where the evaluation of each CN corresponds to a process. In each repeat iteration (lines 4–10, one round), the CN of the highest priority is selected to execute, which retrieves the first un-joined tuple t from the tuple set of the highest priority to identify each potential JTTs in which t can participate. For instance, when the CN_3 in Fig. 3 is selected to execute, p_2 will be retrieved since $\tau(P^Q) > \tau(A^Q)$, and then SQL statement

SELECT * FROM Papers as a, Authors as b,
Write as c WHERE a.PId = c.PId AND b.AId = c.AId AND a.PId = p_2 AND b.AId in
(a_3)

is executed to perform the appropriate joins involving p_2 and the joined tuples of A^Q.

When there are K JTTs in *Results* whose relevance scores are larger than all the $\tau(CN)$s (line 10) Algorithm 1 will stop, and then the largest $\tau(CN)$ is set as θ. The K JTTs are the top-K answers because all the unseen JTTs are of $score^{max} < \theta$.

6 Top-k Answers Maintenance

6.1 Handling Database Modifications

Algorithm 2 shows pseudocode of the top-k answers maintenance process of COKES, which is mainly to deal with two tasks for handling database modifications. One is to recalculate the relevance scores of the stored JTTs (line 2). The other is to find the new JTTs of $score^{max} > \theta$ and delete the expired JTTs (line 4). Updates are modeled as dele-tions followed by insertions. Deleting the expired JTTs is straightforward: all the JTTs that contain the deleted tuples should be deleted. As for finding the new JTTs, we use Algorithm 3 to do that.

Algorithm 2: TopKMaintenance

---

input : Q: a top-k keyword query; S: the stored state of Q; M: database modifications;
output: New top-k answers for Q

1 **if** *All the* $\ln\left(\frac{N+1}{df_w}\right)$ *values do not exceed their upper bounds after applying M* **then**
2   Update the statistics and recompute the relevance scores of the stored JTTs in S ;
3   Find the new JTTs whose $score^{max}$ are larger than θ and insert them into S ;
4   Delete the JTTs that contain the deleted tuples in M from S ;
5   **if** *the number of T in S and that $T.score > \theta$ is not smaller than k* **then**
6 | **return** the top-k JTTs in $S.Results$;
7 Change the $\ln^{max}\left(\frac{N+1}{df_w}\right)$ values and K adaptively ;
8 Reevaluate keyword query Q from scratch and create a new state of Q ;
9 **return** the top-k answers of Q;

There are two conditions for a keyword query needed to be reevaluated from scratch: (a) some $\ln\left(\dfrac{N+1}{df_w}\right)$ values exceed their upper bounds; and (b) the number of found JTTs of $score > \theta$ is smaller than k. Condition (a) is checked at the beginning (line 1). The rationale condition (b) (checked in line 5) is that when it is met the relevance scores of some top-k answers are smaller than the threshold θ, thus the unseen JTTs cannot be omitted due to the possibility of their relevance scores increasing to θ.

6.2 Finding New Top-k Answers

COKES uses Algorithm 3 to compute the JTTs that contain the new tuples of $score^{max}$ $> \theta$. A new tuple is handled differently according to its three possible positions in the tuple sets it belongs to in the order of $tscore^{max}$, which is illustrated in Fig. 4. First, t_{new} is ignored if $t_{new}.tscore^{max}$ is so small that $Max(t_{new}) < \theta$, recall that $Max(t_{new})$ indicates the maximum $score^{max}$ of the JTTs in which t_{new} can participate. Second, t_{new} is joined with the stored joined tuples in the other tuple sets if $Max(t_{new}) > \theta$ (lines 6–8). Finally, if $t_{new}.tscore^{max}$ is so large that $Max(getNext(R_i^Q))$ are higher than θ, t_{new} needs to be joined with the unjoined tuples in the R_i^Q (lines 9–12). In line 12, among the joined tuples of $R(t_{new})^Q$, only t_{new} participate in the joining.

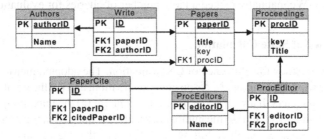

Fig. 4. The DBLP schema graph (PK stands for primary key, FK for foreign key)

Algorithm 3: Insertion

---

input : t_{new}: new tuple; Q: keyword query; S: stored state for Q

1 **if** $R(t_{new})^Q$ *is a new tuple set* **then** generate new CNs;
2 ;
3 $CNSet \leftarrow$ CNs in S that contains $R(t_{new})^Q \cup$ new CNs;
4 **foreach** *CN C in CNSet* **do**
5   **foreach** $R(t_{new})^Q$ *in C* **do**
6   **if** $Max(t_{new}) > \theta$ **then**
7   Insert t_{new} into $R(t_{new})^Q$ as a joined tuple;
8   Join t_{new} with the joined tuples in the other tuple sets of C and add the valid JTTs of $score^{max} > \theta$ into S ;
         // Join t_{new} with the unjoined tuples of C if $t_{new}.tscore^{max}$ is larger
9   **forall** *the other tuple sets* R_i^Q *of C except the root* **do**
10   **if** $Max(getNext(R_i^Q)) > \theta$ **then**
11   Query the unjoined tuples of R_i^Q except the newly inserted tuples that have not been processed ;
12   Join all the unjoined tuples t of $Max(t) > \theta$ in R_i^Q with the joined tuples in the other tuple sets and add the JTTs of $score^{max} > \theta$ into S ;
13   **else if** $R(t_{new})^Q$ *is the root of C* **then** Insert t_{new} into $R(t_{new})^Q$ as a joined tuple ;
14   ;

---

7   Experimental Evaluation

In this section we experimentally study the efficiency of COKES. For the evaluation, we used the DBLP (http://dblp.mpi-inf.mpg.de/dblp-mirror/index.php) data set. The downloaded XML file is decomposed into relations according to the schema shown in Fig. 4. Notice that the two arrows from *PaperCite* to Papers denote the foreign-key-references from *paperID* to *paperID* and *citedPaperID* to *paperID*, respectively. We define two general foreign key references for this database in our experiments: *Papers→Authors* and *Proceedings→ProcEditors*. We retrieve the data in the XML file sequentially until the size of the database is 52 MB. We ran our experiments using the MySQL (v5.1.44) with the default configurations on a Core2 Quad 2.83-GHz PC with 4 GB of RAM. We manually picked a large number of queries for evaluation.

7.1   Efficiency of State Calculation

Here we want to study the efficiency of CN evaluation. The adopted metrics are (1) the time for evaluating the generated CNs on query evaluation, and (2) the number of joined tuples. The parameters that we vary in the experiment are (a) the maximum size *MAXN* of the CNs (from 2 to 5), and (b) the number of results k requested in top-k queries (from 10 to 50). We compared the three following algorithms: the Algorithm 1 of this paper, the CN evaluation algorithm of [13], and the *Global Pipelined* algorithm (*GP*) of [8].

The main experiment results are shown in Fig. 5. In all the experiments, ΔN and Δdf_w are all set to 0.1%.

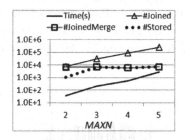

(a) Efficiency of Algorithm 1

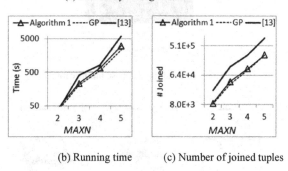

(b) Running time   (c) Number of joined tuples

Fig. 5. Efficiency of CN evaluation algorithms

Figure 5(a) shows the total running time (Time) and the number of all the joined tuples (#Joined) of Algorithm 1 of ten queries on $k = 30$, which grows exponentially as the maximum CN size grows since the number of generated CNs grows exponentially. #JoinedMerge in Fig. 5(a) is the total number of joined tuples of the ten queries if the joined tuples list of the same relation are merged, while #Stored is the total number of stored tuples when the two technologies both are used. Merging the joined tuples of the same relation can highly reduce the number of stored tuple. Figure 5(b) and (c) compare the total running time and the number of all the joined tuples of ten queries of the three algorithms on $k = 50$, respectively. The two metrics of Algorithm 1 are both larger than the GP algorithm and smaller than the CN evaluation algorithm of [13].

7.2 Efficiency of Top-*k* Answers Maintenance

In this experiment, we continue to retrieve data from the DBLP XML file to the database and delete tuples randomly from the database. The two metrics we considered are the time needed to handle each database modification, and the interval between two times of query evaluation. All the queries are maintained by setting $\eta = 600$ s, $MAXN = 3$ and $k = 30$. There are 167,831 database modifications (insertion or deletion) are handled, most of which are unmatched tuples. Figure 6(a) only shows the times that is larger than one second. The peaks in the figure corresponding to reevaluation of some queries. Figure 6(b) presents the distributions of the time intervals between two times of query reevaluations of the six queries, which are from three experiments under deferent insertion and deletion rates. The time intervals disperse around the expected interval η, and more than 87% of them are in the range of [η/2, 2η]. There are some small interval values of the experiment of $I = 3.8D$ for the reason that the Δdf are always be set to zero due to the small rate of deletion.

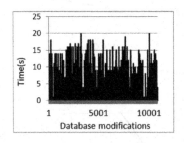

(a)   Times of handling database modifications

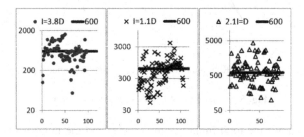

(b) Intervals between two times of query reevaluations
(I stands for insertion rate, and D for deletion rate)

Fig. 6.   Efficiency of top-k answers maintenance

8   Related Work

Keyword search in relational databases has received a lot of research interests in recent years. Existing approaches can be broadly classified into two categories: some based on candidate networks (schema-based) [6–8, 16–22] and others based on Steiner trees (graph-based) [1, 3, 5, 23–27]. Methods of the first category focus on supporting keyword search in an RDBMS using SQL. Since this implies making use of the database schema information to issue SQL queries in order to find structures for an l-keyword query, it is also called the schema-based approach [11]. The latter kinds of methods materialize the database as a data graph, where nodes are tuples of relations and directed edges are the foreign-key references between tuples. Then they find a set of structures (either steiner tree [1], distinct rooted tree [3], r-radius steiner graph [5], or multi-center subgraph [28]) in the database graph for a keyword query, which contain all or some of the keywords of the query. For details, please refer to the authoritative surveys [11, 29], which also provide many references. The materialized data graph should be updated for every database update; therefore, this model is not appropriate for databases that change frequently [29]. Thus our work adopts the query processing framework of the schema-based methods, and can be viewed as a further improvement to the direction of continuous keyword search in relational databases.

One highly related work is *S-KWS* [30], the other one is *KDynamic* [31]. Both of them are focus on finding all the valid JTTs on a high speed large relational data stream and can be classified as the schema-based systems. In this setting, it is necessary to find new JTTs or expire JTTs in order to monitor events that are implicitly interrelated over an open-ended relational data stream for a user-given l-keyword query [11]. The main problem they consider is how to reduce the CUP cost (for evaluating joins) and memory overhead (for intermediate results) in the CN evaluation step while tuples can be inserted/deleted on a high speed. The basic idea of their methods is to share the computational cost by using either the *operator mesh* or the *L*-Lattice. The problem considered in this two papers are totally different from ours, although we all need to response to continuous queries on a dynamic environment. They focus on finding all the valid answers, and answers ranking is not an important issue. In contrary, we need to compute the top-k answers, which have the inertia in response to changes in the database. Therefore, the small amount of most related tuples that are stored in the state are adequate to maintain the top-k answers in most cases.

9   Conclusion

In this paper, we have studied the problem of answering continuous top-k keyword queries in relational databases. We proposed an approach COKES that finds the answers whose upper bounds of future relevance scores are larger than a threshold. Algorithms to maintain the top-k answer list after database modifications were also presented. Our method can efficiently maintain the top-k answers for a query without fully reevaluating the keyword query. COKES can, therefore, be used to solve the problem of continuous keyword search in relational databases with frequent updates.

Acknowledgments. This research was partly supported by the Natural Science Foundation of Shanghai under grant No.~14ZR1427700 and the Shanghai Engineering Research Center for Broadband Technologies & Applications (14DZ2280100).

References

1. Aditya, B., Bhalotia, G., Chakrabarti, S., Hulgeri, A., Nakhe, C., Parag, P.: BANKS: browsing and keyword searching in relational databases. In: VLDB, pp. 1083–1086 (2002)
2. Li, G., Zhou, X., Feng, J., Wang, J.: Progressive keyword search in relational databases. In: ICDE, pp. 1183–1186 (2009)

3. Kacholia, V., Pandit, S., Chakrabarti, S., Sudarshan, S., Desai, R., Karambelkar, H.: Bidirectional expansion for keyword search on graph databases. In: VLDB, pp. 505–516 (2005)
4. He, H., Wang, H., Yang, J., Yu, P.S.: BLINKS: ranked keyword searches on graphs. In: ACM SIGMOD, New York, NY, USA, pp. 305–316. ACM (2007)
5. Li, G., Ooi, B.C., Feng, J., Wang, J., Zhou, L.: EASE: an effective 3-in-1 keyword search method for unstructured, semi-structured and structured data. In: ACM SIGMOD, pp. 903–914 (2008)
6. Agrawal, S., Chaudhuri, S., Das, G.: DBXplorer: a system for keyword-based search over relational databases. In: ICDE, pp. 5–16 (2002)
7. Hristidisand, V., Papakonstantinou, Y.: DISCOVER: keyword search in relational databases. In: VLDB, pp. 670–681 (2002)
8. Hristidis, V., Gravano, L., Papakonstantinou, Y.: Efficient IR-style keyword search over relational databases. In: VLDB, pp. 850–861 (2003)
9. Liu, F., Yu, C., Meng, W., Chowdhury, A.: Effective keyword search in relational databases. In: ACM SIGMOD, pp. 563–574 (2006)
10. Luo, Y., Lin, X., Wang, W., Zhou, X.: SPARK: top-k keyword query in relational databases. In: ACM SIGMOD, pp. 115–126 (2007)
11. Yu, J.X., Qin, L., Chang, L.: Keyword search in relational databases: a survey. Bull. IEEE Tech. Committee Data Eng. **33**(10), 67–78 (2010)
12. Luo, Y.: SPARK: A Keyword Search System on Relational Databases, Ph.D. thesis, The University of New South Wales (2009)
13. Xu, Y., Ishikawa, Y., Guan, J.: Efficient continuous top-k keyword search in relational databases. In: Chen, L., Tang, C., Yang, J., Gao, Y. (eds.) WAIM 2010. LNCS, vol. 6184, pp. 755–767. Springer, Heidelberg (2010). https://doi.org/10.1007/978-3-642-14246-8_71
14. Fagin, R., Lotem, A., Naor, M.: Optimal aggregation algorithms for middleware. J. Comput. Syst. Sci. **66**(4), 614–656 (2003)
15. Burns, A.: Preemptive priority-based scheduling: an appropriate engineering approach. In: Advances in real-time systems, pp. 225–248 (1995)
16. Zeng, Z., Bao, Z., Ling, T.W., Lee, M.L.: iSearch: an interpretation based framework for keyword search in relational databases. In: KEYS, pp. 3–10 (2012)
17. Xu, Y., Guan, J., Ishikawa, Y.: Scalable top-k keyword search in relational databases. In: Lee, S.-g., Peng, Z., Zhou, X., Moon, Y.-S., Unland, R., Yoo, J. (eds.) DASFAA 2012. LNCS, vol. 7239, pp. 65–80. Springer, Heidelberg (2012). https://doi.org/10.1007/978-3-642-29035-0_5
18. Xu, Y., Guan, J., Li, F., Zhou, S.: Scalable continual top-k keyword search in relational databases. Data Knowl. Eng. **86**, 206–223 (2013)
19. de Oliveira, P., da Silva, A.S., de Moura, E.S.: Ranking candidate networks of relations to improve keyword search over relational databases. In: 31st IEEE International Conference on Data Engineering, ICDE 2015, Seoul, South Korea, 13–17 April 2015, pp. 399–410 (2015)
20. Zeng, Z., Bao, Z., Lee, M., Ling, T.W.: Towards an interactive keyword search over relational databases. In: Proceedings of the 24th International Conference on World Wide Web Companion, WWW 2015, Florence, Italy, 18–22 May 2015, Companion Volume, pp. 259–262 (2015)
21. Kargar, M., An, A., Cercone, N., Godfrey, P., Szlichta, J., Yu, X.: Meaningful keyword search in relational databases with large and complex schema. In: 31st IEEE International Conference on Data Engineering, ICDE 2015, Seoul, South Korea, 13–17 April 2015, pp. 411–422 (2015)

22. Zhou, J., Liu, Y., Yu, Z.: Improving the effectiveness of keyword search in databases using query logs. In: Proceedings of 16th International Conference on Web-Age Information Management, WAIM 2015, Qingdao, China, 8–10 June 2015, pp. 193–206 (2015)
23. Ling, T.W., Le, T.N., Zeng, Z.: Towards an intelligent keyword search over XML and relational databases. In: International Conference on Big Data and Smart Computing, BIGCOMP 2014, Bangkok, Thailand, 15–17 January 2014, pp. 1–6 (2014)
24. Torlone, R.: Towards a new foundation for keyword search in relational databases. In: Proceedings of the 8th Alberto Mendelzon Workshop on Foundations of Data Management, Cartagena de Indias, Colombia, 4–6 June 2014 (2014)
25. Lin, Z., Li, Y., Lai, Y.: Improve the effectiveness of keyword search over relational database by node-temperature-based ant colony optimization. In: 12th International Conference on Fuzzy Systems and Knowledge Discovery, FSKD 2015, Zhangjiajie, China, 15–17 August 2015, pp. 1209–1214 (2015)
26. Ling, T.W., Zeng, Z., Le, T.N., Lee, M.: Ora-semantics based keyword search in XML and relational databases. In: 32nd IEEE International Conference on Data Engineering Workshops, ICDE Workshops 2016, Helsinki, Finland, 16–20 May 2016, pp. 157–160 (2016)
27. Yu, Z., Yu, X., Chen, Y., Ma, K.: Distributed top-*k* keyword search over very large databases with map reduce. In: 2016 IEEE International Congress on Big Data, San Francisco, CA, USA, June 27–July 2 2016, pp. 349–352 (2016)
28. Qin, L., Yu, J.X., Chang, L., Tao, Y.: Querying communities in relational databases. In: ICDE, pp. 724–735 (2009)
29. Jaehui, P., Sang-goo, L.: Keyword search in relational databases. Knowl. Inf. Syst. **26**(2), 175–193 (2011)
30. Markowetz, A., Yang, Y., Papadias, D.: Keyword search on relational data streams. In: ACM SIGMOD, pp. 605–616 (2007)
31. Qin, L., Yu, J.X., Chang, L., Tao, Y.: Scalable keyword search on large data streams. In: ICDE, pp. 1199–1202 (2009)

Core Competencies Keywords Discovering Algorithm for Employment Advertisements

Xiaoping Du, Lelai Deng[✉], Xingzhi Zhang, and Qinghong Yang

Beihang University, No. 37 Xueyuan Rd., Haidian District, Beijing, China
{xpdu, denglelai, yangqh}@buaa.edu.cn, zxzbos@gmail.com

Abstract. As librarianship evolves, it is important to understand the changes taken place in its core competencies. One good way to do this is to analyze job advertisements (ads) for professional librarian positions. Most related works are based on manual method; the semi-automatic framework requires a classifier consisting of manual rulesets as input. In this paper, a framework and a multi-label short text clustering algorithm, ICNTC, are proposed to automatically identify core competencies from job ads. Data from the American Library Association (ALA) Joblist from 2009 through 2014 is used to validate the method. The analysis of experiment results shows that the method may identify most of core competencies, with a good performance in evaluating the frequency of each competencies. The accuracy of keyword extraction on ALA dataset is $89 \pm 1.3\%$.

Keywords: Core competency · Keywords discovering · Job advertisement
Text clustering

1 Introduction

This paper focus on the discovering of core competencies from American Librarian Ads. In America, there is a huge demand for new librarians. Thousands of recruitment advertisements were put on the Internet every day. Meanwhile, it's a big headache for both employers and employees. As for employers, since there is often a length limit for every advertisement, nearly 200 words, it's necessary to use certain short words (almost with high frequencies, we named it core competencies) to explain the demand precisely. For employees, it's a waste of time to read through all the advertisements to find an appropriate librarian job. So, it's better to use these core competencies to filter advertisements whose jobs are not suitable for them.

Thus, discovering the core competencies of librarian forms a crucial task in library information science. Core competencies analysis may serve as vital resources in market demand analysis and guidance for both library employers and employees. One basic thesis is, the frequency of competency tags may reflect the significance of them. "Core Competency" is the subset of all occurring competencies that have higher frequency than the others.

However, discovering core competencies often faces two main problems. One is, different from text in traditional text mining, job advertisement only contains less than 200 words, which we named it short text. It's harder to carry out semantics and context

H. Yuan et al. (Eds.): GSKI 2017, CCIS 849, pp. 218–231, 2018.
https://doi.org/10.1007/978-981-13-0896-3_22

analysis based on short text. The other problem is, most core competencies are phrases which two or three words co-exist in the context. Nevertheless, words that often co-exist sometimes are not core competencies but meaningless phrases. For example, in our experiments, "positive attitude" is a high frequency phrase, meanwhile, to employers and employees, it only refers to a basic requirement instead of a core competency.

Adjusted methods based on content analysis [1] have been applied to these problems, which manually extract competency tags from the textual content of job advertisements. Compared to focus group or similar methods, content analysis pro-vides a relatively objective way to extract the core competency tag from job advertisements. Moreover, it provides a quantitative way to provide a relatively objective way to extract the core competency tag from job advertisements. At the same time, scaling such methods is a daunting task since it is labor-intensive and error-prone, especially in big data scenarios. Content Analysis has high accuracy since domain expertise is usually a pre-condition for it. But the huge human expenses of manual content analysis make it incapable to process massive (over thousands) job ads. Debortoli et al. [2] used Latent Semantic Analysis (LSA) to extract competency tags from massive job ads regarding big data (BD, in short) and business intelligence (BI, in short) positions. Data resource of Debortoli's experiment is Huvila's database [3]. The experimental performance is judged by precision (extracted competency tags to actual tags ratio) and recall rate (extracted competency tags to actual competency tags ratio). Experimental result shows that precision is high but recall rate is low. Debortoli's method performs well in discovering tags while unable to precisely filter the competency tags.

Yang et al. [4] introduced a semi-automatic method in 2016, which uses code-book (a multi-tags classifier based on key-word rules) to extract competency tags from coding units (that is, sentences describing competencies in advertisements). Yang's method decrease the laboratory expense since it only relies on initial code-book. However, a shortcoming is that there are many iterations where each requires knowledge from domain experts.

Based on CNTC algorithm, we gave an improved core competency discovering algorithm in this paper, ICNTC. Compared to Yang's method [4], ICNTC can be directly applied to job ads. The result of ICNTC is stable without manual correction in competency clusters. Codebook constructed after ICNTC may serve as initial code-book for Yang's method. It helps iterative development get a better performance.

We summarize our main contributions as follows:

- We propose a framework based on clustering to construct codebook automatically;
- We propose ICNTC, a multi-label short text clustering algorithm, to perform the clustering of recording units;
- We evaluate the efficacy of ICNTC using job advertisements collected from ALA JobList.

2 Related Work

A Most short texts are data spared and ambiguous [1]. Short texts are also lack of word co-occurrence information and contextual information in sentences describing competencies. Traditional text mining methods neglect the semantic relation in words [2–4], and thus may not suitable for analyzing short text in most conditions. To reduce the data sparsity and ambiguity of short texts, LSA or similar word-based short text extension are popular solutions. Another popular solution is to use word similarity to extend the meaning of context.

Theme model is a main tool used in short text mining. Cai [5] tried to use PLSA to extract themes from data. It trained two weak classifiers with raw data separately, then used the integration of these two-weak classifier in further classification. Phan [6, 7] put forward a general framework appending theme name from Latent Dirichlet Allocation (LDA) to the context. It expands the meaning in different segments. Phan's method doesn't consider the themes on different layers. Chen [8] improved Phan's method, extracting themes on multi-granularity. It adds the short text modelling ac-curacy. Yan [11] introduced a BTM theme model, which directly build the word occurrence model on the whole corpora. Yan's algorithm fully used global information. Zhu [9] raised up a non-probabilistic sparse theme coding (STC) method. It directly controls the sparsity of results and reduces topic mixture in probabilistic model.

Semantic similarity is usually calculated by word map. Word map reflects the se-mantic relations of words. Zhang [10] put forward a context similarity measurement method based on word map. In Yang's experiment, Wiki Encyclopedias was the background knowledge resource in discovering semantic relations. Jain [11] put forward a multi-granularity harmonic analysis method based on word-to-word co-occurrence map. This method can represent word in sparse way and determine semantically consistent theme from raw data.

There are some other methods in measuring similarity between words. Bollegala [12] found semantic similarity can be measured through Web information. In Bollegala's experiment, he used web page counting and context segment similarity to measure the word similarity. Sun [13] put forward a simple short text clustering method. He takes majority voting in searching result sample as prediction category. Sahami and Heilman [14] recommended querying with short text, which extends the short text by searching results.

It's a feasible way to model nature language with artificial neural network. After modelling we'll get word vectors as byproduct [15]. Le and Mikolov [16] put forward segment vector algorithm to learn the document feature. Socher [17] raised up a re-current neural network (RNN). It proved to be reliable in sentence representation construction. Wang [18] introduced a new short text modeling method based on semantic clustering and convolution neural network.

Short text clustering is another crux after short text modeling. Shortage in enough word term co-occurrence information and context sharing information usually makes the short text similarity calculation and clustering hard. There are two common solutions to this problem, one is extending the representation of short text, the other is improving clustering algorithms for short text.

Hotho [19] discovered that introducing background knowledge such as Wordnet will greatly improve text clustering performance. Banerjee [20] compared the additionally extended feature representation with Wiki Encyclopedias in conventional word-bag model. Short text clustering accuracy improved after background knowledge introducing. Hu [21] constructed a new framework, which represents the extension reconstruction with three-layer structure. Both the inner semantic and external knowledge of raw context improved the short-text clustering performance.

Errecalde [22] came up with a new algorithm integrating silhouette coefficients at different stages and attraction concepts. Ramgrej [23] compared several clustering algorithms including K-means document clustering methods, singular value decomposition (SVD) methods and map-based methods. Twitter corpus was applied to judge the performance of these algorithms. Experiment result showed that map based clustering algorithm had the best performance in Twitter corpus. Gu [24] put forward a user oriented short text clustering algorithm. During the pretreatment stage, semantic independent word dictionary recognized and removed semantic independent words. These words were then used to classify dictionary specification semantics. Gu pro-posed a K-gram based same position meta similarity calculation method. It uses hierarchical clustering to do text clustering. Finegan-Dollak [25] explored how the context feature of short text influent the similarity measurement and clustering algorithm. He discovered that semantic similarity measurement has better performance than conventional n-grams similarity algorithm. Map based clustering algorithm has better performance on high density data especially.

3   Framework

If we take every job ad as one sample, since there are several competency tags in certain job ad, sentences which describe competencies will interfere with each other. Validity of clustering results becomes lower because of this interfere. In our experiment, coding units are those sentences which describe the requirements of employers. It'll directly tell readers related competencies. A coding unit only describes one competency tag under most situations. By clustering the coding units, we'll get the clusters for competency tags as well.

Figure 1 shows the process of competency list construction and competency recognition. Firstly, clustering the coding units and getting clusters. Then combining the clusters by the realistic meanings of each cluster and constructing competency tags list. Final combination makes sure the one-to-one match between every competency tag and cluster. When clustering is finished, the sample competency tag recognition can be carried out with the relation between clusters and competency tags. Competency tag recognition results could be implanted to count the competency tag frequency in given sample. Tag frequency reveals the importance of every competency tag.

It needs to be stressed that we only took parts of clusters to carry out competency tag construction and left out many non-tag context. Among these non-tag samples, some are indeed non-coding-unit samples while others included coding units. After eliminating interference from tagged samples, this framework helps discover valuable clusters from non-tag samples.

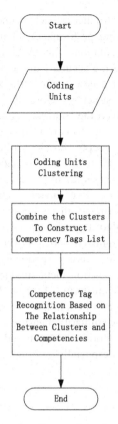

Fig. 1. Extraction process of extraction of competencies in job ad

4   Segment-Based Multi-label Clustering Algorithm

4.1   Preprocess

Before tag clustering, it's necessary to split the job ad into coding units (in word bag model) to extract requirement. The key of recruitment requirements extraction is to detect the beginning and end of recruitment requirement in job ad context. Supposing the employment job ads set is $A = \{a_1, a_2, a_3, ..., a_N\}$, sentences in a_i form a list $Si = [s_{i,\ 1}, s_{i,\ 2}, ..., s_{i,\ j}, ...]$. The rule based classifier is designed according to the structure features of formatted or plain recruitment job advertisement. The start sentence $s_{i,\ js}$ and end sentence $s_{i,\ je}$ of requirement c, $js <= j <= je$. Only when $js <= j <= je$, si, j will be considered as recruitment requirements. In this situation, $S'i = \{si, js, si, js + 1, si, js + 2, ..., si, je\}$.

In preprocess stage, the recruitment job ads will be sorted to two categories: formatted job ads and plain job ads. These two categories will be processed separately.

The most obvious difference between formatted recruitment advertisements and plain recruitment advertisements is that, some special introductive recruitment words such as 'Requirements:' are only contained in formatted recruitment advertisements. If such structure sentences are in Si, the recruitment advertisement will be sorted to formatted recruitment advertisement, sentence is si, js-1. Otherwise, this advertisement is plain advertisement.

If one recruitment is plain advertisement, then there may be several sentences in Si. These sentences include certain words, for example, "require" and "prefer". Else, Si possibly doesn't contain recruitment requirements. Si sometimes has URL which includes more specific information instead. Then we abort these advertisements. When several such sentences inside Si, the first sentence will be marked si, js.

For formatted advertisement, if there are special identifiers in recruitment requirements, then si, je is the last sentence which contains special identifiers. For plain recruitment advertisements, without special identifiers, there may be several sentences in Si. These sentences contain other information identifiers, such as "current CV". Once we find such sentences in Si, the first of them is si, je, otherwise, si, je is the last sentence in Si.

During the above procedure, special structure and identifier is limited in types. This paper constructs regular expressions to carry out judgment works. Until now, we get the start point and end point of requirement in recruitment advertisements. Si represents for the sentences set between start point and end point, also describing recruitment requirements.

4.2   Introduction of RMcut and CNTC

RMCut is an evaluation indicator for the performance of short-text clustering. When using this indicator, we model the short text set R to related weighted undirected graph GR. The n samples in short text set represent n vertexes of graph. Every two points form a side, the weight of this side reflects the similarity between the corresponding short-texts of vertexes. When R is divided into K clusters, every sample only belongs to one cluster, RMCut can be calculated by the following formula:

$$RMCut(R_1, R_2, \ldots, R_k, \ldots, R_K) = \sum_{k=1}^{K} MCut(R_k, R) \tag{1}$$

$$MCut(R_k, R) = \frac{cut(R_k, R - R_k)}{|R_k| \cdot \sum_{r_i, r_j \in R_k} sim(r_i, r_j)} \tag{2}$$

In the formula above, cut(Rk, R–Rk) is the cut of points in Rk and R–Rk. Cut is considered as similarity of different clusters. cut(Rk, R–Rk) equals to the sum of weight of two points, one point in Rk, the other in R–Rk. The calculation formula is:

$$cut(R_k, R - R_k) = \sum_{r_i \in R_k} \sum_{r_j \in R - R_k} sim(r_i, r_j) \tag{3}$$

CNTC algorithm is a short text clustering algorithm. CNTC takes partition strategy, selecting one core item tj in every turn. The partition process of core item cluster is: departing the coding units without core item from current cluster and forming a new cluster. Core items are selected in greedy way, that is, defining a clustering performance evaluation function of clustering result φ:

$$\mathrm{eval}(\varphi_K) = \mathrm{RMCut}(R_0, \ldots, R_K) \tag{4}$$

In the K'+1th iteration in cluster partition, $Cand_{K',I}$ is the core item partition result $\varphi_{K'+1,I}$ of $\varphi_{K'}$. The evaluation function of candidates score $(Cand_{K',i}) = \mathrm{eval}(\varphi_{K'+1,i}) - \mathrm{eval}(\varphi_K)$. Candidate who has the highest score will be considered as core item.

4.3 Feature Extension Based on Frequent Term Sets

Here we choose partition based clustering method to finish clustering. Core thesis is there are keywords in contexts. Contexts which have same key words having high similarity. On the contrast, contexts which have different key words having low similarity. During the extraction process of competency tags, one competency tag may contain plenty of keywords. The co-occurrence of these keywords is not affirmative. They are used to describe the competency tag. For example, 'communication' and 'interpersonal' are both keywords for competency tag 'communication skills'. When there occurs a turn 'communication' is the core word for partition of a certain cluster, among the two new clusters after partition, the cluster without 'communication' will not take 'interpersonal' as the keyword for new cluster. Since the samples contain 'interpersonal' is quite few. Even though we combined clusters artificially, the samples containing 'interpersonal' while excluding 'communication' will not form a single cluster. These samples are also excluded from the competency cluster of 'communication skills'.

The word bag of each coding unit will be seen as an affair in association rules mining. When directly using word bag to construct vector space of coding units, a word term set is a candidate set. For every two-candidate item set <t1, t2> , t1|t2 (only one of t1 and t2 exists in sample text) and t1&t2 (both t1 and t2 exist in sample text) are added in term set. Partition driven by interpersonal| communication could solve some common problems.

Terms having low support, due to the lack of statistical meaning, will be aborted in the feature selection during the construction of competency clusters. We set a threshold for support, min_support, as well. Only frequent one-item set and frequent two-item set were used to construct the corresponding vector space for coding units.

According to the partition strategy of clustering, the realistic meaning of core item (Rk, tj), tj is the keyword for competency cluster Rk. The coding units with tj and units without tj in Rk belong to two different competency tags. So, we set the three necessary conditions for tj:

(1) tj has high word frequency in Rk and the coding units with tj in Rk can form statistically significant competency cluster;
(2) tj is a keyword for certain competency, low word frequency in R–Rk
(3) tj doesn't occur in rule set of Rk

According to TF-IDF, setting Candk, i = (Rk, tj), we can calculate pre-score (Candk, i):

$$\text{pre}_{\text{score}\left(Cand_{K',i}\right)} = \begin{cases} 0, & \text{if } t_j \text{ in the rule set of}, R_{K'} \\ \frac{F\left(t_j, R_{K'}\right)}{idf\left(t_j\right)}, & \text{otherwise} \end{cases} \tag{5}$$

F(tj, Rk) and idf(tj) were got in one traverse. Therefore, the time complicity of calculating O(M) candidate item is O(M).

Standard procedure is the partition procedure under non-candidate selection after K turns of iteration. With the candidate screening principle, if the partition process is aligned with standard procedure when L = Lbase, then when L > Lbase the partion process should be aligned with standard process too. In parameter selection, several possible L values were taken in experiment, if the partition process doesn't change when L beyond a certain threshold, we considered the partition process aligned with standard process. The minimum L-value we got is appropriate parameter.

The number of target competencies is K, taking the above cluster partition strategy, K+1 competencies are got. Among them, R0 is the coding units set doesn't belong to any competency tags. Any other competency cluster Ri except Ri, the coding units inside which will be included in one same competency tag. Then, by rules set in output order, we'll get the coding rule for every cluster, such as librari+experi-commun-work-knowledg+academic".

4.4   Code Rule Extension

When coding the rule "-librari+experi-commun-work-knowledg+academic", ac-cording to partition strategy, "-librari" and "-commun-work-knowledg+academic" are by-products of other cluster partitions. They have low realistic meaning for represent-ing tags. It's reasonable to simplify the rule list, the front of series negative rules, such as "-librari+experi-commun-work-knowledg+academic", can be simplified as "+experi+academic". Only the serial distinct negative rules having the same rules set. There may exist some similar coding units being classified to different clusters. Combination of such competency clusters is necessary. After simplification, there may be several different competency clusters intersecting with rule set classification results aligned. In this way, the strongly interpretative codebook which suits for multi-tag classification is recorded.

5   Experiment

5.1   Dataset

The data source of this paper is ALA Joblist, ranging from year 2009 to 2014. There are 9573 recruitment advertisements from Jan 1st, 2009 to Apr 25th, 2014 in ALA Joblist, full-text and basic description both included. As the first step for data analysis, Fig. 1 shows the data process procedure. After filtering out the Canadian advertisements, 9198 recruitment advertisement were remained as population data. In addition, we made a conventional context analysis based on codebook from 200 recruitment advertisements.

5.2 Design of Experiment

The experiment has two main parts:

(1) Processing recruitment advertisements with recruitment advertisement competency tag extraction method. The output is competency tag list and the frequency of every competency tags in recruitment advertisements.
(2) Making statistical analysis on American librarian core competencies, comparing the results with relative researches to identify the validity of the competency tag extraction method.

The specific process is:

Firstly, employing the advertisement competency tag extraction method in this paper to analyze recruitment advertisements in initial data set to get the codebook and coding results. Then coding the American librarian recruitment advertisements, making statistical analysis on coding results to get the core competencies of American librarians and their changing trends. Finally comparing the statistical result with core competencies in corresponding researches to validate the effectiveness and robustness of INTC.

It needs to be emphasized that there is no open source basic dataset for competency tag recognition results comparison. Since the differences between data sources, simply comparing the competency tags frequencies to other researches is nonsense.

This paper marks the importance of competency tags by the frequency of them in the whole sample. Specific analysis on importance recognition result was compared to relative theory researches on market analysis. If the experimental result is aligned with market demand, the recruitment advertisement competency tag extraction method in this paper will be proved effective.

5.3 Parameters Performance

For parameter min_support was applied to do the text feature expression of coding units, also functioning as basis of further experiment, min_support needs to be confirmed in advance. Excessive low min_support value will lead to dimension explosion. When setting min_support as 1, the scale of term set can reach $O(n2)$, n represents the number of words in word list, approximately 100,000. When min_support is too large, the number of features left will be too few, which makes the feature vectors of coding units sparse. Min_support depends on the supportive calculated amount. In this paper, min_support is set as 3, the scale of term set is 10 thousand.

As is illustrated in correlation theories, when L is approaching positive infinite, in every turn of iteration, there will be a locally optimal solution, standard process. Selecting the appropriate L will not only reducing the runtime of algorithm, but also aligning the partition procedure with standard process.

We could take several L values for parameter selection to determine the influence of L value on runtime and RMCut. In related researches on competency, the number of competency tags in codebook usually is around 20. Table 1 shows the result of experiment. Here is the summary of experiment result:

Table 1. The effect of L value on experiment results

L	15 turns' runtime (s)	15 turns' RMCut	30 turns' runtime (s)	30 turns' RMCut
5	25	118.39	38	1689.59
10	40	92.78	58	1503.03
20	68	74.43	99	1372.67
50	145	74.43	207	1372.67
100	281	74.43	405	1372.67
3000	7873	74.43	12332	1372.67

1. Candidate item selection will greatly reduce the time complexity
2. Time complexity of ICNTC algorithm is in direct proportion to L value
3. Result of clustering gets better with the growth of L value
4. When L value is over 20, both clustering performance and the corresponding process becomes stable
5. Clustering results are approaching stable and partition process is aligned with standard process.

As stated above, when L value is too small, such as 1, the run time will be pretty short while partition process is quite far from standard process. With the increasing of L value, RMCut of partition result is becoming close to standard process, with partition process approaching standard process. The time when L beyond a certain value, partition process will be consistent with standard process, while runtime still far lower than standard process.

So, it's advised to take several small L values to carry out the experiment, when L value over a threshold making the partition process stable, it's the time that partition process is consistent with standard process.

Number of tag clusters K determines the granularity after clustering. Among the clustering algorithms, K-means for example, is usually based on a certain clustering result evaluation function to draw a relation diagram of ration and K value to find the inflection point. K value at inflection point is considered the best K value. In this paper, the iteration process is confirmed and manual taking improvement on clustering result. The redundancy partition in iteration process thus can be restored in manual improvement process. In another word, the increasing of K value has no negative effect on the validity of clustering, only adding the manual improvement work.

We may as well try to use small K values to examine the competency coverage rate of related competency tag list, then gradually increasing the K value. In this paper, we take three K values (20/50/100) to do the experiment. Experiment result shows when K is set as 100, the competency coverage rate of related competency tag list is already 90%. We set K as 100 to carry out further experiments.

5.4   Analysis

In line with the experiment settings and parameter selection above, we take min_-support as 3, L as 50 and K as 100 to conduct the experiment. In the end, we got a competency tags list and the result of competency recognition. To validate the

Table 2. Codebook from competency extraction on huge dataset

Competencies in this paper	Part of coding rules	Hartnett's competencies	Frequency
Minimum degree	+degre-second-addit-advanc	Minimum degree	96%
Communication skills	+commun+interperson	Communication skills, general	57%
Work collaboratively	+work+collabor+work+team	Work collaboratively	40%
Problem solving	+problem+solv+analyt	Analytical, problem solving skills	32%
Change and flexibility	+work+chang+adapt+chang	Change/flexibility	28%
Customer service	+servic+custom+servic+orient	Customer service	24%
Electronic resources	+electron+resource+online+resource	Electronic resources, general	23%
		Technical/system-related, general	20%
Industry trends	+familiar+trend +current+trend	Industry knowledge	15%
		Technical/system-related: website	15%
Technical/system-related: ILS	+librari+system+il	Technical/system-related: ILS	14%
Years of experience: education	+experi+instruct +experi+educ	Years of experience: general	14%
General work experience	+profession+experi+librari		
Years of experience: academic library	+experi+academ	Years of experience: academic library	14%
Technical knowledge, general	+knowledg+techni	Knowledge of technical/system-related, general	13%
		Electronic resources: management/maintenance	12%
		Professional growth and development	12%
Work independently	+work+independ	Work independently	12%
Second degree	+master+second +degree+second	Secondary degree/background	11%
Supervise	+manag+project +experi+supervisori	Project management	11%
		Scholarly & creative activity	10%

codebook, researchers compare competency tags in the codebook with Hartnett's codebook [9], comparison result is shown in Table 2.

There we only provide the competency list (recruitment requirements) whose frequency is over 10% in Hartnett's paper. After comparison, the highest frequency competencies were extracted using the competency extraction method in this paper. Since part of competencies were not extracted, the keywords are distributed.

For example, keywords of "Technical/system-related, website" includes "css", "java" and so on. For the defuzzed model in our clustering algorithm, it's a defection to process several distributed keywords.

6 Conclusions

Competency tags extraction in recruitment advertisement is a vital method in librarian competency research, showing higher objective and reliable than other similar methods. In this paper, a non-supervision competency tags extraction algorithm is put forward. The core concept is construct a codebook suitable for multi-tag classification in non-tag coding units set, realizing the extraction of competency tag in recruitment advertisements. Experiment result shows that the improvement of CNTC algorithm is reasonable and effective. Competency tags extraction method in recruitment advertisement got a realistic librarian competency analysis result. We also constructed a strong accuracy and interpretable codebook.

It's still promotable to do the following improvements in construction of codebook:

- Constructing external knowledge library in Liberian field, introducing external knowledge to the codebook construction replacing human judgement.
- Greedy strategy-based cluster partition in this paper is limited in locally optimal solution. Heuristic search is a promising alternative for partition of clusters.

References

1. Holmberg, K., Huvila, I., Kronqvist Berg, M., WidnWulff, G.: What is library 2.0? J. Documentation **65**(4), 668–681 (2009)
2. Debortoli, S., Mller, O., Brocke, J.V.: Comparing business intelligence and big data skills. Bus. Inf. Syst. Eng. **6**(5), 289–300 (2014)
3. Huvila, I., Holmberg, K., Kronqvistberg, M., Nivakoski, O., Widn, G.: What is librarian 2.0–new competencies or interactive relations? a library professional viewpoint. J. Librarianship Inf. Sci. **45**(3), 198–205 (2013)
4. Yang, Q., Zhang, X., Du, X., Bielefield, A., Liu, Y.Q.: Current market demand for core competencies of librarianship a text mining study of American library association's advertisements from 2009 through 2014. Appl. Sci. **6**(2), 48 (2016)

5. Cai, D., Wang, X., He, X.: Probabilistic dyadic data analysis with local and global consistency. In: Proceedings of the International Conference on Machine Learning, ICML 2009, Montreal, Quebec, Canada, p. 14, June 2009

6. Phan, X.H., Nguyen, C.T., Le, D.T., Nguyen, L.M., Horiguchi, S., Ha, Q.T.: Ahiddentopic-based framework toward building applications with short web documents. IEEE Trans. Knowl. Data Eng. **23**(7), 961–976 (2010)

7. Phan, X.H., Nguyen, L.M., Horiguchi, S.: Learning to classify short and sparse text & web with hidden topics from large-scale data collections. In: Proceedings of the International Conference on World Wide Web, WWW 2008, Beijing, China, pp. 91–100, April 2008

8. Cheng, X., Yan, X., Lan, Y., Guo, J.: BTM: topic modeling over short texts. IEEE Trans. Knowl. Data Eng. **26**(12), 2928–2941 (2014)

9. Zhu, J., Ning, C., Xing, E.P.: Bayesian inference with posterior regularization and infinite latent support vector machines. J. Mach. Learn. Res. **15**(1), 1799–1847 (2012)

10. Zhang, W., Zhang, Q., Yu, B., Zhao, L.: Knowledge map of creativity research based on keywords network and co-word analysis, 1992–2011. Qual. Quant. **49**(3), 1023–1038 (2015)

11. Jain, P.K., Lungu, E.M.: Harmonic analysis of solar radiation data for Sebele, Botswana. In: World Renewable Energy Conference Vi, pp. 2575–2578 (2000)

12. Bollegala, D., Ishizuka, M., Matsuo, Y.: Measuring semantic similarity between words using web search engines. In: International Conference on World Wide Web, pp. 757–766 (2007)

13. Sun, A.: Short text classification using very few words. In: Proceedings of the 35th International ACM SIGIR Conference on Research and Development in Information Retrieval, pp. 1145–1146 (2012)

14. Sahami, M., Heilman, T.D.: A web-based kernel function for measuring the similarity of short text snippets. In: International Conference on World Wide Web, WWW 2006, Edinburgh, Scotland, UK, pp. 377–386, May 2006

15. Basile, P., Caputo, A., Semeraro, G.: Semantic vectors: an information retrieval scenario. In: IIR 2010 Proceedings of the First Italian Information Retrieval Workshop, Padua, Italy, pp. 1–5, January 2010

16. Le, Q.V., Mikolov, T.: Distributed representations of sentences and documents. Comput. Sci. 188–1196 (2014)

17. Socher, R., Huval, B., Manning, C.D., Ng, A.Y.: Semantic compositionality through recursive matrix-vector spaces. In: Joint Conference on Empirical Methods in Natural Language Processing and Computational Natural Language Learning, pp. 1201–1211 (2012)

18. Wang, P., Xu, J., Xu, B., Liu, C., Zhang, H., Wang, F., Hao, H.: Semantic clustering and convolutional neural network for short text categorization. In: Meeting of the Association for Computational Linguistics and the International Joint Conference on Natural Language Processing

19. Hotho, A., Staab, S., Stumme, G.: Wordnet improves text document clustering. In: Proceedings of the Sigrid Semantic Web Workshop, pp. 541–544 (2003)

20. Banerjee, S., Ramanathan, K., Gupta, A.: Clustering short texts using Wikipedia. In: SIGIR 2007: Proceedings of the International ACM SIGIR Conference on Research and Development in Information Retrieval, Amsterdam, The Netherlands, pp. 787–788, July 2007

21. Hu, X., Sun, N., Zhang, C., Chua, T.S.: Exploiting internal and external semantics for the clustering of short texts using world knowledge. In: ACM Conference on Information and Knowledge Management, CIKM 2009, Hong Kong, China, pp. 919–928, November 2009

22. Errecalde, M.L., Ingaramo, D.A.: A new anttree-based algorithm for clustering short text corpora. J. Comput. Sci. Technol. **10**(1), 1–7 (2010)

23. Rangrej, A., Kulkarni, S., Tendulkar, A.V.: Comparative study of clustering techniques for short text documents. In: International Conference Companion on Worldwide Web, pp. 111–112 (2011)
24. Gu, D., Zhang, Z., Zhang, X., Liu, L.: Research on user-oriented short text clustering. In: International Conference on Information Science and Control Engineering, pp. 563–567 (2016)
25. Finegan-Dollak, C., Coke, R., Zhang, R., Ye, X., Radev, D.: Effects of creativity and cluster tightness on short text clustering performance. In: Meeting of the Association for Computational Linguistics, pp. 654–665 (2016)

A Clothing Image Retrieval System
Based on Improved Itti Model

Yuping Hu[1], Chunmei Wang[2(✉)], Hang Xiao[1], and Sen Zhang[1]

[1] School of Information, Guangdong University of Finance and Economics, Guangzhou, China
okhyp@gdufe.edu.cn, 773145296@qq.com, 348167069@qq.com
[2] Department of Internet Finance and Information Engineering,
Guangdong University of Finance, Guangzhou, China
mei_wangchun@163.com

Abstract. Aiming at the problems of Itti visual attention model like inadequate feature extraction, complex feature synthesis process and feature incompatible with existing retrieval system, a better Itti model is proposed to improve the low-level visual features, image segmentation and interesting area in this paper. And then the improved Itti visual attention model is introduce to content based Clothing image retrieval system, the experimental results show our system has obvious advance on the accuracy of retrieval effect than the existing similar system.

Keywords: Image retrieval · Texture character · Image segmentation
Interesting area

1 Introduction

With the development of e-commerce, especially the rise of online clothing, the requirements of image retrieval technology continue to improve. Most of the existing garment image retrieval methods are based on some of the underlying features of the image, such as texture, color, shape and other aspects of the characteristics. These image retrieval methods are universal, and any kind of image retrieval can use such a retrieval method. If not for the inherent characteristics of clothing to retrieve, which will inevitably lead to clothing search results are not ideal, the retrieval efficiency is not high [1, 2].

In the process of visual perception, visual attention has a very important position, many scholars through the physiology, psychology and information science and other fields of knowledge, a great degree of thinking and research, but also gets some theory and model. In the absence of a priori guidance, the visual choice of the target is mainly driven by the bottom-up data in the scene, and whether the goal is focused on its significance. This method is used to extract the initial visual feature of the input image and form a significant graph corresponding to each feature. Among them, the significant graph model of Itti [3] is the most representative, [4–8] Some of the image retrieval methods proposed in [9] are mainly some improvements to the Itti visual attention model. It can be seen from the experimental comparison that these algorithms can improve the content-based image retrieval system to a certain extent.

© Springer Nature Singapore Pte Ltd. 2018
H. Yuan et al. (Eds.): GSKI 2017, CCIS 849, pp. 232–242, 2018.
https://doi.org/10.1007/978-981-13-0896-3_23

In this paper, the Itti attention model is introduced into the content-based garment image retrieval system. In view of the problem that the existing feature extraction is not sufficient, the fusion process of the underlying visual feature is cumbersome and difficult to integrate into the garment image retrieval system. The underlying visual features, image segmentation, and region of interest improved in three aspects of the Itti visual attention model. The texture feature can be reflected in the retrieval system; by dividing the color, brightness, orientation and texture significant graphs respectively, find the color, brightness, orientation and texture interest graph, make the image segmentation result more efficient, Accurate, using the seed point regional growth algorithm, combined with the interest area merger criterion, to obtain a more representative image of the visual area of the visual features, significantly improve the retrieval system recall and precision.

2 Itti Model Inductions

The Itti model [3] first extracts the primary underlying visual features of the three images in color, direction and brightness, and extracts three distinct figures through the central peripheral difference algorithm after extracting the visual features, and then by using the regional growth And segmentation algorithms to obtain multiple interest graphs. Finally, the only interest graph is calculated by pre-established criteria. There are a number of significant features that are detected, and the Winner-take-all mechanism is used to lock the only target of interest. Itti visual attention mechanism model as a data-driven, bottom-up model, the specific algorithm flow shown in Fig. 1:

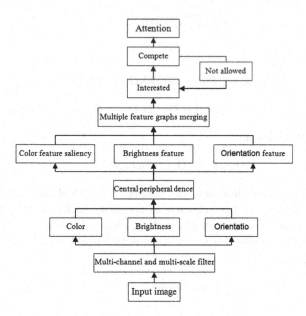

Fig. 1. Data driver attention model

The underlying visual features of the extracted image in the Itti model are: color, brightness, and orientation. And in the image r said red, g said green, b said blue. Then the color is characterized by: red $R = r - (g + b)/2$, green $G = g - (r + b)/2$, blue $B = b - (r + g)/2$ and yellow $Y = (r (R + g + b)/3$, that is, the mean of r, g, b; toward the feature we use Gabor to extract the pattern = $\{0°, 45°, 90°, 135°\}$, the four directions of the component.

The Itti model uses Gaussian differential filters to obtain images of different scales, that is, images with different resolutions. From the original image 1: 1 to 1: 256 the smallest size of the image, that is, from 0 to 8, a total of 9 different sizes of images. Here we use the central peripheral difference to extract the image of the multi-feature significant map. Center c is the pixel of the scale; the surrounding s is the pixel of scale c+, here. Only through the DOG algorithm to calculate the center c and the surrounding s pixels can get the image of the feature map, the specific calculation process is as follows:

$$DOG(x, y) = \frac{1}{2\pi\sigma_c} \exp[-\frac{x^2 + y^2}{2\sigma_c^2}] - \frac{1}{2\pi\sigma_s} \exp[-\frac{x^2 + y^2}{2\sigma_s^2}] \tag{1}$$

In the formula (1), is scale factor for the center c, is scale factor for the surrounding s. By using the nearest pixel interpolation method for small-scale images, the peripheral image s can be obtained. In the following formula, the symbol represents the central peripheral difference algorithm, using the central peripheral difference algorithm to calculate the central c and the surrounding s can be obtained clothing feature map, as follows:

Luminance characteristic map:

$$I(c, s) = |I(c)\Theta I(s)| \tag{2}$$

Color feature map:

$$RG(c, s) = |(R(c) - G(c))\Theta(G(s) - R(s))| \tag{3}$$

$$BY(c, s) = |(B(c) - T(c))\Theta(Y(s) - B(s))| \tag{4}$$

Orientation feature map:

$$O(c, s, \theta) = |O(c, \theta)\Theta O(s, \theta)| \tag{5}$$

Because of the various feature graphs obtained after calculation, the range of pixel values is not uniform, so it is necessary to normalize each feature graph, and then combine the normalized feature graphs with the same dimension, and finally get, and the combined feature graphs. The normalized calculation of brightness, color and orientation is as follows:

$$\tilde{I} = \oplus_c \oplus_s N[I[c, s]] \tag{6}$$

$$\tilde{C} = \oplus_c \oplus_s [N[RG] + N[BY[c, s]]] \tag{7}$$

$$\tilde{O} = \sum_{\theta} N[\oplus_c \oplus_s N[O[c, s, \theta]]] \tag{8}$$

Composite feature map:

$$S = [N[\tilde{I}] + N[\tilde{C}] + N[\tilde{O}]]/3 \tag{9}$$

As can be seen in Fig. 1, the multidimensional feature merging strategy is used to obtain interest graphs. Because it is from different scales, different background visual characteristics of the merger, it may contain a number of different significant areas. But attention to the target can only have one, so must be through a competitive mechanism to select the only goal. Winning the win in the WTA (Winner Take All) mechanism will yield a higher significant coefficient and cycle through the closed loop in Fig. 1 until only a significant area is left, i.e. the only target. There is a mechanism to prohibit the return: when a significant area and target correlation is eliminated, the next round of competition will no longer participate.

3   Clothing Image Retrieval System Based on Itti Improved Model

The Itti visual attention model introduces a psychological threshold to control visual perception, and its size is proportional to the probability of correct or incorrectly identifying the target. That is, the greater the probability of correct or incorrectly identifying the target, the greater the psychological threshold, but the smaller. But this psychological threshold model is independent of the visual task; it is used to explain the whole process of visual perception is clearly wrong. So in order to clarify the application process information process, we will improve the Itti visual attention model as based on data-driven. Figure 2 is a new schematic diagram of the garment image retrieval system based on the Itti improved model. It can be seen from the figure that the whole system includes three parts: the bottom visual feature extraction, the image segmentation and the region of interest extraction:

(1) The bottom of the visual feature extraction: the texture feature by adding the model, the clothing image texture features is reflected in order to improve the accuracy of the search results.
(2) Image segmentation: genetic algorithm to find the optimal threshold of image segmentation, and then use the multi-dimensional significant map segmentation, and finally get multi-dimensional interest map, the garment image segmentation more efficient and accurate.
(3) Region of interest extraction: the use of significant points on the significant map of regional growth, which get the region of interest. Using the pre-defined combination criteria, the significant visual characteristics of the garment image are obtained. This algorithm can obviously improve the precision and recall rate of garment image retrieval system.

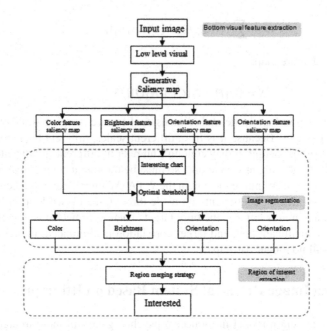

Fig. 2. Garment image retrieval system based on improved Itti model

3.1 Image Segmentation Improvement

Here the image segmentation is mainly to be able to find an appropriate threshold can be the clothing image of the clothing and the background separated. From this point of view, if an image has only background and foreground, then its gray histogram will show a bimodal state, that is, the foreground pixel values and background pixel values will be more uniform around the two extremes, As shown in Fig. 3. For a garment image satisfying such a condition, it is common to divide the garment from the background value of the double-peak valley as the optimum threshold.

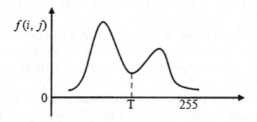

Fig. 3. Bimodal gray scale histogram

But the actual clothing images are not all as mentioned above, some clothing image background there are two different distributions, coupled with clothing, there will be more than three kinds of distribution. Figure 4 shows the gray scale histogram of the three peak images. The gray values at the two peaks are T1 and T2, which are the optimal thresholds.

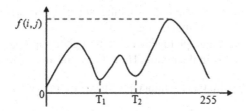

Fig. 4. Multi-peak grayscale histogram

The histogram threshold segmentation method is a direct and efficient image segmentation method, but it requires that the gray scale histogram of the divided garment image has two or more crests. Otherwise, this method cannot be used. At the same time, the histogram segmentation method and the pixel value Has nothing to do with the spatial distribution. If the clothing and the background have the same gray value, then the division cannot achieve the purpose.

3.2 Detection of the Region of Interest

The area of interest is extracted from the conspicuous point of the multidimensional significant graph as the seed, and the region of interest is obtained by using the regional growth algorithm. Finally, using the pre-defined region merging rule, the region of interest region for garment image retrieval is generated.

(1) Seed dot area growth algorithm

The most significant points in the multidimensional salient graphs are preserved before the segmentation is mostly significant, and the most significant points are used as seeds for the segmentation of the significant region, and more multidimensional interest maps can be obtained. The algorithm in this paper is to grow the region in the significant graph after segmentation, that is, to search for a connected area where the largest salient point in the graph is, that is, the only region of the interest graph. Therefore, the algorithm of this paper has a good effect for the detection of only a single target. But for the same time with multiple targets of the image, the algorithm is not applicable. The seed region growth algorithm has the advantages of good real-time and simple and efficient, but the generated area is sometimes not very accurate. In [8], an evolutionary programming algorithm is proposed to carry out the regional growth method, and the ideal effect is achieved. The disadvantage is that the time cost is relatively large. The focus of further research is to find a way to generate a more complete target to be tested, you can add a priori knowledge, time-consuming and efficient regional growth algorithm.

(2) Interesting area merger guidelines

The significant area of the interest graph obtained by the above algorithm is quite different, including the color interest graph, the brightness interest graph, the interest graph, the texture interest graph. Some significant distributions of homogeneous interest maps can have side effects on the final outcome; some significant apparition's show a strong interest graph that contributes greatly to the final outcome. Practical application is not blindly all the interest graph together, but through the appropriate choice, in order to get the image of interest in the region. Here define the area of interest area:

$$S_{regeion} = |\max(x) - \min(x)| \times |\max(y) - \min(y)| \tag{10}$$

Smap is the total area of interest graph, Smap is the area of interest graph, according to experience when Sregion/Smap > 0.6, abandon this interest map, this is the interest area merger criteria.

3.3   Visual Feature Extraction

Based on the Itti model, this algorithm increases the texture features, so that the texture of the image can be reflected in the visual characteristics [10].

Figure 5 on the right for the texture roughness feature map. In the improved Itti model, the texture feature map of the texture roughness will be used as a candidate feature map for the visual prominence region, as opposed to the feature map and the color feature map. The following is given the roughness of the texture parameters of the definition of specific formula calculation method.

Fig. 5. Texture roughness feature map and the original image contrast

A two-dimensional image of size M × N, {f (I, J), v i = 0, 1, 2, ... M; j = 0, 1, 2, ... N}, the roughness is defined as follows:

$$F_{crs} = \frac{1}{M \times N} \sum_{i=1}^{m} \sum_{j=1}^{n} S_{best}(i,j) \tag{11}$$

In the above equation, the calculation of the k-value for each pixel can be obtained by maximizing the E value in the following formula:

$$\begin{cases} E_{k,h}(i,j) = |A_k(i + 2^{k-1},j) - A_k(i - 2^{k-1},j)| \\ E_{k,h}(i,j) = |A_k(i,j + 2^{k-1}) - A_k(i,j - 2^{k-1})| \end{cases} \tag{12}$$

While the average pixel intensity is given by the following formula:

$$A_k(i,j) = \sum_{x=i-2^{k-1}}^{i+2^{k-1}} \sum_{y=j-2^{k-1}}^{j+2^{k-1}} f(x,y)/2^{2k} \tag{13}$$

After the above calculation, it can be obtained image texture roughness map. As shown in Fig. 5, the roughness graph can reflect the granularity of the texture image to a certain extent, and can express the image or region with different texture features. The texture roughness feature can be introduced into the retrieval system, which can improve the precision of the system.

4   Experimental Results and Analysis

In this paper, all the experiments are in the CPU for the Pentium (R) Dual-Core 2.60 GHz, memory 2G, the operating system for Windows7 computer, in order to verify the effectiveness of the proposed method, we made some testing experiments in Matlab R2013a, The test data set is collected from Taobao, Amazon, Jingdong and other e-commerce sites. Selected images are 256 × 256 JPG format, including short T-shirt, long T-shirt, shorts, longs, Polo shirt, each category contains 50 pairs, a total of 2000 images. In this paper, three different retrieval methods are compared: the image retrieval method based on [8], the image retrieval method based on [6], and the improved image retrieval method based on Itti proposed in this paper. Figures 6, 7 and 8 show the comparison of the results of the three methods, in which the first image is the target map to be retrieved and the latter 29 is the garment image of the search result. Figure 6 is used in the literature [8] algorithm to retrieve the results, we can see from the match results 2 began to appear some undesirable results, search the target picture for the long-sleeved collar Polo shirt, and match the results 2 For short-sleeved collarless Polo shirt, in the 29 search results appeared in 20 unwanted results. Figure 7 shows the results of the search [6] algorithm, we can see that the use of Itti model, the 29 search results, the matching results only 13 does not meet the requirements, the accuracy of the search has been greatly improved. Figure 8 shows the results of the improved Itti algorithm retrieval. Of the 29 search results, 22 images meet the requirements and the accuracy of the search is improved.

Fig. 6. Literature [7] algorithm retrieval results

Fig. 7. Literature [5] algorithm retrieval results

Fig. 8. Rretrieval results of this method

The recall rate and the precision rate [11] are the standard evaluation methods of the success rate of information retrieval. More and more of them are used in the content-based image retrieval, in which the recall rate is used to retrieve the relevant image. The quasi-rate for the system to exclude irrelevant images, the formula can be defined as follows:

$$A_k(i,j) = \sum_{x=i-2^{k-1}}^{i+2^{k-1}} \sum_{y=j-2^{k-1}}^{j+2^{k-1}} f(x,y)/2^{2k}$$

$$\text{Recall ratio} = \frac{\text{Retrieved related images}}{\text{All related images}} = \frac{A}{A+C}$$

$$\text{Precision ratio} = \frac{\text{Retrieved related images}}{\text{Retrieved all related images}} = \frac{A}{A+B} \tag{14}$$

Where A is the relevant image retrieved correctly, B is the irrelevant image retrieved, and C is the related image of the missed test. In order to qualitatively evaluate the effectiveness of the proposed method, we randomly selected 10 garment images from each of the styles in the clothing image database. Table 1, Table 2 is the literature [8] algorithm, the literature [6] algorithm, this improved Itti algorithm, respectively, long-sleeved shirts, long-sleeved T-shirts, Polo shirt, short-sleeved shirt and short-sleeved T-shirt recall ratio and precision ratio comparison. It can be seen from Tables 1 and 2 that the retrieval method of this paper has better retrieval effect than the algorithm [8] and the literature [6].

Table 1. Comparison of several algorithms to check the precision ratio

Clothing styles	Long sleeved shirt	Long t-shirt	Polo sweater	Short sleeved shirt	Short t-shirt
Literature [6]	0.375	0.370	0.355	0.326	0.481
Literature [8]	0.526	0.589	0.514	0.604	0.524
Present method	0.651	0.696	0.615	0.625	0.693

Table 2. Comparison of several algorithms to check the recall ratio

Clothing styles	Long sleeved shirt	Long t-shirt	Polo sweater	Short sleeved shirt	Short t-shirt
Literature [6]	0.335	0.362	0.383	0.392	0.395
Literature [8]	0.520	0.547	0.559	0.529	0.618
Present method	0.625	0.635	0.655	0.676	0.687

5   Conclusions

In this paper, the Itti attention model is introduced into the content-based garment image retrieval system. In view of the problem that the existing feature extraction is not sufficient, the fusion process of the underlying visual feature is cumbersome and difficult to integrate into the garment image retrieval system. Bottom visual features, image segmentation and region of interest have improved the Itti visual attention model, which significantly improved the search system recall and precision. But the Itti model also has its shortcomings, which show better results when we use a background-free garment image for a retrieval experiment, indicating that the visual attention mechanism is not well suited to retrieve the target in the image in a background image More suitable for an energy distribution in a uniform image to find a significant area. In order to play the advantage of the visual attention mechanism model in the garment image, we will combine the other algorithms, such as the algorithm, to remove the background interference by dividing the target, so as to better play the advantage of the Itti model.

Acknowledgments. This work was by Guangdong Provincial Scientific Research Fund of China (No. 2016A030313717); Natural Scientific Research Fund of China (No. 61472135).

References

1. Liang, X., Lin, L., Yang, W., Luo, P., Huang, J., Yan, S.: Clothes co-parsing via joint image segmentation and labeling with application to clothing retrieval. IEEE Trans. Multimed. **18**(6), 1175–1186 (2016)
2. Forczmański, P., Czapiewski, P., Frejlichowski, D.: Comparing clothing styles by means of computer vision methods. Comput. Vis. Graph. **86**(7), 203–211 (2014)
3. Schneider, W.: Controlled and automatic human information processing: detection, search and Attention. Psychol. Rev. **84**, 1–66 (1977)
4. Chuanbo, H., Zhong, J.: Image retrieval using multiresolution analysis of visual attention. J. Image Graph. **16**(9), 1656–1663 (2011)
5. Olsllausen, B., Field, D.: Emergence of simple-cell receptive field properties by learning a sparse code for natural images. Nature **1381**(13), 607–609 (1996)
6. Zhang, J., Shen, L., David, D.: A survey of image retrieval based on visual perception. Acta Electronica Sinica **36**(3), 494–499 (2008)
7. Zhang, J., Shen, L.S., Gao, J.J.: Regions of interest detection based on visual attention mechanism. Acta Photonica Sinica **38**(6), 1561–1565 (2009)
8. Zeng, Z., Zhang, X., Cui, J., et al.: A novel image retrieval algorithm based on color and distribution of prominent interest points. Acta Photonica Sinica **35**(2), 308–311 (2006)
9. Itti, L., Koch, C.: Computational modeling of visual attention. Nat. Rev. Neurosci. **2**(3), 194–230 (2001)
10. Karakasis, E., Amanatiadis, A., Gasteratos, A., Chatzichristofis, S.: Image moment invariants as local features for content based image retrieval using the bag-of-visual-words model. Patt. Recogn. **55**, 22–27 (2015)
11. Wei, N., Geng, G.H., Zhou, M.Q.: An overview of performance evaluation in content-based image retrieval. J. Image Graph. **9**(11), 1271–1276 (2004)

Study on a Kind of War Zone Equipment Material's Urgency Transportation Problem for Multi-requirement Points

Peng Dong[✉], Peng Yu, Kewen Wang, and Gongda Yan

Department of Management Science, Naval University of Engineering, Wuhan, Hubei, China
`13627266686@163.com, rocdong@163.com, 18057045897@163.com,`
`yupeng@163.com, 15907118706@qq.com, 704860966@qq.com,`
`15972937528@qq.com, 617691464@qq.com`

Abstract. Equipment material's transportation is one of the most important part in the theater of equipment support work, which decides whether the whole theater's equipment support could be fast and efficient to carry out and successfully completed. Considering the complexity, rapidity and danger of the equipment transportation in the wartime situation, two optimization models of emergency transportation of multi-demand and multi-cargo equipment under different time factors are established. The mathematical model is deduced, and the analytic algorithm is given for the two models. The correctness of the model and the validity of the algorithm are illustrated by concrete examples.

Keywords: Equipment material's urgency transportation
Multi-requirement points · Unlimited transportation ability

1 Introduction

The problem of equipment material's transportation is an important part and a hot spot of Military Logistics [1]; it is also a branch of transportation problem in operations research. Transportation problem is a special kind of linear programming problem in operations research, and the earliest study of such problems is the research taken by American scholar Hitchcock, Later, Koopman, who discussed this issue in detail [2]. Because of the difference between the actual transportation problem and the ideal transportation problem model, the variety or extension model of various transportation problems is put forward: From the point of view of the objective function, we should take into account the minimum transportation cost, the lowest damage rate and the adjustment of unit freight rate. Therefore, the mathematical model and algorithm of multi objective transportation problem are studied [3, 4]; a tabu search algorithm is used to solve the transportation problem with fixed costs [5], the shortest time transportation problem [6], the inverse problem of the optimal transportation problem by adjusting the unit price, etc. From the point of view of the constraint function, there are studies on the problem of uncertainty in the supply and demand in a certain interval [7], researches on the transportation problem with capacity limitation and handling fee [8], transportation

© Springer Nature Singapore Pte Ltd. 2018
H. Yuan et al. (Eds.): GSKI 2017, CCIS 849, pp. 243–253, 2018.
https://doi.org/10.1007/978-981-13-0896-3_24

problems with time windows [9], etc. are considered. Nowadays, several models of military transportation problems in China, the main transportation mode choice model, single kind of material dispatching model, road transport model, wartime transportation model etc. have been studied. However, these models are lack of contact with each other, the whole system is poor, and the assumptions of the model are too idealistic, and it is not consistent with the actual situation.

Single demand point and single cargo equipment material's urgency transportation problems are relatively simple. Taking into account the actual equipment material dispatching process, there is often more than one point demanding materials at the same time. In this paper, on the basis of the research literature [10], to make a further study on the multi-requirement points, multi-goods equipment emergency dispatching problem, the optimization model is put forward, and the analytic algorithm is presented. The correctness and operability of the model and algorithm are proved by a case below.

2 Problem Description

Research on multi requirement points of multi goods equipment emergency dispatching problems, in order to make the model simple, the assumption does not consider the equipment materials capacity constraints. These multi- requirement points of multi-goods without capacity constraints of mathematics urgency transportation equipment materials under the conditions described below:

Set $A_1, A_2, \ldots, A_m$ for the M equipment material demand point, set to M equipment material demand points, $B_1, B_2, \ldots, B_n$ for the n can provide equipment supply point, $S_1, S_2, \ldots, S_l$ for M species equipment supplies, supply Centre B_i for the cargo K maximum equipment material supply for $b_{ik}(b_{ik} \geq 0)$, $i = 1, 2, \cdots, n$, $k = 1, 2 \cdots, l$. Demand point A_j for the demand for the kind of K is $r_{jk}(r_{jk} \geq 0)$, $j = 1, 2, \cdots, m$, $k = 1, 2 \cdots, l$. Equipment and materials of different types have different transport requirements in transportation, such as transportation, transportation safety and transportation ways, their transport time should also be different, but if each kind of equipment and material transporting time are represented by different parameters, so that the constraints of the model too much, increase the complexity of the model solution, the problem is not easy to study, Therefore, we assume that different types of equipment supplies from the supply point B_i, The time required for delivery to the point A_j of demand is all $t_{ij}(t_{ij} \geq 0)$, the loss rate is p_{ij}, from point of B_i supply to demand point A_j the amount of the K type of goods for x_{ijk}. Is the equipment material supply and demand point of each respective equipment provided by the material quantity decision system, so any scheme Φ can be expressed in the form of a collection:

$$\Phi = \begin{bmatrix} \Phi_1 & \Phi_2 & \cdots & \Phi_m \end{bmatrix}^T \tag{1}$$

$$\Phi_j = \left\{ (B_1, X_{1j}), (B_2, X_{2j}), \cdots, (B_n, X_{nj}) \right\} \tag{2}$$

$$X_{ij} = \left\{ x_{ij1}, x_{ij2}, \cdots, x_{ijl} \right\}, j = 1, 2, \cdots, m \tag{3}$$

Equipment and materials dispatching emergency decision-making process still need to consider the time involved, supply points and losses of three decision target: The final equipment delivery time is Φ final delivery time, Use $T(\Phi)$ to represent the final delivery time of program Φ; The number of supply points involved in scheme Φ is expressed as $N(\Phi)$ and the loss is the degree of loss in accordance with plan Φ in the whole process of transportation, which can be expressed as the following $P(\Phi)$:

$$P(\Phi) = \frac{\sum\limits_{i \in N(\Phi)} \sum\limits_{j=1}^{m} \sum\limits_{k=1}^{l} p_{ij} \cdot x_{ijk}}{\sum\limits_{i \in N(\Phi)} \sum\limits_{j=1}^{m} \sum\limits_{k=1}^{l} x_{ijk}} \tag{4}$$

3 Analysis and Establishment of the Model

There are two types of materials and equipment to establish emergency dispatching models.

3.1 Minimum Time, Minimum Number of Supply Points, Minimum Loss

Model objections level is as follows:

(1) the shortest transit time;
(2) minimum number of supply points involved;
(3) the minimum of loss shall not exceed the limit.

Abstract them into a mathematical model (model one):

$$(P_1) \min T(\Phi)$$

$$(P_2) \min N(\Phi) \tag{5}$$

$$(P_3) \min P(\Phi) \tag{6}$$

$$\begin{cases} \sum\limits_{i \in N(\Phi)} (1 - p_{ij}) \cdot x_{ijk} = r_{jk} \\ P(\Phi) \leq P \\ 0 \leq \sum\limits_{j=1}^{m} x_{ijk} \leq b_{ik} \\ x_{ijk} \geq 0 \end{cases} \tag{7}$$

Among $i \in N(\Phi), j = 1, 2 \cdots m, k = 1, 2 \cdots, l$, P for the equipment and materials loss allowance.

3.2 Limited Time, Minimum Number of Supply Points, Minimum Loss

Model objections level is as follows:

(1) Minimum number of supply points involved;
(2) The minimum of loss shall not exceed the limit.

Abstract those into a mathematical model (model two):

$$(P_2) \min N(\Phi)$$

$$(P_3) \min P(\Phi)$$

$$\begin{cases} \sum_{i \in N(\Phi)} (1 - p_{ij}) \cdot x_{ijk} = r_{jk} \\ T(\Phi) \leq T \\ P(\Phi) \leq P \\ 0 \leq \sum_{j=1}^{m} x_{ijk} \leq b_{ik} \\ x_{ijk} \geq 0 \end{cases} \tag{8}$$

Among $i \in N(\Phi), j = 1, 2 \cdots m, k = 1, 2 \cdots, l, T, P$ for the time limit and the loss limit of equipment material.

4 Model Algorithm

4.1 The First Model's Algorithm

Algorithm steps are as follows:

(1) Seek $\min T(\Phi)$.
   Time is the most important factor in decision-making, so think about the time first. Get the t_{ij} sort obtain $\{t^{(1)}, t^{(2)}, \cdots, t^{(n \times m)}\}$, so $\min T(\Phi) \in \{t^{(1)}, t^{(2)}, \cdots, t^{(n \times m)}\}$, the objective function is that the faster the transit time is, the better we can do to minimize the maximum transport time, then take $t_u = \max_i \min(t_{ij})$ as $\min T(\Phi)$.
(2) Seek the minimum combination of supply point $N(\Phi)$.
   When the search to $t^{(z)}$, remember $\Pi = \{(i,j)|t_{ij} > t^{(z)}\}$.

If the supply point of i_0, for the $\forall j$, there are $(i_0, j) \in \Pi$, then from the supply point of the supply point in the elimination of the supply of $B_1, B_2, \ldots, B_n$ points of B_{i_0}.

Remember $p^* = \min(p_{ij})$, from the supply point to find the minimum combination $N(\Phi)$ of $(1 - p^*) \cdot \sum_{i \in N(\Phi)} b_{ik} \geq \sum_{j=1}^{m} r_{jk}$

(3) Seek $\min P(\Phi)$.
   By step (1) and (2), the model can be transformed into:

$$\min P(\Phi)$$

$$s.t. \begin{cases} \sum\limits_{i \in N(\Phi)} (1 - p_{ij}) \cdot x_{ijk} = r_{jk} \\ 0 \le \sum\limits_{j=1}^{m} x_{ijk} \le b_{ik} \\ x_{ijk} \ge 0 \\ i \in N(\Phi) \end{cases} \tag{9}$$

Among $j = 1, 2 \cdots m, k = 1, 2 \cdots, l$.
Because:

$$P(\Phi) = \sum_{i \in N(\Phi)} \sum_{j=1}^{m} \sum_{k=1}^{l} p_{ij} \cdot x_{ijk} / \sum_{i \in N(\Phi)} \sum_{j=1}^{m} \sum_{k=1}^{l} x_{ijk}$$

$$= 1 - \sum_{j=1}^{m} \sum_{k=1}^{l} r_{jk} / \sum_{i \in N(\Phi)} \sum_{j=1}^{m} \sum_{k=1}^{l} x_{ijk} \tag{10}$$

So, min $P(\Phi)$ equivalent to min ($\sum\limits_{i \in N(\Phi)} \sum\limits_{j=1}^{m} \sum\limits_{k=1}^{l} x_{ijk}$)
The model transformed into:

$$\min (\sum_{i \in N(\Phi)} \sum_{j=1}^{m} \sum_{k=1}^{l} x_{ijk}) \tag{11}$$

$$s.t. \begin{cases} \sum\limits_{i \in N(\Phi)} (1 - p_{ij}) \cdot x_{ijk} = r_{jk} \\ 0 \le \sum\limits_{j=1}^{m} x_{ijk} \le b_{ik} \\ x_{ijk} \ge 0 \\ i \in N(\Phi) \end{cases} \tag{12}$$

Among $j = 1, 2 \cdots m, k = 1, 2 \cdots, l$.
Order:

$$M_j = \min \{ (1 - p_{ij})_{i \in N(\Phi)} \};$$

$$E_j = \{ i | (1 - p_{ij}) = M_j \};$$

$$\Gamma_j = \{ i | (1 - p_{ij}) \ne M_j \};$$

According to $\sum\limits_{i \in N(\Phi)} (1 - p_{ij}) \cdot x_{ijk} = r_{jk}$,
thus:

$$\sum_{i \in E_j} (1 - p_{ij}) \cdot x_{ijk} + \sum_{i \in \Gamma_j} (1 - p_{ij}) \cdot x_{ijk} = r_{jk} \tag{13}$$

$$\sum_{i \in N(\Phi)} x_{ijk} + \sum_{i \in \Gamma_j} \left(\frac{(1 - p_{ij})}{M_j} - 1 \right) \cdot x_{ijk} = r_{jk}/M_j \tag{14}$$

$$\sum_{i \in N(\Phi)} \sum_{j=1}^{m} \sum_{k=1}^{l} x_{ijk} + \sum_{i \in \Gamma_j} \sum_{j=1}^{m} \sum_{k=1}^{l} \left(\frac{(1 - p_{ij})}{M_j} - 1 \right) \cdot x_{ijk}$$
$$= \sum_{j=1}^{m} \sum_{k=1}^{l} (r_{jk}/M_j) \tag{15}$$

$$\sum_{i \in N(\Phi)} \sum_{j=1}^{m} \sum_{k=1}^{l} x_{ijk} = \sum_{j=1}^{m} \sum_{k=1}^{l} r_{jk}/M_j$$
$$- \sum_{i \in \Gamma_j} \sum_{j=1}^{m} \sum_{k=1}^{l} \left(\frac{(1 - p_{ij})}{M_j} - 1 \right) \cdot x_{ijk} \tag{16}$$

Order $R_j = \sum_{k=1}^{l} r_{jk}$, $X_{ij} = \sum_{k=1}^{l} x_{ijk}$, $D_i = \sum_{k=1}^{l} b_{ik}$

Then Eq. (16) can be expressed as:

$$\sum_{i \in N(\phi)} \sum_{j=1}^{m} X_{ij} = \sum_{j=1}^{m} (R_j/M) - \sum_{i \in \Gamma_j} \sum_{j=1}^{m} \left(\frac{(1 - p_{ij})}{M_j} - 1 \right) \cdot X_{if} \tag{17}$$

The model can be converted to:

$$\min \left(\sum_{i \in N(\Phi)} \sum_{j=1}^{m} X_{ij} \right) \tag{18}$$

$$s.t. \begin{cases} \sum_{i \in N(\Phi)} (1 - p_{ij}) \cdot X_{ij} = R_j \\ 0 \le \sum_{j=1}^{m} X_{ij} \le D_i \\ i \in N(\Phi) \end{cases} \tag{19}$$

This problem can be transformed into a single-species model, thus could be solved in accordance with the single species solution.

Note y_{ij} as 0,1 variables, when the equipment from B_j to A_i, then $y_{ij} = 1$, otherwise $y_{ij} = 0$. Set up $s_{ij} = X_{ij} \cdot y_{ij}$. Then:

$$\sum_{i \in N(\Phi)} \sum_{j=1}^{m} X_{ij} = \sum_{i \in N(\Phi)} \sum_{j=1}^{m} X_{ij} \cdot y_{ij} = \sum_{i \in N(\Phi)} \sum_{j=1}^{m} s_{ij} \tag{20}$$

$$\sum_{i \in \Gamma_j} (\frac{(1 - p_{ij})}{M_j} - 1) \cdot X_{ij} = \sum_{i \in N(\Phi)} (\frac{(1 - p_{ij})}{M_j} - 1) \cdot X_{ij} \cdot y_{ij}$$

$$= \sum_{i \in N(\Phi)} (\frac{(1 - p_{ij})}{M_j} - 1) \cdot s_{ij} \tag{21}$$

$$\min \sum_{i \in N(\Phi)} \sum_{j=1}^{m} X_{ij} = \min \sum_{i \in N(\Phi)} \sum_{j=1}^{m} s_{ij}$$

$$= \min(\sum_{j=1}^{m} (R_j / M_j) - \sum_{j=1}^{m} \sum_{i \in N(\Phi)} (\frac{(1 - p_{ij})}{M_j} - 1) \cdot s_{ij}) \tag{22}$$

$$= \min(\sum_{j=1}^{m} (R_j / M_j) - \sum_{i \in N(\Phi)} \sum_{j=1}^{m} (\frac{(1 - p_{ij})}{M_j} - 1) \cdot s_{ij})$$

It is obvious that when $\sum_{j=1}^{m} \left[(\frac{(1 - p_{ij})}{M_j} - 1) \cdot s_{ij} \right]$ takes the maximum value, $\sum_{i \in N(\Phi)} \sum^{m} s_{ij}$ has the minimum value. And the maximum value of s_{ij} is obtained when the maximum value of the maximum coefficient corresponds to the maximum value of $\sum_{j=1}^{m} \left[(\frac{(1 - p_{ij})}{M_j} - 1) \cdot s_{ij} \right]$. Thus $\sum_{i \in N(\Phi)} \sum_{j=1}^{m} s_{ij}$ can obtain the minimum value.

Order:

$$N_i = \max \left\{ (\frac{(1 - p_{ij})}{M_j} - 1)_{j=1,2,\cdots,m, i \in \Gamma_j} \right\};$$

$$F_i = \left\{ j | (\frac{(1 - p_{ij})}{M_j} - 1) = N_i \right\};$$

$$H_i = \left\{ j | (\frac{(1 - p_{ij})}{M_j} - 1) \neq N_i \right\};$$

Then:

$$\sum_{j=1}^{m} \left[(\frac{(1 - p_{ij})}{M_j} - 1) \cdot s_{ij} \right]$$

$$= N_i \sum_{j \in F_i} s_{ij} + \sum_{j \in H_i} \left[(\frac{(1 - p_{ij})}{M_j} - 1) \cdot s_{ij} \right]$$

$$= N_i \sum_{j=1}^{m} s_{ij} + \sum_{j \in H_i} \left[(\frac{(1 - p_{ij})}{M_j} - 1 - N_i) \cdot s_{ij} \right] \tag{23}$$

Because $N_i \geq (\frac{(1 - p_{ij})}{M_j} - 1)$, so $(\frac{(1 - p_{ij})}{M_j} - 1 - N_i) \leq 0$ obviously when $s_{ij} = 0 (j \in H_i)$ and $\sum_{j=1}^{m} s_{ij} = D_i$, $\sum_{j=1}^{m} \left[(\frac{(1 - p_{ij})}{M_j} - 1) \cdot s_{ij} \right]$ obtained the maximum value.

In combination $\sum\limits_{i \in N(\Phi)} (1 - p_{ij}) \cdot s_{ij} = R_j$, the equation group is as follows:

$$
\begin{cases}
\sum\limits_{i \in N(\Phi)} (1 - p_{ij}) \cdot s_{ij} = R_j \\
\sum\limits_{j=1}^{m} s_{ij} = D_i \\
s_{ij} = 0 (j \in H_i)
\end{cases}
\tag{24}
$$

Solve the value of s_{ij} and plug it in equation $s_{ij} = X_{ij} \cdot y_{ij}$, and we can get the value of X_{ij}. Plug them into the following equations:

$$
\begin{cases}
\sum\limits_{i \in N(\Phi)} (1 - p_{ij}) \cdot x_{ijk} = r_{jk} \\
\sum\limits_{k=1}^{l} x_{ijk} = X_{ij}
\end{cases}
\tag{25}
$$

Among $j = 1, 2, \cdots, m, k = 1, 2, \cdots, l$.

When there are multiple solutions of the equations, there are many schemes, we can get a set of programs, and compare the loss degree of each scheme, and the minimum (P) of the loss is the optimal solution Φ.

(4) If $P(\Phi) \leq P$, then the scheme is valid. If $P_i > P$, then the scheme is not valid. Order $N(\Phi) = N(\Phi) + 1$, get back to (2) and recalculate until $P_i \leq P$.
(5) When there is no solution to the equation group, take the next $t^{(u+1)}$ as min $T(\Phi)$ in the order of $\{t^{(1)}, t^{(2)}, \cdots, t^{(n \times m)}\}$, and then go back to step (1) to continue to search for the best solution.

4.2 The Second Model's Algorithm

In the second model, the decision point of the minimum supply point and the minimum loss degree is reflected in the condition that the time does not exceed the limit. Therefore, when calculating the model, we first search all the supply points that meet the time limit. And find satisfaction in these supply points:

$$
\begin{cases}
\sum\limits_{i \in N(\Phi)} (1 - p_{ij}) \cdot x_{ijk} = r_{jk} \\
0 \leq \sum\limits_{j=1}^{m} x_{ijk} \leq b_{ik} \\
x_{ijk} \geq 0
\end{cases}
\tag{26}
$$

Condition 1 as the minimum supply point and demand point combination (among $i \in N(\Phi)$, $j = 1, 2 \cdots m, k = 1, 2, \cdots, l$).

5   Calculation Examples

The following examples are shown in Tables 1, 2, 3 and 4 respectively.

Table 1. Loss rate p_{ij} from each supply point to demand point

p_{ij}	B_1	B_2	B_3
A_1	0.01	0.03	0.05
A_2	0.03	0.04	0.03
A_3	0.02	0.02	0.01

Table 2. Delivery time t_{ij} from each supply point to demand point

t_{ij}	B_1	B_2	B_3
A_1	3	2	5
A_2	5	6	7
A_3	4	3	6

Table 3. Availability of each supply point

b_{ik}	B_1	B_2	B_3
S_1	3	6	10
S_2	5	4	5
S_3	6	3	7

Table 4. Requirements of each demand point

r_{jk}	A_1	A_2	A_3
S_1	4	4	2
S_2	5	3	5
S_3	3	5	6

5.1   The First Kind of Decision Goal

Use the first model's algorithm to solve this problem.

When $t_{ij} \leq 5$, A_2 the required goods can only be transported from B_1, while the demand for the A_2 to S_3 is 5 and the maximum supply of B_1 is only 3, which cannot meet the requirements of A_2.

When $t_{ij} \leq 6$, solutions are as follows (The transport matrix from B_i to A_j has been given)

$$
\begin{array}{cc}
\text{Scheme 1:} & \text{Scheme 2:} \\
\begin{bmatrix} 8 & 5 & 1 \\ 4 & 7 & 2 \\ 0 & 0 & 10 \end{bmatrix} & \begin{bmatrix} 8 & 5 & 0 \\ 4 & 7 & 1 \\ 0 & 0 & 12 \end{bmatrix} \\
P = 0.0224 & P = 0.0208 \\
\text{Scheme 3:} & \text{Scheme 4:} \\
\begin{bmatrix} 8 & 5 & 0 \\ 4 & 7 & 2 \\ 0 & 0 & 11 \end{bmatrix} & \begin{bmatrix} 8 & 5 & 0 \\ 4 & 7 & 0 \\ 0 & 0 & 13 \end{bmatrix} \\
P = 0.0211 & P = 0.0205
\end{array}
$$

After comparison, the fourth solution is the optimal one. $T(\Phi) = 6$, $N(\Phi) = 3$, the specific transport scheme is shown in Table 5.

Table 5. Equipment emergency dispatching scheme

	$B_1 \to A_j$			$B_2 \to A_j$			$B_3 \to A_j$		
	A_1	A_2	A_3	A_1	A_2	A_3	A_1	A_2	A_3
S_1	3	0	0	1	4	0	0	1	2
S_2	5	0	0	0	3	0	0	0	5
S_3	0	5	1	3	0	0	0	0	5

5.2 The Second Kind of Decision Goal

According to the second model's algorithm, $T = 6$.

Because $T(\Phi) = 6$ in the first class of decision problems, the calculation process and the results are the same with the first class of the same problem.

6 Conclusion

Based on the previous study of the problem of emergency transportation [12], this paper further discusses the optimization of multi-demand and multi-cargo equipment emergency transportation, and establishes two kinds of optimization models involves multi-demand point and multi-cargo equipment under different time factors. The analytical algorithms are given for the both two models and verified by specific examples.

Single demand point and single cargo equipment material's urgency transportation problems are just an idealized and simple situation for the actual situation, cause there won't be just one demand point and one material transferred generally in actual transfer process. Considering the actual equipment material's urgency transportation, the objective function and the constraint condition of the model are modified to improve the model and algorithm to adapt to multi-demand point and multi-cargo situation, making the problem research more in line with the actual equipment material's urgency transportation problem. This research could improve the entire equipment material's urgency transportation problem process and offer command personnel a quantitative reference.

In order to simplify the model and the calculation, this paper does not consider the military transportation capacity constraints, and assume that the capacity is sufficient. Equipment material's urgency transportation with limited capacity is still a meaningful problem that would be studied in further research.

Acknowledgement. This work is supported by Independent Project of Naval University of Engineering Research under Grant 20161613 and 20161614.

References

1. Wang, Z.X.: Military Logistics Introduction. Haichao Press, Beijing (1994)
2. Hitchcock, F.L.: The distribution of a product from several sources to numerous locations. J. Math. Phys. **20**(4), 224–230 (1941)
3. Gupta, B., Gupta, R.: Multi-criteria simplex method for a linear multiple objective transportation problem. Indian J. Pure Appl. Math. **14**(2), 222–232 (1983)
4. Song, Y.X., Chen, M.Y., Wu, X.P.: The solution of multi-objective transport problem with fuzzy information. J. Fuzzy Syst. Math. **15**(3), 86–89 (2001)
5. Sun, M.H., Aronson, J.E.: A tabu search heuristic procedure for the fixed charge transportation problem. J. European J. Oper. Res. **106**(3), 441–456 (1998)
6. Li, Z.P.: The shortest-limited time transportation problem and its solution. Chin. J. Manag. Sci. **9**(1), 50–56 (2001)
7. Shangtai, L.: The total cost bound of the transportation problem with varying demand and supply. Omega **31**(4), 247–251 (2003)
8. Dong, P., Yang, C., Chen, X.: Capacity-limitation of transportation problem. J. Naval Univ. Eng. **16**(5), 96–99 (2004)
9. Li, J.: A network heuristic algorithm for vehicle scheduling problems with time windows. Syst. Eng. **17**(2), 66–71 (1999)
10. Wei, J., Hu, T., Luo, Z.H.: An optimization model of equipment transport without restriction of transport-power. J. Naval Univ. Eng. **16**(4), 61–64 (2004)

A New Algorithm for Classification Based on Multi-classifiers Learning

Yifeng Zheng[1,2(✉)], Guohe Li[2], and Wenjie Zhang[1]

[1] School of Computer Sciences, Key Laboratory of Data Science and Intelligence Application,
Fujian Province University, Minnan Normal University, Zhangzhou, China
zhengyifengja@163.com, zhan0300@ntu.edu.sg
[2] College of Geophysics and Information Engineering,
Beijing Key Lab of Data Mining for Petroleum Data University, China University of Petroleum,
Beijing, China
lgh102200@sina.com

Abstract. Quality and quantity are the two key factors to influence the accuracy of classification. In order to improve the classification accuracy, in this paper, we propose a new algorithm, called CMCM (Classification based on Multiple Classifier Models), which consists of two classification models. In Model1, we mainly focus on the improvement of quality, thus the best attribute value from both the items and their complements in the training set is selected as the first item of a classification rule. While in Model2, quantity is taken into consideration, so it constructs two candidate sets and uses the one-versus-many strategy to generate several rules at one time. The experiment results show that: (1) Model1 can extract sufficient high quality rules and achieve high classification accuracy. (2) Model2 can extract sufficient information and achieve high classification accuracy. (3) CMCM can achieve higher classification accuracy compare with traditional classification.

Keywords: Data mining · Classification · Ensemble learning
Classification rule

1 Introduction

Classification is an important problem in data mining and machine learning. It has been widely used in many fields, such as oil exploration, mobile communications, medical diagnosis, and so on. Classification consists of two steps: (1) building classification model, (2) using the model to predict unknown objects. In order to improve classification accuracy, two problems have been widely exploited:

(1) How to extract high quality information from the training data?
(2) How to extract as more information as possible?

Traditional rule-based classifications usually adopt greedy strategy to extract classification rules, the best attribute value from the training data is selected to generate the rule. Then after an instance is covered by a rule, it will be removed from the training

H. Yuan et al. (Eds.): GSKI 2017, CCIS 849, pp. 254–262, 2018.
https://doi.org/10.1007/978-981-13-0896-3_25

set. However, due to insufficient information obtained, traditional rule-based classification methods cannot extract high-quality classification rules. As a result, it cannot achieve high classification accuracy in many cases. Associative classification is another method that has also been extensively studied [2, 4, 5]. In such method, if the minimum support and the minimum confidence are set too high, many of potential information will be ignored. However, if these thresholds are set too low, many of redundant rules will be generated. Although associative classification can extract a large number of classification rules, the pruning strategy of rules may affect the classification accuracy. Therefore, the classification accuracy highly depends on the setting of these parameters.

In order to improve the classification accuracy, in this paper, we propose a new algorithm, called CMCM (Classification based on Multiple Classifier Models), which consists of two classification models instead of a single classifier. CMCM exploits the two categories of diversity enhancement strategies [12]. In Model1, the best attribute value of the items and their complements in the training set is selected as the first item of a classification rule. Then Model1 uses the best attribute value from the conditional database of the selected item to generate a rule. The first item of a rule directly influences the quality of the classification rule. An optimal first item will make the training set convergence fastly. Therefore, the quality of the classification rule set can be improved by Model1. Model2 constructs two candidate sets and uses the one-versus-many strategy to generate several rules at one time. After these two models are constructed, CMCM uses the ensemble strategy to combine Model1 and Model2. Therefore, CMCM can effectively resolve the quantity and the quality problem of the classification rule set. The experimental results indicate that CMCM outperforms two popular classification methods: CMAR [10] and CPAR [13] in terms of classification accuracy.

The rest of this paper is organized as follows. Section 2 presents some related works. Section 3 describes the classification algorithm of CMCM in details. In Sect. 4, we discuss how to predict the class label of unknown instances using the two models generated by CMCM. The experimental results are presented in Sect. 5. Finally, some concluding remarks and ideas for future works are given in Sect. 6.

2   Related Work

Constructing diverse and accurate classifiers for large-scale databases is a hot issue in data mining and machine learning. Many classification methods have been proposed in different classification domains. These methods have great difference in building classification model and predicting an unknown object. Our work presented in this paper is related to some existing researches of classification methods.

2.1   Building Classification Model

Associative classification methods have been widely investigated in recent years. CBA employs *Apriori − like* method to discover all of *ruleitems* that meet the *minsup* and *minconf* [5]. CMAR uses the *FP − growth* approach to find all of *ruleitems* and then utilizes the *CR − tree* to store and retrieve classification rules. Meanwhile, all classification rules must satisfy certain user-specified *minsup* and *minconf* [10]. CAEP finds Eps (Emerging Patterns) and then uses these EPs to generate rules [1].

Traditional rule-based classifications usually adopt greedy strategy to extract classification rules. FOIL uses *foil gain* to select the best attribute value and generates a classification rule at one time [8]. It removes instances which are covered by the generated rule. In order to improve the quality of rules, ELEM2 uses the correlation of attribute values with the class label to generate classification rules [9]. It also generates a classification rule at one time. PRM inherits some merits of FOIL for classification. The difference lies in that PRM reserves the instance by decreasing its weight. Thus, each instance may be covered by more than one rule. In order to extract sufficient classification rules, CATW sets the weight of both attribute values and tuples which are matched by the rule [11]. Furthermore, CPAR uses the close-to-the-best strategy to select several attribute values. It can build several rules at one time [13].

2.2 Classification Data

It is a challenging task to effectively use a classification rule set to predict a new object. Different classification methods use different strategies to classify instances. In the process of classification, some methods use one matching classification rule, while others use multiple matching classification rules. For example, CBA uses the confidence and support to rank rules. It selects the best rule to classify a new instance. CMAR uses multiple classification rules and adopts the weighted chi-square to measure the strong of the rule set of different classes. CPAR selects the best k rules and compares the average *LaplaceAccuracy* of each class [3]. ELEM2 defines a new measure to order classification rule. It gives a decision score for each class according to the measure.

In our paper, CMCM uses the same strategy like CPAR to rank rules in Model1 and Model2. In order to improve the classification accuracy in ensemble learning, CMCM fuses two models by using the ensemble strategy [12].

3   Classification Algorithm of CMCM

In this section, we describe the algorithm of CMCM in details. We first give the measure of selecting the best attribute value. Then, we develop the algorithm of the Model1. After that the algorithm of the Model2 is given.

3.1   Improve Correlation Measure

We improve the measure of *foil gain* by selecting the best attribute value. Some traditional classification methods use *foil gain* to select optimal attribute value. They use *foil gain* to select literal p which appends to the current rule. The *foil gain* of p is defined as [13]:

$$gain(p) = |P^*|(\log(|P^*|/(|P^*| + |N^*|)) - \log(|P|/(|P| + |N|))) \qquad (1)$$

where $|P|$ represents the number of positive examples in the training data. $|N|$ is the number of negative examples in the training data. $|P^*|$ means the number of positive examples covered p. $|N^*|$ means the number of negative examples covered p.

If the value of $\log(|P^*|/(|P^*| + |N^*|)) - \log(|P|/(|P| + |N|))$ is too small and the value of $|P^*|$ is too large, then $|P^*|$ influences the selection of the best attribute value. We divide *foil gain* into two parts as follows:

$$g_1(p) = \log(|P^*|/(|P^*| + |N^*|)) - \log(|P|/(|P| + |N|)) \tag{2}$$

$$g_2(p) = |P^*| \tag{3}$$

$g_1(p)$ can measure the correlation of the p with the class label. $g_2(p)$ can measure the class support of the p. Given two literals $p1$ and $p2$. If $p1$ is better than $p2$, we say that $p1 > p2$. There are two cases for $p1 > p2$, that is

If $g_1(p1) > g_1(p2)$, then $p1 > p2$.
If $g_1(p1) = g_1(p2)$ and $g_2(p1) > g_2(p2)$, then $p1 > p2$.

3.2   Constructing Model1

The algorithm of Model1 has three special points. Firstly, Model1 selects the best item from both all attribute values and their complements in the training data as the first item of a rule. Secondly, Model1 utilizes the improved correlation measure to select the best attribute value from the conditional database of the first item to generate the rule. It is worth to mention that Model1 does not use the complement of attribute value in the conditional database of the first item. Finally, in order to get more classification rules, Model1 sets the weight of both attribute values and tuples. After a rule is generated, Model1 finds all instances which are covered by the rule in positive examples. Then, Model1 decreases the tuple weight of these instances by multiplying the tuple weight factor. If the tuple weight of the instance is less than the given end threshold, Model1 removes this example from the training data. If we set a small end threshold, many of redundant rules will be generated. On the contrary, if we set a large end threshold, many of potential information will be ignored. Thus different thresholds have different impacts on classification accuracy. After the rule is generated, Model1 can reduce the importance of attribute value by using the weight of attribute value. Thus, Model1 can get many of potentially useful information to generate more high quality rules. The details of how to construct Model1 is shown in Alogrithm 1.

ALOGRITHM1: Construct_ Model1

Input: Training set $D = P \cup N$ (P and N are the sets of all positive and negative examples, respectively)

1: *attributeWeight* $\leftarrow \alpha$, *tupleWeight* $\leftarrow \beta$,

   tupleThreshold $\leftarrow \lambda$, *rules* $\leftarrow$ *null*

2: while $|P| > 0$

3:    $N' \leftarrow N$, $P' \leftarrow P$,

     rule $\leftarrow$ *null* , *negativeFlag* $\leftarrow$ *true*

4:     while $|N'| > 0$ and *rule.length* < *max_rule_length*

5:       if *negativeFlag = true* then

6:         *Cav* $\leftarrow$ Get Attribute values and their complements in P'

7:         *av* $\leftarrow$ *GetBestValue(measure, Cav)*

8:         *negativeFlag* $\leftarrow$ *false*

9:       else

10:        *Cav* $\leftarrow$ Get Attribute values in P'

11:        *av* $\leftarrow$ *GetBestValue(measure, Cav)*

12:      end

13:     *rule.add(av)*

14:     $P' \leftarrow P' - \{$ all examples not satisfying *rule* in $P'\}$

15:     $N' \leftarrow N' - \{$ all examples not satisfying *rule* in $N'\}$

16:    end

17:    *rules* $\leftarrow$ *rules* $\cup \{rule\}$

18:    *RemoveInstance(P, rule)*

19: end

3.3 Constructing Model2

In order to generate several high quality rules simultaneously, Model2 constructs two candidate sets and uses the one-versus-many strategy.

(1) Model2 obtains the best first item from the training set like Model1 as seed. Then, it chooses several close-to-the-best attribute values as a global candidate set. Meanwhile, Model2 constructs the conditional candidate set according to the seed.
(2) Model2 sorts these two sets according to the score of their elements. And then, it selects three of the best elements from each candidate set to generate candidate set.
(3) Model2 connects the seed with the candidate set to generate the pattern set.

If the patterns have greater information gains than the given threshold, they will be reserved. If the confidence of the pattern is 100%, then the rule is directly generated. Otherwise, in the conditional database of each pattern, Model2 selects the best attribute value to generate a rule. After the rule is generated, the weight of both attribute values and tuples will be decreased as that in the Model1. Model2 repeats this process until all patterns generate the rules. Therefore, Model2 can generate several rules at one time. The details of how to construct Model2 is shown in Alogrithm 2.

ALOGRITHM2: Construct_Model2

Input: Training set $D = P \cup N$ (P and N are the sets of all positive and negative examples, respectively)

1:    *attributeWeight* $\leftarrow \alpha$, *tupleWeight* $\leftarrow \beta$, *tupleThreshold* $\leftarrow \lambda$, *rules* $\leftarrow$ *null*

2:    while $|P'| > 0$

3:      $N' \leftarrow N , P' \leftarrow P$, *subRules* $\leftarrow$ *null* , *patternSet* $\leftarrow$ *null*

4:      *patterSet* $\leftarrow$ *GeneratePattern(P', measure)*

5:      for each pattern p in *patternSet*

6:        $N' \leftarrow N , P' \leftarrow P$

7:        while $|P'| > 0$

8:          *rule* $\leftarrow$ *null*

9:          *rule.add(p)*

10:          if *rule.confidence* = 1 then

11:            *subRules* $\leftarrow$ *subRules* $\cup \{rule\}$, continue

12:          end

13:          while $|N'| > 0$ and *rule.length* < *max_rule_length*

14:        *AR* $\leftarrow$ Get Attribute values in P' according the antecedent of *rule*

15:          *av* $\leftarrow$ *GetBestValue(measure, AR)*

16:          *rule.add(av)*

17:          $P' \leftarrow P' - \{$all examples not satisfying *rule* in $P'\}$

18:          $N' \leftarrow N' - \{$all examples not satisfying *rule* in $N'\}$

19:        end

20:        *subRules* $\leftarrow$ *subRules* $\cup \{rule\}$

21:        *RemoveInstance(P', r)*

22:      end

23:     end

24:    *rules* $\leftarrow$ *rules* $\cup$ *subRules*

25:    for each rule r in *subRules*

26:      *RemoveInstance(P, r)*

27:    end

28: end

4   Prediction of the Algorithm CMCM

CMCM constructs two classification models. Before making any prediction, Model1 and Model2 use the Laplace expected error estimate [3] to evaluate the quality of rules respectively.

LaplaceAccuracy is defined as follow:

$$LaplaceAccuracy = (n_c + 1)/(n_{tot} + k) \tag{4}$$

where k is the number of classes, n_{tot} is the total number of examples satisfying the antecedent of rule, among which n_c examples belong to c

In the process of predicting an unknown instance, if the instance is matched by several rules at one time in each model [6, 7], [14]. CMCM uses the following steps:

(1) In each model, if all of the rules have the same class label, we assign the label to the model.
(2) In each model, if all of the rules belong to different classes, we calculate the average *LaplaceAccuracy* of each class. Then, the class label with the highest average value is assigned to the model.
(3) If Model1 and Model2 have the same class label, CMCM assigns that label to the instance. Otherwise, if Model1 and Model2 belong to different classes, CMCM selects the model which has higher score and assigns its label to the instance.

5   Experimental Analysis

In this section, we provide experimental results to compare the performance of our proposed CMCM with two popular classification methods: CMAR and CPAR. All experiments are performed on 18 different datasets from the UCI data collection. All datasets are conducted using stratified ten-fold cross-validation. For CMAR, the support threshold is set to 1% and the confidence threshold is set to 50%. The database coverage threshold of CMAR is set to 4 and the confidence difference threshold is set to 20%. For CPAR, the threshold δ is set to 0.05. The threshold α of CPAR is set to $2/3$ and the threshold of minority gain is set to 0.7. For CMCM, the threshold of *attributeWeight* is set to 0.667 and the threshold of *tupleWeight* is set to 0.75.

Table 1 compares the classification accuracy achieved by our proposed CMCM as well as CMAR and CPAR. CMAR and CPAR are implemented by their authors. From Table 1, we can see that both Model1 and Model2 can achieve higher accuracy than CMAR and CPAR in most cases. This is because that Model1 selects the best attribute value from both the items and their complements in the training set as the first item of a classification rule. And Model2 constructs two candidate sets and uses the one-versus-many strategy to generate several rules at one time. Therefore the quality and quantity of classification can be improved, which results in better classification accuracy. Furthermore, since CMCM uses the effective ensemble strategy to combine Model1 and Model2, it can achieve higher accuracy than the single classifier.

Table 1. Comparison of test accuracy on CMCM

Dataset	CMAR	CPAR	Model1	Model2	CMCM
anneal	0.973	0.984	0.9927	0.9865	0.9922
austral	0.861	0.862	0.827	0.8222	0.8681
auto	0.781	0.82	0.8297	0.8247	0.8348
breast	0.964	0.96	0.9499	0.9561	0.9728
cleve	0.822	0.815	0.8155	0.8191	0.8447
diabetes	0.758	0.751	0.7643	0.7657	0.7695
glass	0.701	0.744	0.7479	0.7481	0.7383
heart	0.822	0.826	0.8056	0.8214	0.8407
hypo	0.984	0.981	0.987	0.9856	0.9889
iono	0.915	0.926	0.92	0.9324	0.9515
iris	0.94	0.947	0.9583	0.95	0.96
labor	0.897	0.847	0.9021	0.8862	0.9133
led7	0.725	0.736	0.7283	0.7279	0.7309
lymph	0.831	0.823	0.8662	0.8454	0.8729
pima	0.751	0.738	0.7572	0.7544	0.7618
tic-tac	0.992	0.986	0.969	0.9793	0.976
vehicle	0.688	0.695	0.7039	0.6949	0.7388
wine	0.95	0.955	0.9649	0.965	0.9667
Average	0.8531	0.8553	0.8605	0.8592	0.8734

6   Conclusions

The quality of classification rule is one of the most important factors for the accuracy of classification. There are many methods to improve the quality of the classification rule, for example the support of the classification rule, the length of the classification rule, and so on. The other important factor is the quantity of the classification rule. If the number of the classification rules is too small, it may influence the classification accuracy. In this paper, we present a new approach by constructing two classification models. In Model1, we mainly focus on the quality, thus attribute value and its complements are used. In Model2, quantity is taken into consideration, so it constructs two candidate sets and uses the one-versus-many strategy to generate several rules at one time. Meanwhile, to address the issue of ranking the base classifiers and combining the outputs of these classification models, CMCM uses the ensemble strategy to combine Model1 and Model2. The results of our experiment indicate that CMCM can generate enough number of high quality classification rules and achieve higher classification accuracy than the single one.

Acknowledgments. This work is supported by Natural Science Funds of China (Nos. 61701213), Scientific Research Foundation for the Returned Overseas Chinese Scholars, State Education Ministry, the Program for Excellent Talents of Fujian Province, the Special Research Fund for

Y. Zheng et al.

Higher Education of Fujian (No. JK2015027), and the Research Fund for Educational Department of Fujian Province (No. JA15300).

References

1. Dong, G., Zhang, X., Wong, L., Li, J.: CAEP: classification by aggregating emerging patterns. In: Arikawa, S., Furukawa, K. (eds.) DS 1999. LNCS (LNAI), vol. 1721, pp. 30–42. Springer, Heidelberg (1999). https://doi.org/10.1007/3-540-46846-3_4
2. Veloso, A., Meira Jr., W., Zaki, M.J.: Lazy associative classification. In: ICDM 2006, pp. 645–654 (2006)
3. Clark, P., Boswell, R.: Rule induction with CN2: some recent improvements. In: Kodratoff, Y. (ed.) EWSL 1991. LNCS, vol. 482, pp. 151–163. Springer, Heidelberg (1991). https://doi.org/10.1007/BFb0017011
4. Brin, S., Motwani, R., Silverstein, C.: Beyond market: generalizing association rules to correlations. In: SIGMOD 1997, pp. 265–276 (1997)
5. Liu, B., Hsu, W., Ma, Y.: Integrating classification and association rule mining. In: KDD 1998, pp. 80–86 (1998)
6. Liu, R., Yuan, B.: Multiple classifiers combination by clustering and selecting. Inf. Fus. 2(2001), 163–168 (2001)
7. Windeatt, T.: Diversity measures for multiple classifier system analysis and design. Inf. Fus. 6(2005), 21–36 (2005)
8. Quinlan, J.R., Cameron-Jones, R.M.: FOIL: a midterm report. In: Brazdil, Pavel B. (ed.) ECML 1993. LNCS, vol. 667, pp. 1–20. Springer, Heidelberg (1993). https://doi.org/10.1007/3-540-56602-3_124
9. An, A.: Learning classification rules from data. Int. J. Comput. Math. Appl. 45(2003), 737–748 (2003)
10. Li, W., Han, J., Pei, J.: CMAR: accurate and efficient classification based on multiple class-association rules. In: ICDM 2001, pp. 369–376 (2001)
11. Zheng, Y., Huang, Z., He, T.: Classification based on both attribute value weight and tuple weight under the cloud computing. Math. Prob. Eng. 2013(2013), 1–7 (2013)
12. Zhou, Z.H.: Ensemble Methods: Foundations and Algorithms, p. 2012. CRC, Boca Raton (2012)
13. Yin, X., Han, J.: CPAR: classification based on predictive association rules. In: Proceedings of the 2003 Society for Industrial and Applied Mathematics (SIAM) International Conference on Data Mining (2003)
14. Wang, G., Sun, J., Ma, J., Xue, K., Gud, J.: Sentiment classification: the contribution of ensemble learning. Decis. Support Syst. 57(2014), 77–93 (2014)

An Information Distance Metric Preserving Projection Algorithm

Xiaoming Bai[1] and Chengzhang Wang[2(✉)]

[1] Information School, Capital University of Economics and Business, Beijing, China
xmbai@cueb.edu.cn
[2] School of Statistics and Mathematics, Central University of Finance and Economics,
Beijing, China
czwang@cufe.edu.cn

Abstract. This paper proposes a novel dimensionality reduction algorithm. The algorithm, coined information distance metric preserving projection (IDPP), aims to identify the complicated intrinsic property of high dimensional space. IDPP employed geodesic information distance to evaluate the relationship between each pair-wise data points. It yielded a distance preserving projection to map sample data from high dimensional observation space to low dimensional feature one. IDPP preserves intrinsic structure of high dimensional space globally. It possesses explicit projection formula which makes it easily to be used for new sample data. Unsupervised and supervised approaches constructed on the basis of IDPP was evaluated on financial data. Experimental results show that trustworthiness of IDPP is almost the same as ISOMAP, and it performs much better than the rival algorithms.

Keywords: Dimensionality reduction · Manifold learning · Financial analysis

1 Introduction

Many manifold learning algorithms have been proposed for data analysis in recent years. Manifold learning is an approach of dimensionality reduction. Real data, such as financial data, is composed of many important factors, such as financial ratio, inventory turnover ratio, cash ratio, etc. According to [1], some of the factors are correlated. For example, when cash flows of a listed company are less than adequate, its debt levels will be high. If these correlated factors cannot be evaluated precisely, actual information contained in the original data may be overlapping and ambiguous. Replace the original data by a lower dimensional representation obtained via subspace approximation can reduce the disadvantage effect of factors' correlation [2].

There are two typical categories of manifold learning algorithms: linear and nonlinear ones. Principal component analysis (PCA) is the most popular linear manifold learning algorithm, and has been applied in financial data analysis [3, 4]. By calculating the eigenvectors of covariance matrix of the original data, PCA linearly transforms a high dimensional input vector into a low dimensional one whose components are uncorrelated. However, financial data is located in a nonlinear manifold embedded in high

© Springer Nature Singapore Pte Ltd. 2018
H. Yuan et al. (Eds.): GSKI 2017, CCIS 849, pp. 263–272, 2018.
https://doi.org/10.1007/978-981-13-0896-3_26

dimensional observation space. Linear methods are bound to ignore some importantly intrinsic information of the original data. To overcome the disadvantage of linear dimensionality reduction methods, many nonlinear manifold learning algorithms are proposed to analyze data. Isomap [5] and LLE [6] are two earliest proposed nonlinear manifold learning algorithms. Isomap tries to capture the intrinsic geometry of observation space by preserving geodesic distance between all data points. Whereas, LLE tries to seek the intrinsic nonlinear structure through preserving locally linear relationship between data points within one's neighborhood. These two nonlinear methods do yield impressive results on data analysis, however, they cannot present any map from high dimensional space to low dimensional one. How to produce correspondent representation in low dimensional space for new sample data is an obstacle for these two classical algorithms in application. To tackle the problem, Locality Preserving Projection (LPP) [7] is proposed. LPP aims to generate linear projection explicitly which preserves the intrinsic geometry of nonlinear manifold structure by optimizing the linear approximation of eigenfunctions of the Laplace Beltrami operator on data set. Algorithms as mentioned above all use geometric space distance to characterized inherent relationship between data points. As for financial data analysis, information characteristics of data set, i.e. probability distributions, are very important. Geometric space distance is not suitable to measure the distance between financial data points. Information distance metric [8] is proposed to describe the distance between financial data points.

In this paper, a new manifold learning algorithm, named Information Distance Metric Preserving Projection (IDPP), is proposed to implement dimensionality reduction. IDPP is a globally nonlinear manifold learning approach. Advantage of global approach is it tends to give more faithful representation of data set's structure, and it is easy to understand theoretically. IDPP generates projection from original high dimensional observation space to low dimensional one explicitly. Information distance metric between data points is preserved in low dimensional space. So the low dimensional embedding can reflect nonlinear properties of original data. Experiments using financial data of small and medium-sized companies from China A-share Stock Market are designed to validate effectiveness of the proposed algorithm. The rest of the paper is organized as follows: Sect. 2 introduces information distance metric. Section 3 describes the proposed algorithm IDPP. Section 4 reports experimental results on financial data analysis. Conclusions are presented in last section.

2 Information Distance Metric

The key of manifold learning algorithm is how to analyze the intrinsic structure of the manifold. Most of classical manifold learning algorithms, such as Isomap [5], LLE [6], just use Euclidean distance to obtain geometric structure of the manifold. The advantage of Euclidean distance is that it is direct and easy to compute, as most of the data are represented on Euclidean space. However, if the data are distributed on a statistical manifold, Euclidean distance would not properly measure geometric information between pair-wise data. According to [9], distance between pair-wise data on statistical manifold can be measured by information divergence, such as Kullback-Leibler (KL). Information distance metric has been used on financial data analysis [8], visualization in demography analysis [10].

For a statistical manifold M, suppose $f_1(x)$, $f_2(x) \in M$ are two probability distributions, then information distance between f_1, f_2 can be approximated with KL divergence [10] as:

$$\mathrm{Dis}(f_1, f_2) \approx \frac{1}{2}\left(\sqrt{KL(f_1 \| f_2)} + \sqrt{KL(f_2 \| f_1)} \right) \tag{2.1}$$

Where

$$KL(f_1 \| f_2) = \int f_1(x) log \frac{f_1(x)}{f_2(x)} \tag{2.2}$$

As the statistical manifold M is a nonlinear subspace, points far apart may appear deceptively close as measured by their straight-line information distance using (2.1), the pair-wise geodesic distance should be approximated along the manifold. For nearby points, information distance can be regarded as geodesic distance on the manifold. For faraway points, geodesic distance can be approximated by adding up a sequence of "short hops" between nearby points [5].

For a probability distribution set $F = \{f_i | i = 1 \dots n\}$, to approximate geodesic information distance between all pairs of probability distributions, a connected graph is constructed, then geodesic information distance is computed in following steps:

(1) Define parameter $k(1 < k \leq n)$ of k-nearest neighborhood. For probability distribution f_i, if f_j is one of the k-nearest neighbor of f_i, set the edge length between f_i and f_j to be the information distance between f_i and f_j, that is $l^1(i, j) = \mathrm{Dis}(f_i, f_j)$; otherwise, define $l^1(i, j) = +\infty$.

(2) Use Warshall algorithm to compute the shortest distance between all pairs of probability distributions. For each value $s = 1, \dots, n$, calculate:

$$l^s(i, j) = \min\left\{ l^{s-1}(i, j), l^{s-1}(i, h) + l^{s-1}(h, j) \right\} \tag{2.3}$$

Where $i = 1, \dots, n, j = 1, \dots n$. The final value $l^n(i, j)$ is the shortest path between probability distribution f_i and probability distribution f_j, and can be approximated to the geodesic information distance between f_i, f_j, so one can define the information distance metric of F to be $Dis_G = (l^n(i, j))_{n \times n}$.

3   IDPP Algorithm

The proposed information distance metric preserving projection algorithm (IDPP) aims to preserve intrinsic manifold structure through preserving Euclidean distance relationship of each pair-wise data in low dimensional space to be the same as information distance relationship between corresponding pair-wise data in high dimensional space. That is nearby data points in high dimensional space is still kept nearly in low dimensional space, at the same time, far away data points in high dimensional space is still kept fairly in low dimensional space.

Our proposed IDPP algorithm is different from other manifold learning algorithms in the following aspects:

(1) IDPP aims to generate a projection explicitly from high dimensional space to low dimensional one. Using the projection, it is very convenient to find location of new data point in low dimensional space. So IDPP algorithm can be used for the task of pattern recognition, classification, etc.

(2) Unlike LPP [7], IDPP is constructed on the basis of information distance, not Euclidean distance. The information distance metric is more suitable to be used on statistical manifold. Information divergence is generally more relevant to statistical discrimination performance rather than Euclidean distance [10].

(3) IDPP is a global algorithm. Principal advantage of the global approach is that it tends to produce a more faithful representation of the manifold's global structure, and it is easy to be understood theoretically [11].

For a collection of data set $X = \{x_i | x_i \in R^n, i = 1, \ldots, n\}$, IDPP is proposed to generate a projection α, which satisfies: $y_i = \alpha x_i$. Where $y_i \in R^d (d < n)$ is the corresponding low dimensional representation of x_i. As mentioned above, data in low dimensional space should keep the relative information distance between each pair of data in high dimensional one. It can be achieved by optimizing the following function:

$$\min \sum_{i,j} \left\| y_i - y_j \right\|^2 S_{ij}, \quad s.t \ y_i \neq y_j \tag{3.1}$$

Where S_{ij} is punishment factor, and value of S_{ij} is related to the geodesic information distance between x_i and x_j. S_{ij} can be defined by heat kernel or cosine kernel function. In this paper, heat kernel function is adopted as: $S_{ij} = e^{-I^n(i,j)/2}$. $I^n(i,j)$ is geodesic information distance between x_i and x_j defined in Eq. (2.3).

To solve the optimization problem as (3.2), one can get

$$\min \sum_{i,j} \left\| y_i - y_j \right\|^2 S_{ij} = tr(YLY^T), \quad s.t \quad YDY^T = 1 \tag{3.2}$$

Where $L = D - S, S = (S_{ij})$, D is a diagonal matrix whose entries are column sum of S, that is $D_{ii} = \sum_{j=1}^{n} S_{ji}$. For $Y = \alpha f(X), F = (f(x_i))$, using Lagrangian multiplier method, one can get: $FLF^T \alpha^T = \lambda FDF^T \alpha^T$. FDF^T is nonsingular and the above eigenfunction problem can be stably solved [12]. α is eigenvector.

4 Experimental Results

To verify the effectiveness of the proposed IDPP algorithm, three experiments are conducted using dataset from China A-share Stock Market.

4.1 Dataset

Annual financial data of 2090 listed companies between year 2008 to 2014 from China A-share stock market are exploited in the work. All data are come from Wind Financial Terminal. 23 financial indexes are selected to reflect 6 aspects of the listed companies's financial status. All indexes are shown in Table 1.

Table 1. Financial indexes

Aspect	Variable	Factor
Solvency	x_{i1}	Current ratio
	x_{i2}	Quick ratio
	x_{i3}	Account payable turnover ratio
Growth ability	x_{i4}	Operating income growth rate
	x_{i5}	Growth rate of net assets
	x_{i6}	Net profit margin
Management ability	x_{i7}	Inventory turnover
	x_{i8}.	Accounts receivable turnover rate
	x_{i9}	Turnover rate of current assets
	x_{i10}	Fixed asset turnover
	x_{i11}	Turnover ratio of total assets
Cash flow ratio	x_{i12}	Cash ratio
	x_{i13}	Net operating cash flow/current liabilities
	x_{i14}	Cashaturity debt ratio
Profitability	x_{i15}	Operating profit margin
	x_{i16}	Return on equity
	x_{i17}	Return on total assets
	x_{i18}	Gross profit
	x_{i19}	Net profit
Capital composition	x_{i20}	Equity ratio
	x_{i21}	Fixed assets
	x_{i22}	Total assets
	x_{i23}	Asset-liability ratio

4.2 Experimental Settings

To verify effectiveness of the proposed algorithm, IDPP, experiments are carried out on financial data to illustrate the promising character of it. First, we present rust degree of the algorithms using trustworthiness measure. Second, on the basis of IDPP, unsupervised learning algorithm is constructed and evaluated using some classification measures. Such as Precision and Error type, are used in low dimensional space to evaluate the classifying ability of the algorithms. Last, a supervised learning approach is constructed by combining IDPP with LDA to improve the accuracy.

4.2.1   Trustworthiness of the Algorithm

Trustworthiness [13] measures the trust degree of a projection which maps high dimensional data onto low dimensional space. A projection is trustworthy if the k-nearest neighbors of each data point in low dimensional space are also distance-close in high dimensional space. Trustworthiness measurement is defined as:

$$M(k) = 1 - \frac{2}{Nk(2N - 3k - 1)} \sum_{i=1}^{N} \sum_{j \in U_k(i)} (r(i,j) - k) \tag{4.1}$$

Where $U_k(i)$ is the set of k-nearest neighbors of the *i-th* point in low dimensional space. $r(i, j)$ is the rank of the *j-th* point by ordering distance from *i-th* point in the original data space. The maximum value of M(k) is 1. More trustworthy of one projection, value of M(k) more closes to 1. Trustworthiness of IDPP, PCA and ISOMAP are computed respectively, results are shown in Fig. 1.

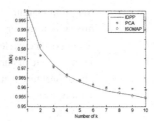

Fig. 1.   Trustworthiness with k-nearest neighbor.

Experimental results show that three algorithms all present good trustworthy property. As the number k increases, trustworthiness of the algorithms decreases. Whereas trustworthiness of PCA decreases more slowly than the others, the difference is less than 0.005. IDPP achieves almost the same good trustworthiness as ISOMAP which is above 0.955.

4.2.2   Unsupervised Learning Algorithm

For China A-share stock market, 'ST' or '*ST' will be appointed before a company's stock name if it is in an abnormal financial condition. In our experiment, ST and *ST company is assigned to 1, otherwise –1. K-means algorithm is employed to implement the classification task in low dimensional space. To verify the performance of IDPP, Recall and Precision, Error type I, Error type II are calculated respectively. Recall reflects the efficiency of how many healthy companies can be classified to be 'healthy' by the classifier and Precision is the ratio that how many companies that classified to be 'healthy' are healthy companies in reality. Error type I represent the number of companies classified as abnormal when in reality they are healthy divided by the total number of health companies, and Error type II represents number of samples classified as healthy when they are observed to be abnormal, divided by number of abnormal companies. Results are shown in Fig. 2.

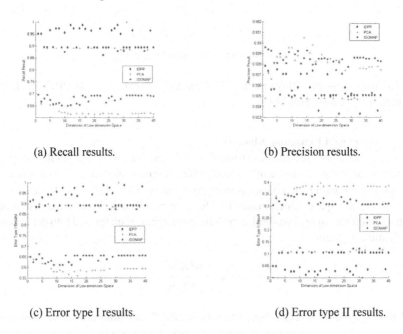

(a) Recall results.   (b) Precision results.

(c) Error type I results.   (d) Error type II results.

Fig. 2. Performance of the algorithms.

Experimental results show that IDPP algorithm achieves better performance in the aspects of Recall and Error type II than the rival algorithms. As to Precision and Error type I results, IDPP performs not so good compared with PCA and ISOMAP.

Generally, results of recall and precision of one algorithm could not achieve the best performance simultaneously. So as to the results of error type I and type II. To evaluate the over-all performance, F_1-score is usually adopted as the criteria. F_1-score is a measure of a test's accuracy. The greater F1-score is, the better performance of one algorithm is. Calculation results of F_1-score are shown in Fig. 3.

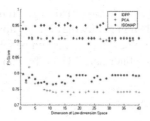

Fig. 3. Results of F1-score of the algorithms.

Experimental results illustrate that the over-all performance of IDPP is much better than that of PCA and ISOMAP.

4.2.3 Supervised Learning Algorithm

To get more accurate classification results, supervised approach is generally adopted to accomplish the task. In this work, a supervised learning algorithm is constructed by combining IDPP with Linear Discriminant Analysis (LDA). LDA seeks to map original data onto feature space which makes the distance between different classes maximum and that within the same class minimum. The algorithm is transformed into the following optimization problem:

$$w_{opt} = argmax \frac{w^T S_b w}{w^T S_w w} \tag{4.2}$$

Where S_b is between-class divergent matrix, and S_w is within-class divergent matrix. W is projected vector. Because of using category prior knowledge, data in the feature space can obtain more accurate classification results. In our experiment, financial data of 2090 companies from China A-share stock market are divided into two datasets randomly, training set and test one. Training set includes 1500 company's data, and the rest of 590 company's data are included in test set.

In the training process, IDPP is first used to get the projection α, which can map high dimensional data x_i onto low dimensional space (as shown in Eq. 3.1). Then LDA is employed in the low dimensional space to get the projection W, which would project the data from low dimensional space onto feature space by $z_i = wy_i$. In the test process, new sample data x_i is project into feature space as: $z_i = wax_i$. Nearest neighborhood approach is used in the feature space to classify the test sample into normal company or abnormal one. Experimental results are shown in Fig. 4.

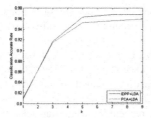

Fig. 4. Accumulation accuracy of the algorithms.

Experimental results show that our proposed algorithm, IDPP+LDA, can achieve much better classification accuracy than PCA+LDA, which indicates that IDPP has the potential to reveal intrinsic geometry of high dimensional dataset and is more suitable to classify complicated samples such as financial data.

5 Conclusions

In this paper, we proposed a new nonlinear dimensionality reduction approach named Information Distance Metric Preserving Projection (IDPP) algorithm. IDPP exploits information distance to evaluate local relationship of the data points. Geodesic distance is employed in IDPP to size up the global geometry of the nonlinear manifold. In addition, IDPP generates projection explicitly which makes it more easy and faster to map novel data points to low dimensional space than other traditional nonlinear dimensional reduction algorithms.

Experimental results on financial dataset of China A-share stock market show that IDPP possesses the following properties. Firstly, IDPP is a trustworthy projection. The nearest relationship in high dimensional space can be kept in low dimensional space. IDPP achieves almost same trustworthiness as ISOMAP. Secondly, IDPP can reveal the intrinsic attributes of the high dimensional dataset effectively. Unsupervised binary classification algorithm can be used directly on the low dimensional space to get promising results. Thirdly, IDPP can be combined easily with other algorithm such as LDA to construct supervised approach and achieve more excellent classification accuracy.

Acknowledgments. This work is supported partly by the Beijing Social Science Foundation (NO. 16SRB021), Beijing Philosophy and Social Science Foundation (NO. 16YJB029).

References

1. Moyer, R.C., McGuigan, J., Rao, R.: Contemporary Financial Management. Cengage Learning, Ohio (2012)
2. Berrya, M.W., Brownea, M., et al.: Algorithms and applications for approximate nonnegative matrix factorization. Comput. Stat. Data Anal. **52**, 155–173 (2007)
3. Yu, L., Wang, S., Lai, K.: A neural-network-based nonlinear meta-modeling approach to financial time series forecasting. Appl. Soft Comput. **9**, 563–574 (2009)

4. Canbas, S., Cabuk, A., BilginKilic, S.: Prediction of commercial bank failure via multivariate statistical analysis of financial structures: the Turkish case. Eur. J. Oper. Res. **166**, 528–546 (2005)
5. Tenenbaum, J.B., de Silva, V., Langford, J.C.: A global geometric framework for nonlinear dimensionality reduction. Science **290**(5500), 2319–2323 (2000)
6. Roweis, S., Saul, L.: Nonlinear dimensionality reduction by locally linear embedding. Science **290**(5500), 2323–2326 (2000)
7. He, X., Yan, S., et al.: Face recognition using Laplacian faces. IEEE Trans. Pattern Anal. Mach. Intell. **27**(3), 328–340 (2005)
8. Huang, Y., Kou, G.: A kernel entropy manifold learning approach for financial data analysis. Decis. Support Syst. **64**, 31–42 (2014)
9. Carter, K.M., Raich, R., et al.: FINE: fisher information non-parametric embedding. IEEE Trans. Patt. Anal. Mach. Intell. **31**(11), 2093–2098 (2009)
10. Carter, K.M., Raich, R., et al.: Information-geometric dimensionality reduction. IEEE Sig. Process. Mag. **28**, 89–99 (2011)
11. de Silva, V., Tenenbaum, J.B.: Global versus local methods in nonlinear dimensionality reduction. In: Advances in Neural Information Processing Systems, vol. 15, pp. 705–712 (2003)
12. Cai, D., He, X., Han, J.: Spectral regression for efficient regularized subspace learning. In: ICCV 2007 (2007)
13. Venna, J., Kaski, S.: Local multi-dimensional scaling with controlled trade-off between trustworthiness and continuity. In: Workshop of Self-Organizing Maps, pp. 695–702 (2005)

Bug Patterns Detection from Android Apps

Waheed Yousuf Ramay[1(✉)], Arslan Akbar[1], and Muhammad Sajjad[2]

[1] School of Computer and Communication Engineering,
University of Science and Technology Beijing, Beijing, China
waheedramaycs@gmail.com, engr.arslanakbar050@gmail.com
[2] Department of Computer Science, Government Degree College, Sahiwal, Pakistan
sajjad@gcs.edu.pk

Abstract. Android has become the most popular OS because of its user-friendly environment, free-ware licensing and thousands of available applications. It is an open source for contributors and developers. The challenging problem in Android apps is to handle the bugs those are generated because of code segment (code constructs) written by developers to fix the reported bug. so code change management is also as critical task, as bug tracking. We have investigated all available previous history of Android bug reports and code changes to identify bug introducing changes. Apply the chi square test to observe the buggy construct. This study will help the reviewers, contributors, developers and quality assurance testers to concentrate and take special care while making or accepting changes to those constructs where it is most likely to induce a bug, which will lead to improve the quality of services provided by Android platform, and ultimately will get more satisfied user.

Keywords: BD (Bug Detection) · SCM (Software Coding Management)
AOS (Android Open Source Apps)

1 Introduction

Mining Software Repositories is one of the active research areas in the field of software engineering. There are many open source software projects including Android, Eclipse, and Mozilla etc. which maintain a version control system for the management of software revisions. Revisions in different versions are managed in Software Configuration Management (SCM) system including CVS, SVN and Git hub. Whereas the bugs and issues are managed in JIRA, Bugzilla, and Google code etc. Data from these version control systems and issue tracking systems are available for the researchers, developers, bug reporters and bug triages to mine and extract useful information for better development and management of the software. In this study we have been able to find out the most sensitive and error prone programming constructs in the code and pattern of bugs introducing code changes. Changes made in the software in different revisions may induce a bug in the code [1] which is overlooked or remained un-noticed in the testing phase and committed in the next version. Such changes in the code are known as bug introducing changes (BICs) [1, 3]. These changes containing bugs remain in the code until reported by the end user. Such reports are managed and gathered using an issue

© Springer Nature Singapore Pte Ltd. 2018
H. Yuan et al. (Eds.): GSKI 2017, CCIS 849, pp. 273–283, 2018.
https://doi.org/10.1007/978-981-13-0896-3_27

tracking or bug tracking system [2, 4]. The Android Open Source Project maintains a public issue tracker where end users may report bugs and request features for the core Android software stack [5]. In this study we mine Bug Introducing Changes (BICs), bug reports, change histories and software repositories to find the most error prone programming constructs and bug patterns in the BICs. To be more specific we have found the answers of the following research questions;

Which are the most sensitive and error prone programming constructs in the code?
What is the pattern of bugs in code changes?
Remaining part of this paper is arranged as follows. In Sect. 2 we mention the related work. Section 3 shows overall approach adopted for study. In Sect. 4 we give some of our findings with a brief discussion in Sect. 5. Section 5 Concludes this paper and Sect. 6 is about the future work.

2 Related Work

Changes made to source code are initiated by bug reporters who use Google online issue tracking system to report the bugs they encounter while using the Android. Bug reports were linked to the revisions in which these issues were fixed to identify the changes introducing the bugs. By analyzing 20169 bugs and 16118 defects [4]. Locate the lines of code that are buggy and the files that contain the buggy code. Successfully identifying the problem areas in the source code where making changes is more risky. Most fixes are found on Tuesday whereas most bugs introducing changes were made on Saturday [6]. Automatic Identification of Bug-Introducing Changes [5] by using annotation graph tells us (i) About which developers and what type of changes in the source code produced the more bugs. (ii) Validation was performed to determine the fixes as legitimate or not by manual inspection. This is to make sure no outlier's i.e. false positives or false negatives are included in the detection process. After determining the BICs further analysis were performed to find the signature changes and micro pattern changes. Find out the correlations between signature changes and BICs. Change history of Android was mined [7] from 1998–2016, revealed that Android Open Source Project (AOSP) consists of 5 sub-projects i.e. kernel, platform, device, tools and tool-chain. Each file of AOSP has been modified average 8.7 time on average where kernel is totally C based, is the top most in terms of changes made to its files i.e. 78.8%. There are total 1563 contributors, 86 contributed to more than one sub-projects. Google leads with 78% contribution for device, 100% for tool-chain and 77% for tools. To help the end user to specify the components of a new bug correctly and enable triggers to predict the buggy component, following were main contribution [8]. (A) To evaluate the impact of incorrectly specified bugs on triggers and developers of Eclipse project with the help of statistical analysis. (B) To predict bugs' components via mining historical bug reports. All fixed bugs were classified [8], based on support vector machines and Naïve Bayes classifiers. Approach predicted and localized the components correctly that were buggy. Automatic Recovery of Root Causes from Bug Fixing Changes [8, 9]. Root causes of a particular bug are a line of code in the previous revision that may or may not be the part of essential changes. Reverse engineering approach has been adopted which is a combination of machine learning and code analysis techniques to track the root causes of a bug. Approach mainly consists of two steps as follows; (i) apply machine learning and code analysis to automatically recover the root causes. (ii) Comparing the root causes with 200 manually extracted golden set of root causes for evaluation. Finding the fix inducing changes has been the task in the analysis of software changes. This approach replaces annotation graphs used by [7], with line- number mappings. This was to tracked lines of source code changes over the lifetime of the software; secondly, DiffJ, a syntax aware diff tool was used to ignore formatting changes and comments. Changes that are fixes means those changes which are clean and resulted in no bugs. Chadd Williams and Jaime Spacco [9]. Introduced an algorithm base on SZZ, Sliweski, Zimerman and Kim [10], automatically identify the fix-inducing changes. It also uses diffj a java based syntax aware diff tool which provides the changes ignoring the comments and formatting changes. In this approach Java-syntax aware diff tool was used to ignore a large number of different types of formatting changes. Most of the efforts were put in to find out the bug introducing changes [10, 11], buggy components problematic code segments [12], root causes of fixes [9], days of week more bugs introduced, classification of BICs, finding topic trends in the discussion forum and prediction of buggy components or development activities [11]. When compared our work with related work. This is a new and novice idea to find the buggy programming constructs along with bug patterns from two widely used programming languages for coding the Android Open Source Project. To our knowledge no such attempt was made in the history, so this is the baby step towards the new dimension of analyzing the bug inducing changes in the software configuration management system.

3   Methodology

Bug reports can be viewed and downloaded from Google code i.e. current issues/bug reports ("Issues - Android - Android Open Source Project - Issue Tracker - Google Project Hosting," n.d.). These are about 23202 bug reports where there are many useful information was observed like type of bug, status, owner, reporter's message. This information was very important for the analysis as this was considered to match the bug IDs with Bug references found in the Gerrit code changes ("Android/issues, fix, merged Android-review. googlesource Code Review," n.d.). Keeping in view of the objectives of the research it is more convenient to use the 'Gerrit code review' for reviewing the changes made as a result of bug reports. Gerrit provides many facilities including list of fixes made in the code, query tool, diff tool, comments and staring the changes you review. It is easy to extract the bug report reference for Android issues, change id, committer name and email, commit message, code branch, project, commit date and code changes. Files that are changed in a commit are indicated with green and red colors where green color shows the changed lines in the current revision of the code and red color represents those buggy lines which have been changed in the previous revision Fig. 1.

Fig. 1. Bug inducing changes and fixes in Gerritcode review. (Color figure online)

The big problem faced was to clean the data. For that purpose commit messages were carefully studies and only considered those changes where a bug was fixed and which has the status open. In the open status we consider only those changes who has the sub status as merged, release, or future release. Preprocessing the millions of code changes, the built-in search utility of 'Gerrit' was used i.e. the search was refined like status: open, Android/issues, fix, bug, merged. In this way only those changes were projected where bug was fixed. Out of these confirmed bug fixes, each change was manually observed by using diff tool and compared with previous revision to identify the bug inducing changes. See the Fig. 1 where the change in the left pan was responsible for bug-fix i.e. BIC. Right pan shows the bug-fix change.

3.1 Extraction of Bug Patterns

After identification of changes that are involved in inducing the bugs, these lines are extracted to a database table. So that queries may be applied easily to mine the buggy programming constructs and patterns from the source code chunks called change deltas. Change deltas were extracted along with metadata information e.g. bug Id, Change Id, project name, type of file and bug reference. We gathered total 1011 bug introducing changes from 208 commits and 988 files of Java and C language code changes. Programming constructs like for loop, do loop, while loop, if-else, switch-case, Type declaration, Pointers, Classes, Arrays, Return and include/import files are extracted by applying precise queries on the database. These are the commonly used programming constructs in computer languages like Java and C++. Such programming constructs are counted and profiled according to the number of occurrences of each in the Experimental Results section.

Bug patterns are mined from the extracted constructs by finding the associations with each other. Again this was accomplished by designing search queries on the stored code changes in a database table. Following is an example query designed to find the association of 'IF' with 'IF' itself to find nesting of 'IF' construct; SELECT Count (changes. [Code]) AS Total_IF FROM changes WHERE (((changes. Code) Like "* if * if *")) Our methodology is shown in Fig. 2, to find the most error prone programming constructs and Patterns of bugs in the code changes from Android Project consists of following steps.

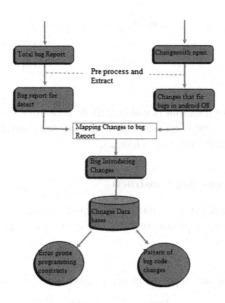

Fig. 2. Methodology for extraction of buggy constructs and patterns

i. Bug reports from code.google.com/issues to view and locate the bugs which has the status release or future release for only defects, ignoring feature request and others reports.
ii. Bug fix information and changes are viewed and preprocessed from Gerrit code review, to select only those changes where bugs are fixed and belonged to Android issues.
iii. Searching those changes which has the status merged in the Gerrit code review.
iv. Map the changes by looking the commit message where bug information is matched with the bug ID in the issues.
v. Copy these changes which are responsible for inducing the bugs from the Gerrit code review to database along with metadata information.

Designing and applying the queries to extract the buggy constructs and patterns from the code changes.

4 Experiments and Results

In this section we present our results for mining bug patterns from Android project. The data gathered for the experiments are obtained from the 'Gerrit code review' for google/Android/issues. Change deltas are collected manually and carefully to be stored in a database table as described in Sect. 4. The analysis is performed to profile the error prone programming constructs in the code changes. On the basis of the analysis on these constructs, we found some patterns of bugs which will be discussed here in detail. We have gathered a total of 1011 sample code changes from 208 commits and 988 files of 'java' and 'C' programming languages see Table 1 and Graph 1.

Table 1. Code change

	C file changes	Java file changes	Total changes
Count	317	694	1011
% age	31.7	68.6	

Using our sample corpus that is gathered from code review system of Android, it was discovered that most bugs are detected from Java code changes about 69% and 31% of the bugs are detected from C code changes.

4.1 Extracted Programming Constructs

Table 2 Shows the combined 'java' and 'C' files buggy constructs. As it is evident from the Graph 2 that most error prone programming construct is 'IF' conditions that also

Table 2. Summary of programming constructs and results of Chi-sq test.

Buggy constructs	Java	% age	C	% age	Total
FOR	101	9%	17	3.2%	118
	79.54		38.46		
DO WHILE	32	3%	81	9.3%	49
	54.60		26.40		
WHILE	8	1%	5	0.9%	13
	8.76		4.24		
IF ELSE	242	22%	101	19.1%	343
	231.21		111.79		
SWITCH CASE	19	2%	8	1.5%	27
	18.20		8.80		
TYPE DECLARATIONS	132	12%	116	22.0%	248
	167.17		80.83		
POINTERS	15	1%	114	21.6%	129
	86.96		42.04		
CLASSES	228	21%	25	4.7%	253
	170.54		82.46		
ARRAY	58	5%	25	4.7%	83
	55.95		27.05		
RETURN	146	13%	43	8.1%	189
	127.40		61.60		
INCLUDE/IMPORT	111	10%	25	4.7%	136
	91.67		44.33		
TOTAL	1092		528		1620
CHI-SQ	334.175				
DF	10				
P-VALUE	0.000				

includes the 'ELSE' part of the statement. Whereas the 2nd highest number of occurrence for the buggy construct is the 'CLASS' definition of a member function or data member of a class. The 3rd largest occurrences of bugs are in data type declarations which involves INT, FLOAT, CHAR, DOUBL. There are 528 buggy programming constructs of type C as shown in Table 2. It is clearly visible that detection rate of 'TYPE DECLARATIONS' and 'POINTERS' are higher in C changes. Which are the most sensitive code changes in the C files. So it is better to take care while declaring a variable and use of pointers in C language code to avoid bug inducing changes. Beside the type declarations and pointers the next largest population of buggy constructs as expected is 'IF' conditions which are not only the overall problematic construct but it is also one of the problematic area of the C language code changes as well. If we talk about the java language we extracted 1092 buggy constructs out of total 1620. 'IF' condition happened to be most buggy construct in java code changes, it is found to be 242 in the java changes. This area of programming languages is the most problematic for the code reviewers and developers. As java is totally based on object orientation, that is why the errors percentage is also very high in 'classes' with 228 counts. Beside this 'TYPE DECLARATIONS' and 'RETURN' also show good enough detection as 132 and 146 respectively. It is observed that 'WHILE' and 'DO' loops are least bothered area of programming language.

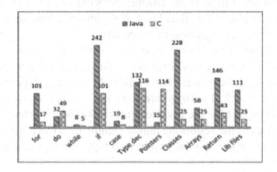

Graph 2.   Comparison of buggy constructs in java and C

4.2   Statistical Analysis

Table 3 shows that average change in the buggy constructs is found to be 101.84 and the percentage variations for the total buggy constructs is found to be 69.15%. If we discuss it separately for java and C changes we can observe that average changes in java is 82.73 which is greater than C change, which are 42.2 on average. Their respective coefficients of variation are 83.34% and 87.93%. The maximum difference in overall constructs is found to be 330 and the maximum disturbance caused by 'IF' is 343 whereas minimum for 'WHILE' equals 30 for our sample data.

Table 3. Bug patterns from code changes

	Total	%	Java	%	C	%
Nested if	73	41.7%	56	38.4%	17	58.6%
Nested for	28	16.0%	26	17.8%	2	6.9%
Nest while	0	0.0%	0	0.0%	0	0.0%
If – for	28	16.0%	26	17.8%	2	6.9%
For – if	40	22.9%	34	23.3%	6	20.7%
If – while	0	0.0%	0	0.0%	0	0.0%
While – if	0	0.0%	0	0.0%	0	0.0%
If - case	4	2.3%	3	2.1%	1	3.4%
Cse – if	2	1.1%	1	0.7%	1	3.4%
For – while	0	0.0%	0	0.0%	0	0.0%
While – for	0	0.0%	0	0.0%	0	0.0%
Total	175		146	83.4%	29	16.6%

4.3 Chi Square Test

This test is used to check the association between the two computer languages and observed buggy construct in their file changes detected as bug inducing. If the results are significant that P value is less than level of significance then we can conclude that the above two attributes are significantly associated.

Expected counts are printed below observed counts, Table 2 also shows the results of Chi-Sq test in which observed and expected counts for different buggy constructs are given for both Java and C languages. The overall Chi-sq test statistical value is 334.175 with degree of freedom $k-1 = 10$ where k is the number of categories of buggy constructs. The Chi-sq test has the P value equals 0.000 which is less than any level of significance. That means the results are highly significant. Hence we can conclude that both the languages show strong relationship with type of buggy constructs.

4.4 Pattern of Bugs in the Extracted Constructs

But pattern are mined from already extracted programming constructs by associating them with each other and finding a relationship between them. We have been able to detect the bug pattern from the constructs, please take a look at the Table 4 and Graph 3. A total of 175 bug patterns are discovered in both Java and C files. Whereas in Java code constructs alone there are 146 bug patterns out of 694 code changes and 1092 programming constructs which is 22% of total java code changes. As compared to Java, C has only 29 out of 317 sample code changes which is just 9% of total C code changes. It is found that nested 'if' structures are the most likely the errors prone pattern Besides the nested if structure it is also evident from the graph that when 'for' is used with 'if' it is also an area of concern for the developers and code reviewers. We can deduce that changes in java files must be carefully reviewed before accepting them. Similarly developers must take special care while changing java files and playing with 'IF' statements more importantly the nested 'IF' structures. While developers who are intended to make changes in the C language, changes that involve pointers and nested if structures are the most sensitive and error prone patterns.

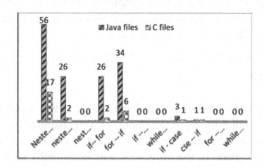

Graph 3. Comparison of bug patterns in Java and C constructs

5 Conclusion

In this study the buggy code changes were mined to understand the programming constructs involved in most of the changes. Total buggy construct found were 1620 in the 1011 bug introducing changes, in which 1092 constructs found in Java file changes and 528 in C file changes. Out of these buggy constructs some patterns of bugs were also mined using the text searching criteria in Specially designed queries. Bug patterns in the code were discovered by finding the association of the buggy constructs with each other e.g. use of IF with IF, IF—FOR, IF – WHILE, IF—FOR, FOR—IF, WHILE— IF, FOR—WHILE, WHILE— FOR etc. as already describe in experimental section of this paper. We profile the buggy constructs and bug patterns found in two types of programming languages (Java and C) used widely in developing the code for Android Open Source Project.

We then perform statistical analysis using Chi-sq test to show the relationship of these constructs for java and C programming language. We conclude that both the languages show strong relationship with type of buggy constructs.

Now let's conclude our findings. When we look at the java files code changes the population of having the most bugs are present in the 'IF' construct. The 2nd largest amount of bugs are detected in the java classes or the code involved in a class. It is another problematic area for the java code developers. Again it is also obvious that 'FOR' loop is the mostly used iteration structure not only in java but C language as well. This makes 'FOR' loop the widely used loop in programming languages. Number of occurrences of functions returning a value and importing the library files in java code is also very high that means these are also considerable buggy constructs which a developer and code reviewer must take into consideration. As for as patterns of bugs are concerned, the nested 'IF' is found to be the most erroneous bug pattern in the java code changes. Similarly the use of 'IF with FOR' is also a high profile bug pattern in java. As compared to C language code changes where we found more bugs in DATA TYPE DECLARATIONS and use of POINTERS i.e. 7.16% and 8.15% respectively. Here 'IF' construct has shown a little less percentage of bugs i.e. 6.23% as compared to Java where it is 14.94%, still very considerable buggy construct in C as well. Use of 'RETURN' statement in the functions is another problematic area in Java buggy codes, but it is not alarming in C code changes. But in case of java files it is pretty high i.e. 13% changes are involved in bugs due to use of RETURN statement.

6 Future Work

When compared our work with related work in the Sect. 2, this is a new and novice idea to find the buggy programming constructs along with bug patterns from two widely used programming languages for coding the Android Open Source Project. To our knowledge no such Attempt was made in the history, so this is the baby step towards the new dimension of analyzing the bug inducing changes in the software configuration management system. Our work may be fragile but it would definitely show a direction to a new horizon of analysis in the field of mining software repositories. Firstly we have gathered the bug introducing changes manually. It has been a hectic and time consuming effort since there are millions of code changes and thousands of bug reports to be examined. It would be more beneficial if our approach with some automated tool for extracting the buggy code changes from all the revisions of the project files. Secondly the buggy constructs and patterns are Mined with database query tool. Our approach uses samples where 1011 code changes were gathered to draw some conclusion.

Although the corpus volume is reasonably large but it does not cover all the bug reports and changes made to the files. In future we intend to mine all the bug fix changes and change history of the Android project to show more accurate. We also intend to include all the sub projects of Android using automated tool.

References

1. Android/issues, fix, merged Androidreview. googlesource Code Review. Accessed 19 Jan 2016
2. Aversano, L., Cerulo, L., Grosso, C.D.: Learning from bug-introducing changes to prevent fault prone code. In: Ninth International Workshop on Principles of Software Evolution: in Conjunction with the 6th ESEC/FSE Joint Meeting, IWPSE 2007, p. 19 (2011)
3. Fiaz, A.S.S., Devi, N., Aarthi, S.: Bug tracking and reporting system, no. 1, pp. 42–45 (2012). Issues - Android - Android Open Source Project - Issue Tracker - Google Project Hosting
4. Kim, S., Zimmermann, T., Pan, K., Whitehead Jr., E.: Automatic identification of bug introducing changes. In: 21st IEEE/ACM International Conference on Automated Software Engineering (ASE 2006), pp. 81–90 (2006)
5. Lamkanfi, A., Perez, J., Demeyer, S.: The Eclipse and Mozilla defect tracking dataset: a genuine dataset for mining bug information. In: 2013 10th Working Conference on Mining Software Repositories, pp. 203–206 (2013)
6. Martie, L., Palepu, V.K., Sajnani, H., Lopes, C.: Trendy bugs topic trends in the Android bug reports, pp. 120–123 (2012)
7. Shihab, E., Kamei, Y., Bhattacharya, P.: Mining challenge 2012: the Android platform. In: 9th IEEE Working Conference on Mining Software Repositories, pp. 112–115 (2012)

8. Sinha, V.S., Mani, S., Gupta, M.: MINCE: mining change history of Android project. In: 2012 9th IEEE Working Conference on Mining Software Repositories (MSR), pp. 132–135 (2012)
9. Śliwerski, J., Zimmermann, T., Zeller, A.: When do changes induce fixes? ACM SIGSOFT Softw. Eng. Notes **30**(4), 1 (2005)
10. Thung, F., Lo, D., Jiang, L.: Automatic recovery of root causes from bug-fixing changes. In: 20th Working Conference on Reverse Engineering, pp. 92–101 (2013)
11. Wang, D., Zhang, H., Liu, R., Lin, M., Wu, W.: Predicting bugs' components via mining bug reports. J. Softw. **7**(5), 1149–1154 (2012)
12. Whitehead, E.J.: Classifying software changes: clean or buggy? IEEE Trans. Softw. Eng. **34**(2), 181–196 (2008)

An Improved PHD Filter Based on Dynamic Programming

Meng Fang[✉], Wenguang Wang, Dong Cao, and Yan Zuo

School of EIE, Beihang University, Beijing 100191, China
fangmeng_buaa@163.com, wwenguang@buaa.edu.cn,
749849251@qq.com, yzuo@hdu.edu.cn

Abstract. Traditional PHD filter for detecting and tracking weak targets does not work well in the case of low detection probability. In this paper, an improvement of PHD filtering based on dynamic programming is proposed. The method takes advantage of the correlation among the multi-frame data. The result of dynamic programming is applied to PHD filter for getting stable detecting and tracking effect. Monte Carlo simulation results show that the improved method is superior to the PHD filter under low detection probability.

Keywords: Weak targets · PHD filter · Dynamic programming

1 Introduction

Detection and tracking technology is widely used in national defense and civilian areas. Civilian application include traffic surveillance, air traffic control, navigation and positioning, etc., while military applications mainly include the detection and tracking of military targets such as ships, aircraft and missiles. The harsh environment of military applications always leads the detection technology to a higher level. The rapid development of highly mobile UAVs and stealth technologies has stimulated the development of target detection and tracking of multi-target, weak-target and high-maneuvering target domains. In general, target detection and tracking contains two kinds of thought. The first one is the classic thought called tracking after detecting which extract target by suppression of clutters before tracking. The other one is called tracking before detecting. This thought advocate that the confirmation of targets should not be finished after processing single frame data. On the contrary, the result of detecting is based on integration multi frame data. The first thought is suitable for high SNR conditions with low computational complexity. However, the information loss caused by threshold detection may lead to failure in strong clutter environment or fluctuating targets. Compared with tracking after detecting, the latter is more suitable for the detection and tracking of weak targets [1].

The tracking before detecting algorithm focuses on research association among multi frame data, such as 3-D matched filter and multiple hypothesis tracking. These algorithms can achieve certain effect, but they do not deal with scenarios with dense clutter or crossing target. In recent years, Mahler et al. applied the random finite set theory to multi-target tracking detection, and proposed the probability hypothesis

© Springer Nature Singapore Pte Ltd. 2018
H. Yuan et al. (Eds.): GSKI 2017, CCIS 849, pp. 284–293, 2018.
https://doi.org/10.1007/978-981-13-0896-3_28

density (PHD) filter. This method avoids issues about the data association. As the result, it has some advantage in processing multi-target tacking before detecting [2]. However, when the target detection probability is low, the detection effect of PHD filtering algorithm declines rapidly, and the missed alarm rate and false alarm rate cannot meet the requirements.

2 PHD Filter Algorithm

Related algorithm based on random finite set develops rapidly for handling the problem of target detection and tracking under the condition of complex environment and large amount of targets. However, these algorithms did not have huge impact on practical engineering applications for that they were too complicated in computational calculation to be realized until VO research group made the important contributions. This team proposed two PHD filter solutions contain particle filter form and Gauss mixed form, which make it possible to apply random finite set to actual project [3, 4]. The main principle and implementation method of PHD filtering algorithm are introduced briefly as followed.

2.1 Multi-target Random Finite Set Model

Random finite set is used to describe a finite set whose elements count and states are unknown. Thus, the random finite set theory is suited to build the multi-target motion model scene within the designated field of view. This model is first proposed by Mahler which is a recursive approach based on Bayesian model.

For a single target motion scene, the target's motion state can be denoted as x and its measurement can be denoted as z. Similarly, in the multi-target scene the target i's true state at moment k is denoted as x_k^i. To integrate all the N_k targets in the field of view at moment k, multi-target state can be described with random finite set as $X_k = \{x_k^1, x_k^2, x_k^3, \ldots, x_k^{N_k}\} \in F(\chi)$. And M_k measurements at the moment k can be described by $Z_k = \{z_k^1, z_k^2, z_k^3, \ldots, z_k^{M_k}\} \in F(\psi)$. The random finite set of observation includes not only those of true targets but also of false alarm caused by the interference of clutter and so on. What's more, the observation set may miss targets as well. $F(\chi)$ and $F(\psi)$ represent the set of all finite subsets of real targets' state space and observation space respectively.

From moment $k - 1$ to moment k, there may be different changes of targets' state in the field of view, including death, rebirth, survival and so on. Thus, the following state set can be used to characterize the above state changes. Assuming that the multi-target state set at moment $k - 1$ can be described as X_{k-1}, the multi-target state set at moment k can be denoted as follows:

$$X_k = \Gamma_k \cup \left| \underset{x \in X_{k-1}}{\cup} S_{k|k-1}(x) \right| \cup \left| \underset{x \in X_{k-1}}{\cup} B_{k|k-1}(x) \right| \tag{1}$$

Γ_k means the set of targets newborn independently at moment k. $S_{k|k-1}(x)$ represents the set of targets which exist at moment $k-1$ and survive at moment k. And $B_{k|k-1}(x)$ denotes the set of targets at moment k derived from targets at moment $k-1$. The set of observation may miss targets or receive measured value from clutter. Thus, the set of observation can be described as follows:

$$Z_k = \left| \bigcup_{x \in X_k} \Theta_k(x) \right| \cup K_k \tag{2}$$

$\Theta_k(x)$ represents the set of observation from real targets, and $K_k(x)$ indicates the set of false alarms from clutters [5].

2.2 PHD Filter

The core of the PHD filter is to recursive with random finite set's posterior first order statistical moments which mean the posterior hypothesis density D. The computation load of the method is low because its integral process is based on every single target's motion state independently. The main process of iteration is as follows:

$$D_{k-1|k-1}(x|Z_{1:k-1}) \overset{predict}{\rightarrow} D_{k|k-1}(x|Z_{1:k-1}) \overset{update}{\rightarrow} D_{k|k}(x|Z_{1:k}) \tag{3}$$

Assume that targets and clutters satisfy four basic conditions [6]:

(1) The motion of each target and its measurement are independent of each other;
(2) The appearance of clutter in each measurement data follows Poisson distribution and is independent of the target measurement;
(3) The state of the predicted multi-target random sets follows Poisson distribution;
(4) The target newborn follows Poisson distribution and is independent of the target survival.

The implementation of the above iterative process is mainly consisted of the prediction process and the update process. The equations for prediction and update are shown in the following Eqs. (3) and (4).

$$D_{k|k-1}(x|Z_{1:k-1}) = \gamma_k(x) + \int \left(b_{k|k-1}(x|\xi) + e_{k|k-1}(\xi) f_{k|k-1}(x|\xi) \right) \\ D_{k-1|k-1}(x_{k-1}|Z_{1:k-1}) dx_{k-1} \tag{4}$$

$\gamma_k(x)$ represents the PHD of random finite set of targets newborn at moment k. $b_{k|k-1}(\cdot|\xi)$ denotes the PHD at moment k derived from target with state ξ at moment $k-1$. $e_{k|k-1}(\xi)$ is the probability that target which existed at moment $k-1$ still survives at moment k. $f_{k|k-1}(\cdot|\cdot)$ indicates the state transition probability from moment $k-1$ to moment k.

$$D_{k|k}(x|Z_{1:k}) = \left[\sum_{z \in Z_k} \frac{P_{D,k}(x) g_k(z|x)}{\lambda_k c_k(z) + \int P_{D,k}(x) g_k(z|x) D_{k-1}(x|Z_{1:k-1}) dx} \\ + 1 - P_{D,k}(x) \right] D_{k|k-1}(x|Z_{1:k-1}) \tag{5}$$

$P_{D,k}(x)$ means the detection probability at moment k . $g_k(z|x)$ describes the likelihood probability of the measurement z caused by the targets in state x . $\lambda_k s$ and $c_k(x)$ represent the average number and probability density of clutters in each frame of the measurement respectively [7].

It is difficult to achieve the analytic solution of multiple integral in the iterative process of standard PHD filter. Sampling method is used to approximate the posterior probability density distribution of nonlinear functions. The motion states of potential targets are represented by a large amount of particles with different weights. If the particles are enough, the particle filter approaches Bayesian optimal estimation gradually. The particle filter is advantageous for that it is not constrained by the assumption of linear and Gaussian model. PHD filter with particle is achieved by five main steps including initialization, prediction, update, resampling and estimation of target. And the final result is obtained after several times of iteration.

3   Improved Phd Method

The relevance between two frames of observation turns worse as the detection probability gets lower. Thus, it is difficult to achieve effective aggregation of particles characterizing true targets' states with conventional PHD filter. To solve the problem, this improved method is proposed to enhance the association of targets among multi frames of observation by accumulation with dynamic programming. And the result of accumulation is applied to conventional PHD filter as a coefficient term adjusting the confidence of measurement.

The flow chart of improved method is shown in Fig. 1 which is consisted of module of data preprocessing based on dynamic programming and module of PHD filter processing.

According to the flow chart, the first module of accumulating the observation based on dynamic programming is subdivided into three steps [8].

Initialization: Select observation points from first frame of data which is in the neighborhood of the second frame. Record the direction and combination of amplitude.

Accumulation: To the input data, select the neighborhood points from last frame. And it is necessary to consider the rationality of trajectory angle. Observation from

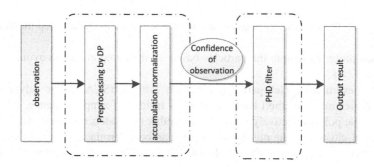

Fig. 1. Flow chart of improved method

trajectory with large fluctuation of angles cannot be accumulated. The accumulation is realized by summing coherent points in different frames. The operation is executed iteratively for several times to get the accumulation at moment k.

Normalization: The accumulation results of each observation is normalized which is used in the PHD filter framework later as the confidence level $\{cl(z_m^k)|m \leq M_k\}$ of each measurement.

The PHD filter is realized with particle filer which is divided into five steps as follows [9].

Initialization: Take a few particles characterizing the prior target distribution like Eq. (5). Where each target's state is described by L_0 particles with weight ω_0.

$$D_0(x_k) = \sum_{i=1}^{L_0} \omega_0 \delta_{x_k^{(i)}}(x_k) \tag{6}$$

Prediction: Predict the next state of each particle with survival probability and state transfer function, and the PHD after predicting is as follows:

$$D_{k|k-1}(x) = \begin{cases} \sum_{i=1}^{L_{k-1}} \tilde{\omega}_{k|k-1}^{(i)} \delta(x - \tilde{x}_k^{(i)}) \\ \sum_{i=L_{k-1}+1}^{L_{k-1}+J_k} \tilde{\omega}_b^{(i)} \delta(x - \tilde{x}_k^{(i)}) \end{cases} \tag{7}$$

Where $\tilde{x}_k^{(i)}$ denotes the particles' states at moment k which come from step of re-sampling originally. And this particles need to be put into state transfer function.

Update: The weight of each particle can be re-calculated according to the observation at moment k, the confidence level of observation $\{cl(z_m^k)|m \leq M_k\}$ and other prior information. The weight after update is as follows:

$$\tilde{\omega}_k^{(i)} = [\sum_{z \in Z_k} \frac{cl(z)P_{D,k}(\tilde{x}_k^{(i)})g_k(z|\tilde{x}_k^{(i)})}{\lambda_k c_k(z) + \sum_{i=1}^{L_{k|k-1}} cr(z)P_{D,k}(\tilde{x}_k^{(i)})g_k(z|\tilde{x}_k^{(i)})\tilde{\omega}_{k|k-1}^{(i)}} + 1 - P_{D,k}(\tilde{x}_k^{(i)})]\tilde{\omega}_{k|k-1}^{(i)} \tag{8}$$

Where all the parameters above share the same means as update step mentioned at Sect. 2.2.

Re-sampling: Resample the particles based on their importance to avoid degradation of particles.

Target estimation: Get particles clustered with DBSCAN. The advantage of DBSCAN lies in the method based on density instead of simple distance, which can remove noise points effectively without the number of clusters specified. According to the result of clustering, the number of targets can be determined by clustering centers and the state of every target can be obtained from the mean of each pile of particles.

4 Simulation

To verify the effectiveness of the improved method, simulation experiments are designed as followed: given that the simulation is conducted within the scope of $[-1500, 1500]$ m $\times$ $[0, 2000]$ m and the radar is located in $[0, 0]$ m which provides the observation result every other second. The observation contains the information about angle and distance, which may be caused by true targets or clutters. And the standard deviations of angle and distance in observation data are $(2 * \pi/180)rad$ and 10 m separately. According to the framework of PHD filter, assume that the probability that true targets are observed in single measurement is 0.8. The average number of clutters existing in every observation is 60, and all the clutters are distributed in the field of view uniformly. The Radar monitors the whole view for 130 s. And four independent point targets moved with angle changing in the field whose trajectories are crossed of adjacent. Their simulation parameters are shown in Table 1.

Table 1. Targets motion parameters

Target	TA/s	TD/s	PA/m	IV/$m \cdot s^{-1}$	AV/$rad \cdot s^{-1}$
1	1	120	[-1100, 430]	[10, 10]	0.00785
2	20	130	[-950, 1480]	[12, -10]	-0.00785
3	30	130	[50, 400]	[-15, 3]	0.00785
4	30	130	[-20, 1250]	[-8, -8]	0.00785

Where TA means time appear, TD means time disappear, PA represents position appear, IV denotes initial velocity and AV means angular velocity.

The conventional PHD filter is chosen as a comparison. And the simulation is conducted with the two methods in same conditions. Single simulation result is shown in Figs. 2 and 3.

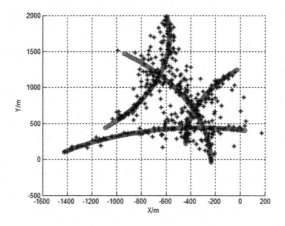

Fig. 2. Conversional PHD estimation (Color figure online)

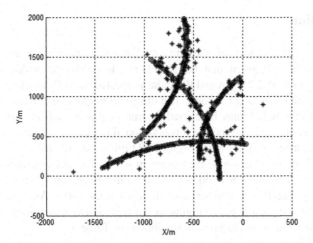

Fig. 3. Improved method estimation (Color figure online)

Where orange dots characterize the true targets' trajectories and the black stars are the estimation of targets at each moment. According to the result of statistic, there are 0.5 false alarms per frame in conventional PHD simulation on average while there are 0.3 false alarms in improved PHD on average. And there are 50 frames of data which misses targets in conventional PHD simulation while 22 frame of data in improved PHD simulation.

For verifying the advantages of the improved method over the original PHD method, Monte Carlo simulation is performed on the above experiments. The simulation process focuses on three aspects: the false alarm rate, the missed alarm and OSPA distance. A target is detected if the distance between the truth and the estimation

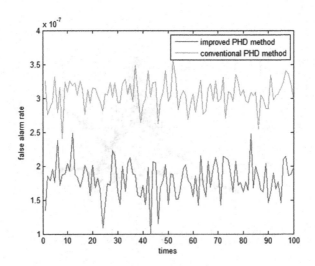

Fig. 4. False alarm rate comparison (Color figure online)

is less than a specified threshold. The estimation is judged as false alarm if there is no true target near the estimation. The miss alarm rate is counted with the number of miss targets in every frame of data. And the false alarm rate is counted with the number of false alarm in every estimation. The results of 100 times of Monte Carlo experiments are shown in Figs. 4 and 5.

According to Figs. 4 and 5, the red lines representing improved PHD method are generally lower than the green lines representing conventional PHD method. The average miss alarm rate and false alarm rate of conventional PHD method are 0.47 and 3.06e-7, while the improved PHD method's miss alarm rate and false alarm rate are 0.34 and 1.80e-7.

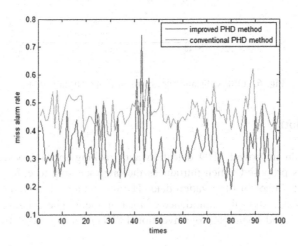

Fig. 5. Miss alarm rate comparison (Color figure online)

Optimal sub pattern assignment (OSPA) distance is used generally in simulations about random finite set for describing the distance of true target set and estimation set [10]. OSPA integrates the penalty of miss alarm, false alarm and the deviation of location between actual targets and estimation values, which makes it reflect the performance of the PHD filter intuitively. The comparison about OSPA between two methods is displayed in Fig. 6.

The average value of green lines which represents conventional PHD method is 60 m while the average value of red lines representing improved PHD method is 47 m. Thus, it is proved that the improved method is superior to conventional PHD method in detecting targets and suppressing false alarms.

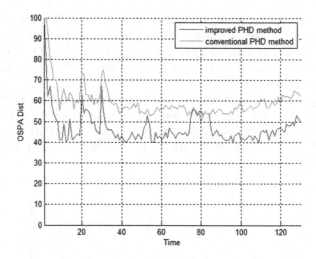

Fig. 6. OSPA distance comparison (Color figure online)

5 Conclusion

In this paper, an improved PHD detection and tracking method based on dynamic programming is proposed which introduces the preprocessing to enhance the relation among adjacent frames of observation data. The integration of dynamic programming can be used for adjusting the confidence of measurement. The simulations prove that the improved method is superior to conventional PHD filter in false alarm rate and miss alarm rate.

Acknowledgments. The work is supported by NSFC (No. 61771028 and No. 61673146).

References

1. Yang, W., Fu, Y., Pan, X.G., Zhang, Z., Li, X.: Track-before-detect technique for dim targets: an overview. Acta Electronic Sinica **42**(09), 1786–1793 (2014)
2. Mahler, R.: A theoretical foundation for the Stein-Winter probability hypothesis density (PHD) multi-target tracking approach. In: Proceedings of the MSS National Symposium on Sensor and Data Fusion, San Antonio, TX, pp. 99–117 (2000)
3. Vo, B.-N., Ma, W.-K.: The Gaussian mixture probability hypothesis density filters. IEEE Trans. Sig. Process. **54**(11), 4091–4104 (2006)
4. Vo, B.-N., Singh, S., Doucet, A.: Sequential Monte Carlo methods for multi-target filtering with random finite sets. IEEE Trans. Aerosp. Electron. Syst. **41**(4), 1224–1245 (2005)
5. Han, C., Zhu, H., Duan, Z.: Multi Sensor Information Fusion. Tsinghua University Press, Beijing (2010)
6. Hu, Z.: A Study of Multi-target Tracking Based on Random Finite Set Using Radar. Xidian University (2015)
7. Zhang, H.: Probability Hypothesis Density Filter Algorithm and its Application in Multi-Targets Tracking. Harbin Engineering University (2012)

8. Wan, Y., Wang, S., Weihua, W.: Dynamic programming track before detect for maneuvering dim targets. J. Sig. Process. **29**(05), 548–590 (2013)
9. Tian, S., Wang, G., He, Y.: Multi-target tracking with probability hypothesis density particle filter. J. Nav. Aeronaut. Eng. Inst. (04), 417–420 + 430 (2007)
10. Jing, P., Shiyou, X., Li, X., Chen, Z.: Performance evaluation of multiple target tracking: a survey. Syst. Eng. Electron. **36**(1), 2127–2132 (2014)

Type Analysis and Automatic Static Detection of Infeasible Paths

Fuping Zeng, Wenjing Liu[✉], and Xiaodong Gou

School of Reliability and Systems Engineering, Beihang University,
Beijing, China
{zfp, gou_xiaodong}@buaa.edu.cn, heroolwj@163.com

Abstract. Infeasible paths are a common type of defect in software testing, which can cause failure of software system and lead to problems about software reliability and safety. In this paper, infeasible paths are divided into three types, which are control infeasible paths, logic infeasible paths, constraint infeasible paths. For each type, details and examples are given to find out the defects of infeasible paths during software testing. In order to improve the detection efficiency, automatic static detection method is given based on three types of infeasible paths. The experimental results show that the proposed method can detect the infeasible paths of code accurately and effectively.

Keywords: Software testing · Infeasible paths · Type analysis
Checking tool

1 Introduction

The infeasible path refers that no input can execute the code in any case. The infeasible path is a kind of defect which is easy to appear in software development, and it is also one of the most important defects in software white box testing. Many software industry employees, especially developers, consider that the infeasible paths have little impacts on software quality, only increase the storage capacity of the code and reduce the readability of the code. In fact it's not true, it is impossible to design infeasible paths without special requirements, so there should be no any infeasible path in general code. Moreover, some infeasible paths are often the symptoms of some logical problems, which can lead to software failures. For the software such as aviation, aerospace and other industries, these software failures often lead to disastrous consequences, which cause software reliability and safety problems. Therefore, it is important for software testers to find out existing infeasible paths comprehensively, and it is necessary to analyze and research the infeasible paths.

At present, through scholars' continuous study, there have many research achievements such as literature [1–7]. However, these literatures focus on a specific infeasible detection technique rather than introduce the types of infeasible paths, and lack of the overall introduction about infeasible paths. In fact, the detection techniques for the different type of infeasible paths are different, and one detection technique is difficult to detect all infeasible paths. Based on many-years experiences of software testing, the different types of infeasible paths are analyzed as far as possible. The details

© Springer Nature Singapore Pte Ltd. 2018
H. Yuan et al. (Eds.): GSKI 2017, CCIS 849, pp. 294–304, 2018.
https://doi.org/10.1007/978-981-13-0896-3_29

and examples about each type of infeasible paths are given to get a clearer understanding of infeasible paths. For large software with hundreds thousands or even millions lines code, it is often inefficient to rely only on manual detection of infeasible paths. Therefore, this paper presents an automatic static detection method based on each type of infeasible paths.

2　Type Analysis of Infeasible Paths

What are the forms of infeasible paths and how to classify them? Based on many-years experiences of software development and testing, infeasible paths are classifies into three main categories: control infeasible paths, logic infeasible paths, constraint infeasible paths.

2.1　Control Infeasible Paths

Control infeasible path refers to the codes that are not passed by any path in the control flow graph. It is divided into two categories: "isolated island" code and "be skipped" code.

2.1.1　"Isolated Island" Code

Description" Isolated island" code is absolutely isolated code that has no association with any other code. It can be a function, class, or file. It is different between "isolated island" code and isolated island in the sea, because that even though islands in the sea are isolated to the mainland, but it still can be arrived by transport such as boats and planes. It is often thought that "isolated island" code does not exist, but for large-scale software, especially for the software with research properties, the "isolated island" code is not uncommon.

2.1.2　"Be Skipped" Code. Description

Description "Be skipped" code refers to the code between the jump statement and the jump target statement, including goto, break, return, infinite loop.

Listing 1: The code that was skipped after goto:

```
1 if (a>b)
2 {
3   goto Label1;
4   a=a+1; //skipped code
5 }
6 Label1:
......
```

Listing 2: The code that was skipped after return:

```
1 int sub1(int x)
2 {
3   int z;
4   z=x+1;
5   return z;
6   z=z*z //skipped code
7 }
```

Listing 3: The code that was skipped after infinite loop:

```
1 int sub2 (int x)
2 {
3   int y=x;
4   while (1) {
5     y+=1;
6   }
7   y=x+1; //skipped code
8 }
```

Listing 4: The code that was skipped after break:

```
1 int sub3 (int x)
2 {
3   int y=x;
    ......
4   switch (x) {
5   case 1:
6   {
7     y=0;
8     break;
9     y+=x; //skipped code
10  }
11  case 2:
12  {
13    y=4;
14    break;
15  }
16  default:
17    return 0;
18  }
19  return y;
20 }
```

2.2   Logic Infeasible Paths

Logic infeasible path means that although the path coverage exist, but the code still infeasible because of logical entry conditional value of their own branches forever false or the values of former branch are always true. It can be divided into three parts: "this block" infeasible path, "brother and sister" infeasible path, "compatriot" infeasible path.

2.2.1   This Block Infeasible Path

Description: The value of the branch entry condition or condition combination is always false, resulting in "this block" infeasible path and is called "this block" infeasible path.

```
1  int sub2 (int x)
2  {
3    int y=x;
4    while (1) {
5      y+=1;
6    }
7    y=x+1; //skipped code
8  }
```

Listing 1: The branch condition is calculated as always false:

The expression $(5 + 3 < 4)$ && $(a > (a + 1))$ in "if $(5 + 3 < 4)$ && $(a > (a + 1))$" can be directly calculated, the calculated value is 0, the value of block entry combination is always false, so line 3 is infeasible code.

Listing 2: There is a contradiction between branch conditions:

Line 3 is infeasible code because $(a > b)$ and $(a < (b - 1))$ are contradictory, and the value of $(a > b)$ && $(a < (b - 1))$ is false.

Listing 3: The branch condition by data flow analysis is always false:

```
1  int a=10;
2  int b;
3  if(a==5)
4  {
5    b=3;
6  }
```

The expression a == 5 with the variable a will be the integration of a = 10 in the path, and the original variable conditional expression 10 == 5 is obtained whose value is false, so the line 5 is infeasible code.

2.2.2 Compatriot Infeasible Path

Description: The relationship between every branch in branch statement is like brotherhood. If the entrance condition in some branch is always true, then in addition to block of this branch, the code of other brother block is infeasible, called compatriot infeasible path.

Listing: Compatriot infeasible path in switch-case statement:

```
1  ef_fruit= APPlE;
2  switch(ef_fruit)
3  {
4    case APPlE:
5    {
6      ......
7      break;
8    case PEAR:
9    {
10     ......
11     break;
12   }
13   default:
14   {
15     ......
16     break;
17   }
18 }
```

ef_fruit = APPlE causes the branch of case APPlE always true, so the codes of line 8–17 are infeasible, called compatriot infeasible path.

2.2.3 Brother and Sister Infeasible Path

Description: The relationship between every branch of branch statement is like the relationship between brother and sister. If entry condition of some branch is always true, the code of other brother and sister block is infeasible except for this branch, called brother and sister infeasible path. In addition, if the entry condition of some branch is a subset of the previous or a certain association entry conditions, so this condition is a stronger than the condition of the previous entry condition. Because of the order of execution, the code of this entry condition is infeasible, also called brother and sister infeasible path.

Listing 1: Entry condition of if statement is always true:

```
1  int a=10;
2  int b;
3  if(a>5)
4  {
5    b=3;
6  }
7  else if(a<-7)
8  {
9    b=6;
10 }
11 else
12 {
13   ...
14 }
```

The value of line 3 "a > 5" is always true, so the code of line 7–14 is unfeasible, called brother and sister infeasible path.

Listing 2: Entry condition of if statement is stronger than previous branch:

```
1  int a;
2  int b;
3  if(a>5)
4  {
5    b=3;
6  }
7  else if(a>7)
8  {
9    b=6;
10 }
```

a > 7 of line 7 is stronger than a > 5 of line 3, so the code of line 9 is infeasible, also called brother and sister infeasible path.

2.3   Constraint Infeasible Paths

Description: Variables generally have a clear range of values, so the range for the entry condition expression of branch including the variables is determined. If the value ranges of branch lead to the condition of corresponding branch always false, resulting in the code that is never infeasible to the branch, that is constraint infeasible paths. Logic infeasible path is a subset of constraint infeasible path.

Listing: The code is as follows:

```
1 float get_BMI_of_man(float f_height,float f_weight)
2 {
3   float f_ret;
4   ......
5   f_ret= f_weight/(f_height*f_height)
6   ......
7   if((f_ret<0.5)||(f_ret>4000))
8   {
9     printf("not a normal man");
10  }
11  ......
12  return fRet;
13 }
```

In practical applications, the value of f_height is (0.5,3) m, and the value of f_weight is (5,1000) kg. Used the constraint solving techniques, the value of (f_ret < 0.5)||(f_ret > 4000) is always false, so code on line 9 is infeasible, called constraint infeasible paths.

3   Automatic Static Detection of Infeasible Paths

For the three types of infeasible paths, the control infeasible path is usually checked first, and then the logic infeasible path is checked. If conditions are met, the constraint infeasible path is checked finally. The method of the automatic static detection is shown in Fig. 1.

Step1:   Preprocessing source code. The source code is formatted, and the lexical and syntax is initial analyzed to obtain basic information and get the preprocessed code file.

Step2:   Lexical analysis and syntax parsing, and detect the 'skipped' code. The syntax tree, data flow chart, control flow graph and function call graph of the program are generated, and the static information related to morphology, syntax and semantics is extracted after the preprocessing program is fully lexical analysis, syntax paring and semantic analysis. In the process of lexical analysis and syntax parsing, it can be determined whether some code belongs to the 'skipped' code by detecting whether the code behind the jump keyword belongs to the same block as the jump keyword.

Step3:   Detect 'isolated island' code. After the completion of the source program preprocessing, based on the generated syntax tree and control flow graph, the 'isolated island'code can be detected by combining the function call analysis and the object call analysis.

Step4:   Detect logic infeasible paths. Based on lexical analysis, syntax parsing and function call, combined with control flow analysis and data flow analysis, a complete constraint condition expression for each branch condition can be

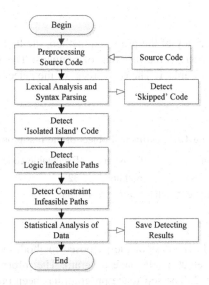

Fig. 1. Method of automatic detection of infeasible paths

obtained. Logic infeasible path is detected by analyzing and calculating conditional expressions for each branch entry.

Step5: Detect constraint infeasible paths. If the range of the input data of the operation state can be obtained, the constraint condition of the range is added to the constraint of whether the branch statements are infeasible in the previous stage, and then the set of constraint infeasible paths is obtained by applying the constraint solving technology.

Step6: Analyze and save result data. The error information is recorded in the result file if the matching infeasible paths are found, and the detection result file is saved finally. The result file includes some relevant information of infeasible paths, such as file name, line number, function name, error type and so on. The infeasilbe path information report is generated from the result file, and the error information is returned back to the user.

4 Experiments Result and Analysis

On the basis of the method in this paper, a program infeasible path detection tool called PLTip (PL Tool of infeasible path) is implemented for C/C++ language. The PLTip tool not only can automatically detect infeasible paths, but also can give the type of infeasible paths: control infeasible paths, logic infeasible paths or constraint infeasible paths, which greatly reduce the work intensity of the white-box software tester and provide support for improving the code quality.

In order to evaluate the method of this paper, a Siemens open source program and a self-made project are selected as the experimental object to detect the infeasible paths in the program.

(1) Experiment design

In order to verify the accuracy of the proposed method, the first group experiment was designed to detect the open source program of Siemens. The information of experimental object is shown in Table 1. The correctness of the detection results is judged by manual analysis.

Table 1. Experimental object of the first group

No	File name	Function	Constraint	Executable code lines after formatting
1	tcas.c	alt_sep_test()	nothing	32
2	tot_info.c	InfoTbl(r, c, f, pdf)	r > 1, c > 1	108

In order to verify the effectiveness of the proposed method, the second group experiment was designed to detect a self-made program. The information of experimental object is shown in Table 2. The self-made program has been pre-injected into various types of infeasible paths, so it is easier to obtain a considerable number of detection results in the experiment. The self-made program pre-injected 1 control infeasible path, 3 logic infeasible paths and 3 constraint infeasible paths. The correctness of the detection results is judged by comparing the detected results with the number of pre-injected infeasible paths.

Table 2. Experimental object of the second group

No	Self-made program	Function	Constraint	Executable code lines after formatting
1	unreache1.c	unreach_sync(int n_param)	n_param	232

(2) Experiment results

Table 3 shows the results of the first group experiment. The "number of the existed infeasible paths" is the number of infeasible paths existed in code. The "number of the detected infeasible paths" is the number of infeasible paths detected by PLTip tool. From the experimental results, it can be seen that the infeasible paths in the program can be completely detected by the tool, the detection rate is 100% and the correct rate is 100%.

Table 3. The results of the first group experiment

No	Program	Function	Number of the existed infeasible paths	Number of the detected infeasible paths
1	tcas.c	alt_sep_test()	3 (logic infeasible paths)	3
2	tot_info.c	InfoTbl(r, c, f, pdf)	4 (constraint infeasible paths)	4

Table 4. The results of the second group experiment

No	Self-made program	Function	Number of the existed infeasible paths	Number of the detected infeasible paths
1	unreache1.c	unreach_sync (int n_param)	7 (control infeasible path:1 logic infeasible path:3 constraint infeasible path:3)	7 (control infeasible path:1 logic infeasible path:3 constraint infeasible path:3)

Table 4 shows the results of the second group experiment. It can be seen from the experimental results that the pre-injected infeasible paths can be completely detected by the tool with the detection rate of 100% and the correct rate of 100%.

In summary, the proposed method can detect infeasible paths in the program accurately and effectively, so the detection efficiency of infeasible paths can be improved and the test resources can be saved.

5 Conclusion

In this paper, the various types of infeasible paths are fully analyzed with details and examples. A complete automatic static detection method for infeasible paths is proposed. Based on the research results, an infeasible path detection tool called PLTip is developed for C/C++ language, which has a strong practical value.

Of course, it does not mean that all the infeasible paths can be detected by the proposed method and tool. From a technical perspective, the detection of constraint infeasible paths mainly depends on the constraint solving technique. However, the constraint solving technology is not perfect which leads to some infeasible paths cannot be detected. Therefore, for the detection of "constraint infeasible paths", testers need to check the specific code manually besides the use of PLTip tool, which is the direction of further research in the future.

References

1. Arlt, S., Schäf, M.: Joogie: infeasible code detection for Java. In: Madhusudan, P., Seshia, Sanjit A. (eds.) CAV 2012. LNCS, vol. 7358, pp. 767–773. Springer, Heidelberg (2012). https://doi.org/10.1007/978-3-642-31424-7_62
2. Chen, R., Zhang, G., Xiaowei, L.I.: Detection of infeasible path in procedure. Comput. Eng. **32**(16), 86–88 (2006)
3. Ding, S., Tan, H.B.K.: Detection of infeasible paths: approaches and challenges. In: Maciaszek, L.A., Filipe, J. (eds.) ENASE 2012. CCIS, vol. 410, pp. 64–78. Springer, Heidelberg (2013). https://doi.org/10.1007/978-3-642-45422-6_5
4. Gong, D., Yao, X.: Automatic detection of infeasible paths in software testing. Softw. IET **4**(5), 361–370 (2010)

5. Hedley, D., Hennell, M.A.: The Causes and Effects of Infeasible Paths in Computer Programs, pp. 259–267 (1985)
6. Wang, H.Y., Jiang, S.J., Wang, X.Y., Ju, X.L., Zhang, Y.M.: An approach for detecting infeasible paths based on sub-path expansion. Tien Tzu Hsueh Pao/Acta Electronica Sin. **43**(8), 1555–1560 (2015)
7. Yu, Q.-Y., Luo, Y., Yang, H.: Improved static approach of infeasible paths in program. J. Univ. South China (Sci. Technol.) **4**, 68–73 (2014)

A New Perspective on Evaluation Software of Contribution Rate for Weapon Equipment System

Huadong Yang[1,2(✉)], Fang Liu[1], and Yongdun Yan[2]

[1] Naval Research Academy, Wuhan, China
control_beijing@sina.com, jzbliufang@163.com
[2] Naval Armament, Beijing, China
my0liver97@sohu.com

Abstract. In view of the difficulty of quantitative evaluation of the contribution rate for each member in the equipment system, the challenges of the rate assessment for system contribution were analyzed in detail, and the basic concepts and main contents of the system contribution rate assessment were expounded. In the context of system confrontation, the main key technologies were analyzed. A new perspective of quantitative assessment of system contribution rate was put forward from the perspectives of capability, mission, structure and evolution. In terms of evaluating the role and contribution rate of equipment in the operational system, the method has achieved relatively good results. The results provide a new solution for the research on the equipment system and the contribution rate assessment.

Keywords: Weaponry · System design · Contribution rate · Assessment

1 Introduction

System confrontation is a significant feature of modern warfare. Any type of equipment in the system is an indispensable part of the system and plays an indispensable role. Accompanied high degree of informationization of weaponry and equipment with long construction period and large investment, the development of a type of equipment is not only depend on whether it has advanced technical indicators for warfare, but more on the contribution rate of such equipment to the operational system[1]. If only the warfare performance indicators are emphasized, but the question that how to form a system is placed insufficient attention, as the result, the equipment development cannot well adapt to the characteristics of modern war system confrontation.

The development of weapons and equipment needs to go through a process of needs analysis and argumentation and cannot be arbitrarily decided by subjective assumptions. Argumentation is the result of an analysis of one or a set of indicators to help decision-makers make the right decision-making process [2]. In the development of new equipment, we first need to compare a variety of equipment design to determine the most economically reasonable, tactical and technically feasible optimal system solutions, and then need to evaluate the type of equipment and performance in the

© Springer Nature Singapore Pte Ltd. 2018
H. Yuan et al. (Eds.): GSKI 2017, CCIS 849, pp. 305–312, 2018.
https://doi.org/10.1007/978-981-13-0896-3_30

entire battle the role of the system and the contribution rate. Therefore, starting from the operational requirements, the analysis method targeting the contribution rate of the system plays an important role in the equipment development demonstration, design, manufacturing and testing [3]. Especially under the premise of effective military investment, the contribution rate of the system is more we should serve the system decision-making issues for the development, demonstration and research and development of new types of weapons and equipment.

As for the contribution rate of equipment system, scholars such as Lyu [4–6], Chang [7, 8] and Luo [9–11] studied the evaluation theory of contribution rate of the system and the construction method of assessment model deeply; they provide some effective methods for assessing the contribution rate of the weapon system. It is of great significance to the demonstration of the development of equipment, such as the building of operational capability of the system, the carrying out of operational tests, the guarantee of operational use, and actual combat training and so on. Based on the above researches, this paper systematically reviews the key technologies and challenges faced in the assessment of the contribution rate of the equipment system, and put forward a new perspective for evaluating the contribution rate of the system.

2 Related Concepts

2.1 System Contribution Rate Related Concepts

(1) Equipment system

The equipment system is a higher-level system consisting of various weaponry and equipment systems that are functionally interconnected and interacting to accomplish certain operational tasks under certain strategic guidance, combat command and support conditions. Different types, different systems, and even different ages of weapons and equipment establish mutual relations and roles mainly through information.

(2) Combat system

The concept of combat system is gradually established with the advancement of military informatization and the development of systematic science. Combat body is composed of a variety of operational systems (elements) in accordance with certain command relations, organizational relations and operational mechanism of the organic whole.

(3) Contribution

In the analysis of equipment architecture, the contribution is the percentage of a certain type of equipment or system in the complete set of equipment of the completely combat system, and which is used to describe the share of this type of equipment or system in all the components of a combat system.

(4) Contribution degree

In the field of weapons and equipment, the contribution is the incremental value of a certain type of equipment or system. As a percentage of the incremental value of the full complement of combat equipment, it is used to describe the incremental value of this type of equipment or system in the full complement of all operational system equipment. The share of value is an indicator of the change in stock structure intensity.

(5) Contribution rate

In the field of weapons and equipment, "contribution rate" is used as a measure of the value of a type of equipment, which is used as an indicator. Mainly referring to the specific role or contribution and investment in resources and the sum of the protection of resources, which means the combat effectiveness and the manpower and material resources ratio.

The formula is:

$$\text{Contribution(output)}/\text{input(consumption)}.$$

The contribution rate can also be used to analyze the role of each factor in economic growth, which comprehensively reflects the contribution of each factor in economic growth.

The formula is as follows: increase amount (increment) of a certain type of equipment or system/increase of complete amount of equipment of a combat system.

(6) System contribution rate

Drawing on the concept of contribution rate in the field of economics, the system contribution rate of weaponry and equipment refers to the position and function of a single piece (or single type) of equipment in the system. It can also be understood as the degree to which the equipment contributes to the overall function of the system (such as operational capability or operational effectiveness) in the operational system.

2.2   The Main Content of the System Contribution Rate Assessment

The rate assessment of system contribution mainly aims at the contribution rate of the equipment to the combat system, and is usually evaluated from the following three aspects:

Firstly, the effectiveness evaluation is mainly based on the perspective of the effectiveness of the operational system. It is designed to assess the equipment during the project development and commissioning. The effectiveness of a typical combat system plays the role including the completion of combat missions, perception and detection, command and control, communications and transport, combat operations, equipment damage, casualties and other aspects of the impact.

Secondly, in terms of capability assessment, the main purpose of the assessment is to assess the changes in the capabilities of the operational system in a static manner, and to assess the contribution of the equipment to the operational system by assessing the impact on the operational capabilities of the system before and after the addition of equipment. Relative to the effectiveness evaluation, In terms of tasks, the assessment of competence is broader and the conclusions converge more.

Thirdly, in the aspect of structural assessment, the influence and contribution of equipment performance are mainly evaluated with quantity and service time on the equipment architecture from the point of view of the change of pros and cons of equipment architecture. It is characterized by continuous service in equipment and continuous Assessment, thus, the evolution of the contribution rate of equipment to combat system can be fully demonstrated.

2.3   System Contribution Rate Evaluation of Key Technologies

(1) Construction of operational capability / performance indicators for rate assessment of system contribution

This technology is mainly used to support the combat system to build operational capabilities and operational effectiveness indicators, which are used to evaluate the evaluation equipment before and after the operational system, put into combat systems and combat effectiveness changes in order to assess the contribution rate of system services.

(2) Operational system operational capability requirements analysis techniques

Those techniques are mainly used to support the analysis of combat system operational needs. According to the equipment to be assessed before and after joining the operational system, the system to combat the ability to meet the needs of the ability to change the degree of combat capability from the perspective of assessment system contribution rate.

(3) Combat deduction technology

It is used in the early stages of simulation experiments to analyze the operational determination, the design of the main tactics and the tactics of using force. The technique is used to refine the sequence of military actions. By this way, we can playback through the battle process to identify problems and sort out the key link. After explicitly influencing elements and external environmental conditions, and design an expanded operational action plan, and change the technology for the latter part of the large sample simulation comparative evaluation experiment to lay the foundation technology. Usually, deduction is conducted in a "face-to-face study" or "back-to-back game" in an experimental environment in which "people are in the loop".

(4) Combat simulation technology

For the problem of quantitative analysis in the process of deduction, the combat simulation supports the iterative optimization of the scheme by carrying out large sample simulation experiments in the simulation system and comparing the impact of different schemes on the combat process and the results.

(5) Value Analysis Technology

The value-centered decision-making analysis method is usually adopted by field experts to analyze and assess the military value of weapons and equipment that need to be developed in the future through a combination of qualitative analysis and quantitative analysis. In the system of contribution, rate assessment is mainly used to support the system from the perspective of operational capabilities to assess the contribution rate of the system.

(6) System Evolution Simulation Technology

Discrete event simulation method is adopted to simulate the execution process of planning plan, which can dynamically output the proportion structure of weaponry and equipment in different periods in the future and analyze, evaluate and optimize the planning and planning plan. The contribution rate of the system is mainly used to support the assessment of the contribution rate of the system from the perspective of structural assessment.

3 Challenges

How to measure the contribution rate of the system is more difficult. It is mainly due to the multi-layered combat system and the complex and comprehensive evaluation of the contribution of weaponry and equipment. It is necessary to consider the combat of various weapon units in the system under various conditions, such as different environments, different missions, different tactical tactics, different forces and weapon configurations, thus, effectiveness and system modeling are very complicated. The traditional evaluation methods based on mathematical analysis and data statistics are difficult to solve the problem of system contribution evaluation. The challenges of the equipment to the rate research of system contribution are as follows:

(1) Due to the difficulty of modeling, it is difficult to obtain a comprehensive evaluation of the contribution of the equipment system by the traditional mathematical methods, and a new measure of contribution needs to be found.
(2) The contribution rate evaluation does not distinguish between the combat system and the equipment system, and it is difficult to evaluate the different types of tasks scientifically.
(3) There are many elements of the operational system, the relationship of the cross-linked structure of all weapons in the system is complex, and there is a lack of system design method and overall performance simulation supporting platform.
(4) The operational system is large in scale, and the means of system operational effectiveness simulation are outdated. The key parameters of each factor in the system are difficult to be valued.

4 New Perspective

Equipment system contains a large number of equipment nodes; the relationship between the complex equipment is a complex system. The factors that influence the contribution rate of equipment to the system are numerous, and the meaning of the contribution rate is different for different equipment systems. Therefore, the connotation of the contribution rate of equipment to the system is not of a single but of many aspects. Evaluation contribution rate must be conducted from the equipment on the system from multiple angles. Analyzing the contribution from a single perspective will result in one-sidedness of the result and reduced credibility. As can be seen from the description of the weapon and equipment system, the "quality" and the structure of the system's constituent elements (equipment and equipment) have a significant impact on the system. At the same time, the external factors of the system, the adaptability of the system to the external environment and the characteristics of the evolution and evolution of the system are also very significant.

Therefore, the role or value of equipment on the system can be analyzed from the following four perspectives:

4.1 Ability Point of View

The traditional thinking of the development of the threat-based equipment system is not suitable for the requirements of the modern warfare system. Therefore, the U.S military proposed the development of a capability-based equipment system [4]. Weaponry system capability is the ability to complete the task, depending on the composition of the system structure and equipment properties (tactical indicators/performance parameters) with the number, and has nothing to do with operational activities, but also has nothing to do with the specific operational tasks. From the goal of building a weapon system, the system of weaponry and equipment should be able to accomplish its strategic objectives under different operational scenarios and against different threats in the battlefield. Equipment system is a process of continuous development and changes, so the weaponry and equipment system should be adaptable to ensure that the system can meet the mission requirements for a long period.

The contribution of equipment to the system's capabilities mainly lies in the following aspects: The system's ability is composed of completeness, there is no obvious shortcoming in ability and there is no obvious lack of capacity. With the combination of reasonable ability and high and low ability of the system, Long-range, difficult targets have a threat. Ability is not efficiency, not with the changes in the specific use of combat targets and equipment. If the contribution of equipment to the system is analyzed from the perspective of ability, it will be confirmed that the weaponry system can meet the actual needs better more. In response to the new military threat, there are no shortcomings in ability, but also in line with the "capacity-based" system construction thinking, reflecting the requirements of the system adaptability.

4.2 Mission Perspective

The basic use of weaponry is to accomplish combat missions. The mission of the weapon and equipment system "stems from" operational tasks. The implementation of operational tasks supports the mission of the system. In the equipment system, the contribution of equipment to the system is directly reflected in the implementation of the equipment on the task. For example, missiles can perform long-range strike missions. If there is a missing missile in the equipment system, long-range precision strike missions in the system's combat missions cannot complete. The missile's contribution to the system lies in the missile's support of the system's mission. The extent of each equipment supporting the operational system in fulfilling its mission is its contribution to the mission of the operational system. The level of implementation of the modified equipment mission can be used to describe the extent to which the equipment supports the mission.

4.3 Structural Points of View

Equipment system contains a large number of equipment, all kinds of equipment combined together to form a variety of structures, equipment, and the hierarchical structure of the functional structure. In the equipment system, each equipment plays a role in it and is an integral part of the equipment architecture, contributing to the completion of the structure of the entire equipment system. The structural contribution of equipment to the system is reflected in the structural rationality of the equipment structure.

4.4 Evolutionary Perspective

Equipment system is not of a static structure, but of keeping constantly changing over time, with the maintenance of equipment, the level of training changing. A mature equipment system from the perspective of development should be able to maintain a certain degree of stability. The main body of the equipment system, key equipment in the equipment system cannot be drastic changed. Describing the evolutionary properties of individual equipment toward the entire system, including "the stability of the equipment structure" and "the persistence of system capabilities" requires the contribution of the single outfit to the evolution of the system from a developmental perspective.

The evolution of the equipment system is an inherent characteristic of the system development. The contribution rate of the equipment to the system cannot be simply considered from the existing time point. Most of the equipment service life is more than decades. There are constantly new equipment added to the system with the development of equipment system, but also there still have the old equipments out of the equipment system, the new equipments from the conceptual are designed to service use, which needs a few year or even ten years time. The equipment development process needs to consider the role of time. At the same time in the equipment development process, the enemy's equipment is constantly changing repeatedly. Analyzing the evolution of the contribution rate of equipment to the system is not only from one's own side, but also from the situation evolved over time by both the enemy and ourselves.

5   Concluding Remarks

Modern war fight is systematic; the design of system is the design of the war. The contribution rate of the system should mandatorily conduct as the criterion in the future development and construction of equipment. System research and construction will face unprecedented opportunities and challenges. In the past 20 years, the system research and construction have achieved remarkable results. The top level of the scientific system and the construction of an advanced verification platform are the keys. Therefore, facing the system confrontation under the complex environment, it is necessary to carry out in-depth system top-level design, carry out conceptual modeling in the field of systems, and conduct a systematic study on the application of equipment. There should establish an integrated support platform for integrated systems, including requirements analysis, system design, system verification, system evaluation and so on. There must make clear the position and contribution rate of each weapon and equipment in the system and provide the basic technical accumulation for the research on the weapon and equipment system and the contribution rate assessment.

Acknowledgments. I would like to express my gratitude to my collaborators, thanks for their outstanding work. I gratefully acknowledge the help of all those who helped me during the writing of this thesis.

References

1. Guan, Q., Yu, X.: Research on evaluation of equipment's contribution to system Warfighting. J. Equip. Inst. **3**, 1–5 (2015)
2. Ren, X., Tu, Z.: Research on an assessment method of equipment to system contribution rate. J. New Technol. New Process **9**, 49–53 (2016)
3. Jian, C.: Research on contribution rate of aerospace equipment system. J. Sci. Technol. Dev. **5**, 358–362 (2017)
4. Lyu, H., Zhang, W., Lyu, Y.: Comprehensive evaluation and analysis method of the contribution rate of weapons and equipment system. J. Ordnance Eng. Coll. **29**(2), 33–38 (2017)
5. Lyu, H., Wu, Q., Zhang, W.: Equipment system contribution evaluation based on gray evidence theory. J. Mil. Transp. Univ. **5**, 22–27 (2017)
6. Lyu, H., Zhang, W., Lyu, Y.: Establishment of multi-perspective assessment index system of weaponry system contribution rate. J. Equip. Inst. **28**(3), 62–66 (2017)
7. Chang, L.: Research on evaluation method of technical contribution of weaponry system. National University of Defense Technology, Changsha (2010)
8. Chang, L., Zhang, X., Li, M.: Weapon system technology contribution evaluation based on grey target theory. J. Ordnance Ind. Autom. **29**(10), 13–15 (2010)
9. Luo, X., He, R., Zhu, Y.: Evaluation of contribution of weaponry architecure. J. Armored Force Eng. Coll. **4**, 1–6 (2016)
10. Luo, X., Zhu, Y., He, R.: Research on evaluation method of contribution to system war fighting for weapons and equipment system based on complex network. J. Fire Control Command Control **42**(2), 83–87 (2017)
11. Luo, X., Yang, J., Rong, H.: Research and demonstration on contribution evaluation of weapon equipment system based on task-capability-structure-evolution. J. Equip. Inst. **3**, 7–13 (2016)

Research on Sentiment Analysis of Online Public Opinion Based on Semantic

Zhengtao Jiang[✉] and Lu Liu

School of Computer Science, Communication University of China,
Beijing, China
z.t.jiang@163.com, liulu3295@163.com

Abstract. In this paper, we combine the traditional analysis method based on sentiment dictionary and two kinds of text sentiment based on semantic pattern. We then propose an improved text sentiment analysis technology, including constructing an emotional dictionary, and designing 4 kinds of calculation rules based on dependency syntax and 3 kinds of calculation rules based on complex sentences. Finally, we construct the emotional semantic relation tree to calculate the value of text sentiment. Experimental results show that the accuracy rate, recall rate and F-measure of our method are significantly better than traditional algorithms.

Keywords: Network public opinion · Affective tendency analysis
Affective lexicon · Semantic model · The affective tendency value

1 Introduction

Internet public opinion refers to the public opinion or speech that has some influence and tendentious opinion on a "focus" or "hot topic". This paper mainly studies one of the core technologies of online public opinion analysis – sentiment analysis technique of online public sentiment, which aims to realize the sentiment orientation of text by means of Natural Language Processing technology.

Domestic and foreign research on text sentiment orientation analysis technology is very extensive. Bo Pang first used the machine learning method in the analysis of text sentiment classification [1]. Whitelaw constructed a linear space model for characterizing text, and used adjectives and their modifiers as affective features, and finally constructed SVM classifier [2]. He put forward a text sentiment calculation method based on syntax structure analysis for blog text [3]. Wei extracted the subject words, emotional words, associated words and degree adverbs in the text, and transformed the semantic chunk model into two or three semantic analysis models and calculated affective orientation results [3]. Feng Shi proposed a kind of sentiment orientation analysis method based on dependency relation model, the affective tendency values are calculated by the relational emotion computation, and the influence of grammatical distance and modifier on the affective tendency is also discussed in detail [4].

This paper puts forward a kind of affective tendency analysis method with emotion dictionary combined semantic model according to the characteristics of the network public opinion, and designs a network public opinion sentiment analysis system.

© Springer Nature Singapore Pte Ltd. 2018
H. Yuan et al. (Eds.): GSKI 2017, CCIS 849, pp. 313–321, 2018.
https://doi.org/10.1007/978-981-13-0896-3_31

Finally, this paper proves that the system can effectively recognize the emotional tendency of text by experiments.

2 Sentiment Analysis System of Online Public Opinion

Network public opinion analysis system structure as shown in Fig. 1. Text preprocessing is necessary before analyzing emotion, including word segmentation, part of speech tagging, removing stop word and so on. And then enter the emotion analysis process, Firstly, analyze the emotional words. This process is to extract keywords from the text after preprocessing, and then obtains the sequence of emotional feature words by matching the emotional dictionary and calculating the words affective orientation based on the seed lexicon. Next, analyze the sentences further combining semantic patterns. This process is to extract the emotion prone syntactic structure to construct the dependency sequence of sentences, and identify the related words to match complex sentence patterns, and then construct the emotional semantic relation tree. Finally, calculate sentiment tendency value of the text by emotional semantic relation tree.

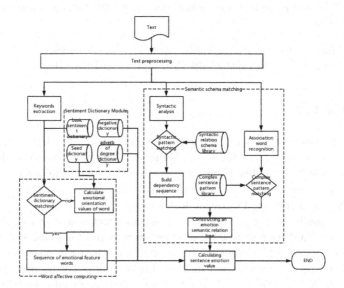

Fig. 1. Flow chart of software reliability evaluation based on BP neural network

2.1 Text Preprocessing Module

The text preprocessing module implements a series of processing of text, including the segmentation of the text, the tagging of the part of speech and the removal of the dead word. At present, there are many open word segmentation systems in the market. In the end, we choose to call the stuttering participle system to realize the process.

2.2   Module Sentiment Dictionary Module

The sentiment dictionary module includes the basic sentiment dictionary, the seed dictionary and the modifier dictionary. The basic sentiment dictionary contains the basic sentiment dictionary, the network sentiment dictionary and the domain sentiment dictionary. Seed dictionary is used to calculate the emotional intensity of words. Modifier dictionary includes negative word dictionary and adverb of degree dictionary.

2.3   Module Sentiment Dictionary Module

Affective computing module can be divided into three parts: Lexical Emotional Orientation calculation, dependency parsing and complex sentence recognition, and semantic pattern emotion calculation rules.

3   Sentiment Dictionary Combined with Semantic Model

For the simple sentence structure, the emotional tendency of keywords represents the emotional tendency of the sentence. Actually, the comment text is composed of sentences with many grammatical relations and the emotional expression of different interdependent relationships has certain regularity. In addition, people often use complex sentence patterns to express their emotional attitudes. Complex sentence pattern have specific semantic structure, and the associated clauses tend to embed different emotions, so in order to accurately identify the true emotion tendency in complex sentence patterns, we should also excavate the rules of emotion expression in complex sentence patterns.

In this paper, semantic pattern analysis is divided into two parts, which are syntactic dependency parsing and complex sentence analysis. Complex sentence analysis mainly analyzes the correlation between clauses. The relation structure among the components of sentences is the basis of sentence semantic model analysis. Mining the association between clauses further after determining the emotional tendency of the clause can achieve the correction of the overall emotional tendency of the sentence.

3.1   Affective Orientation Calculation Rules Based on Part of Speech and Dependency Syntax

Dependency parsing reveals its grammatical structure by analyzing the dependency between sentence components. Figure 2 is an example of syntactic analysis [5].

Fig. 2. Syntax analysis example

The language technology platform developed by Research Center for Social Computing and Information Retrieval generalized 15 dependency parsing tagging relationships. It is not considered that all dependent syntactic relations have affective tendencies. This paper finally summarizes 6 kinds of emotional tendency that have obvious affective orientation, which are respectively ATT (attribute relation), ADV (adverbial relation), SBV (subject-verb relation), VOB (verb-object relation), CMP (complement relation) and WP (punctuation relation).

Owing to the part of speech of the emotional feature words in different relation types is not fixed, and the relationship between emotional words and modifiers in different syntactic structure will affect the emotional tendency of sentences. It is found that the syntactic patterns that express obvious emotional attitudes mainly include nouns, verbs, adjectives and adverbs. Combined with the relationship between syntactic structures, this paper summarized 5 kinds of affective orientation calculation rules as follows.

Rule 1: the dependent syntactic relation between noun and emotional word. This model mainly appears in ATT (attribute relation), SBV (subject-verb relation) and VOB (verb-object relation). The method of calculation is shown in Table 1, where word stands for emotional word and n stands for noun.

Table 1. Affective orientation calculation rule of emotional word and noun

Noun	Value
Neuter	$Orientation(word)$
Affective word	$Polarity(word) * Polarity(n) * sqrt(Strength(n) * Strength(word))$

Rule 2: the dependent syntactic relation between adverb and emotional word. This pattern appears in ADV (adverbial relation) and CMP (complement relation). Adverb plays the role of modifying emotional words. Thereinto, adverbs of degree can strengthen or weaken the emotional intensity of emotional words; negative adverbs can change the polarity of emotional words and the emotional intensity of emotional words. The method of calculation is shown in Table 2, where $Degree\ (adv)$ stands for the modified strength coefficient of the degree adverbs and the weighted coefficient of the negative word is uniformly defined as -1.

Table 2. Affective orientation calculation rule of emotional word and adverb

Adverb	Value
Degree Adverb + sentiment word	$Orientation(word) * Degree(adv)$
Negative words + emotional words	$-0.7 \times Orientation(word)$
Negative word + degree adverb + emotional word	$0.7 \times Orientation(word) * Degree(adv)$
Degree Adverb + negative word + sentiment word	$-Orientation(word) * Degree(adv)$

Rule 3: the dependent syntactic relation between adjective and emotional word. This form is divided into two cases. One is that adjectives and emotional words are juxtaposed then calculate the affective tendency values of two words separately, and add them. The other is that there is a dependency between adjectives and emotional words usually are ADV (adverbial relation) and CMP (complement relation). The method of calculation is shown in Table 3, where word stands for emotional word and adj stands for adjectives.

Table 3. Affective orientation calculation rule of emotional word and adjective

Relation	Adjective	Value
Parataxis	Affective word or neutral word	$Orientation(word) + Orientation(adj)$
Attribution	Affective word	$Polarity(word) * sqrt(Strength(adj) * Strength(word))$
	Neutral word	$Orientation(word)$

Rule 4: the dependent syntactic relation between verb and emotional word. This form is divided into two cases. One is that verbs and emotional words are juxtaposed then calculate the affective tendency values of two words separately, and add them. The other is that there is a dependency between verbs and emotional words usually are VOB (verb-object relation) and CMP (complement relation). When verb is also emotional word, the two are closely related and should consider whether the verb has reversal characteristics. The method of calculation is shown in Table 4, where word stands for emotional word and v stands for verb.

Table 4. Affective orientation calculation rule of emotional word and verb

Relation	Adjective	Value
Parataxis	Affective word or neutral word	$Orientation(word) + Orientation(v)$
Dependence	Affective word	$Polarity(word) * Polarity(v) * sqrt(Strength(v) * Strength(word))$
	Neutral word	$Orientation(word)$

Rule 5: Punctuation processing. Although punctuation itself has no emotional tendency, it affects the emotional intensity of the original sentence. The method of calculation is shown in Table 5.

Table 5. Affective orientation calculation rule of punctuation

Punctuation	Value
Exclamatory mark	$2 \times Orientation(word)$

3.2 Affective Orientation Calculation Rules Based on Complex Sentence Patterns

As the grammatical relation between neutron sentences is mainly reflected by related words, so we mainly analyze the influence of related words on the emotional tendency of sentences. This paper sums up three kinds of sentence patterns that affect the emotional tendency of sentences. The first is the progressive sentence pattern which the emotional tendency of all clauses is consistent and the emotion of the latter clause is stronger than the previous one. The second is the transitional sentence pattern which the emotional tendency of the latter and previous are inconsistent and the real emotional attitude of the sentence is often the emotional attitude after the transition. The third is the rhetorical question sentence pattern which is usually in the form of questions to emphasize positive opinions. The actual emotional attitude of a sentence is opposite to the clause it leads to, and more strongly than the emotional attitude of the general sentence.

A complex sentence consists of clauses which generally separated by the associated words. This paper uses s_1, s_2 and so on to represent clauses. The calculation rules of complex sentence patterns are as follows (Table 6).

Table 6. Affective orientation calculation rule of complex sentence patterns

Relation	Value
Progressive sentence pattern	$Value = Orientation(s_1) + 1.5 \times Orientation(s_2)$
Transitional sentence pattern	$Value = 0.8 \times Orientation(s_1) + 1.5 \times Orientation(s_2)$
Rhetorical question sentence pattern	$Value = -1.5 \times Orientation(s_1)$

4 Figures/Captions Experiment and Result Analysis

The performance of the system is tested by contrast experiments which can verify whether the optimization of the algorithm has achieved the desired effect, and whether the accuracy of text orientation has been improved.

4.1 Evaluating Indicators

This paper select three basic evaluation indexes to evaluate the system performance. They are accuracy rate, recall rate and F value. For sentiment classification systems, the higher the accuracy rate and recall rate, the better the system performance. Since there is an inverse interdependence between accuracy and recall, the most common approach is to compute F-measure in order to consider their effects.

4.2 Test Corpus

Experiments on system performance testing require statistical analysis of the accuracy of results; therefore, it is necessary to prepare a standard dataset, that is, an artificially annotated corpus of emotion. In this experiment, we have prepared two kinds of corpus which are positive and negative polarity annotation, then processed by duplicate removal and emotion classification correction. Finally, the test data set is obtained.

4.3 Comparison of Experimental Results

(1) The influence of sentiment dictionary expansion on system performance. This experiment uses the algorithm proposed in this paper, but only the sentiment dictionary is loaded differently. The final results of affective orientation recognition are shown in Table 7.

Table 7. Comparison of results using different sentiment dictionaries

Corpus	Emotional tendency	Evaluating indicators	Basic sentiment dictionary	Extended sentiment dictionary
Hotel reviews	Positive	Accuracy rate	0.84	0.92
		Recall rate	0.81	0.93
		F-measure	0.82	0.92
	Negative	Accuracy rate	0.82	0.93
		Recall rate	0.85	0.91
		F-measure	0.85	0.92
Labtop reviews	Positive	Accuracy rate	0.86	0.93
		Recall rate	0.80	0.90
		F-measure	0.83	0.91
	Negative	Accuracy rate	0.81	0.91
		Recall rate	0.87	0.93
		F-measure	0.84	0.92

The results show that the adjunction of network sentiment dictionary, domain sentiment dictionary and modified dictionary can improve the performance of the algorithm and improve the accuracy of text classification.

(2) Performance comparison of the sentiment orientation classification based on sentiment dictionary and the algorithm proposed in this paper. In order to verify the performance of the improved algorithm, using traditional analysis method based on emotion dictionary and the analysis method presented in this paper to conduct the sentiment classification experiments. The final results of the two methods are shown in Table 8.

The results show that the algorithm proposed in this paper is better than the traditional algorithm based on sentiment dictionary. The accuracy rate, recall rate and F-measure were significantly increased, which means that the affective patterns of text can be more accurately identified by analyzing the influence of semantic patterns on the basis of considering affective words.

(3) Performance comparison of the sentiment orientation classification algorithm based on sliding window and the algorithm proposed in this paper. The principle of the

Table 8. Comparison of results of the two method

Corpus	Emotional tendency	Evaluating indicators	Sentiment dictionary algorithm	Improved algorithm
Hotel reviews	Positive	Accuracy rate	0.74	0.92
		Recall rate	0.76	0.93
		F-measure	0.75	0.92
	Negative	Accuracy rate	0.75	0.93
		Recall rate	0.74	0.91
		F-measure	0.74	0.92
Labtop reviews	Positive	Accuracy rate	0.77	0.93
		Recall rate	0.71	0.90
		F-measure	0.74	0.91
	Negative	Accuracy rate	0.73	0.91
		Recall rate	0.78	0.93
		F-measure	0.75	0.92

sentiment orientation classification algorithm based on sliding window and context semantic modification is, taking the emotional words in the sentence as the center, the window size as the search scope as the center, to find modifiers within the window area before and after emotional word [6]. Then, the emotional value of the emotion words is revised according to the modifier, and finally the emotional orientation value of the sentence is obtained. Through the contrast experiment, the validity of the semantic pattern analysis method can be verified. The final results of the two method are shown in Table 9.

Table 9. Comparison of results of the two method

Corpus	Emotional tendency	Evaluating indicators	Sliding window algorithm	Improved algorithm
Hotel reviews	Positive	Accuracy rate	0.87	0.92
		Recall rate	0.81	0.93
		F-measure	0.84	0.92
	Negative	Accuracy rate	0.83	0.93
		Recall rate	0.88	0.91
		F-measure	0.85	0.92
Labtop reviews	Positive	Accuracy rate	0.82	0.93
		Recall rate	0.80	0.90
		F-measure	0.81	0.91
	Negative	Accuracy rate	0.81	0.91
		Recall rate	0.83	0.93
		F-measure	0.82	0.92

The results show that the algorithm proposed in this paper is better than the sentiment orientation classification algorithm based on sliding window. The sliding window algorithm roughly defines the modification range of emotion words by defining the window size, and the modified relationship matched by window size is not accurate. In this paper, we use the dependency syntax analysis to get the context semantic relation of emotion words. The emotion modification relation obtained is more accurate and the performance of the algorithm is improved obviously.

5 Conclusion

This paper mainly studies the existing text sentiment analysis technology, discusses the analysis methods and puts forward a kind of improved sentiment dictionary combining sentiment semantic pattern analysis algorithm. It is shown that the he performance of algorithm proposed in this paper is improved obviously. The next research can be improved in the following aspect, such as the perfection of sentiment dictionary, the setting of emotion classification threshold and automatic recognition and monitoring of network public opinion.

Acknowledgments. This work was financially supported by the National Natural Science Foundation of China (61103199), the Engineering Program Project of CUC (3132015XNG1541, JXJYG1603) and the outstanding young teacher training project of CUC, Natural Science Basic Research Plan in Shaanxi Province of China (No. 2016JM6002) and the National Cryptography Development Fund of China (No. MMJJ20170208).

References

1. Bo, P., Li, L., Vaithyanathan, S.: Thumbs up? Sentiment classification using machine learning techniques. In: Acl-2002 Conference on Empirical Methods in Natural Language Processing, pp. 79–86. Association for Computational Linguistics (2002)
2. Whitelaw, C., Garg, N., Argamon, S.: Using appraisal groups for sentiment analysis. In: ACM International Conference on Information and Knowledge Management, pp. 625–631. ACM (2005)
3. He, F.Y.: Orientation analysis for Chinese blog text based on semantic comprehension. Comput. Appl. **31**(8), 2130–2137 (2011)
4. Feng, S., Fu, Y.C., Yang, F., Wang, D.L.: Blog sentiment orientation analysis based on dependency parsing. J. Comput. Res, Dev. **11**(49), 2395–2406 (2012)
5. Research Center for Social Computing and Information Retrieval. Language Technology platform [EB/OL]. http://www.ltp-cloud.com/intro/#dp_how
6. Yang, P., Tao, L.I., Zhao, K.: Quantitative method for analyzing public opinions on internet. Appl. Res. Comput. **3**(26), 1065–1066 (2009)

A New Method of Dish Innovation Based on User Preference Multi-objective Optimization Genetic Algorithm

Zijie Mei$^{(\boxtimes)}$ and Yinghua Zhou

Chongqing University of Posts and Telecommunications, Chongqing, China
357777519@qq.com, zhouyh@cqupt.edu.cn

Abstract. With the improvement of living level, people put forward new requirements for the diversification of diet and greater demand for new dishes. However, it is hard to make food collocation to meet specific requirement, since there are too many foodstuffs, while their nutrition ingredients and incompatibility are not well known to the ordinary people. To solve this problem, food collocation and dish creation to meet the user's requirement or preference are studied in the paper. First, the data of food composition are collected, the different food guides are referenced and the food component incompatibility is studied. Second, a food nutrition evaluation model is constructed and an improved non-dominated sorting genetic algorithm is proposed. A probability operator is introduced, by analyzing the existing recipes, to control the number of foodstuffs of a dish. A strategy to model user preference is also proposed and the non-dominated solutions are filtered by using the preference model. Third, the experiments are carried out and the experiment results show that the proposed algorithm and nutrition evaluation model can meet the requirements of user preferred dish creation and multi-objective optimization, and has better convergence speed than the original algorithm.

Keywords: Dish innovation · Multi-objective optimization · Genetic algorithm

1 Introduction

In recent years, the innovation on food gets a lot of attention. A variety of TV media are interested in cuisine. Many cyber citizens also share their experiences, opinions, attitude about cooking, and recipes through the online communities and forum websites [1]. Some websites collected these recipes [2] and some proposed recipe improvements according to people's comment on recipes [3]. Others are making diet menu for specific groups based on the existing recipes [4] or make recommendation [5].

In this paper, a model of dish innovation to meet requirements and preferences of user is constructed, combined with the intrinsic elements of ingredients, such as nutrient intake requirements. Besides, the taboo of food collocation is also considered.

The way on judging the quality of a dish is mainly depended on the nutritional value of the dish and the health preserving effect. However, the nutrient component in different ingredients is quite different. For a group of dishes, multiple nutritional goals

© Springer Nature Singapore Pte Ltd. 2018
H. Yuan et al. (Eds.): GSKI 2017, CCIS 849, pp. 322–333, 2018.
https://doi.org/10.1007/978-981-13-0896-3_32

sometimes fail to achieve the optimum result at the same time. In addition, the number of combinatorial schemes could be large due to the number of optional ingredients. The strategy to find the best combination of new dishes relying on Chef's experience only will take a long time, and the individual factors of chef may lead to similar style of dish. Therefore, it is an effective way for dish innovation by building the model of ingredients collocation with the computer. At present, the research on dish innovation or the ingredients collocation is rare, but the algorithm of this kind of multi-objective combination optimization problem is maturity.

Dealing with the multi-objective optimization problem which the number of objectives is large, usually greater than four, is far more difficult than 2-objective or 3-objective problems. And the main challenge as follows [6].

For a large number of objectives, most of the solutions in the population become non-dominated very soon in evolutionary search [7, 8], resulting in the loss of pressure to drive the population toward the Pareto front [9]. That is to say, the existence of different dominance among different individuals in the population is greatly increased. Furthermore, in order to associate with the coverage of the Pareto front, the number of solutions required to approximate the Pareto front grows exponentially with the number of objectives. This will make it very difficult to capture the whole front for a large number of objectives, even with a reasonably large population size. In addition, it's hard to find a suitable way to visualize the Pareto front [10].

To solve high dimension problem on literature [11] an evolutionary algorithm based on set, treating hyper volume [12], distribution, and ductility as new goals was proposed. This algorithm transformed the original optimization problem into a set of three objective optimization problems, including preference description, algorithm design and performance evaluation, and unified them in a framework. The literature [13] proposed a new algorithm based on sparse feature selection. It used the geometrical structural characteristics and SBX [14] to construct a graph representing the original problem. A sparse projection matrix mapping the high dimensional data into low dimensional space was then learned by a sparse regression model, which was used to measure the importance of each objective. The method has high accuracy and is less influenced by the quality of the approximate solution. According to the concept of immune memory and the principle of clonal selection, literature [15] proposed preference rank immune memory clone selection algorithm (PISA) to solve multiple objective optimization problems with a large number of objectives. The non-dominated antibodies are proportionally cloned by their preference ranks, which are defined by their preference information. It is beneficial to increases election pressure and speed up convergence to the true Pareto-optimal front. Literature [16] pointed out that the traditional crowded distance method of NSGA-II cannot measure the diversity of Pareto front solutions in some cases. It proposed a new method to preserve diversity and extreme value solutions based on the hierarchical clustering methods. This method chooses solutions from all regions of the Pareto frontier, rather than choosing two closer solutions. Compared with the existing NSGA-II method, this method has better diversity.

2 Datasets

For the establishment of dish innovation model in this paper, a series of related basic data are needed to support our research. However, the public and comprehensive dataset that contains the data needed is not constructed, due to the fact that there are few studies in this field. However, some related datasets on recipes which is used for image recognition [17] are constructed. Amaia Salvadorian (http://im2recipe.csail.mit.edu/) established a dataset named Recipe1 M, which includes 1029720 recipes and 887706 dishes pictures. Using Recipe1 M, the related recipes by identifying pictures of dishes are retrieved and then the cooking steps on how to make the dishes are shown. In addition, Chen [18] has also built a recipe dataset for Chinese cuisine, including 65284 recipes, 353 ingredients, and 110241 pictures of the dishes.

To meet the research needs, 1365 kinds of common food ingredients and the daily intake standard of nutrition for Chinese people are collected. Following is the detailed description of how to set up the dataset for this paper.

2.1 Sources of Data

VireoFood-172 dataset [19] was used as the diet dataset, which contains 64874 recipes. The data of food nutrient component are compiled from the Food Nutrition Network (http://www.neasiafoods.org). However, the quantity of ingredients in food nutrition network dataset does not match with VireoFood-172. To supplement the data, the missing ingredients was acquired from other Food Nutrient websites (http://www.boohee.com) (http://fitness.39.net). The nutrition intake standard [20] is developed by Chinese Nutrition Society and we use it as our intake standard dataset.

2.2 Data Structure

VireoFood-172 dataset records the name of the recipe, the ingredients and the cooking steps. The food nutrient dataset divided the food into 21 categories, and recorded the contents of 24 nutrients, such as calories, protein, fat, carbohydrates and dietary fiber. The intake standard datasets recorded different populations in different ages of above various nutrient intake demand, including EAR (Estimated Average Requirement), RNI (Recommended Nutrient Intake) or AI (Adequate Intakes) and UL (Tolerable Upper Intake Level).

2.3 Analysis

According to the quantity of recipe ingredients in VireoFood-172 dataset, the probability of adding ingredients to control the quantity of ingredients in a dish can be calculated. The nutrient intake standard and heat intake standard from the intake standard dataset is used to calculate the INQ (Index of Nutrition Quality), with the total component of various nutrients for different combination of ingredients, as one of the evaluation functions.

3   Multi Objective Optimization Model Establishment

Index of Nutritional Quality is an important index to evaluate the nutritional value of food. The nutritive value of food can be evaluated by the ratio of nutrients that can meet the needs of human nutrition, also called nutrient density, and the ratio of the same food that can meet the needs of human energy, also called heat density. The nutritional value of food is the ratio of nutrient density and heat density.

$$\text{INQ} = \frac{n}{N} \cdot \frac{H}{h} \tag{1}$$

Where n is the nutrient content in food, N is the nutrient intake standard, h is the energy provided by food, and H is the recommended energy intake. When INQ < 1, it means the nutrient content of food is insufficient. INQ = 1 means the nutrient content of food is up to the standard. INQ > 1 means the food has a higher content of nutrient.

The nutrient content of the recipe is an important factor to judge the combination of a group of food materials. A dietary target can be determined by the intake of one or more nutrients. In a reasonable intake range, the greater nutrient you eat the greater effect on its effectiveness. According to Chinese dietary intake standard, the absorption and metabolism of nutrients for a man are limited. That is to say, even with excessive intake of nutrients, the promotion of the effect will not be changed. By analyzing the relationship between nutrients and target efficacy, the sigmoid function is introduced to map the promotion effect of nutrients on efficacy to (0, 1). As a sub objective function, f_1 can be expressed as.

$$f_1 = \frac{1}{1 + e^{-\left[\sqrt{I(U,N)-1}\right]}} \tag{2}$$

Where $I\ (U,\ N)$ is the INQ of a nutrient in some kind of population. U is the particular population, and N is the nutrient which promotes the target efficacy. This objective function can be used for different efficacy targets.

4   Dish Innovation Algorithm Based on Improved NSGA- II

The formula (2) above is used on the improved NSGA- II, as a sub objective function, to build the dish innovation optimization model on food collocation by improving the traditional genetic algorithm. It can satisfy all sub objective functions, to some extent. And a set of solutions are obtained to meet the needs of user.

The improved non-dominated sorting genetic algorithm in this paper is mainly presented as follows.

(a) A probability operator P (P1, P2…) is introduced according to the quantity of recipe ingredients in VireoFood-172 dataset. It means the probability of adding the ingredients in order to limit the individual expressiveness gene and control the quantity of the ingredients.

Supposing each recipe is likely to choose n food, n = 1, 2, 3... And the upper limits of n can be counted in VireoFood-172 dataset.

$$\prod_{j=1}^{i} P_j \cdot (1 - P_{i+1}) = N_i \quad i = 1, 2, \ldots, n - 1 \tag{3}$$

$$N_i = \frac{n_i}{\sum_{i=1}^{n} n_i} = 1, 2, \ldots, n \tag{4}$$

Where n_i is the number of recipes which select i ingredients. N_i means the probability of the number of ingredients in the recipe is i, and P_i is the probability of selecting the i th ingredients. $P_1 = 1$, $P_{n+1} = 0$.

(b) The crowding operator is to filter the non-dominated solutions in traditional NSGA2, but the user's preference of the goal cannot be represented. In this paper, the linear summation of the objective function values according to weights set by user is calculated to transform the multi-objective problem into a single objective optimization problem. The specific formula is

$$F(x) = \sum_{i=1}^{n} \omega_i \times f_i(x) \tag{5}$$

Where ω_n are the weights of nth objective, $f_i(x)$ is the fitness of nth objective.

A preference model is presented to solve the problem that user cannot provide weights of objectives. First of all, all solutions is divided into several level by running the fast non-dominated sorting algorithm. Then for the non-dominated solutions in the same level, the preference tendency is decided by the order of sub functions ($\omega_1 > \omega_2 > \ldots > \omega_n$). The decreasing amplitude U is determined by the target number n.

$$U \in \left(0.1U_{max}, U_{max} = \frac{2}{n(n-1)}\right), n = 1, 2, \ldots \tag{6}$$

Supposing the number of objectives is n, $\mu_n \in U$ is a group of random number.

$$\omega_n - \omega_{n+1} = \mu_n, n = 1, 2, 3, \ldots n - 1 \tag{7}$$

$$\sum_{i=1}^{n} \omega_i = 1, n = 1, 2, 3, \ldots \tag{8}$$

Where μ_n is the weight difference between the nth objective and $n + 1$ th objective.

(c) To avoid the problems that parent chromosomes have the same offspring after crossover operator, a phenotype gene (assuming in binary encoding, the "1" is phenotype, "0" is hidden) replacement crossover method is introduced to guarantee the diversity of the solutions and expand the coverage of solution space. Firstly, two individuals are selected from parent population randomly, denoted as P1, P2. And a phenotype gene position is chose randomly from P1 and P2 respectively, denoted as S1, S2. Finally, the gene on the position of S1, S2 from P1, P2 is exchanged. And the two new chromosomes are added to the offspring population.

The algorithm used the existing recipes and the preference of users as the constraint conditions and evaluation criteria. In population initialization process, a probability operator to control the phenotype gene of individual is introduced. In the selection stage, an adaptive target weights to transform the multi-objective problem into a single objective optimization problem is added. The convergence speed is improved by the algorithm and the new populations have a higher fitness (Fig. 1).

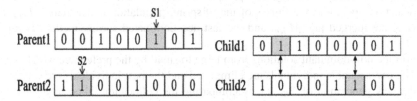

Fig. 1. Expressive crossover operator

The process of this algorithm is as follows (Fig. 2).

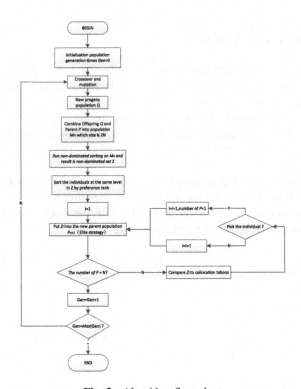

Fig. 2. Algorithm flow chart

1. In population initialization process, the method of Chromosome coding for selected ingredients is binary coding. The "1" is phenotype, which represents the ingredient is selected. The "0" is hidden, indicating the ingredient isn't selected. The number of each individual phenotype gene deciding by the probability operator is saved to generate the location of phenotype gene randomly and get the initial population P_0. Next is to calculate the fitness of population, and set the generation time $Gen = 0$.
2. Genetic operation: all individuals in P_{Gen} are selected to run the crossover operation and some individuals randomly are chose to run the mutation operation. Result is the offspring Q_{Gen}. (This paper adopts the crossover way of phenotype gene, and the mutation strategy is to take the opposite between "0" and "1").
3. Selection operation: the fitness of the offspring population is calculated. P_{Gen} and Q_{Gen} are merged into M_{Gen}, and the fast non-dominated sorting method is run on M_{Gen}.
4. Sort the non-dominant solutions from large to small by the preference weight score.
5. The unreasonable individuals are eliminated and the best individuals are selected as the new generation of P_{Gen+1} by comparing the collocation taboo tables with the individuals in M_{Gen}.
6. When it reach the maximum number of iterations, that is, $Gen = Gen + 1$, the cycle ends, or else go to 2;
7. A set of Pareto optimal solutions are obtained.

5   Experiment and Analysis

The two purposes in this experiment are to verify the rationality of the improved NSGA-II algorithm. The other is to inspect the effectiveness of the algorithm in this paper by comparing with the traditional NSGA-II. Judging a dish's quality can be considered from many aspects. On the aspects of nutritional value, the goals on effect can be multiple. In this experiment, the sub objective functions, $f1$ and $f2$, were used to express two effects on bone growing and enriching blood. The corresponding nutrients are calcium and iron.

The Elitist preservation (EP) strategy is used in the experiment. First, the parent and offspring population are mixed, then the selection operation is executed to ensure the diversity of individuals. The crossover probability is 1, the mutation probability is 0.2, the population size is 100, and the generation time is 200.

N	Gen	Pc	Pm	Goal 1	Goal 2
100	200	1	0.2	Ca	Fe

User Information:

Sex	Age	Physiological stage
Male	25	None

5.1   The Expressive Crossover Operator

In order to verify the rationality of adding the expressive crossover operator, comparing with the traditional single point crossover operator, the average fitness of these two groups on two dimensional goals are calculated. The x axis represents the population evolution times, and the y axis represents the fitness of the sub objective function. By comparing the average fitness of each generation, the influence of the two kinds of crossover operators was presented on the experiment. The statistical results are shown in Figs. 3 and 4.

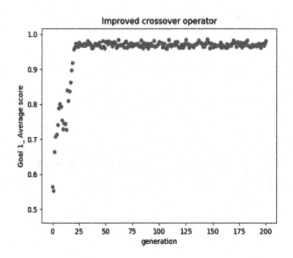

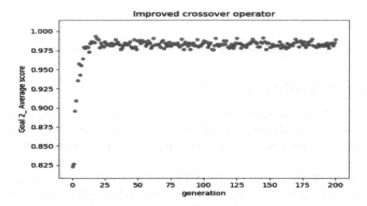

Fig. 3. Population fitness in expressive crossover operators

As shown in Figs. 3 and 4, the average fitness of the population by using the expressive crossover operator is higher, and the populations have better similarity after convergence. It shows that the expressive crossover operator is more likely to get rid of the local optimal solution and get a better Pareto optimal set.

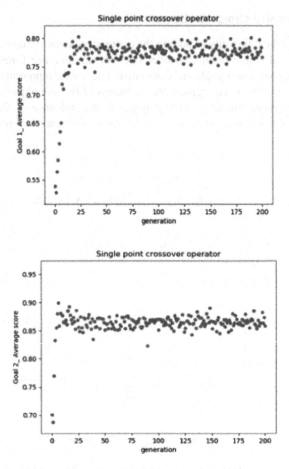

Fig. 4. Population fitness in single point crossover operators

5.2   Screening Search Space

To verify the influence of search space on the convergence speed of the algorithm, the top 100 ingredients which nutrient component is abundant are picked up as the selected food. And the average fitness of the population under the two dimensional goals are calculated.

Compared with Figs. 3 and 5, the speed of convergence was significantly improved after limiting the quantity of ingredients to be selected, while maintaining higher population fitness. For high dimensional objective, it could effectively improve the convergence speed of the algorithm.

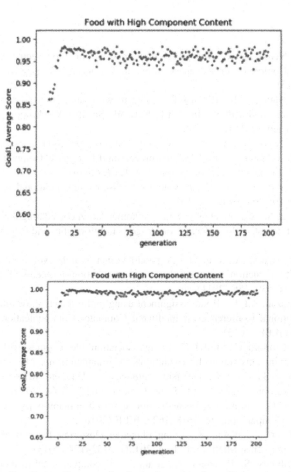

Fig. 5. Population fitness under limited number ingredient to be selected

6 Summaries

In this paper, a multi-objective mathematical model of dish innovation is established and a multi-objective optimization algorithm based on improved NSGA-2 is proposed. As a result, a satisfactory matching scheme is provided in nutritional objectives. The feasibility of the algorithm is verified by experimental analysis. This algorithm has two main advantages. 1. Preference weights are added to meet the specific needs of users. 2. An expressive crossover operator is introduced to increase the space search capability and get a better approach the Pareto front.

The experimental results can obtain a set of optimal solutions. These combinations of innovative dishes can be referenced by users. On the other hand, this method has not yet considered about the other aspects of dish innovation as evaluation indicators, such as color matching, smell, and cost and that will be the direction of further research.

References

1. Pugsee, P., Niyomvanich, M.: Suggestion analysis for food recipe improvement. In: International Conference on Advanced Informatics: Concepts, Theory and Applications, 1–5. IEEE (2015)
2. Kular, D.K., Menezes, R., Ribeiro, E.: Using network analysis to understand the relation between cuisine and culture. In: IEEE Network Science Workshop, pp. 38–45. IEEE Computer Society (2011)
3. Pugsee, P., Niyomvanich, M.: Comment analysis for food recipe preferences. In: International Conference on Electrical Engineering/Electronics, Computer, Telecommunications and Information Technology, pp. 1–4. IEEE (2015)
4. Gagliardi, I., Artese, M.T.: Create your menu discovering traditional recipes. In: Digital Heritage, pp. 195–196. IEEE (2016)
5. Mao, X., Yuan, S., Xu, W., et al.: Recipe recommendation considering the flavor of regional cuisines. In: International Conference on Progress in Informatics and Computing, pp. 32–36. IEEE (2017)
6. Singh, H.K., Isaacs, A., Ray, T.: A pareto corner search evolutionary algorithm and dimensionality reduction in many-objective optimization problems. IEEE Trans. Evol. Comput. **15**(4), 539–556 (2011)
7. Chira, C., Bazzan, A.L.C.: Route assignment using multi-objective evolutionary search. In: IEEE International Conference on Intelligent Computer Communication and Processing, pp. 141–148. IEEE (2015)
8. Raschip, M., Croitoru, C., Stoffel, K.: Using association rules to guide evolutionary search in solving constraint satisfaction. In: Evolutionary Computation, pp. 744–750. IEEE (2015)
9. Li, M., Yang, S., Liu, X.: Diversity comparison of Pareto front approximations in many-objective optimization. IEEE Trans. Cybern. **44**(12), 2568 (2014)
10. He, Z., Yen, G.G.: An improved visualization approach in many-objective optimization. In: Evolutionary Computation, pp. 1618–1625. IEEE (2016)
11. Guo, X., Wang, Y., Wang, X.: Using objective clustering for solving many-objective optimization problems. Math. Prob. Eng. **2013**(1), 133–174 (2013)
12. Maitre, J., Gaboury, S., Bouchard, B., et al.: A new computational method for stator faults recognition in induction machines based on hyper-volumes. In: IEEE International Conference on Electro/Information Technology, pp. 216–220. IEEE (2015)
13. Chen, X.H., Li, X., Wang, N.: Objective reduction with sparse feature selection for many objective optimization problems. Acta Electronica Sinica **43**(7), 1300–1307 (2015)
14. Hamdan, M.M.: Revisiting the distribution index in simulated binary crossover operator for evolutionary multi objective optimization algorithms. In: Fourth International Conference on Digital Information and Communication Technology and its Applications, pp. 37–41. IEEE (2014)
15. Yang, D.D., Jiao, L.C., Gong, M.G., et al.: Clone selection algorithm to solve preference multi-objective optimization. J. Softw. **21**(1), 1–6 (2010)
16. Vachhani, V.L., Dabhi, V.K., Prajapati, H.B.: Improving NSGA-II for solving multi objective function optimization problems. In: International Conference on Computer Communication and Informatics, pp. 1–6. IEEE (2016)
17. Güngör, C., Baltacı, F., Erdem, A., et al.: Turkish cuisine: a benchmark dataset with Turkish meals for food recognition. In: Signal Processing and Communications Applications Conference, pp. 1–4. IEEE (2017)

18. Chen, J., Ngo, C.-W: Deep-based ingredient recognition for cooking recipe retrival. ACM Multimed. (2016)
19. Chen, J., Ngo, C.W.: Deep-based ingredient recognition for cooking recipe retrieval. In: ACM on Multimedia Conference, pp. 32–41. ACM (2016)
20. Yao, Y.: Chinese Dietary Reference Intake. DRIs. Acta Nutrimenta Sinica **36**(04), 308 (2014). (in Chinese)

Algorithm for Calculating the Fractal Dimension of Internet AS-Level Topology

Jun Zhang[1(✉)], Hai Zhao[1], and Wenbo Qi[2]

[1] School of Computer Science and Engineering, Northeastern University,
Shenyang, China
zhangjun1@mail.neu.edu.cn
[2] School of Materials Science and Engineering, Northeastern University,
Shenyang 110819, China

Abstract. A box-covering algorithm to calculate the fractal dimension of Internet topology at AS-level was introduced. The algorithm first selects some nodes that have big degree and put them into different boxes, and then uses the node as seed in each box to cover the network. The purpose is to ensure that the boxes to cover the network are as little as possible. By analyzing a large number of the actual measurement data of AS-level topology, we found the relationship between the number of the nodes that were first selected as seeds and the size of the network. The number of the boxes to cover the network obtained by this algorithm is very close to the minimum number of boxes needed to cover the entire network. The results show that the algorithm can get the near-optimal solutions to cover the Internet network at AS-level without an exhaustive search, and thus effectively saves the time for calculating the fractal dimension of Internet topology at AS-level.

Keywords: Complex network · Box-Covering · Fractal dimension
AS-Level topology

1 Introduction

Being a prototypical instance of complex network, the analysis on Internet microscopic topology has become a hot topic at present and has attracted more and more attention of academia. Recent studies show that Internet macroscopic topology has got self-similarity [1–6]. The self-similarity of Internet macroscopic topology reflects the overall properties of the network topology, that is, a feature does not depend on the local technical details. For understanding the architecture of Internet, finding the inherent laws in it, studying the self-similarity of Internet topology is a meaningful topic in the fields of complex network.

Fractal scaling recently observed in real-world scale-free networks has opened a new perspective in complex network theory and modeling. Song et al. [7] creatively described the self-similarity of complex networks with the fractal dimension of the fractal theory which provides a new perspective for people to study the complex network. Fractal dimension can characterize the intrinsic properties of objects by simple statements, and reflect the essence of the research object by a small amount of information. Using the innate superiority of fractal theory in the research of the self-similarity, we can give an overall characterization of Internet topology. It can survey network characteristics without the aid of the excessive statistical features. It is a possible way to study Internet from the overall by studying the self-similarity of Internet topology through fractal geometry theory.

In order to unfold the universal scaling properties of Internet topology, we study the fractal dimension of it at AS-level using the dimension measurement algorithm based on the algorithm proposed by Song et al. [7]. In the paper, we first analyzed the typical algorithm for calculating the fractal dimension, the box-covering method. Then we designed a new algorithm which could obtain the approximate minimal number of boxes for covering the network without an exhaustive search, and applied it to the Internet AS-level topology. The results show that it greatly reduced the workload, and made it efficient to calculate the fractal dimension of Internet AS-level topology.

2 Research Method

2.1 Box-Covering Method

Fractal scaling refers to a power-law relationship between the minimum number of boxes $N_B(l_B)$ needed to cover the entire network and the lateral size of the boxes l_B, i.e.

$$N_B(l_B) \sim l_B^{-d_B} \tag{1}$$

where d_B is the fractal dimension [8]. This method is called the box-covering method.

In fractal geometry, box-counting is the primary way to evaluate the fractal dimension of a fractal object [9, 10]. However, it is not clear how to apply box-counting to complex networks, due to the lack of embedding onto Euclidean space. A major breakthrough has been made by Song et al. who introduced a generalized box-covering method for complex networks using the intrinsic metric of chemical distance which corresponds to the number of edges on the shortest path between two nodes in networks [7]. From then, the researchers have carried out a lot of researches on the calculation of fractal dimension of complex networks [11–23] and made considerable progress.

But how to get the minimum number of boxes for cover the network among all the possible tiling configurations? It can be mapped onto a graph coloring problem in computer science. Its solution is known to be NP-hard. In principle, the optimal solution should be identified by testing exhaustively all possible solutions. Nevertheless, for practical purposes, this approach is unfeasible since the solution space with its 2^N solutions is too large. Finding the actual minimum number over all configurations is a challenging task. Until now how to cover a network with the fewest number of boxes of a given size is still an unsolved problem in network and computer science. Researchers are trying their best to get the near-optimal solutions to cover the network.

2.2 Burning Algorithm

For a given box size l_B, a box is a set of nodes where all distances l_{ij} between any two nodes i and j in the box are less than l_B. It is possible, then, to grow a box from a given central node, so that all nodes in the box are within distance less than a given box radius r_B (the maximum distance from a central node). For the original definition of the box, l_B corresponds to the box diameter (maximum distance between any two nodes in the box) plus one. That is,

$$l_B = 2r_B + 1 \tag{2}$$

This method is called burning algorithm [14]. The central node in each box is called the seed node.

In order to get the minimum number of boxes for covering the network, it is necessary to ensure that each box which covers the network contains nodes as much as possible. To achieve this purpose, the key point is the choice of the seed node in each box. So far, there are two methods that are usually adopted for selecting the seed node. The first one is selecting the seed node randomly, which is called the random sequential (RS) box-covering method [22]. The other one is selecting the node with the biggest degree as the seed (P-BC method) [23]. RS method is with a lot of randomness. Different realizations of the procedure may yield different numbers of boxes covering the network. P-BC method can ensure to make more nodes attribute to a box. And then make the number of the boxes to cover the network fewer. But it is still not ideal.

P-BC method can only ensure that the first box contains nodes as much as possible, but not ensure that the subsequent boxes also contain nodes as much as possible. This is because it is likely to put some nodes with bigger degree into the same box, and makes the left network become broken, so that the boxes to cover the entire network are increased. It can be illustrated by Fig. 1. In which, Fig. 1(a) is the original network, and Fig. 1(b) is the result of P-BC method. The entire network is covered by four boxes which marked by different color and line style. It is clear that the result is not fine. The optimal covering should be the result shown as Fig. 2.

Figure 1(a) is the original network. The degree of the nodes 1–10 in it is 6, 4, 1, 1, 1, 1, 1, 1, 1, 1 respectively. Sorting them in descending order by their degree, we obtained a node queue: 1, 2, 3, 4, 5, 6, 7, 8, 9, 10. In which, the order of node 3 to 10 is random, because the degree of them are equal. According to P-BC algorithm, we first chose node 1 as the seed in a new box, and put the nodes that are less than or equal to 1 edges away from it into the box. Then we obtained the box colored by blue, shown in Fig. 1(b), which contained 7 nodes of 1, 2, 3, 4, 5, 6, and 7. Next we created a new box, chose node 8 as seed in it to cover the network, and obtained the box colored by red. Continue to cover the network in the same way, we then obtained two boxes colored by orange and green separately. At last, we got the result illustrated by Fig. 1(b). The network is covered by four boxes.

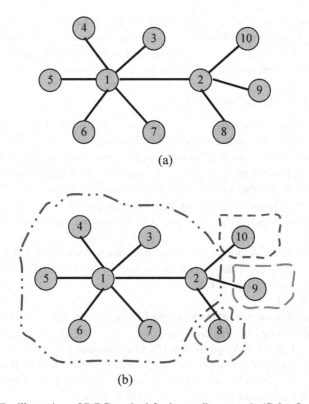

(a)

(b)

Fig. 1. The illustration of P-BC method for box radius $r_B = 1$. (Color figure online)

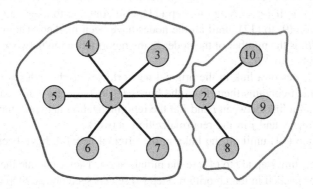

Fig. 2. The optimal covering result of Fig. 1(a) for box radius $r_B = 1$. (Color figure online)

2.3 Improved Box-Covering Method

For obtain the optimal solution for covering the network, it must ensure that each box for covering the network contains nodes as much as possible. So we consider to choose several nodes that have the biggest degree and put them into different boxes. Then in each box, choose the node as seed, and put all the nodes that are less than or equal to r_B distance to it into the box and mark them. So that makes the number of the nodes in each box as much as possible, and thus leads to the number of the boxes for covering the network as little as possible, and then get the near-optimal solution to cover the network.

The algorithm is described as followed:

(1) Read the network topology to a two-dimensional array, *Links*, and record the number of the links with a variable, *Linksnumber*;

(2) Statistic the nodes contained in the topology and calculate the degree of them. Store the nodes into an array, *Nodes*, according to their degree from big to small, and record the number of the nodes with a variable, N;

(3) Calculate the distance l_{ij} between any pair of nodes i and j;

(4) Set the initial value of r_B, the radius of the box. Set the state of each node as unmarked;

(5) Choose the first CN nodes, $n_1 \sim n_{CN}$, from array *Nodes* and put them into CN boxes, $H_1 \sim H_{CN}$ separately. Then set the state of them as marked. Set the number of the boxes NB equals to CN;

(6) Set $j = CN + 1$;

(7) If the state of node n_j is unmarked, and $l_{ij} \leq r_B (i = 1 \sim CN)$, then put the node n_j into the according box, H_i, then mark it;

(8) Set $j = j + 1$; If $j <= N$, go to step (7), else continue to execute the next step;

(9) If there are unmarked nodes in array *Nodes*, create a new box H and set $NB = NB + 1$. Then choose a node n_k with the biggest degree from the unmarked nodes in the array and put it into box H, then mark it;

(10) Set $j = k + 1$;

(11) If node n_j is unmarked, and $l_{kj} \leq r_B$, put the node into box H, and mark it;

(12) Set $j = j + 1$; If $j <= N$, go to step (11), else continue to execute the next step;

(13) Repeat step (9) to (12), until all the nodes have been marked. The number of the boxes, NB, is the number of the nodes in the renormalization network. Number the nodes with 1 to NB;

(14) For two nodes of a link in the original network, search the indexes i and j of the boxes which contains them from the boxes H_1 to H_{NB}. If i is not equal to j, and there is not a link between i and j in the renormalization network, then add a new link between i and j in the renormalization network;

(15) Repeat step (14) until all the links in the original network have been treated.

In the algorithm, step (1) to (4) are the initialization. They calculate the initial value of the variables needed in the algorithm. Step (5) selects seed nodes. Step (6) to (8) use seed nodes to generate the boxes for cover the network. Step (9) to (13) continues to cover the left network until the entire network has been covered completely. Step (14) and (15) generalize the links in the renormalization network.

3 Results and Discussion

3.1 Choose of Seed Nodes

In the above algorithm, how much the seeds we first choose is suitable? It is varied with the scale and structure of the network topology. We analyzed it on Internet topology at AS-level. Through trials repeatedly on large amount of measurement data of Internet AS-level topology from CAIDA ARK, we draw the conclusion that the number of the seed nodes, CN, has the relationship with the box radius, r_B, as followed:

$$CN = N * 6/10^{r_B+1} \tag{3}$$

where N is the size of the network, i.e. the number of the nodes in the network.

3.2 The Comparation of the Results

According to the three methods of selecting the seed nodes, we covered Internet AS-level topology in Feb, 2011 obtained from CAIDA ARK with boxes of radius $r_B = 1, 2, 3, 4, 5$, the results are listed in Table 1.

Table 1. The number of boxes for cover Internet AS-level topology obtained by the three methods

Original network	Algorithm proposed in the paper	P-BC method	RS method
25804	3258	16051	17415

The number of boxes obtained by our algorithm is 3258, and it is 16051 and 17415 respectively obtained by the other methods. It is clear that the number of the boxes covering Internet AS-level topology obtained by our algorithm is far superior to the other methods. It is more close to the mininum number of boxes for covering the network.

3.3 Fractal Dimension of Internet AS-Level Topology

For calculate the fractal dimension of Internet AS-level topology, it needs to remormalize it using the above algorithm. Using the algorithm to cover Internet AS-level topology in Feb, 2011 obtained from CAIDA ARK with boxes of radius $r_B = 1, 2, 3, 4, 5$ respectively, the results are listed in Table 2.

Table 2. The renormalization network of Internet AS-level topology in Feb, 2011

Original network	Renormalization network				
	$r_B = 1$	$r_B = 2$	$r_B = 3$	$r_B = 4$	$r_B = 5$
$N = 25804$	$N = 3258$	$N = 368$	$N = 33$	$N = 3$	$N = 1$
$L = 60852$	$L = 18698$	$L = 2655$	$L = 122$	$L = 2$	$L = 0$

Notes: N reflects the nodes in the network, and L reflects the links in the network.

According to formular (1), for calculate the fractal dimension d_B, it should fit the number of the nodes in the renormalization network, $N_B(l_B)$, and the size of the box, l_B, linear under the logarithm coordinates. The result is illustrated in Fig. 3.

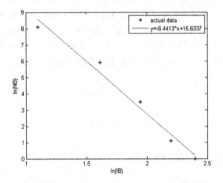

Fig. 3. The fractal dimension of Internet AS-level network topology

The horizontal coordinate is the logarithm of l_B which is the size of the box, and the vertical coordinate is the logarithm of $N_B(l_B)$ which is the number of the boxes to cover the network. The linear expression of the fitness result is:

$$y = -6.4413x + 15.6337 \qquad (4)$$

The coefficient of determination is $R^2 = 0.986$ which shows that the Goodness of Fit is fine. Thus we calculated the fractal dimension of Internet AS-level topology, $d_B = 6.4413$. We exceed to calculate the fractal dimension of Internet AS-level topology with the different data in the other month of 2011, and obtained the similar results, shown as Fig. 4.

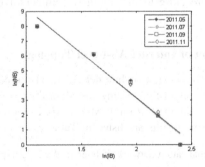

Fig. 4. The fractal dimension of the AS-level network topology in the other month of 2011

4   Conclusion

We applied the classical box-covering method of the geometry to Internet AS-level Topology. By deeply analyzed the algorithm proposed by Song et al., we designed an algorithm which suits to calculate the fractal dimension of Internet AS-level topology. The method can find the near-optimal solution of the minimum number of boxes needed to cover the Internet network at AS-level without an exhaustive search. The algorithm proposed in the paper has got lower time complexity which makes it possible for calculate the fractal dimension of Internet AS-level topology within the shorter time. The experiment results show that the algorithm proposed in the paper is effective in the calculation of the fractal dimension of Internet AS-level network topology.

Although our purpose of designing the algorithm is for calculating the fractal dimension of Internet AS-level network topology, the algorithm can easily be extended to the other complex networks. Only the ratio number of the nodes that are first chosen as the seed nodes is different. So the method provides a reference for the other kind of complex networks.

References

1. Zhang, J., Zhao, H., Yang, B., Sun, H.L.: Fractal characteristics of internet router-level topology. J. Northeastern Univ. **32**(3), 372–375 (2011)
2. Caldarelli, G., Marchetti, R., Pietronero, L.: The fractal properties of Internet. Europhys. Lett. **52**(4), 386–391 (2000). http://stacks.iop.org/0295-5075/52/i=4/a=386
3. Zhang, J., Zhao, H., Yang, B.: Fractals on IPv6 network topology. Telkomnika **11**(2), 577–582 (2013)
4. Mi, X., Zhu, J., Zhao, H.: Analysis of fractal characteristic of Internet router and IPv6 level topology. J. Northeastern Univ. **35**(1), 43–46 + 55 (2014)
5. Zhang, W.B., Zhao, H., Sun, P.G., Xu, Y., Zhang, X.: Research on Internet topology evolution and the fractal of average degree of nodes. Acta Electronica Sin. **34**(8), 1438–1445 (2006)
6. Kitsak, M., Havlin, S., Paul, G., Riccaboni, M., Pammolli, F., Stanley, H.E.: Betweenness centrality of fractal and nonfractal scale-free model networks and tests on real networks. Phys. Rev. E **75**(5), 056115 (2007). https://doi.org/10.1103/physreve.75.056115
7. Song, C.M., Havlin, S., Makse, H.A.: Self-similarity of complex network. Nature **433**(7024), 392–395 (2005). https://doi.org/10.1038/nature03248
8. Feder, J.: Fractals. Plenum Press, New York (1988)
9. Viquez, S., Rodriguez-Lugo, V., Vazquez-Polo, G., Castano, V.M.: Measuring two-dimensional fractal patterns: the role of the definition of dimension. Comput. Mater. Sci. **4**(2), 172–180 (1995). https://doi.org/10.1016/0927-0256(95)00020-q
10. Feeny, B.F.: Fast multifractal analysis by recursive box covering. Int. J. Bifurcation Chaos **10**(9), 2277–2287 (2000). https://doi.org/10.1142/s0218127400001420
11. Schneider, C.M., Kesselring, T.A., Andrade, J.S., Herrmann, H.J.: Box-covering algorithm for fractal dimension of complex networks. Phys. Rev. E **86**(1), 016707 (2012). https://doi.org/10.1103/physreve.86.016707
12. Kim, J.S., Goh, K.-I., Kahng, B., Kim, D.: A box-covering algorithm for fractal scaling in scale-free networks. Chaos **17**(2), 26116/1–6 (2007). https://doi.org/10.1063/1.2737827

13. Zhou, W.X., Jiang, Z.Q., Sornette, D.: Exploring self-similarity of complex cellular networks: the edge-covering method with simulated annealing and log-periodic sampling. Phys. A **375**(2), 741–752 (2007). https://doi.org/10.1016/j.physa.2006.10.025

14. Song, C.M., Gallos, L.K., Havlin, S., Makse, H.A.: How to calculate the fractal dimension of a complex network: the box covering algorithm. J. Stat. Mech., 03006 (2007). https://doi.org/10.1088/1742-5468/2007/03/p03006

15. Gao, L., Hu, Y.Q., Di, Z.R.: Accuracy of the ball-covering approach for fractal dimensions of complex networks and a rank-driven algorithm. Phys. Rev. E **78**(4), 046109 (2008). https://doi.org/10.1103/physreve.78.046109

16. Zhou, Y.W., Liu, J.L., Yu, Z.G., Zhao, Z.Q., Anh, V.: Fractal and complex network analyses of protein molecular dynamics. Phys. A **416**(12), 21–32 (2014). https://doi.org/10.1016/j.physa.2014.08.047

17. Sun, Y.Y., Zhao, Y.J.: Overlapping box covering method for the fractal dimension of complex networks. Phys. Rev. E **89**(4), 042809 (2014). https://doi.org/10.1103/physreve.89.042809

18. Kuang, L., Zhao, Z.Y., Wang, F., Li, Y.X., Yu, F., Li, Z.J.: A differential evolution box-covering algorithm for fractal dimension on complex networks. In: Proceedings of 2014 IEEE Congress on Evolutionary Computation, Beijing, China, 06–11 July, 2014, pp. 693–699 (2014). https://doi.org/10.1109/cec.2014.6900383

19. Zhang, H.X., Hu, Y., Lan, X., Mahadevan, S., Deng, Y.: Fuzzy fractal dimension of complex networks. Appl. Soft Comput. J. **25**, 514–518 (2014). https://doi.org/10.1016/j.asoc.2014.08.019

20. Shanker, O.: Algorithms for fractal dimension calculation. Mod. Phys. Lett. B **22**(7), 459–466 (2008)

21. Tao, S.H., Zhang, Z.L., Tian, S.L.: Properties of self-similarity networks. J. Comput. **5**(10), 1582–1589 (2010). https://doi.org/10.4304/jcp.5.10.1582-1589

22. Kim, J.S., Goh, K.I., Kahng, B., Kim, D.: Fractality and self-similarity in scale-free networks. New J. Phys. **9**(6), 177 (2007). https://doi.org/10.1088/1367-2630/9/6/177

23. Yao, C.Z., Yang, J.M.: Improved box dimension calculation algorithm for fractality of complex networks. Comput. Eng. Appl. **46**(8), 5–7 (2010)

An Improved GPSR Routing Algorithm Based on Vehicle Trajectory Mining

Peng Zhou[✉], Xiaoqiang Xiao, Wanbin Zhang, and Weixun Ning

Computer School, National University of Defense Technology,
Changsha 410073, People's Republic of China

Abstract. The taxi GPS trace data has great potential value for the development of intelligent transportation. By analyzing the data, the social attributes of vehicles can be found, and the excavated information could play a guiding role in VANETs routing designing. In this paper, an improved GPSR Routing Algorithm based on Vehicle Trajectory Mining algorithm is proposed. The algorithm can effectively improve the routing performance by eliminating the unreliable forwarding node and improving the perimeter forwarding strategy in the GPSR algorithm by comparing the social attributes of these nodes. The simulation experiment shows that our algorithm can improve the packets delivery ratio and reduce the average end-to-end delay.

Keywords: VANET · Trajectory mining · GPSR algorithm · Social attribute
Simulation

1 Introduction

In the Vehicle Ad-hoc Network (VANET), the vehicle is regarded as a mobile wireless node or router. Using the short distance communication of nodes within hundreds of meters, the VANET can realize a wide range of wireless self-organized network. It has the features of quickly changed network topology and limited capacity, making the establishment of communicating links random and unstable. Therefore, the routing techniques determine the performance of entire network, and the routing protocols become one of the major challenges for the study of VANET.

As the popularity of vehicular positioning equipment, the vehicle movement trajectory data can be collected and studied. Information, such as the hot areas or traffic status on the road, can be driven by analyzing these data. In addition, the excavation of vehicle trajectory data can reveal the hidden social relationships among nodes. We can improve the routing algorithm and the performance of network communication reasonably by using these relationships [1]. The Greedy Perimeter Stateless Routing (GPSR) algorithm is based on the geographic location information and greedy strategy, which is a typical location-based routing algorithm in the VANET. We choose GPSR as a target algorithm for comparing the performance enhancement after introducing social relationship.

The remainder of this paper is organized as follows. We analyze the GPS trajectory data from taxis in a city and extract the social relationships among the taxis. Then we

© Springer Nature Singapore Pte Ltd. 2018
H. Yuan et al. (Eds.): GSKI 2017, CCIS 849, pp. 343–349, 2018.
https://doi.org/10.1007/978-981-13-0896-3_34

modify the GPSR routing algorithm based on those social relationships and evaluate the performance of the new routing algorithm by simulation.

2 Related Work

2.1 Social Properties Mining Methods

Community Detection Algorithm. The Clique Percolation Method (CPM) is a typical algorithm in community detection, which is based on the group penetration theory and claims that community is a set of fully associated sub graphs with shared nodes [2]. The nodes in community connect closely and can easily form clique with high edge density. The CPM algorithm finds communities by finding cliques in the network by which we can divide the vehicle social network into communities. Vehicles in the same community obviously have the higher possibility to meet each other, so by selecting nodes which are in the same community with the target nodes as the relay on routing can be expected to improve the performance of algorithm.

Calculate the Centralities. The degree centrality reflects the level of connection about one node to the others [3]. The node with high degree centrality is associated with many other nodes, showing that this node occupies the central position in the network. As to VANET, the high degree centrality of nodes implies the high possibility of direct or indirect association with the target node. It should improve the transmitting performance when we choose this node as the relay.

The closeness centrality shows the approaching degree of a node and others in the network [3]. The high centrality of a node can be more efficient in transmitting messages with other nodes. When messages are transmitting into community of the target node in VANET, we need find a node which is more closely associated or more efficient in communication with the target node. Therefore, it is necessary to get the closeness centrality in community.

2.2 Research About Related Protocols

As mentioned above, we choose GPSR algorithm as the basis to be compared with. With GPSR, when source node gives out a message with the target node location information, the node receiving the message first forwards the message to the neighbor node which is located closer to the destination until the message arrives at the destination. Once this greedy strategy is invalid, GPSR will adopt the perimeter forwarding strategy which chooses its neighbor node as the next hop or relay [4].

However, the update of location messages is hysteresis due to the dynamic topology of VANET, which may cause communication failure between nodes which decreases the arriving rate of messages. Besides, the border greedy strategy may cause the routing hole [5].

In order to improve the transmitting reliability of GPSR routing protocol, GPSR-R is proposed [6]. This protocol presents a computing model of link reliability, combines the current moving rate with direction to ensure the reliability of links according to the probability function of rate distribution. If the reliability of the link exceeds the threshold set in advance, it can be used as the relay, and then the closest point from the target node is the forwarding node.

To avoid the routing hole in GSPR, Easy Modeling Greedy Routing (EMGR) algorithm is proposed [7]. It introduces the concept of virtual coordinates, uses the empty border detecting packet to collect the message of border nodes and establish a model to improve the routing efficiency while decrease the network delay.

3 Vehicle Trajectory Data Mining

The movement trajectory can be used to analyze the encounter relationships among vehicles. If two vehicle nodes are within the communication range, these two nodes are considered as encountered. Based on those encounter information, we can establish a weighted network by regarding the frequency of encounter as the edge weight and thus can obtain the social attributes and relationships just like analyzing the centrality and community of social network [8].

3.1 Encounter Judgment of Nodes

Considering the same direction movement of two nodes, when their distance stays at parameter d, which is less than the vehicle communication range r, we declare these two nodes are encountered. Due to the different sampling time points of trajectory data, we need to take the median of two sampling time and compute the distance according to the speed and moving direction of nodes to decide whether communication link can be found between these two nodes.

In Fig. 1, N_1 and N_2 separately represent two nodes' positions in the moment t_1 and t_2 respectively. The circles denote the communication range of nodes. As the sampling time points are different, we suppose $t_1 < t_2$ and take $\Delta t = t_2 - t_1$. N_1' and N_2' are the positions of nodes at $(t_1 + t_2)/2$, when the two nodes distance is less than the communication range, which are denoted as d and r, we judge that two nodes are encountered. It should be noticed that in this method these two nodes should move with the constant speed. So, we need to limit Δt in a small range to make sure the speed of nodes is kept unchanged. If we regard the sampling time interval as ΔT, we can approximately consider the node's speed V during $(T - \Delta T/2, T + \Delta T/2)$ is same as the speed at T. Then the value of Δt must be less than $\Delta T/2$. The encounter judgment of nodes is shown as the Eq. (1), where x and y separately represent the coordinates of nodes.

$$\begin{cases} r > \sqrt{((x_1 - x_2) + \Delta t/2 * (V_1 - V_2))^2 + ((y_1 - y_2) + \Delta t/2 * (V_1 - V_2))^2} \\ \Delta t < \Delta T/2 \end{cases} \quad (1)$$

To analyze the vehicle trajectory data and take all vehicle nodes into consideration according to the encounter judgment method, we can finally get the encounter frequency between vehicles and constitute a weighed social network.

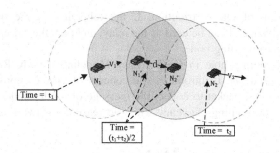

Fig. 1. The judgment of encounter of N_1 and N_2.

3.2 Obtaining the Social Attributes of Vehicles

Result of Community Division. After obtaining the network of the vehicle nodes, the nodes can be divided according to the k-clique algorithm described above. Since k is an input parameter value, the value of k will affect the final community discovery results of the CMP algorithm [9].

Closeness centrality of Nodes. The degree centrality of nodes in the whole network is easy to calculate. However, as the center of the right network, the distance between nodes not only is based on the number of hops connected between nodes, but also need to consider the weight of the edge [3].

4   GPSR Algorithm Based on Trajectory Mining

Based on the trajectory data mining and social attribute analysis, we develop an improved GPSR routing protocol called GPSR Algorithm based on Trajectory Mining (GPSR-TM). There are five main steps in GPSR-TM shown in Fig. 2.

First, source node obtained the position and social attribute message of target node and then store at the head of the data packets. Then the beacon will be broadcasted to make the neighbor nodes within one hop are able to obtain the position, velocity and social attribute message of the source node;

Second, source node or forwarding node takes the action of checking whether the target node is in the neighbor nodes. For the target node is in the neighbor nodes, the routing comes to the end, else the routing action take the third step;

Third, source node or forwarding node excludes the unreliable nodes from neighbor nodes under the message of neighbor nodes and then choose the relay in line with the greedy strategy in GPSR algorithm. When choosing step doesn't satisfy the greedy strategy, the routing action take the forth step;

Forth, source node or forwarding node computes the nodes which satisfy the border condition according to the border forwarding strategy in GPSR algorithm, obtain the set of alternative nodes and then continue to execute the final step;

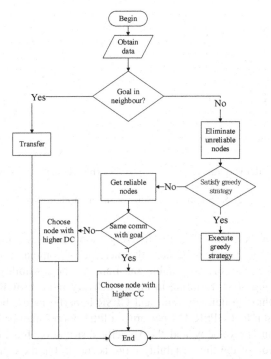

Fig. 2. The procedure of GPSR-TM algorithm.

Finally, the social attributes between target nodes and alternative nodes are compared. Once there is a node from alternative nodes that is in the same community with target nodes, then the routing algorithm choose the node of the highest closeness centrality as the relay. Otherwise, the routing algorithm chooses the node of the highest degree centrality as the relay from alternative nodes.

5 Simulation Results

In order to evaluate the performance of the routing algorithm, we use simulator to simulate the routing algorithm and obtain the value of average delay and average message delivery ratio in different VANET scenarios.

The ONE simulator is a kind of open source simulator written in java, it can be applied to the analysis of many VANET routing protocols. Its' advantages of object-oriented, discrete event-driven, ability to simulate real network, some existing moving models and routing algorithms, and friendly GUI make it easy to extend and provide lots of reports and analysis model for further data analysis and simulation [10].

We compare the delivery ratio and the average end-to-end delay from GPSR, GPSR-R, EMGR and GPSR-TM in different communication range. The simulating results are shown in Fig. 3.

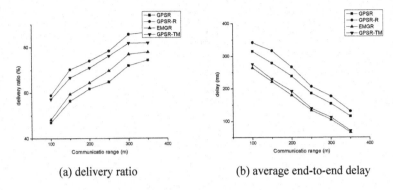

(a) delivery ratio   (b) average end-to-end delay

Fig. 3. Simulation results of different algorithms.

In Fig. 3(a), we can find that the delivery ratio increases with the increase of communication range, which is because the increase of communication range makes the selection of the relay more available and improve the possibility of finding more available forwarding node, resulting in higher delivery ratio. EMGR performs worse than other algorithms in delivery ratio and GPSR-R performs the best. Compared to GPSR-R, the reason that GPSR-TM performs a little poorer may be that the GPSR-R considers both current velocity and the velocity distribution function of nodes and make the prediction of the link reliability more accurate. On the contrary, GPSR-TM runs faster and computes less.

In Fig. 3(b), we can find that the average end-to-end delay decrease with the increase of communication range, that is because the increase of communication can effectively reduce the amount of hops for data transmission. GPSR-R selects nodes more reliable but results in higher average delay compared to GPSR. For EMGR, its improvement of routing hole makes average delay upgrading from GPSR. As for GPSR-TM, in spite of demands of link reliability increase the transmission delay, the full usage of social attributes to solute the forwarding strategy in border status makes the whole average delay difference not obvious compared with EMGR and the whole computing overhead is small.

6   Conclusion

Routing algorithm is one of the key technologies in VANET, and the social relationship between vehicles is helpful to improve the performance of routing algorithm. Aiming at the problems existing in GPSR routing algorithm, this paper proposes a modified GPSR routing algorithm called GPSR-TM, based on mining the real vehicle trajectory data and finding the social attributes of vehicle nodes.

Firstly, the relationship between vehicles is expressed by the form of social network. By using more social information, the transmission of the routing message is more reliable. The performance of the routing algorithm has also been improved. After simulation with the ONE, based on the comparison of the original GPSR algorithm and some enhanced GPSR algorithms such as GPSR-R and EMGR, we find that GPSR-TM has better delivery rate and smaller routing delay.

In the future, our attention will focus on the modification and performance evaluation of other types of VANET routing algorithms by introducing the social attributes.

Acknowledgments. The work is financially supported by the National Science Foundation of China under Grant No. 61272485.

References

1. Feng, H., Xu, Y.: An empirical study on evolution of the connectivity for VANETs based on taxi GPS traces. Int. J. Distrib. Sens. Netw. **2016**(3), 1–11 (2016)
2. Li, J., Wang, X., Cui, Y.: Uncovering the overlapping community structure of complex networks by maximal cliques. Phys. Stat. Mech. Appl. **415**, 398–406 (2014)
3. Stanley, W., Katherine, F., Chen, Y. (Trans.): Social Network Analysis: Methods and Applications. China People's Publishing House, pp. 131–138 (2011). (in Chinese)
4. Karp, B., Kung, H.T.: GPSR: greedy perimeter stateless routing for wireless networks. In: International Conference on Mobile Computing and Networking, pp. 243–254. ACM (2000)
5. Huang, W.J.: The Research and Improvement of GPSR Routing Protocol in Vehicular Ad Hoc Network. Chongqing Jiaotong University (2015). (in Chinese)
6. Shelly, S., Babu, A.V.: Link reliability based greedy perimeter stateless routing for vehicular ad hoc networks. Int. J. Veh. Technol. **2015**, 1–16 (2015)
7. Fan, S.J., Xie, S.W., Jiang, Y., Gao, P.: An improved geographic routing algorithm based on hole modeling. Chin. J. Sens. Actuators **25**(11), 1556–1561 (2012)
8. Castro, P.S., Zhang, D., Chen, C., et al.: From taxi GPS traces to social and community dynamics: a survey. ACM Comput. Surv. **46**(2), 1167–1182 (2014)
9. Clusters & Communities [EB/OL]. http://www.cfinder.org/. Accessed 20 Aug 2017
10. Desta, M.S.: Evaluating (Geo) content sharing with the ONE simulator. In: ACM International Symposium on Mobility Management and Wireless Access, pp. 37–40. ACM (2013)

Design and Implementation of a Self-powered Sensor Network Node

Jun Jiao[1,2], Moshi Wang[1,2], and Lichuan Gu[1,2(✉)]

[1] College of Information and Computer, Anhui Agricultural University,
Hefei 230036, Anhui, People's Republic of China
jiaojun2000@sina.com, 871743861@qq.com,
gulichuan@ahau.edu.cn
[2] Key Laboratory of Agricultural Electronic Commerce,
Ministry of Agricultural, No. 130 Changjiang West Road, Shushan District,
Hefei, Anhui, People's Republic of China

Abstract. For the applications of Wireless Sensor Networks (WSN) randomly deployed in the complicated environment, the most important challenge is to design sensor networks that require long system lifetime and some metrics for the Quality of Service (QoS). Therefore, in this paper, we proposed the self-powered WSN node system based on MC9S12XS128 and LTC6803-4, designed the hardware circuits like charging and discharging of lithium ion battery pack, temperature measure, voltage acquisition and equilibrium control, compiled the corresponding underlying software, compared the accuracy of the sampling values and measured values of battery voltage, charging and discharging current, battery temperature, and tested the effects of equilibrium control. The test results showed that the designed photovoltaic charging management system was safe and reliable, which could provide stable energy sources for WSN node in future.

Keywords: MC9S12XS128 · Lithium ion battery pack · LTC6803-4
Equilibrium control

1 Introduction

Solar energy resources is abundant, green and inexhaustible [1]. The lithium battery has the characteristics of no memory effect, small volume, and storing the electrical energy from solar panel in lithium battery pack, so it has become an indispensable key technology for battery management system to carry out reasonable management and protection of Sensor Network Node.

There are a number of studies in China. Zhao et al. [2] designed the energy management control research for solar electric car, which applied the management and protection of lithium battery into the field of electric vehicles. Zhang et al. [3] conducted research on solar illumination controller based on the Maximum Power Point Tracking (MPPT), which applied the management and protection of lithium battery pack to lighting equipment. Xiong et al. [4] made design on power supply for the transmission line on-line monitoring equipment, which applied the charging-discharging management and

© Springer Nature Singapore Pte Ltd. 2018
H. Yuan et al. (Eds.): GSKI 2017, CCIS 849, pp. 350–363, 2018.
https://doi.org/10.1007/978-981-13-0896-3_35

protection of lithium battery pack to on-line monitoring equipment. In view of the existing literature about the application in farmland environment detection [5–8], there is still no application of the charging-discharging management and protection of lithium battery pack in Sensor Network Node.

To Design and Implementation of a Self-powered sensor Network Node, a set of photovoltaic charging management system was developed based on MC9S12XS128 and LTC6803-4, which could charge the lithium batter pack by the electrical energy converted from solar energy, and realized the effective management of lithium battery pack.

1.1 Overall System Function Analysis

The photovoltaic charging management system based on MC9S12XS128 (Freescale) and LTC6803-4 charges the lithium battery pack using the electrical energy converted from the solar panel. The lithium battery pack is in series connection of 8 cells. Since there is production variance and continuous charging and discharging of a single battery, which could result in the difference in battery voltage, charging-discharging circuits and equilibrium control circuit are designed to ensure the safe running of the lithium battery. Thus, the service life of the battery can be extended [9].

The system mainly includes battery pack charging-discharging module and control module, temperature acquisition module, battery voltage collection and equilibrium control module.

The battery pack charging-discharging measure and control module is composed of collection and control circuits. Freescale is in real-time acquisition of battery charging and discharging current, and Field-Effect Transistor (FET) controls the charging and discharging process as the switch, avoiding the over-charging (more than 2 A) and over discharging (over 2 A) of the battery pack, which could destroy the battery performance and could even cause risks for security.

The temperature measure and control module consists of collection and control circuits. Freescale is in real-time acquisition of the working temperature of each battery and the temperature of LTC6803-4, and field-effect transistor (FET) controls the charging and discharging process as the switch. When the working temperature of the battery is over 45 °C or the working temperature of LTC6803-4 is over 85 °C, the charging or discharging switch will turn off.

The core of the battery voltage acquisition and equilibrium control modules is in real-time acquisition of the voltage of each lithium battery, and transmit it to Freescale. The equilibrium control is to judge the maximum voltage and the minimum voltage difference of a single battery in the battery pack in real time. When the difference is over 0.2 V, key S1–S8 is to discharge to the corresponding maximum value. The node diagram is shown in Fig. 1.

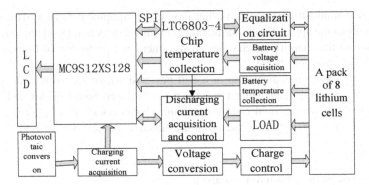

Fig. 1. System block chart.

2 Hardware Circuit

2.1 Charging Circuit and Discharging Circuit

2.1.1 Charging Circuit

The principle of the charging circuit is to use the Freescale processor to collect the charging current in real time, and compare the current value to the preset value (2A) to decide whether the irf4905 field-effect transistor is connected and control the charging of the lithium battery pack. Specific implementations are shown in Fig. 2, the battery pack is connected to the positive and negative poles of the solar panel through U10, and LM2576HV-ADJ is used as an adjustable switching regulator. The following formula is used to make the calculation:

$$V_{out} = V_{ref}(1 + \frac{R50}{R52})\tag{1}$$

$$R50 = R52(\frac{V_{out}}{V_{ref}} - 1)\tag{2}$$

Where, V_{ref} is reference voltage with the value of *1.23* V; *R52* is 1 K, and the calculated *R50* is *25* K, while the measured V_{out} is *32.35* V, meeting the charging voltage requirements.

For the collection of charging current, the current signal should be converted into voltage signal. As shown in Fig. 3, when a precision resistance *R53* of *10* mΩ is connected to the circuit, the voltage range is *0–0.03* V, so the circuit is amplified. The double operational amplifier LM158 is used, which amplifies the voltage at both end of *R53* by *51 (R41/R43)* times, *R41/R43 = R49/R47*, to ensure that the output current is independent of load resistance R45, ensuring the accuracy of measurement. The amplified voltage signal is connected to the Freescale PAD12 pin. The output current of the solar panel is calculated by collecting the voltage value of PAD12. The switch is the field-effect transistor irf4905 of enhanced PNP type [10], and the circuit is shown in Fig. 2.

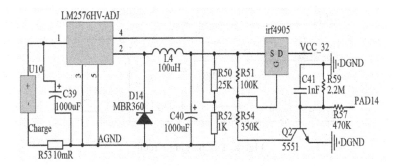

Fig. 2. Charging circuit

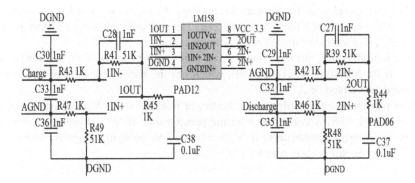

Fig. 3. Amplification circuit

If the charging current is greater than 2 A, then irf4905 turns off through Freescale PAD14. VCC_32 is the voltage of the battery pack, AGND is analog ground, and DGND is digital ground.

2.1.2 Discharging Circuit

The principle of discharging circuit is the same with the principle of charging. Freescale processor is used to collect the discharging current in real time, and compare the current value to the preset value (2 A) to decide whether irfs3607 is connected and control the discharging of the lithium battery pack.

As shown in Fig. 4, same as the charging process, the collection of discharging current also uses a precision resistance R62 of 10 mΩ, and it also uses LM158 to amplify the circuit by 51 times. The amplified voltage signal is connected to the Freescale PAD06 pin. The discharging current is calculated by collecting the voltage value of PAD06. The load is connected by J1, and the irfs3607 field-effect transistor.

If the discharging current is greater than 2 A, then irfs3607 turns off through Freescale PAD07 (Fig. 4).

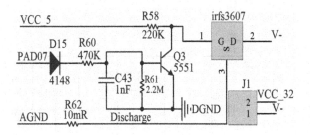

Fig. 4. Discharging circuit

2.2 Battery Voltage Acquisition Circuit

The battery voltage acquisition circuit uses the battery pack monitoring chip LTC6803-4, developed by Linear Technology Corporation, C1–C8 is used for real-time acquisition of battery voltage input. The real time voltage of battery pack is transmitted to Freescale through SPI communication.

The lithium battery pack is connected in series with 8 battery cells, and the lithium battery is the Samsung ICR18650-26F, which has the battery capacity of 2600 mAh, and standard voltage of *3.7* V.

The real-time voltage value of the battery at working status V_n(Voltage(n)) (n is a integer from 1 to 8) is compared with the preset value. If V_n is lower than *3* V, the battery is charged immediately; if V_n is above *4* V, charging stops by turning off irf4905. The circuit is shown in Fig. 5:

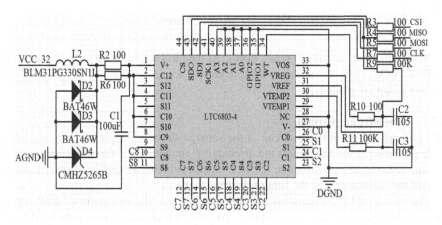

Fig. 5. Voltage acquisition circuit

2.3 Equilibrium Control Circuit

Equilibrium control is the successive series connection of the 8 battery cells, in which AGND is connected to the negative pole of the first cell, CELL1 to the positive pole of the first cell and the negative pole of the second cell, CELL2 to the positive pole of the second cell and the negative pole of the third cell, until the positive pole of the eighth cell is connected with VCC_32. The S1-S8 of LTC6803-4 chip is used to equalize the voltage of each cell in the battery pack. C1–C8 collects the voltage of single battery in real time, and when the difference between the maximum value and minimum value of a single battery is larger than *0.2* V, equilibrium control starts, which uses the power resistor of *33* Ω to discharge the battery with the maximum value, thereby equalizing the battery voltage [11]. The circuit is shown in Fig. 6:

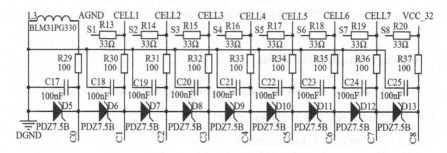

Fig. 6. Equilibrium control circuit

2.4   Battery Temperature Data Collection and Chip Temperature Data Collection Circuit

The lithium battery generates heat during operation, and NTC thermistor is used to sense the temperature of the lithium battery in real time. When the temperature is over *45* °C, the charging or discharging switch is switched off.

In the process of equilibrium control of the battery pack, NTC thermistor is also used to sense the temperature of LTC6803-4 chip in real time. When the temperature is greater than *85* °C, the charging or discharging switch is switched off (Fig. 7).

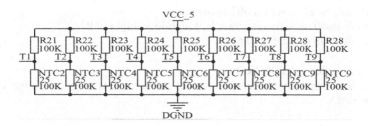

Fig. 7. Temperature acquisition circuit

2.5   Software Design

Software functions mainly include charging-discharging current acquisition, temperature collection, battery voltage collection and equilibrium control.

The software part completes the initialization of the system, collects the charging and discharging current in real time, judges whether the acquisition value exceeds the preset value (2 A), so as to turn on or shut off the charging switch. In addition, it collects the battery temperature value, chip temperature value, battery voltage value in real time, and judges whether the total voltage exceeds the preset value, thereby determining whether to close the charging switch. The collected parameters are displayed on the LCD in real time. If the voltage value of a single battery is smaller than 3 V, then the charging switch turns on, otherwise, it determines whether to conduct equilibrium control. If the voltage value of a single battery is greater than 4 V, then the charging switch turns off, otherwise continuing the charging. The software flow chart is shown in Fig. 8.

3   Software Implementation

3.1   Main Codes for System Initialization and Charging and Discharging

The node software structure is shown below:

```
void ATD0_Init ()  //AD initialization
void LTC6803_Init ()  //LTC6803 chip initialization
void SPI0_Init ()   //SPI0 bus initialization
void LCD_Init()   //LCD initialization
uchar  charge value  //PAD12 pin, corresponding to the voltage signal at both ends
of amplified R53
DDR0AD0=0x40     // set PAD14 as output
PT0AD0=0x40    // Charging switch
while (!ATD0STAT2H_CCF12)
{ ; }
charge_value = ATD0DR12L;
ChongDianPanDuan(convert_value) //determine whether charging current greater
than 2A
uchar discharge_value //PAD06, corresponding to the voltage signal at both ends
of amplified R62
DDR1AD0=0x80 // set PAD07 as output
PT1AD0=0x80     //Charging switch of high-low output of PAD07
while (!ATD0STAT2H_CCF6)
{;}
discharge_value = ATD0DR6L;
Fang Dian Pan Duan (disconvert_value) //determine whether discharge current
greater than 2A
```

Where ATD0_Init() is Initialization of AD conversion, LTC6803_Init() is Initialization of LTC6803, SPI0_Init() is Initialization of SPI bus, LCD_Init() is Initialization of LCD, ChongDianPanDuan() determines whether the charging current is greater than 2 A, so as to decide whether to turn on or off the charging switch, Fang Dian Pan Duan() determines whether the discharge current is greater than 2 A, so as to determine whether the discharge switch is switched on or off.

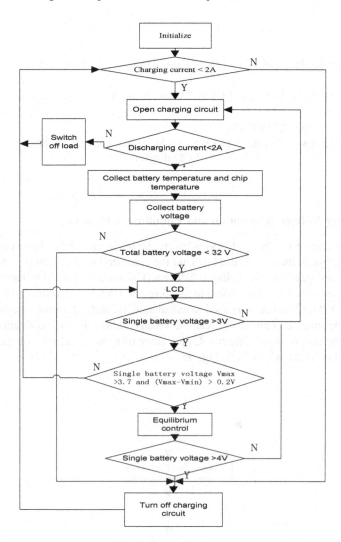

Fig. 8. Software process

3.2 Battery Temperature and Chip Temperature Collection

In this paper, the subscript is inquired according to the corresponding AD value using look-up table method. In other words, the elements in the NTC_Tab1 [86] form of temperature values all are the corresponding AD voltage values. The GFunc_NTC-Query () function is used to obtain the corresponding subscript of the real-time collected voltage value, namely, the corresponding temperature value of the battery, which is displayed in real time.

Key code:
    unsigned char NTC_Tab1[86]={191188186...... 25,24,23,22};
                        // NTC_Tab1
    while (!ATD0STAT2L_CCF0) // Wait for the AD conversion to complete
{;}
    convert_ue = ATD0DR0;
    Temperature =GFunc_NTCQuery (NTC_Tab1, convert_ue, 86);
    ......   / / LCD display

3.3   Battery Voltage Acquisition and Equilibrium Control

The initialization of LTC6803-4 begins before the beginning of the main function, and then ltc_sendbyte() function is used to send the command to start battery voltage ADC conversion and read battery voltage. SPIRead() is used to read the battery voltage register values, which are then stored in the Original_CVR1 [12] array, and then CRC8 (Original_CVR1,12) function is used to calculate CRC and determine whether CRC is correct. If incorrect, it continues to read the voltage value until the verification is right. If correct, the actual stored Original_CVR1 array of a single battery voltage is calculated. The flow chart is shown in Fig. 9:

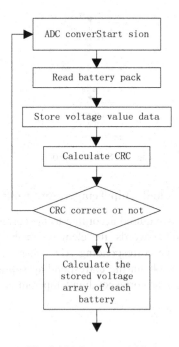

Fig. 9. Voltage acquisition

Equilibrium control is find the maximum and minimum values of a single battery. If the maximum value of a single battery is greater than 3.7 V and the difference between the maximum value and minimum value is greater than 0.2 V, then equilibrium control starts [12]. The flow chart of equilibrium control is shown in Fig. 10.

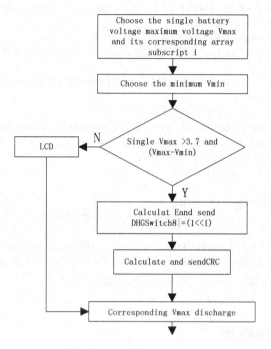

Fig. 10. Equilibrium control

Key code:

```
ltc_sendbyte(0x10 ) // Send monitoring battery voltage command
......
for(i=0;i<12;i++)
{Original_CVR1[i]=SPIRead();}//Pass each battery voltage to the Original_CVR1
CRC_Cal=CRC8(Original_CVR1,12)//Calculate the check value and judge
```
whether the check value is correct
```
if(CRC_Cal==Original_CVR1[12]) //If the check is correct
{ Cell_CVR1[0]=((Original_CVR1[1]&0x0F)<<8)+Original_CVR1[0];
......
Cell_CVR1[7]=((Original_CVR1[11]<<4)+((Original_CVR1[10]&0xF0)>>4));
  for(i=0;i<8;i++)
{Cell_CVR1[i]=((Cell_CVR1[i]-512)*3)>>1; }
}    // The value of the battery voltage register group is converted to the actual
```
voltage value of the battery pack.
```
if((Vmax>=3.7)&&((Vmax-Vmin)>0.2))
DHGSwitch8|= (1<<k) {};
else
{DHGSwitch8&amp=~ (1<<k);
......                    / / Each battery voltage is displayed
}
ltc_sendbyte (DHGSwitch8)//Battery discharge with maximum voltage
CRC_Temp=CRC8 (DHGSwitch8,1) //calculate the CRC of CFGR unit

Ltc_sendbyte (CRC_Temp)    // Write CRC check byte
```

4 Test and Analysis

The real object of the design is shown in Fig. 11.

Fig. 11. Photovoltaic conversion equipment

The first thing to test was the accuracy of the battery voltage in the battery pack. The voltage values collected by LTC6803-4 was compared with the measured values of (Table 1).

Table 1. Comparison of measured values of battery voltage

Battery No.	Measured single battery voltage (V)	Actual single battery voltage (V)	Error (mV)
1	3.82	3.82	0
2	3.81	3.81	0
3	3.83	3.82	10
4	3.79	3.80	10
5	3.80	3.80	0
6	3.83	3.82	10
7	3.82	3.82	0
8	3.82	3.82	0

As shown in Table 1, the measured voltage of the single cell voltage was very close to the actual value, and the error was about 3‰, indicating that the measurement of battery management chip to the battery voltage is accurate, which can meet the requirements of the design.

The temperature was measured using DT-8380 non-contact infrared thermometer, which was measured every 10 min. Two battery cells were selected from the battery pack to measure the temperature (Table 2).

Table 2. Comparison of measured and actual values of batteries

No.	Measured value of battery 1 (°C)	Actual value of battery1 (°C)	Error (°C)	Measured value of battery2 (°C)	Measured value of battery 2 (°C)	Error (°C)
1	17	17	0	16	17	1
2	20	19	1	20	20	0
3	24	23	1	23	23	1
4	23	23	0	23	24	1
5	24	24	0	23	23	1

As shown in Table 2, battery temperature became higher and higher during the working status of the battery, and it was mainly caused by charging and discharging, which finally reached a stable value with the measured error of about 4%, indicating that the measurement of battery temperature is accurate, which could meet the requirements of the design.

And then, the charging and discharging current values were measured, and the measured values were compared with the measured values using multimeter. The results are shown in Table 3.

Table 3. Measured values of battery charge and discharge system and the measured values of multimeter

Charging current	System measured value (A)	Multimeter measured value (A)	Error
1	0.25	0.25	0
2	0.46	0.46	0
3	0.98	0.97	0.01
Discharging current	System measured value (A)	Multimeter measured value (A)	Error
1	0.15	0.15	0
2	0.25	0.25	0
3	0.46	0.46	0

As shown in Table 3, the measuring error of the system in charging and discharging current was at *1%* or so, relatively accurate, which could meet the requirements of the design. Moreover, the effect of equilibrium control was tested. First, one of the cell was charged separately, making its voltage reach *3.76* V, which was higher than the voltage value of other 3 cells (*3.12* V, *3.01* V, *2.90* V, respectively), and then the charging started. During the charging process, the voltage values of the 4 cells were recorded every *2* min, and marked as points. As shown in Fig. 12 when charging, the minimum voltage was *2.90* V, and the maximum was *3.75* V, and after charging, the voltage of all batteries almost reached the same, indicating that equilibrium control was effective, which could ensure the batteries in the pack could work in a consistent state.

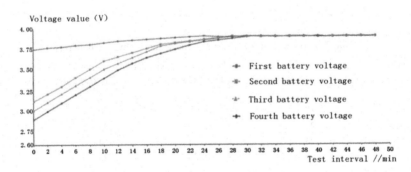

Fig. 12. Equilibrium control test results.

As shown in Fig. 12, at the end of charging, the battery voltage changes slowly, close to *4* V, because the charging switch switched off when reaching *4* V, indicating that the whole control was accurate, which can meet the requirements of the design.

5   Conclusion

The photovoltaic charge management based on MC9S12XS128 and LTC6803-4 achieved the collection and control of charging-discharging current, collection and control of temperature, collection and equilibrium control of battery voltage, and the test results showed that the d system was safe and reliable, which could provide stable energy sources for WSN node in future. Further research will focus on an automatic tracking solar azimuth control scheme, and designed a feasible method for improving solar photovoltaic conversion efficiency.

Acknowledgments. We thank the reviewers for their thoughtful comments and suggestions. This work was supported by the National Natural Science Foundation of China (Grant No. 31671589, 31771679, 31671589, 31371533), the Special Fund for Key Program of Science and Technology of Anhui Province, China (Grant No. 15czz03131, 16030701092); Project supported by the Natural Science Foundation of the Anhui Higher Education Institutions of China (Grant No. kJ2016A836).

References

1. Jun, J., Ma, H., Qiao, Y., Du, Y.L., Kong, W.: Design of farm environmental monitoring system based on the internet of things. Adv. J. Food Sci. Technol. **6**(3), 368–373 (2014)
2. Zhao, R.F., Ge, B.M., Bi, D.Q., et al.: Energy management control research for solar electric car. Adv. Technol. Electric. Eng. Energy **5**(05), 32–37 (2014)
3. Zhang, K.S., Cheng, P.: Research on solar illumination controller based on the MPPT. J. Shaanxi Univ. Sci. Technol. (Nat. Sci. Ed.) **1**, 160–164 (2015)
4. Xiong, L., He, Y.Z., Song, D.J., et al.: Design on power supply for the transmission line on-line monitoring equipment. High Volt. Eng. **36**(9), 2252–2257 (2010)
5. Jiao, J., Ma, H., Qiao, Y., et al.: Design of farm environmental monitoring system based on the Internet of Things. Adv. J. Food Sci. Technol. **6**(3), 368–373 (2014)
6. Wang, Q., Jiao, J., Kong, W., et al.: The simulation of wireless sensor networks which includes fixed nodes and mobile node based on NS2. J. Hefei Univ. (Nat. Sci. Ed.) **25**(2), 24–28 (2015)
7. Kong, W., Jiao, J., Wang, Q., et al.: Real-time detection of chlorophyll and nitrogen content in tomato leaves and 3G transmission based on ARM. J. Anhui Agric. Sci. **43**(30), 347–350 (2015)
8. Jiao, J., Cao, J., Pan, Z., et al.: Farm environmental online monitoring system based on Internet of Things. Agric. Eng. **06**(06), 19–22 (2014)
9. Wang, Z.B.: Design of WSN node power supply system with automatic switching function. Sci. Technol. Eng. **14**(08), 190–194 (2014)
10. Li, P.J., Zhang, W.J., Zhang, Q.F., et al.: Nanoelectronic logic circuits with carbon nanotube transistors. Acta Phys. Sin. **2**(02), 1054–1060 (2007)
11. Feng, F., Song, K., Lu, R.G., et al.: Equalization control strategy and SOC estimation for LiFePO4 battery pack. Trans. China Electrotechnical Soc. **01**(01), 22–29 (2015)
12. Lv, J., Song, W.J., Lin, S.L., et al.: Research on signal acquisition technology of battery management system based on LTC6803-4. Measur. Control Technol. **32**(1), 23–27 (2013)

Mining Association Rules from Multidimensional Transformer Defect Records

Yi Yang[1(✉)], Yujie Geng[1], Yi Ju[2], Xuan Zhao[3], and Danfeng Yan[3]

[1] State Grid ShanDong Electric Power Research Institute, Jinan, China
waiwai814@126.com, gengyujie1225@126.com
[2] State Grid Jinan Power Supply Company, Jinan, China
snakejuyi@sina.com
[3] State Key Laboratory of Networking and Switching Technology,
Beijing University of Posts and Telecommunications, Beijing, China
{zhaoxuan,yandf}@bupt.edu.cn

Abstract. There are various types of transformer device defects and the formation reasons are complex. Exploring the influencing factors and occurrence of transformer devices defects is a focus in the field of power transmission and transformation devices state inspection and evaluation. This paper proposes an analysis method, multidimensional FP-Growth algorithm (MDFPG) to mine association rules from multidimensional transformer defect records. The method combines records from different system of power grid to construct multidimensional records first. Then, the records are preprocessed and encoded into single dimension form. The MDFPG method speeds up the mining process by adding a pruning step. Experiments show that MDFPG method has a better performance than FP-Growth algorithm on large data sets. Some conclusions can be learned from the experiment result, which has a certain value for making equipment maintenance plans and exploring defect occurrence regularity.

Keywords: Transformer · Association rule mining · FP-Growth

1 Introduction

Transformers are important equipment in power grid. The device status of transformer has great influence on the condition of the whole power system. Power companies paid a lot for the maintenance of the transformers every year, which occupied a main part of the total maintenance cost of the power system. Therefore, it is meaningful to research how to evaluate the transformer state and analyze the causes and laws of the equipment defects. Based on the analysis results, power companies could make effective maintenance plan of power equipment, reduce cost and ensure the power system operating safely, which has positive significance.

At present, the researchers have made a series of achievements in the field of transformer state evaluation and many effective methods have been put forward. For example, Yang et al. [1] and Zhang et al. [2] used improved three ratio methods in technologies of analysis of dissolved gas in oil to judge the nature of the device faults.

© Springer Nature Singapore Pte Ltd. 2018
H. Yuan et al. (Eds.): GSKI 2017, CCIS 849, pp. 364–374, 2018.
https://doi.org/10.1007/978-981-13-0896-3_36

Ruan et al. [3] and Gong et al. [4] employed neural networks to diagnosis transformer faults, and Song and Wang [5] applied fuzzy clustering method to improve the performance of the BP neural network. These methods have achieved certain results in practical application. However, these studies mainly focus on the detection and analysis on the fault of transformer. Defects data of the equipment are hard to process and analyze due to large volume, variety and diverse formats, and have not been used effectively. In fact, the deepening of defects degree and the superposition of various defects may lead to the occurrence of equipment failure [6]. Analyzing the defect data and finding out the regular pattern and potentially causes is helpful for making daily maintenance plan, prevention of defects occurrence and reduce the loss.

The essence of the research on the causes of the device defects is to study the relationship between the defect phenomenon and factors that may lead to the occurrence of defects. The existing methods for analyzing these relationships roughly include methods depends on the experience of experts, traditional statistical methods, structural defects tree method [7] and applying the classical association rules algorithms [8, 9]. There are some shortcomings of these methods: the methods rely on expert experience to find the reasons for occurrence of defects are limited by the experts' experience level, and may not be able to fully tap the potential relationship of various factors. What's more, experts' opinions have strong subjectivity and lack of objectivity and convincing. Causes of transformer equipment defects are result of the combined action of many factors in complex conditions, which is very complicated. In this situation, the traditional statistical methods are blind in selection of statistical object, and always need large workload. Fault tree analysis needs complete and correct data to construct the fault tree, which is hard to realize in practical problems, and is unable to handle new defect type. The association rules algorithm is widely used to find association between things. However, the classical association rule algorithms, such as Apriori and FP-Growth, are commonly applied for processing Boolean data for single dimension, and are not ideal in dealing with multi-dimensional data in various types [10, 11].

On the basis of the above analysis, this paper proposes a multidimensional FP-Growth algorithm (i.e. MDFPG) to mine association rules on multidimensional transformer equipment defects data. First, collect the equipment basic information, the original equipment defects records and the meteorological index monitoring data from different systems of the power grid. Then preprocess and combine these data to construct multidimensional equipment defect records. Finally, apply FP-Growth algorithm to mine association rules between possible cause factors and the equipment defects, and reach some valuable conclusions like the most influential factor and the potential law of occurrence of defects.

The rest of the paper is organized as follows. Section 2 presents a brief introduction to association rule mining algorithms. Section 3 describes the proposed method MDFPG in detail. Experiments and discussion of the results are presented in Sect. 4. The conclusions are finally made in the last section.

2 Association Rule Mining

2.1 Definitions

Association rule mining is one of the major tasks in data mining, which is used to mine the implicit correlations between frequent items. The concept of association rules was first proposed by Agrawal et al. [12] in 1993. Define $I = \{I1, I2, \ldots, In\}$ represents the set of all items, and any subset A of I is called an item set. Particularly, if the number of items contained in A is k, then A is called a k item set. Let transaction database $D = \{T1, T2, \ldots, Tm\}$, where Ti is a nonempty set of item set I, defines the degree of support of item set A in D as (1).

$$S(A|D) = \frac{|\{T_i|A \subseteq T_i\}|}{|D|} \tag{1}$$

The support degree means the percentage of the transactions containing the item set A in total transactions in D. In particular, if the support degree of A is greater than the minimum support threshold $Smin$, item set A is termed of a frequent item set on D.

An association rule is expressed in the form of $X \rightarrow Y$, where X and Y are nonempty subsets of item set I and satisfy $X \cap Y = \varphi$. X is usually called the antecedent and Y is termed of the consequent. The definition of the support and confidence degree of association rule $X \rightarrow Y$ in D are shown in (2) and (3).

$$S(X \rightarrow Y|D) = \frac{|\{T_i|X, Y \subseteq T_i\}|}{|D|} \tag{2}$$

$$C(X \rightarrow Y|D) = \frac{|\{T_i|X, Y \subseteq T_i\}|}{|\{T_j|X \subseteq T_j\}|} \tag{3}$$

Higher support degree indicates that the rule is more general and not accidental, and is more likely to happen again in the future. Confidence degree indicates the intensity of the implication. The higher the confidence degree, the stronger the degree of association between X and Y is.

The support and confidence degree are classical framework to evaluate an association rule. Association rules are called strong association rules if satisfy both the minimum support threshold Smin and the minimum confidence threshold $Cmin$ at the same time. Finding the strong rules in dataset is exactly the purpose of association rule mining.

2.2 Algorithms

The Apriori algorithm and FP-Growth algorithm are two kinds of classical association rule mining algorithms, which have been widely used in association rule mining problems in different fields.

The Apriori algorithm was proposed by Agrawal et al. in 1994. The method is consist of two main steps: the first step is to find all the frequent item sets in database iteratively and the second step is to construct rules that satisfies the minimum confidence threshold from the frequent sets. It is based on the theory that any nonempty subset of a frequent item set must also be frequent, which is usually called the Apriori property. This limitation makes it possible to construct $k + 1$ item set from k item sets, which avoids the generation of redundant item sets. The Apriori algorithm has advantages such as easy to program and has high reliability, and the Apriori property makes pruning during the generation of frequent item sets and improves efficiency to a certain extent. However, since the method needs to scan the whole database for times and needs lots of memory to save the candidate frequent item sets, the algorithm has a great deal of resources cost, and becomes inefficiency on large dataset.

Aiming at the deficiency of Apriori algorithm, Han et al. [13, 14] proposed a more efficient method termed of FP-Growth algorithm. A skillfully designed data structure called frequent pattern tree (FP-Tree) is employed to improve the efficiency. The FP-Tree is a special prefix tree consists of frequent item sets table and prefix tree of items. The FP-Growth method scans the database only twice. The first scan calculates the support of each item and constructs the item table. Then scan the database again and for each transaction insert the items into the frequent pattern tree. The FP-Growth algorithm is more efficient and less resource consumption compared to the Apriori algorithm, but it also has some shortcomings such as is complex and hard to realize [15, 16].

Association rules can be divided into single dimensional association rules and multidimensional association rules according to the data dimension involved in the rules. Both the Apriori and FP-Growth algorithms are designed for handling the single dimensional data [17]. Considering the fact that data are always multidimensional in real world problems, this paper proposed a method to encode the original data and turn it to single dimension form, then FP-Growth algorithm was chosen to mine association rules.

3 The Proposed Method

The flow diagram of mining association rules on transformer defect records is shown in Fig. 1.

There are three main steps of the analysis process:

- Collecting data. To find the potential cause factors of equipment defects, data such as equipment basic information, the original defects records and weather condition records are needed. These records are stored in different systems in power grid and have to be collected first.
- Preprocessing and encoding. The data collected in the first step may have various types of attributes. For example, the equipment type is a categorical attribute and the temperature attribute in weather condition records is numerical. Records may also have some missing or invalid values. Therefore, pretreatment methods such as discretization and de-noising have to be applied. What's more, in order to use FP-Growth algorithm to find rules, all attributes have to be encoded to a single dimension form in this step.

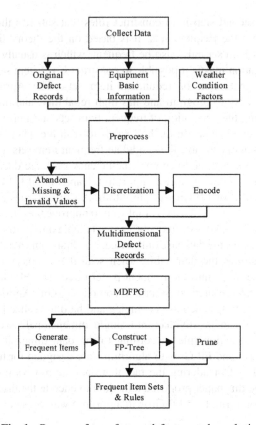

Fig. 1. Process of transformer defect records analysis.

• Mining association rules. In this step, the proposed method MDFPG is applied to mine association rules on the multidimensional equipment defect records. From the analysis results, some conclusions on the importance of the factors and relationships between causes and phenomenon can be reached.

3.1   Construct Multidimensional Defect Records

According to the data provided by the State Grid Shan Dong Power Research Institute, original equipment defect records are main consist of fields including device ID, component, defect property, device type, and happen time.

It is obvious that the original defect records only contain a few of attributes and can reflect limited amount of information. Therefore, in order to deeply explore the possible causes of equipment defects and the occurrence law, it is necessary to expand the defect records.

Considering the actual operation of the power system and related statistical data [18], the following assumptions are proposed:

- With the increase of the running time, the transformer equipment would inevitably lead to the aging problems of components.
- By the influence of production process and technical level, the same type of transformer equipment produced by the same manufacturer in the same period may show a similar running state.
- Transformers belongs to the same station may have similar state because of the same environment factors, and the defects occurrence may have some relevance to these factors.

To verify these assumptions, basic information of the transformer equipment is collected and added to multidimensional defect records.

A number of studies have shown that weather conditions have a certain impact on the operation of transformer equipment. For example, extreme weather like lightning and strong wind may cause damage to the insulator of transformer [19], heavy rainfall may lead to winding insulation resistance and hot weather may affect the internal temperature of the oil immersed transformer [20]. With the support of these theories, weather condition factors are also appended to the multidimensional defect records. The final multidimensional defect records set has three categories of a total of 15 attributes for each record, containing both categorical and numerical type of data.

3.2   Preprocessing and Encoding

For various reasons, such as sensor faults and human errors, the records in power systems may have some missing and invalid values for every attribute. The common methods to handle this situation include abandoning these values as noise, filling the missing values with the specified value or the average value of the attribute. Because defect records have many categorical attributes, it is not suitable to apply the average filling method. There is a huge amount of defect records in power grid, and drop a few of them may have little influence. Therefore, records that contain missing or invalid value are filtered and removed from the records set in this paper.

The FP-Growth algorithm is suitable for single dimensional and categorical data, so the multidimensional defect records with both categorical and numerical attributes need to be encoded first before mining the association rules.

First, discretize the numerical attribute to categorical form. There are several discretization methods such as separation methods with equal width, equal depth or equal frequency, K-means partition method and supervised discretization method. Among these methods, the supervised discretization method has the best performance but it needs labeled train set to train the model. The equal width separation method is easiest to realize but may not have good result because the values of the attributes often have uneven distribution. Separation methods with equal depth or frequency and K-means partition method are scientific methods and have a trade-off between effects and ease of use. Therefore, equal depth separation method is used in this paper.

Then encode each attribute in a record and turn the multidimensional defect records to single dimensional format. As shown in Fig. 2, each attribute is represented by three parts. The first part indicates which category this attribute belongs to. Letters D, I and W are used to represent original defect records, equipment basic information and weather condition factors. The second part stands for the attribute number. Since there are 15 attributes in total, letters from A to O are used to represent these attributes. The last part indicates the specific value of the attribute with an integer i, where i means the attribute takes the i_{th} category for categorical attributes and i_{th} interval for numerical attributes after discretization.

Attribute 1			...
Category	No.	Value	...
D	A	i1	...

Fig. 2. Record encoding format.

For example, after encoding, the item *DA1* represents the device ID attribute in origin defect records with the first category value, and the item *WK2* represents the max wind speed attribute in weather condition factors and the attribute value falls in the second interval.

3.3   Multidimensional FP-Growth

When the multidimensional defect records set is prepared, FP-Growth algorithm is employed to mine the frequent item sets and rules on these sets. The FP-Growth algorithm scans the whole dataset twice. All the frequent item sets are found in the first scan and the FP-Trees are generated during the second scan. This paper proposes an improved multidimensional data oriented FP-Growth algorithm, MDFPG. The MDFPG method adds a pruning step after constructing the FP-Tree, which could improve the efficiency to a certain extent. The pruning step is introduced in detail as follows.

In this problem, the main purpose is to find the correlations between defects and causes factors, so the frequent item sets should contain at least one attribute that belongs to the original defect records. To reduce useless search procedure, a pruning step is added before generating the frequent item sets. In this step, the algorithm traverses every path from the root node to leaf nodes for each FP-Tree, and store the category symbol of each item. After the traversal, paths that do not contain symbol D, which stands for attributes belong to the original defect records, would be deleted from the FP-Tree. The pruning process is shown in Fig. 3.

4   Experiments

In this section, a series of experiments were conducted to evaluate the performance of the proposed method MDFPG. The Apriori algorithm and the standard FP-Growth algorithm were chosen to do the controlled experiments and time consumptions of these two methods were compared with the one of MDFPG. The statistic results of frequent item sets mined by MDFPG were given and the results showed meaningful information on the importance of each kind of cause factors.

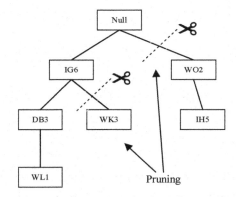

Fig. 3. Prune the redundant path from the FP-Tree.

The experiments data was provided by the State Grid Shan Dong Electric Power Research Institute, which was collected from the different systems of power grid during 2010 to 2015. All algorithms were implemented with Python, and all experiments were conducted on a desktop PC with Intel Core i5 processor and 8 GB RAM.

4.1 Efficiency Tests

In this part, experiments on different scale data sets were conducted and results were compared.

As shown in Fig. 4, this paper took ten groups of tests on different scales of records from 5000 to 50000 to compare time consumption of Apriori algorithm and FP-Growth method. The parameters of these two methods were set to the same value, as minimum support threshold of 0.01 and minimum confidence threshold of 0.6. For each scale, this paper repeated the test 10 times and took the mean value of these results to avoid the randomness and guarantee the objectivity. From the figure it can be concluded that the time cost of the Apriori algorithm grows fast with the data scale increasing. By comparison, the run time of the FP-Growth algorithm grows quite smoothly. With the largest data scale of 50000 records, the FP-Growth algorithm takes 29 s to mine all the frequent item sets while the Apriori algorithm costs 743 s to do the same work, which is nearly 26 times to the FP-Growth method.

Experiments have shown that the FP-Growth algorithm has a better performance than Apriori, especially on large data set. It proves that the paper chose FP-Growth as the association mining algorithm is scientific and correct.

This paper also conducted experiments between the standard FP-Growth algorithm and the proposed method MDFPG. When the data scale is small, the time cost of MDFPG is slightly higher than the original FP-Growth method. This is because the MDFPG method has an extra pruning step which needs to scan each path of the FP-Tree. When processing the small data set, the efficiency improvement brought by the pruning step is not obvious, so the final result seems not ideal compared to FP-Growth method with no pruning. However, with the data set scale increasing, from the figure when it is over 25000, the MDFPG starts to have better performance. When

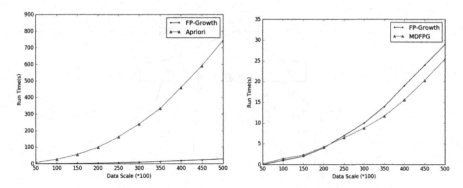

Fig. 4. Comparison between different methods.

there is a large amount of records, the generated FP-Tree grows large too and there are more redundant paths. In this situation, the pruning step can substantially reduce the FP-Tree scale and speed up the mining process.

4.2　Causes Factors Analysis

In this part, the MDFPG method was employed to mine frequent item sets on 2000 records. The results contained 125 item sets in total. The statistics of each factor in the results are listed in Table 1.

Table 1. Statistics of factors in the result.

Category	Attribute	Count	Percentage
Original defect records	Device ID	26	0.208
	Component	45	0.360
	Defect property	53	0.424
	Device type	78	0.624
	Happen time	0	0
Equipment basic information	Manufacturer	44	0.352
	Date of production	29	0.232
	Running time	29	0.232
	Voltage level	60	0.480
	Station ID	33	0.264
Weather condition factors	Max wind speed	0	0
	Max temperature	75	0.600
	Min temperature	66	0.528
	Max humidity	52	0.416
	Precipitation	59	0.472

From the table it can be concluded that weather condition factors are the most influential category to occurrence of transformer defects. Environment temperature and precipitation are factors most closely related to defects, which verifies the hypothesis that transformer defects occurrence has relations with extreme weather. Moreover, the conclusions such as the defect prone component, device type and voltage level can also be learned from the results. In our future work, we will try to forecast the occurrence of equipment defects based on these conclusions.

5 Conclusions

This paper proposes a multidimensional data oriented association rules mining method MDFPG. The proposed method designs an encoding format to turn the multidimensional data into single dimension form, then mines frequent item sets with improved FP-Growth algorithm. By adding a pruning step after generating the FP-Tree, the MDFPG method reduces the FP-Tree scale and speeds up the mining process to a certain extent, which has a better performance than FP-Growth algorithm on large data sets. The paper used MDFPG method to analyze correlations between transformer defects occurrence and potential cause factors, and the results have a certain value for making equipment maintenance plan and exploring defect occurrence regularity.

Acknowledgments. This paper is supported by "National 863 project (No. 2015AA050204)" and "State Grid science and technology project (No. 520626170011)".

References

1. Yang, T.F., Pei, L., Jing-Lu, L.I., et al.: New fault diagnosis method of power transformer by combination of FCM and IEC three-ratio method. High Volt. Eng. **33**(8), 66–70 (2007)
2. Zhang, W., Yuan, J., Zhang, T., et al.: An improved three-ratio method for transformer fault diagnosis using B-spline theory. **34**(24), 4129–4136 (2014)
3. Ling, R., Xie, Q., Gao, S., et al.: Application of artificial neural network and information fusion technology in power transformer condition assessment. High Voltage Eng. (2014)
4. Gong, R.K., Liang, M.A., Zhao Y.J., et al.: Fault diagnosis for power transformer based on quantum neural network information fusion. Power Syst. Prot. Control **39**(23), 79–84+88 (2011)
5. Song, Z.J., Jian, W.: Transformer fault diagnosis based on BP neural network optimized by fuzzy clustering and LM Algorithm. High Volt. Apparatus **49**(5), 54–59 (2013)
6. Wang, Y., Chen, B.: An integrated life estimation model of power transformer based on hierarchical architecture and health index. Power Syst. Technol. **38**(10), 2845–2850 (2014)
7. Zhou, J.K., et al.: Research on optimal transformer maintenance scheme based on LS-SVM. Zhongguo Dianji Gongcheng Xuebao/Proc. Chin. Soc. Electr. Eng. **32**(22), 94–103 (2012)
8. Li, L.I., Deng, Z., Xie, L., et al.: A condition assessment method of power transformers based on association rules and variable weight coefficients. Proc. Chin. Soc. Electr. Eng. **24** (2013)
9. Li, L., Cheng, Y., Xie, L.J., et al.: An integrated method of set pair analysis and association rule for fault diagnosis of power transformers. IEEE Trans. Dielectr. Electr. Insul. **22**(4), 2368–2378 (2015)

10. Dai, K., Wang, Z.J., Zhang, R.P.: Research and improvement of Apriori algorithm for mining association rules. Comput. Appl. Soft. **43**, 916–921 (2009)
11. Mao, Y.X., Chen, T.B., Shi, B.L.: Efficient method for mining multiple-level and generalized association rules. J. Soft. **22**(12), 2965–2980 (2011)
12. Agrawal, R., Imielinski, T., Swami, A.: Database mining: a performance perspective. IEEE Trans. Knowl. Data Eng. **5**(6), 914–925 (1993)
13. Han, J., Kamber, M.: Data Mining: Concepts and Techniques. Data Mining Concepts Models Methods & Algorithms, 2nd edn. **5**(4), 1–18 (2000)
14. Han, J., Pei, J., Yin, Y., Mao, R.: Mining frequent patterns without candidate generation: a frequent-pattern tree approach. Data Min. Knowl. Disc. **8**(1), 53–87 (2015)
15. Xiao-Dong, H.E., Liu, W.G.: Comparison of association rules mining methods in data mining. Comput. Eng. Des. (2005)
16. Feng, J., Tao, H.C.: Analysis and comparison of representative algorithms for mining association rules. Comput. Technol. Dev. (2007)
17. Qiong, H.E., Liu, T.R., Guo, P.: Multi-dimension and multi-level association rule mining algorithm on data cube. Comput. Appl. **24**(3), 85–88 (2004)
18. Wang, M.L.: Statistic analysis of transformer's faults and defects at voltage 110 kV and above. Distribution & Utilization (2007)
19. Sima, W., Sun, P., Wu, J., et al.: Accumulative effect characteristics of transformer oil impregnated paper under repeated lightning impulses. High Volta. Eng. **42**(2), 589–597 (2016)
20. Chen, W.G., Su, X.P., Chen, X., et al.: Influence factor analysis and improvement of the thermal model for predicting transformer top oil temperature. High Volta. Eng. **37**(6), 1329–1335 (2011)

A Modeling Algorithm to Network Flows in OTN Based on E1 Business

Fei Xia[1(✉)], Fanbo Meng[2], Zongze Xia[1], Xiaobo Huang[1],
and Li Song[1]

[1] State Grid Liaoyang Electric Power Supply Company,
Liaoyang 111000, China
merry_99@sina.com
[2] State Grid Liaoning Electric Power Company Limited, Shenyang
110006, China

Abstract. Recently, Optical Transport Networks (OTN) have been extensively deployed and applied in communication networks. Compared with traditional transport networks, OTN can provide much larger traffic transport ability. However, the properties and characteristics of network flows in OTN are not deeply studied and this is still a larger gap between theory analysis and practical applications. This paper studies the modeling problem of network flows in OTN. We propose a Walsh transform-based modeling method to describe end-to-end traffic amount of network flows in OTN. Firstly, the end-to-end traffic is denoted as a independent identically distributed random time-varying series. Then the Walsh transform theory is used to characterize the end-to-end traffic of network flows. By calculating the corresponding parameters, the proposed model is build correctly. Simulation results show that our approach is feasible and effective.

Keywords: End-to-end traffic · Walsh transform · Traffic modeling
Optical transport networks · Traffic engineering

1 Introduction

With the increasing development of network transport requirements and new applications, Optical Transport Networks (OTN) have extensively deployed in current communication networks. Traffic amount of network flows in OTN exhibits new features. This leads to a new challenge for transport network performances and traffic engineering [1, 2]. As mentioned in [3], to accurately characterize and model traffic amount of network traffic in OTN has an important impact on improving OTN performance. Moreover, network traffic in OTN holds self-similarity nature, auto-correlations, heavy-tailed distribution and so on. This also has an important impact on network optimization and routing [3, 4]. The traffic amount of network flows in OTN characterizes the network-wide behaviors from a global view. Hence, modeling the end-to-end traffic in OTN has received an extensive attention from researchers, operators, and developer all around the world [5].

The end-to-end network traffic behaviors in communication networks embody the path-level and network-level features in the network. This is able to be used to describe

© Springer Nature Singapore Pte Ltd. 2018
H. Yuan et al. (Eds.): GSKI 2017, CCIS 849, pp. 375–382, 2018.
https://doi.org/10.1007/978-981-13-0896-3_37

network status and nature, such as path loads, throughput, network utilization, and so on. The statistical approaches are exploited to denote and describe the model of network traffic from the source node to the destination node [1, 3]. The gravity model [4], generic evolvement [6, 7], mix method [2], and compressive sensing are utilized to capture the properties of the end-to-end network traffic. These methods can attain the better prediction and estimation of the end-to-end traffic by performing a modeling process. However, these methods want the additional information from link loads or a prior information about the end-to-end network traffic. This necessarily increases the computational complexity and overhead for attaining the model parameters. The time-frequency domain analysis method can be used to capture the multi-scale features and dynamic nature [1, 8]. The neural network is employed to model the network traffic [7, 8]. The prior distributions of link counts [9], link weights [10], and information theory [11] were used to analyze network traffic. These approaches can build the model to denote the end-to-end network traffic, while it is very difficult to exactly capture and seize their features and to build the accurate and appropriate network traffic model for traffic engineering in communication networks. Specially for highly energy-efficient communication requirements [12–15], they face new challenges.

This paper propose a modeling method to describe the features of the traffic amount of network flows in OTN based on E1 business, where E1 denotes the E1 interface. Generally, it is significantly difficult to directly build the model about them due to their complex properties. Different form previous methods, we use the Walsh transform to construct the model about the end-to-end traffic of network flows in OTN. Firstly, we denote the end-to-end network traffic as a independent identically distributed random time-varying series. In the random process, there are several parameters to be estimated accurately. This is very difficult for the limited traffic information. Secondly, to this end, we use the Walsh transform to characterize the end-to-end network traffic. By calculating the parameters with statistical methods, the model is determined correctly. Additionally, the model about the end-to-end network traffic is correctly built. Thirdly, we propose a new algorithm to build the model. Simulation results show that our approach is feasible and effective.

The rest of this paper is organized as follows. Our method is derived in Sect. 2. Section 3 presents the simulation results and analysis. We then conclude our work in Sect. 4.

2 Problem Statement

The Walsh function is a complete, normalized orthogonal system defined as $[0, 1]$, denoted as $wal(n, k)$, where n is the order rate and k is the independent variable, and its value is only $+1$ and -1. The Walsh function is a non-sinusoidal function, and any time function $f(t)$ is a period of 1 and in the $[0, 1)$. The time-varying network traffic can be decomposed into the weighted sum of a series of Walsh functions. Accordingly, we can obtain the following equation for any continuous time function $f(t)$:

$$f(t) = A_0 wal(0, t) + A_1 wal(1, t) + A_2 wal(2, t) + \ldots$$

$$= \sum_{k=0}^{\infty} A_k wal(k, t) \tag{1}$$

where $A_k = \int_0^1 f(t)wal(k, t)dt, k = 0, 1, 2, \ldots$

The Walsh transform for $f(t)$ is denoted as

$$f(t) = \sum_{k=0}^{\infty} F(k)wal(k, t)$$

$$F(k) = \int_0^1 f(t)wal(k, t)dt, k = 0, 1, 2, \ldots \tag{2}$$

This is a Walsh transform pair.

For a discrete case with N sampling points, the Walsh transform pair is:

$$x_i = \sum_{k=0}^{N-1} X_k wal(k, i), \ i = 0, 1, \ldots, N - 1$$

$$X_k = \frac{1}{N} \sum_{i=0}^{N-1} x_i wal(k, i), \ k = 0, 1, \ldots, N - 1 \tag{3}$$

The methods involved in this paper are based on the following assumptions: In the measurement interpretation model, the network traffic is uniform and stable in a short time, so the measurement curve can be approximated as a rectangular wave in the short term.

The network flow data obtained by the measuring instrument is actually a nonlinear function which is influenced by the instrument response function, environmental condition and so on. And it is often the true value for the network traffic. Accordingly, the following equation can be attained:

$$y(t) = f[x(t)] = \int_{\tau_1}^{\tau_2} x(t - \tau)h(\tau)d\tau \tag{4}$$

Where x denotes the true value of the measurement; h is the instrument response function; $[\tau_1, \tau_2]$ indicates the filter window length; t represents the time.

Hence, we can attain the below discrete form:

$$y(k) = \sum_{i=i_1}^{i_2} x(k - i)h(i),$$

$$k = 0, 1, \ldots, N - 1 \tag{5}$$

Where $[i_1, i_2]$ denotes the filter window length; k indicates the time-sampled marker; and N is the number of sampling points in the window.

The purpose of the measurement curve inversion is to remove the influence of the instrument response function h, the environmental condition and so on from the measured value y to recover the estimated $\tilde{x}$ of the real value x of the flow, so that the mean square errors of $\tilde{x}$ and x are the same. Walsh transform is more accurate than Fourier transform to reflect the essential characteristics of the time-varying traffic. Therefore, we use the Walsh transform based measurement curve inversion technique to describe network traffic. The least squares method is used to obtain the estimate $\tilde{x}$ of the true value of the measurement.

According to the previous assumptions, $x(k-i)$ takes its Walsh inverse transformation and finishes the equation as:

$$y(k) = G_k^T X = \sum_{n=0}^{N-1} X_n G_n(k), \ k = 0, 1, \ldots, J-1 \tag{6}$$

Where $G_k = (G_0(k), G_1(k), \ldots, G_{N-1}(k))^T$; $X = (X_0, X_1, \ldots, X_{N-1})^T$ is the Walsh transformation of $x(k-i)$; J is the total number of sampling points; $G_n(k) = \sum_{i=i_1}^{i_2} h(i) wal(n, k-i)$.

The solution of X_n can be estimated using the least squares method. According to the Walsh inverse transformation, we can obtain the estimation value of network flow x. This can denoted as

$$\begin{cases} \min & Q(X_0, X_1, \ldots, X_{N-1}) \\ s.t. & \frac{\partial Q(X_0, X_1, \ldots, X_{N-1})}{\partial X_n} = 0 \\ & n = 0, 1, \ldots, N-1 \end{cases} \tag{7}$$

Equation (7) makes the error sum of the squares $Q(X_0, X_1, \ldots, X_{N-1}) = \sum_{K=0}^{J-1} \left[y(k) - G_k^T X \right]^2$ take the minimum value of X_n.

It has been proved that the model with the least squares solution under the Walsh transform has the highest resolution, and the exact solution x of network traffic can be obtained without considering the influence of the ambient noise, and the interpretation result is close to the obtained data value. Now we propose our algorithm, called Walsh transform Traffic Modeling Algorithm (WTMA), to the end-to-end network traffic according to the above analysis and derivation, namely:

Step 1: According to the network flow measurement instrument, obtain the measured value in the network, and write the true value of the network flow of nonlinear function as shown in Eq. (4).

Step 2: The nonlinear function formula (4) is written as a discrete form $y(k)$ according to Eq. (5).

Step 3: According to the Walsh transformation theory, the measurement curve is retrieved by Eqs. (2)–(3), and the influence of the instrument response, environmental conditions and so on are removed from the measured value y.

Step 4: Using the least squares method, achieve the error sum of squares $Q(X_0, X_1, \ldots, X_{N-1})$ to obtain the minimum value of X_n by Eq. (7).

Step 5: The X_n is evaluated by the inverse of Walsh to obtain the estimated value $\tilde{x}$ of the real value x of network flows.

Step 6: Use estimation errors to correct the model. If the traffic at all the time slots are handled, exit and save the result to the file, or go back to Step 1.

3 Simulation Result and Analysis

In this section, we conduct some tests to demonstrate our algorithm WTMA. In order to verify the accuracy of our algorithm, we need to use real network data. The real data needed in the simulation experiment is collected by the network nodes; we use the real data from the real Abilene backbone network in the United States to validate WTMA. Matlab2010 is exploited performed the detailed simulation experiments. PCA [3], WABR [7], and HMPA [2] algorithms for the network flows modeling have been reported as the better performance. Hence, we compare WTMA with them in detail. In the following, the prediction results of the end-to-end network traffic are analyzed for WTMA algorithm. The average relative errors for the end-to-end network traffic are indicated for four algorithms. Finally, we also evaluate the performance improvement of WTMA against PCA, WABR, and HMPA. In our simulation, the data of the first 500 time slots are used to train the models of four approaches, while other data are exploited to validate their performance.

Figure 1 shows the estimation values of network flows 67 and 107, where network flows 67 and 107 are selected randomly from the 144 end-to-end network flow pairs in the Abilene backbone network. As shown in our simulation experiments, other end-to-end network flow pairs denote similar results. Without loss of generality, we only discuss the network flows 67 and 107 in this paper. Additionally, here the end-to-end network flow is equal to the Origin Destination (OD) pair. Figure 1(a) shows that WTMA can effectively seize the dynamic changes of end-to-end network flow 67. For different time slots, the real end-to-end network flow exhibits the significant time-varying nature. From Fig. 1(a), we have seen that WTMA can capture the trend of the end-to-end network flow. Likewise, the end-to-end network flow 107 exhibits the irregular and dynamic changes over the time as indicated in Fig. 1(b). From Fig. 1(a), it is very clear that although WTMA holds the larger estimation errors for the end-to-end network flow 67, it can still capture its change trend. This further demonstrates that BTMA can effectively estimate the change of the end-to-end network traffic over the time.

Next, we discuss the estimation errors of four algorithms. Generally, the time-varying nature of the end-to-end network flows over the time is difficult to be captured only via the model. To further validate our algorithm, we compare the relative estimation errors over the time for all algorithms. To avoid the randomness in the simulation, we perform 500 runs to calculate the average relative estimation errors.

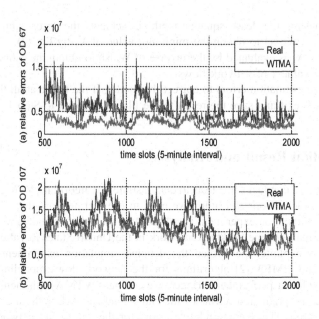

Fig. 1. Prediction results of end-to-end traffic flows 67 and 107.

The average relative estimation errors over the time for the end-to-end network traffic are defined as:

$$e(t) = \frac{1}{N} \sum_{i=1}^{N} \frac{||\hat{x}_i(t) - x_i(t)||_2}{||x_i(t)||_2} \tag{8}$$

Where $i = 1, 2, \ldots, N$, N is the number of runs in the simulation process, $||\cdot||_2$ is the norm of L_2, and $\hat{x}_i(t)$ indicates the end-to-end traffic estimation value of run i at time slot t.

Figure 2 illustrates the average relative estimation errors of four algorithm over the time for end-to-end network flows 67 and 107. It is very interesting that for end-to-end network flows 67 and 107, WABR, HMPA, and WTMA show the lower relative errors while PCA holds the larger estimation deviation. At the same time, Fig. 2 also indicates that WTMA holds the lowest relative errors. This tells us that in contrast to PCA, WABR, and HMPA, WTMA holds the better estimation ability for the end-to-end network flows, while WTMA indeed has the best estimation ability. More importantly, WABR, HMPA, and WTMA exhibit the lower fluctuation over the time in terms of relative errors than PCA. This shows that compared with other three algorithms, WTMA can more effectively model the end-to-end network flows with dynamic and time-varying features.

Now, we analyze the improvement of WTMA to other three algorithms for the end-to-end network flows. Figure 3 plots the improvement ration of end-to-end traffic flow 67 and 107. For End-to-end traffic flow 67, WTMA attains the performance improvement of about 4.95%, 2.11%, and 3.39% against PCA, WABR, and HMPA,

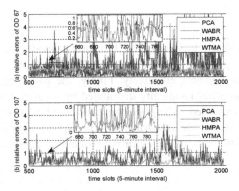

Fig. 2. Average relative errors for end-to-end traffic flows 67 and 107.

respectively. Similarly, for end-to-end traffic flow 107, WTMA obtains the performance improvement of about 19.5%, 12.9%, and 5.0% against PCA, WABR, and HMPA, respectively. This definitely demonstrates that in contrast to PCA, WABR, and HMPA, our algorithm WTMA can indeed model the end-to-end network traffic more effectively. From Fig. 3, we also see that relative to PCA, WTMA can reach the largest performance improvement. For WABR, WTMA only achieve the smaller improvement. However, WTMA holds the lowest improvement against HMPA, namely less than 5%. As mentioned in Fig. 2, this further shows that WABR, HMPA, and WTMA hold the better modeling capability for the end-to-end network traffic. Moreover, WTMA and HMPA hold the similar performance. Therefore, WTMA can correctly model the end-to-end traffic.

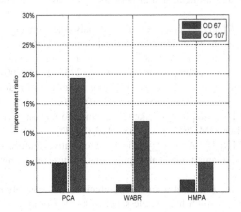

Fig. 3. Improvement ratio of end-to-end traffic flows 67 and 107.

4 Conclusions

This paper propose a Walsh transform-based method to model the end-to-end network flow. Different from previous methods, the Walsh transform is used to infer and establish the model parameters effectively. Firstly, the end-to-end network traffic is described as an independent identically distributed time-varying series. Secondly, the Walsh transform is exploited to capture the end-to-end network flow features. By calculating the parameters, we construct the corresponding network traffic model. Simulation results show that our approach is feasible and effective.

References

1. Jiang, D., Nie, L., Lv, Z., et al.: Spatio-temporal Kronecker compressive sensing for traffic matrix recovery. IEEE Access **4**, pp. 3046–3053 (2016)
2. Jiang, D., Xu, Z., Xu, H.: A novel hybrid prediction algorithm to network traffic. Ann. Telecommun. **70**(9), 427–439 (2015)
3. Soule, A., Lakhina, A., Taft, N., et al.: Traffic matrices: balancing measurements, inference and modeling, In: Proceedings of SIGMETRICS 2005, vol. 33(1), 362–373 (2005)
4. Zhang, Y., Roughan, M, Duffield, N., et al.: Fast accurate computation of large-scale IP traffic matrices from link loads. In: Proceedings of SIGMETRICS 2003, vol. 31(3), 206–217 (2003)
5. Takeda, T., Shionoto, K.: Traffic matrix estimation in large-scale IP networks. In: Proceedings of LANMAN 2010, pp. 1–6 (2010)
6. Yingxun, F.: The Research and Improvement of the Genetic Algorithm. Beijing University of Posts and Telecommunications, Beijing (2010)
7. Jiang, D., Zhao, Z., Xu, Z., et al.: How to reconstruct end-to-end traffic based on time-frequency analysis and artificial neural network. AEU-Int. J. Electron. Commun. **68**(10), 915–925 (2014)
8. Jiang, D., Yuan, Z., Zhang, P., et al.: A traffic anomaly detection approach in communication networks for applications of multimedia medical devices. Multimed. Tools Appl. (2016)
9. Vaton, S., Bedo, J.: Network traffic matrix: how can one learn the prior distributions from the link counts only. In: Proceedings of ICC 2004, pp. 2138–2142 (2004)
10. Lad, M., Oliveira, R., Massey, D., et al.: Inferring the origin of routing changes using link weights. In: Proceedings of ICNP 2007, pp. 93–102 (2007)
11. Tune, P., Veitch, D.: Sampling vs sketching: an information theoretic comparison. In: Proceedings of INFOCOM 2011, pp. 2105–2113 (2011)
12. Jiang, D., Li, W., Lv, H.: An energy-efficient cooperative multicast routing in multi-hop wireless networks for smart medical applications. Neurocomputing **2017**(220), 160–169 (2017)
13. Jiang, D., Xu, Z., Li, W., et al.: An energy-efficient multicast algorithm with maximum network throughput in multi-hop wireless networks. J. Commun. Netw. **18**(5), 713–724 (2016)
14. Jiang, D., Xu, Z., Liu, J., et al.: An optimization-based robust routing algorithm to energy-efficient networks for cloud computing. Telecommun. Syst. **63**(1), 89–98 (2016)
15. Jiang, D., Zhang, P., Lv, Z., et al.: Energy-efficient multi-constraint routing algorithm with load balancing for smart city applications. IEEE Internet of Things J. **3**(6), 1437–1447 (2016)

Computing Offloading to Save Energy Under Time Constraint Among Mobile Devices

Xiaomin Zhou[✉], Yong Zhang, and Tengteng Ma

School of Electronic Engineering, Beijing University of Posts
and Telecommunications, Beijing, China
{lindazhou,yongzhang}@bupt.edu.cn,
buptteng@foxmail.com

Abstract. The recent advancement in wireless communication has motivated increasing number of mobile applications, including computing-intensive tasks. However, it takes resource-limited mobile devices a lot of energy to execute these tasks. Computing offloading is helpful in the scenario, where mobile device offloads part of the task to available devices. In this paper, we propose an algorithm AOA (Alternately Optimizing Algorithm) to alternatively optimize task and power allocation in order to achieve the minimum system energy consumption under given time constraint. KM (Kuhn-Munkres) algorithm in graph theory is adopted to get the optimal task assignment. And we get the optimal solution for power allocation via mathematical derivation. Simulations have shown that the proposed algorithm can give a global optimal task and power allocation solution.

Keywords: Computing offload · Mobile Edge Computing
Resource allocation

1 Introduction

With the rapid development of wireless communication technique, the transmission speed of mobile devices has increased significantly. This motivated increasing number of applications to be executed on mobile devices, including computing- complex applications. However, mobile devices have limited battery power, storage and processing speed. The limited capability of mobile devices can't guarantee Qos requirements of applications. Instead of single machine processing, we can offload some computing tasks to an external platform through wireless network to enable collaborative computing. There are several concepts related to this field.

First, Wireless Distributed Computing (WDC). In [1], WDC means exploiting wireless connectivity to share processing-intensive tasks among multiple devices. In [2], the resources allocation for OFDMA based WDC System is studied. It is mentioned that OFDM/OFDMA physical layer is the ideal candidate for implementing WDC because of the advantages of high data rate and robust to multipath fading. Second, Mobile Cloud Computing (MCC) has been a potential computing paradigm. In [3], the definition of MCC is that the data processing and storage of mobile application are moved from the mobile device to powerful and centralized computing platforms

© Springer Nature Singapore Pte Ltd. 2018
H. Yuan et al. (Eds.): GSKI 2017, CCIS 849, pp. 383–391, 2018.
https://doi.org/10.1007/978-981-13-0896-3_38

located in clouds. Computing offloading is an import feature of MCC to improve battery lifetime and improve applications performances. However, the data has to go through a long backhaul to reach remote cloud server, which will cause non-ignorable latency. Third, Mobile Edge Computing (MEC) was first proposed by ETSI in 2014 and was defined as a new platform that provides IT and cloud-computing capabilities within the RAN in close proximity to mobile subscribers [4]. In contrast to MCC, MEC pushes mobile computing, network control and storage to network edges. Fourth, Fog Computing transfers the computing tasks to the fog nodes. Anything with computation capabilities around us can be called fog nodes, such as routers, BS, set-up boxes, wearable devices etc. In 5G times, various devices will be densely deployed. MEC and Fog Computing are similar in many ways, and are often used alternatively.

A lot of research work focusing on resources allocation [5–9] has been done. Different offloading policies under different models are proposed. There are also some studies about task partition. In [10], a partition scheme that uses a cost graph to statically divide the program is given. In this paper, we creatively represent the task allocation problem as a graph match problem. And jointly solve the computation and communication problem.

In this paper, we consider a computing offloading scenario with a single offloading node and multi cooperative nodes. The optimization problem is to achieve minimization energy consumption under given time constraint. The remainder is organized as follows, Sect. 2 presents system model and object problem. Section 3 introduces our algorithm to solve the problem. Section 4 gives the simulation results and analysis. Section 5 concludes the article.

2 System Model and Problem Formulation

2.1 System Model

Consider an offloading scenario consisting of a single offloading node and multi cooperative nodes in Fig. 1. We call the offloading node Master and the cooperative nodes Slaves. Master is a resource-constraint mobile device. Slaves are mobile devices or other available devices with computing capability. Master has a computing-intensive task, which can be partitioned into several independent subtasks. Master communicates with slaves over wireless link.

2.2 Task Model

Consider single computing-intensive task on Master. Assume the task has already been partitioned into N independent subtasks $\{T_1, T_2, \ldots\ldots, T_N\}$. The sub-tasks can be executed locally or offloaded. We describe sub-task T_i as (D_i, X_i).

D_i: the data size of T_i, measured by bit.

X_i: the computing density of T_i, average CPU cycles cost of processing per bit, measured by cycles/bit.

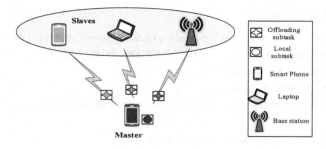

Fig. 1. System model

2.3   Network Model

We use the central control network mode. Master starts the offloading and sends subtasks to relevant slaves. Slaves begin executing after receiving the complete data. Results usually consist of small amount of data, so returning time and energy are negligible. Assume master is equipped with multiple antennas, it can send subtasks in parallel. Total delay depends on the slowest returning subtask. The time order is presented in Fig. 2.

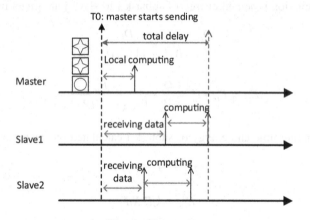

Fig. 2. Time order

As for the wireless communication techniques, we would like to base on the reliable 4G/5G standards, which have high data rate, achieve very less interference. In the coming 5G, there will be densely deployed cellular network and D2D (Device to Device) communications, which perfectly suit the application scenario.

2.4   Computing Model

Slaves process the task in a blocking mode, executing won't start until the transmission of data is completed. We have a set of slave nodes {slave1, slave2, ..., slaveM}. The number of slaves is M. Describe slave j as (F_j, k_j).

F_j: the CPU frequency of slave j.
k_j: the parameter related to computing energy consumption of slave j.

Master also has these two parameter, note as (F_0, k_0).

2.5   Problem Formulation

In this paper, we set the minimum energy cost under given time constraint as an objective. Assume slaves keep stable during the offloading stage. According to Shannon's theorem, the max transmission data rate from master to slave j:

$$R_j = B * log_2\left(1 + HP_{tr}^i/\delta^2\right) \tag{1}$$

B is the bandwidth. H is the channel gain. P_{tr}^i is the transmit power that master assigns to subtask i. δ^2 is noise power.

The transmission time and energy of subtask i to slave j are given by

$$t_{tr}^{ij} = \frac{D_i}{R_j} = \frac{D_i}{B*log_2\left(1 + HP_{tr}^i/\delta^2\right)} \tag{2}$$

$$E_{tr}^{ij} = P_{tr}^i * t_{tr}^{ij} = \frac{D_i}{B} * \frac{P_{tr}^i}{log_2\left(1 + HP_{tr}^i/\delta^2\right)} \tag{3}$$

The computing time and energy of subtask i calculated on slave j are written as

$$t_{cp}^{ij} = D_i * X_i/F_j \tag{4}$$

$$E_{cp}^{ij} = k_j D_i X_i F_j^2 \tag{5}$$

Suppose the given time constraint is τ. There are two variables to optimize in problem $\mathcal{P}$. One is the subtask assignment, deciding each subtask is assigned to which device, and we use a match M to note. The other is the transmission power of each subtask $P_{tr}^* = \left[P_{tr}^1, P_{tr}^2 \ldots P_{tr}^N\right]$. Thus the problem $\mathcal{P}$ can be formulated as:

$$\mathcal{P}: \quad min \sum_{i=1}^{N}\left(E_{tr}^i + E_{cp}^i\right) \tag{6}$$

Subject to:

$$t^i_{tr} + t^i_{cp} \leq \tau, \quad \forall i \in \{1, 2, \ldots N\} \tag{7}$$

$$\sum_{i=1}^{N} P^i_{tr} \leq P_{max} \tag{8}$$

(6) means the goal is minimal transmission and computing energy cost of subtasks. (7) guarantees each subtask finished in time constraint. (8) means sum transmission power should not exceed master's max transmission power.

3 Solution and Algorithm

We can easily find $\mathcal{P}$ is a MINLP problem as the subtask assignment match variable is a N * (M + 1) integer matrix, each element in the matrix is 0 or 1 representing offloading decision and $P^*_{tr} = \left[P^1_{tr}, P^2_{tr}, \ldots P^N_{tr}\right]$ consists of continuous variables. It's a challenging work to jointly optimize. We propose an Alternately Optimizing Algorithm (AOA) to alternately solve the problem.

3.1 AOA—Task Allocation

Kuhn-Munkres (KM) algorithm in graph theory is effective in finding an optimal assignment for a given cost matrix. Subtasks $\{T_1, T_2 \ldots, T_N\}$ and the devices $\{master, slave1, \ldots, slaveM\}$ are regarded as vertices set of bipartite graph. Figure 3 is an example bipartite graph. The energy cost matrix is regarded as edge weight, given in (9).

$$\text{Edge}[i][j] = \begin{cases} E^{i0}_{cp}, & j = 0 \\ E^{ij}_{tr} + E^{ij}_{cp}, & j! = 0. \end{cases} \tag{9}$$

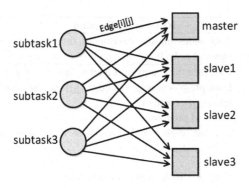

Fig. 3. Bipartite graph

Edge[i][j] means the energy cost of the i-th subtask assigned to the j-th device. When j = 0, the subtask is processed by master, transmission energy is 0. In simulation, we found that the transmission energy E_{tr} is rather smaller than computing energy E_{cp}. It can be calculated from Table 1, $E_{cp} \approx 10^{-2}J$, $E_{tr} \approx 10^{-5}J$. So we can roughly think Edge[i][j] = E_{cp}^{ij}.

Table 1. Relevant parameters

Parameter	Value and meaning
$\{D_i\}$	{3, 2, 4, 5} Kbit
	Subtask data size randomly chosen from 2–8 Kbit
$\{X_i\}$	{1008, 987, 1109, 1114} cycles/bit
	Computing density randomly chosen from 800–1200
$\{F_j\}$	{2.05, 2.45, 1.24, 1.22, 1.67, 1.02} GHz
	CPU frequency randomly chosen from 1–2.5 GHz
K	10^{-26}
	Computing energy parameter
W	1 MHz
	Total bandwidth
δ^2	−77 dBm
	Noise power
P_{max}	400 mW
	Master's max transmit power
H	{1.33e−7, 1.45e−6, 8.53e−6, 2.05e−6, 9.34e−8}
	Channel gain generated from distance

Details of the algorithm is given in Fig. 4. This section is the first part of AOA algorithm, it gives the optimal task assignment scheme. The Computing Energy is thus the lowest.

	AOA—task allocation
Input:	Task nodes, master, slave nodes, time constraint τ, P_{tr}^*.
Output:	Optimal task allocation match.
Step1:	Calculate the energy cost matrix, time cost matrix.
Step2:	Data pre-processing, set Edge[i][j] as a big number if time[i][j] exceeds τ.
Step3:	Run KM program.
Step4:	Get the result match. Otherwise there is no feasible match under τ.

Fig. 4. AOA—task allocation detail steps

3.2   AOA—Power Allocation

After Sect. 3.1, the Computing Energy $\sum E_{cp}$ achieves the minimal, and problem $\mathcal{P}$ turns to be

$$min \sum_{i=1}^{N} E_{tr}^{i} = \sum_{i=1}^{N} \frac{D_i}{B} * \frac{P_{tr}^{i}}{log_2\left(1 + HP_{tr}^{i}/\sigma^2\right)} \tag{10}$$

Conditions (7) and (8) keep the same.
We will get the solution by math deduction:

① Note $A = H/\sigma^2$, make a function

$$f(x) = \frac{x}{log_2(1 + Ax)} \tag{11}$$

② The first derivative of f(x) is:

$$f'(x) = \frac{log_2(1 + Ax) - \frac{Ax}{(1+Ax)ln2}}{log_2^2(1 + Ax)} \tag{12}$$

It can be proved that $f'(x) > 0$ when x > 0.
So f(x) increases with x.

$$\sum E_{tr}^{i} = \sum \frac{D_i}{B} * f\left(P_{tr}^{i}\right) \tag{13}$$

$\sum E_{tr}^{i}$ increases with P_{tr}^{i}. We can figure out in order to make the object function minimum, P_{tr}^{i} should be minimum under conditions (7) and (8). Then get the analytical solution of P_{tr}^{*} in (14).

$$P_{tr}^{i} = \left(2^{\frac{D_i}{(\tau - t_{cp}^{i})B}} - 1\right)\sigma^2/H_i \tag{14}$$

4   Simulation Results

Set the number of subtasks N = 4, the number of slaves M = 5. Relevant parameters are given in Table 1.

Without offloading, delay is 7.5 ms. We get different matches under different τ as shown in Table 2. When τ is strict (less than 3 ms), there is no feasible match.

From Fig. 5, there is a tradeoff between energy and time. When τ is strict, offloading will choose devices with high CPU frequency to reduce time, as a consequence, energy cost rises. When $\tau > 7.5$ ms, the result will keep the same. The line is segmented flat, because in some time interval, for example, 5–6 ms, the match keeps the same, so total energy and time don't change.

Table 2. Result match

τ	3 ms	4 ms	5 ms	6 ms	7 ms
Subtask1		Slave3	Slave5	Slave5	Slave2
Subtask2		Slave5	Slave2	Slave2	Slave4
Subtask3		Slave4	Slave3	Slave3	Slave5
Subtask4		Master	Slave4	Slave4	Slave3

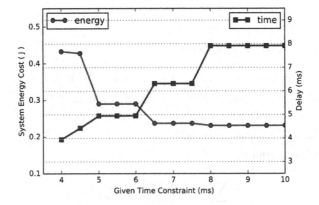

Fig. 5. The influence of time constraint on energy and time

Form Fig. 6, the initial line is transmitting energy cost under $P_{tr}^* = [100\,\text{mW},$ $100\,\text{mW}, 100\,\text{mW}, 100\,\text{mW}]$. We get the optimal power allocation according to (13). Figure 6 shows there is a significant reduction in transmit energy cost.

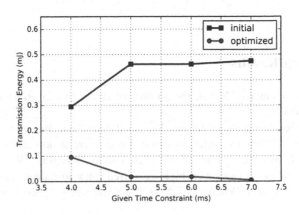

Fig. 6. Optimized transmission energy

5 Conclusion

Computing offloading is a promising paradigm in saving energy and reducing delay. This work focuses on energy saving and gives a single user multiple cooperative partners model. Task is partitioned into several independent subtasks. The proposed algorithm AOA optimizes task and transmit power allocation to achieve the minimum system energy cost. We would like to research on more complex model and try other optimization methods in the future work.

Acknowledgements. This work is supported by National Natural Science Foundation of China (No. 61171097 and No. 61771072). We thank the reviewers and editors for their helpful comments.

References

1. Datla, D., et al.: Wireless distributed computing: a survey of research challenges. IEEE Commun. Mag. **50**(1), 144–152 (2012)
2. Ramji, T., Ramkumar, B., Manikandan, M.S.: Resource and subcarriers allocation for OFDMA based wireless distributed computing system. In: IEEE International Advance Computing Conference IEEE, pp. 338–342 (2014)
3. Dinh, H.T., et al.: A survey of mobile cloud computing: architecture, applications, and approaches. Wirel. Commun. Mob. Comput. **13**(18), 1587–1611 (2013)
4. Mao, Y., et al.: Mobile Edge Computing: Survey and Research Outlook. https://arxiv.org/pdf/1701.01090v1.pdf
5. Mao, Y., Zhang, J., Letaief, K.B.: Joint task offloading scheduling and transmit power allocation for mobile-edge computing systems. In: Wireless Communications and Networking Conference, pp. 1–69. IEEE (2017)
6. Ramji, T.: Adaptive resource allocation and its scheduling for good tradeoff between power consumption and latency in OFDMA based wireless distributed computing system. In: International Conference on Computation of Power, Energy Information and Communication, pp. 0496–0501. IEEE (2015)
7. Dinh, T.Q., et al.: Adaptive computation scaling and task offloading in mobile edge computing. In: Wireless Communications and Networking Conference. IEEE (2017)
8. Mao, Y., et al.: Stochastic joint radio and computational resource management for multi-user mobile-edge computing systems. IEEE Trans. Wirel. Commun. **16**, 5994–6009 (2017)
9. You, C., et al.: Energy-efficient resource allocation for mobile-edge computation offloading. IEEE Trans. Wirel. Commun. **16**(3), 1397–1411 (2017)
10. Xie, Y., et al.: Computing offloading strategy based on joint allocation in mobile device cloud. In: 2nd International Conference on Communications, Information Management and Network Security, Beijing (2017)
11. Li, Z., et al.: Computation offloading to save energy on handheld devices: a partition scheme, pp. 238–246 (2001)

A New Weighted Connection-Least Load Balancing Algorithm Based on Delay Optimization Strategy

Guangshun Li[⊠], Heng Ding, Junhua Wu, and Shuzhen Xu

School of Information Science and Engineering, Qufu Normal University,
Jining, China
30752585@qq.com, 656093478@qq.com,
7182829@qq.com, 2460923107@qq.com

Abstract. The load balancing problem of edge computing networks is resear-ched in this paper. Edge nodes can process information collaboratively, which may reduce the workload of the cloud data centers, and improve the quality of experience of users. A new weight connection-least load balancing algorithm based on delay optimization strategy with the user time constraint is proposed. A new weight setting method of server is put forward to measure the perfor-mance of servers, which can adjust the data forwarding times of each edge node as soon as possible. Experimental results show that our method can improve the performance of edge computing networks significantly.

Keywords: Load balancing · Edge computing · Cloud data centers
Delay optimization strategy

1 Introduction

Cloud computing [1] is a style of computing in which dynamically scalable and often virtualized resources are provided as a service over the Internet. With the rapid devel-opment of the Internet of Things [2] and the Mobile Internet, it becomes very common and popular to access cloud services by using Various access devices. However, the increasing amount of data will not only occupy a large number of network bandwidth, but also aggravate the burden of the data center, and may make data transmission and information acquisition worse and worse. Edge computing [3] extends the cloud com-puting paradigm to the edge of the network and is closer to the end user. This distributed infrastructure has the ability of computing, storage and control by exploiting local computing resources. Edge computing has obvious characteristics such as low latency and location awareness, more extensive geographical distribution, supporting more edge nodes, and adapting to mobility applications. The data originally sent to the cloud data center can be directly processed and stored at the edge of the network, which can greatly reduce the pressure of the cloud data center and effectively offload network traffic. Thereby the cloud data center can provide services for more users.

Edge computing load balancing [4] is mainly to solve the problem that how to reasonably store data, allocate tasks and schedule resources among multiple servers.

© Springer Nature Singapore Pte Ltd. 2018
H. Yuan et al. (Eds.): GSKI 2017, CCIS 849, pp. 392–403, 2018.
https://doi.org/10.1007/978-981-13-0896-3_39

A number of scholars have studied the load balancing problem between edge computing nodes and user devices, and many scholars have studied the load balancing problem between edge computing nodes and cloud datacenters. They put forward many solutions to improve the utilization of edge computing resources, and improve the availability and reliability of the network.

The reminder of this paper is organized as follows. The related works are introduced in Sect. 2. We describe the delay optimization strategy and load balancing algorithm in Sect. 3. In Sect. 4, we describe the algorithm analysis. The experiment results are presented in Sect. 5. Section 6 concludes the paper.

2 Related Work

Verma et al. [5] proposed an efficient load balancing algorithm for a Fog-Cloud based architecture. They use data replication technology for maintain data in fog networks, which reduces overall dependency on big data centers. The ultimate goal is to balance load, reduce the reliance on cloud and make data close to the user end through fog networks. In the algorithm, when the fog servers cannot response to the request, the request is forwarded to a nearest fog server node whose load is less than the set threshold. The algorithm does not consider the real-time load capacity of single edge node, which will lead to overload or light load problem of partial fog nodes. Moreover, frequent data replication cache will increase the system overhead.

Xiao et al. [6] proposed a distributed optimization algorithm based on distributed alternating direction method of multipliers (ADMM). They use variable splitting to achieve the optimal workload allocation solution that maximizes users' quality of experience under the given power efficiency. Numerical results show that their proposed approach significantly improves the performance of fog computing networks.

Cardellini et al. [7] proposed a distributed QoS-aware scheduler for DSP systems based on Storm, which can operate in a distributed fog computing environment. The results show that the distributed QoS-aware scheduler outperforms the centralized default one, it improves the application performance and enhances the system with runtime adaptation capabilities. However, complex topologies involving many operators may cause some instability and decrease the DSP application availability.

Deng et al. [8] studied the tradeoff between power consumption and delay in a cloud-fog computing system. Simulations and numerical results show that the sacrifice of modest computing resources can save communication bandwidth and reduce transmission latency, and fog computing can significantly improve the performance of cloud computing.

The least connection algorithm (LC) is a dynamic algorithm. When users send requests, the number of current connections of every server needs to be obtained, and the new arrival request is always allocated to the server with the smallest number of connections. The LC algorithm does not consider differences in performance among servers, it is applicable to the systems with small differences in server performance.

Weighted Least Connection algorithm (WLC) [9] increases the weight setting. The algorithm needs to calculate the ratio of the server connection number to server weight each time, and selects the server with the lowest ratio to receive the new user request.

The WLC algorithm takes into account the performance differences of each server and the impact of the current server connection number on the server load. However, the weight parameter setting that reflects server performance is still not flexible enough. It can not reflect the load state of servers exactly only by the number of server connections. The algorithm needs to calculate the ratio of the number of server connections to the weights of all servers each time, and the cost of the algorithm is large.

On the basis of network architecture and load balancing algorithm proposed by Verma et al. [5], we propose a new weighted connection-least load balancing (WCLB) algorithm based on delay optimization strategy. Compared with LC and WLC algorithm, the server weight of the WCLB algorithm is expressed by the ratio of the server idle load to the total load. We take full account of the impact of server connections and current server load on global load balancing, rather than only looking within the ratio of the server connection number to server weight. Since the calculation of each current server information is distributed computing and can be performed locally without real-time calculation in cloud-edge architecture, so the system overhead is smaller.

3   Delay Optimization Strategy and Load Balancing Algorithm

3.1   Delay Optimization Strategy

Yang Yang, manager of the keynote network technical support, said at the 2013 China Internet Conference that when 100% of the users access the server, 74% of the users wait for 5 s to give up waiting, and the number of APP is 50%. However, all the 1/3 users who give up waiting will go to other websites or other similar applications to access, which will lead to loss of users. How to reduce the delay time, improve the user experience and retain customers is an urgent problem to be solved.

In the cloud-edge architecture, when user sends a request to the nearest edge node, if the user's request can be processed by the edge node, the processing result is returned to the user. If it's completed by other edge nodes, the data will be forwarded to the edge node that nearest the user and then sent to the user. If it's completed by cloud servers, the data will be forwarded to the edge node that nearest the cloud servers and then sent to the edge node that nearest the user, the processing result is returned to the user finally. We define T as the user acceptable communication delay time, define X as the number of edge nodes, define D_1 as the communication delay time between edge nodes and cloud servers, define D_2 as Communication delay time between edge nodes and terminal users, define $Dz_1z_i (i = 1,2...X)$ as communication delay between edge nodes, the communication delay time of each edge node only considers the communication delay between the device that receives the task and the task distribution device. The average communication delay between edge nodes ave can be calculated as:

$$ave = \frac{\sum_{i=1}^{X} D_{z_1 z_i}}{X} \qquad (1)$$

Within the time T, when the user requests can be processed at the edge nodes without sending requests to cloud servers, the maximum number of data forwarding hop_1 between edge nodes can be defined as:

$$\frac{T - 2D_2 - ave}{ave} \leq hop_1 \tag{2}$$

Within the time T, in order to ensure the user requests can be processed in time and be sent to cloud servers, we remove the communication delay time between the edge nodes and the cloud servers. The maximum number of data forwarding hop_2 between the edge nodes in the remaining time can be defined as:

$$\frac{T - 2D_1 - 2D_2 - ave}{ave} \leq hop_2 \tag{3}$$

When the communication delay between edge nodes and cloud servers is large, and the number of edge nodes is enough, the bandwidth occupancy rate of cloud server processing user requests will be increased and the communication delay will be greater, the revenue of edge nodes that successfully handle user requests will be improved. When the number of data forwarding of edge nodes reaches hop_2, it send the user requests to the cloud servers, meanwhile, continue to access the edge nodes that has not accessed. During the time that edge nodes send the request to the cloud server and get the response from cloud server, the maximum number of data forwarding hop_3 between edge nodes can be defined as:

$$\frac{2D_1 - D_2 - ave}{ave} \leq hop_3 \tag{4}$$

The hop_1, hop_2, hop_3 satisfies the following equation:

$$hop_2 + hop_3 \leq hop_1 \tag{5}$$

3.2 Load Balancing Algorithm

We chose CPU utilization $L(c_i)$, memory utilization $L(m_i)$ and network bandwidth utilization $L(b_i)$ three parameters to measure servers load. The three parameters are all percentages, indicating the ratio of the current occupying resources to the total resources. When any of the three values reaches 95%, it is determined that the node is an overloaded node, and the task request is stopped. The integrated load of server i $L(s_i)$ can be expressed as:

$$L(s_i) = k_1 \times L(c_i) + k_2 \times L(m_i) + k_3 \times L(b_i) \tag{6}$$
$$i = 1, 2 \ldots X, \sum k = 1$$

Where k_1, k_2, k_3 are represent server weight coefficients and $k_1 + k_2 + k_3 = 1$.

The idle load of server i $P(s_i)$ can be expressed as:

$$P(s_i) = k_1 \times L(1 - c_i) + k_2 \times L(1 - m_i) + k_3 \times L(1 - b_i) \, i = 1, 2....X, \sum k = 1 \quad (7)$$

The weight of server i $W(s_i)$ is defined as:

$$W(s_i) = \frac{P(s_i)}{P(s_i) + L(s_i)} \times 10 \tag{8}$$

The initial weight of each server is 10.
The system total load $L(sum)$ is defined as:

$$L(sum) = \sum_{i=1}^{X} L(s_i) \tag{9}$$

The system total weight $W(sum)$ is defined as:

$$W(sum) = \sum_{i=1}^{X} W(s_i) \tag{10}$$

The total connection number of system servers $C(sum)$ is defined as:

$$C(sum) = \sum_{i=1}^{X} C(s_i) \tag{11}$$

Where $C(s_i)$ indicates the number of connections of the i th server.

We calculate the ratio of $L(s_i)$ to $W(s_i)$, and compared with the ratio of $L(sum)$ to $W(sum)$, then calculate the ratio of $C(s_i)$ to $W(s_i)$, and compared with the ratio of $C(sum)$ to $W(sum)$, there will be four cases:

$$\text{case}(1) : \frac{L(s_i)}{W(s_i)} \leq \frac{L(sum)}{W(sum)} \, \frac{C(s_i)}{W(s_i)} \leq \frac{C(sum)}{W(sum)}$$

$$\text{case}(2) : \frac{L(s_i)}{W(s_i)} \leq \frac{L(sum)}{W(sum)} \, \frac{C(s_i)}{W(s_i)} \geq \frac{C(sum)}{W(sum)}$$

$$\text{case}(3) : \frac{L(s_i)}{W(s_i)} \geq \frac{L(sum)}{W(sum)} \, \frac{C(s_i)}{W(s_i)} \leq \frac{C(sum)}{W(sum)}$$

$$\text{case}(4) : \frac{L(s_i)}{W(s_i)} \geq \frac{L(sum)}{W(sum)} \, \frac{C(s_i)}{W(s_i)} \geq \frac{C(sum)}{W(sum)}$$

In case (1), it means that the server is a light load node. In case (2) and case (3), due to the difference of server performance, user request load and user request duration, it will result in a large number of server connections while the actual load is small, or the number of server connections is small while the actual load is larger. In case (4), it means that the server is a heavy load node.

We set array *arr* to store the server identifiers that satisfy the case (1) and case (2). When the requests of user arrive, the servers corresponding to the identifier stored in the array *arr* are sequentially accessed until the request is processed. When the array is empty, each value is recalculated according to the above method, and the eligible server identifier is stored in the array *arr*.

The flow chart of the WCLB algorithm is shown as follows (Fig. 1).

The WCLB algorithm pseudo code is described as follows:

Algorithm: WCLB algorithm

```
1:  Input: User request ci mi bi
2:  Output: Server access sequence
3:    L=array(ci,mi,bi,);
4:    int i,X,Csum,C[si];
5:    double k1,k2,k3,Lsum,Wsum,L[si],P[si],W[si];
6:    k1+k2+k3=1;
7:    sequence(L,k1,k2,k3,X,Csum,Lsum,Wsum){
8:    L[si]=k1*L[ci]+k2*L[mi]+k3*L[bi]      //i=1,2,...,X
9:    P[si]=k1*L[1-ci]+k2*L[1-mi]+k3*L[1-bi]   //i=1,2,...,X
10:   W[si] = (P[si]/(P[si]+L[si]))*10
11:     for (i=0, i<=X, i++)
12:       Lsum=Lsum+L[si];
13:     for (i=0, i<=X, i++)
14:       Wsum=Wsum+W[si];
15:     for (i=0, i<=X, i++)
16:       Csum=Csum+C[si];
17:     Array result1,result2;
18:     for (i=0, i<=X, i++){
19:     if(L[si]/W[si]<=Lsum/Wsum){
20:       if(C[si]/W[si]<=Csum/Wsum){
21:          result1.append(i)
22:          }elseif(C[si]/W[si]>Csum/Wsum){
23:          result2.append(i)
24:          }
25:     }else{
26:       //do nothing
27:          }
28:        }
29:     return merge(resutl1,result2)  //Server access sequence
30:       }
31:   Array arr = function(L,k1,k2,k3,X,Csum,Lsum,Wsum);
32:   if (arr.length==0)
33:     {
34:     L = reget_L_asset(ci,mi,bi)      //Initialization
35:     arr = function(L,k1,k2,k3,X,Csum,Lsum,Wsum);
36:     }
37:       return arr
```

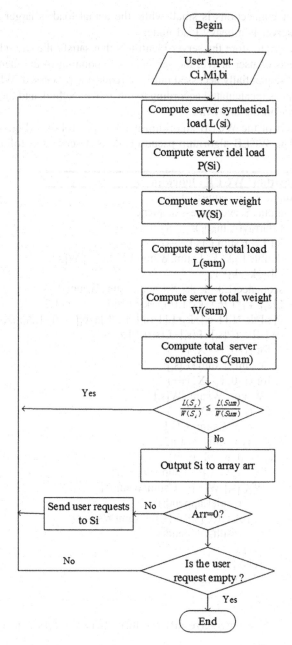

Fig. 1. Flow chart of WCLB algorithm

4   Algorithm Analysis

The delay strategy takes into account the users acceptable communication delay time, which restricts the data forwarding times of edge nodes. For different systems and requirements, user acceptable communication delay time can be set with different values. In the cloud-edge architecture, the cloud servers computing power is stronger but the transmission delay is large, the edge nodes computing power is relatively weak but the transmission delay between the edge nodes is small. In order to improve the users response speed, we hope that user requests are completed at the edge nodes as much as possible. We consider the maximum number of data forwarding between edge nodes in three cases under the given user waiting time constraint.

Compared with LC and WLC algorithm, the WCLB algorithm considers the performance differences between servers and the impact of current server connections on server load. We use CPU utilization, memory utilization and network bandwidth utilization as the performance index to measure the server load state. The server weight is set as the ratio of the current idle server load to the total server load, and it changes dynamically with the change of the server load. Compared with fixed weights or the weights that adjusted manually by administrator, the weight setting is more flexible and can more accurately measure the server load state. Because the WLC algorithm calculates the ratio of the server connection number to server weight each time, and selects the server with the lowest ratio to receive the new user request, the overhead of the algorithm is large. Due to the difference of server performance, user request load and user request duration, it will result in a large number of server connections while the actual load is small, or the number of server connections is small while the actual load is larger. In WCLB algorithm, we use the current server connection number and current server load to reflect the load state of servers. Because the edge computing nodes consist of the devices which the computing power are relatively weak, in order to avoid overload of single server node and maintain the whole system in a relatively stable state, we hope that the load occupancy rate of each edge node always fluctuates around the average of the whole system. We set the average ratio of total load to total weight of the whole system as the load threshold, set the average ratio of total connection number to total weight of the whole system as the connection number threshold. Then we select the light and heavy load nodes by comparing the corresponding value of each edge node with the two threshold values. With the processing of user requests, when the light load node receives the new user request, the load proportion will increase, on the contrary, when the heavy load node completes the user request, the load proportion will reduce. The load occupancy rate of each edge node always fluctuates around the average of the whole system.

5   Experimental Results

The experimental platform adopts MATLAB, the experimental data refer to the literature [11]. We set the number of the edge computing nodes X as 10, the user waiting time T as 5 s, the communication delay between Z_1 and the cloud server as 0.7 s, the communication delay between Z_1 and the terminal user as 0.04 s, and the computing power of the cloud data center as 10 GHz. The computing power of each edge node Vz_i and the one-way communication delay $Tz_1z_i (i = 1, 2...10)$, are shown in Table 1, the communication delay between device and task assignment is considered only.

Table 1. The parameters of edge computing nodes

Parameters	$Vz_i(GHz)$	$Tz_1z_i(s)$
Z_1	2	0
Z_2	1	0.1
Z_3	3	0.09
Z_4	0.5	0.12
Z_5	0.4	0.08
Z_6	0.7	0.09
Z_7	0.6	0.07
Z_8	0.3	0.06
Z_9	0.5	0.11
Z_{10}	1	0.14

The delay optimization strategy proposed in this paper is applied in cloud-edge architecture, which adjust the data forwarding times of each edge node under the constraint of user waiting time to reduce communication delay time. We compared the delay time between cloud architecture and cloud-edge architecture, the experimental results are shown in Fig. 2. With the increasing amount of processing data, cloud-edge computing network can reduce the processing delay of users more effectively than traditional cloud computing networks. Since cloud servers have strong computing power, the delay time for computation in cloud computing is relatively small. The delay time in cloud computing is mainly caused by the communication between the edge devices and the cloud servers. With the increasing amount of data and the impact of network bandwidth and ultra long distance communication, the communication delay will increase greatly. However, the edge computing delay is mainly caused by the data forwarding between edge nodes, our delay strategy effectively reduces the delay time for this problem.

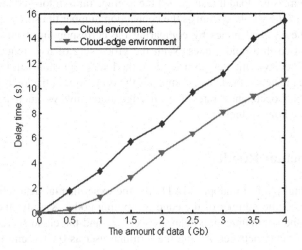

Fig. 2. Delay contrast in cloud environment and cloud-edge environment

The amount of data requested by users is generated randomly, and is measured by occupying the server integrated load. When the user requests arrive, they access the servers according to LC, WLC, and the WCLB algorithm proposed in this paper. Due to the different access policies, it may cause the different server load occupancy rates. We compare the system average idle load ratio of the three algorithms. The experimental results as shown in Fig. 3:

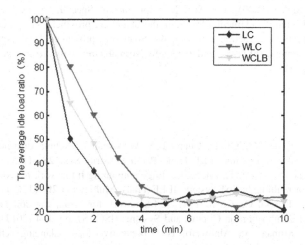

Fig. 3. Average idle load ratio of the three algorithms

Figure 3 shows that the average idle load rate of WCLB algorithm decreases most stable compared with LC algorithm and WLC algorithm. The decrease of LC algorithm is relatively faster than that of the WLC algorithm. Since LC algorithm only considers the number of server connections and does not consider the performance difference between services, it is easy to cause partial server node load overweight. WLC algorithm increases the weight factor, but the weight parameter that reflect server performance is still not flexible enough. It may lead to the error of the ratio of the connection number to the weight, and can not accurately measure the state of the server load. In the WCLB algorithm, the number of server connections and weights of the every server is always in the average state of the whole system, and the change of the load is more stable.

6   Conclusion

In this paper, we propose anew weighted connection-least load balancing (WCLB) algorithm based on delay optimization strategy. The algorithm can offload part or all the workload originally targeted to the cloud data centers. We consider the maximum data forwarding number between edge nodes in three cases under the given user waiting time constraint. We make server idle load ratio as server weight parameter, and use the current server connection number and current server load to reflect the load state of servers. The goal of the algorithm is make the load occupancy rate of each edge node always fluctuates around the average of the whole system. Numerical results show that our proposed approach significantly improves the performance of edge computing networks.

Acknowledgments. This work is supported by the National Natural Science Foundation of China (61672321, 61771289), the Shandong provincial Graduate Education Innovation Program (SDYY14052, SDYY15049), the Shandong provincial Specialized Degree Postgraduate Teaching Case Library Construction Program, the Shandong provincial Postgraduate Education Quality Curriculum Construction Program, the Shandong provincial University Science and Technology Program (J16LN15), and the Qufu Normal University Science and Technology Project (xkj201525).

References

1. Jonathan, A., Ryden, M., Oh, K., Chandra, A., Weissman, J.: Nebula: distributed edge cloud for data intensive computing. IEEE Trans. Parallel Distrib. Syst. **28**(11), 3229–3242 (2017)
2. Long, C., Cao, Y., Jiang, T., Zhang, Q.: Edge computing framework for cooperative video processing in multimedia IoT system. IEEE Trans. Multimedia **20**, 1126–1139 (2017)
3. Yang, S.W., Tickoo, O., Chen, Y.K.: A framework for visual fog computing. In: IEEE International Symposium on Circuits and Systems (ISCAS), pp. 1–4 (2017)
4. Beraldi, R., Mtibaa, A., Alnuweiri, H.: Cooperative load balancing scheme for edge computing resources. In: Second International Conference on Fog and Mobile Edge Computing, pp. 94–100. IEEE (2017)
5. Verma, S., Yadav, A.K., Motwani, D., Raw, R.S., Singh, H.K.: An efficient data replication and load balancing technique for fog computing environment. In: International Conference on Computing for Sustainable Global Development, pp. 2888–2895 (2016)
6. Xiao, Y., Krunz, M.: QoE and power efficiency tradeoff for fog computing networks with fog node cooperation. In: IEEE INFOCOM 2017 - IEEE Conference on Computer Communications, pp. 1–9. IEEE (2017)
7. Cardellini, V., Grassi, V., Presti, F.L., Nardelli, M.: On QoS-aware scheduling of data stream applications over fog computing infrastructures. In: Computers and Communication, pp. 271–276. . IEEE (2015)
8. Deng, R., Lu, R., Lai, C., Luan, T.H.: Towards power consumption-delay tradeoff by workload allocation in cloud-fog computing. In: IEEE International Conference on Communications, pp. 3909–3914. IEEE (2015)
9. Tong, X., Shu, W.: An efficient dynamic load balancing scheme for heterogenous processing system. In: International Conference on Computational Intelligence and Natural Computing, pp. 319–322. IEEE Computer Society (2009)
10. Yi, S., Hao, Z., Qin, Z., Li, Q.: Fog computing: platform and applications. In: Third IEEE Workshop on Hot Topics in Web Systems and Technologies, pp. 73–78. IEEE Computer Society (2015)
11. Zhang, H., Xiao, Y., Bu, S., Niyato, D.: Fog computing in multi-tier data center networks: a hierarchical game approach. in: IEEE International Conference on Communications, pp. 1–6. IEEE (2016)
12. Wang, P., Xu, H., Niu, Z., Han, D., Xiong, Y.: Expeditus: congestion-aware load balancing in clos data center networks. In: ACM Symposium on Cloud Computing, pp. 442–455. ACM (2016)

13. Chen, X., Zhang, J.: When D2D meets cloud: hybrid mobile task offloadings in fog computing. In: IEEE International Conference on Communications, pp. 1–6. IEEE (2017)
14. Chen, Z., Kang, L., Li, X., Li, J., Zhang, Y.: Constructing load-balanced degree-constrained data gathering trees in wireless sensor networks. In: IEEE International Conference on Communications, pp. 6738–6742 (2015)
15. Zhang, J., Zhang, Z., Guo, H.: Towards secure data distribution systems in mobile cloud computing. IEEE Trans. Mob. Comput. **16**, 3222–3235 (2017)
16. Dinitz, M., Fineman, J., Gilbert, S., Newport, C.: Load balancing with bounded convergence in dynamic networks. In: IEEE INFOCOM 2017 - IEEE Conference on Computer Communications, pp. 1–9. IEEE (2017)

An Extensible PNT Simulation Verification Platform Based on Deep Learning Algorithm

Shuangna Zhang[(⊠)], Li Tian, and Fuzhan Yue

Space Star Technology Co., Ltd.,
2nd Zhi Chun Road, Hai Dian District, Beijing, China
zhangshn@spacestar.com.cn

Abstract. In this paper, a simulation platform for multi-source PNT (Positioning, Navigation and timing) means is designed. The platform, which adopts a distributed simulation architecture to transmit data through the network, provides a test environment for multi-source PNT users and performs performance evaluation. Through in-depth learning of the output data of various PNT tools collected by different types of users in different scenarios, the platform can achieve parameter settings of multi-source PNT based on user characteristics. Seen from the test results can give the simulation platform, weight value will affect the comprehensive results, deep learning can make the weight value distribution is more close to the human judgment through a large amount of data to judge the artificial experience, so as to realize the autonomous PNT multi-source fusion.

Keywords: PNT · Simulation platform · Deep learning algorithm
Distributed architecture

1 Introduction

Based on BDS satellite navigation system, the PNT (positioning navigation timing) system includes a variety of positioning navigation and timing means of mutually reinforcing, complement, backup, and fusion methods. PNT system is the national information infrastructure, which can provide spatial information services for our civilian and army users [1]. PNT simulation verification platform is committed to the research and follow-up verification of the PNT system in China.

The platform can be divided into 4 processes, including signal source simulation, simulation of signal processing, information processing and data simulation application. System level simulation of PNT, design verification, and PNT products testing can realized by this platform.

Currently, due to the lack of unified PNT simulation platform, the performance of multi-source PNT products cannot be verified during the design phase. In addition, the current single method simulation verification platform is based on the experience of the designer or the actual collection data of a certain time, and cannot realize the automatic configuration. This platform realizes the automatic simulation data generation of the scene through the deep learning of existing data acquisition methods.

© Springer Nature Singapore Pte Ltd. 2018
H. Yuan et al. (Eds.): GSKI 2017, CCIS 849, pp. 404–413, 2018.
https://doi.org/10.1007/978-981-13-0896-3_40

2 PNT System

The main contents and aims of PNT system are to build a unified time and space standards system framework of positioning, navigation and timing. The purpose of the National Positioning, Navigation and Timing (PNT) Architecture effort is to help guide future PNT system-of-systems investment and implementation decisions. PNT touches almost every aspect of people's lives today [2].

Navigation satellite system is the cornerstone of the PNT system. Together with augmentations to BDs, and back-up capabilities, BDS are getting better to meet growing national, homeland, and economic security needs. Develop a new generation of satellite navigation system characterized by airspace-based high-performance navigation services, highly autonomous constellation stable operation, excellent system security and navigation warfare, and expansion services based on the global network of BDS. Build a full-link PNT verification platform is committed to cooperate with our country PNT system research and follow-up verification of PNT products.

3 Deep Learning Methods

Deep learning is a class of machine learning algorithms that [3] use a cascade of multiple layers of nonlinear processing units for feature extraction and transformation. Each successive layer uses the output from the previous layer as input. Build a deep model with many hidden layers. For PNT scenarios simulation and evaluation are usually complicated, we have to use multi-class categorization, which is a kind of boosting method. Compared with binary categorization, multi-class categorization looks for common features that can be shared across the categories at the same time. They turn to be more generic edge like features. During learning, the detectors for each category can be trained jointly. Gradually extract from the bottom to the top form the input-data and establish the mapping from the bottom signal to the higher layer. Eventually improve the classification or prediction accuracy. It can constantly change to learn again for the uncertain problems. In addition, deep learning, independent of human design, is a pattern (feature) that automatically extracts multiple levels of repetition [4, 5].

4 PNT Simulation Verification Platform

4.1 Architecture

The PNT simulation verification platform uses the distributed simulation architecture as the underlying support tool. The platform is extensible and flexible to adapt to the new PNT means of efficient access and can meet the fast and flexible PNT system-level simulation verification, multi-angle assessment and other related applications. The platform can cover the entire system chain, structure is showed in Fig. 1.

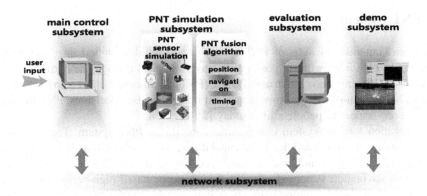

Fig. 1. Architecture of PNT simulation platform

Simulation verification platform includes main control subsystem, PNT simulation subsystem, performance evaluation subsystem, demonstration and display subsystem and network subsystem. The main control subsystem includes operation control and promotion software, scenario planning and simulation software and data logging and parsing software. PNT simulation subsystem includes signal source software and position solution software. The position solution software includes satellite navigation, land navigation, VLBI navigation, star map matching and inertial navigation. Performance evaluation subsystem includes availability accuracy evaluation software and navigation means contribution evaluate software. Demonstration and display subsystem includes demonstration software and projection system. Demonstration software conducts a comprehensive demonstration of the operation control information, scene, and navigation information and evaluation results. Network subsystem includes data exchange control software and statue monitoring software.

The process of PNT full-link simulation verification system are as follows: according to user needs, the main control subsystem determines the scene and the user trajectory, starts the corresponding PNT methods, and transfers user point file data and basic parameters to drive PNT system level simulation. PNT simulation subsystem generates the involved sensor measurement and output sensor analog measurements. Data fusion of original measurement output from different PNT means can achieve integrated navigation, position and timing service. All kinds of data are transmitted through network subsystem. According to the result data and the process data of each part simulation platform analysis performance, including the system availability and accuracy prediction of system level simulation results, contribution degree analysis of the user each navigation means track. The results of the effectiveness evaluation and the system and user related demo and display content in the simulation process are projected and showed.

4.2   PNT Performance Evaluation Method Based on Depth Learning Algorithm

PNT fusion algorithm gets the location and state information of the target by multi-navigation and positioning technology. It includes satellite navigation, inertial navigation, very long baseline interferometry (VLBI) navigation [6], land navigation, visual navigation etc. [2]. Through the fusion analysis method, perceive the physical state of the dynamic target. Provide more accurate data for navigation, trajectory planning and positioning tracking system [3]. Artificial intelligence deep learning method mimics the hierarchical model structure of the human brain. By building a deep model with many hidden layers, gradually extract the characteristic from the bottom to the top of input-data and establish the mapping from the bottom signal to the higher layer. Collect the output data of all kinds of PNT methods used by different types of users in different scenarios. Platform can set parameters according to user characteristics of multi-source PNT methods. Results show that the simulation platform of weight values will affect the comprehensive results. Through deep learning of a large number of data judged by artificial experience, we can make weight value assignment closer to human judgment. Achieve autonomous PNT multi-source fusion. Deep learning enables the allocation of weight values closer to human judgment, thus realizing autonomous PNT multisource fusion.

Compared with the traditional weight coefficient estimation of multi-source navigation means technique, introduce deep learning into the weight coefficient evaluation of the PNT multi-source navigation means technology research. Deep learning with good nonlinear expression ability can better describe the rich internal information of various navigation means and can provide a theoretical basis for effective navigation, position and timing. Multi-feature ability of deep learning can analysis different means of navigation feature space in different scenarios. It also can provide the support for the multiple levels of time and integration. Independent feature extraction ability of deep learning can adapt to different scenes of different means of navigation in different dimensions of the positioning accuracy.

Therefore, the proposal of deep learning provides a valuable opportunity for the study of the integrated evaluation of PNT navigation means large data.

5   Simulation Test of Typical Scene

The platform is verified by two scenarios of deep space exploration and aviation. Scenarios are modeled separately with the aid of STK (Satellite Tool Kits) simulation tools. Under in-depth learning of PNT methods data collected during the task of low earth orbit, medium earth orbit, stationary orbit satellites, the platform achieve parameter settings of multi-source PNT based on user characteristics.

5.1   Aviation Airborne Scenario

There are 4 kinds of PNT means used in aviation airborne: ground-based navigation, inertial navigation, satellite navigation, and satellite based augmentation system. The simulation Table 1 shows the configuration aviation airborne scene, which has 3 phases. During the take-off phase, the aircraft in the scope of action of satellite ground enhanced reference station so that the weight of satellite foundation reinforcement mean is larger. As the flight distance increases, the enhanced reference station loses its effect and other navigation means are used for fusion positioning. Interference sources are set in the coastal area. When the interference source is single interference, the airborne loading into the interference area has anti-interference function (the receiver under test adopts anti-single interference receiver). When the interference source is three, satellite navigation and land-based navigation is not available, this time inertial navigation as the main navigation means. Aviation airborne scene simulation results are shown in Fig. 2.

Table 1. Aviation scenario parameters

Stage	Aircraft parameters	Navigation means	Navigation means main parameters
Take off	Take off speed in 80 m/s; 540 m/s within 100 s;	Satellite carrier phase difference and MEMS inertial navigation	Enhanced station position: longitude: 92.928°, latitude: 39.34° high: 0 km
Fly	540 m/s	Satellite navigation, MEMS inertial navigation	Interference source position: 1. longitude: 109.52°, latitude: 33.531°, power: 30 W 2. longitude: 107.526°, latitude: 32.531°, power: 35 W 3. longitude: 110.373°, latitude: 27.904°, power: 35 W high: 0 km
Land	150 s landing	Satellite navigation, bi-directional range finding subgrade navigation, MEMS inertial navigation	Land station position: 1. longitude: 107.526°, latitude: 32.531° 2. longitude: 113.5736°, latitude: 23.695° 3. longitude: 116.065°, latitude: 23.339° 4. longitude: 115.066°, latitude: 24.982° 5. longitude: 110.688°, latitude: 24.671° 6. longitude: 117.459°, latitude: 24.172° 7. longitude: 114.827°, latitude: 27.778° high: 0 km, power: 26.8 W

Fig. 2. Airborne aerial scenario

5.2 Lunar Exploration Scenario

The lunar exploration satellite mainly uses five kinds of navigation methods: star map matching, VLBI, inertial navigation, satellite navigation and satellite enhancement, including three stages of star rocket separation, earth transition and lunar flight. The lunar exploration satellite scene parameters are shown in Table 2.

Table 2. Deep space scenario parameters

Stage	Satellite parameters	Navigation means	Navigation means main parameters
Star rocket separation	Perigee 200 km, apogee 5100 km	VLBI, star map matching, MEMS inertial navigation	VLBI position: 1. longitude: 116.388° latitude: 39.9289
Earth transition	flight 114 h distance from the 200 km surface of the moon		2. longitude: 102.718° latitude: 25.0389 3. longitude: 121.368° latitude: 31.1094
Lunar flight	A circular orbit with a period of 127 min and a height of 200 km		4. longitude: 102.718° latitude: 39.5 high: 0 km Star map matching information: CCD camera parameters: dimensional pixel N = 256; field angle: 35°; pixel size 10 μm

During the orbit around the Earth, stars and arrows with three times of orbit separate to enter the orbit with a period of 48 h. The satellite is ready to change orbit in perigee into the earth and moon transfer orbit. During the Earth's transitional phase, the satellite is orbited in the perigee and made a midway amendment after 17 h flight, reaching the nearest point of 200 km from the lunar surface. During the phase of lunar orbit, the satellite makes three brakes to close the moon and enter the lunar orbit (Fig. 3).

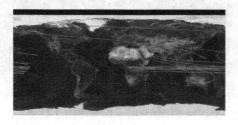

Fig. 3. Lunar exploration satellite scenario

The PNT signal source simulation system includes satellite navigation, satellite enhancement navigation and simulation of various complementary backup navigation methods (inertial navigation, land-based navigation, radio astronomy navigation and star map matching). The software is showed in Fig. 4.

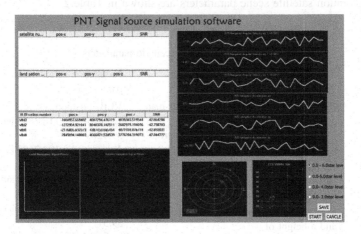

Fig. 4. PNT signal source software

PNT positioning solution simulation subsystem covers alone positioning solution and navigation fusion simulation including satellite navigation, satellite enhancement navigation, radio astronomy, star map matching, and inertial navigation. The results of single-source PNT products and multi-source PNT products can be prepared in the same window. As it showed in Fig. 6, after learning from aviation data collected before, the platform calculate the weight of every PNT methods. INS and BDs are the main PNT method used in airplane (Fig. 5).

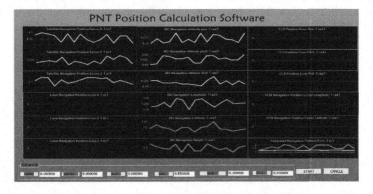

Fig. 5. PNT position calculation software

PNT availability and precision estimation software can evaluate the effect of each PNT methods. The various contribution degree of each PNT means to the user scene is obtained. As it is showed in Fig. 6, when the location of the user is not satisfied with the PNT application conditions, the output of some PNT means is empty.

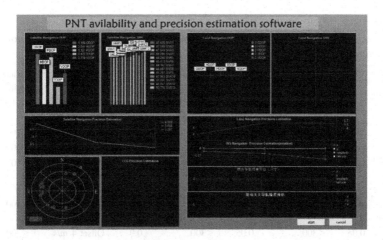

Fig. 6. PNT availability and accuracy estimation software

Table 3. In aviation scenario the influence of the contribution of depth learning error on position results

Stages	Satellite enhance navigation		Satellite navigation		Land navigation		MEMS inertial navigation		Interference source number	Fusion positioning accuracy (m)
	Weight	Positioning accuracy (m)	Weight	Positioning accuracy (m)	Weight	Positioning accuracy (m)	Weight	Positioning accuracy (m)		
Take off	0.1	≤1	–	–	0.9	≤2 (ground station)	–	–	0	≤2
	–	–	0.3	≤6	0.7	≤2 (ground station)	–	–		≤10
	–	–	0.19	≤6	0.8	≤2 (ground station)	0.01	≤80 (calibration in 20 s)		≤6
Fly	–	–	0.89	≤6	–	–	0.11	≤80 (calibration in 20 s)	0	≤6
	–	–	0.89	≤6	–	–	0.11	≤80 (calibration in 20 s)	1 (Anti-interference)	≤6
	–	–	–	–	–	–	1	≤80 (calibration in 20 s)	3 (interference)	Deviation
	–	–	0.95	≤6	–	–	0.05	≤80 (calibration in 20 s)	0	≤5
Land	–	–	–	–	1	≤2	–	–	0	≤2
	–	–	0.15	≤6	0.8	≤2	0.05	≤80 (calibration in 20 s)	0	≤3

Through deep learning algorithm, the input-data can be gradually extracted from bottom to top so that the mapping from the bottom signal to the higher layer can be well established. Depth learning algorithm is adopted to extract the error eigenvalues of available navigation means. The influence of error eigenvalues on multi-source fusion navigation positioning results is analyzed by PNT positioning software. Simulation results is showed in Tables 3 and 4.

Table 4. In deep space scenario scene the influence of the contribution of depth learning error on position result

Stage	VLBI		Star map matching		MEMS inertial navigation		Fusion positioning accuracy (m)
	Weight	Positioning accuracy (m)	Weight	Positioning accuracy (m)	Weight	Positioning accuracy (m)	
Star rocket separation	1	≤100	–	–	–	–	≤100
	–	–	1	≤300	–	–	≤300
	0.1	≤100	0.05	≤300	0.85	≤80 (calibration in 20 s)	≤80
Earth transition	0.15	≤300	0.05	≤300	0.8	Offset 4 m/s increase	≤300
	0.05	≤300	0.05	≤300	0.9	Offset 4 m/s increase	≤300
Lunar flight	0.2	≤1000	0.1	≤300	0.7	Offset 4 m/s increase	≤300
	0.15	≤1000	–	≤300	0.85	Offset 4 m/s increase	≤300

In aerial scenes, without the use of aircraft auxiliary self-sensors at take-off phase, to get a high precision, fusion software adopts land navigation. The comforting thing is that chosen of platform is the same with pilot. With the change of the aircraft scene, the weight of various PNT means in the fusion algorithm also changes. Therefore, through the deep learning of large data, the performance of the automatic calculation method of weight is consistent with the artificial judgment.

In deep space scenario, we can see that the positioning accuracy of star map matching play an important role in the deep space environment far away from the earth. During the fusion process of the three PNT means, the results obtained by the platform algorithm are consistent with the results of the engineers.

6   Conclusion

In this paper, a simulation verification platform is proposed. At the same time, the test results are given, which show that the weight determination method based on deep learning in this platform is consistent with the judges of human brain at present. Through further research and optimization, the platform can be applied to the effectiveness evaluation of the PNT system, the evaluation of the independent running effect of PNT products and so on.

Acknowledgments. Our thanks to Beijing Municipal Science and Technology Commission for supporting us to develop the platform.

References

1. Li, N., Zhang, Y., Xi, H.: Some cognition on the new PNT technology under designed by USA. Satell. Appl. **12**, 34–37 (2015)
2. Zhang, F., Ou, M., Liu, D., Zhen, W.: Future potential PNT review. GNSS World China (2015)
3. Deng, L., Yu, D.: Deep Learning: Methods and Applications (PDF). Foundations and Trends in Signal Processing, P1-200 (2014)
4. Nei, Z., Jia, D.: Overview of research on deep learning. Tech. Innov. Rev. **30**(2), 224–226 (2015)
5. Zhou, G.: Research on Deep Learning Based Image Recognition Application. Beijing University of Technology (2016)
6. Zhu, Y.: Research on Very Long Baseline Interferometry Applied to Precise Orbit Determination. University of Electronic Science and Technology of China (2012)

A Binary Translation Backend Registers Allocation Algorithm Based on Priority

Jun Wang$^{(\boxtimes)}$, Jianmin Pang$^{(\boxtimes)}$, Liguo Fu, Zheng Shan, Feng Yue, and Jiahao Zhang

State Key Laboratory of Mathematical Engineering and Advanced Computing, Zhengzhou 450001, China
wj_xd@foxmail.com, jianmin_pang@126.com

Abstract. As most binary translation systems don't consider the difference of register requirements of basic blocks, which brings redundant memory access instructions caused by unnecessary registers overflow. To solve this problem, a binary translation backend registers allocation algorithm based on priority (BTBRAP) is proposed. Firstly, local global register is allocated statically to reduce the global register maintenance overhead, according to the statistical features of registers on the source platform. Then, the number of every register requested in basic blocks is determined, according to the relationship between intermediate representation and the source platform registers. So the priority of registers allocation is obtained. Conclusively, allocate the registers dynamically based on the priority to reduce the registers overflow. As the test results of nbench, representative recursive programs and SPEC2006 show, the algorithm effectively reduces the redundant memory access of local code, and improves the program performance with an average increase of 7.94%.

Keywords: Binary translation · Register allocation · QEMU · TCG

1 Introduction

Binary translation [1] is a kind of instantaneous compiling technology, whose main goal is to convert an architectural sequence of instructions into another executable sequence of instructions. It has been widely used in software security analysis [2], program behavior analysis [3], software reverse engineering, system virtual etc. And has become one of the mainstream software transplantation technologies. Binary translation can be divided into three parts: frontal decoding, intermediate optimization and backend encoding. The main work of frontal decoding is similar to the disassembly, who separates each source instruction and translates the source executable program into the intermediate code. The intermediate optimization simplifies the intermediate code by analyzing the organization relation of the intermediate code. The common used methods of eliminating redundant code include constant propagation [4], variable activity analysis [5] and condition code optimization [6]. The backend encoding's main work is generating the local target code, who converts the optimized intermediate code into a locally executable code sequence that contains register allocation.

© Springer Nature Singapore Pte Ltd. 2018
H. Yuan et al. (Eds.): GSKI 2017, CCIS 849, pp. 414–425, 2018.
https://doi.org/10.1007/978-981-13-0896-3_41

The purpose of registers allocation is to save the value in the register as many as possible, so as to minimize the number of memory accesses and improve the efficiency of the program. The key point of registers allocation optimization is how to deal with register overflow problem. At present, the main register allocation methods are register graph coloring, linear scanning, and the optimized variants based on the two methods. In binary translation, especially dynamic binary translation, the registers allocation method based on linear scan is the most frequently.

At present, many scholars have paid attention to the registers allocation in binary translation. Alei [7] describes the management and allocation mechanism of QEMU (quick emulator) register in detail, but it doesn't give an effective method to improve it. Wu [8] explains that the intermediate representation reduces the performance of binary translation by comparing experiments when translating ARM programs on X86 platform. The register direct mapping strategy is adopted to improve the translation efficiency. However, this method needs to modify the translation mechanism of QEMU greatly and it is not universal. When Wen [9] translates the PowerPC program on the Alpha platform, he proposes a combination method of segmented mapping and special register clipping, achieved some optimization results, but the register clipping function is more complex and less optimized code. Liao [10] uses the direct mapping strategy when the X86 platform registers are simulated on the MIPS platform. He mapped the 8 general registers of X86 directly to the general register of MIPS, according to the characteristic of the large number of general-purpose registers in the local platform, to reduce the code expansion rate. But the method depends on the specific hardware, meanwhile, the versatility and portability are not very good. Cai [11] proposes a simple register graph coloring method in cross-bit system. Three linked lists are used to collect the reference information of fixed value variables in the method, to construct active variables into a conflict graph. The graph would be restructured if a register overflow is encountered. However, this approach increases translation overhead and improves overall efficiency limitedly. Liang [12] uses a linked list to store the life cycle and usage of variables through analyzing the values and references of variables based on the QEMU intermediate representation TCG (tiny code generator), which reduces the number of intermediate expression instructions. But it needs to traverse many times to collect the fixed value and reference information of variables in the basic block, and the algorithm, with higher complexity, does not have good transplantation.

In this paper, the translation process of QEMU, the relationship between the temporary variables and the registers allocation in TCG intermediate represents was elaborated firstly. Then, the registers allocation mechanism [7] in QEMU was introduced. After that, a binary translation backend registers allocation algorithm based on priority was proposed, with the idea of global register static allocation and local register dynamic allocation [13]. Lastly, the efficiency of the registers allocation algorithm is proved by the experiments.

2 Related Work

QEMU is a widely used dynamic binary translation system. The dynamic translation process of QEMU is shown in Fig. 1. And the work of registers allocation is at the backend decoder of the QEMU translator.

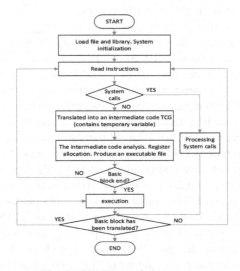

Fig. 1. QEMU translation process

In order to achieve multi-source to multi-objective translation, QEMU uses a machine independent intermediate representation called TCG (short for tiny code generation). With the help of TCG, QEMU can realize the translation from multi-source to target platform just changing the frontal decoder, without changing the backend encoder. The principle of dynamic translator QEMU is to translate the instructions of source system programs into one or more TCG intermediate representations by using semantic equivalence of instruction transformation. Then, the TCG intermediate representation is transformed into one or more instructions of the target platform. So the semantics of the instructions in the two transformations are consistent, and the equivalence of instructions on different platforms is achieved.

TCG instructions is similar to RISC instructions, and also has the instructions of data transfer, arithmetic operation, logic operation, program control instruction and other instructions [14].

The operands of the TCG command are called temporary variables, forming the basis of the TCG intermediate representation, which is the bridge between the source machine instruction operands and the target machine instruction operands. According to the different division of the temporary variable life cycle, TCG defines 4 temporary variable type, common variable, ordinary local variable, global variable and global register variable.

The life cycle of global variable and the global register variable is the whole translation process, whose assigned address is recovered when the program exits. The global register variable is typically allocated a fixed allocation on the host, used to hold the pointer of the source machine CPUState structure, which can accelerate the data reading of source machine status and speed up the program execution. The life cycle of common variable is a basic block, and the variable is marked as release when the block execution is over, to prepare for another basic block. The life cycle of ordinary local variable is a function, and it is necessary to write the basic block execution information back to preserve the data flow information at the end of some basic blocks in the function, which is different from the common variable.

Temporary variable is stored in the static array static_temps in the TCG context. The global variable and global register variable adopt a one-time allocation strategy to establish the runtime environment, and it will not be assigned in the future translation process. For example, the runtime environment ENV of source machine platform, a global variable, is generally represented by global register variable. Common variables and ordinary local variables are dynamically allocated according to the source machine instructions, stored in the back of the array. And the space would be assigned a tag to mark if it is allocated to a variable.

3 Registers Allocation in Quick Emulator

The main object of the registers allocation [15] in QEMU includes two parts: one is the memory virtual registers, and the other is the temporary variables used by the TCG intermediate code. A set of virtual registers is a contiguous memory area, mainly mapped from the source system registers. Take translating x86 code as an example, as shown in Fig. 2.

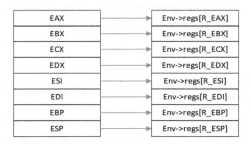

Fig. 2. Map from source register to TCG virtual register

For memory virtual registers, QEMU uses a static direct mapping method, using a fixed binding method to achieve the registers mapping from the source system registers to the local target registers. For example, when the x86 host uses *ebp* register to point to *env*, we can get the whole virtual registers by the offset of *ebp* register.

The temporary variables used in the TCG intermediate code are similar to the virtual registers in the traditional compilers. For translation programs, there is no difference between the temporary variables and the general registers, but its mapping method to the local target registers is more complex.

For the temporary variables used in the TCG intermediate code, its registers allocation is based on a linear scan static fixed allocation mechanism, that is, "first-mean-busy, FMB", allocating the local target registers by the register array index provided by scanning the target system lineally. The specific registers allocation process is as follows: Firstly, determine the range of the registers can be assigned when the intermediate variables need to be allocated local registers, according to the intermediate instruction operation code and the intermediate variable position; Then, traverse from the beginning of the array, a register is assigned and its state will be set *busy* when it is in *idle* state, and the register will be released when the corresponding intermediate variable is released. If all the registers in array is *busy*, then overflow a register as a specified allocation register through traversing the register index array lineally. As the spilled register holds the value of the previous temporary variable, to ensure that the value in the register is not lost, the value in the register needs to be written back into memory when the register is released.

4   The Defects of Registers Allocation Mechanism

According to the analysis of the TCG registers allocation mechanism, the registers allocation of the variables in TCG instruction adopts the priority method, using the number of operands to allocate the priority of registers allocation to make sure every operands can get the register resource when there is registers allocation competition. The registers allocation mechanism between instructions takes a simple linear scan and overflow method, which ignores the optimization of registers allocation among instructions. If registers allocation competition occurs, it's obviously unreasonable to overflow a *busy* register optionally regardless of whether there is an *idle* register or not. As shown in Fig. 3, take translating x86 executable program on Shenwei platform as an example.

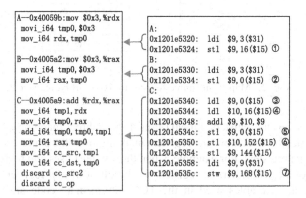

Fig. 3. TCG and local instruction after translation

In Fig. 3, the left is the TCG intermediate code, and the right is the Shenwei local instructions generated after binary translation. Each Shenwei local instruction corresponds to the corresponding intermediate instruction. In the example, the part A and B of the instructions both allocate the local register *$9* to tmp0, and the part C of the instructions allocates the registers *$9* and *$10* to tmp0 and tmp1 respectively. QEMU does not actually consider the different requests of the registers among instructions. And it has done a reply-writing operation before each registers is released in instruction, considering the possible occurrence of registers overflow, which brings redundant memory access instructions ①②③④. These redundancy memory access instructions is produced mainly because QEMU ignores the connection among instructions at the time of registers allocation. Furthermore, if the next instruction or block continue to use the value of *RDX* and *RAX*, the memory access instructions ⑤⑥⑦ is also redundant and can be eliminated.

To reduce the redundancy memory access caused by registers overflow and improve the execution efficiency of local target program, a binary translation backend registers allocation algorithm based on priority (BTBRAP) is proposed, absorbed the idea of global register static allocation and local register dynamic allocation. Firstly, the static global register allocation is performed according to the statistical characteristics of the source x86 used registers to reduce the maintenance overhead of the global register. Then, with the aid of the variable activity analysis, the number of register requested by instruction operands in basic block is analyzed, to reduce unnecessary register overflows in order to reduce the expansion rate of local code and improve the execution efficiency of local target program.

5 BTBRAP Algorithm

The TCG registers allocation mechanism used in QEMU only solves the competition of the operands assignment in the instructions by allocating the optimal register to the operands. But it uses a fixed registers allocation order for the inter-instructions, ignoring the instructions composition of the basic block and the different register requirement among blocks. In fact, the fixed-order registers allocation inter-instructions with the optimal registers allocation in an instruction don't achieve the optimal allocation of registers in the whole basic block or the whole program.

The key to improve registers allocation efficiency is how to minimize the overhead of register overflows. Considering simple direct mapping method, mapping from the most common registers used on the source platform to the register of the local machine directly, can effectively avoid excessive memory access operation and improve the translation program performance, it's useful to get what registers used in x86 program mostly. So, statistics on the usage of registers on x86 platform is carried out. Take Linux-0.2 boot as an example, is shown in Table 1.

Table 1. Register usage statistics on X86 program

X86 general registers	EAX	EBX	ECX	EDX	ESP	EBP	EDI	ESI
Percentage of visits/%	29.6	12.6	8.1	13.3	16.0	4.8	6.5	9.1

Combined the statistical data of registers used in x86 application programs, the most commonly used registers in x86 architecture are *EAX*, *EBX*, *EDX* and *ESP*. When the x86 program is translated to the local target machine, the registers *EAX*, *EBX*, *EDX* and *ESP* can firstly be mapped to the Shenwei registers *$9*, *$10*, *$11* and *$12*. When the *EAX*, *EBX*, *EDX* and *EXP* register is encountered in translation process, the corresponding fixed mapped register *$9*, *$10*, *$11* and *$12* can be used directly, without loading from the virtual memory registers, to improve the efficiency of the program.

On the basis of registers static global allocation, the local dynamic registers allocation is carried out. Firstly, estimate the registers requested by the operands in TCG intermediate instruction within a basic block through the variable activity analysis. Then the registers allocation priority is determined based on the estimated number of requested registers. The larger of the estimated number of the requested register is, the more intense demand to the register of the instructions in the basic block, and the higher priority of the register allocation. A register with the highest priority will be assigned firstly. Relatively, the lowest priority register will be allocated the most slowly of all. Thus, the possibility of residual instructions needs the register to become smaller, which can reduce the possibility of registers overflow and reduce the cost of register overflow. The specific algorithm is shown in Fig. 4.

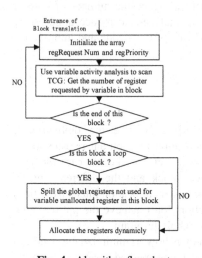

//Function: Get the number of registers requested by variables in this block
//Input: TCG Intermediate representation
Procedure:
GetRegRequestNum(TCGContext *s)
{
    while(op_index > 0)//The number of opcode in this block
    {
        op = gen_opc_buf[op_index]; //Get the opcode
        def = &tcg_op_defs[op]; //Get the operand
        switch(op) //opcode
        {
            case INDEX_op_call:
                nb_iargs = args[0] & 0xffff; //Get the input parameters
                nb_oargs = args[0] >> 16; //Get the output parameters
                Get the number of registers requested according to opcode, input and
                    output parameters, and update the array s->regRequestNum
            case INDEX_op_set_label:
            case INDEX_op_debug_insn_start: Special intermediate instruction,
            case INDEX_op_nopn: no input parameters, such
            case INDEX_op_discard: instruction is not processed

            default:
                nb_iargs = def->nb_iargs;
                nb_oargs = def->nb_oargs;
                Get the number of registers requested according to opcode, input
                    and output parameters, and update the array s->regRequestNum
        }
        op_index--;
    }
}

Fig. 4. Algorithm flowchart   **Fig. 5.** Pseudo-code algorithm

Firstly, TCG, as the link between the frontal decoder and the backend decoder in QEMU, records the number of global variables and basic block jump information in a basic block. On this basis, the registers demand array regRequestNum is added to record the demand registers by TCG variables in basic block. And the registers priority array regPriority is added to mark the priority of every requested registers in basic block. At the beginning of translating each basic block, the two arrays will be initialized.

Then, count the number of the required registers according to variable activity analysis to scan the TCG instructions in basic block linearly. The global variable which has been allocated a register is not treated as a variable, but will be marked *busy*. For other variables, the counter of registers allocation can be completed just through accumulating the regRequestNum corresponding to the required registers in the TCG instructions iteratively. The pseudo code of the iterative accumulation algorithm is shown in Fig. 5.

After that, the register demand array regRequestNum is sorted in descending order. The former position of the variables is, the greater demand of register it is in the basic block. Keeping priority to allocate the forward variables registers can effectively reduce the overhead of register overflow in basic block. If the value is 0, the variable has been assigned a fixed global register or the variable does not need a register.

Thus, the utilization of register can be improved, and the overhead of register overflow will be reduced. Also, the efficiency of the program will be improved.

6 Experiments and Results

The experiments was carried out on the binary translator QEMU. Firstly, use the QEMU to translate the source program to the local target program in the default register allocation mechanism in QEMU. Then, use the QEMU to translate the source program to the local target program in the improved registers allocation mechanism proposed in this paper. Comparing the running time of the translated program, the actual optimization effect of the dynamic and static combined registers allocation algorithm will be evaluated.

Making T_{before} and T_{after} represent the execution time of the local target program translated before the use of registers allocation optimization algorithm and after. Thus, the speedup ratio after the use of the algorithm is:

$$Ratio = \frac{1/T_{after}}{1/T_{before}} - 1 = \frac{T_{before} - T_{after}}{T_{after}}. \tag{1}$$

In the actual tests, the proposed algorithm was evaluated through correctness test, cyclic hot code test, recursive hot code test and overall performance test.

6.1 The Experiment Environment

The target platform: domestic Shenwei platform. The operating system is linux3.8.0. The compiler is gcc-4.5.3.

The source platform: x86 platform. The operating system is linux2.6.29.4. The compiler is gcc-4.6.4.

The test set: nbench-2.2.3, the manual typical recursive algorithm and SPEC2006 set.

6.2   Correctness Test

Firstly, compiled nbench, recursive program and SPEC2006 test set on x86 platform. Then, translated these test sets with QEMU on the domestic Shenwei processor platform, and ran the local executable program. The experimental results are shown in Table 2.

Table 2.   Correct test

Tests	Before optimization	After optimization	Tests	Before optimization	After optimization
NUMERIC_SORT	✓	✓	FIBONACCI	✓	✓
STRING_SORT	✓	✓	QUICKSORT	✓	✓
BITFIELD	✓	✓	MERGESORT	✓	✓
FP EMULATION	✓	✓	N-QUEEM	✓	✓
FOURIER	✓	✓	BZIP2	✓	✓
IDEA	✓	✓	MILC	✓	✓
HUFFMAN	✓	✓	SPECRAND	✓	✓
NUEURAL NET	✓	✓	MCF	✓	✓
LU DECOMPOSITION	✓	✓	LBM	✓	✓

The experimental results show that, the results of the local target program translated before and after optimization is the same as the results executed on the source x86 platform, which indicates that the dynamic and static combined registers allocation algorithm can perform the correct translation. The algorithm can ensure the equivalent translation of the program, with high credibility.

6.3   Cyclic Hot Code Test

The performance test of the cyclic hot code test was mainly completed through the nbench test set. The main function of the nbench test is to evaluate the performance of a system by calculating the cycle iterations of individual test code blocks within a certain time (generally 5 s). Every test block is a typical cyclic hot code, and the functions of the nbench test set is shown in Table 3.

Table 3.   nbench tasks

Test case	Tasks
NUMERIC_SORT	Sorts an array of long integers
STRING_SORT	Sorts an array of strings of arbitrary length
BITFIELD	Executes a variety of bit manipulation functions
FP EMULATION	A small software floating-point package
FOURIER	A numerical analysis routine for calculating series approximations of waveforms
ASSIGNMENT	A well-known task allocation algorithm
IDEA	A text and graphics compression algorithm
HUFFMAN	A relatively new block cipher algorithm
NUEURAL NET	A small but functional back-propagation network simulator
LUDECOMPOSITION	A robust algorithm for solving linear equations

Using the registers allocation optimization algorithm to translate the nbench test to the local target code by QEMU. Compare the execution time on the domestic Shenwei processor, the speedup after optimization is shown in Fig. 6. As shown in Fig. 6, for different nbench test items, the speedup ratio obtained after the registers allocation optimization is also different.

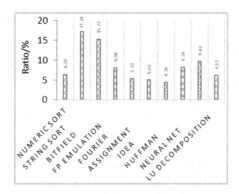

Fig. 6. Speed ratio on cyclic hot code after optimization

6.4 Recursive Hot Code Test and Overall Performance Test

Recursive algorithm is the code that will be executed over and over. In fact, there is a large number of recursive code, which would produce a large number of function calls and return instructions as it has a big number of repeated calls to a single or some functions. At this time, how to deal with the allocation and overflow of registers also directly affects the efficiency of program execution. So some typical recursive algorithms were tested in this paper, and the test results were shown in Fig. 7.

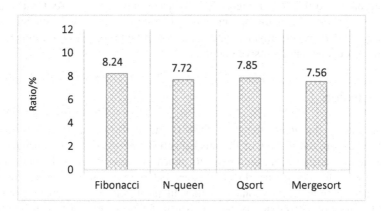

Fig. 7. Speed ratio on recursive algorithms after optimization

The SPEC2006 test set is the program commonly used in our lives. The execution results of SPEC2006 can reflect the overall performance of a translation system. In the actual experiments, some common test applications in SPEC2006 were chosen to be translated to the local target programs by QEMU, to verify the efficiency of the registers allocation optimization algorithm. The performance improvement of these SPEC2006 programs were shown in Fig. 8.

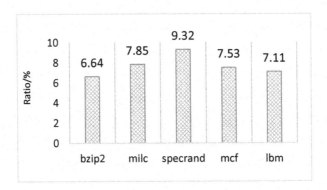

Fig. 8. Speed ratio on part of SPEC2006 after optimization

6.5   Analysis of Experimental Results

Through the tests of different programs, according to the results of Figs. 6, 7 and 8, all local target programs have good performance improvement after improving the registers allocation. Among them, the STRING_SORT and BITFIELD in nbench have the most improved performance, most up to 17.24%.

After the registers allocations optimization, the performance of nbench test items increased 4.35% to 17.24%, improved 8.56% averagely, according to the results of Fig. 6; The performance of typical recursive program test items improved 7.56% to 8.24%, averagely 7.84%, according to Fig. 7; The performance of SPEC2006 test items improved 6.64% to 9.32%, averagely 7.71%, according to Fig. 8. As the test results show, the registers allocation optimization algorithm is effective with an average increase of 7.94% on performance, and it has much better optimization effect for the program with cyclic and recursive code.

7   Conclusion

After introducing the binary translator QEMU and analyzing its TCG registers allocation mechanism, the defects of the mechanism is pointed out in this paper. So, an efficient binary translation backend registers allocation algorithm based on priority was proposed, with the idea of the global registers static allocation and the local registers dynamic allocation in the traditional compiler. In the algorithm, the global registers was allocated statically according to the statistical features of registers used in x86 applications. Considering the difference of registers requirements among the basic blocks, the mapping relationship between the opcode and the local registers was used to count the requested times of local registers in the basic block, and the priority order of local registers was assigned to allocate the registers better dynamically. Lastly, the algorithm was tested by nbench, some classical recursive programs and SPEC2006 programs. The results show that, the registers allocation optimization algorithm can effectively improve the execution efficiency of the local target program. In fact, the algorithm has little dependence on the specific target platform, and has a good cross-platform characteristics.

The study of register allocation, whether for traditional translation or binary translation, it is of great significance to play the performance of CPU better and improve the performance of the program.

References

1. Altman, E.R., Kaeli, D., Sheffer, Y.: Welcome to the opportunities of binary translation. J. Comput. **33**(3), 40–45 (2000)
2. Ma, J., Li, Z., Hu, C., et al.: A reconstruction method of type abstraction in binary code. J. Comput. Res. Dev. **50**(11), 2418–2428 (2013)
3. Chen, J.S., Lan, X.H., Wei, Z.: Software transplant based on instruction simulation. J. Electron. Instrum. Customer (2010)
4. Muth, R.: Register liveness analysis of executable code. Manuscript, Department of Computer Science, the University of Arizona, December 1998
5. Ma, X., Wu, C., Tang, F., et al.: Two condition code optimization approaches in binary translation. J. Comput. Res. Dev. **42**(2), 329–337 (2005)
6. Liang, A., Guan, H., Li, Z.: A research on register mapping strategies of QEMU. In: 2nd International Symposium on Intelligence Computation and Application (2007)
7. Wen, Y., Tang, D., Ql, F.: Register mapping and register function cutting out implementation in binary translation. J. Softw. **20**(2), 1–7 (2009)
8. Liao, Y., Sun Z.G., Jiang, H., et al.: All registers direct mapping method in dynamic binary translation. J. Comput. Appl. Softw. **28**(11), 21–24 (2011)
9. Cai, Z., Liang, A., Qi, Z., et al.: Performance comparison of register allocation algorithms in dynamic binary translation. In: International Conference on Knowledge and Systems Engineering, pp. 113–119. IEEE (2009)
10. Liang, Y., Shao, Y., Yang, G., et al.: Register allocation for QEMU dynamic binary translation systems. Int. J. Hybrid Inf. Technol. **8**(2), 199–210 (2015)
11. Bellard, F.C.: QEMU, a fast and portable dynamic translator. In: Conference on Usenix Technical Conference, p. 41. USE-NIX Association (2005)
12. Jiang, J., Wang, C., Wei, H.: An optimization strategy for local register allocation. J. Comput. Appl. Softw. **12**, 215–217 (2013)
13. Zhang, X., Guo, X., Zhao, L.: Study on TCG dynamic binary translation technique. J. Comput. Appl. Softw. **30**(11), 34–37 (2013)
14. Dai, T., Shan, Z., Lu, S., et al.: Register allocation algorithm of dynamic binary translation based on priority. J. Zhejiang Univ. (Eng. Sci.) **50**(1), 158–165 (2016)
15. Smith, T.F., Waterman, M.S.: Identification of common molecular subsequences. J. Mol. Biol. **147**, 195–197 (1981)

Applications of Geo-Informatics in Resource Management and Sustainable Ecosystem

A New Information Publishing System for Mobile Terminal by Location-Based Services Based on IoT

Li Zhu[1,2,3] and Guoguang Ma[4(✉)]

[1] Hubei Collaborative Innovation Center for High-Efficient Utilization of Solar Energy, Hubei University of Technology, Wuhan, China
julianabiding@126.com
[2] Hubei Key Laboratory for High-Efficiency Utilization of Solar Energy and Operation Control of Energy Storage System, Hubei University of Technology, Wuhan, China
[3] Hubei Power Grid Intelligent Control and Equipment Engineering Technology Research Center, Wuhan, China
[4] Shenzhou Rent Screen (Xiamen) Network Technology Company Limited, Xiamen, China
maguoguang@x-link.com.cn

Abstract. In this paper, a new information publishing system based on Internet of things is proposed. It mainly consists of three parts: the screen side, the service side and the client side. And all of them connect each other by network. The screen side has realized the internet of screens in which geographically dispersed independent screens are connected to the internet by the customized set-top boxes. The server cluster provides high performance application services and manages the promptly increasing multimedia publishing information to users on the service side. Meanwhile MQTT protocol is deployed to implement a lightweight broker-based publish and subscribe messaging mechanism in our constrained environments to solve the bandwidth bottleneck. On the client side, the mobile terminal user can release information with dedicated software by location-based services. The paper has realized a prototype SzIoScreen, and give some related test results.

Keywords: Information publishing system · Location-based services
Internet of things · Screen · Set-top box

1 Introduction

With the popularity of various kinds of display devices such as plasma displays and LED displays, information releasing by screens increasingly be widely used in a variety of scenarios, public service, government agency, education sector, medical system,

L. Zhu—Doctor, Graduate advisor, Wuhan City, 430068, Hubei Province, People's Republic of China.

H. Yuan et al. (Eds.): GSKI 2017, CCIS 849, pp. 429–436, 2018.
https://doi.org/10.1007/978-981-13-0896-3_42

finance industry, hotel service, exhibition hall, for example. It can not only provide timely, comprehensive, high-quality and efficient information services, but also greatly improves a new culture and a beautiful environment, which is the development trend of the building industry in the future [1].

The existing information publishing system can send the text, sound, graphics, images, animation, video and other multimedia information to the terminal display equipment by the servers through public or private networks. It realizes the remote centralized management and updating at any time for the released information. The audience could receive the freshest information in first time. This kind publishing system widely used in all walks of life [2–5]. There are two main types of using forms for the player terminal screens. One is the screens bought directly by enterprises, departments or individuals. These screens have different prices, and some of them even are expensive. The information issue range is very limited, and the information transmission efficiency is relatively low because of the fixed screens' position. The published content is usually monotonous and repeated, and the actual utilization rate of the screens is not high. The other is the screens chosen freely and rent from the owners. This mode greatly reduces the releasing cost, which is the main method of information distribution now. But there are still many problems.

Firstly, the publishers are usually the government organizations or the large-scale enterprises. It has nothing to do with the masses. The published information is less interesting, less attractive and less interaction. Secondly, the widespread of the information is also limited unless the geographically dispersed screens are used. Thirdly, there are a mountain of repetitive operations related to screen renting and information management because the multiple chosen screens always have different owners or belong to different platforms. The more screens, the more work. At last, there is no unified platform for that the screen renters are independent each other and management systems are standalone.

In this paper, a new multimedia information publishing system for Mobile Terminal by Location-based services (LBSs) based on IoT is proposed to solve the industry issues mentioned above. A unified platform is realized to manage screens and release information through connecting geographically dispersed independent screens to the internet by LBSs [6] and adopting the IOT technique [7], MQTT technique [8] and cloud storage technique [9].

2 The New Information Publishing System Architecture

The proposed information publishing system mainly consists of three parts: the screen side, the service side and the client side. And all of them connect each other by network. The whole architecture of information publishing system as shown in Fig. 1. The service side is the core of the whole information publishing system. It maintains the normal operation and upgrade of the platform, providing various services to the users. On the client side, the customers from all walks of life implement related operations of information release by dedicated software. The screens will be identified by separate addresses, managed and connected to the network on the screen side.

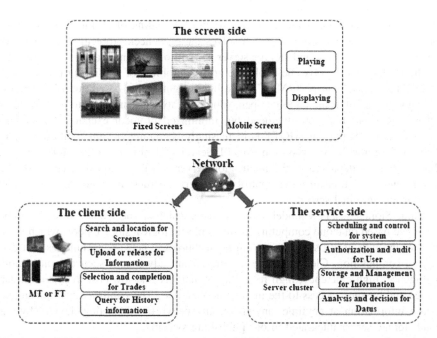

Fig. 1. The block diagram of the information publishing system. It mainly consists of three parts: the screen side, the service side and the client side. And all of them are connected each other by network.

In Fig. 1, the screen side has realized the internet of screens in which geographically dispersed independent screens are connected to the internet by the customized set-top boxes. The server cluster provides high performance application services and manages the promptly increasing multimedia publishing information to users on the service side. Meanwhile MQTT protocol is deployed to implement a lightweight broker-based publish and subscribe messaging mechanism in our constrained environments to solve the bandwidth bottleneck. On the client side, different application client software is designed and applied respectively for the mobile terminal and the fixed terminal.

2.1   The Service Side with Server Cluster

The service side is the core of our multimedia information publishing system based on Internet of things. It is a server cluster system, including application server, MQTT server, database server, cloud storage server, big data server, etc. These servers are mainly used for: (1) system scheduling and control; (2) user information management, authorization and audit; (3) publishing information storage and transmit; (4) big data analysis and decision making.

The application server provides the website services for the users and converts commands from the users into command that can be interpreted and executed by MQTT Client. Database server stores user information, controlling information, etc.

The MQTT server realizes the transmission and forwarding of all kinds of messages that control the screen terminal, which solves the bottleneck problem of the network service bandwidth. The cloud storage server is used to store and manage vast amounts of multimedia data to solve the explosive growth problem of publishing information.

MQ Telemetry Transport (MQTT) is a lightweight broker-based publish/subscribe messaging protocol designed to be open, simple, lightweight and easy to implement. It generates a small transport overhead but minimized protocol exchanges to reduce network traffic. At present, MQTT is increasingly becoming an important component of the IOT protocol. In our system, MQTT Server is deployed on the MQTT server. MQTT Client is deployed in the application server and the terminal screens. MQTT Server filters and transmits the control and query instructions from the application server to the terminal screen.

Cloud Storage is a new model of data storage, which has been a new direction to be developed based on cloud computing. It stores files in logical storage pools which work together through utility software by cluster technology, network techniques and distributed computation. Cloud Storage has significant advantages such as automation, intelligence, high-efficiency, high-reliability, scalability and low cost. It provides data storage and business access to the internet applications. The publisher can upload and release information at anytime, anywhere, any network- connecting devices by the cloud storage server integrated in our publishing system.

2.2   The Screen Side Based on Internet of Things

In order to realize our information publishing system based on the Internet of things, one of the most critical challenges is how to connect all kinds of screens to the Internet. Existing screens are divided into two categories. One is the screens with operating system, such as Internet TV, IPAD, mobile phone, media advertising machine, etc. The other is the screens without operating system, such as LCD monitors, LED screens, and liquid crystal Mosaic TV walls, etc. The former can be directly connected to network using customized software and identified by the information publishing system. The latter has to be connected to the internet by the customized set-top box for that it is only display device.

The customized set-top box is a micro system. It can help the ordinary display becoming an intelligent networking item with some processing capability. The upgraded terminal screens can connect to the internet, play the information and display pictures by customized software. MQTT Client is also configurated in the micro system and perform the control and query instructions from MQTT Server forwarded by the application server.

2.3   The Client Side Based on Location-Based Services

The client side is related closely to the specific applications of the information release system. Its main functions include: define the adoptive network protocols and methods, and realize the corresponding client software. With the rapid development of broadband wireless access technology and mobile terminal technology, mobile internet come into being and the mobile phone becomes the largest internet terminal.

To meet the needs of different occasions, the application client is divided into MT and FT. According to different operating systems, the terminals are divided into Android versions, Apple versions, Microsoft versions, and Linux versions. Among them, MT APP is the most important access mode to our information publishing system. Users can use MT APP to issue multimedia information easily at any time and in any place, even at the moving route. All kinds of the terminals have the same functions, searching for the suitable screens, publishing the relevant information, querying and managing historical information, etc. This system is widely applied to every fields in the modern society, such as education, entertainment, display, military, advertising and public service.

LBSs are IT services for providing information that has been created, compiled, selected, or filtered taking into consideration the current locations of the users or those of other persons or mobile objects. In our system, one of the most important work is the location of the screens, which is directly influences the services price, screen utilization, service efficiency and system performance. So, the screens at different locations are organized managed and searched by map. Figure 2 shows the search interface for the screens in MT APP.

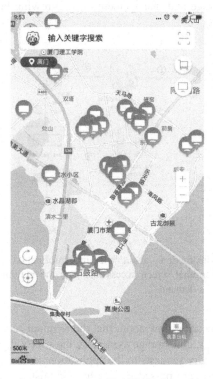

Fig. 2. The search interface for the screens in MT APP. The searching scope can least be limited to a city. User can slide or zoom the map on the phone to search his interesting screens.

The searching scope can least be limited to a city. The blue circles represent the screens available for rent in the picture. User can search his interesting screens by sliding or zooming the map on the phone. Then the user can click on the selected screen and enter some relevant release information. User can also add their own screens information in specific functional modules. The new added screens could been shown in the interface after approval.

3   The Transaction Processing Flow

In our information release system of the Internet of things, the control link of the service requests and the transmission link of the file are separated. In the control link, the application server receives the service request from the user, and then forwards the request to the MQTT server. MQTT server processes the request message and transmit to the terminal screen, which reduces the overhead transmission bandwidth of the network. In the file transmission link, when the corresponding control command is completed, the user directly uploads the multimedia files to the cloud storage system. The terminal screen also directly downloads the multimedia files from the cloud storage system to solve the storage and management of the growing huge amounts of multimedia datum (Fig. 3).

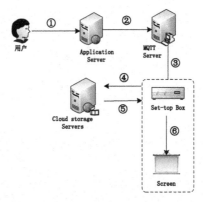

Fig. 3. The users send instructions about releasing information to the externally facing applications server. The terminal screen access and play the multimedia file from the cloud storage system on the user's demand.

The transaction processing flow about that the terminal screen access and play the multimedia file from the cloud storage system on the user's demand is as follows: ① The publishers make service requests to the application server through the MT APP or FT; ② After the requests are passed by system administrator, the application server forwards the service requests to MQTT server via MQTT Client; ③ The MQTT server packages user requests into smaller messages by some filtering rules to the screen terminal; ④ The terminal screen sends data access requests to the cloud storage server according to the list of playlists; ⑤ The cloud storage server verifies the validity of the playlists and establishes the transmission connection. ⑥ The terminal screen obtains the true multimedia files from the cloud storage server. Meantime it completes the broadcast and display of the published information.

4 The Prototype and Test Results

In this paper, a prototype system SzIoScreen for self-service information publishing system is designed. The performance of the server cluster system in it is preliminarily tested. The test environment is as follows: three servers are considered respectively as application server, MQTT server, and database server. They all have dual-core CPU, 4 GB memory, CentOS 7.2 operating system. Application programs and MQTT Client are installed and configured on the application server. Mqtt-broker is installed and configured on the MQTT server. Mysql-community-server is installed and configurated on the database server. Otherwise there are five user computers for making application requests, P4 3. 0G CPU, 2 GB memory, Windows7 operating system.

The performance parameters of the MQTT server are included under different load conditions which gradually increased, such as memory occupancy, CPU utilization, average delay of pushing messages, pushing success rate, etc. A large-scale user simulated on user computers initiate connection requests to the application server. Every user computer can mostly simulate 10000 users, and four user computers can simultaneously participating in the test. The test results are shown in Table 1.

Table 1. Test results of parameters.

Number of connections	CPU utilization (%)	Memory occupancy (M)	Average delay of pushing all messages(s)	Pushing success rate (%)
5000	8.35	16	6.8	100
10000	13.22	23	11.4	100
20000	21.63	47	26.7	100
30000	31.27	72	41.3	100
40000	39.72	96	67.5	100

Table 1 depicts that, all the pushing success rate reached 100%. Single MQTT server is enough to support 50000 connections. The memory occupancy and CPU utilization are all in the acceptable range, which shows the MQTT server has a certain compressive ability and robustness. Furthermore, the average delay of pushing all messages can be accepted. In addition, the files which will be played on the terminal screen will be normally downloaded from the cloud storage server.

5 Conclusion

In this paper, a new information publishing system is proposed, which is composed of three parts: the screen side, the service side and the client side. And all of them connect each other by network. The screen side has realized the internet of screens in which geographically dispersed independent screens are connected to the internet by the customized set-top boxes. The server cluster provides high performance application services and manages the promptly increasing multimedia publishing information to users on the service side. Meanwhile MQTT protocol is deployed to implement a lightweight broker-based publish and subscribe messaging mechanism in our constrained environments to solve the bandwidth bottleneck. On the client side, the mobile terminal user can release information with dedicated software by LBSs.

Acknowledgments. This work was financially supported by the National Natural Science Foundation of China (61471162, 61501178); Science and Technology Research Program of Hubei Provincial Department of Education (Q20171401); Open Foundation of Hubei Collaborative Innovation Center for High-efficiency Utilization of Solar Energy (HBSKFMS2014032); Program of International science and technology cooperation (2015DFA10940).

References

1. Liu, C., Zhao, C.: Research on group enterprise multimedia information publishing system. In: MATEC Web of Conferences, ICMAA 2017, pp. 1–4 (2017)
2. Ji, X.-Y., Xd, Z.: The Design and implementation of teaching aids information publishing system based on glossy display. In: International Conference on Computer Science and Technology, pp. 1134–1141 (2017)
3. Yázici, A., Koyuncu, M., Yilmaz, T., Sattari, S., Sert, M., Gulen, E.: An intelligent multimedia information system for multimodal content extraction and querying. Multimedia Tools Appl. **1**, 1–36 (2017)
4. Zhang, J.: Design and Implementation of Information Distribution System Based on Internet of Vehicles. South China University of Technology (2014)
5. Zhang, X., Wang, C.: The construction of transaction information release system based on WebGIS for house property. Sci. Surv. Mapp. **3**(42), 169–173 (2017)
6. Küpper, A.: Location-based services: fundamentals and operation. JCMS J. Common Mark. Stud. **49**(5), 923–947 (2005)
7. Miorandi, D., Sicari, S., Pellegrini, F.D., Chlamtac, I.: Internet of Things. Ad Hoc Netw. **10**(7), 1497–1516 (2012)
8. Hunkeler, U., Hong, L.T., Stanford-Clark, A.: MQTT-S—A publish/subscribe protocol for Wireless Sensor Networks. In: International Conference on Communication Systems Software and Middleware and Workshops, pp. 791–798 (2008)
9. Zeng, W., Zhao, Y., Ou, K., Song, W.: Research on cloud storage architecture and key technologies. In: International Conference on Interaction Sciences: Information Technology, pp. 1044–1048 (2009)

An Improved Spatial-Temporal Interpolation and Its Application in the Oceanic Observations

Huizan Wang[1,2(✉)], Ren Zhang[2], Hengqian Yan[2], Shuliang Wang[3], and Lei Liu[2]

[1] State Key Laboratory of Satellite Ocean Environment Dynamics, Second Institute of Oceanography, State Oceanic Administration, Hangzhou 310012, China
wanghuizan@126.com
[2] Institute of Meteorology and Oceanography, National University of Defense Technology, Nanjing 211101, China
[3] School of Software, Beijing Institute of Technology, Beijing 100081, China

Abstract. An improved spatial-temporal interpolation method, which can eliminate suspicious interpolated values effectively and consider both direction anisotropy and angle-based weight, is proposed to overcome the insufficiency of the traditional spatial-temporal interpolation. By using the traditional and improved spatial-temporal interpolation respectively, different weekly products of ocean temperature fields from surface to 2000 m are reconstructed in the Pacific Ocean for interpolated test based on the Argo observations, and then the reconstructed products are validated in comparison with other gridded product and in-situ observations. The results show that the error of reconstructed data by the improved method is smaller than that of the traditional method apparently, and the improved interpolation can eliminate the suspicious estimated data effectively and improve the interpolated results greatly. The improved interpolation method is very effective to interpolate scattered data onto regular grids for data reconstruction.

Keywords: Spatial-temporal weighted interpolation · Argo observation
Anisotropy · Data reconstruction · Angle-based weight

1 Introduction

Because of the limitations of the observation instruments and observation environment, continuous and homogeneous observation data are usually difficult to obtain and insufficient to meet the needs of scientific research. Therefore, the reconstruction of

---

Project supported by the National Natural Science Foundation of China (41206002, 41706021 and 41775053), Strategic Priority Research Program of the Chinese Academy of Sciences (XDA 11010103), Jiangsu Natural Science Foundation (BK20151447) and China Postdoctoral Science Foundation (2014M551711).

© Springer Nature Singapore Pte Ltd. 2018
H. Yuan et al. (Eds.): GSKI 2017, CCIS 849, pp. 437–446, 2018.
https://doi.org/10.1007/978-981-13-0896-3_43

uniform gridded fields from irregular observations is of great importance. Since observed sampling is strongly inhomogeneous in time and space, scattered observations should be interpolated with objective methods to provide regular and uniform gridded fields [1–4]. However, in the traditional interpolation of scattered data, the observations within the same temporal bin but at different observed time are often considered as the observations at the same time and then only spatial interpolation is performed [5]. In order to take the observed time into account more reasonably, various types of interpolation methods based on both spatial and temporal weight are proposed to fill in the spatial gaps of observations [5–7].

An objective analysis method, namely spatial-temporal weighted interpolation, was proposed by Zeng et al. [5], which can be used to generate the gridded data from scattered spatial and temporal data. In comparison with the traditional interpolation method (e.g., optimal interpolation and the successive corrections method), there are some advantages in this spatial-temporal method as follows. Firstly, the spatial-temporal interpolation does not require a prior knowledge of the variable. Secondly, the spatial-temporal interpolation is very economical in computation time and thus with the large data base could be used operationally. The spatial-temporal interpolation method has been applied to many data reconstruction aspects [8]. However, there are still some shortages in the traditional spatial-temporal method. It couldn't consider different spatial influence radius for different directions (i.e. isotropy) and also couldn't consider the angle-based density of observations with different azimuths. At the same time, there are also some unreasonable interpolated values such as extrapolated values.

In order to overcome the insufficiency of the traditional spatial-temporal weighted interpolation, an improved spatial-temporal interpolation method is proposed in this study and then interpolated test and comparative analysis are carried out based on the Argo scattered observations. This paper is organized as follows. In Sect. 2, the traditional spatial-temporal weighted interpolation is introduced. Section 3 presents the improved spatial-temporal interpolation. The application of the improved method in Argo gridded data reconstruction and comparative analysis are shown in Sect. 4. Finally, a brief conclusion is given in Sect. 5.

2 Basic Idea of the Traditional Spatial-Temporal Weighted Interpolation

The spatial-temporal weighted interpolation method proposed by Zeng et al. [5] can be used to generate gridded data from scattered data. Suppose the value of one grid point at a certain location with longitude x_g, latitude y_g and time t_g need to be evaluated, the scheme will search for observed values within a horizontal (spatial) influence radius D, and a temporal influence radius T (Fig. 1).

Then the value q_g at (x_g, y_g, t_g) is estimated as a linear combination of the K observed values $q_i(i = 1,\ldots, K)$ found, namely [5, 8]:

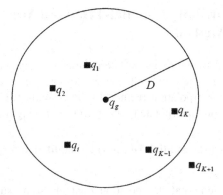

Fig. 1. Schematic diagram of irregularly distributed observations (squares), and a radius of spatial influence D around a grid point g marked with a black circle.

$$q_g = \frac{\sum\limits_{i=1}^{K} w_{i,g} q_i}{\sum\limits_{i=1}^{K} w_{i,g}} \tag{1}$$

$$w_{i,g} = \frac{2 - \left[\frac{d_{i,g}^2}{D^2} + \frac{(t_i - t_g)^2}{T^2} \right]}{2 + \left[\frac{d_{i,g}^2}{D^2} + \frac{(t_i - t_g)^2}{T^2} \right]} \tag{2}$$

$$d_{i,g} = \sqrt{(x_i - x_g)^2 + (y_i - y_g)^2} \tag{3}$$

where $w_{i,g}$ is a weighted function between the point of gridded value (denoted by subscript g) and the ith selected point of observed value q_i within the radius defined by D and T, $d_{i,g}$ is the horizontal distance between them, K denotes the number of selected observations, (x, y, t) denotes their corresponding longitude, latitude and time respectively. The resulting field is slightly sensitive to the choice of D and T. They are selected as the compromise between the desired smoothness of the gridded field and the number of observations in the influence radius. Increasing the two parameters will increase the number of available observations but will result in smoother fields, while decreasing them will produce accurate fields containing more small-scale information but will reduce the number of available observations and generate more missing values in the reconstructed results.

3 Improved Algorithm of Spatial-Temporal Weighted Interpolation Method

Although the traditional spatial-temporal interpolation has many advantages compared with other interpolations, there are still some shortages as is described above. We proposed an improved interpolation method by introducing two processing schemes, i.g., eliminating suspicious interpolated values and improving the interpolated values.

3.1 Eliminate Suspicious Spatial-Temporal Weighted Interpolated Values

The traditional spatial-temporal interpolation contains some suspicious interpolated values. The extrapolation often takes some unreasonable values at the extrapolated points, and thus the spatial or temporal extrapolated gridded values should be identified as suspicious data and then be eliminated.

a. Eliminate the temporal extrapolated gridded value. For some gridded position, if the observations in the temporal influence radius are only located on one side, the gridded value is considered to be suspicious. That is, the condition below should be satisfied: $\max(t_i) \geq t_g, \min(t_i) \leq t_g, i = 1, \ldots, K$.

b. Eliminate the spatial extrapolated gridded value. The value on the grids located outside of influence radius is considered to be suspicious.

3.2 Improve the Interpolated Values

Different Spatial Influence Radii for Different Directions. In the traditional spatial-temporal interpolated method, the spatial influence radius D is uniform both in the meridional and zonal direction [9]. But as we all know, the influence radius often has a different value in the zonal direction than in the meridional one. Let us suppose that the influence radii D are different in different directions, the meridional influence radius is D_y and the zonal influence radius is D_x (Fig. 2). The influence radii in different directions constitutes a closed curve, suppose that the closed curve is an ellipse.

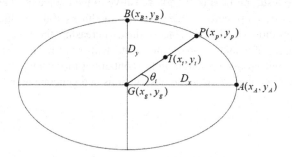

Fig. 2. Schematic diagram of different spatial influence radii for different directions.

In the calculation of weighted value, the value of term $d_{i,g}/D$ should be equal to one in the ellipse, while it should be equal to zero in the point G. The point $I(x_i, y_i)$ is one of the observations. Suppose the values of the term $d_{i,g}/D$ in formula (2) are linearly changed from the point G to be point P. When we consider the different influence radii in different directions, weighted function (2) can be rewritten as:

$$w'_{i,g} = \frac{2 - \left[\frac{(x_i-x_g)^2}{D_x^2} + \frac{(y_i-y_g)^2}{D_y^2} + \frac{(t_i-t_g)^2}{T^2}\right]}{2 + \left[\frac{(x_i-x_g)^2}{D_x^2} + \frac{(y_i-y_g)^2}{D_y^2} + \frac{(t_i-t_g)^2}{T^2}\right]} \tag{4}$$

Let

$$q'_i = q_i \times \frac{w'_{i,g}}{\frac{1}{K}\sum_{i=1}^{K} w'_{i,g}} \tag{5}$$

Note that the weight coefficients have been normalized here. We can think q'_i as the observed value at grid A_i after considering the influence of distance. Following formulas (1), (4) and (5), the estimated value at point G can be represented by the average of $q'_i (i = 1,\ldots,K)$:

$$q_g = \frac{1}{K}\sum_{i=1}^{K} q'_i \tag{6}$$

Consider Different Angles of Observations by Angle-Based Weight. From the algorithm described above, we can find that the estimated value at grid point in the spatial-temporal interpolation method is only simply averaged by q'_i (see the formula (6)), which only considers the distance between the observations and gridded position, but not takes the angle between observations into consideration. However, as we all know, the angle also plays an important role in the interpolation. Apparently, when one observation is very close to the other observations, that is, one's angle is very similar to other's, and then their weighted value should be reduced to avoid redundancy. So if we can consider the spatial distribution density of the observations simultaneously, the interpolation result may be improved. How to consider the angle and quantify its influence on the gridded value? Now we have introduced an angle-based weight to solve it. Figure 3 is taken as a schematic diagram to describe it and deduce the formulas.

In Fig. 3, the observed value at grid A_i is $q'_i (i = 1,\ldots,K)$ and its corresponding angle is θ_i. The angle between two adjacent observations (q'_i, q'_{i+1}) is α_i. Suppose the values between two adjacent observations are linearly changed with angle. The lines joining the points (θ_i, q'_i) and (θ_{i+1}, q'_{i+1}) are straight lines. We can easily find that the weighted mean height of observed values are just the reasonable estimated value at grid G. The area of the polygon under the straight lines between adjacent observations is the

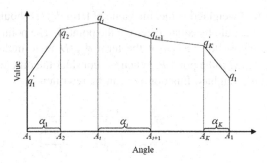

Fig. 3. Schematic diagram of angle-based weight

sum of the trapezoids, the gridded estimated value is equal to the mean height of polygon:

$$q_g = \frac{1}{\sum\limits_{i=1}^{K} \alpha_i} \left[\frac{\alpha_1(q_1' + q_2')}{2} + \cdots + \frac{\alpha_i(q_i' + q_{i+1}')}{2} + \cdots + \frac{\alpha_K(q_K' + q_1')}{2} \right] = \sum_{i=1}^{K} \left(q_i' \times \frac{\gamma_i}{2\pi} \right)$$

(7)

where

$$\gamma_i = \begin{cases} \frac{\alpha_1 + \alpha_K}{2}, & i = 1 \\ \frac{\alpha_i + \alpha_{i-1}}{2}, & 2 \leq i \leq K \end{cases}$$

(8)

According the above analysis and formula derivation, we have obtained the improved spatial-temporal interpolation method, which can get more appropriate and accurate gridded value from observations by using formulas (4), (5), (7) and (8).

4 Application of the Improved Spatial-Temporal Interpolation Method to the Oceanic Data Reconstruction

4.1 Data and Reconstructed Procedure

In order to validate the effect of the proposed method, Argo profiles in the Pacific Ocean for the period from January 2004 to April 2010 were used for interpolated test. Argo floats are free-drifting over the upper ocean, their drift trajectories are irregular, which mainly depend on the local ocean currents [10]. As the horizontal positions of Argo floats are very scattered, it is very important to reconstruct the Argo gridded product. Three dimensional weekly temperature products were reconstructed by spatial-temporal interpolation based on the Argo temperature profile observations in this paper. The spatial resolution of reconstructed products is 1° × 1°; area coverage is 120.5°E-89.5°W, 89.5°S-60.5°N. We carry out an extra quality control to check the position of profile and do the spike test [10]. The Argo temperature profile data were linearly interpolated to 36 vertical standard levels.

The improved spatial-temporal weighted interpolation method introduced in the Sect. 3 is an objective analysis method for irregular spatial and temporal observed data. The scattered Argo temperature data at each standard level can be interpolated into regular weekly gridded products by the spatial-temporal weighted interpolation method described in Sects. 2 and 3. In the present study we adopted 5° and 3° for the values of D in the zonal and meridional directions, respectively, which are similar to the values adopted by Wang et al. [9] and Kubota et al. [11]. As we mainly focus on the improvement of improved interpolation in this paper, the selection of influence radius didn't discuss in detail here.

4.2 Validation of the Improved Spatial-Temporal Interpolation with Anisotropy and Angle-Based Weight

The in-situ daily temperature data from the Tropical Atmosphere Ocean (TAO) observations [12] are used in an independent check for the reconstructed fields. In order to validate the effect of reconstructed data by considering anisotropy, the mean absolute errors (MAE) between the three reconstructed temperature data (i.e., the traditional interpolations with $D = 3°$, the traditional interpolations with $D = 5°$ and the improved interpolation with $D_x = 5°$ and $D_y = 3°$) and TAO observations at different depths are shown in Fig. 4a.

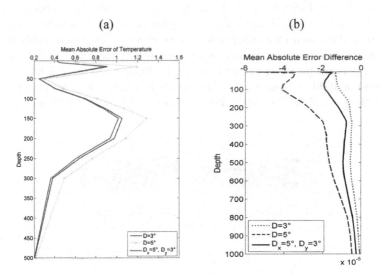

Fig. 4. (a) MAE between the reconstructed temperature data and TAO observations. (b) Difference of MAE between angle-dependent weight and angle-independent weight.

It can be seen clearly that the MAE of the reconstructed product made by the improved interpolation with $D_x = 5°$ and $D_y = 3°$ is smaller than those by the traditional interpolations with both $D = 3°$ and $D = 5°$ in comparison with the TAO observations on the whole, which shows that the improved interpolation based on anisotropy is more effective for data reconstruction. These results show that the reconstructed product considering anisotropy can produce better the interpolation results than that considering isotropy.

In order to further validate the reconstructed data considering angle-based weight, we estimate the temperature values in the original scattered positions from the reconstructed Argo products both angle-dependent weight and angle-independent weight method, and then calculated the errors between the estimated values and observations. Figure 4b shows the difference of MAE between angle-dependent weight and angle-independent weight and their corresponding numbers for computing comparative errors at different depths. The values of angle-based weight minus angle-independent weight at different depths are negative on the whole, which means that the MAE of angle-weighted method is smaller than those angle-independent weight method. These comparative results show that the reconstructed products based on angle-dependent weight perform better than those based on angle-independent weight.

4.3   Comparison the Reconstructed Gridded Data with WOA09 Data

The annual mean World Ocean Atlas 2009 (WOA09) temperature climatology is used in an independent check for the reconstructed fields by improved method. The reconstructed annual climatology was calculated by averaging the temperature data of 330 weeks for each spatial point. Figure 5 compares the reconstructed product and annual WOA09 annual mean temperature at 10 m and 1000 m. Generally the large scale features in temperature for our product are well defined. The spatial correlation coefficient between the reconstructed product and WOA09 can reach 0.9991 at surface and 0.9984 at 1000 m, respectively. The root mean square errors between the reconstructed product and WOA09 are 0.458 at surface and 0.0562 at 1000 m.

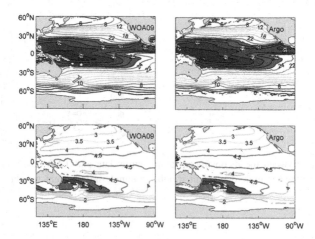

Fig. 5. Annual mean temperature climatology at 10 m (top) and 1000 m (bottom). (a): WOA09 data; (b): Reconstructed Argo data.

5   Conclusion

In this study, we propose an improved spatial-temporal interpolation which can improve the interpolation results effectively. Against the insufficiency of the traditional interpolation method, the main advantages of improved interpolation method are as below: (1) it can eliminate some suspicious values and remain the reliable values; (2) it can consider direction anisotropy, that is, the meridional influence radii can be different from the zonal influence radii; (3) it can improve interpolation result by considering the different azimuths of observations based on angle-dependent weight.

To investigate the reliability of improved spatial-temporal interpolation, we have compared the gridded products with WOA09 data, TAO, which shows that the improved reconstructed product is very reliable and the error of the product reconstructed by the improved spatial-temporal interpolation method is smaller than that of the products reconstructed by the traditional interpolation method in total. Therefore, the improved interpolation method is very economical in computation time and effective to interpolate scattered data onto regular grids for data reconstruction.

Acknowledgments. The Argo data used in this paper were collected and made freely available by the International Argo Program. Discussion with Prof. Wang Guihua at Fudan University is appreciated.

References

1. Li, D., Wang, S., Li, D.: Spatial Data Mining: Theory and Application. Springer, Heidelberg (2016). https://doi.org/10.1007/978-3-662-48538-5
2. Wang, H.Z., Zhang, R., Liu, W., Wang, G.H., Jin, B.G.: Improved interpolation method based on singular spectrum analysis iteration and its application to missing data recovery. Appl. Math. Mech. **29**, 1351–1361 (2008)
3. Wang, H.Z., Zhang, R., Wang, G.H., An, Y.Z., Jin, B.G.: Quality control of Argo temperature and salinity observation profiles. Chin. J. Geophys. **55**(2), 577–588 (2012)
4. Wang, H.Z., Zhang, R., Liu, K., Liu, W., Wang, G.H., Li, N.: Improved Kriging interpolation based on support vector machine and its application in oceanic missing data recovery. In: International Conference on Computer Science and Software Engineering, pp. 726–729. IEEE Computer Society (2008)
5. Zeng, L., Levy, G.: Space and time aliasing structure in monthly mean polar-orbiting satellite data. J. Geophys. Res. **100**(D3), 5133–5142 (1995)
6. Patoux, J., Levy, G.: Space-time interpolation of satellite winds in the tropics. J. Geophys. Res. Atmos. **118**(18), 10–405 (2013)
7. Levy, G., Brown, R.A.: A simple, objective analysis scheme for scatterometer data. J. Geophys. Res. **91**(C4), 5153–5158 (1986)
8. Zhang, H.-M., Bates, J.J., Reynolds, R.W.: Assessment of composite global sampling: sea surface wind speed. Geophys. Res. Lett. **33**, L17714 (2006). https://doi.org/10.1029/2006GL027086
9. Wang, G., Zhang, R., Chen, J., Wang, H., Wang, L.: The correlation length-scale optimized by baroclinic Rossby radius of deformation and its improvement to optimum interpolation. Acta Oceanologica Sinica (in Chinese) **36**(1), 109–118 (2014)

10. Wang, H.Z., Wang, G.H., Chen, D., Zhang, R.: Reconstruction of three-dimensional pacific temperature with argo and satellite observations. Atmos. Ocean **50**(sup1), 116–128 (2012)
11. Kubota, M., O'Brien, J.J.: Variability of the upper tropical pacific ocean model. J. Geophys. Res. **93**(C11), 13930–13940 (1988). https://doi.org/10.1029/JC093iC11p13930
12. McPhaden, M.J.: The tropical atmosphere ocean array is completed. Bull. Am. Meteor. Soc. **76**, 739–741 (1995)

The Spatial-Temporal Simulation of Mankind's Expansion on the Tibetan Plateau During Last Deglaciation-Middle Holocene

Tianyun Xue[1(✉)], Changjun Xu[2,3], and Sunmei Jin[4]

[1] The Second Surveying and Mapping Institute of Qinghai Province,
Xining 810001, Qinghai, China
709462217@qq.com
[2] Geomatics Technology and Application Key Laboratory of Qinghai Province,
Xining 810001, China
[3] Provincial Geomatics Center of Qinghai, Xining 810001, China
[4] School of Life and Geographic Science, Qinghai Normal University,
Xining 810000, China

Abstract. Attributed by vast territory, extremely harsh physical environment, and comparatively integrated geographical unit, the Qinghai-Tibet Plateau has become a valuable site to investigate adaptation regime of prehistoric human to extreme environment. Which is currently focused on single dependent site in most studies, where a integrated research that coves complete scope the plateau is needed. to better understand expansion logic of prehistoric human moving towards the Plateau. This paper build a comprehensive index to indicate the characteristics of natural environment by using GIS software, which is composited with elevation, vegetable type, level of river system, and accumulated temperature of 0 °C etc., combined with the archaeological ages of 69 gathered microlithic sites, followed by environmental adaptation and spreading hypothesis, namely the doctrine of the time of human expansion was broadly consistent in the regions where the natural environments were similar. We simulated the spatial and temporal process of prehistoric human's migration and expansion on the plateau during Last Deglaciation- Middle Holocene. The results of our study indicated that during the Last Glacial Maximum(24–16 ka B.P., LGM), human activities were very weak, which is mostly likely distributed in the Huang River Valley area of northeastern margin of Tibet Plateau and Yarlung Zangbo River valley of southern Tibet, where elevation was 1,640 m on average; During 15–13 ka B.P., the microlithic hunter-gatherer activities became strong, which had expanded to Qinghai Lake-Gonghe basin of the northeast of Tibet Plateau, and Hengduan Mountains valleys in the east, where elevation was 2,800 m on average. The area of activity region accounted for 5.5% in the Tibet Plateau. Also, during the periods of 13–11 ka B.P., prehistoric human expanded towards higher zones along the valleys of Yellow River, Ya-lung River, Yangtze River and Yarlung Zangbo River, where elevation was 3,658 m on average, the increased expansion area accounted for 11.4% in the Tibet Plateau. The expansion was relatively obvious; During 11–9 ka B.P., with the rapid improvement of environmental conditions, hunter-gatherers expanded to the principal part of the Tibet Plateau. The elevation of expansion area was 3,971 m on average. The increased expansion area accounted for 11.5% in the Tibet Plateau. During 9–7 ka B.P., the human expansion speed was the fastest. During the periods, the expansion area was wide, and the area was maximum in the period. Human activities rapidly expanded to the hinterland of the Tibet Plateau, including the northern Tibet Plateau, the source regions of the Yangtze and Yellow Rivers and Kunlun Mountains. Many regions among them were depopulated zones nowadays. But the locations where some microlithic sites were found, The increased expansion area accounted for 52.2%, in the Tibet Plateau during 9–7 ka B.P. The elevation of expansion area was 4,700 m on average during the periods. And the expansion and occupation of prehistoric human towards the Tibet Plateau was basically completed by then. But regions (accounting for 19% of the plateau) with extreme environmental conditions, such as cold mountain area, desert plateau in Northern Tibet, salt desert in Qaidam Basin had not been occupied. Migration and expansion of prehistoric human towards Tibet Plateau in prehistoric period occurred multiple times. The human expansion during 15–7 ka B.P. was oriented by hunter-gatherers, which happened from the west to the east, from low to high, from the margin to the principal part of Tibet Plateau. The environmental evolution acted as important driver of hunter-gatherers expansion towards the Tibet Plateau during the Last Deglaciation- Middle Holocene. Yellow River and Yangtze River valleys were important passages of prehistoric human expansion towards the Tibet Plateau.

Keywords: Tibet Plateau · Hunter-gatherer · Expansion simulation

1   Introduction

The Qinghai-Tibet Plateau is known as the "roof of the world", with an average elevation of 4400 m, the highest plateau in the world, increasing altitude, oxygen pressure is reduced, For example, at an altitude of 4270 m, the oxygen pressure is only 58% of the sea level, the human body will lead to significant hypoxia [1]; The Qinghai-Tibet Plateau dry and cold climate variability, strong radiation, is one of the world's most extreme harsh environment of the region. Predecessors in the Qinghai-Tibet Plateau widely discovered Paleolithic and microlithic sites, indicating that of the late in the Late Pleistocene human beings have set foot on the plateau [2–5]. In recent years, because of global warming and other climate crises and environmental problems, to promote human thinking about global changes and human response and adaptation, The Qinghai-Tibet Plateau is undoubtedly a test of the human face of extreme harsh environmental response and adaptation model, especially prehistoric human migration and expansion in the Qinghai-Tibet Plateau process and power by the scientific community of widespread concern [6].

2 Data and Method

2.1 Data

The data used in this paper are from the National Earth System Science Data Sharing Platform (http://www.geodata.cn); Including: the Qinghai-Tibet Plateau range and boundary data; China 1000 m resolution DEM (2000); China 1: 250,000 Grade 1, 3, 4 and 5 River Classification Data sets (2002); China 1:10 million lake database (2000); China 1:10 million desert (sand) distribution map. Vegetation data for the Chinese Academy of Sciences Resources and Environment Science Data Center of China 1 million vegetation type spatial distribution data (http://www.resdc.cn/data.aspx?-DATAID=122); accumulated temperature of 0 °C using the Chinese Academy of Agricultural Sciences Agricultural Natural Resources and Agricultural Planning Institute completed the Chinese ecological environment background level temperature and humidity data level construction database.

2.2 Method

In this paper, the geographical factor - combined with the archaeological ages of sites, methods to simulate the hunter-gatherer population migration and expansion to plateau.

(1) Geographic factors and natural environment comprehensive index

The natural environment of the Qinghai-Tibet Plateau is constructed by means of the reclassification and grid calculator tools in the spatial analysis of ARCGIS, which are based on different geographical factors, such as altitude, vegetation type, water level (river and lake), ≥ 0 °C accumulated temperature Comprehensive index, used to characterize the comprehensive situation of the natural environment of the Qinghai-Tibet Plateau, in order to overcome the shortcomings of a single indicator of the lack of representation. Take the elevation as an example: the human into the Qinghai-Tibet Plateau, first faced with the increase in oxygen content with elevation; In general, the elevation of 1600–2400 m, the body may be hypoxia reaction, but the basic normal, the reaction is not obvious; Altitude of 3000–3600 m or more, the body's hypoxia significantly, if there is a reasonable altitude ladder and enough time to gradually adapt; More than 4500 m above sea level, atmospheric pressure near the sea level of 1/2 when the human body appears obvious hypoxemia, and cause significant physiological response and a series of clinical problems; higher than 5500 m above, the body function will be a serious decline, some damage will not be recovery, mankind will not be able to adapt with the long-term survival [1]. According to this can be assigned to the elevation of 0–9 (Table 1), known as the altitude index, the following similar, the lower the assignment, the more difficult to adapt and survival.

According to AHP analytic hierarchy process [7], altitude (0.296), river-lake (0.17), vegetation (0.205), ≥ 0 °C accumulated temperature (0.169) and longitude factor (0.16) according to the importance of each factor. Build the relationship:

Table 1. The classification and evaluation of geographical factors

Typical vegetation types	Evaluation	Altitude/m	Evaluation	River
Temperate deciduous shrub	9	<1600	9	1–5
Temperate grass, miscellaneous grass meadow grassland	8	1600–2000	8	1–7.5
Temperate coniferous forest, subtropical and tropical mountain coniferous forest, temperate deciduous leaflets	7	2000–2400	7	1–10
Subtropical coniferous forest, broad-leaved mixed forest, temperate deciduous broad-leaved forest	6	2400–2800	6	3–5
Cold temperate and temperate mountain coniferous forest, alpine meadow and so on	5	2800–3200	5	3–10
Subtropical evergreen broadleaved forest	4	3200–3600	4	4–5
Subtropical hardwood evergreen broad-leaved forest	3	3600–4100	3	4–10
Tropical rain forest and so on	2	4100–4600	2	5–5
Low semi-arbor desert, shrub desert, cushioned dwarf half shrub alpine desert Alpine sparse vegetation and so on	1	4600–5500	1	5–10
Alpine swamp, desert, bare land, snow, salt and so on	0	>5500	0	>10
Typical vegetation types	Evaluation	Accumulated temperature of 0 °C/°C	Evaluation	Longitude/°E	Evaluation
Temperate deciduous shrub	9	≥6500	9	101.8–105.0	9
Temperate grass, miscellaneous grass meadow grassland	8	5300–6500	8	98.6–101.8	8

(*continued*)

Table 1. (*continued*)

Typical vegetation types	Evaluation	Accumulated temperature of 0 °C/°C	Evaluation	Longitude/ °E	Evalu-ation
Temperate coniferous forest, subtropical and tropical mountain coniferous forest, temperate deciduous leaflets	7	4200–5300	7	95.4–98.6	7
Subtropical coniferous forest, broad-leaved mixed forest, temperate deciduous broad-leaved forest	6	3500–4200	6	92.2–95.4	6
Cold temperate and temperate mountain coniferous forest, alpine meadow and so on	5	2000–3500	5	89.0–92.2	5
Subtropical evergreen broadleaved forest	4	1500–2000	4	85.8–89.0	4
Subtropical hardwood evergreen broad-leaved forest	3	1000–1500	3	82.6–85.8	3
Tropical rain forest and so on	2	800–1000	2	79.4–82.6	2

(*continued*)

Table 1. (*continued*)

Typical vegetation types	Evaluation	Accumulated temperature of 0 °C/°C	Evaluation	Longitude/ °E	Evalu- ation
Low semi-arbor desert, shrub desert, cushioned dwarf half shrub alpine desert Alpine sparse vegetation and so on	1	500–800	1	76.2–79.4	1
Alpine swamp, desert, bare land, snow, salt and so on	0	<500	0	73.0–76.2	0

*Vegetation types are only selected typical representative list, the river classification meaning 5–10: 5 on behalf of the river level, 10 on behalf of the distance within the river 5–10 km range, the same with the same.

$$I = 0.296 * H + 0.17 * R + 0.205 * P + 0.169 * T + 0.16 * L \tag{1}$$

In the formula, I is the comprehensive index of the natural environment of the plateau (hereinafter referred to as the environmental index), H is the altitude index, R is the hydrological index, P is the vegetation index, T is ≥ 0 °C accumulated temperature index, L is the longitude index. Environment index higher, it means more suitable for survival, the more easily enter and occupation.

(2) The age of grinding stone sites

At present, more than 100 grinding stone sites are found in the Qinghai-Tibet Plateau, mainly for the gathered microlithic sites, and some of them have been scientifically appraised. This article focuses on the earlier sites in the region, the earlier years of the site. Identify the same or similar environmental index areas in earlier generations, with human occupation and approaching time roughly the same or close. According to the earliest years of regional relics, and environmental indicators to do the relevant analysis and regression, and the environmental index classification of 15 ka B.P., 13 ka B.P., 11 ka B.P., 9 ka B.P. and 7 ka B.P. was determined according to this regression relationship.

3 Results

3.1 Environmental Factor Classification

According to the environmental factors of the Qinghai-Tibet Plateau elevation, river, vegetation and ≥ 0 °C accumulated temperature, it can be seen from Fig. 1 that the elevation is decreasing from east to west and from the southeast to the northwest. River grading shows a distinct eastern high and low western features; Vegetation grading is characterized by high coverage in the northeastern part of the plateau and the south, the central part of the north, the poor pattern of the north; The accumulation temperature in the southern part of the Qinghai-Tibet Plateau is the highest, indicating that the heat conditions are better and gradually decrease from the edge of the plateau to the inside.

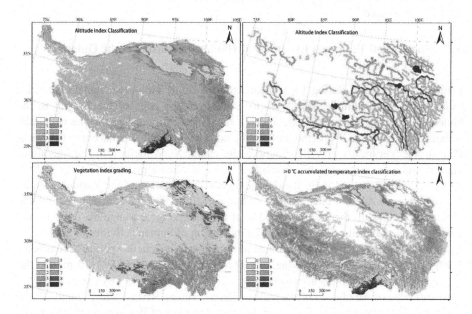

Fig. 1. The index grade of environmental factors on the Tibet Plateau

3.2 The Relationship Between Environmental Index and Ages of Sites

The environmental factors were graded according to the formula (1), and ages of typical ruins was compared with the environmental index (Table 3). It is found that there are some changes in the age of the LGM $\sim$ Middle Holocene, the typical ruins and the environmental index, that is, the higher the environmental index, the relatively old sites, in other words, the more suitable the environment, the earlier the human activity; The LGM sites are distributed in the area of environmental index >7; The Last Deglaciation appeared in the northeastern and eastern parts of the Qinghai - Tibet Plateau with high altitude, and the environmental index was 6.0–4.5. At the beginning of the Holocene, the environmental index is about 3.5, and the environmental index of the early and middle of the Holocene is between 2 and 4. Using the environmental index of the typical ages of ruins and the environmental index of the region, the establishment of relations between the two polynomial regression:

$$I = 6 \times 10 - 8Y2 - 0.0009Y + 6.7443 \qquad (2)$$

Where I is the environmental index, Y is the age, the relationship R2 is 0.928. In the regression analysis, the sample size is too small to reveal the statistical relationship between things and phenomena. Blind pursuit of large sample size, will increase the unnecessary data collection costs, may also cause data on the conflict and interference, but not conducive to the resulting statistical laws. It is pointed out that the early human activities of the Qinghai-Tibet Plateau are still relatively weak and the sites of the scientific dating are limited by various conditions. Therefore, the relationship (2) can be used as a reference.

3.3   Spatial and Temporal Evolution of Human Expansion in the Qinghai Tibet Plateau

Figure 2 can be seen during Last Deglaciation- Middle Holocene, human activities from low to high altitude, from east to west, from the edge of the plateau to the hinterland continue to expand. Specifically, the plateau did not find the site of human activities during the LGM period, only in the northeastern margin adjacent to the Loess Plateau, the Yellow River valley found a site called XiaWangjia [28], but the simulation results show that the lower reaches of the northeastern margin of the Yellow River valley, and located in the southern Qinghai-Tibet Plateau of the Yarlung Zangbo Valley, does not rule out the existence of human activities in the period, but the scope of activities is small, the area is only 1% of the plateau area, Range 62–3180 m, the average activity elevation of 1640 m. The expansion of human activities in the last ice age (15–13 ka BP) is obvious. The range of human activities in this period accounts for 5.5% of the whole plateau area, the simulated expansion area is 88–4179 m, and the average activity elevation is also increased to 2800 m; Human activity expanded to the northeast edge of the plateau of the Yellow River - Huang River Valley, Qinghai Lake basin, the Republican basin, Tao River and upper reaches of Bai Longjiang valley, the eastern plateau and Hengduan mountain valleys, while the Yangtze River and the Lancang River may become an important channel into the hinterland of the Qinghai-Tibet Plateau; The activities of the southern part of the Qinghai-Tibet Plateau also expanded rapidly, and the whole of southern Tibet could be expanded by human beings and could enter the hinterland of the plateau along the Yarlung Zangbo River. During 13–11 ka B.P. human activities in the previous foundation has a certain expansion, the new expansion area of 11.4% of the plateau, but the expansion area is limited, and may along the river (including the Yellow River, Yarlung Zangbo River, Yangtze River, Brahmaputra) to the upstream Expanded; Altitude range of 1202– 5254 m, the average elevation increased to 3658 m. 11 to 9 ka B.P. The expansion of human activities is limited and the expansion range is similar to that of the previous period. The new expansion area accounts for 11.5% of the plateau, mainly concentrated in the northeast and east of the plateau, and slightly expanded on the original basis. But the period is the human to get rid of the elevation of 3000–4000 m, to 4000 m into the critical period, to achieve the main body into the plateau across the expansion area in the range of 1693–5946 m, the average elevation of human activities 3971 m. 9–7 ka B.P., the rapid expansion of human activities to the hinterland of the plateau, the new expansion area increased rapidly, reaching 52.2% of the plateau area, the altitude range of 2450–6605 m, the average elevation of the expansion area reached 4700 m; Including the northern Tibet Plateau, the Qinghai-Tibet Plateau hinterland of the Yangtze River - the Yellow River source area, Kunlun Mountains and other more harsh environment; But the alpine mountain, the Tibetan plateau desert, the Qaidam Basin salt desert zone and other areas of the environment is not difficult to survive (about 19% of the plateau area, these areas are also no mana area); Can be found in some of these expansion areas for today's no man's land, also found some microlithic sites, the discoverer is speculated that the early Holocene remains [32]; Therefore, the period since the Last Deglaciation is the most significant expansion, the largest expansion of the area of the period, bringing the human race has basically completed the March with the expansion of the Qinghai-Tibet Plateau.

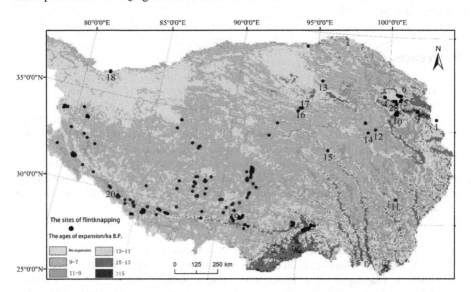

Fig. 2. The spatial-temporal simulation of mankind's expansion and chipped - microlithic sites on the Tibetan Plateau during Last Deglaciation-Middle Holocene

1. Xiawangjia [8] (17.4 ka B.P.), 2. JXG1 [9] (14.6 ka B.P.), 3. HZYC1 [10] (13.5 ka B.P.), 4. HMH1 [11] (13.1 ka B.P.), 5. 10HTHS [10] (12.3 ka B.P.), 6. BWC3 [10] (12.1 ka B.P.), 7. GH1 [10] (11.2 ka B.P.), 8. YWY1 [10] (8.6 ka B.P.), 9. SLK [10] (8.3 ka B.P.), 10. LYH [12] (7.6 ka B.P.), 11. Luhuoxialatuo [13] (13.5 ka B.P.), 12. Xiadawu1 [14] (11.2 ka B.P.), 13. XCD [15] (9.2 ka B.P.), 14. NZH [16] (8.5 ka B.P.), 15. Canxionggashuo [17] (8.0 ka B.P.), 16. Bison ditch [18] (7.6 ka B.P.), 17. XDT2 [7] (6.4 ka B.P.), 18. YC [10] (7.4 ka B.P.), 19. CS [10] (8.4–7.4 ka B.P.), 20. UYT sites [16] (6.6 ka B.P.).

4 Conclusion

During the period of LGM, the area and scope of human activities in the plateau were very limited, accounting for less than 1% of the plateau area, which was confined to the valley of the northeastern margin of the plateau and about 1640 m above sea level in southern Tibet. 15–13 ka B.P., hunting activity began to be active, human activities expanded to the northeast and east of the plateau, the expansion area accounted for 5.5% of the plateau, the average activity elevation of 2800 m; 13–11 ka B.P. expansion significantly, the expansion area of 11.4% of the plateau, the average elevation of 3658 m expansion area; 11–9 ka B.P. human began to altitude 4000 m plateau into the new expansion area accounted for 11.5% of the plateau, the expansion area average elevation of 3971 m; 9–7 ka BP to the hinterland of the plateau to further expand, this period is the Last Deglaciation- Middle Holocene expansion of the most rapid period, the new expansion area reached 52.2% of the plateau, including today's no man's plateau Regions have been expanded, But the conditions are extremely harsh alpine mountain, the Tibetan Plateau desert, Qaidam Basin salt desert zone, in the period has not been occupied.

References

1. Wu, T.Y.: J. Med. Res. **35**(10), 1–2 (2006). (in Chinese)
2. Tang, H.S.: Archaeology **5**, 44–54 (1999). (in Chinese)
3. Madsen D.B., Perreault, C., Rhode, D.: Early foraging settlement of the Tibetan Plateau highlands. Archaeol. Res. Asia **11**, 15–26 (2017). https://doi.org/10.1016/j.ara.2017.04.003
4. Rhode, D., Zhang, H.Y., Madsen, D.B.: J. Archaeol. Sci. **34**(4), 600–612 (2007)
5. Brantingham, P.J., Gao, X., Madsen, D.B., et al.: Geoarchaeology **28**(5), 413–431 (2013)
6. Chen, F.H., Dong, G.H., Zhang, D.J., et al.: Agriculture facilitated permanent human occupation of the Tibetan Plateau after 3600 BP. Science (2014). https://doi.org/10.1126/science.1259172
7. Xu, J.H.: Mathematical Methods in Contemporary Geography, pp. 1–457. Higher Education Press, Beijing (2004)
8. Xie, J.Y.: Acta Anthropologica Sinica **10**(1), 27–33 (1991). (in Chinese)
9. Sun, Y.J, Lai, Z.P., Madsen, D., et al.: Quat. Geochronol. **2**(5), 107–110 (2012). (in Chinese)
10. Rhode, D., Brantingham, P.J., Perreault, C., et al.: J. Archaeol. Sci. **52**, 567–577 (2014)
11. Madsen, D.B., Ma, H.Z., Brantingham, P.J., et al.: J. Archaeol. Sci. **33**(10), 1433–1444 (2006)
12. Gai, P., Wang, G.D.: Acta Anthropologica Sinica **2**(1), 49–59 (1983). (in Chinese)
13. Shi, S.: Tibetan Stud. **2**, 33–39 (2003). (in Chinese)
14. Hou, G.L, Cao, G.C., C, Y.E., et al.: Acta Geographica Sinica **71**(7), 1231–1240 (2016). (in Chinese)
15. Sun, Y.J., Lai, Z.P., Long, H.: Quat. Geochronol. **5**(2), 360–364 (2010). (in Chinese)
16. Hudson, A.M., Olsen, J.W., Quade, J., et al.: Quat. Res. **86**(1), 13–33 (2016)
17. Dong, G.H., Jia, X., Elston, R., et al.: J. Archaeol. Sci. **40**(5), 2538–25463 (2013). (in Chinese)
18. Tang, H.S., Zhou, C.L., Li, Y.Q., et al.: Chin. Sci. Bull. **58**(3), 247–253 (2013). (in Chinese)

Remote Environmental Information Real-Time Monitoring and Processing System of Cow Barn

Faquan Yang[1(✉)], Chunsheng Zhang[2], and Ling Yang[3]

[1] School of Electrical Information Engineering,
Foshan University, Foshan 528000, China
Yafaquan.fosu@163.com
[2] Guangdong Radio and Television Station, Guanzuo 523138, China
[3] Xinhua College of Sun Yat-sen University, Guanzuo 523133, China

Abstract. Hot and humid weather in southern China lead the modern dairy farming into trouble. If the temperature, humidity and illumination of the cow house, and the noxious gas including carbon dioxide, ammonia and hydrogen sulfide from the breaths of the cows and decomposition of the organic can be monitored in the real time, the trouble because of the weather in the modern dairy farming can be solved. So this paper focuses on the wireless network, though applying the MSP430F149 and Nrf905 chips as the wireless network module, and LTM8901 as the sensing devices, the real-time monitor and processing system for the cow house can be established to solve the trouble of modern cow farming in the south of China. This system has low operating cost and stable property so that it is extremely fit for the hilly terrain in the south of China. Meanwhile, it can be also used in monitoring environmental pollution in the real time.

Keywords: Wireless sensor network · Sensor · Router · Monitoring center
Remote cow house environment pollution monitoring

1 Introduction

It is well known that milk is nourishable and it can offer the absorbed and digested calcium for people. Therefore, the large-scale farming can be seen in many rural areas of southern of China even under the hot and humid weather condition. However, the larger the scale of farm is, the higher the internal environment of the cow house request. As the result, without the real-time of monitor and process for the cow house, the breeding benefit can be decreased so as to impact on the surrounding ecosystem [1].

The environmental factors of the cow house contain temperature, humidity, illumination, carbon dioxide, ammonia gas and hydrogen sulfide [2]. When these harmful gases including carbon dioxide, ammonia gas and hydrogen sulfide exceed the normal level, it will result the disease reduced, which causes infectious diseases and even death. In addition, only when the temperature, humidity, and light are appropriate, the cows will grow healthily and the utilization of fodder will be highest. However, for the current rural cattle breeding in our country, especially in the rural south area, the scale

© Springer Nature Singapore Pte Ltd. 2018
H. Yuan et al. (Eds.): GSKI 2017, CCIS 849, pp. 457–465, 2018.
https://doi.org/10.1007/978-981-13-0896-3_45

is generally small, the technology is least advanced, and the environment in the barn lacks of information monitoring system, which affects the scientific cattle breeding and even affects the surrounding ecological environment. With the increasing breeding scale, more and more subtle levels of the management, higher demand of the internal barn environment, building the real-time and reliable cowshed environmental information monitoring system is very important because this system can prevent various diseases, improve the yield and quality of the cattle farming, promote the development of cattle breeding industry in rural areas [3].

The international and Chinese journals related to the application of wireless sensor network in environmental pollution monitoring system can be seen frequently. For example, the article [4] introduced the design of monitoring system based on the wireless sensor network which is used for monitoring the behavior characteristics of the cows. The article [5] also presented the application of wireless sensor network on wireless sensor network in the pig breeding. The article [6] talked about the application of wireless sensor network in automatic monitoring the birdhouse. The article [7] showed the design of environmental monitoring system based on wireless sensor network for cow barn environment. The monitoring system based on wireless sensor network scheme presented in above articles is feasible and the system performance is stable. However, the monitoring system talked in above articles only has monitoring function cannot deal with the monitoring information in the real-time. Meanwhile, these designs are only used for small scale of farm but not for the whole farming area because they all apply the wireless transmitting module of power parameter estimate. This paper are based on the principles of the system and apply the real-time monitoring and processing system which is composed by the wireless sensor network module with MSP430F149 and nRF905 chip and the sensors such as LTM8901 etc. so as to collect and deal with the environmental information in cow barn. When remote monitoring the cow barn in real-time, if the environment data monitored exceeds extremely, then emergency response plans for the environment will be automatically started so that effective measures can be taken and the accident can be quickly dealt with. Meanwhile, this system can keep the barn environment clean and highlight scientific and advanced nature of the breeding for cows.

2 Real-Time Monitoring Systems of Hardware

The hardware system consists of sensor nodes, router nodes, local monitoring centers, gateway nodes, and remote monitoring centers as shown in Fig. 1.

Based on wireless sensor network, through the design of the hardware and software system, building a remote cow barn environmental monitoring system, the system is mainly composed of sensor nodes, the router nodes, local monitoring center, gateway nodes and remote monitoring center, etc. For this system, the sensor network which is the terminal equipment of wireless network put in the monitoring area and is responsible for acquisition and sending data of temperature, humidity, light, CO_2 concentration, ammonia concentration and the concentration of hydrogen sulfide, and other environmental information. The local monitoring centers and various sensors nodes make up the local subnets and all kinds of data that sent from the sensors nodes

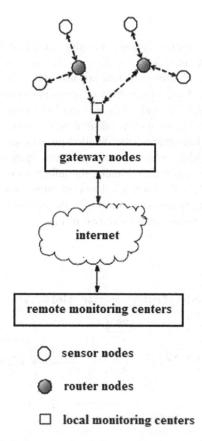

gateway nodes

internet

remote monitoring centers

○   **sensor nodes**

●   **router nodes**

□   **local monitoring centers**

Fig. 1. The block diagram of real-time monitoring systems of hardware

can be obtained, which achieves the local environmental monitoring. When the environmental data exceeds bid badly by real-time monitoring, emergency response plans for the environment will be immediately started and the effective measures for the cow barn environment can be quickly taken, such as automatic start ventilation exhaust system. In addition, the local monitoring center data is transmitted to remote monitoring center via network node. The monitoring center is responsible for display storage and analysis of the information data, and control the environmental adjustment device so as to get a good internal environment.

We would like to draw your attention to the fact that it is not possible to modify a paper in any way, once it has been published. This applies to both the printed book and the online version of the publication. Every detail, including the order of the names of the authors, should be checked before the paper is sent to the Volume Editors.

2.1 Sensor Nodes

Sensor nodes are at the forefront of system monitor, including different types of sensor modules, microprocessor modules, wireless communication modules and power modules. Different types of sensor module are used for collecting the data for temperature, humidity, light, CO2 concentration, ammonia concentration and the concentration of hydrogen sulfide, and other real-time environmental information data. Microprocessor module is mainly used for dealing with information data from different types of sensor module information, the detailed process such as data compression, source coding, multiplexing, channel coding. These processes can improve the anti-jamming of the information data. Finally, the information data which is processed by microprocessor module will be sent wireless communication module, monitoring by the antenna to the routing nodes send real-time information to the environment. The block diagram of sensor node circuit as shown in Fig. 2.

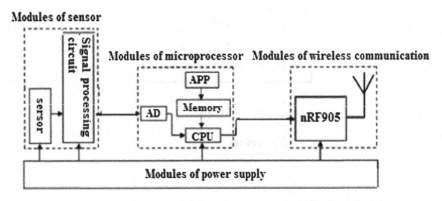

Fig. 2. The block diagram of sensor node circuit

In order to achieve low power consumption design, the MSP430F149 produced from TI company can be applied for the microcontrollers of each node. MSP430F149 is 16-bit microprocessor which has high level of integration, rich peripheral module function. Ultra-low power consumption (can provide 5 kinds of low power consumption mode, power down electric is only 0.1 μA). Its internal integration has 8 channels of AD input, 2 SPI interfaces, 60 KB program storage space and 2 KB of RAM. For the wireless communication module, 433/868/915 MHz transceiver chip nRF905 which is launched by Norwegian Nordic Semiconductor has a strong anti-jamming capability, adjustable frequency, low power consumption, and long transmission distance [8].

2.2 Nodes of Router

The collected information from all sensor nodes in the wireless sensor network are sent to the router node through a wireless launch module. Therefore, the router node plays an important part in the remote real-time monitoring and processing system for cow barn environment which is designed in this article. Its functions include:

① Receiving the data information from each sensor network node
② Merging the data
③ Sending the merged data to the local data monitoring center to display system and gateway nodes.

The router node structure diagram is shown in Fig. 3.

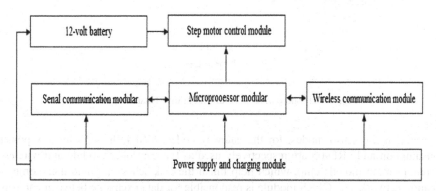

Fig. 3. The structure diagram of router node

In order to achieve reliable long-distance communication with the sensing nodes which are spread evenly in the monitoring area of parties, the router node can be adjusted to directional antenna and the stepper motor can be used to control the router node in the horizontal direction so that it has the function of multidirectional directional sending and receiving. For the problem of limited energy in wireless sensor networks [9, 10], the solution can be as follows: when the lithium battery of each router nodes is used in this system to supply for power supply, timing dormant arousal mechanism can also be used in the system network to decrease the energy consumption. As a result of the large energy consumption of router nodes and gateway nodes, the solar panel is used in this paper and lithium battery can be charged through BQ2057w so as to compensate for the overly energy consumption and extend the life of the network.

2.3   Gateway Nodes and Local Monitoring Centers

Gateway node is mainly responsible for receiving, collecting and storing network data, and data will be sent to the Internet through GPRS module network transmission to internet network, and then to the remote monitoring center server. When the cow barn environment data monitored exceeds certain limits, the gateway can also send early warning messages to the farmers through the GPRS network [11, 12] and then the ventilation exhaust system will be automatically started. The gateway node hardware structure consists of the processor module, the wireless communication module, the serial port module, GPRS module, SD storage module and the power management module [13]. The related structure diagram is shown in Fig. 4.

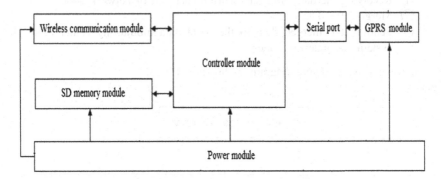

Fig. 4. The hardware structure diagram of gateway node

Same as the sensor nodes, for the gateway nodes, MSP430F149 with low power consumption and nRF905 are respectively used as the controller module and wireless communication module chip, which help finish the task scheduling and data communication network, etc. GPRS module is responsible for data exchange between gateway and external network, and the sending of alarm message. In this system, MC55 from Siemens is applied as the main control chip of GRS communication module. This module has the advantages of stable data transmission, low price and easy development. The GPRS, the common SD card is applied as the data storage medium so that the network data can be back up and the data integrity can be guaranteed.

The gateway node is identical to the sensor node power supply module. It also needs two lithium batteries in series. After conversion of voltage, it can supply electricity for GPRS module and other modules respectively. The gateway can control the switch of GPRS module and other modules through relay so as to extend the lifetime of gateway node. For the local monitoring center, real-time monitoring the cow barn environment can be achieved after the received data from route is demodulated, decoded and sent to the display output system.

3 Software Systems of Real-Time Monitoring

3.1 Sensor Node Software Systems

The sensor node is responsible for the collection of field data, the wireless delivery of collected data package through wireless communication module, and the modular design of programme. The program flow chart is shown in Fig. 5.

This program is mainly composed of initialization, the system time synchronization, data acquisition, wireless communication and other modules. The sensor node periodically acquire data and the data acquisition cycle is set to 30 min. For the network, the dormant arousal mechanism is applied, and the node enter into a dormant

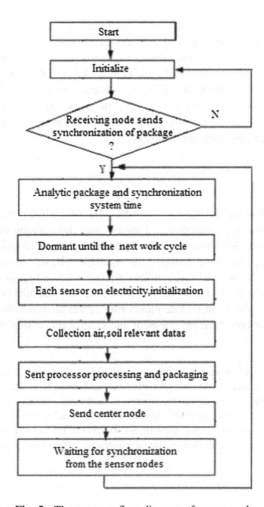

Fig. 5. The program flow diagram of sensor node

state during the synchronization system time after receiving the synchronous package. After the wake up time, the node can be waked up, begin collecting and packing data information so as to send the data to the sensor nodes. If receiving the sensor node synchronization packet, the node can enter into the next work cycle. If not receiving the synchronization packet, the node will wait until receiving the synchronization packet.

3.2 Routing Node Software Systems

For the sensor node, its main task is receiving the data of all sensor nodes, merging the data, and sending the merged data to the local data monitoring center and gateway node. The routing nodes are located in the network center, and are equipped with directional antenna. By applying the stepping motor, the directional antenna can be controlled so that the data package of each sensor node can be received. Then, each sensor node wakes up regularly and send the collected data to the routing nodes. In the meantime, the routing node wakes up and the directional antenna begins rotating by four phase eight racquet speed. After the routing node receives a data packet of sensor node, it immediately returns the synchronization package to the sensor node, and then the directional antenna continues to roll so as to receive the next sensor node data, until receiving the data from all sensor nodes. After the sensor node receives the synchronization package of the routing node, it will enter into the periodically dormant and the wake-up time will begin from the next cycle.

4 Conclusion

In this paper, by choosing LTM8901, On9658, MH-Z14, MQ137 and ME4-H2S and other sensor modules, the temperature, humidity and illumination of the cow house, and the noxious gas including carbon dioxide, ammonia and hydrogen sulfide from the breaths of the cows and decomposition of the organic can be monitored in the real time. Collecting data can be finished through fusion processing and remote transmission of the router nodes which are based on the MSP430F149 and nRF905 chips and the gateway nodes. The local and remote monitoring center analyzes data, which realizes real-time monitoring cow barn environment and control processing the environmental control equipment.

Acknowledgements. This work was supported by The Projects of Science and Technology Plan Guangdong Province under Grand (2014A010101284) and Projects of The Public Welfare and Capacity Enhancement of Foshan (2016AB00041).Thanks my classmates and friends in our laboratory such as Dr. Zhongxian PAN, Xinyin XIANG, Ganchao LIU, Dr. Jie Zheng et al. Meanwhile, thanks for support from a grant from Co., LTD of Foshan middle south agricultural science and technology and the department of electronic information engineering in Foshan University.

References

1. Sheng, J., Weixing, W.: Design and implementation of wireless monitoring system of water quality for intensive aquaculture. J. Agric. Netw. Inf. **41**(11), 17–20 (2013)
2. Fangming, T., Weichunbo, W.: Design of cold and standardized cow shed environment parameters acquisition system. J. Jiangsu Agric. Sci. **41**(6), 371–373 (2014)
3. Tingjiang, W., Lishan, Y.: Design of monitoring system for environment of large scale dairy farm in the shed—based on ZigBee technology. J. Agric. Mech. Res. **37**(2), 210–213 (2015)
4. Zhaojun, X., Chunxin, G.: Research and implementation of wireless sensor network in precision agriculture. J. Mech. Electr. Eng. **2**(03), 38–46 (2015)
5. Siyuan, L., Yanling, J.: Design of piggery environment monitoring system based on ZigBee. J. Hubei Agric. Sci. **54**(16), 4041–4044 (2015)
6. Congxi, Z.: Research on Poultry House Environmental Monitoring System Based on ZigBee Technology. Jilin Agricultural University (2013)
7. Canghai, W., Huojiao, X., Huanliang, X., Dong, H.: Design of remote monitoring system of dairy farm based on RFID and ZigBee. J. Agric. Mech. Res. **35**(2), 163–166 (2014)

8. Faquan, Y., Zan, L., Benjian, H., Jie, Z.: A new method of modulation recognition of block orthogonal amplitude modulation. J. Commun. **9**(9), 693–698 (2014)
9. Hang, S.: Clustering algorithm of wireless sensor network in intelligent traffic. J. Traffic Inf. Secur. **26**(03), 16–21 (2017)
10. Jun, L., Qian, S., Shaohua, L.: Topology control algorithm based on directional antenna in wireless ad hoc networks. J. Northeast. Univ. Nat. Sci. **33**(9), 1257–1260 (2012)
11. Heng, Z., Dongyi, C., Bing, L.: Research on the orientation of antenna in WSN. J. Univ. Electron. Sci. Technol. Chin. **39**(8), 85–88 (2010)
12. Salim, T., Haiyunnisa, T.: Design and implementation of water quality monitoring for eel fish aquaculture. In: International Symposium on Electronics and Smart Devices, vol. 25, pp. 208–213 (2016)
13. Yan, L., Weichunbo, W.: Research of cold and cow barn to wireless monitoring system. Jiangsu Agric. Sci. **42**(5), 358–361 (2014)

The Application of Big Data Technology in Competitive Sports Research

Xiaobing Du[✉]

Public Sports Department of Sports Institute, Han Shan Normal University,
Chaozhou 521041, China
duxiaobingshifan@126.com

Abstract. With the coming of the big data era, a new proposition that how the competitive sports system should conform to the times development is put forward. Based on the analysis of the importance of big data technology in competitive sports, this paper puts forward a competitive sports analysis framework based on big data analysis. Opportunities and challenges faced by competitive sports in the age of big data are illustrated with concrete examples.

Keywords: Big data technology · Competitive sports · Data analysis

1 Introduction

With the development of human society, the era of big data [1, 2] has come. The popularization of mobile Internet [3], cloud computing [4, 5] and Internet of things [6] affects the way of life and habits of the future human beings. The vast amount of data that science and technology will pick up everywhere is presented to the public in an intelligent and visual way, and the development and application of it to the sports field. This has brought unprecedented opportunities and challenges for the entire sports industry, including sports industry, competitive sports events and sports communication modes.

Competitive sports [7, 8] are an important part of world sports. Nowadays, sensors, 3D radars, and wearable devices on athletes' bodies collect large amounts of data. Professional sports, whether it's tennis, football, golf or basketball, is recorded and analyzed every time you hit, toss, and swing. Teams of athletes and coaches are increasingly relying on data analysis to make their skills and tactics more perfect. The game, when the state of the athletes, or tactical layout consideration of the coaches, referees of cutting way, or pitch audience's experience, now more and more role of science and technology. Data collection has become a common practice. The professional sports community has turned it into an insight by analyzing big data. This has laid a more solid foundation for the success of sports, as well as a personalized experience for sports fans around the world.

Looking for correlations from a large number of data reveals previously unknown and critical breakthroughs. This is the key to winning in the face of the veneer, the password that determines the outcome of the competition. That's why big data is so

H. Yuan et al. (Eds.): GSKI 2017, CCIS 849, pp. 466–471, 2018.
https://doi.org/10.1007/978-981-13-0896-3_46

popular in the world of competitive sports. At the national level, sports are becoming digital warfare, and future sports must be digital.

2 Concepts and Characteristics of Big Data

Big data refers to data sets with large capacity, multiple types, fast access speed and high application value. It is the behavior of collecting, storing and analyzing the data collected, stored and correlated in a large quantity, scattered and diverse sources. It is also a new generation of information technology and service industry to discover new knowledge, create new value and enhance new capabilities. Technical features include the following aspects.

(1) It is a kind of data set with large capacity, fast growth, type and low value.
(2) It is a new generation information system architecture and technology for data collection, storage and correlation analysis of large quantity, scattered sources and diverse formats.
(3) It is a new scientific paradigm that finds new knowledge, creates new value, promotes new energy, and forms the universal cognitive world and the ability to transform the world.

In the era of big data explosion, we should rely on big data to find the right direction, seize the key points and put forward countermeasures. Therefore, it can accurately grasp the characteristics and change process of competitive sports, and make an objective and comprehensive evaluation. But the traditional method is only subjective, scattered, one-sided to speculate or stay in the description of the surface nature of things. The application of big data can reveal the relationship that traditional technology is difficult to excavate. This not only helps coaches and athletes analyze every game, but also the merits of each training, and can identify trends in data analysis.

3 Competitive Sports Analysis Framework Based on Big Data Analysis

The economic sports analysis architecture based on big data analysis is shown in Fig. 1. It is mainly divided into the data source layer, management layer, analysis layer and presentation layer.

(1) Data source layer. The main function of this layer is to collect competitive sports data, including time information, location information, sensor data and so on. The presentation mode of information carrier is mainly non-structural data, including pictures, audio, video information, etc.
(2) Management layer. The data of data source layer are extracted and integrated, data aggregation and correlation method is adopted to process the data, and the data is stored uniformly. It includes the following aspects.

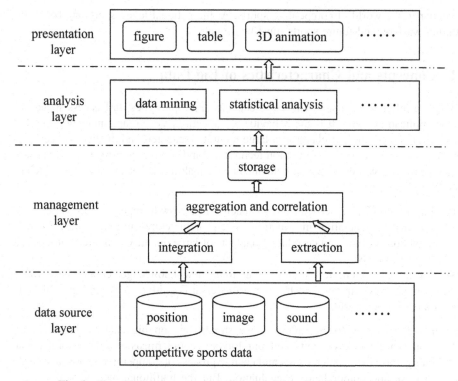

Fig. 1. Competitive sports analysis framework based on big data analysis

A. Data cleaning (to noise and irrelevant data).
B. Data integration (combining data from multiple data sources in a consistent data store).
C. Data transformation (conversion of raw data into a form suitable for data mining).
D. Data specification (main methods include: data cube aggregation, dimensional reduction, data compression, numerical reduction, discretization and concept stratification, etc.).

(3) Analysis layer. This layer provides a large number of data analysis algorithms that can classify and cluster data and realize linkage mining and rule mining. This layer is the core of the whole system, which can realize the mining analysis of key event information and find out the relation between events.

(4) Presentation layer. The analysis results can be displayed by means of table, figure and 3D animation, and can be stored in various data formats according to user's requirements.

4 Opportunities and Challenges Faced by Competitive Sports in the Age of Big Data

4.1 Case Analysis

Traditional competition analysis is based on observation and mathematical statistics. With the rise of network technology, the demand of reducing artificial input and competitive tactics has promoted the production of motion acquisition and athlete evaluation system. The introduction of big data analysis gives coaches and athletes the opportunity to analyze sports from another dimension and gain insight into their own. Then adjust the strategy, and then make scientific and reasonable training plan. Take the American professional basketball league for example. According to statistics, the average winning percentage of teams that hire data analysts is 59.3%, compared with 40.7% for teams without analysts. Since the 1980s, players' performance and data have been quantified in the database. It is now possible to analyse any player's strengths and weaknesses immediately, and help the coach in terms of tactics and training.

In the 2013 Chinese tennis open, li na's game against serena Williams, IBM passed the intelligent analysis platform SlamTracker to give li's winning strategy (Key to the match) three indicators. (1) First serve scoring rate over 69%. (2) The score in the 4–9 shot is more than 48%. (3) Serve 30–30 or 40–40, the scoring rate is more than 67%. Li completed one of three indicators. Li completed one of three indicators, and Williams completed two of the three indicators. Li finally lost the game.

Let's take the second index given by IBM and try to find out what's behind it. The analysis of the batting position of the 4–9 was found to be in the bottom line. Most of the loss due to the distance of the ball from the ball resulting in the failure of the ball. With the exclusion of venue, technology, and psychological problems, we can determine that the pace and the flexibility of footwork have led to li's lack of a second indicator. In the following training, you can achieve the batting effect of the 4–9 by stepping up your footwork ability. For example, leg strength exercises, the shift of center of gravity, stability of the core area and the control of body posture.

The above examples show that big data technology brings new opportunities and challenges to traditional competitive sports.

4.2 Big Data Technology Presents New Opportunities for Traditional Competitive Sports

The traditional sports field is relatively closed. Sports intelligence, training methods and winning rules are relatively conservative and hidden. In order to maintain competitive advantage, the organizers and implementers will try their best to seal their information channels. With the advent of the era of big data, the closed "system" will be broken. The environment for competitive sports has also become more complex. In the field of competitive sports, such as selection, technical analysis and running track, which rely on experience, can now be achieved by relying on big data technology. For example, big data technology can effectively realize the prediction of the selection of materials in competitive sports.

The arrival of the big data era has brought an open impact to the original "relatively conservative" competitive sports field. The traditional methods of "secrecy" and the mastery of the rules of success are gradually being proved by the "prediction" theory produced by big data operation. Under the influence of big data, the external environment of competitive sports is gradually becoming more complicated and informative. The competitive environment and competitive landscape of the world sports world are also becoming more scientific, systematic and complicated. Therefore, the traditional training theory of selection, training means, status diagnosis and information intelligence gathering before the competition can all produce innovative thinking methods and methods. In the context of big data, the theory and practice related to competitive sports will also be innovated.

4.3   Traditional Competitive Sports Selection, Training, Competition and Other Ways of Thinking Face Challenges

The application of big data technology to sports is the inevitable trend of sports science and technology and modernization. The complexity of sports and sports competitions brings new challenges to the storage and acquisition of big data. The prediction, training and real-time technology tracking and analysis of athletes in competitive sports have become an important part of the development of competitive sports training in the big data era. Big data technology will help with high levels of training and competition. The athletes' training and competition features will transmit data in real time through the sensor, and the transmission of these real-time data will provide reference for coaches' training decisions. The technology of big data is closely combined with high level athletic training. Traditional training fields, such as selection, training and competition, are facing challenges. In addition, data collection and analysis related to sports events are facing challenges. The world's level of sports meets thousands of spectators every game, and the people who pay attention to the media outside the field are even more massive. There are huge amounts of data including a amount of load, running speed, running track, troop deployment, tactical configuration, other data produced by the stars and coaches and comments from viewers and netizens. The acquisition and storage of these data will pose considerable challenges to relevant departments.

5   Conclusion

The big data era has come. Vast amounts of data are produced, shared and used all the time. Sports information is also included. With the development of science and technology, we are able to collect more and more tools for data analysis, and the results of these data and analysis data are more important in the field of sports. This paper first introduces the concept and characteristics of big data. Based on this, a competitive sports analysis framework based on big data analysis is proposed. Finally, opportunities and challenges faced by competitive sports in the age of big data are analyzed.

References

1. He, X., Ai, Q., Qiu, R.C., Huang, W.: A big data architecture design for smart grids based on random matrix theory. IEEE Trans. Smart Grid **8**(2), 674–686 (2017)
2. Sookhak, M., Gani, A., Khan, M.K., Buyya, R.: Dynamic remote data auditing for securing big data storage in cloud computing. Inf. Sci. **380**, 101–116 (2017)
3. Xu, X., Thong, J.Y.L., Tam, K.Y.: Winning Back technology disadopters: testing a technology readoption model in the context of mobile internet services. Soc. Sci. Electron. Publishing **34**(1), 102–140 (2017)
4. Sookhak, M., Gani, A., Khan, M.K., Buyya, R.: Dynamic remote data auditing for securing big data storage in cloud computing. Inf. Sci. **380**, 101–116 (2017)
5. Xia, Z., Wang, X., Zhang, L.: Privacy-preserving and copy-deterrence content-based image retrieval scheme in cloud computing. IEEE Trans. Inf. Forensics Secur. **11**(11), 2594–2608 (2016)
6. Botta, A., Donato, W.D., Persico, V.: Integration of cloud computing and internet of things. Future Gener. Comput. Syst. **56**(C), 684–700 (2016)
7. Caya, O., Bourdon, A.: A framework of value creation from business intelligence and analytics in competitive sports. In: Hawaii International Conference on System Sciences, pp. 1061–1071 (2016)
8. Veliz, P., Boyd, C.J., Mccabe, S.E.: Nonmedical use of prescription opioids and heroin use among adolescents involved in competitive sports. J. Adolesc. Health **60**(3), 346–349 (2017)

UMine: Study on Prevalent Co-locations
Mining from Uncertain Data Sets

Pingping Wu[1($\boxtimes$)], Lizhen Wang[2], Wenjing Yang[1], and Zhulin Su[1]

[1] Dianchi College of Yunnan University, Kunming, China
fjwpingping@126.com
[2] School of Information Science and Engineering, Yunnan University,
Kunming, China
lzhwang2005@126.com

Abstract. We can collect a large amount of spatial data by utilizing sensor positioning technology and wearable devices. However, most of the acquired data are uncertain because of the gaps in data collection or to maintain subject privacy. Thus, we investigate co-location pattern mining problem in the context of uncertain data. The prevalent co-location pattern under uncertain environments has two different definitions. The first definition, referred as the expected prevalent co-location, employs the expected interest degree of co-location to measure whether this pattern is frequent. The second definition, referred as the probabilistic prevalent co-location, uses the probabilistic formulations to measure frequency. Here a novel system called UMine is proposed to compare this two different definitions with a user-friendly interface. The core of a system such as this is the mining algorithm, and UMine is integrated with the expected mining method, probabilistic mining method, and approximate mining method. In this paper, the system is introduced in detail, and the comparison between these two types of definitions is implemented. The experimental results show that the difference between these two definitions' result sets changes as the threshold changes. By flexibly adjusting the parameters, users can observe interesting patterns in the data. In addition, the demonstration provides data generation and preprocessing function while showing its practicality for either real-world or synthetic data sets. The study can also provide support for the further uncertain Co-location patterns mining research.

Keywords: Spatial co-location patterns · Uncertain data · Possible worlds
Visualization

1 Introduction

A spatial co-location pattern represents a subset of spatial features whose instances are frequently located within a given spatial neighborhood [1]. A typical example of such a pattern: there are orchids in 80% of the area where the middle-wetness green-broad-leaf forest grows. Since the concept of spatial co-location patterns was first proposed, many investigations have been conducted on mining algorithms and their applications. Paper [2] used Apriori-like method, proposed Join-Base algorithm. Paper [3, 4] put forward Partial-Join method and Join-Less method respectively based on paper [2]. Paper [5]

© Springer Nature Singapore Pte Ltd. 2018
H. Yuan et al. (Eds.): GSKI 2017, CCIS 849, pp. 472–481, 2018.
https://doi.org/10.1007/978-981-13-0896-3_47

provided an Order-Clique-Based algorithm, which is used for mining maximal prevalent co-locations, avoiding both outputting a large amount of smaller-size prevalent patterns and storing a mass of table instances. In some specific applications, we focus on infrequent patterns, such as the regional co-location patterns in paper [6] and the negative co-location patterns in paper [7]. Pattern mining has a wide range of applications. For example, paper [8] used the real data of China's Wuhan to study the relationship between crime and different functional areas. Experiments have yielded many inspired patterns which can help police to target and deploy in different functional areas to reduce crime.

In traditional co-location mining, whether a feature's instance is present in, or absent from, a location in the area is known. However, in reality, owing to instrument errors, damaged hardware, transmission problems, and privacy, spatial data has a very high level of uncertainty. Hence, mining co-locations from these uncertain data sets has become an interesting and important task.

Before finding prevalent patterns from uncertain data sets, the definition of the prevalent co-location pattern is the most essential issue. In deterministic data, it is clear that a pattern is prevalence if and only if the participation index (interest degree) of this pattern is not smaller than a specified minimum threshold [2]. However, different from the deterministic case, the definition over uncertainty case has two different semantic explanations: expected prevalent co-location [9, 10] and probabilistic prevalent co-location [11, 12]. In the definition of the expected prevalent co-location, the expectation of participation index is defined as the measurement, a pattern is prevalence if and only if the value of expectation of such pattern is no less than a specified minimum prevalent threshold (*min_prev*). In the definition of probabilistic prevalent co-location pattern, the probabilistic formulations is used to measure frequency. The pattern is prevalence if and only if the probability that the frequency of pattern is not less than *min_prev* is greater than or equal to the minimum probabilistic threshold (*min_prob*).

We note that the ensemble learning that have been proposed, such as [13, 14], do not focus on uncertainties. In this paper, we propose a new prototype system, named UMine, to mine prevalent co-location patterns from uncertain data sets. In order to verify the relationship between these two definitions, this system is integrated with the expected mining method and probabilistic mining method which are novel, practical, and derived from recent research. Taking into account the user's real-time needs, the demonstration also provides an approximate algorithm that proposed in our previous research [11] which can run in polynomial time at the expense of accuracy. It is worth noting that the system model the uncertain data set by using the possible world model [15] which is one of the most widely used data models. In the possible world model, any legal combination of each instance constitutes a possible world, and the probability of the possible world can be calculated from the probability of the relevant instance.

2 System Architecture

The general system architecture, shown in Fig. 1, comprises three layers. The bottom layer is a data management layer. This layer is responsible for data collection and data preprocessing. Because spatial data comes from a variety of sources, data preprocessing is necessary. Then, the second is the pattern mining layer which provides three pattern mining methods: an expected mining method and two probabilistic mining methods; The third is the analysis layer. This layer involves the analysis of efficiency and comparative analysis of these three methods. To help users to explore interesting patterns, we provide a visual interface which is simple and easy to learn.

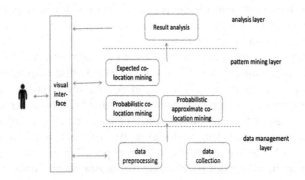

Fig. 1. System architecture.

3 The Basic Definitions

This section introduces the definitions of expected prevalent co-location and probabilistic prevalent co-location.

Definition 1. Given an uncertain spatial instance set S of spatial feature set $F = \{f_1, f_2, \ldots, f_n\}$, and a size k co-location c with W as its space of all possible worlds containing all instances of spatial features in c. In a possible world $w \in W$, the participation ratio $PR_w(c, f_i)$ for feature type f_i in the co-location c is the fraction of instances of feature type f_i which participate in table instance of c in w, that is,

$$PR_w(c, f_i) = \frac{|\pi_{f_i}(table\_ins\,tan\,ce_w(c))|}{|table\_ins\,tan\,ce_w(\{f_i\})|}$$

Where π is the relational projection operation with duplication elimination. $table\_ins\,tan\,ce_w(c)$ is the table instances of co-location c in the possible world w.

Definition 2. The expected participation index $EPI(c)$ of a k-size co-location c is used to measure the prevalence of the co-location c in the spatial uncertain data, it is defined as

$$EPI(c) = \sum_{w \in W} P(w) \times \min_{i=1}^k PR_w(c, f_i)$$

where $P(w)$ is the probability of the possible world w.

Definition 3. Given a minimum prevalent threshold *min_prev*, a co-location c is a expected prevalent co-location if its expected participation index *EPI(c)*exceeds *min_prev*.

Definition 4. Given an spatial uncertain data set D (that is a spatial feature set F and an uncertain spatial instance set S) with W is its space of all possible worlds, the probabilistic participation index *PPI(c)* of a k-size co-location c is used to measure the prevalence of the co-location c in the spatial uncertain data, it is defined as

$$PPI(c) = \sum_{w \in W, \min_{i=1}^k PR_w(c, f_i) > min\_prev} P(w)$$

Definition 5. A co-location c is a (*min_prev*, *min_prob*)-probabilistic prevalent co-location if its probabilistic participation index *PPI(c)* is above a given probabilistic threshold *min_prob*.

4 Demonstration Scenarios

UMine was developed in C# in the Windows 10 operating system. Now, we will give a detailed introduction to three layers: data management layer, pattern mining layer, analysis layer.

4.1 Data Management

The main functions of data management are to generate, display, and preprocess the data. The interface is shown in Fig. 2.

(1) Display and save. UMine uses a coordinate diagram for displaying spatial features and instances to provide an intuitive, clear interface. Data can also be stored as a streaming file for repeated use.

(2) Data generating. With uncertain data, the mining results are affected by the instances number of features. The dataset's total number of instances is the product of the number of features and the number of instances. For example, for a 30 * 10 and 10 * 30 dataset, the total numbers of instances for both datasets is equal to 300; however, in the possible world model, mining the 10 * 30 dataset will required more time than the 30 * 10 dataset [11]. Therefore, it is not enough to simply use the total number of features as parameter. The prototype system use the number of instances and number of features as parameters that allowed the user to set as needed.

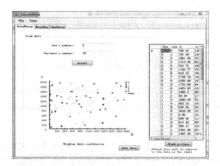

Fig. 2. Data management interface.

(3) Data preprocessing. If the user suspects that their data set contains incorrect data, then they can perform data cleaning. The UMine system provides several simple operations to clean incorrect data, including insertion of a new record, deletion of an incorrect record, and alteration of an incorrect value. The user can observe the processing result in a coordinate diagram.

4.2   Pattern Mining

The pattern mining interface is shown in Fig. 3.

Fig. 3. Mining algorithm interface.

(1) Main classes

Instance class (feature id, instance id, x coordinates, y coordinates, probability, adjacent instance collection, clique instances)

Pattern class (features, table instance set, possible world)

In these two main classes, adjacent instance collection is performed in the ascending order according to the corresponding feature id. The clique instance is used to calculate the feature's table instances through an order-clique-based method. The possible world stores a set of instances that are possible worlds for the pattern.

(2) Mining algorithms

- All three algorithms generate a table instance through a prefix tree using the method in the paper [5]. This method is proven to greatly reduce instance storage and repeat access.
- To reduce memory pressure, our demonstration pushes the calculations into the possible world generation process. At the same time, it stores only recent rows of data, quickly releases the node space and returns it to the buffer pool When calculating probabilistic mining method.

Track and cancel functions are available while the algorithm is running. Figure 4(a) shows an example output from a tracking option. Example mining results are shown in Fig. 4(b). The user can save the results according to their need.

(a) algorithm track

(b) mining results

Fig. 4. Result interface.

4.3 Mining Analysis

The mining analysis layer provides two functions: mining efficiency analysis and results statistics analysis. The user can load a dataset and then set the related parameters, as shown in Fig. 5(a). Finally, the user can select multiple algorithms they desire to compare. Through the analysis, the user can determine the difference between the algorithms being compared and how long is the maximal prevalence co-location pattern in the dataset. An example of results from an analysis of this type is shown in Fig. 5(b).

First of all, we compare the parameters of the three algorithms, as shown in Table 1. The expected mining algorithm requires the least number of parameters, while the approximate algorithm requires the user to input four parameters. It is well known that choosing the right parameters is difficult for the user. Therefore, in the future, we can consider using statistical learning and exploring methods to help users find suitable parameters.

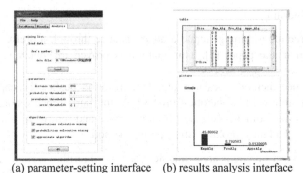

(a) parameter-setting interface   (b) results analysis interface

Fig. 5. Mining analysis interface.

Table 1. The parameters of the three algorithms

	Distance threshold	Prevalence threshold	Probability threshold	Error threshold
Expected co-location mining	√	√	–	–
Probabilistic co-location mining	√	√	√	–
Approximate co-location mining	√	√	√	√

Then, we compared the result sets of expected prevalent and probabilistic prevalent mining algorithm. The index of dissimilarity is used to measure the difference between the two result sets and defined as follows:

$$\text{Index of dissimilarity } ID = \frac{|M \oplus N|}{|M \cup N|} \tag{1}$$

M and N are two result sets of mining algorithm, the numerator of the fraction is the number of patterns that appear in the set M but does not appear in the set N or appear in the set N but not appear in the set M, and the denominator is the number of patterns that appears in the set M or appears in the set N. The numerator is equal to 0 when the two mining results are the same, then the index of dissimilarity is minimized.

Figure 6 shows the change in the value of ID as the threshold *min_prob* changes. The horizontal axis represents the value of *min_prob*, and the vertical axis is the value of ID. The experimental results show that the difference between the two mining results is small when the value of *min_prob* is small, then with the increasing of the *min_prob*, the influence of *min_prob* on the probabilistic mining algorithm is larger. Therefore, with the increase of the value of *min_prob*, the value of index of dissimilarity shows a trend of increasing. It is also found from the experiment that as the *min_prev* value increases, there will be a small number of patterns that are not expected prevalent co-location but are probabilistic prevalent co-location. The main reason for this situation is that there are some possible worlds with a large probability of occurrence in where the degree of interest is not less than *min_prev*.

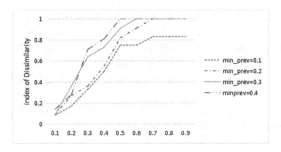

Fig. 6. Index of dissimilarity

Finally, the experiment also uses random data to verify the efficiency and accuracy of the probabilistic approximate mining method. The data in Table 2 shows that the mining time of the probabilistic mining algorithm and the probabilistic approximate mining algorithm in different cases when the error threshold is 0.005, and in the course of this experiment, the index of dissimilarity of these two result sets is zero. In the possible world model, the number of possible worlds is much higher than the size of the uncertainty database, or even the exponential of the latter, which is the biggest difficulty faced by uncertain data management techniques. while the experiment shows that probabilistic approximate mining algorithm effectively avoids traversing all legal combination that makes it greatly improves efficiency and makes it suited to real time systems that allow errors.

Table 2. Running time in seconds

min_prev	0.2	0.4	0.6	0.8
Probabilistic co-location mining	14.8	9.15	4.58	0.22
Approximate co-location mining	0.1	0.005	0.002	0.002

5 Summary

In this paper, we study on the two prevalent co-location pattern definitions from the uncertain data: expected prevalent co-location and probabilistic prevalent co-location. The experiment compares these two definitions from three aspects: parameter, result set dissimilarity and running time. It is found that the dissimilarity between expected prevalence and probabilistic prevalence is small when the threshold is small. As the probability threshold increases, the probability prevalent pattern decreases and becomes a subset of the expected prevalent result sets. On the other hand, the probabilistic approximate co-location mining algorithm effectively avoids traversing all the combinations which is more suitable for real-time systems owing to its faster runtime than the probabilistic mining algorithms.

To study the prevalent co-locations mining, this paper presents a visual, easy-to-learn prototype demonstration. The demonstration comprises three modules: (1) mining methods that are novel, practical, and derived from recent research, (2) a data management module that cleans the raw data and supplies missing points, and (3) a mining analysis module that facilitates the broad application of spatial co-location mining. In general, this research extends the application of possible world models and supports subsequent investigations and research in spatially uncertain data mining.

Acknowledgment. This paper was supported by the Research Foundation of Educational Department of Yunnan Province (No. 2016ZZX304).

References

1. Morimoto, Y.: Mining frequent neighboring class sets in spatial databases. In: Proceedings of SIGKDD, pp. 353–358 (2001)
2. Huang, Y., Shekhar, S., Xiong, H.: Discovering colocation patterns from spatial data sets: a general approach. IEEE Trans. Knowl. Data Eng. (TKDE) **16**(12), 1472–1485 (2004)
3. Yoo, J.S., Shekhar, S.: A Partial Join approach for mining co-location patterns. In: Proceedings of the 12th Annual ACM International Workshop on Geographic Information Systems, pp. 241–249. ACM Press (2004)
4. Yoo, J.S., Shekhar, S., Celik, M.: A Join-Less approach for co-location pattern mining: a summary of result. In: Proceedings of the 5th IEEE International Conference on Data Mining (ICDM), pp. 813–816. IEEE Press (2005)
5. Wang, L., Zhou, L., Lu, J., Yip, J.: An order-clique-based approach for mining maximal Co-locations. Inf. Sci. **179**(19), 3370–3382 (2009)
6. Deng, M., Cai, J., Liu, Q., et al.: Multi-level method for discovery of regional co-location patterns. Int. J. Geograph. Inf. Sci. **31**, 1–25 (2017)
7. Jiang, Y., Wang, L., Lu, Y., et al.: Discovering both positive and negative co-location rules from spatial data sets. In: International Conference on Software Engineering and Data Mining, pp. 398–403. IEEE (2010)
8. Yue, H., Zhu, X., Ye, X., et al.: The local colocation patterns of crime and land-use features in Wuhan, China. Int. J. Geo-Information **6**(10), 307 (2017)
9. Wang, L., Chen, H., Zhao, L., Zhou, L.: Efficiently mining co-location rules on interval data. In: Cao, L., Feng, Y., Zhong, J. (eds.) ADMA 2010. LNCS (LNAI), vol. 6440, pp. 477–488. Springer, Heidelberg (2010). https://doi.org/10.1007/978-3-642-17316-5_45
10. Ye, L.U., Wang, L., et al.: Spatial co-location patterns mining over uncertain data based on possible worlds. J. Comput. Res. Dev. **47**(Supp 1.), 215–221 (2010). (in Chinese with English abstract)
11. Wang, L., Wu, P., Chen, H.: Finding probabilistic prevalent colocations in spatially uncertain data sets. TKDE **25**(4), 790–804 (2013)
12. Liu, B., Chen, L., Liu, C., Zhang, C., Qiu, W.: Mining co-locations from continuously distributed uncertain spatial data. In: Li, F., Shim, K., Zheng, K., Liu, G. (eds.) APWeb 2016. LNCS, vol. 9931, pp. 66–78. Springer, Cham (2016). https://doi.org/10.1007/978-3-319-45814-4_6

13. Wang, L., Lu, Y., Chen, H., Xiao, Q.: Prefix-tree-based spatial co-location patterns mining algorithms. J. Comput. Res. Dev. **47**(Suppl.), 370–377 (2010). (in Chinese with English abstract)

14. Wang, L., Bao, Y., Lu, J., et al.: A web-based visual spatial co-location patterns' mining prototype system (SCPMiner). In: International Conference on Cyberworlds, pp. 675–681. IEEE (2009)

15. Green, T.J., Tannen, V.: Models for incomplete and probabilistic information. In: IEEE Data Engineering Bulletin, pp. 278–296 (2006)

Research for Distributed and Multitasking Collaborative Three-Dimensional Virtual Scene Simulation

Jing Zhou[✉]

School of Mathematics and Computer Science, Jianghan University,
Wuhan 430056, Hubei, China
zhjl31@jhun.edu.cn

Abstract. Currently most research of virtual scene simulation focus on the establishment algorithm of three-dimensional terrain model in the scene, but rarely consider the communication mechanism, multi-thread synchronization, dynamic loading issues of the distributed three dimensional virtual scenes. In this paper, the simulation engine based on vega prime is achieved by multi-threading technology, and communication protocol is implemented by winsocket technology, then the network architecture with high cohesion and low coupling control/running terminals are built. Combined with dynamic loading model reuse technology, three-dimensional virtual scene system based on distributed network communication is achieved. Based on the algorithm interface reserved in the system, the multitasking cooperative swarm intelligent pathfinding algorithms can be integrated. Then the communication model, multi-thread synchronization, dynamic loading and pathfinding problems are solved in the distributed multitasks three-dimensional visual scene system. The simulation results show that network data communication and the routing algorithm simulation are realized in three-dimensional virtual environment, and the effectiveness and feasibility of the algorithm can be verified, thereby the cost and risk of late operation are reduced.

Keywords: Multi-threading · Dynamic loading · Distributed communication
Three-dimensional virtual scene · Cooperative multitasking algorithm

1 Introduction

Studies with respect to the distributed virtual scene simulation mostly focused on the establishment algorithms of three dimensional terrain model [1–4]. And the issues with communication mechanisms, multithread synchronization, and dynamic loading in the distributed network communication environment are rarely considered.

Research for mission planning focus on single mission planning methods. From domestic technology novelty and literature search results, the research literatures for multitasking collaboration planning issue are rarely. Most modeling scene is based on the simplified model, which is not satisfying the real three-dimensional space constraints, and the simulation properties of real-time and interactivity are poor.

© Springer Nature Singapore Pte Ltd. 2018
H. Yuan et al. (Eds.): GSKI 2017, CCIS 849, pp. 482–491, 2018.
https://doi.org/10.1007/978-981-13-0896-3_48

To solve these problems, the technologies of multi-threading, network communication protocols, dynamic model reuse, multitasking swarm intelligence planning algorithm [5–8] are adopted. The three-dimensional models are established, which satisfy the real three-dimensional space constraints. And the three dimensional distributed multitask virtual visual simulation system with multi channels are achieved based on the network environment. The Network data communication and routing algorithms simulation in three dimensional virtual environment can be achieved on the simulation system, and the effectiveness and feasibility of the algorithm can also be verified, thereby the cost and risk of late operation are reduced.

2 Network Communication Module Design

2.1 Multi-thread Design

In the distributed simulation system, computing resources are very tight. The scene rendering, path generation and collision detection will be carried out in the system. Child thread can be started to perform the time-consuming tasks or time-urgent tasks, without tying up the main thread. Child thread is often used in server applications to immediately respond to incoming requests, without waiting for the completion of the previous request. Front interface response and data communication in background can be processed separately when the multi threads are applied, and too much CPU resources are not occupied by another.

Multi-mission planning with multi-threading is shown in Fig. 1. A worker thread is created to implement VP program, and then VP initialization is called and main loop is executed in main function of the thread. The main program of worker thread is a global function, which returns a 32-bit UINT-type value (declared as LPVOID) as a parameter. Each child thread shown in Fig. 1 can be used when the thread starts, wherein the system main thread is responsible to handle user input and transmit data to the thread. VP child thread is used to calculate and update the position of each object with intelligent routing algorithm, and the communication child thread is used to update and transfer the position of each object in real time between the server and the client.

To alleviate the burden of network communication, the status information of the virtual object controlled by each client in a distributed system can be communicated on the network. The final scene is generated and rendered independently on each client. When objects between clients interact, the client only need to send the state of the corresponding object to the server, and the server will send the results back to the clients after arbitration, thus the each client synchronization is completed. Multi-thread communication mechanism used in the whole process based on thread pool is shown in Fig. 2.

Resource sharing issues are brought when multiple threads is used to handle tasks, that is thread synchronization. Due to the size and performance, MFC objects are thread-safe only at the class level. So the synchronization objects and wait functions are used to realize the multiple threads synchronization.

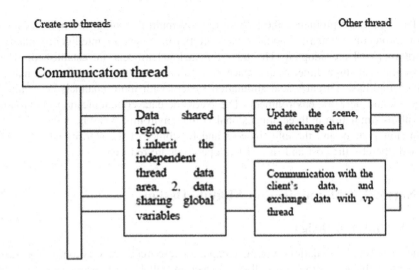

Fig. 1. Schematic diagram for multi-mission planning with multi-thread

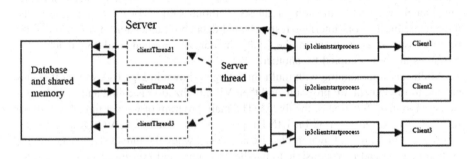

Fig. 2. Multi-thread communication mechanisms

2.2 Communication Framework Design Based on the Control Terminal and Operation Terminal

The specific purpose simulation is accomplished in a distributed network environment with a number of servers and clients which work cooperatively. As shown in Fig. 3, the underlying communication framework is designed for distributed simulation system. The data (such as coordinate information, the object status, environmental information, etc.) can be sent between the server and the client.

Communication between the server and client is realized by the Winsock communication method as shown in Fig. 3. In the server communication unit, the communication serves as a separate thread. Client works as same as the server side, but the client does not establish the communication thread pool. The fixed port number of data communication is given from the server. The polling for a long connection is the way of win-socket communication, which can be adopted to connect the connected clients and complete the communication. After communication connection for the server and

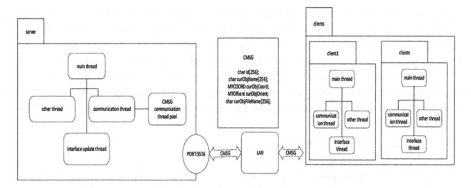

Fig. 3. Data communication unit architecture for server and client

client is established, server establishes a memory table (msglist table) to find access to the client id, and communicate with the client. Msglist is used to maintain communication information table of the connected clients. By operating msglist table, you can get data transferred from the client and the server.

Simulation scheduling is completed by the server in distributed simulation system, and database is regularly scanned. Server traverses the state information of operation terminals in the database, and finds the connected operation terminals. Work-flow of server monitor unit is shown in Fig. 4.

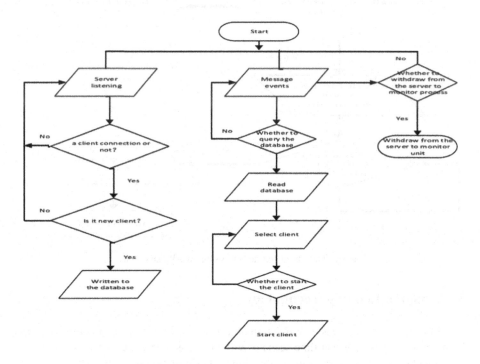

Fig. 4. Flow chart of the server monitor unit

Runtime system of client will gather environmental information (such as IP, port etc.) into the database to the server for query. The environmental information is used by server to assign different models on the client IP automatically. After the distribution, model data information is sent to the client system through the socket communication, background client operating system receives the data information and then starts the load model, and control the movement of model, and communication of the network data is implemented. The client operation system work process is shown in Fig. 5.

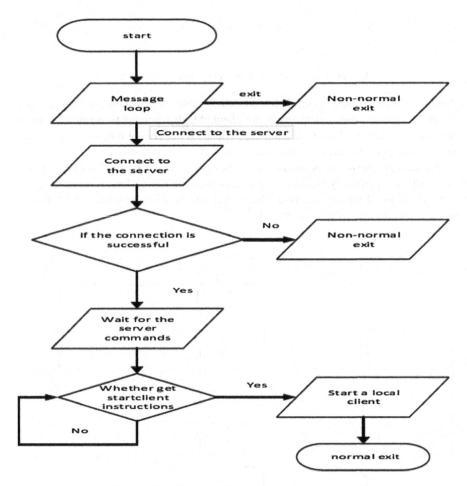

Fig. 5. The client operation system work flow chart

3 Dynamic Loading Technology

The 3d models and all kinds of simulation objects are loaded in the simulation program in the scene to generate real-time scene of virtual scene. The virtual visual system can dynamically generate and loaded all kinds of simulation objects. The dynamic generation and virtual object loading technology has realized in this paper. By use of copy-object methods, make the original object stay put, and a copy of the object produced by the object can move through the search path algorithm for regular. In system development, through to instantiate an object, and then use the object to copy the original object, and then change the position of the copy object, and the new copy is added into the container, which is set to the children of scene, so as to realize the dynamic load model.

The dynamic loading technology can also be used for dynamic load model file, and use the Win32 API function–'Create Process' to create a new process and its main thread, and the new process run a specified executable file. The second parameter of function is the command line parameters, which is used for the incoming different model file path. The file path is get from the command line by string copy function, and then it is copied to global variable, that is 'strcpy (acfName, str)'. Through the different model file, the exe file can be made into the model of the car, or tanks, or plane.

4   Multitasking Path Planning Based on Particle Swarm Optimization (PSO) Algorithm

For multitasking multi-agent NP problem [9–12] of path planning, known that the key for task allocation decision is to determine: the agent arrived at which target respectively in the scene. Thus, constructs a U-dimension space corresponds to U agents' task allocation problem, and everyone in the group includes a U-dimension vector, which X_i corresponds to serial number of the target location of the agent to arrive at. For example, set up six agents to reach 3 goals, the position vector X of a subgroup as shown in Table 1.

Table 1. Target position vector of each subgroup

Number	x_i
1	1
2	2
3	1
4	2
5	3
6	3

From Table 1, subgroup 1 and 3 collaboratively arrive at target 1, and subgroup 2 and 4 cooperatively arrive at target 2, and subgroup 5 and 6 arrive at target 3 cooperatively.

Steps of multi-tasking planning which is achieved by intelligent algorithm based on the division of subgroups are as follows.

Step 1: Initialization.

(1) The whole group is divided into some overlapping subgroups.
(2) Each dimension of target position vector X within each subgroup is randomly selected from integer 1 to T. Numbers 1-T (target numbers) represent the serial number of the target.
(3) Initialize the speed and position of each individual in subgroup.
(4) All objective function values of individuals are evaluated, and the initial individual position is set as the optimal solution of individual [5].

Step 2: Repeat the following steps until the destination is found or the iterations number exceeds maximum.

(5) The transition probabilities are calculated for each individual to select the next position(X, Y). When (X, Y) exceeds its scope, the next position equals to the boundary [5].
(6) Compare the fitness function value of each individual with its history best value, and then update the optimal value.
(7) Find the nearly optimal solutions in each subgroup and the approximate optimal solution of the total swarming.

Based on the above subgroup algorithm, the targets and tasks of each agent are decomposed for each subgroup in the system, and the targets and tasks are assigned to different levels, thus the reasonable hierarchical planning tasks are accomplished, as shown in Table 1.

5 The Simulation Results and Analysis

The server of the distributed virtual visual system controls multiple clients, through the thread pool technology to manage the connection on the client. After the client end connect the IP on the server, the client's tanks will follow the plane movement on the server, at the same time the server dynamic loads the model of the tanks. The tank has been below the plane with the following movement on the server side. When close the client, tanks disappears. On each client nodes in simulation system, multitask path planning based on particle swarm intelligence algorithm can be realized.

Initial interface of the virtual visual system is shown in Fig. 6. The left exe file is the client side, and the right exe file is the sever side. Socket network programming technology is adopted for system communication, and data communications follow the TCP/IP protocol. When IP are properly set, the multiple computers (multiple clients) can be connected.

As shown in Fig. 7, in the client's dialog box, enter the IP address, port number and nickname for each text box.

Click "connect" button, then the client tank can get the plane location data passed by the server to move. Switch the server side view, from the original tank view to plane view, as shown in Fig. 8. The tank model of the client is dynamic loaded to the server, and moves following the server-side plane model, which indicates that the network communication is successfully. So the client model movement is controlled by the server-side.

Fig. 6. Initialization of client (left window) and server (right window)

Fig. 7. Fill the IP address and port number information for the server

Fig. 8. Tank is loaded to the server side dynamically and moves following the aircraft

Click the "off" button on the left side client, and the client will close, as shown in Fig. 9. When the client is turned off, only the server runs, at the same time the server tank model disappears.

Fig. 9. Close the client, and the server side tanks disappears

On the clients in a virtual visual system, according to the task allocation in Table 1, the 6 objects are allocated to 3 target position by clicking on the radio buttons. Goal 1 (590,490) is assigned to object 1 and 3, and goal 2(700,680) is assigned to object 2 and 4, target 3(200,300) is assigned to object 5 and 6. After the target assignment is completed, the objects will arrive at the assigned target position, then every path will be draw real-time in the overlooking channel of virtual visual system. Switch to the overlook view, the planned various paths of each tank on the server side when performing multitasking collaborative planning are as shown in Fig. 10.

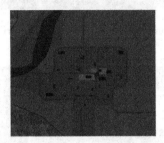

Fig. 10. Client multitasking path planning result

The Fig. 10 shows that when the agents are located in the dense regions of obstacles, multitasking planning algorithm can also plan the viable path.

6   Conclusions

Conduct the three dimension visual simulation system in the distributed network environment, multithreading technology is used to process different tasks and solve the problem of throughput and responsiveness. This paper adopts multithreading technology to design and implement three-dimensional virtual visual simulation engine based on Vega Prime. Build high poly and low coupling control/operation of the network architecture through the network communication mechanism. Implement model reuse combined with dynamic loading technology. Then swarm intelligence algorithm of multitasking collaborative planning is proposed to realize 3d multipath search program. The implementation of distributed collaborative 3d visual system is proved be effective and practical by the simulation results.

Acknowledgments. This paper is sponsored by teaching and research fund of Wuhan education Bureau (2017008).

References

1. Peng, L.: The real-time image formation in 3D simulation and distributed system research. Thesis for of Master's Degree in Huazhong University of Science and Technology, pp. 28–38, May 2012
2. Yao, F.F., Liang, Q., Xu, R.J., Du, J.: Study of three-dimensional virtual battlefield large terrain dynamically generated based on vega prime. J. Syst. Simul. **24**(9), 1900–1904 (2012)

3. Liu, S.S.: Research on key techniques of heterogeneous parallel computing for virtual reality simulation platform. Doctor Dissertation of Ocean University of China, pp. 20–32, May 2014
4. Zhao, B.S., Feng, K.P., Luo, L.H.: The implementation of multi-channel three- dimensional simulation system based on vega prime. J. Graph. **33**(5), 73–77 (2012)
5. Zhou, J., Fu, X.C.: New particle swarm optimization algorithm for path planning simulation of virtual character. J. Comput. Appl. **34**(9), 2562–2565 (2014)
6. Wang, B.G.: The research of unmanned aerial vehicles mission planning system. Thesis for Master's degree in ShenYang Aerospace University, pp. 23–46, January 2013
7. Zhou, J., Peng, C.: Research and analysis of path planning simulation system for three-dimensional complex scene. Comput. Simul. **32**(6), 364–367 (2015)
8. Sun, D.D., Zhang, H.X.: A routing cooperative selection method based on ant colony optimization algorithm. In: International Conference on Cyberspace Technology (2014). CP656
9. Huang, H., Zhu, D.Q., Ding, F.: Dynamic task assignment and path planning for multi-AUV system in variable ocean current environment. J. Intell. Rob. Syst. Theor. Appl. **74**(3), 999–1002 (2014)
10. Zhu, D.Q., Huang, H., Yang, S.X.: Dynamictask assignment and path planning of multi-AUV system based on an improved self-organizing map and velocity synthesis method in three-dimensional underwater workspace. IEEE Trans. Cybern. **43**(2), 504–514 (2013)
11. Moon, S.W., Oh, E.M., Shim, D.H.: An integral framework of task assignment and path planning for multiple unmanned aerial vehicles in dynamic environments. J. Intell. Rob. Syst. Theor. Appl. **70**(4), 303–313 (2013)
12. Sahingoz, O.K.: Flyable path planning for a multi-UAV system with Genetic Algorithms and Bezier curves. In: 2013 International Conference on Unmanned Aircraft Systems, pp. 41–48 (2013)

Comparisons of Features for Chinese Word Segmentation

Xiaofeng Liu[✉]

School of Software Engineering,
Huazhong University of Science and Technology,
Luoyu Road 1037, Wuhan, China
liuxf@hust.edu.cn

Abstract. Machine learning based approach is the most important one among Chinese word segmentation, and feature selection is very crucial to it. This paper overviews feature sets used in a few machine learning based approaches for Chinese word segmentation closed task. The comparison of these feature sets is made on the SIGHAN corpora and the same machine learning framework – maximum entropy model. Based on this model, two new efficiency measures are presented, i.e. the numbers of unique events and predicates. The experimental results for the impacts of feature sets on effectiveness and efficiency are shown, according to which the suggestion for feature selection is presented when building machine learning based Chinese word segmentation system.

Keywords: Chinese information processing · Chinese word segmentation
Closed task · Feature selection

1 Introduction

Chinese word segmentation is an important step of Chinese information processing, the performance of which has a marked impact on the subsequent steps of Chinese information processing, such as part-of-speech tagging, syntactic parsing, semantic parsing, and so on. Moreover, Chinese word segmentation would influence other Chinese NLP tasks, e.g. information retrieval, machine translation, information extraction, and so on. Therefore, it has been studied in many literatures, and a great many of approaches has been proposed.

Nowadays, the state-of-the-art approaches for Chinese word segmentation are based on machine learning, and they have the best performance. Among them the discriminate methods perform better than the generative methods. The maximum entropy model and conditional random field are widely used in the discriminate methods, in which the parameters of models are learned based on the specific feature sets.

In SIGHAN Bakeoff the features that can be used by discriminate methods are dependent on the segmentation task. Only the features extracted from the training corpus are available in the closed task, while in the open task any additional information and knowledge can be used. Therefore, the features in the Chinese word segmentation closed task are determinate and comparable, but they are very different in the open task. So we choose the features in the closed task as our research object.

© Springer Nature Singapore Pte Ltd. 2018
H. Yuan et al. (Eds.): GSKI 2017, CCIS 849, pp. 492–499, 2018.
https://doi.org/10.1007/978-981-13-0896-3_49

In the closed task, it is obvious that the feature sets of discriminate methods have a significant impact on the effectiveness and efficiency of Chinese word segmentation, so researchers choose different features to train models according to their understanding. As we know, so far there has been no wok that compares the effectiveness and efficiency of different feature sets and studies their impacts by the same experimental setting. In this paper, on the SIGHAN corpora we compare these feature sets using the same machine learning framework – maximum entropy model, present the experimental results for their impacts on effectiveness and efficiency and give some advice about feature selection for building a Chinese word segmentation system.

2 Feature Sets in the Close Task

Although the features that can be used in the closed task are relatively determinate, there exist a few different feature sets in the literature, which are shown in Table 1. The current character is denoted as C_0, the ith character before C_0 as $C_{-i}(i = 1, 2)$, the ith character after C_0 as $C_i(i = 1, 2)$, and the position tag of C_{-i} as T_{-i}. There is a special feature prefix C_0 in [10] which means for each feature in the feature set, a feature is generated by adding C_0 to its head. For example, if C_1C_0 is a feature for the model, then $C_0C_1C_0$ also is. Note that there exist different machine learning frameworks for the feature sets in Table 1, e.g. the maximum entropy model and conditional random field.

Firstly, it is shown in Table 1 that the current, previous ant next characters are used in features by all papers, but how to combine them into features is slightly different. Secondly, there is no agreement with C_{-2} and C_2, and they are ignored in a few papers. Thirdly, the position tags are hardly used in feature sets, which only appeared in [1].

Table 1. Feature sets in the closed task

Feature	Paper [1]	Paper [2, 8]	Paper [3]	Paper [4]	Paper [6]	Paper [7]	Paper [5, 9, 11–13]	Paper [10]
C_{-2}	✓			✓	✓	✓	✓	✓
C_{-1}	✓	✓		✓	✓	✓	✓	✓
C_0	✓	✓	✓	✓		✓	✓	✓
C_1	✓	✓	✓	✓	✓	✓	✓	✓
C_2	✓				✓	✓	✓	✓
$C_{-2}C_{-1}$	✓			✓	✓		✓	✓
$C_{-1}C_0$	✓	✓	✓	✓	✓	✓	✓	✓
C_0C_1	✓	✓	✓	✓	✓	✓	✓	✓
C_1C_2	✓		✓				✓	✓
$C_{-1}C_1$	✓	✓		✓		✓	✓	
$C_{-2}C_0$				✓				
$C_{-1}C_0$ C_1					✓			
$T_{-2}T_{-1}$	✓							
Prefix C_0								✓

Although the SIGHAN Bakeoff corpora are widely chosen for training and testing in previous work, the machine learning frameworks are different. Thus, it is necessary for feature selection in Chinese word segmentation to compare the effectiveness and efficiency of features with the same learning framework.

3 Experimental Settings

The SIGHAN2005 Bakeoff corpora are chosen for experiments, which contain four corpora, i.e. PKU, MSR, CITYU and AS. The statistics for corpora are shown in Table 2. For each x/y in the table, x is for the training corpus and y for the test corpus.

Table 2. The statistics for the training and testing corpora

Corpus	MSR	PKU	CITYU	AS
# of sentences	86,924/3,985	19,056/1,945	53,019/1,493	708,953/14,432
# of word types	88,119/12,923	55,303/13,148	69,086/9,001	141,338/18,811
# of word tokens	2,368,391/106,873	1,109,947/104,372	1,455,630/40,936	5,449,581/122,610
# of character types	5,167/2,838	4,698/2,934	4,922/2,702	6,115/3,707
# of characters	4,050,469/184,355	1,826,448/172,733	2,403,354/67,690	8,368,050/197,681
Average word length (characters per word)	1.71/1.72	1.65/1.65	1.65/1.65	1.54/1.61
Average sentence length (words per sentence)	27.25/26.82	58.25/53.66	27.45/27.42	7.69/8.50
Average sentence length (characters per sentence)	46.60/46.26	95.85/88.81	45.33/45.34	11.80/13.70
OOV rate	2.6%	5.8%	7.4%	4.6%

All experiments are based on the maximum entropy model framework and implemented by Apache OpenNLP 1.7.0 as well as Java 8. The number of iterations for training is 100, and the cutoff of the number of events is 3. We adopt 4-tag set which contains S (single character word), B (the begin of multiple characters word), M (the middle of multiple characters word) and E (the end of multiple characters word).

The effectiveness measures for experiments are recall R, precision P, F measure, Riv, $Roov$ and sentence accuracy SA, where SA is defined as follows:

$$SA = \frac{\# \text{ of sentences segmented correctly}}{\# \text{ of sentences}} \tag{1}$$

Sentence accuracy SA is a coarse-grained effectiveness measure, which is directly influenced by F measure and correlate with the average sentence length. Let l be the average sentence length, then SA is calculated as: $SA = F^l$.

The efficiency measures for experiments are the number of predicates denoted as $PRED$ and the number of unique events denoted as UE. In the maximum entropy model, let Y be the outcome set, i.e. $Y = \{S, B, M, E\}$, and F be the feature set. For each character in a sentence, there exists a corresponding event $e = (F_e, y), y \in Y, F_e \subseteq F,$

where F_e is called a context. When two events have the same outcome and context, they are duplicate events.

On the period of training, the sentences are converted into the intermediate event set, which is a compact representation of training set. According to paper [14], the training cost of the maximum entropy model is $O(NTA)$, where N is the size of training set, T is the size of outcome set and A is the average number of features in an event. Since reducing the number of unique events is to reduce the size of training set, the smaller is UE, the smaller is the training cost.

For each $f \in F$ and $y \in Y$, (f, y) is a predicate, the weight of which is learned during training phase and used to compute the probability of segmentation. Therefore, the number of predicates $PRED$ has a direct impact on the training time and segmentation speed. The smaller is the $PRED$, the smaller is the training cost and the faster is the segmentation speed.

Compared with the training time and segmentation speed, UE and $PRED$ are accuracy and independent of the platform and experimental runs. So, they are used as efficiency measures.

4 Comparison of Segmentation Effectiveness

For each feature set in Table 1, the character based maximum entropy models are trained and tested on the SIGHAN 2005 Bakeoff corpora and the effectiveness measures are shown in Table 3. The figures with bold and underline style are the biggest ones amongst all feature sets.

(1) **The best segmentation effectiveness.** In terms of F and SA, paper [2, 8] have the best performance in corpus PKU, while paper [10] does in other three corpora. Moreover, the F and SA of paper [10] are slightly smaller than those of paper [2] and [8] in PKU. It is obvious from Table 3 that SA and F are highly relevant.

(2) **The relation between effectiveness and corpora.** Among all corpora, F and SA are the smallest in corpus PKU, in that it has the smallest training set, the biggest average sentence length and the highest OOV rate. SA in corpus AS is the biggest, which is due to the smallest average sentence length. F, P, Riv and $Roov$ in corpus MSR are the biggest, because its training set is bigger, its average word length is the biggest and its OOV rate is the smallest.

(3) **The relation between effectiveness and the size of feature set.** The effectiveness is more relevant with the combination of features than with the size of feature set. The feature set of paper [1] is a superset of those of paper [2, 3, 5, 8, 9, 11–13], but in all corpora there is no effectiveness measure that is bigger. In the same way, the feature set of paper [5, 9, 11–13] includes those of paper [2, 3, 7, 8], while all their effectiveness measures in all corpora except $Roov$ in corpus MSR are smaller. We also find out that although the feature set of paper [3] is the smallest, in all corpora except MSR its F is not the smallest.

Table 3. Effectiveness for existing feature sets

Corpus	Measure	Paper [1]	Paper [2, 8]	Paper [3]	Paper [4]	Paper [6]	Paper [7]	Paper [5, 9, 11–13]	Paper [10]
PKU	P	0.9267	0.9325	0.9318	0.9251	0.9192	0.9300	0.9300	**0.9337**
	R	0.9159	**0.9242**	0.9177	0.9146	0.9110	0.9192	0.9178	0.9222
	F	0.9213	**0.9283**	0.9247	0.9198	0.9151	0.9246	0.9239	0.9279
	RIV	0.9367	**0.9435**	0.9425	0.9361	0.9356	0.9401	0.9381	0.9424
	ROOV	0.5766	**0.6076**	0.5120	0.5636	0.5070	0.5769	0.5859	0.5909
	SA	0.2900	**0.3090**	0.2838	0.2751	0.2735	0.2972	0.2910	0.3033
MSR	P	0.9549	0.9531	0.9515	0.9538	0.9546	0.9554	0.9568	**0.9601**
	R	0.9531	0.9513	0.9504	0.9503	0.9553	0.9528	0.9535	**0.9572**
	F	0.9540	0.9522	0.9509	0.9520	0.9550	0.9541	0.9552	**0.9587**
	RIV	0.9609	0.9603	0.9598	0.9584	**0.9644**	0.9608	0.9611	0.9650
	ROOV	0.6681	0.6218	0.6037	0.6518	0.6239	0.6578	**0.6748**	0.6698
	SA	0.5626	0.5476	0.5355	0.5471	0.5739	0.5571	0.5691	**0.5910**
CITYU	P	0.9307	0.9339	0.9295	0.9291	0.9222	0.9336	0.9346	**0.9367**
	R	0.9348	0.9392	0.9343	0.9335	0.9311	0.9381	0.9375	**0.9408**
	F	0.9328	0.9366	0.9319	0.9313	0.9266	0.9359	0.9361	**0.9387**
	RIV	0.9553	0.9612	0.9577	0.9544	0.9563	0.9592	0.9571	**0.9614**
	ROOV	0.6791	0.6636	0.6411	0.6722	0.6160	0.6735	0.6926	**0.6821**
	SA	0.4099	0.4481	0.4059	0.4159	0.3972	0.4374	0.4287	**0.4461**
AS	P	0.9295	0.9343	0.9304	0.9301	0.9236	0.9339	0.9331	**0.9421**
	R	0.9487	0.9507	0.9471	0.9469	0.9461	0.9502	0.9496	**0.9513**
	F	0.9390	0.9424	0.9387	0.9384	0.9347	0.9419	0.9413	**0.9467**
	RIV	0.9646	0.9671	0.9644	0.9634	0.9652	0.9660	0.9653	**0.9691**
	ROOV	0.5985	0.5882	0.5641	0.5825	0.5254	0.5995	0.6036	**0.6132**
	SA	0.7497	0.7609	0.7438	0.7452	0.7286	0.7566	0.7518	**0.7622**

(4) **The relation between F and other measures**. From Table 3, the correlation coefficients of other effectiveness measures with F are derived and shown in Table 4. Because F is the mean of P and R and SA can be derived from F with Eq. (1), P, R and SA are more relevant with F than other measures, among which P is the most relevant. Among all measure, $Roov$ is the least relevant with F, which is less relevant than Riv.

Table 4. The correlation coefficients of other measure with F

Corpus	Measure	Coeff.	Corpus	Measure	Coeff.
PKU	P	0.9807	CITYU	P	0.9912
	R	0.9758		R	0.9826
	Riv	0.8949		Riv	0.7250
	Roov	0.6637		Roov	0.7825
	SA	0.8901		SA	0.9190
MSR	P	0.9642	AS	P	0.9914
	R	0.9587		R	0.9275
	Riv	0.8507		Riv	0.8077
	Roov	0.6447		Roov	0.8379
	SA	0.9811		SA	0.9335

5 Comparison of Segmentation Efficiency

The statistics about UE and PRED for experiments are shown in Table 5.

Table 5. Efficiency for existing feature sets

Corpus	Measure	Paper [1]	Paper [2, 8]	Paper [3]	Paper [4]	Paper [6]	Paper [7]	Paper [5, 9, 11–13]	Paper [10]
PKU	UE	154.85	88.22	119.62	132.38	154.44	154.46	154.46	154.46
	PRED	49.45	31.29	26.95	53.02	39.00	32.06	49.45	120.02
MSR	UE	327.28	162.77	246.02	267.45	325.58	325.62	325.62	325.62
	PRED	86.94	55.71	46.73	95.03	72.25	56.60	86.94	221.72
CITYU	UE	209.99	122.41	162.94	181.94	209.42	209.47	209.47	209.47
	PRED	65.82	41.78	36.00	70.77	51.38	42.61	65.82	159.52
AS	UE	639.65	309.87	470.92	518.20	634.98	635.66	635.66	641.24
	PRED	147.48	94.53	80.81	160.13	126.30	95.59	147.48	320.13

(1) **The relation between efficiency and the size of feature set.** Different from the relation between effectiveness and the size of feature set, as feature set A contains feature set B, *UE* and *PRED* of set A are bigger than those of set B. This implies that the bigger is the size of feature set, the slower are the training speed and segmentation speed.

(2) **The relation between *UE* and feature set.** Basically, if the size of one feature set is bigger, then its *UE* is bigger. However, this relation is not strict. For example, the size of feature set in paper [10] is the biggest, while its *UE* is not the biggest. The reason is that for the limited corpus *UE* increases as the size of feature set increases. But the increase of *UE* finally becomes smaller and smaller.

(3) **The relation between *PRED* and feature set.** *PRED* highly correlate with the size of feature set. With the increase of the size of feature set, *PRED* keeps growing. This means that as more and more features are included, the training time will get longer and the segmentation speed will become slower.

6 Trade-off for Feature Selection

From the above experiments, it is shown that paper [10] almost has the best effectiveness, however, the worst efficiency, i.e. the biggest *UE* and *PRED*. So, we cannot obtain a Chinese word segmenter whose effectiveness and efficiency both are the best, and a balance for them must be made.

Firstly, for a Chinese word segmentation system position tags, such as T_{-2} and T_{-1}, have no positive impact on the performance, and they should be discarded. Secondly, C_2 and C_{-2} have different and slight impact on the effectiveness, and they could be deliberately exploited. Thirdly, the most important features are C_1, C_0 and C_{-1}, and it is crucial for system to combine them in various ways.

7 Conclusion

Based on the same learning framework and data set, the effectiveness and efficiency of existing feature sets for Chinese word segmentation are compared and their impacts on effectiveness and efficiency are also examined. Due to their different impacts, we give some advice to help to make a balance on feature selection.

References

1. Xue, N., Shen, L.: Chinese word segmentation as LMR tagging. In: Proceedings of the Second SIGHAN Workshop on Chinese Language Processing, vol. 17. Association for Computational Linguistics, pp. 176–179 (2003)
2. Wang, Z., Huang, C., Zhu, J.: The Character-based CRF segmenter of MSRA&NEU for the 4th Bakeoff. In: IJCNLP, pp. 98–101 (2008)
3. Fang, Y., Li, Z.W.S., et al.: Soochow university word segmenter for SIGHAN 2012 bakeoff. In: CLP, pp. 47–50 (2012)
4. Tseng, H., Chang, P., Andrew, G., et al.: A conditional random field word segmenter for SIGHAN bakeoff. In: Proceedings of the Fourth SIGHAN Workshop on Chinese Language Processing, pp. 168–171 (2005)
5. Low, J.K., Ng, H.T., Guo, W.: A maximum entropy approach to Chinese word segmentation. In: Proceedings of the Fourth SIGHAN Workshop on Chinese Language Processing, pp. 448–451 (2005)
6. Peng, F., Feng, F., McCallum, A.: Chinese segmentation and new word detection using conditional random fields. In: Proceedings of the 20th International Conference on Computational Linguistics. Association for Computational Linguistics, pp. 562–568 (2004)
7. Zhao, H., Huang, C., Li, M., et al.: Effective tag set selection in chinese word segmentation via conditional random field modeling. In: PACLIC (2006)
8. Zhao, H., Huang, C.N., Li, M.: An improved Chinese word segmentation system with conditional random field. In: Proceedings of the Fifth SIGHAN Workshop on Chinese Language Processing (2006)
9. Wang, K., Zong, C., Su, K.Y.: A character-based joint model for Chinese word segmentation. In: Proceedings of the 23rd International Conference on Computational Linguistics. Association for Computational Linguistics, pp. 1173–1181 (2010)

10. Jiang, W., Huang, L., Liu, Q., et al.: A cascaded linear model for joint chinese word segmentation and part-of-speech tagging. In: Proceedings of the 46th Annual Meeting of the Association for Computational Linguistics (2008)
11. Jiang, W., Huang, L., Liu, Q.: Automatic adaptation of annotation standards: Chinese word segmentation and POS tagging: a case study. In: Proceedings of the Joint Conference of the 47th Annual Meeting of the ACL and the 4th International Joint Conference on Natural Language Processing, pp. 522–530 (2009)
12. Li, X., Zong, C., Su, K.: A unified model for solving the OOV problem of chinese word segmentation. ACM Trans. Asian Low-Resour. Lang. Inf. Proces. **14**(3) (2015). 12
13. Wang, K., Zong, C., Su, K.Y.: Integrating generative and discriminative character-based models for Chinese word segmentation. ACM Trans. Asian Lang. Inf. Proces. (TALIP), **11** (2) (2012). 7
14. Ratnaparkhi, A.: A maximum entropy model for part-of-speech tagging. In: Proceedings of the Conference on Empirical Methods in Natural Language Processing, vol. 1, pp. 133–142 (1996)

Forecasting of Roof Temperature in a Grey Prediction Model with Optimal Fractional Order Accumulating Operator

Yuan Zhang$^{(\boxtimes)}$, Xiaoyong Peng, and Wei Hu

School of Civil Engineering, University of South China, Hengyang, China
zhangyuanzy1015@163.com, HWdreams@163.com,
pengxiaoyong@126.com

Abstract. Building roof temperatures mainly affected by solar radiation. With the solar radiation intensity changing, the change of roof temperature also occurs constantly. It has an uncertainty to a high degree, so the grey system can be combined with data analysis for researches. Based on the classical NDGM model, this paper introduced the fractional order $NDGM^{\frac{r}{p}}$ model to study the important properties of the model and used the PSO particle swarm optimization algorithm to optimize the fractional order. Finally, the two representative measuring points, namely, the maximum solar radiation and the second solar radiation points, were taken as the experimental objects. The experimental results show that the mean absolute percentage error (MAPE) of the optimized fractional order $NDGM^{\frac{r}{p}}$ model for the roof temperature is several percentage points higher than that of the classical GM, DGM and NDGM models, as well as the minimum error of the model can reach 2.4247%.

Keywords: Discrete grey model · Optimized fractional order
Roof temperature · PSO algorithm

1 Introduction

At present, a large number of scholars at home and abroad have done a lot of researches on reducing roof temperature [1–7], steady state and unsteady heat transfer analysis [8] and roof structure optimization [9–11], but there are few studies on roof temperature prediction and simulation. Roof temperature is mainly affected by solar radiation, and solar radiation has great uncertainty. It is difficult to accurately grasp the role of factors and mechanisms, so the grey system can be combined with data analysis to carry out researches.

The grey prediction model is simple and adaptable. It not only can handle better mutation parameter changes but also does not require many data points for prediction and update. Since 1982, Professor Deng [12], a famous Chinese scholar, has put forward the grey system theory. It has been widely used in many fields, such as industry, agriculture, transportation and so on [13–18], for more than three decades of grey model researches. The systematic studies were conducted on the grey prediction model from the initial value and the background value [19–27], which promoted the

© Springer Nature Singapore Pte Ltd. 2018
H. Yuan et al. (Eds.): GSKI 2017, CCIS 849, pp. 500–512, 2018.
https://doi.org/10.1007/978-981-13-0896-3_50

development and improvement of the grey prediction model theory system. The classical GM and DGM models were mainly used to simulate and predict homogeneous for approximately homogeneous data, and the effect was betterr. However, if the classical GM and DGM models are used for the roof temperature data in a parabolic way, the effect was poor. NDGM model was approximately constructed based on the non-homogeneous index trend, and it is not suitable to simulate parabolic data, Therefore, Wu [28] defined the actual data with fractional order accumulation and defined the NDGM model with fractional order accumulation (abbreviated as $NDGM_p^{\frac{q}{p}}$). But in his findings, it is not found which order number was the best or how to obtain the best order number for the $NDGM_p^{\frac{q}{p}}$ model and other properties.

In this paper, the important properties of fractional order model were studied and the PSO particle swarm algorithm was used to optimize the fractional order [29]. Finally, two sets of data in the measured data were taken as the objects of the optimized fractional model. The two sets of data represented the temperatures at the maximum solar radiation and the second largest solar radiation, and they were the highest temperature in all the measuring points.

In Sect. 2, the basic theory of grey systems was introduced. In Sect. 3, the important properties of the fractional order $NDGM_p^{\frac{q}{p}}$ were studied and the fractional order using the PSO particle swarm optimization algorithm was optimized. In Sect. 4, set of data in the measured roof temperature were used as experimental subjects for experimental analysis. In Sect. 5, the conclusions were presented.

2 The Basic Theory of Grey System

Assume that a sequence is

$$X^{(0)} = (x^{(0)}(1), x^{(0)}(2), \cdots, x^{(0)}(n)) \tag{1}$$

$X^{(1)}$ is the accumulating generation operator sequence of $X^{(0)}$, and

$$X^{(1)} = (x^{(1)}(1), x^{(1)}(2), \ldots, x^{(1)}(n)) \tag{2}$$

where $x^{(1)}(k) = \sum_{i=1}^{k} x^{(0)}(i), \quad k = 1, 2, \cdots n.$

$$z^{(1)}(k) = 0.5(x^{(1)}(k) + x^{(1)}(k-1)), k = 2, 3, \cdots, n. \tag{3}$$

be the mean sequence generated by consecutive neighbors.

Definition 2.1
Assuming that $X^{(0)}$, $X^{(1)}$ and $Z^{(1)}$ are showed respectively as (1), (2), (3)

$$x^{(0)}(k) + az^{(1)}(k) = b \tag{4}$$

is called the grey differential equation of GM(1,1), which is $\begin{pmatrix} a \\ b \end{pmatrix} = (B^T B)^{-1} B^T Y$,

$$B = \begin{pmatrix} -z^{(1)}(2) & 1 \\ -z^{(1)}(3) & 1 \\ \vdots & \vdots \\ -z^{(1)}(n) & 1 \end{pmatrix}, \quad Y = \begin{pmatrix} x^{(0)}(2) \\ x^{(0)}(3) \\ \vdots \\ x^{(0)}(n) \end{pmatrix},$$

The time response sequence of grey different Eq. (4) is given by

$$\hat{x}^{(1)}(k+1) = [x^{(1)}(1) - \frac{b}{a}]e^{-ak} + \frac{b}{a}, k = 1, 2, \cdots, n.$$

Definition 2.2

Assuming that $X^{(0)}, X^{(1)}$ are showed respectively as (1), (2), the following equation

$$x^{(1)}(k+1) = \beta_1 x^{(1)}(k) + \beta_2,$$

is called the grey differential equation of DGM (1, 1) model, which is $\begin{pmatrix} \beta_1 \\ \beta_2 \end{pmatrix} = (B^T B)^{-1} B^T Y$,

$$B = \begin{pmatrix} x^{(1)}(1) & 1 \\ x^{(1)}(2) & 1 \\ \vdots & \vdots \\ x^{(1)}(n-1) & 1 \end{pmatrix}, \quad Y = \begin{pmatrix} x^{(1)}(2) \\ x^{(1)}(3) \\ \vdots \\ x^{(1)}(n) \end{pmatrix}$$

The restored values of $\hat{x}^{(0)}(k+1)$ can be formulated as

$$\hat{x}^{(0)}(k+1) = \beta_1^k(x^{(0)}(1) - \frac{\beta_2}{1 - \beta_1}) + \frac{\beta_2}{1 - \beta_1}, k = 1, 2, \ldots, n - 1$$

Definition 2.3

Assuming that sequences $X^{(0)}, X^{(1)}$ are showed respectively as (1), (2), the equations

$$x^{(1)}(k+1) = \beta_1 x^{(1)}(k) + \beta_2 k + \beta_3$$

is the NDGM(1,1) model, the recurrence function

$$\hat{x}^{(1)}(k+1) = \beta_1^k \hat{x}^{(1)}(1) + \beta_2 \sum_{j=1}^{k} j\beta_1^{k-j} + \frac{1 - \beta_1^k}{1 - \beta_1} \beta_3, k = 1, 2, \cdots, n - 1. \quad (5)$$

3 The Properties of $NDGM_{p}^{q}$ Model

3.1 NDGM Model with Fractional Order Accumulation

First of all, introduce the basics of the NDGM model, details as follows:

Definition 3.1

The order accumulate degenerating operator $\frac{p}{q}\left(0<\frac{p}{q}<1\right)$ of the original non-homogeneous index sequence $X^{(0)}$ be $X^{\left(\frac{p}{q}\right)}$, for

$$C_{\frac{p}{q}}^0 = 1, C_{k-1}^k = 0$$

then

$$x^{\left(\frac{p}{q}\right)}(k) = \sum_{i-1}^{k} C_{k-i+\frac{p}{q}-1}^{k-i} x^{(0)}(i), k = 1, 2, \ldots, n \tag{6}$$

$$C_{k-i+\frac{p}{q}-1}^{k-i} = \frac{\left(\frac{p}{q}+k-i-1\right)\left(\frac{p}{q}+k-i-2\right)\ldots(r+1)\frac{p}{q}}{(k-i)!}$$

$\frac{p}{q}$ order inverse accumulate degenerating operator of $X^{(0)}$ is

$$x(\frac{p}{q})x(0) = \alpha^{(1)}x(1-\frac{p}{q})$$
$$= \{\alpha^{(1)}x^{\left(1-\frac{p}{q}\right)}, \alpha(1)^{(1)}x^{\left(1-\frac{p}{q}\right)}(2), \ldots, \alpha^{(1)}x^{\left(1-\frac{p}{q}\right)}(n)\}$$

Definition 3.2

The equation

$$\hat{x}^{\left(\frac{p}{q}\right)}(k+1) = \beta_1\hat{x}^{\left(\frac{p}{q}\right)} + \beta_2 k + \beta_3 \tag{7}$$

The sequences $X^{(0)}$ and $X^{\left(\frac{p}{q}\right)}$ are defined as Eqs. (2) and (6). $\hat{x}^{\left(\frac{p}{q}\right)}(k)$ is the simulative value of $x^{(1)}(k)$ and $\hat{x}^{\left(\frac{p}{q}\right)}(1)$ is the iterative value of the NDGM model. β_1, β_2, β_3 are parameters of $NDGM_{q}^{p}$ model.

That is least square method. So we can get the expressions of parameters in Proposition 3.1.

Proposition 3.1
Based on the least square method the first level parameters β_1, β_2, β_3 satisfy to the matrix equation

$$\begin{pmatrix} \beta_1 \\ \beta_2 \\ \beta_3 \end{pmatrix} = (B^T B)^{-1} B^T Y,$$

$$B = \begin{pmatrix} x_q^{(\ell)}(1) & 1 & 1 \\ x_q^{(\ell)}(2) & 2 & 1 \\ \vdots & \vdots & \vdots \\ x_q^{(\ell)}(n-1) & n-1 & 1 \end{pmatrix}, \ Y = \begin{pmatrix} x_q^{(\ell)}(2) \\ x_q^{(\ell)}(3) \\ \vdots \\ x_q^{(\ell)}(n) \end{pmatrix}$$

Proof. According to the least square method, we can get (7), we have

Proposition 3.2
Let

$$C = \sum_{k=1}^{n-1} \left(x_q^{(\ell)}(k) \right)^2, D = \sum_{k=1}^{n-1} k x_q^{(\ell)}(k),$$

$$D = \sum_{k=1}^{n-1} x_q^{(\ell)}(k), D = \sum_{k=1}^{n-1} k^2, G = \sum_{k=1}^{n-1} k,$$

$$H = \sum_{k=1}^{n-1} x_q^{(\ell)}(k) x_q^{(\ell)}(k+1),$$

$$I = \sum_{k=1}^{n-1} k x_q^{(\ell)}(k+1), I = \sum_{k=1}^{n-1} x_q^{(\ell)}(k+1),$$

$$N = n - 1,$$

then

$$(B^T B)^{-1} = \frac{1}{CFN + 2DEG - CG^2 - ND^2 - FE^2}$$
$$\times \begin{pmatrix} FN - G^2 & EG - DN & DG - EF \\ EG - DN & CN - E^2 & DE - CG \\ DG - EF & DE - CG & CF - D^2 \end{pmatrix}, (B^T Y) = (H, I, M)^T.$$

For (5), we have

Proposition 3.3

The recursive function of $NDGM^{\frac{q}{p}}$ model

$$\hat{x}^{(\frac{p}{q})}(k+1) = \beta_1 \hat{x}^{(\frac{p}{q})}(1) + \beta_2 \sum_{j=1}^{k} j\beta_1^{k-j} + \frac{1-\beta_1^k}{1-\beta_1}\beta_3, k = 1, 2, \ldots, n \qquad (8)$$

Thus $\frac{p}{q}(0 < \frac{p}{q} \leq 1)$ model order inverse accumulated generating operator is

$$\hat{x}^{(0)} = \alpha^{(1)}\hat{x}^{(1-\frac{p}{q})}(k) = \alpha^{(1)}\hat{x}^{(1-\frac{p}{q})}\left(1 - \frac{p}{q}\right)$$

$$= \left\{\alpha^{(1)}x^{(1-\frac{p}{q})}(1), \alpha^{(1)}x^{(1-\frac{p}{q})}(2), \ldots, \alpha^{(1)}x^{(1-\frac{p}{q})}(n)\right\}$$

3.2 Optimization of the Order Number of the $NDGM^{\frac{q}{p}}$ Model by Particle Swarm Optimization Algorithm (PSO)

PSO (particle swarm optimization) algorithm, is a new optimization technology which is widely used, and it came from the simulation of biological predation in nature. PSO algorithm can determine the initial positions and initial speeds of the particles, and then the fitness value was determined by the objective function. When the particle flight in the multi-dimensional space, its speed and location would also change, that is, the particles would follow the optimal particles and then searched for the optimal solution direction, finally, they can get the optimal solution.

In order to determine the best cumulative order of the $NDGM^{\frac{q}{p}}$ model, the value of MAPE was often used to judge the merits of modeling, making the MAPE of the model theoretically minimal. The mean absolute percentage error is as follow.

$$M \inf(r) = \frac{1}{n-1}\sum_{k=2}^{n}|\frac{x^{(0)}(k) - \hat{x}^{(0)}(k)}{x^{(0)}(k)}|, r \in R^+$$

In this paper, the PSO particle swarm optimization algorithm was used to design the Matlab program to optimize the fractional order of models. Specific steps can be done according to literature [29].

4 Case Analysis of NDGM Model

4.1 Actual Measurement of Roof Temperature

As shown in Fig. 1, the roof of the teaching building was divided into 15 measuring points, and each measuring point was separated by 5 m. From 9 a.m. to 18 p.m, an infrared radiation thermometer was used to measure each point at each time point.

In the summer, because the roof is seriously exposed to solar radiation, the roof surface temperature is particularly high. In order to meet the high temperature conditions and the accuracy of the simulation, we must choose the two highest temperature data as experimental research objects, so data of the two measuring points (7 and 8) were selected as the first and second sets of data, respectively. These two points represented the temperatures at which the roof was exposed to the maximum solar radiation and the second solar radiation. They were the highest temperatures and the most representative of all measuring points temperatures.

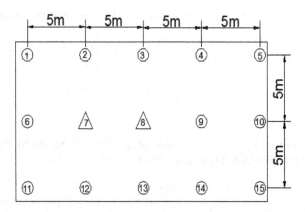

Fig. 1. Roof temperature measuring point layout

4.2 Prediction of Roof Temperature Using $NDGM_p^q$ Model

From Table 1 and Fig. 2, it can be seen that in the 9:00–18:00 period, the roof temperature of the teaching building first increased and then decreased. At 14:00 pm, the roof temperature reached the maximum, the first group was 65.4 °C, and the second group was 62.4 °C. In 9:00–14:00, with the increase of solar radiation intensity, the roof temperature increased gradually. In 14:00–18:00, the roof temperature decreased with the decrease of solar radiation intensity. Since the roof has a heat storage characteristic, after a day of solar irradiation, the minimum temperature was 45.4 °C, which was higher than the temperature at the beginning of the measurement time (9:00). To sum up, this suggested that the temperature of the roof has the parabolic characteristics.

Table 1. Original data of the roof temperature

Time	First temperature/°C	Second temperature/°C
9:00	40.6	40.2
10:00	49	48.2
11:00	53.2	50.8
12:00	59	57
13:00	58.4	57.2
14:00	65.4	62.4
15:00	57.2	56
16:00	55.8	53.4
17:00	48	47.2
18:00	46.4	45.4

According to Table 1, the steps are modeled as follows.

Step 1. Data calculation process, original data were listed as follows.
Step 2. According to the method in literature [29], the parameters were obtained.
Step 3. The second order parameters of the structure parameters were calculated.

$$\beta_1 = 0.8991, \ \beta_2 = -1.9260, \ \beta_3 = 28.1312$$

Step 4. The values of the parameters obtained in Step 3 were substituted into (8).
Step 5. The simulation, prediction and error values from Step 4 were calculated.

$x^{(0)}(k)$ was the original data of step 1. MAPE was defined as:

$$MAPE = 100\% \frac{1}{n} \sum_{k=1}^{n} \left| \frac{x^{(0)}(k) - \hat{x}^{(0)}(k)}{\hat{x}^{(0)}(k)} \right|,$$

where $x^{(0)}(k)$ referred to the original data, $\hat{x}^{(0)}(k)$ referred to the simulation values.

The simulated values and absolute percentage error for $NDGM_r^a$ model, GM model, DGM model and NDGM model were showed in Tables 2 and 3.

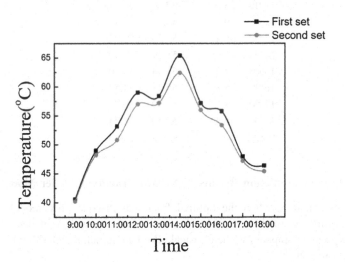

Fig. 2. Two sets of roof temperature changed with the time

Table 2. Simulation of roof temperature using four models (first set of data)

Time	Initial data	GM	DGM
9:00	40.6	40.6	40.6
10:00	49	56.80	56.96
11:00	53.2	56.27	56.39
12:00	59	55.74	55.82
13:00	58.4	55.22	55.25
14:00	65.4	54.70	54.69
15:00	57.2	54.18	54.14
16:00	55.8	53.68	53.59
17:00	48	53.17	53.05
18:00	46.4	52.67	52.51
MAPE	0	9.1557	9.1559

Table 3. Simulation of roof temperature using four models (first set of data)

Time	Initial data	NDGM	$NDGM^{0.3302}$
9:00	40.6	40.6	40.6
10:00	49	54.86	49.30
11:00	53.2	55.08	55.47
12:00	59	55.23	58.81
13:00	58.4	55.33	59.96
14:00	65.4	55.39	59.40
15:00	57.2	55.44	57.50
16:00	55.8	55.47	54.54
17:00	48	55.49	50.73
18:00	46.4	55.50	46.24
MAPE	0	9.038	2.873

4.3   Analysis of Prediction Results of NDGM Fractional Order Model

From Tables 2 and 3, when the optimal fractional discrete grey model is used to simulate the first set of data, the MAPE was 2.873%, as well as it decreased a few percentage points, compared to the classical GM(1,1) model, the DGM(1,1) model and NDGM(1,1) model.

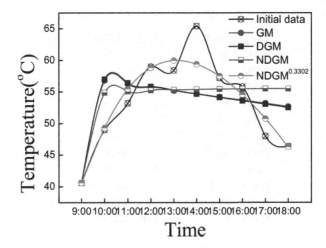

Fig. 3. Comparison of the first set of data in different mathematical models

Table 4. Simulation of roof temperature using four models (second set of data)

Time	Initial data	GM	DGM
9:00	40.2	40.2	40.2
10:00	48.2	54.96	55.10
11:00	50.8	54.48	54.58
12:00	57	54.00	54.07
13:00	57.2	53.53	53.57
14:00	62.4	53.05	53.05
15:00	56	52.59	52.55
16:00	53.4	52.13	52.06
17:00	47.2	51.67	51.56
18:00	45.4	51.21	51.08
MAPE	0	8.7427	8.7432

As can be seen from Fig. 3, compared with the other three kinds of classic grey models, the model curve was closest to the original data curve, and its simulation effect was the best.

Similarly, the simulation values for the second set of data were listed in Tables 4 and 5.

As can be seen from above, when the optimal fractional discrete grey model is used to simulate the second set of data, the MAPE is 2.4247%. Compared to the classical GM(1,1) model, the DGM(1,1) model, NDGM(1,1) model, it reduces a few percentage points. From Fig. 4, we can learn more about the comparison of several models.

Table 5. Simulation of roof temperature using four models (second set of data)

Time	Initial data	NDGM	NDGM$^{0.4498}$
9:00	40.2	40.2	40.2
10:00	48.2	53.28	47.78
11:00	50.8	53.42	53.54
12:00	57	53.52	56.77
13:00	57.2	53.58	58.01
14:00	62.4	53.63	57.66
15:00	56	53.66	56.00
16:00	53.4	53.69	53.23
17:00	47.2	53.70	49.52
18:00	45.4	53.71	44.98
MAPE	0	8.7746	2.4247

Figure 4 showed that the simulation results were better than those of the other three classic gray models, and they were closest to the actual value. Therefore, the simulation by the optimized NDGM model has a higher accuracy and a smaller error.

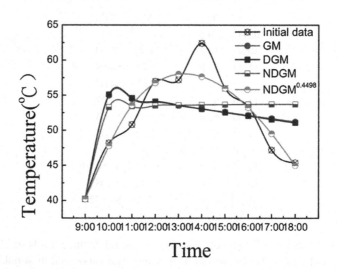

Fig. 4. Comparison of the second set of data in different mathematical models

5 Conclusion

Based on the classical NDGM model, this paper introduced the fractional order $NDGM_p^q$ model to study the important properties of the model, and used the PSO particle swarm optimization algorithm to optimize the fractional order. Finally, two sets of roof temperature data were selected as the research objects, and the conclusions were obtained as follows.

(1) By studying the important properties of fractional order $NDGM^{\frac{p}{q}}$ model, the three-level parameter package of this model was obtained, and the fractional order of model was optimized by PSO particle swarm optimization.

(2) The data characteristics of roof temperature were analyzed, and then the fractional order $NDGM^{\frac{p}{q}}$ model was selected. The optimized fractional discrete grey model was compared with GM, DGM and NDGM models, the results showed that the optimized fractional discrete grey model had the highest precision and the smallest error.

(3) Based on the analysis and demonstration of this paper, the optimized fractional discrete grey model was feasible for the roof temperature simulation, which can provide the theoretical basis for roof temperature measurement.

References

1. Shen, H., Tan, H.W.: Effect of solar reflective coatings on factory building energy saving in hot summer and warm winter zone. Build. Sci. **3**, 50–53 (2009)
2. Zhao, H.Z., Huang, C.: Study on roof energy saving of air conditioning system for main exhibition buildings of Shanghai Exo. HVAC **12**, 96–99 (2008)
3. Li, Y.X., Li, B.M.: Effects of shading and roof sprinkling in venlo-type greenhouse in summer. Trans. CSAE **5**, 127–130 (2002)
4. Zhao, H.Z., Huang, C.: Similar experimental study on roof sprinkling of large space atrium. In: International Conference on Energy and Environment Technology, pp. 309–312 (2009)
5. Guo, Q.H., Xia, F., Li, J.: Application of the intelligent sun shading louvers in glass roof. J. Shandong Univ. Sci. Technol. (Nat. Sci.) **3**, 18–19 (2006)
6. Feng, J.Q.: Study on effect of air temperature on the roof by simple flat roof greening. Xi'an University of Science and Technology, Xi'an (2012)
7. Li, X.G.: Attached PV roof's temperature with FEM simulation. Build. Energ. Saving **8**, 22–24 (2015)
8. Tan, W.J.: Analysis and calculation of unsteady heat transfer of roof in Ji'nan. Shan XI Architecture, pp. 241–242, August 2009
9. Fu, C.J.: Numerical simulation of the indoor thermal environment and thermal insulation characteristic of light weight roof. Chongqing University, Chongqing, May 2015
10. Tang, H.Q.: The Applied research of the solar power thermo compression ventilation roof. Chongqing University, Chongqing, October 2008
11. Zuo, Z.Y., Mao, H.P., Zhang, X.D.: Forecast model of greenhouse temperature based on time series method. J. Agric. Mechanization **41**(11), 173–177 (2010)
12. Deng, J.: Estimate and Decision of Grey System. Huazhong University of Science and Technology Press, Wuhan (2002)
13. Wu, L.F., Liu, S.F., Yang, Y.J.: Grey double exponential smoothing model and its application on pig price forecasting in China. Appl. Soft Comput. **39**, 117–123 (2016)
14. Bezuglov, A., Comert, G.: Short-term freeway traffic parameter prediction: application of grey system theory models. Expert Syst. Appl. **62**, 284–292 (2016)
15. Wang, Z.X.: AGM (1, N)-based economic cybernetics model for the high-tech industries in China. Kybernetes **43**(5), 672–685 (2014)

16. Zeng, B., Guo, C., Liu, S.F.: A novel interval greyprediction model considering uncertain information. J. Franklin Inst. **350**, 3400–3416 (2013)
17. Ren, X.W., Tang, Y.Q., Li, J., et al.: A prediction method using grey model for cumulative plastic deformation under cyclic loads. Nat. Hazards **64**(1), 1–7 (2012)
18. Zhao, Z., Wang, J.: Using a grey model optimized differential evolution algorithm to forecast the per capita annual net income of rural households in China. Omega **40**, 525–532 (2014)
19. Wang, Y., Liu, Q., Tang, J.: Optimization approach of background value and initial item for improving precision of GM (1,1) model. J. Syst. Eng. Electron. **1**, 77–82 (2014)
20. Yang, Y., Liu, S., John, R.: Uncertainty representation of grey numbers and grey sets. IEEE Trans. Cybern. **44**, 1508–1517 (2014)
21. Chen, L.H., Guo, T.Y.: Forecasting financial crises for an enterprise by using the Grey Markov forecasting mode. Qual. Quant. **45**, 911–922 (2011)
22. Tian, G., Li, N., Liu, S.: Grey forecasting of logistics demand based on parameter optimize model. East China Econ. Manage. **25**, 155–157 (2011)
23. Wang, Z.X.: Multivariable time-delayed GM (1, N) model and its application. Control Decis. **30**(12), 2298–2304 (2015)
24. Mao, S., Chen, Y., Xiao, X.: City traffic flow prediction based on improved GM (1,1) model. J. Grey Syst.-UK **24**, 337–346 (2012)
25. Xie, N.M., Liu, S.F.: Interval grey number sequence prediction by using non-homogenous exponential discrete grey forecasting model. J. Syst. Eng. Electron. **26**(1), 96–102 (2015)
26. Xie, N.M., Liu, S.F.: Discrete grey forecasting model and its optimization. Appl. Mathe. Model. **33**, 1173–1186 (2009)
27. Liu, J., Xiao, X.P.: The relationship of discrete grey forecasting model DGM and GM (1,1) model. J. Grey Syst. **26**(4), 14–31 (2014)
28. Wu, L.F., Liu, S.F., Cui, W., et al.: Non-homogenous discrete grey model with fractional-order accumulation. Neural Comput. Appl. **25**, 1215–1221 (2014)
29. Meng, W., Zeng, B.: Research on Fractional Operator and Gray Forecasting Model. Science Press, Beijing (2016)

Wa Language Syllable Classification Using Support Multi-kernel Vector Machine Optimized by Immune Genetic Algorithm

Meijun Fu, Wenlin Pan[✉], Hua Yang, and Huazhen Dong

School of Mathematics and Computer Science, Yunnan Minzu University,
Kunming, Yunnan, China
{779685578,2497821757,1248571027}@qq.com,
panwenlin@sina.cn,com

Abstract. A novel Wa syllable classification method based on multi-kernel support vector machine (MKSVM) optimized by immune genetic algorithm (IGA) is proposed in this paper. First, use vowel main body extension (VMBE) to extract the first dynamic characteristic parameter, pitch frequency. Then, use adaptive variational mode decomposition (AVMD) to extract the second dynamic characteristic parameter, formant frequency. Next, extract the mean values, standard errors, minima and maxima from the pitch frequency sequence and the first three formant frequency sequences respectively. Again, the feature sets with the mean values, standard errors, minima, maxima and label information, are inputted to IGA optimized MKSVM for analysis mode identification. Theoretical analysis demonstrates that MKSVM can approximate any multivariable function. The global optimal parameter vector of MKSVM can be rapidly identified by IGA parameter optimization. The experimental result of Wa syllable classification shows that, the proposed method significantly increases the accuracy of syllable classification and enhances the generalization of its application, and that, therefore, is feasible and effective on Wa language syllable classification.

Keywords: Wa syllables · Vowel Main Body Extension Method (VMBE)
Adaptive Variational Mode Decomposition (AVMD)
Multi-kernel Support Vector Machine (MKSVM)
Immune Genetic Algorithm (IGA)

1 Introduction

The Wa nationality [1, 2] is one of Chinese nations. They live mainly in the southwest border of Yunnan Province, China and northern Myanmar. And the native language they use to communicate with each other is Wa language. Wa language belongs to Va-De'ang branch, Mon-Khmer languages, Austro-Asiatic family. China Wa language can be divided into three kinds of dialects that are "Barao dialect", "Lawa dialect" and "Wa dialect". Currently, Wa language is based on the Barao dialect and the voice of YanShuai is standard pronunciation. The speech corpus used here was all recorded in YanShuai.

© Springer Nature Singapore Pte Ltd. 2018
H. Yuan et al. (Eds.): GSKI 2017, CCIS 849, pp. 513–523, 2018.
https://doi.org/10.1007/978-981-13-0896-3_51

It is well known that pitch and formant frequencies [3–5] are the two most important parameters of speech signal. Pitch frequency describes an important feature of speech excitation source. The pitch changing pattern is called pitch tone that plays a very important role in distinguishing the meaning of different syllables. We used VMBE for pitch period detection, which can effectively reduce the number of "outliers" that they obtain in the transition zone, are often integer multiplies or a half of the actual pitch period, this is mainly due to the wave forms in the forward transition zone exhibit incomplete periodicity. Formant includes two important parameters, resonant frequency and its width of band width (bandwidth), which are important parameters that can distinguish different vowels, including voiced consonants. In general, there are about five formants that can be told in the voiced, the first three of which have a critical effect on distinguishing the different voiced sound. We used the improved VMD [6] (Adaptive Variational Mode Decomposition, AVMD) to achieve the extraction of the formant.

With the development of artificial intelligence theory, syllable classification technology has made great progress in practical applications. Syllable classification, in essence, still belongs to pattern recognition [7], which can be summarized as "feature extraction → syllable pattern recognition". Syllable pattern recognition is the key problem in syllable classification in this paper.

Support vector machine (SVM) [7] is a kind of machine learning models established on Vapnik-Chervonenkis dimension theory and structural risk minimization principle. SVM is the optimal compromise between model complexity and learning ability using limited samples. It overcomes the drawback that traditional machine learning models easily get trapped in local minima. It has enormous potential to accurately classify the signal into multiple levels. Therefore, SVM has been used widely in all kinds of nonlinear pattern recognition problems [8]. However, in complicated cases, especially when the data are heterogeneous [9] and samples are unevenly distributed [10], or samples are in large scales [11], SVM begins to lose its advantages in accomplishing the tasks [12]. Multi-kernel support vector machine (MKSVM) refers to combining individual kernels by weights based on traditional single kernel SVM. It inherits the generalization and learning ability of single kernel SVM. Meanwhile, it reasonably adjusts the weight of each individual kernel and improves the adaptability and robustness of single kernels [13]. However, in the signal identification process using MKSVM, the identification performance of MKSVM is directly determined by the choice of the function parameters of individual kernels and their weights. Traditional methods, including trial and error or traversing optimization, are not only complicated in computation, but also unable to acquire global optimal solution. Therefore, the pattern recognition ability of MKSVM still needs further improvements. Immune genetic algorithm (IGA) [14] finds optimal solutions by synthetically considering the information interaction between antibodies of populations. Based on genetic algorithm [15], it integrates a series of mechanisms of biological immune system, such as antigen recognition, antibody diversity, density control, and elitist strategy. It greatly helps to avoid immature convergences and meanwhile preserves the global stochastic parallel searching character of genetic algorithm [14, 16]. Taking computational efficiency, stability, and global optimality factors into consideration, IGA is used to optimize the penalty parameter, weight factor, and kernel parameters of MKSVM, in order to improve the accuracy and stability of signal classification, and enhance the applicability of MKSVM.

Wa language is a tone language. For every Wa-language syllable, after speech signal preprocessing, we extract its each frame of pitch frequency and of the first three formant frequencies. Then, we take the mean values, standard errors, minima and maxima belonging to pitch frequency sequence and the first three formant frequency sequences respectively, to form a 16-dimensional feature vector as its classification pattern. We will classify these obtained syllable classification patterns using multi-kernel support vector machine optimized by immune genetic algorithm (IGA-MKSVM).

The rest of this paper is organized as follows. In Sects. 2, the main steps to extract Wa language classification patterns are stated. And the data set is obtained according to these steps. In Sect. 3, the theories of support vector machine (SVM) and multi-kernel support vector machine (MKSVM) are firstly reviewed, and then the immune genetic algorithm (IGA) optimized MKSVM (IGA-MKSVM) method is presented. In Sect. 4, the experiment of Wa language syllable classification by multi-kernel support vector machine based on immune genetic algorithm (IGA-MKSVM) is implemented. In Sect. 5, the feasibility and effectiveness of syllable classification strategy is discussed finally.

2 Extract Wa Language Syllable Classification Patterns to Form Data Set

The main steps to extract Wa syllable classification patterns are demonstrated in the following (Fig. 1):

(1) Selecting all the Wa language syllables speech signal from the corpus.

(2) Preprocessing Wa language syllables, including eliminating direct current (DC) components, eliminating trend items by least squares polynomial fitting, framing, windowing, and pre-emphasising for formant extraction.

(3) Endpoint detection by improved spectral entropy method.

(4) Pitch extraction by VMBE and formant extraction by linear predictive coding (LPC) method based on AVMD.

(5) For any given Wa language syllable, taking the mean values, the standard errors, minima and maxima belonging to pitch frequency sequence and the first three formant frequency sequences respectively to form a 16-dimensional feature vector as its syllable classification pattern.

We take 29 Wa language syllables from the corpus, most of which were recorded at least 5 times. In total, we have 159 pieces of speech signal. According to the above 6 steps (Fig. 1), we obtain the data set, composed of 159 16-dimensional feature vectors (except classification label), corresponding to 159 syllable classification patterns.

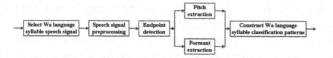

Fig. 1. Extraction process of syllable classification patterns

3 Multi-kernel Support Vector Machine Optimized by Immune Genetic Algorithm (IGA - MKSVM)

3.1 Support Vector Machine (SVM)

Let two classes of linearly separable sample sets be $\{(x_i, y_i)\}_{i=1}^{l}$, where $x_i \in R^n$ and $y_i \in \{+1, -1\}$. Here, y_i is the category label corresponding to the i-th input n dimensional eigenvector $x_i(i = 1, \cdots, l)$. The general form of decision functions is $f(x) = \omega \cdot x + b$, and the decision surface equation is as follows:

$$\omega \cdot x + b = 0 \tag{1}$$

After being normalized, the left side of Eq. (8) has the property with all the samples satisfying the inequality $|f(x)| \geq 1$. Certainly, the samples closest to the decision surface satisfy the equality $|f(x)| = 1$. The decision surface who correctly classifies all samples meets the following condition:

$$y_i(\omega \cdot x_i + b) \geq 1, i = 1, \cdots, l \tag{2}$$

Support vectors refer to the samples such that the equality sign holds in Inequality (9) and the classification margin $(1/2)\|\omega\|^2$ attains the minimum. All the support vectors are on the lines of both H_1 and H_2, and H is the optimal classification hyperplane. Under the constraint of (9), the problem of optimal classification surface can be expressed as follows:

$$\begin{aligned} \min \phi(\omega) &= (1/2)\|\omega\|^2 \\ s.t. \quad y_i(\omega \cdot x_i + b) - 1 &\geq 0, i = 1, \cdots, l \end{aligned} \tag{3}$$

If we want to find an optimal hypersurface such that the average classification error for the entire training sample set reaches the minimum, then we have to introduce a nonnegative relaxation factor ξ and allow the existence of misclassified samples. That is to say, the decision surface $\omega \cdot x + b = 0$ satisfies

$$\min \phi(\omega, \xi) = (1/2)\|\omega\|^2 + c \sum_{i=1}^{l} \xi_i$$

$$s.t. \quad \begin{cases} y_i(\omega \cdot x_i + b) \geq 1 - \xi_i, \\ \xi_i \geq 0, \end{cases} i = 1, \cdots, l \tag{4}$$

Here, $c \sum_{i=1}^{l} \xi_i$ is a penalty term, where $c > 0$ is a penalty factor.

Using Lagrange optimization method, we convert the above optimal classification surface problem into the following dual problem of convex quadratic programming optimization:

$$\max \quad \sum_{i=1}^{l} a_i - (1/2) \sum_{i=1}^{l} \sum_{j=1}^{l} a_i a_j y_i y_j (x_i \cdot x_j)$$

$$s.t. \begin{cases} a_i \geq 0, i = 1, \cdots, l \\ \sum_{i=1}^{l} a_i y_i = 0 \end{cases} \tag{5}$$

By solving Problem (12) above, we can find the optimal solution $\alpha^* = (\alpha_1^*, \cdots, \alpha_l^*)^T$, where T represents transpose of matrix (the same below). Take a positive component α_j^* from α^* satisfying the inequality $0 < \alpha_j^* < c$, then we can get

$$b^* = y_j - \sum_{i=1}^{l} y_i \alpha_i^* K(x_i, x_j) \tag{6}$$

Here, (x_j, y_j) corresponds to the above determined α_j^*. Thus, the optimal decision function is obtained as follows:

$$f(x) = \text{sgn} \left\{ \sum_{i=1}^{l} \alpha_i^* y_i K(x_i, x) + b^* \right\} \tag{7}$$

Similarly, we can obtain a multi-class support vector machine by modifying directly the above objective function. Certainly, on the other hand, we can construct a multi-class support vector machine by combining some binary class support vector machines. Here, we will use multi-class support vector machine.

3.2 Multi-kernel Support Vector Machine

Because of different kernel functions corresponding to different decision functions, the selection of kernel functions plays a very important role in syllable identification by SVM, and it directly affects the identification accuracy of SVM.

The kernel functions of SVM mainly include local kernel functions and global kernel functions. The Gaussian kernel function is a typical local kernel function that is described as follows:

$$K_{rbf}(x_i, x_j) = \exp\{-g||x_i - x_j||^2\} \tag{8}$$

Polynomial function is a typical global kernel function, which is described as follows:

$$K_{poly}(x_i, x_j) = (x_i \cdot x_j + 1)^d \tag{9}$$

Local kernel functions have strong learning ability but weak generalization ability while global kernel functions have strong generalization ability but weak learning ability. In order to achieve better learning and generalization abilities of SVM, multi-kernel support vector machine (MKSVM) is constructed by the convex combination of local kernels and global kernels:

$$K_{mix}(x_i, x_j) = aK_{rbf}(x_i, x_j) + (1 - a)K_{poly}(x_i, x_j) \tag{10}$$

Where x_i and x_j are feature vectors of input space; g and d are the parameters of kernel functions; $a(0 < a < 1)$ is a weight factor. MKSVM combines the advantages of each single kernel and possesses the better classification and identification performance.

3.3   Multi-kernel Support Vector Machine Optimized by Immune Genetic Algorithm (IGA - MKSVM)

In immune genetic algorithm, we regard respectively the object problem to be solved as biological invasion antigen and the feasible solution of the problem as antibody. The searching process of the optimal solution is viewed as the process of seeking maximum antigen affinity antibodies by biological systems. The suppression and promotion of antibodies can ensure the diversity of antibodies in the population and improve the local searching ability of GA. Crossover and mutation of antibodies can ensure that the antibody population evolves towards the direction of high fitness and maintain the diversity of the population. The memory unit accelerates searching by constantly updating with better solutions, which improves the global searching capability of the algorithm. The flowchart of IGA algorithm is shown in Fig. 2. Refer to [18, 19] for more details of IGA.

In IGA – MKSVM, IGA algorithm is used to optimize the weight factor, penalty parameter, and kernel parameters. First, for the above reason, an antibody gene vector X is defined, which is composed of the weight factor a, penalty parameter c, and parameters g and d of kernel functions:

$$X = [a, c, d, g] \tag{11}$$

In order to minimize the square error between the actual output and the expected output of MKSVM, the fitness function $h(x_i)$ of MKSVM is defined as the classification accuracy $E(x_i)$ of the i-th training sample (the i-th antibody) x_i:

$$h(x_i) = E(x_i) \tag{12}$$

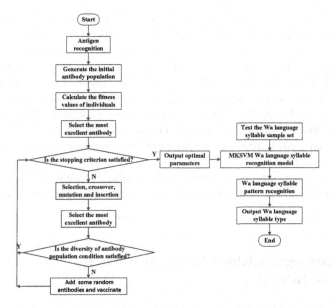

Fig. 2. Immune genetic algorithm (IGA)

When the diversity of antibody population is not satisfied, the fitness of the i-th antibody is modified as follows:

$$h^*(x_i) = h(x_i) \exp(-kC_i) \tag{13}$$

Here, C_i is the density [26] of the i-th antibody, and $k > 0$ is a positive constant. The above $h^*(x_i)$ is called the polymer fitness of the i-th antibody.

The flowchart of IGA – MKSVM algorithm is shown in Fig. 2, and the detailed steps are as follows:

(1) Initialize the similarity [17] threshold A_0, maximum iteration number, and the antibody population size N. Generate the initial vector of each antibody within the ranges of penalty parameter and kernel parameters.

(2) According to (19), compute the fitness value $h(x_i)$ of each antibody in the current antibody population. Choose the antibody with the highest fitness value as the most excellent antibody, and save it.

(3) Judge whether the stopping criterion is satisfied. If yes, output the results and the algorithm ends; otherwise, go to the next step.

(4) Perform selection, crossover, mutation and insertion operations for the current antibody population based on their fitness values.

(5) Repeat Step (2).

(6) According to the similarity definition, compute the similarity A of the current antibody population.

(7) Judge whether $A < A_0$ holds. If yes, return to Step (3). (That is to say, the condition of the antibody population diversity is satisfied.) Otherwise, go to the next step.

(8) Generate $P = 0.4N$ random antibodies and add them to the current antibody population, forming a new antibody population composed of $P + N$ antibodies.

(9) According to the similarity [26] definition, compute the similarity A_i and the density C_i [26] of each antibody x_i in the antibody population. Then compute the polymer fitness value $h^*(x_i)$ of each antibody by Formula (20)

(10) Take N antibodies from the current antibody population based on the polymer fitness value $h^*(x_i)$

(11) Choose a gene segment randomly from the most excellent antibody saved, and vaccinate for all the antibodies in the current antibody population. Then, return to Step (3).

4 Wa-Language Syllable Classification Based on IGA-MKSVM

4.1 Divide the Data Set into Training Set and Test Set

29 classes of Wa language syllables correspond to 159 syllable classification patterns from the above data set. And each class is divided into two groups, one of which belongs to training set, and the other test set. The box plot of the data set is shown in Fig. 3, which offers us some information such as abnormal values and so on.

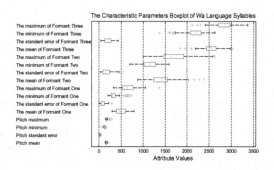

Fig. 3. The boxplot of Wa-language syllables

4.2 The K-Crossover Validation Method (K – CV)

To obtain the optimal values of parameters a, c, g and d in Expression (11), we need to introduce the K-crossover validation method (K – CV). Firstly, the data set are divided into K groups, one of which is used as test set and the remainder as train set. For any given a, c, g and d, we will get K predicted accuracies corresponding to test sets, thereby obtain the average value of the above K accuracies. After searching a, c, g and *d* within a certain range of values, according to the specific step sizes, we can pick out the largest from all the average accuracies. Then the values *a*, *c*, *g* and *d* corresponding to the largest is exactly the best parameter values we want to search for. The above method to search the best parameter values is called the K-crossover validation method (K-CV). Here, take K = 5.

4.3   Optimize the MKSVM Parameters by IGA

In order to improve the classification accuracy of MKSVM, we use IGA to optimize parameters *a*, *c*, *g* and *d* in Expression (11) by the training set (normalized into the interval [0,1]) and the K – CV method. All the operation parameters in IGA algorithm are shown in Table 1 in this paper.

Table 1. The parameters setting in **IGA**

Antibody Population Size N	50
Maximum Generation	100
The number binary bits of each variable	20
Crossover probability	0.7
Mutation probability	0.01
Generation probability	0.95
The similarity threshold A_0	0.1
The constant k in Formula (13)	0.8
Range of the weight factor a	(0,1)
Range of the penalty parameter c	(0,100]
Range of the parameter g in radial basis function	(0,1000]
Range of the polynomial order d	[1, 10]

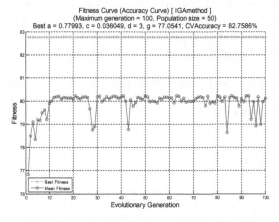

Fig. 4. The fitness (Accuracy) curve based on IGA

The optimized result is shown in Fig. 4. From it, we obtain the optimal parameter values $a = 0.77993$, $c = 0.036049$, $d = 3$, and $g = 77.0541$. The average classification accuracy (under the K-CV sense) is 82.7586%.

4.4   The Experimental Results and Comparison

Build the MKSVM using the above parameter values optimized by IGA, and train our MKSVM by the training set (normalized into the interval [0, 1]). Finally by the test set to test our IAG-MKSVM, the predictive accuracy is 93.0233%. In order to verify the advantage, SVM with Gaussian kernel (GSVM) and SVM with polynomial kernel (GSVM) are chosen for comparison, which respectively correspond to the cases of $a = 1$ and $a = 0$ in (10). Using the optimized parameter values correspondingly, the classification accuracy of IGA-MKSVM, GSVM and PSVM on the test set is respectively shown in Table 2.

Table 2. The classification accuracy of IGA-MKSVM, GSVM and PSVM on the test set

IGA-MKSVM	93.0233%
GSVM	86.0465%
PSVM	74.1379%

5   Conclusion

In this paper, we proposed the MKSVM method based on IGA (IGA-MKSVM) to classify Wa language syllables. From the comparison of the above experimental results, the classification accuracy of IGA-MKSVM achieves higher if data set is normalized, and SVM is equipped with combining kernel composed of Gaussian kernel and polynomial kernel, using the best parameter values obtained by IGA. This results shows that our method is feasible and effective on Wa language syllable classification. In addition, from Fig. 10, the abnormal values from pitch extraction and formant extraction are many, causing the syllable classification accuracy to be less than 95%, meaning that we have to further improve the methods to extract both pitch and formant to raise the syllable classification accuracy in the future.

Acknowledgments. This work is financially supported by Yunnan Provincial Department of Education Science Research Fund Project (2016YJS078), Yunnan Minzu University Overseas Masters Program (3019901).

References

1. Fang, T.: The study of Wa. National Lang. **3**, 23 (1995)
2. Qing, X.: A review of studies on Qinghua and Wa language studies. National Translation (2014). (1)
3. Kong, J.: Experimental Phonetics Basic Course. Peking University Press, Beijing (2015)

4. Zhao, L.: Speech Signal Processing, 2nd edn. Mechanical Industry Press (2009)
5. Song, Z.: Application of MATLAB in Speech Signal Analysis and Synthesis. Beijing University of Aeronautics and Astronautics Press, Beijing (2013)
6. Dragomiretskiy, K., Zosso, D.: Variational mode decomposition. IEEE Trans. Signal Process. **62**(3), 531–544 (2014)
7. Tartakovsky, D.M., Broyda, S., Vapnik, V.N.: The nature of statistical learning theory (2000)
8. Ao, H., et al.: A roller bearing fault diagnosis method based on LCD energy entropy and ACROA-SVM. Shock Vib. **2014**(1), 1–12 (2014)
9. Ben-Hur, A., Noble, W.S.: Kernel methods for predicting protein-protein interactions. Bioinformatics **21**(Suppl 1), 38–46 (2005)
10. Zheng, D., Wang, J., Zhao, Y.: Non-flat function estimation with a multi-scale support vector regression. Neurocomputing **70**(1), 420–429 (2006)
11. Rakotomamonjy, A., Bach, F., Grandvalet, Y.: More efficiency in multiple kernel learning (2007)
12. Schölkopf, B.: Choosing multiple parameters for support vector machines (2008)
13. Lee, W.-J., Verzakov, S., Duin, R.P.W.: Kernel combination versus classifier combination. In: Haindl, M., Kittler, J., Roli, F. (eds.) MCS 2007. LNCS, vol. 4472, pp. 22–31. Springer, Heidelberg (2007). https://doi.org/10.1007/978-3-540-72523-7_3
14. Luo, J.W., Wang, T.: Motif discovery using an immune genetic algorithm. J. Theor. Biol. **264**(2), 319–325 (2010)
15. Holland, J.H.: Adaptation in natural and artificial systems: an introductory analysis with applications to biology, control, and artificial intelligence. Q. Rev. Biol. **6**(2), 126–137 (1975)
16. Sakthivel, V.P., Bhuvaneswari, R., Subramanian, S.: Artificial immune system for parameter estimation of induction motor. Expert Syst. Appl. **37**(8), 6109–6115 (2010)
17. Zhao, L., Yang, S.: A novel immune genetic algorithm based on quasi-secondary response. In: AIAA/ISSMO Multidisciplinary Analysis and Optimization Conference (2008)

A Novel Method for Detecting the Degree of Fatigue Using Mobile Camera

Qing Yu[1], Ludi Wang[1], Ying Xing[1], Xiaoguang Zhou[1(✉)],
and Wei Zhou[2]

[1] Automation School, Beijing University of Posts
and Telecommunications, Beijing, China
zxg_bupt@126.com
[2] Department of Neuroscience, Uppsala University, Uppsala, Sweden
wzhoukina@gmail.com

Abstract. This paper presented a novel method for detecting human fatigue using mobile camera and cloud techniques. Photoplethysmography technique and detrended fluctuation analysis (DFA) method are used to fatigue detection. The experimental results confirm the correctness of the proposed method. The proposed method has realistic significance.

Keywords: Fatigue · Component · Detrended fluctuation analysis (DFA)
Photoplethysmography technique

1 Introduction

Human body fatigue measurement is an effect method to prevent the overwork, but there are few direct measures, with most measures of the outcomes of fatigue rather than of fatigue itself [1]. Probably the only direct measure of fatigue involves self-reports of internal states, however there are a number of problems in using any self-report measure due to the influence of demand effects or motivational influences [2].

In the previous researches, some different techniques are used in the monitoring systems to detect human fatigue. Kim et al. [3] proposed a visual fatigue monitoring system based on eye-movement and eye-blink detection. It analyzes the eye-movement and number of blinks based on the assumption that saccade movement of the eye decreases and the number of eye blink increases when visual fatigue of viewer is accumulated. However, this method has high requirement for hardware and poor flexibility, so it does not apply to the home detections for normal users. Gu and Ji [4] presents an efficient approach to recognition of facial expressions of interest. They applied a task-oriented framework to the detection of fatigue. Compared their work, our method does not rely on the face recognition but on the heart rate variability which can be used with low using cost.

The heart receives the commands of brain through the autonomic nervous system (ANS), and some researches have found that individual differences in heart rate variability (HRV) can reflect the performance of ANS. It has been noted that emotional

H. Yuan et al. (Eds.): GSKI 2017, CCIS 849, pp. 524–530, 2018.
https://doi.org/10.1007/978-981-13-0896-3_52

stress, pain, or fatigue have a particularly pronounced autonomic response. As a result, this paper tries to detect the fatigue of human body by analyzing the HRV signal.

In this paper, the HRV signal is calculated by the heart rate signal obtaining by smart phone, for the sake of getting more data for investigation, we design an application for volunteers to use every time and everywhere. More specifically, this application uses smart phones and finger photoplethysmography (PPG) to detects changes in pulses from variations in skin color. It has been widely used in health application, such as pulse oximeters, digital beat-to-beat blood pressure measurement systems and vascular diagnostics. Nowadays, PPG has also been used in smart phone applications. PPG is most often employed non-invasively and operates at a red or a near infrared wavelength. The most recognized waveform feature is the peripheral pulse, and it is synchronized to each heartbeat. Therefore, our application can continuously obtain data about the brightness of the fingertip skin and calculate a pulse wave based on luminance change. Then, we detect the RR interval from the pulse waveform, then estimate the spectrum of data by using the detrended fluctuation analysis [5], finally calculate the evaluation indices for investigation.

This paper presents a human fatigue detection method using mobile camera based detrended fluctuation analysis. We evaluate the accuracy of the estimation on 48 samples from 29 subjects (14 males, 15 females), and receive great results. This novel method can meet the requirements of portability in the home detection of human fatigue.

Figure 1 shows the process of the application and cloud platform, which can provide people real-time monitoring of their body fatigue.

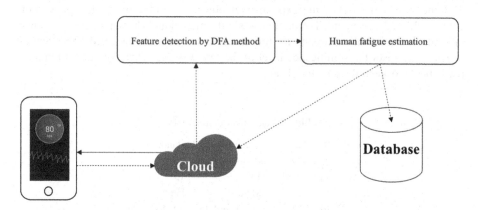

Fig. 1. Process of the application and cloud platform

2 Evaluation Index

In last decades, the detrended fluctuation analysis (DFA) invented by Peng [5] has been used as an effective tool for the detection of long-range correlations in time series. In the field of researches of heart rate dynamics [6–9], it has successfully been applied.

Briefly, the time series to be analyzed (with N samples) is first integrated. Secondly, the integrated time series is divided into boxes of equal length, n. In each box of length n, a least squares line is fit to the data. As a result, the y coordinate of the straight line segments is denoted by $y_n(k)$.

In the next step, the $y(k)$ can be detrended by subtracting the local trend, $y_n(k)$, in each box. Next, we calculated the mean-square fluctuation of this integrated and detrended time series as follows [5]:

$$F^2(n) = \frac{1}{N} \sum_{k=1}^{N} [y(k) - y_n(k)]^2$$

This computation is repeated over all time scales (box sizes) to characterize the relationship between $F(n)$, the average fluctuation, and the box size, n. Typically, $F(n)$ will increase with box size. A linear relationship on a log-log plot indicates the presence of power law (fractal) scaling. Under such conditions, the fluctuations can be characterized by a scaling exponent, the slope of the line relating log $F(n)$ to log n.

3   Database and Method

3.1   Data Acquirement

In this study we performed analysis based on the autonomic nervous system data of 29 people (male: 14, female: 15). In order to eliminate the interference of other factors, for example, age and disease, the experimental object is limited in healthy population between 18 to 25 years old. The participants' information and characteristics are shown in Table 1. Statistical processing for this study was done using the IBM SPSS Statics Version 22. Also, the significance level of the test was 5%. This experiment required participants to keep their finger clean.

Table 1. Participant demographics

Parameter	Value (mean ± standard deviation)	
Total sample number	14	15
Sex	Male	Female
Age (years)	21.80 ± 2.45	22. 58 ± 2.6
Height (cm)	178.06 ± 5.08	161.88 ± 2.80
Weight (kg)	73.20 ± 14.95	54.77 ± 6.34
BMI	23.12 ± 4.96	20.88 ± 2.198

We acquire a PPG signal from a single-point measurement on the finger using an Android application. We filter the signal first and then find the peaks based on smooth Savitzy-Golay [10] polynomials. Savitzky-Golay [10] smoothing effectively removes local signal noise while preserving the shape of the signal. It locally smooths a signal by fitting a polynomial, in a least square sense, to a sliding window of data. At last, the RR interval waveform (peak interval waveform) is obtained. Figure 2 is the data acquisition method and Fig. 3 is the overview of our application.

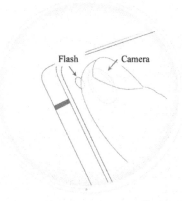

Fig. 2. Data acquisition method

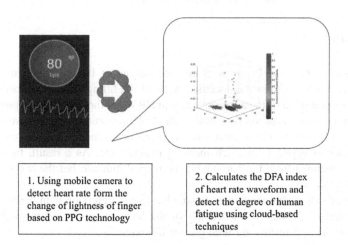

Fig. 3. Overview of the application

PPG waveform and heart rate data were collected in 30-s length every day. We then compared these values between different days. The participants answered a short questionnaire after each collection to record their degree of fatigue.

3.2 Detrended Fluctuation Analysis (DFA) of HRV Signal

We use HRV to quantify autonomic nervous system responses for detecting human fatigue, which were measured using our application. After collecting data, we use MATLAB (MATLAB; MathWorks, Inc.) to compute a using DFA method. Figure 4 shows the flow chart of the fatigue detection.

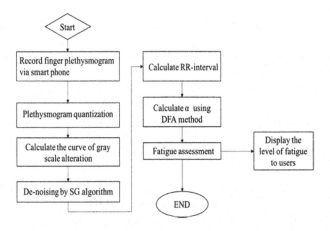

Fig. 4. Flow chart of the fatigue detection

4 Results

Figure 5 shows the correlation of α and the degree of fatigue collecting from the participants. Table 2 shows the specific results of the fitting. The experimental results confirm the correlation of the a calculated from HRV and the degree of fatigue, and also confirm the correctness of the proposed method. We present a simple questionnaire for each of the subjects and the result of that questionnaire is the level of fatigue, such as 0 (which means energetic) 1 (which means yawning), etc. As a result, the degree of fatigue we obtained from the participants is integral number, but the α computing by DFA method is not.

The results show that the human fatigue has linear regression with the α computing by DFA method. However, on account of the level we presented to participants is integral number, the results are with greater discreteness.

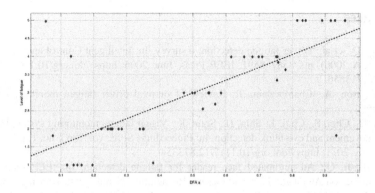

Fig. 5. Correlation of α and the degree of fatigue

Table 2. Result of the linear model

Parameter	Value
Linear model	fatigue = p1 * a + p2
Coefficients (with 95% confidence bounds)	p1 = 3.554 (2.608, 4.5) p2 = 1.217 (0.6674, 1.767)
SSE (Sum of Squares for Error)	36.98
R-square	0.5542
Adjusted R-square	0.5445
RMSE (Root Mean Squared Error)	0.8966

5 Conclusions and Future Works

This paper proposes a new method to detect the degree of human fatigue using DFA method and a phone camera. It uses only mobile phone for the capture and transmission of data and Cloud for the computation. Such configuration is well suited for the real world applications.

The ongoing research is focused on the optimization of the proposed method in order to implement it on a smartphone allowing fast and easy detection of human fatigue anywhere and anytime.

Acknowledgments. This work is supported by Engineering Research Center of Information Networks, Ministry of Education.

References

1. Wang, Q., et al.: Driver fatigue detection: a survey. In: Intelligent Control and Automation (WCICA 2006), pp. 8587–8591. IEEE Press, June 2006. https://doi.org/10.1109/WCICA.2006.1713656
2. Williamson, A., Chamberlain, T.: Review of on-road driver fatigue monitoring devices (2005)
3. Kim, D., Choi, S., Choi, J., Shin, H., Sohn, K.: Visual fatigue monitoring system based on eye-movement and eye-blink detection. In: Proceedings SPIE, vol. 7863, no. 1, pp. 159–172 February 2011. https://doi.org/10.1117/12.873354
4. Gu, H., Ji, Q.: An automated face reader for fatigue detection. In: IEEE International Conference on Automatic Face and Gesture Recognition, Seoul, South Korea, pp. 111–116 May 2004. IEEE Computer Society. https://doi.org/10.1109/AFGR.2004.1301517
5. Peng, C.K., Mietus, J.E., Hausdorff, J.M., Havlin, S., Stanley, H.E., Goldberger, A.L.: Long-range anti-correlations and non-gaussian behaviour of the heartbeat. Phys. Rev. Lett. **70**(9), 1343–1346 (1993). https://doi.org/10.1103/PhysRevLett.70.1343
6. Peng, C.K., Havlin, S., Stanley, H.E., Goldberger, A.L.: Quantification of scaling exponents and crossover phenomena in nonstationary heartbeat time series. Chaos **5**(1), 82–87 (1995). https://doi.org/10.1063/1.166141
7. Peng, C.K., Hausdorff, J.M., Havlin, S., Mietus, J.E., Stanley, H.E., Goldberger, A.L.: Multiple-time scales analysis of physiological time series under neural control. Phys. A Stat. Mech. Appl. **249**(1–4), 491–500 (1998). https://doi.org/10.1016/S0378-4371(97)00508-6
8. Bunde, A., Havlin, S., Kantelhardt, J.W., Penzel, T., Peter, J.H., Voigt, K.: Correlated and uncorrelated regions in heart-rate fluctuations during sleep. Phys. Rev. Lett. **85**(17), 3736–3739 (2000). https://doi.org/10.1103/PhysRevLett.85.3736
9. Papasimakis, N., Pallikari, F.: Correlated and uncorrelated heart rate fluctuations during relaxing visualization. EPL **90**(4), 1303–1324 (2010). https://doi.org/10.1209/0295-5075/90/48003
10. Savitzky, A., Golay, M.J.E.: Smoothing and differentiation of data by simplified least squares procedures. Anal. Chem. **36**, 1627–1639 (1972). https://doi.org/10.1021/ac60214a047

WPNet: Wallpaper Recommendation with Deep Convolutional Neural Networks

Hang Yu[1], Quan Cheng[2], Jiejing Shao[1], Boyang Yu[1], Guangli Li[1], and Shuai Lü[1(✉)]

[1] College of Computer Science and Technology, Jilin University, No. 2699, Qianjin Street, Changchun, China
{yuhang2115, shaojj2115, yuby2115, gl1i15}@mails.jlu.edu.cn, lus@jlu.edu.cn
[2] College of Software, Jilin University, No. 2699, Qianjin Street, Changchun, China
chengquan5515@mails.jlu.edu.cn

Abstract. The recommendation quality of new users plays an increasingly important role in recommender systems. Collaborative Filtering cannot handle the cold-start problem, while the content-based approach sometimes can achieve recommendation with new items. To recommend in the wallpaper field, this paper proposes a content-based recommender system and extracts the features of wallpaper via the deep learning approach. The first part of the recommendation model is the convolution layers, and the model takes the output of full connection layer as features to employ. In order to improve the scalability, the model adopts deep neural network as non-linear dimension reduction method to reduce the image features. Taking the recommended results into account, this paper compares the feature similarities of user images and those in the image library. Finally, the model sorts them via cosine similarity, and presents the recommendation results using Top-K list. In the experiment, our model is trained with selected wallpapers on MIRFLICKR dataset, and uses VGG on ImageNet for feature extraction. The experimental results indicate that WPNet will have higher hit rates with different K if the image division of some wallpapers can be improved, and achieve a better performance in less time under the recommendations of new items.

Keywords: Recommender system · Content-based recommendation
Deep learning

1 Introduction

In recent years, the personalized recommendation becomes increasingly popular in modern recommender system, many sites adopt the method of recommending relevant content to reduce the cost as well as increase the accuracy. The most commonly used approaches are Collaborative Filtering (CF) and content-based (CB) recommendations, both of which have advantages and disadvantages. Collaborative Filtering [1] uses the user's previous interactions to recommend the most relevant content. While another

© Springer Nature Singapore Pte Ltd. 2018
H. Yuan et al. (Eds.): GSKI 2017, CCIS 849, pp. 531–543, 2018.
https://doi.org/10.1007/978-981-13-0896-3_53

major method is content-based recommendation [2] which employs the features to recommend new items to users based on the feature similarity. Generally speaking, the CF method requires a large number of users history of interaction (i.e. user-item ratings in some cases) to ensure the recommendation accuracy. The accuracy tends to be very low even cannot recommend in the case of insufficient user ratings or the "cold start" [3] problem, which is CF's limitations. That is why the traditional CF method cannot give high-quality recommendations for new users. On the other hand, the content-based recommendation seems different. After extracting user features or item features, the new items can be recommended due to the comparison of feature similarity. For instance, there are two articles with the same topic, one user prefers one of them, then another article can be recommended to him/her; or there are two users with the same sex or age, one user prefers an item, and this item can be recommended to another user. Therefore, content-based recommendation is able to solve the cold-start problem of new items. In the process of content-based recommendation, there exists an important problem in feature extraction, where may be handling text or image features. The accuracy of different features is also different. So how to extract features is crucial in content-based approach.

Given that the specific scene in wallpaper recommendation, it is difficult to obtain the corresponding user ratings. In this case, the accuracy of CF method only is not satisfying. We use the image content as item features rather than other categories of feature to recommend. So that the computational complexity of recommendation can be reduced when offering users preferred images, and there will be also easier to obtain user features, such as browsing history [4]. All of them can be regarded as input user features to recommend in the form of pictures. Here we assume that the user has browsed a number of wallpapers as rich user features. Then the user gives one of the preferences, and we present the former K wallpapers with the highest similarity as the recommended result based on user's previous browsing history and current preferences. In the process of extracting image features, this paper adopts the deep learning approach to extract advanced features. CNN [5] is suitable for processing images and maybe we could increase the convolution layers to improve the recommendation accuracy. We use the VGG-16 [6] currently with better effect for feature extraction, and the previous convolution layers stacking makes the fitting ability stronger.

After multiple convolution and multi-layer connection, we obtain the feature vector with high dimension. If not addressed well, time cost will increase and system scalability gets worse. Therefore, how to choose the dimension reduction method is also very important. In this paper, the Autoencoder (AE) in deep learning approaches is used to reduce dimension [7], and process the extracted high-dimensional eigenvector. By constructing a bi-directional deep neural network with multiple intermediate layers, we transform high-dimensional vectors into low-dimensional vectors to achieve non-linear reduction and reduction after the reconstruction. Finally, we present the former K pictures as the recommendation result based on the order of the cosine similarity from high to low.

2 Related Work

There are many kinds of recommended fields, such as movies, text and pictures. Here we choose wallpaper recommendation, a specific area, to do our research. Many articles have studied on the field of image recommendation, and we will mainly elaborate some representative approaches in the following sections.

The general recommendation method can be divided into collaborative filtering and content-based recommendation. The collaborative recommendation system uses similar user preferences to recommend items, including some methods include Nearest Neighbor [1], Matrix Completion [8], Bayesian matrix factorization [9] and Restrictive Boltzmann machine [10]. Among these methods there are item collaborative filtering, user collaborative filtering, and user-item collaborative filtering. In [1], the user CF calculates the similarity between users according to the different user preferences, and then calculates the user-item pair according to the score of similar users. In [8], the item CF gives the items that all users prefer and calculates the similarity between items to recommend. The user-item CF mainly bases on the user-item rating matrix in recommendation, where a common method is the matrix factorization [9]. However, the drawback of CF may be unable to deal with new items.

Another major method is content-based recommendation. This method extracts the item features and calculates the similarity according to the extracted feature, then it comes to recommend due to the given user features. It is generally assumed that the user's preference habit is similar to that before. In [11], it is suggested that a query is created for some item features to retrieve what the user might have liked. In [2], it is modeled to extract topic features from news, and then recommended to users with similar contexts. In [12], RBM in deep learning is used to calculate the similarities between items. [13] proposes a Bayesian-based method to deal with text features related to different topics, which achieves better performance. The content-based method above can solve the cold –start problem with new items.

In general, in the process of wallpaper recommendation, there are two methods including keyword-based recommendation and image content-based recommendation. The typical method based on keywords is the bag-of-features model. The image is regarded as the document and the keyword-based feature vectors are constructed by TF-IDF. Thus the similarity comparison is made according to the Euclidean distance. This method does not take into account the advanced features of image and the relationship between features, which affects the recommendation accuracy. On the other hand, the similarity is calculated from the low-level features such as pixel level, color and texture, to some advanced features like HOG in the content-based method. The deep learning approach has recently been proposed to apply in the field of recommender system and [14] uses the deep neural network in music feature extraction in order to implement the content-based recommendation. For many recommender systems, an effective way is to use the incentive function [15] for ranking to present better recommendation results.

3   The Deep Neural Network Recommendation Model

3.1   VGG-16 for Image Classification

The CNN in deep learning performs well for extracting image features. We will introduce the basic composition of CNN and the structure of VGG-16 used in our model as follows.

The unique parts of CNN are the convolution layers and pooling layers. The input image obtains the partial features through the convolution layer, and then the features after convolution are pooled through the pool layer. The features after pooling can be more easily classified, where the max-pooling sampling will not change the image features when reducing the complexity. The characteristics of CNN are local perception and weight sharing. Partial connection can be used to extract the local features of small areas in the image at the same time when compared to full connection. Due to the greater relevance of nearer pixels in the image, the local perception is more suitable for processing the image.

As is shown in the Fig. 1, VGG [6] is the CNN image recognition model proposed by Oxford. The top-5 test on ImageNet can achieve 92.7% accuracy, so we choose the deep neural network above as the feature extraction part in the recommendation model.

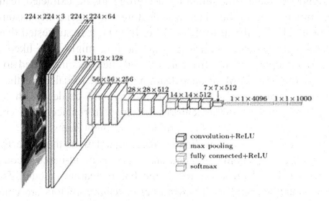

Fig. 1. The structure schematic of VGG-16 [6]

The scale of VGG-16 convolution kernel is 3*3, the first 13 layers is the stack of convolution layer followed by three full connection layers, and the last layer is the softmax layer. The convolution layers with a number of smaller convolution kernels can replace the layer with larger convolution kernel, which reduces the amount of parameters as well as allows the network to characterize more features.

For the full connection layers, x is the input eigenvector, y is the output vector, l_i is the i-th hidden layer, W is the i-th layer weight matrix, and b_i is the bias of the i-th layer $(i = 1, \ldots, N - 1)$, then

$$l_1 = W_1 x$$
$$l_i = f(W_i l_{i-1} + b_i), \ i \neq 1 \tag{1}$$
$$y = f(W_N l_{N-1} + b_N)$$

For each hidden layer l_i and the last full connection layer, we use modified linear unit *ReLU* as the activation function:

$$f(x) = \max(0, x) \tag{2}$$

we map the high-dimensional feature to the (0,1) interval via the multi-classifier softmax function, and give the corresponding scores for each category:

$$y_c = \varsigma(z)_c = \frac{e^{z_c}}{\sum\limits_{d=1}^{C} e^{z_d}} \qquad (c = 1, \ldots, C) \tag{3}$$

where $y_1 + y_2 + \ldots + y_C = 1$, the softmax function values is expressed by c neurons. The input is c-dimensional vector $\{z\}_1^c$, here denotes the extracted image features, the output is c-dimensional vector $\{y\}_1^c$, here denotes the probability of different classification.

3.2 Dimension Reduction with Autoencoder

The deep learning methods require tremendous training data and high dimensional features. In order to improve the system scalability, dimension reduction is necessary. Here are some methods commonly used in many studies, and we will describe the non-linear dimension reduction method Autoencoder (AE) used in our model.

The dimension reduction methods are generally divided into linear and non-linear. The most widely used linear method is PCA [16]. PCA constructs a low-dimensional representation to describe as many variables as possible in the original vector and map them to low-dimensional subspaces. However, PCA has some faults where the correlation coefficient matrix is proportional to the dimension of the original data, so the computational complexity is high when dealing with such high dimension eigenvectors. Plus, PCA does not consider the correlation between the data. When the high-dimensional data does not have a linear structure or Gaussian distribution, PCA and other methods have poor performance. At this time, non-linear dimension reduction methods should be used, such as Autoencoder [7] in the Neural Network. The reduction dimension function can be achieved when the number of intermediate nodes is much smaller than input nodes. Therefore, the deep neural network with multiple middle layers is constructed to reduce the dimension, and finally the output low-dimensional eigenvectors will be used to compare similarity. Hinton and Salakhutdinov [5] used a two-layer network called RBM to obtain the appropriate initial weights from the encoded network and train it with Back Propagation (BP).

Autoencoder (AE) is divided into two parts for encoding and decoding, as shown below. Encoder belongs to the dimensionality reduction part, where the function is to reduce the high-dimensional raw data to a certain dimension of the low-dimensional nested structure; Decoder belongs to the reconstruction part, which can be regarded as the reverse structure of encoder, the role is to reduce the low-dimensional nested points into high-dimensional data. There is also an intersection between the encoder and the decoder that is called the "code layer", which is the core of the whole AE network. It can reflect the essential rules of the high-dimensional dataset with nested structure, and determine the essential dimension of the high dimensional dataset (Fig. 2).

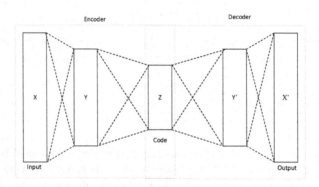

Fig. 2. Autoencoder structure diagram

AE works as follows: First, initialize the weights of the encoder and decoder network, and then train the AE network based on the principle of minimizing the error between the original training data and the reconstructed data. If the initial weight of AE network is close to the optimal solution, the gradient descent can be used to achieve satisfying training performance.

3.3 The Establishment of WPNet

Through the dimension is reduced by encoder part, the low-dimensional (in our experiment is 10) eigenvectors can be obtained as the final image features. Then we calculate the eigenvectors after mapping in the vector space of input images and the images in the library, and compare the similarity between the images by similarity measure. The smaller the value of similarity measure, the smaller the similarity between individuals. In contrast, the larger the value of similarity measurement is, the greater the difference will be. Here we choose the vector space cosine similarity [17]. The cosine similarity is used as a measure of the magnitude of the difference between two individuals in the cosine of the two vectors in the vector space. The closer the cosine value is to 1, the closer the angle is to $0°$, i.e., the more similar the two vectors are. This is called "cosine similarity". The formula shows as follows:

$$sim(X, Y) = \cos \theta = \frac{\sum\limits_{i=1}^{n} (x_i * y_i)}{\sqrt{\sum\limits_{i=1}^{n} (x_i)^2} * \sqrt{\sum\limits_{i=1}^{n} (y_i)^2}} \tag{4}$$

where X is the feature vector of input image after processing, and Y is the feature vector in the image library. For each of the library images corresponding to the vector Y_i, We calculate the cosine similarity $sim(X, Y_i)$ of the vector X corresponding to the input image and sort vectors to present the recommendation list.

In summary, we propose the *WPNet* recommendation model. This model uses the 13 convolution layers and the first full connection layer of VGG-16 as the image feature extraction part, and uses the encoder part of Autoencoder (AE) as the dimension reduction part. The last part of our model is to calculate the value of cosine similarity to present the image recommendation list. Finally we combine the above sections into the *WPNet* model. The recommendation model *WPNet* is shown in the following Fig. (3).

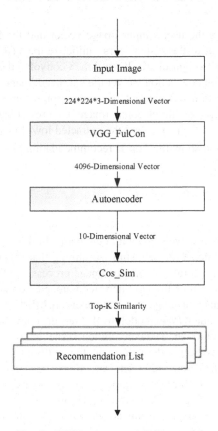

Fig. 3. WPNet recommendation model

According to *WPNet* recommendation model, we present the specific overall predicting procedure as follows:

Algorithm 1 Predicting Procedure of *WPNet*

1: **Input:** User image feature vector $X = \{x_i\}_1^n$,

     Image   library   feature   vector   set
$Y = \{Y_1, Y_2, ..., Y_m\}$

2: Initialize *VGG* and *Autoencoder*

3: $X' = VGG\_FulCon(X)$

4: $X'' = Enc(X')$

5: **for** $i = 1$ to m

6:    $\cos[i] = COSINE(X'', Y)$

7: **end for**

8: $\{P_1, P_2, ..., P_K\} = ChsTpK(\cos)$

9: **Output:** Recommendation list $P = \{P_1, P_2, ..., P_K\}$

The algorithm takes the user's input image vector and the library vector set $Y = \{Y_1, Y_2, ..., Y_m\}$ as input to the system. First, initialize the *VGG* trained on ImageNet and *AE* trained with the weight matrix W, and then convolve the input image vector X through *VGG*, after a full connection we get the extracted image feature. Moreover, we take the extracted high-dimensional features as the input of encoder part to reduce the dimension, and get the low-dimensional image features. Finally, we calculate the cosine similarity between the results and the extracted low-dimensional feature vectors of the picture library, and show the Top-K recommendation list $\{P_i\}_1^K$ according to the similarity measure.

4 Experiment

The cold-start problems involve some with new items. In this case, our model presents a Top-K list of similar items for new stuff. Assuming that the user gives a new item, this paper uses the deep neural network for image processing. The Top-K list is given by similarity comparison, thus the new item recommendation can be achieved.

We selected a number of images as wallpapers in MIRFLICKR dataset and used 10,000 of them to train our *WPNet* model. In *WPNet*, the convolution structure of CNN is the same as that of VGG-16. The convolution kernel adopts structure of 3 * 3. The activation function uses Sigmoid function in the multi-layer Autoencoder, and the parameters in encoder part are set as 4096-1024-256-64-32-10. Then the high-dimensional image features are extracted to 10-dimensional vector. Finally, we compare the similarity and give the recommendation results.

Some of the recommendation results are shown in the following Figs. 4 and 5, and given in the form of Top-K picture list (K = 5).

Fig. 4. Top-K recommendation results

Fig. 5. Top-K recommendation results

Similar to the mean reciprocal rank (MRR) that appears in other studies, we regard the reciprocal of correctly predicted item in the proportion of other items as our evaluation index.

Because of the insufficiency of user data, we address this problem by image division. Our approach is to randomly select a number of pictures and divide them into 1 : 3 ratios. We assume that a quarter of subgraphs denotes the choice of user. Then we give the Top-K picture list via WPNet model (experimental K = 3, 5, 10), and calculate the ratio of images appeared in Top-K to the total images Top-K list in the remaining 75% images. Finally, the ratio is regarded as evaluation index.

The evaluation results are shown in the Table 1 below:

Table 1. Evaluation results and hit rate

Images	Top-K	
	Top-5	Top-10
100	0.45	0.65
1000	0.191	0.269

We randomly select n images in training set of 10,000. Each image is divided into four blocks, so that we get 4*n images. Then we randomly choose each of four blocks in images as input, and recommend it in the range of 4*n pictures. If the recommended block is consistent with the input block, it hits. The experimental results of 100 images are shown below (Fig. 6).

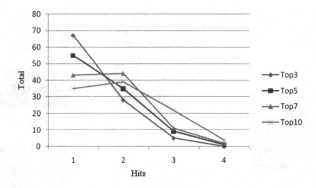

Fig. 6. The total number of hits

It can be seen from the figures above, for the cases with different k value, the times that four subgraphs only hit their own gradually reduced in each group, and cases with more hits gradually increase, i.e. the increase of overall hit rate. On the other hand, for the case of 100 divided images, the number per group with more hits tend to increase with bigger k value, which means the overall hit rate increases. So our model in this paper has a better effect for small-scale wallpaper recommendation.

When the number of images reaches 1000, the hits are shown in the table above. In 1000 groups of pictures, 941 groups of pictures can be hit successfully. With the increase of K value in Top-K, the number of groups that can hit multiple times increases, indicating that the recommendation effect is improved. In this case, our model in this paper can guarantee a certain degree of recommendation results as the volume of data grows.

From the Fig. 7 and Table 2 we can see that sometimes the subgraph hits better (more than 75%), but most of the time it gets an ordinary performance (less than 50%). According the corresponding statistics on image tags, we find the subgraphs hit poorly when the wallpaper theme is portrait and objects. On the contrary, the hit rate gets higher when the wallpaper theme is low-rank landscape. The reason why the performances differ may be our approach of image division. The difference between subgraphs is more obvious when the theme is portrait or object, thus the effect of hitting is poor. On the other hand, many of the landscape wallpapers divided in the same way can still maintain a higher similarity which means it hits better. Therefore, the next step should improve how to divide the images of portrait and object, and thus enhance the overall recommendation effect.

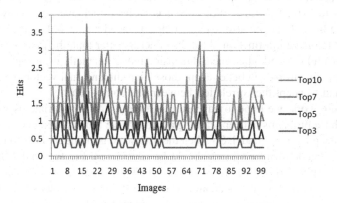

Fig. 7. The distribution of hits in 100 images

Table 2. The total number of hits in 1000 images

Top-K	Hits			
	1/4	2/4	3/4	4/4
Top3	791	142	8	0
Top5	761	162	15	2
Top7	737	171	26	7
Top10	689	210	32	10

5 Conclusion

This paper presents a recommender system in wallpaper area, and builds a recommendation model based on deep learning. We use CNN to achieve the extraction of image features, and obtain the initial high-dimensional image features. Then we adopt Autoencoder to reduce dimension and get low-dimensional image features. Input the users' preference of wallpapers, we give a Top-K list of recommended images by calculating the cosine similarity.

In contrast to recommender systems based on CF, the sparse rating matrix may result in very low recommendation accuracy for the explicit ratings of user are difficult to obtain. Our system only needs to determine the preference of user, and then we can offer the Top-K recommendation list which also solves the cold-start problem of new items. Compared to the traditional image features extraction, there are many advantages using CNN to extract features. Not only it is easier to achieve (e.g. the well-trained VGG on the ImageNet), but also to extract the advanced features of image which better represents the image information. Also, its effect is better than the pixel level features. Compared with PCA and other linear dimension reduction methods, using Autoencoder to reduce the dimension can better adapt those high-dimensional vectors without linear structure, and to adapt the correlation between the components.

For future work, we hope to have more sufficient and appropriate user data. Plus, similar to those problems in deep learning approach, we found a tremendous amount of data in the deep learning model. So when the user scale is enlarged, how to improve the scalability of recommender system should be considered. For the cold-start problem, this paper can give Top-K lists for selection when new items come. In fact, the model could not give a valid recommendation yet when the new user does not provide any information. This paper only achieves the content-based recommendation, how to design a hybrid recommender system combined with CF will be an improvement.

References

1. Bell, R.M., Koren, Y.: Improved neighborhood-based collaborative filtering. In: KDD 2013 CUP (2007)
2. Liu, J., Dolan, P., Pedersen, E.R.: Personalized news recommendation based on click behavior. In: IUI 2010, pp. 31–40 (2010)
3. Zhou, K., Yang, S.-H., Zha, H.: Functional matrix factorizations for cold-start recommendation. In: SIGIR 2011, pp. 315–324 (2011)
4. Elkahky, A.M., Song, Y., He, X.: A multi-view deep learning approach for cross domain user modeling in recommendation systems. In: WWW 2015, pp. 278–288 (2015)
5. Hinton, G., Salakhutdinov, R.: Reducing the dimensionality of data with neural networks. Science (2006)
6. Simonyan, K., Zisserman, A.: Very deep convolutional networks for large-scale image recognition. In: ICLR (2015)
7. Wang, W., et al.: Generalized autoencoder: a neural network framework for dimensionality reduction. In: CVPRW 2014, pp. 490–497 (2014)
8. Jain, P., Netrapalli, P., Sanghavi, S.: Low-rank matrix completion using alternating minimization. In: STOC 2013, pp. 665–674 (2013)

9. Liu, J., Wu, C., Liu, W.: Bayesian probabilistic matrix factorization with social relations and item contents for recommendation. Decis. Support Syst. **55**, 838–850 (2013)
10. Salakhutdinov, R., Mnih, A., Hinton, G.: Restricted boltzmann machines for collaborative filtering. In: ICML 2007, pp. 791–798 (2007)
11. Jannach, D.: Finding preferred query relaxations in content-based recommenders. In: Chountas, P., Petrounias, I., Kacprzyk, J. (eds.) Intelligent Techniques and Tools for Novel System Architectures, pp. 81–97. Springer, Heidelberg (2008). https://doi.org/10.1007/978-3-540-77623-9_5
12. Gunawardana, A., Meek, C.: Tied boltzmann machines for cold start recommendations. In: RECSYS 2008 (2008)
13. Wang, C., Blei, D.M.: Collaborative topic modeling for recommending scientific articles. In: KDD 2011 (2011)
14. Van den Oord, A., Dieleman, S., Schrauwen, B.: Deep content-based music recommendation. In: NIPS 2013, pp. 2643–2651 (2013)
15. Lee, J., Bengio, S., Kim, S., Lebanon, G., Singer, Y.: Local collaborative ranking. In: WWW 2014, pp. 85–96 (2014)
16. Hotelling, H.: Analysis of a complex of statistical variables into principal components. J. Educ. Psychol. **24**(6), 417–441 (1933)
17. Steinbach, M., Karypis, G., Kumar, V.: A comparison of document clustering techniques. In: KDD Workshop on Text Mining vol. 400, no. 1, pp. 525–526 (2000)

Equipment Maintenance Support Decision Method Research Based on Big Data

Ziqiang Wang[✉] and Yuanzhou Li

Armored Force Engineering Institute, Beijing 100072, China
wzq166@126.com, lyzl56@126.com

Abstract. Facing huge amounts of data in the field of equipment maintenance support, this paper studies the technique of equipment maintenance support data analysis and decision, formed information analysis technology and relevant methods for stages of Data acquisition, data integrate, theme data, online analysis and data mining, which is theory and practice basis of equipment maintenance support data analysis and decision support method research; It puts forward the trinity system framework for the technology of data storage, analysis and show. Through constructing safe and reliable storage environment, designing intelligent and efficient analysis algorithm, provide intuitive display form, it provides technical support for scientific decision based on the data.

Keywords: Equipment support · Big data · Decision support

1 Introduction

1.1 Demand

With the acceleration development of military information construction, and a lot of information system installed in the armed forces, the use of these management systems make the quality and benefits have been a lot of ascension for equipment maintenance support management, each equipment management department has collected and stored a large amount of raw data. But the accumulation of various units of various data utilization rate is not high, often failed to perform its huge value, mainly displays in the storage technology lag behind, lack of efficient data processing method, and facing the situation of hardware and software localization accelerating technology reserve is insufficient, need to carry out related technical research.

1.2 Research Content

Firstly, It is to build huge amounts of data analysis application framework, research on massive amounts of data storage technology, set up huge amounts of data analysis and auxiliary decision support environment; Secondly, it is to study equipment maintenance support of data analysis, data processing and decision method, comprehensive analysis of equipment maintenance support data, analysis and decision method research equipment maintenance, set up a corresponding decision model. Using of intelligent computing, heterogeneous data conversion, data retrieval, data statistics analysis, data

H. Yuan et al. (Eds.): GSKI 2017, CCIS 849, pp. 544–551, 2018.
https://doi.org/10.1007/978-981-13-0896-3_54

mining and data visualization technology, it forms a huge amounts of data analysis and decision support environment.

1.3 Research Significance

In view of the huge amounts of data in the field of equipment maintenance support, the file explores the huge amounts of data analysis and processing technology, studies large amounts of data storage, analysis and processing methods, builds software and hardware platform based on the commercial platform and localization environment; On the other hand, research and design specifically for equipment maintenance support business of multidimensional data analysis, intelligent optimization and auxiliary decision algorithm, visualization in the development of the huge amounts of data analysis and processing results explain tools, able to form a multiple perspectives, multiple granularity, multidimensional visualization of equipment maintenance support data analysis and display, provide support for the equipment maintenance support scientific decision-making.

2 Technical Route

2.1 Equipment Maintenance Support Data Analysis and Decision Method

Based on the achievement of information construction, through in-depth study of equipment technical status, running parameters and fault conditions, as well as the equipment maintenance support business process records, video, and environmental monitoring, the article finds out the historical data characteristics and laws firstly, then establishes the correlation analysis model and algorithm analysis model. These methods and models can be used to evaluate health equipment, predict equipment failure, build drive relationship between equipment maintenance equipment demands and supplies, and realize decision-making support strongly based on the data of equipment maintenance support. Equipment maintenance support data analysis and research on typical decision method as shown in the Fig. 1 below.

(1) Data BGF

Through to extraction, cleaning, transform and load, summary and comprehensive data on demand between departments and the business, build data warehouse for decision analysis, multidimensional analysis and data mining.

(2) Subject Data

According to the decision of leaders and institutions demand, on the basis of the data warehouse, build subject data for subsequent conduct online analysis and data mining, such as maintenance planning data, maintenance power data, maintenance training data, technical status.

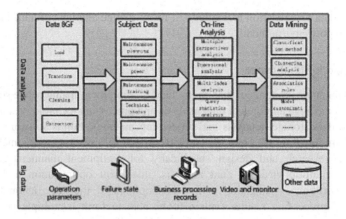

Fig. 1. Equipment support data analysis and research on typical decision algorithm

(3) On-line Analysis

According to the geographical, time, forces organizational system, unit category of equipment business data for multiple dimensions such as drilling, rotation, slice, multi-angle analysis, realizes the local data and global data correlation analysis, the influence analysis of static data and dynamic data, the contrastive analysis of the historical data and current data, implement flexible query statistics analysis.

(4) Data Mining

Using the typical mining such as clustering, classification and correlation algorithm to dig deep analysis of equipment business history data, dig up the implicit, previously unknown, having potential value, patterns and trends, and the knowledge and rules used for decision-making model training and optimization. According to the requirements of the prototype system decision analysis, establish typical decision model in the aspects of the equipment management security analysis, trend prediction, comprehensive ability evaluation.

2.2 Mass Data Analysis Application Technology System Framework

The technical architecture of Equipment maintenance support decision support system based on big data, is divided into foundation platform layer, data storage layer and analysis platform layer. Among them, the platform layer is composed of cloud server and virtual service software, the data storage and analysis platform layers are mainly composed of HDFS, Hbase, Hive, Sqoop (TL tools), Pig, Mahout, MapReduce and Ambari management tool. The overall technology architecture is shown in Fig. 2.

(1) Data Storage Technology Architecture

With the increasing amount of data, data storage and maintenance costs rise sharply. The traditional disk array is not only expensive, but maintenance and extension faces many difficulties, it is difficult to store expansion was achieved by simple way. And in the industry, has achieved mass data storage scheme based on cloud storage technology,

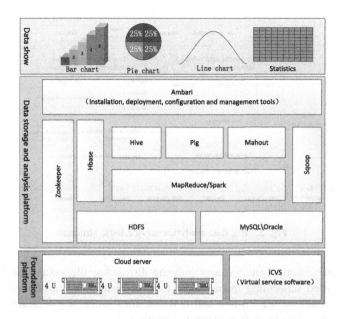

Fig. 2. Overall technical framework system

through the application cluster, grid technology, or function of the distributed file system, the network of a large number of various types of storage devices set up by applying the software to work together, common external provide access to data storage and business functions of a service system.

(2) Data Analysis Technology Architecture

Big data analysis service, depending on the type and the size of the data, using the database cluster MPP architecture and distributed computing systems architecture, one each for high density of structured data and low density value of unstructured data, provide such as distributed data acquisition, ETL processing, distributed retrieval and online analysis, data mining and so on core competence, huge amounts of heterogeneous data offline batch analysis and online real-time analysis, for the analysis of the upper cloud services provide strong support. The overall design as shown in Fig. 3.

(1) Data acquisition and ETL process. Mainly through the methods of extraction, transformation and loading, form data warehouse or distributed file system.
(2) Data management. Mainly using both database and distributed computing cluster system architecture handle huge amounts of heterogeneous data.

Based on the data of database cluster processing architecture includes large-scale parallel database, operational data storage, data warehouse (mart). Data warehouse operated on the database cluster, through the ETL processing tools, according to the analysis of the theme, takes the data into the data mart.

Based on distributed computing system architecture of data processing mainly includes distributed file systems, resource scheduling management tools, distributed computing, distributed computing framework and distributed memory engine and flow

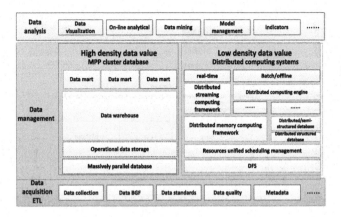

Fig. 3. Big data analytics service logic structure

computing framework. Data extracts into the distributed file system firstly through resources unified scheduling management tool for distribution, according to the different size as well as the off-line and real-time data processing requirements, using different analysis engine or framework for processing.

(3) Data Analysis and Auxiliary Decision-making Model

(1) Equipment support data analysis and processing model

Through the analysis of large amounts of equipment maintenance support data and decision requirements, designs huge amounts of data analysis and decision support algorithm, builds huge amounts of data analysis and decision models based on Hadoop, as shown in Fig. 4.

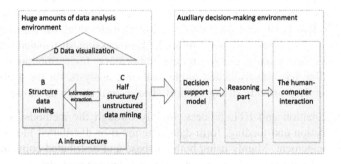

Fig. 4. Data analysis and auxiliary decision-making model

• Huge amounts of data analysis model

Huge amounts of data analysis includes the infrastructure, the structure of data mining, half structure/unstructured data mining and data visualization components, and the results of the analysis provide for the use of auxiliary decision-making environment. The structured data mining model is shown in Fig. 5.

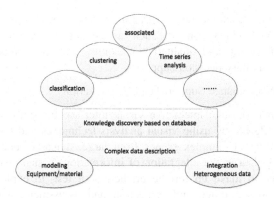

Fig. 5. Structured data mining model

The file researches EM algorithm, STREAM tree algorithm, the Apriori algorithm, FP - frequency set algorithm, GMDH algorithm and other commonly used algorithm, and according to the characteristics of equipment support data optimize it. Half/unstructured data mining model structure as shown in Fig. 6.

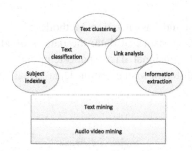

Fig. 6. Half structure/unstructured data mining model

- Auxiliary decision-making model

Auxiliary decision model includes decision support model, reasoning mechanism, human-computer interaction and other parts. Part of the decision support model including model base and its management system, rational part consists of knowledge base, knowledge base management system and reasoning units; The human-computer interaction part is the decision support system for human-computer interaction interface, to receive and test the user requests, call system internal software for decision service function, make the model run, data calls and knowledge reasoning to organically unify, effectively solve the decision problem.

In view of semi-structured and unstructured data preliminary study text under-standing, audio and video content, such as deductive reasoning and research, non-monotonic reasoning and qualitative reasoning, the rule engine, through data provide effective auxiliary decision support.

(4) Equipment Maintenance Support Data Visualization

Data visualization is through interactive visual interface for analysis, reasoning and decision making. People by using visual analysis techniques and tools, can obtain a deeper understanding of complex scenes from large, dynamic, uncertain, and even contain conflicting data in the integration of information. Visual analysis technology that allows people to make up for the prediction of test, to explore the unknown information, provides a quick and inspection and assessment, and provide more effective means of communication.

(1) the principle of data visualization

- accuracy: It is best to use a mathematical formula, according to the Numbers, and then use the same proportion in the graphics. Instead of drawing shapes.
- creativity: creativity is reflected from the simple graphs. Don't be afraid to use typography, illustrations, ICONS or other design elements.
- simplicity: simple is actually need to transform some complex data into some simple data forms.

(2) Data Classification and Visualization Methods

According to the characteristics of data, the data is divided into correlation data, hierarchical data, multi-dimensional data, spatio-temporal data, different methods of data classification using different visualization. Data visualization design as shown in Fig. 7.

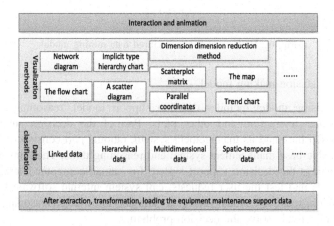

Fig. 7. Data visualization design

In the actual process of visualization, the single visualization method often cannot meet the needs. More and more visualization system is built by combining different data visualization methods, which provides a consistent and coherent interaction means, the visual system is able to provide the necessary increasingly complex data analysis ability.

3 Summaries

Research results can be applied to the army troops promotion, and it can provide simple and reliable method for huge amounts of data storage, including support the large capacity data storage environment; It can provide commonly used algorithms about data processing and analysis, and visualization tools, realize the data of multiple perspectives, multiple granularity, multi-dimensional visualization analysis and demonstration; Can provide huge amounts of data application environment based on localization of software and hardware platform.

References

1. Wang, F., Liu, J.C.: Networked wireless sensor data collection: issues, challenges, and approaches. IEEE Commun. Surv. Tutor. **13**, 673–687 (2011)
2. Shi, J.H., Wan, J.F., Yan, H.H., et al.: A survey of cyber-physical systems. In: Proceedings of International Conference on Wireless Communications and Signal Processing, Nanjing, pp. 1–6 (2011)
3. White, T.: Hadoop: The Definitive Guide. O'Reilly Media Inc., Newton (2012)
4. Zikopoulos, P., Eaton, C.: Understanding Big Data: Analytics for Enterprise Class Hadoop and Streaming Data. McGraw-Hill Osborne Media, New York (2011)
5. Meijer, E.: The world according to LINQ. Commun. ACM **54**, 45–51 (2011)
6. Borkar, V.R., Carey, M.J., Li, C.: Big data platforms: what's next? XRDS: crossroads. ACM Mag. Students **19**, 44–49 (2012)
7. Bryant, R.E.: Data-intensive scalable computing for scientific applications. Comput. Sci. Eng. **13**, 25–33 (2011)
8. Wang, X.Q.: Semantically-aware data discovery and placement in collaborative computing environments. Dissertation for Ph.D. Degree. Taiyuan University of Technology, Taiyuan (2012)
9. Middleton, S.E., Sabeur, Z.A., Löwe, P., et al.: Multi-disciplinary approaches to intelligently sharing large-volumes of real-time sensor data during natural disasters. Data Sci. J. **12**, WDS109–WDS113 (2013)

Research on a New Density Clustering Algorithm Based on MapReduce

Yun Wu$^{(\boxtimes)}$ and Zhixiong Zhang

BaoTou Teacher's College, Baotou, China
`wy-xxz@yeah.net, nmyahoo@163.com`

Abstract. The empirical solution parameters for the Density-Based Spatial Clustering of Applications with Noise(DBSCAN) resulted in poor Clustering effect and low execution efficiency, An adaptive DBSCAN algorithm based on genetic algorithm and MapReduce programming framework is proposed. The genetic algorithm (minPts) and scanning radius size (Eps) optimized intensive interval threshold, at the same time, combined with the similarities and differences of data sets using the Hadoop cluster parallel computing ability of two specifications, the data is reasonable of serialization, finally realizes the adaptive parallel clustering efficiently. Experimental results show that the improved algorithm (GA) - DBSCANMR when dealing with the data set of magnitude 3 times execution efficiency is improved DBSCAN algorithm, clustering quality improved by 10%, and this trend increases as the amount of data, provides a more precise threshold DBSCAN algorithm to determine the implementation of the method.

Keywords: DBSCAN · MinPts · Eps · Genetic algorithm · MapReduce

1 Introduction

The density cluster DBSCAN algorithm has always had two problems: Setting threshold (minPts, Eps) can only rely on experience to result in the quality of clustering results cannot be guaranteed, It is inefficient to process large data sets. At present, scholars have put forward many suggestions for improving the quality of clustering. Chen gang and other people have proposed an adaptive DBSCAN algorithm based on gaussian distribution to improve the accuracy of minPts and Eps [1]; Feng et al. proposed the Greedy DBSCAN: An improvement on multidimensional clustering of DBSCAN algorithm, using the greedy strategy to find out the parameters of Eps radius, improved clustering accuracy [2]; Ester and other people have proposed the density based cluster concept to optimize DBSCAN algorithm [3]; Wang et al. proposed the adaptive spatial clustering based on the density, according to the characteristics of the data structure, by constantly changing the value of minPts to determine the optimal solution of Eps to achieve the process of adaptive solution [4]; In order to deal with the time-consuming problem of large data sets, Uncu et al. proposed GRIDBSCAN: The spatial clustering algorithm based on grid density is used to reduce the computation time [5]; Liu et al. proposed the DBSCAN algorithm based on grid cells, and by the grid cell division of data space, the most time-consuming regional query process in DBSCAN algorithm is optimized to improve the operation efficiency of the whole algorithm [6].

© Springer Nature Singapore Pte Ltd. 2018
H. Yuan et al. (Eds.): GSKI 2017, CCIS 849, pp. 552–562, 2018.
https://doi.org/10.1007/978-981-13-0896-3_55

With the advent of cloud computing and Hadoop platform, it provides a new way to solve the low computing efficiency. According to the research of DBSCAN algorithm based on cloud computing, the algorithm of DBSCAN clustering algorithm based on the MapReduce framework is used to encapsulate the DBSCAN clustering algorithm, which effectively improves the operation efficiency of the algorithm [7]; Ya-jun et al. proposed adaptive density clustering algorithm based on graphs, normalization of data processing, and the data after processing block finally on the division of each data block is improved ADC algorithm for clustering is applied respectively [8]; He et al. proposed an efficient parallel density clustering algorithm based on MapReduce, and implemented the four-level MapReduce paradigm by using the rapid zoning strategy to improve the efficiency of the algorithm [9]. However, the above improvement works still can't really realize the reasonable threshold value (minPts and Eps) of the data set efficiently. Based on the above research, this paper, by using Genetic Algorithm (based Algorithm, GA) improved DBSCAN Algorithm, by dynamically adjust the fitness function to improve the precision of the threshold, and combining with the Hadoop platform for GA - provides guarantee the execution efficiency of DBSCAN Algorithm.

2 GA-DBSCAN Algorithm Design and Improvement

DBSCAN algorithm is a density based classical clustering algorithm, which can detect clusters of arbitrary shapes and filter the noise of data concentration [10]. Traditional algorithm completely rely on experience to set the value of the parameters of the Eps and minPts the experiential is directly affect the credibility of the clustering results and application of diversity, at the same time run through all objects in the process of data points will consume a lot of time. Aiming at the problem of threshold precision, GA is introduced in this paper to improve the traditional algorithm to realize the adaptive threshold problem, In order to improve the quality of clustering and the MapReduce framework of Hadoop cluster, it successfully solves the time-consuming problem of improving algorithm and elaborates the concrete improvement process.

2.1 Genetic Algorithm Improvement Scheme

The design of GA-DBSCAN in this paper mainly includes coding strategy, group setting, fitness function setting and algorithm end condition. Aiming at the coding problem, this paper USES the real number encoding method to directly encode the solution space form. The advantages of this paper are to restrict the value of individual parts or all components according to specific problems, The genetic manipulation of the original parameters is used to make the optimal solution can be filled with the possible space of the optimal solution, so as to facilitate the large space search and not get into local extremum. Aimed at the problem of setting groups and group size affect the end result of a genetic optimization and execution efficiency, this paper set the optimal solution of the space distribution in the whole problem space, and set within the scope of the initial population. The specific approach is as follows: to set up the data set point distance matrix D, dij represents the distance between the data concentration points and points, as follows:

$$D = \begin{bmatrix} 0 & d_{21} & \cdots & d_{n1} \\ d_{12} & \ddots & & d_{n2} \\ \vdots & & \ddots & \vdots \\ d_{1n} & \cdots & \cdots & 0 \end{bmatrix}$$

For scanning radius to solve the problem, can the statistics matrix D frequency have overlapping distance from close range at the midpoint, set distance overlap high frequency range for [a, b], tinkering with D as follows:

$$d'_{ij} = \begin{cases} 1 & a \leq d_{ij} \leq b \\ 0 & others \end{cases}$$

From this, we can obtain the 0-1 matrix of the core point to be selected, and the initial group of GA is the collection of the kernel points to be selected.

GA's fitness function directly affects the performance of genetic algorithm. The number of groups is n. According to the distance of matrix D and high overlap frequency interval, the fitness function of each point distance is set as follows:

$$f_{ij} = \begin{cases} d_{ij} / \sum_{i}^{n} d_{ij} & d'_{ij} = 1 \\ 0 & d'_{ij} = 0 \end{cases} \quad (i = 1, 2, \ldots, n)$$

Thus, the fitness of the selected core points in the initial group can be obtained:

$$f_i = \sum_{j=1}^{n} f_{ij} \quad (i = 1, 2, \ldots, n)$$

2.2   GA - DBSCAN Algorithm

If you can't find the optimal core point in the search process through several generations, note that in the previous generations, only the parents selected in the previous generations were not able to find the best advantage, GA constantly regenerates and causes the group to continuously join the parent, to increase the proportion of non-optimal individuals in the group, genetic drift, finally converges to local optimal solution. Therefore, the improvement of traditional GA algorithm needs to take into account the dynamic adjustment while considering the group fitness while choosing the parent.

The specific steps of the improved algorithm are as follows:

(1) Define the adjustment coefficient alpha and threshold theta, where alpha and theta are positive decimals, and set the adjustment period for K generation. The number of selected groups to be selected is n, and the fitness function is f.

(2) Perform the following operations for the initial group:

(a) The individual fitness of the initial group was found and the following operations were performed:

$$\max_{i=1}^{n} f_i \rightarrow f_1$$

(b) Backup the initial group so that you can recover in a local polar hour.
(c) The probability that the individual I was selected as the core point in the initial group is:

$$P_i = f_i / \sum_{i=n}^{n} f_i$$

Select the core point using the probability Pi and make a backup of the elected individual.

(3) Initialization of renewable generation calculator I = 0, carried out in accordance with the DBSCAN algorithm clustering, and according to the traditional GA algorithm for genetic operation, and was elected emphasis for backup, if find the optimal solution algorithm ended; Otherwise I = I + 1.
(4) Remove the visited core points in the current population and pay the maximum fitness value to f2,

$$\max_{i=1}^{n} f_i \rightarrow f_2$$

If the search process is still progressing in the direction of optimization, the individual in the current group is replaced by the individual in the reserved group, and f2 is transferred to f1, and then to (3).

If the convergence process is slow, it might get into the local optimal Now we're replacing the current population with the retention population, in order to restore the population to the pre-k state, and the determined minPts and Eps were replaced by the value of the previous population, the selection of the individuals who have been selected as fathers in the previous k-generation regeneration and the selection probability of the similar individuals with the father are reduced, that is:

$$P_i = \alpha P_i$$

go to (3).

(5) Determining the number of individuals in a group is an approximation of the threshold value of minPts. The largest dij in the data set point distance matrix D of this group is the value of Eps.

3 MapReduce Parallel GA-DBSCAN

We propose a ga-dbscan algorithm based on MapReduce programming framework, reducing the time of DBSCAN algorithm in order to improve minPts and Eps accuracy. Adopting FPRBP algorithm [11] using grid division and data box technology to accurately divide the original data sets to ensure that there is no overlap zone, on this basis, using Map and Reduce functions can be used to parallelize the algorithm, this solves the problem of low efficiency of algorithm execution [12] Among them, song jie and others proposed a task distribution algorithm to optimize the energy consumption of MapReduce system, To Reduce the overall energy consumption of MapReduce system by dynamically adjusting the Map task and Reduce task size [13]; Wang and others propose the MapReduce data balancing method based on incremental partitioning strategy, which can better solve the problem of balance after data partitioning [14]; Xunyaling et al. proposed the data placement strategy in the MapReduce cluster environment, and summarized and analyzed the research and progress of the optimization method of data placement in the current MapReduce cluster environment [15].

3.1 The Map Process

Each data node (including the Namenode and Datanode) is a ga-Dbscan cluster for the assigned tasks, the intermediate clustering results are output in <P, FCBCo> (<key, value>). P is the number of the data object and is unique in the whole data set, which can represent key values. Value (F, C, B, Co) consists of four parts, where F represents the partition number and is assigned when the partition function FPRBP is executed; C means cluster number; B represents the boundary data object; Co indicates whether it is a core object. The specific process is shown in Fig. 1.

The formal description is as follows:

(1) The initial variable Cid value is 1, and the ga-dbscan algorithm for the data set is performed to determine minPts and Eps;

(2) Select a data object, p, and mark the p value, if the cluster number of p is not empty, jump to step (7);

(3) If p is the core object, the cluster number of p is assigned to Cid, otherwise, p is temporarily determined as the noise point, and the cluster number is assigned to 0;

(4) Traverse from p can reach all the objects directly, and determine its not a boundary object, includes the object cluster of cluster number is empty number assignment for Cid, deposited in the queue Q, previously marked as noise (cluster number 0) object cluster number assignment for Cid, and judged boundary object;

(5) If queue Q is empty, go to step (7), otherwise, take out the queue header element q;

(6) If the data object q is the core object, the step (5) is executed, otherwise the value of the value of the boundary object is determined, and the variable Cid value is added 1;

(7) If all data objects have a category tag, output the intermediate clustering result that reduce process from <key, value> to the end the Map process, otherwise return to step (2).

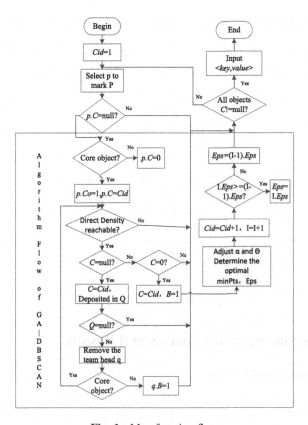

Fig. 1. Map function flow

3.2 The Process of Reduce

The Reduce processor receives the intermediate data generated by the Map <P, FCBCo>, reduce is divided into two parts, the algorithm flow is shown in Fig. 2: Its formal description is as follows:

(1) select the data object p to judge whether it belongs to the noise set or the boundary object;

(2) Do the following according to the value of p:
  (a) if the data is marked as noise and it is not a boundary object, then it is marked as noise data;
  (b) if the data neither the noise nor the data of the boundary object, find all the data objects whose cluster number is the same;
  (c) all the data that marked as a boundary object, to the boundary data processing function for further processing;

(3) If there is an unprocessed data object, return to step (1);

(4) According to the result of the merging of the boundary processing functions, the cluster number of the cluster in the whole data set is re-numbered so as to obtain a

unified cluster number, end the Reduce process and output the final result of <P, FCBCo>.

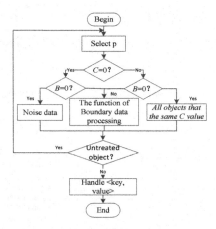

Fig. 2. Reduce fuctional process

4 Analysis Summary of Experimental Results

4.1 Experiments and Results

Data from the 30 GB Baidu Encyclopedia data that Nutch crawler to obtain, after the data encoding of similar to the data, the sample data points to do experiments of clustered simulation. Using the improved algorithm to repeat the experiment 5 times, after getting the average, certain relationship between the parameters a and & can been found, shown in Fig. 3-left. When improved algorithm choice of the parent, not only consider the group fitness at the same time, but also the dynamic adjustment into the category, introduction of adjustment coefficient α and threshold θ. After repeated experiments can be found that it can avoid minPts and Eps into local optimal solution when adjustment of α and θ in the iterative process. It can be concluded from the experimental data that the relationship between the parameters θ and minPts is shown in Fig. 3-right. The accuracy of the algorithm will be higher and higher when the iterative process is optimized, but when θ increases to a certain extent, as the θ continues to increase, the accuracy rate drops linearly. This is because the value of θ beyond a certain value, resulting in the difference between the parent generation infinitely smaller, no longer replace, that is, the first selected population directly identified as the final solution of the population, and minPts solution process is considered to be completed, making the minPts and Eps solution accuracy decline.

Record the experimental process and found when the parameters of α and θ values shown in Table 1, the clustering effect is optimal, when the accuracy of clustering as shown in Table 2, the study can be seen that although the amount of data is growing, but the improved algorithm has always maintained the correct direction of clustering to ensure the implementation effect, thus improving the accuracy of clustering.

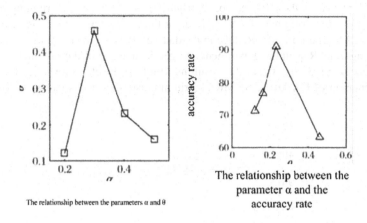

The relationship between the parameters α and θ

The relationship between the parameter α and the accuracy rate

Fig. 3. Relationship diagram of parameters and accuracy

Table 1. Parameters of α and θ values

Data size	α	θ	minPts	Eps
3400	0.3	0.21	5	0.348
9880	0.3	0.43	4	0.268
14886	0.4	0.50	4	0.869
20350	0.4	1.68	3	0.932
24650	0.2	2.89	4	1.895

Table 2. Accuracy of clustering

Data size	DBSCAN	GA-DBSCAN	GA-DBSCANMR
3400	98.61	99.98	99.47
9880	96.37	99.26	98.86
14886	93.22	98.16	97.75
20350	89.93	96.87	96.39
24650	83.29	94.56	94.24

From the data of Table 1, it is found that the accuracy of DBSCAN algorithm clustering tends to decrease with the increase of data volume. With the improved algorithm, the clustering effect has maintained a high accuracy rate. At the same time, it can be seen that although the amount of data is increasing, the improved algorithm has maintained the correct clustering direction and ensured the implementation effect, thus improving the accuracy of clustering.

In order to verify the efficiency of the algorithm, we compare the running time and accuracy of the original DBSCAN algorithm, GA-DBSCAN algorithm and GA-DBSCAN algorithm MapReduce in the data set. In order to ensure the reliability of the running time, Repeat the experiment and get the average of the run time. When the parameters $\alpha = 0.3$, $\theta = 0.21$, the resulting run-time results shown in Fig. 4, the implementation of GA-DBSCANMR algorithm clustering results shown in Fig. 5:

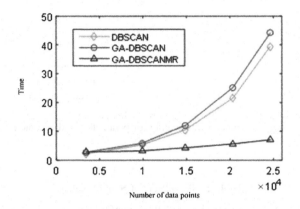

Fig. 4. Runtime comparison

It can be seen that the GA-DBSCAN algorithm of MapReduce is less time-consuming than the original algorithm, which is more time-consuming than the original algorithm because of the implementation of the partition function FPRBP and the assignment of tasks to the nodes Time, will consume a certain amount of time. And with the increasing amount of data, the execution time of the DBSCAN algorithm under the single machine shows a trend of linear growth, and the improved algorithm is basically stable in the running time, which shows that the improved algorithm fully exploits the Hadoop cluster processing large data Time, the data segmentation and distribution to a number of nodes to deal with the advantages, thereby greatly improving the GA-DBSCAN algorithm implementation efficiency.

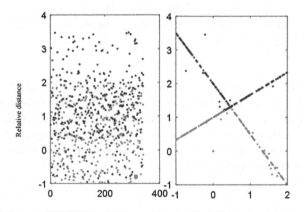

Fig. 5. Results of clustering results

5   Conclusion

In this paper, the algorithm of the DBSCAN algorithm is improved, and the algorithm is improved by using the genetic algorithm and the MapReduce programming framework. The original algorithm and the improved algorithm are compared experimentally. From the research process and the experimental results The following conclusions are drawn: based on the combination of genetic algorithm, can be adapted to determine the minPts and Eps height approximation, instead of relying on experience to set the threshold, and thus greatly improve the accuracy of clustering; aiming at the problem of time-consuming algorithm, this paper combines the MapReduce programming framework to hand over the large data set to the Hadoop cluster. Through the experimental conclusion, the improved algorithm still maintains the high efficiency when the data volume increases.

Through the improvement of the classical DBSCAN algorithm, the efficiency of the algorithm is greatly improved while the accuracy of the algorithm is improved. However, the improved algorithm is still time-consuming for high-dimensional data, and the future work will be High-dimensional data set, the algorithm for further transformation, so that the algorithm to achieve a wide range of applications.

References

1. Chen, G., Liu, B.Q., Wu, Y.: An adaptive DBSCAN algorithm based on gaussian distribution. Microelectron. Comput. **30**(03), 27–30 (2013)
2. Feng, Z., Qian, X., Zhao, N.: Greedy DBSCAN: a DBSCAN improvement algorithm for multi-density clustering. Comput. Appl. Res. (9) (2016)
3. Ester, M., Kriegel, H.P., Sander, J., et al.: A Density-based algorithm for discovering clusters in large spatial databases with noise. pp. 226–231 (2008)
4. Wang, W.T., Wu, Y.L., Tang, C.Y., et al.: Adaptive density-based spatial clustering of applications with noise (DBSCAN) according to data. In: International Conference on Machine Learning and Cybernetics, IEEE (2015)
5. Uncu, O., Gruver, W.A., Kotak, D.B., et al.: GRIDBSCAN: grid density-based spatial clustering of applications with noise. vol. 4, pp. 2976–2981 (2006)
6. Shufen, L., Dongxue, M., Xiaoyan, W.: Study on DBSCAN Algorithm Based on Grid Element. J. Jilin Univ. Eng. Sci. **44**(4), 1135–1139 (2014)
7. Luo, Q.: DBSCAN algorithm based on cloud computing. Wuhan University of Technology (2013)
8. Yang, Y.: Study on adaptive density clustering algorithm based on MapReduce. Tianjin University (2013)
9. He, Y., Tan, H., Luo, W., et al.: MR-DBSCAN: an efficient parallel density-based clustering algorithm using MapReduce. In: IEEE 17th International Conference on Parallel and Distributed Systems, IEEE Computer Society 2011, pp. 473–480 (2011)
10. Lei, L., Nie, R., Wang, J., et al.: Improved DBSCAN algorithm based on MapReduce. Comput. Sci. (s2) 396–399 (2015)
11. Li, L., Xi, Y.: Research on clustering algorithm and its parallelization strategy. In: International Conference on Computational and Information Sciences, pp. 325–328 (2011)
12. Design, application and application of data clustering algorithm based on MapReduce. J. East China Inst. Technol

13. Song, J., Xu, S., Guo, C., et al.: A task distribution algorithm for optimizing energy consumption of MapReduce system. J. Comput. **39**(2), 323–338 (2016)
14. Wang, Z., Chen, Q., Li, Z., et al.: MapReduce data equalization method based on incremental partition strategy. J. Comput. (1) 19–35 (2016)
15. Yaling, X., Jifu, Z., Xiao, Q.: Data placement strategy in MapReduce cluster environment. J. Softw. (8), 2056–2073 (2015)

Bounded Correctness Checking for Extended CTL Properties with Past Operators

Fei Pu[✉]

College of Computer and Information Engineering,
Zhejiang Gongshang University, Hangzhou, China
pufei@zjgsu.edu.cn

Abstract. Bounded semantics of a certain temporal logic is a basis to develop bounded model checking algorithms for finding errors in system designs. Traditional temporal logics are used in formal verification to predicate about the future evolutions of dynamic systems, both with a linear time model or a branching time model. This paper we further study bounded semantics of extended CTL formulas with past operators ($PeCTL$) which not only allows some sort of fairness but also could reason about the past behaviors of the systems being verified. Since QBF (quantified boolean formula) is exponentially more succinct in expressing specifications, we thus develop a QBF encoding of $PeCTL$ from the proposed bounded semantics. Finally, we present a bounded correctness checking algorithm for $PeCTL$ formulas and apply the bounded semantics of $PeCTL$ to derive a QBF-based characterization of $PeCTL$ properties.

Keywords: Bounded semantics · $PeCTL$
Bounded correctness checking

1 Introduction

Model checking is a popular automated verification technique used to check properties of the finite-state systems [1]. The model checking result is either a counterexample at the source level showing how the system could violate the property or a statement that the system respects the property. The counterexample returned by a model checker can help in understanding the symptom related to the error. Bounded model checking (BMC) as a complementary approach to BDD based symbolic model checking [3,12] applies satisfiability checking to the verification of temporal properties, especially, for efficient error detection. Given a finite transition system M, an LTL formula ϕ, and a natural number k, a BMC procedure decides whether there exists a computation in M of length k or less that violates ϕ. SAT-based BMC is performed by generating a propositional formula, which is satisfiable if and only if such a path exists. The main problem

© Springer Nature Singapore Pte Ltd. 2018
H. Yuan et al. (Eds.): GSKI 2017, CCIS 849, pp. 563–573, 2018.
https://doi.org/10.1007/978-981-13-0896-3_56

of this kind approach is the definitions of bounded semantics of temporal logics (or fragments of such logics) that are appropriate with respect to the potential usefulness as a basis for developing bounded model checking algorithms. Semantic translation for BMC is in general more efficient, as it results in smaller CNF formulas, and it potentially eliminates redundancies in the property of interest. Such a bounded semantics need to be sound and complete in general.

Due to the successes of bounded model checking, there are a lot of works on bounded semantics for various (fragments of) temporal logics such as LTL, $ACTL$, $ECTL$, and $ACTL^*$ [2–10,16–28]. Navarro-Perez et al. [28] presented an encoding of LTL bounded model checking problems within the Bernays-Schonfinkel fragment of first-order logic. This fragment allows a natural and succinct representation of both a software/hardware system and the property that one wants to verify. Oshman and Grumberg [6] proposed a new approach to bounded model checking for universal branching-time logic in which they encode an arbitrary graph and allow the SAT solver to choose both the states and edges of the graph that could significantly reduce the size of the counter-example produced by BMC. Wimmer et al. [25] applied bounded model checking to generate counterexamples when invariant properties of Markov chains are violated. By returning not simply flat paths, but paths which are annotated with loops, they make not only the algorithm more efficient, but also the counterexamples more useful for the designer.

Wenhui [16] proposed QBF-based bounded correctness checking for extended CTL (extended Computation Tree Logic) [15]. QBF has exponentially more succinct representations of the checked formulas than SAT [2,14]. Wenhui [17] also presented characteristics of bounded semantics for clarifying the concept of bounded semantics and provided a QBF-based bounded correctness checking algorithm for CTL under the given bounded semantics. As reported in [17], there is no bounded semantics which is sound and complete for CTL^* and $ACTL^*$ properties. Wozna [22] proposed a BMC method for $ACTL^*$ consists in combining a translation of a model M to several symbolic paths, which can start at arbitrary states of the model, with a translation of the negation of a formula. Xu et al. [18] further studied $ACTL$ formulas which have linear counterexamples using bounded semantics, and applied them to SAT-based verification, in particular, they presented a bounded correctness checking algorithm of $ACTL$ properties. There are many advantages over the existing approaches at both semantic and algorithmic levels, in particular, at the semantic level, it may gain at least a polynomial factor on the size of bounded models for verifying a property in certain cases and at the algorithmic level, their approach can be exponentially better than the existing one in certain cases.

Traditional temporal logics are used in formal verification to predicate about the future evolutions of dynamic systems. The introduction of past operators enables to produce more natural formulation of a wide class of properties of reactive systems, compared to traditional pure future temporal logics. Heljanko et al. [4] presented an incremental and complete bounded model checking method for the full linear temporal logic with past (PLTL). The advantage of their method is that their encoding is incremental and is better than the previously compact encoding for PLTL. Cimatti et al. [23] proposed a new encoding of past LTL into propositional logic, based on the use of separated normal form for past LTL which yields encodings that are smaller (in terms of clauses) and that are solved much more easily by the propositional solver.

In this paper, we are interested in extending CTL formulas to $eCTL$ with past operators($PeCTL$), after presenting a sound and complete bounded semantics we develop a QBF encoding of $PeCTL$ from the proposed bounded semantics and then present an algorithm for bounded correctness checking of $PeCTL$ properties. The rest of this paper is organized as follows. Section 2 introduces the definitions of relevant logics and concepts. Section 3 discusses properties of $PeCTL$, and a bounded semantics for $PeCTL$ is given. In Sect. 4, the bounded correctness checking algorithm for $PeCTL$ is developed, and Sect. 5 presents the QBF-based characterization of $PeCTL$ properties. Section 6 is concluding remarks.

2 Preliminaries

We introduce the definition of transition system models and that of the extended computation tree logic with past operators.

2.1 Transition Systems Model

Let AP be a set of atomic propositions. A finite transition system is represented by a Kripke structure which is a quadruple $M = < S, T, I, L >$, where S is a finite set of states, $T \subseteq S \times S$ is a transition relation which is total (i.e., for every $s \in S$, there is $s' \in S$ such that $(s, s') \in T$). $I \subseteq S$ is a set of initial states and $L : S \rightarrow 2^{AP}$ is a labeling function that maps each state to a subset of propositions of AP. A Kripke structure is also called a model.

Paths and computations. An infinite path of M an infinite sequence $s_0 s_1 \ldots$ such that $(s_i, s_{i+1}) \in T$ for $i \geq 0$. A computation of M is an infinite path $s_0 s_1 \ldots$ of M such that $s_0 \in I$. A finite path is a finite prefix of an infinite path. Given a path $\pi = \pi_0 \pi_1 \ldots$, we use π^i to denote the subpath of π starting at π_i, use $\pi(s)$ to denote a path with $\pi_0 = s$. Then $\exists \pi(s).\varphi$ means that there is a path π with $\pi_0 = s$ such that φ holds, and $\forall \pi(s).\varphi$ means that for all path π with $\pi_0 = s$, φ holds.

2.2 Extended Computation Tree Logic with Past

Properties of a Kripke structure may be represented by temporal logic formulas. Extended computation tree logic [15] is a propositional branching time logic that extends the computation tree logic (CTL) with possibility to express fairness constraints. For brevity, the extended computation tree logic is hereafter denoted $eCTL$. $PeCTL$ is a specification logic with both past and future temporal operators.

Syntax. Let AP be a set of propositional symbols. Let p range over AP. Let ϕ be state formula and ψ be the path formula. The set of $PeCTL$ formulas over AP is defined as follows:

$$\phi ::= p \mid \neg\phi \mid \phi \wedge \phi \mid \phi \vee \phi \mid A\psi \mid E\psi$$
$$\psi ::= X\phi \mid F\phi \mid G\phi \mid F^{\infty}\phi \mid G^{\infty}\phi \mid \phi U \phi \mid \phi R \phi$$
$$Y\phi \mid Z\phi \mid O\phi \mid H\phi \mid \phi S \phi \mid \phi T \phi$$

The past operators Y, Z, O, H, S and T, which are the temporal duals of the future operators allow us to express statements on the past time instants. The Y (for Yesterday) operator is the dual of X and refers to the previous time instant. At any non-initial time, $Y\phi$ is true if and only ϕ holds at the previous time instant. The Z (the name is just a mnemonic choice) operator is very similar to the Y operator, and it differs in the way the initial time instant is dealt with. At time zero, $Y\phi$ is false, while $Z\phi$ is true. The O (for Once) operator is the dual of F (sometimes in the future), so that $O\phi$ is true iff ϕ is true at some past time instant (including the present time). Similarly, H (for Historically) is the past-time version of G (always in the future), so that $H\phi$ is true iff ϕ is always true in the past. The S (for Since) operator is the dual of U (until), so that $\phi_1 S\phi_2$ is true iff ϕ_2 holds somewhere in the past and ϕ_1 is true from then up to now. Finally, we have $\phi_1 T\phi_2 = \neg(\neg\phi_1 S\neg\phi_2)$ (T is called the Trigger operator).

Definition 1 *(Semantics of PeCTL). Let p denote a propositional symbol, ϕ_0, ϕ_1 denote state formulas, ψ_0, ψ_1 denote path formula. Let s be a state and π be a path of M. The relation $\models$ is defined as follows:*

$M, s \models p$	iff $p \in L(s)$.
$M, s \models \neg p$	iff $M, s \not\models p$
$M, s \models \phi_0 \wedge \phi_1$	iff $(M, s \models \phi_0)$ and $(M, s \models \phi_1)$
$M, s \models \phi_0 \vee \phi_1$	iff $(M, s \models \phi_0)$ or $(M, s \models \phi_1)$
$M, s \models A\psi_0$	iff $\forall \pi(s).(M, \pi \models \psi_0)$
$M, s \models E\psi_0$	iff $\exists \pi(s).(M, \pi \models \psi_0)$
$M, \pi^m \models \phi_0$	iff $M, \pi_m \models \phi_0$
$M, \pi^m \models \psi_0 \wedge \psi_1$	iff $M, \pi^m \models \psi_0 \wedge M, \pi \models \psi_1$
$M, \pi^m \models \psi_0 \vee \psi_1$	iff $M, \pi^m \models \psi_0 \vee M, \pi \models \psi_1$
$M, \pi^m \models X\psi_0$	iff $M, \pi^{m+1} \models \psi_0$
$M, \pi^m \models G\psi_0$	iff $\forall i \geq 0.(M, \pi^i \models \psi_0)$
$M, \pi^m \models F\psi_0$	iff $\exists i \geq m.(M, \pi^i \models \psi_0)$
$M, \pi^m \models G^{\infty}\psi_0$	iff $\exists i \geq m.\forall k \geq i.(M, \pi^k \models \psi_0)$
$M, \pi^m \models F^{\infty}\psi_0$	iff $\forall i \geq m.\exists k \geq i.(M, \pi^k \models \psi_0)$
$M, \pi^m \models \psi_0 U\psi_1$	iff $\exists j \geq m.(M, \pi^j \models \psi_1$ and $(\forall m \leq i < j.(M, \pi^i \models \psi_0))$
$M, \pi^m \models \psi_0 R\psi_1$	iff $(\exists j \geq m.(M, \pi^j \models \psi_0$ and $\forall 0 \leq i \leq j.(M, \pi^i \models \psi_1))$
	or $\forall j \geq m.(M, \pi^j \models \psi_1)$
$M, \pi^m \models Y\psi_0$	iff $m > 0$ and $M, \pi^{m-1} \models \psi_0$
$M, \pi^m \models Z\psi_0$	iff $m = 0$ or $M, \pi^{m-1} \models \psi_0$
$M, \pi^m \models O\psi_0$	iff $\exists 0 \leq j \leq m.\ M, \pi^j \models \psi_0$
$M, \pi^m \models H\psi_0$	iff $\forall 0 \leq j \leq m.\ M, \pi^j \models \psi_0$
$M, \pi^m \models \psi_0 S\psi_1$	iff $\exists 0 \leq i \leq m.(M, \pi^i \models \psi_1$ and $(\forall i < j \leq m.\ M, \pi^j \models \psi_0))$
$M, \pi^m \models \psi_0 T\psi_1$	iff $\forall 0 \leq i \leq m.(M, \pi^i \models \psi_1$ or $(\exists i < j \leq m.\ M, \pi^j \models \psi_0))$

Although the use of past operators in $PeCTL$ does not enhance expressive power, it allows us to formalize properties more naturally.

Definition 2. Let φ be a $PeCTL$ formula. $M \models \varphi$ iff $M, s \models \varphi$ for all $s \in I$.

3 Bounded Semantics

To define the bounded semantics one needs to represent infinite paths in a model in a special way. To this aim, we define the notions of k-paths and loops.

k-paths. Let M be a model, $k \geq 0$, and $0 \leq n \leq k$. A k-path of M is a path $\pi(k) = (s_0, s_1, ..., s_k)$ (also denoted by π) with length $k+1$. A k-path may start at any state of M in the model. A k-path π is a loop $\pi_{rs}(k, n)$ if $n < k$ and $\pi_k = \pi_n$. As in the definition of bounded semantics, we need to define the satisfiability relation on suffixes of k-paths, we denote $\pi^m(k)$ by the k-path $\pi(k)$ starting at point π_m, where $0 \leq m \leq k$. We denote k-path $\pi(k)$ starting at s by $\pi(k)(s)$.

Bounded models. The k-model of M is a structure $M_k = <S, ph_k, I, L>$, where Ph_k is the set of all different k-paths of M. M_k can be considered as an approximation of M. The k-model M_k is a special unique (k, n)-model of M with $n = |Ph_k|$.

The encoding of the BMC problem for $PeCTL$ when the bounded path has no loop is fairly straightforward. The case when loops are allowed in bounded paths becomes more complicated.

Definition 3. *The past operator depth for a PeCTL formula ϕ (denoted by $\delta(\phi)$) is inductively defined as:*

$$
\begin{aligned}
\delta(\phi) &= 0 & \text{for } \phi \in AP \\
\delta(\circ\phi) &= \delta(\phi) & \text{for } \circ \in \{\neg, X, F, G\} \\
\delta(\circ\phi) &= \delta(\phi) & \text{for } \circ \in \{F^\infty, G^\infty\} \\
\delta(\phi_0 \circ \phi_1) &= max(\delta(\phi_0), \delta(\phi_1)) & \text{for } \circ \in \{\vee, \wedge, U, R\} \\
\delta(\circ\phi) &= 1 + \delta(\phi) & \text{for } \circ \in \{Y, Z, O, H\} \\
\delta(\phi_0 \circ \phi_1) &= 1 + max(\delta(\phi_0), d(\phi_1)) & \text{for } \circ \in \{S, T\}
\end{aligned}
$$

Definition 4. *Let d be the current d-unrolling of the loop $\pi_{rs}(k, n)$. Let l_i be the boolean variable such that it is true only if $i = n$ on the loop $\pi_{rs}(k, n)$. Let ϕ be PeCTL formula. For any state i in the current d-unrolling of $\pi_{rs}(k, n)$, $M, \pi^i \models_k^d \phi$ means that ϕ holds on the k-path π^i where state i is in the current d-unrolling of $\pi_{rs}(k, n)$. The case where $d = 0$ corresponds to the original k-path.*

Theorem 1. *Let ϕ be a PeCTL formula, π be a $\pi_{rs}(k, n)$ loop. For any state i in the current d-unrolling of $\pi_{rs}(k, n)$ where $d > \delta(\phi)$, $M, \pi^i \models \phi$ iff $M, \pi^j \models \phi$, where $j = i - (d - \delta(\phi))(k - n + 1)$.*

Definition 5 (*Bounded Semantics of PeCTL*). *Let p denote a propositional symbol, ϕ_0, ϕ_1 denote state formulas, and ψ_0, ψ_1 denote path formulas. Let s be a state of M and π be a k-path of ph_k. Let $M, s \models_k \varphi$ denote the relation that φ holds on s of M_k. Let $d(\pi)$ the current d-unrolling of the loop-path $\pi_{rs}(k, n)$. Let $\delta(\phi)$ be the depth of ϕ. The relation $\models_k$ is defined as follows.*

$M, s \models_k p$	iff $p \in L(s)$
$M, s \models_k \neg p$	iff $M, s \not\models_k p$
$M, s \models_k \phi_0 \wedge \phi_1$	iff $(M, s \models_k \phi_0)$ and $(M, s \models_k \phi_1)$
$M, s \models_k \phi_0 \vee \phi_1$	iff $(M, s \models_k \phi_0)$ or $(M, s \models_k \phi_1)$
$M, s \models_k A\psi_0$	iff $\forall \pi(k)(s).(M, \pi \models \psi_0)$
$M, s \models_k E\psi_0$	iff $\exists \pi(k)(s).(M, \pi \models \psi_0)$
$M, \pi^m \models_k \phi_0$	iff $M, \pi_m \models_k \phi_0$
$M, \pi^m \models_k \psi_0 \wedge \psi_1$	iff $M, \pi^m \models_k \psi_0 \wedge M, \pi^m \models_k \psi_1$
$M, \pi^m \models_k \psi_0 \vee \psi_1$	iff $M, \pi^m \models_k \psi_0 \vee M, \pi^m \models_k \psi_1$
$M, \pi^m \models_k X\psi_0$	iff $(m < k$ and $M, \pi^{m+1} \models_k \psi_0)$ or $(m = k$ and $\pi_{rs}(k, n)$ and $M, \pi^{n+1} \models_k \psi_0)$
$M, \pi^m \models_k G\psi_0$	iff $n < k, \pi_{rs}(k, n)$ and $(\forall min(m, n) \leq j \leq k$ and $M, \pi^j \models_k \psi_0)$
$M, \pi^m \models_k F\psi_0$	iff $(\exists m \leq j \leq k, M, \pi^j \models_k \psi_0)$ or $(n < m$ and $\pi_{rs}(k, n)$ and $(\exists n < j < m, M, \pi^j \models_k \psi_0))$
$M, \pi^m \models_k G^\infty \psi_0$	iff $\exists i \geq m, \forall i \leq l \leq k.(n < k, \pi_{rs}(k, n)$ and $(\forall min(l, n) \leq j \leq k$ and $M, \pi^j \models_k \psi_0))$
$M, \pi^m \models_k F^\infty \psi_0$	iff $\forall i \geq m, \exists i \leq l \leq k.((\exists l \leq j \leq k, M, \pi^j \models_k \psi_0)$ or $(n < l$ and $\pi_{rs}(k, n)$ and $(\exists n < j < l, M, \pi^j \models_k \psi_0)))$
$M, \pi^m \models_k \psi_0 U\psi_1$	iff $(\exists m \leq j \leq k, M, \pi^j \models_k \psi_1$ and $(\forall m \leq i < j, M, \pi^j \models_k \psi_0))$ or $(n < m$ and $\pi_{rs}(k, n)$ and $(\exists l \leq j \leq m, M, \pi^j \models_k \psi_1)$ and $(\forall l < i < j, M, \pi^i \models_k \psi_0)$ and $(\forall m \leq i \leq k, M, \pi^i \models_k \psi_0))$
$M, \pi^m \models_k \psi_0 R\psi_1$	iff $(\forall m \leq j \leq k, M, \pi^j \models_k \psi_1$ or $(\exists m \leq i \leq j, M, \pi^i \models_k \psi_0))$ or $(n < m$ and $\pi_{rs}(k, n)$ and $(\exists n < j < m, M, \pi^j \models_k \psi_0)$ and $(\forall n < i \leq j, M, \pi^i \models_k \psi_1)$ and $(\forall m \leq i \leq k, M, \pi^i \models_k \psi_1))$ or $(n < k$ and $\pi_{rs}(k, n)$ and $(\forall min(m, n) \leq j \leq k, M, \pi^j \models_k \psi_1))$
$M, \pi^m \models_k Y\psi_0$	iff $(d = 0, 1 \leq m \leq k, M, \pi^{m-1} \models_k \psi_0)$ or $(1 \leq d \leq \delta(Y\psi_0), 1 \leq m \leq k, (l_m \wedge M, \pi^k \models_k^{d-1} \psi_0) \vee (\neg l_m \wedge M, \pi^{m-1} \models_k^d \psi_0))$
$M, \pi^m \models_k Z\psi_0$	iff $m = 0$ or $((d = 0, 1 \leq m \leq k, M, \pi^{m-1} \models_k \psi_0)$ or $(1 \leq d \leq \delta(Y\psi_0), 1 \leq m \leq k, (l_m \wedge M, \pi^k \models_k^{d-1} \psi_0) \vee (\neg l_m \wedge M, \pi^{m-1} \models_k^d \psi_0)))$
$M, \pi^m \models_k O\psi_0$	iff $(d = 0, 1 \leq m \leq k, \exists 0 \leq j \leq m.M, \pi^j \models_k \psi_0)$ or $(1 \leq d \leq \delta(O\psi_0), 1 \leq m \leq k, (l_m \wedge \exists 0 \leq j \leq k.M, \pi^j \models_k^{d-1} \psi_0)$ or $(\neg l_m \wedge \exists 0 \leq j \leq m.M, \pi^j \models_k^d \psi_0))$
$M, \pi^m \models_k H\psi_0$	iff $(d = 0, 1 \leq m \leq k, \forall 0 \leq j \leq m.M, \pi^j \models_k \psi_0)$ or $(1 \leq d \leq \delta(H\psi_0), 1 \leq m \leq k, (l_m \wedge \forall 0 \leq j \leq k.M, \pi^j \models_k^{d-1} \psi_0) \vee (\neg l_m \wedge \forall 0 \leq j \leq m.M, \pi^j \models_k^d \psi_0))$
$M, \pi^m \models_k \psi_0 S\psi_1$	iff $(d = 0, \exists 0 \leq i \leq m.(M, \pi^i \models_k \psi_1 \wedge (\forall i < j \leq m.M, \pi^j \models_k \psi_0)))$ or $(1 \leq d \leq \delta(\psi_0 S\psi_1), M, \pi^m \models_k^d \psi_1 \vee (M, \pi^m \models_k^d \psi_0 \wedge ((l_m \wedge M, \pi^k \models_k^{d-1} \psi_0 S\psi_1) \vee (\neg l_m \wedge M, \pi^{m-1} \models_k^d \psi_0 S\psi_1))))$
$M, \pi^m \models_k \psi_0 T\psi_1$	iff $(d = 0, \forall 0 \leq i \leq m.(M, \pi^i \models_k \psi_1 \vee (\exists i < j \leq m.M, \pi^j \models_k \psi_0)))$ or $(1 \leq d \leq \delta(\psi_0 T\psi_1), M, \pi^m \models_k^d \psi_1 \wedge (M, \pi^m \models_k^d \psi_0 \vee ((l_m \wedge M, \pi^k \models_k^{d-1} \psi_0 T\psi_1) \vee (\neg l_m \wedge M, \pi^{m-1} \models_k^d \psi_0 T\psi_1))))$

4 Bounded Correctness Checking

Since the number of k-paths in the k-model is large, to verify more efficiently, we focus on using submodels with smaller size of the k-model M_k. A (k, n)-model of M is a structure $N = <S, ph'_k, I, L>$, where ph'_k is a multi-set with the size $|ph'_k| = n$ and all paths of ph'_k are in Ph_k. A (k, n)-model is then considered as a submodel of M_k. The k-model M_k is a special unique (k, n)-model of M with $n = |ph_k|$. Let $N' = <S, ph''_k, I, L>$, if $ph'_k \subseteq ph''_k$, then $N \leq N'$.

Definition 6 Let ψ_0, ψ_1 be PeCTL formulas over the set of atomic propositions AP, $f_k^a(\phi)$ and $f_k^e(\phi)$ is defined as follows.

$f_k^a(\phi_0) = f_k^e(\phi_0)$	$= 0$ if ϕ is propositional	
$f_k^a(\phi_0 \wedge \phi_1)$	$= \max(f_k^a(\phi_0), f_k^a(\phi_1))$	
$f_k^a(\phi_0 \vee \phi_1)$	$= f_k^a(\phi_0) + f_k^a(\phi_1)$	
$f_k^a(AX\phi_0)$	$= f_k^a(\phi) + 1$	
$f_k^a(AY\phi_0)$	$= f_k^a(\phi) + 1$	
$f_k^a(AZ\phi_0)$	$= f_k^a(\phi) + 1$	
$f_k^a(AG^\infty \phi_0)$	$= f_k^a(\phi_0) + 1$	
$f_k^a(AF^\infty \phi_0)$	$= k \cdot f_k^a(\phi_0) + 1$	
$f_k^a(A(\phi_0 R\phi_1))$	$= k \cdot f_k^a(\phi_0) + \max(f_k^a(\phi_0), f_k^a(\phi_1)) + 1$	
$f_k^a(A(\phi_0 U\phi_1))$	$= f_k^a(\phi_1) + k \cdot \max(f_k^a(\phi_0), f_k^a(\phi_1)) + 1$	
$f_k^a(A(\phi_0 T\phi_1))$	$= k \cdot f_k^a(\phi_0) + \max(f_k^a(\phi_0), f_k^a(\phi_1)) + 1$	
$f_k^a(A(\phi_0 S\phi_1))$	$= f_k^a(\phi_1) + k \cdot \max(f_k^a(\phi_0), f_k^a(\phi_1)) + 1$	
$f_k^e(\phi_0 \wedge \phi_1)$	$= f_k^e(\phi_0) + f_k^e(\phi_1)$	
$f_k^e(\phi_0 \vee \phi_1)$	$= \max(f_k^e(\phi_0), f_k^e(\phi_1))$	
$f_k^e(EX\phi)$	$= f_k^e(\phi) + 1$	
$f_k^e(EY\phi_0)$	$= f_k^a(\phi) + 1$	
$f_k^e(EZ\phi_0)$	$= f_k^a(\phi) + 1$	
$f_k^a(EG^\infty \phi_0)$	$= k \cdot f_k^a(\phi_0) + 1$	
$f_k^a(EF^\infty \phi_0)$	$= f_k^a(\phi_0) + 1$	
$f_k^e(E(\phi_0 U\phi_1))$	$= f_k^e(\phi_1) + k \cdot f_k^e(\phi_0) + 1$	
$f_k^e(E(\phi_0 R\phi_1))$	$= f_k^e(\phi_0) + f_k^e(\phi_1) + k \cdot \max(f_k^e(\phi_0), f_k^e(\phi_1)) + 1$	
$f_k^e(E(\phi_0 S\phi_1))$	$= f_k^e(\phi_1) + k \cdot f_k^e(\phi_0) + 1$	
$f_k^e(E(\phi_0 T\phi_1))$	$= f_k^e(\phi_0) + f_k^e(\phi_1) + k \cdot \max(f_k^e(\phi_0), f_k^e(\phi_1)) + 1$	

Theorem 2 (Soundness and Completeness)

(1). Let ϕ be an APeCTL formula, $n = f_k^a(\phi)$. $M, s \models_k \phi$ iff there is a (k, n)-model N such that $N, s \models_k \phi$.

(2). Let φ be an EPeCTL formula, $n = f_k^e(\varphi)$. $M, s \models_k \varphi$ iff there is a (k, n)-model N such that $N, s \models_k \varphi$.

5   QBF Characterization of *PeCTL*

From the bounded semantics, a QBF-based characterization of *PeCTL* formulas, can be developed as follows.

Let $k \geq 0$. Let $u_0, \ldots, u_k$ be a finite sequence of state variables. The sequence $u_0, \ldots, u_k$ (denoted by $\overrightarrow{u}$) is intended to be used as a representation of a k-path of M.

Definition 7. *Let $k \geq 0$.*

$$P_k(\overrightarrow{u}) := \bigwedge_{j=0}^{k-1} T(u_j, u_{j+1})$$

Every assignment to the set of state variables $u_0, \ldots, u_k$ satisfying $P_k(\overrightarrow{u})$ represents a valid k-path of M. The (k, n)-model of M can be encoded as $[[M]]_k^n := \bigwedge_{i=1}^n P_k(\overrightarrow{u_i})$. Let $rs_k(\overrightarrow{u})$ denote that there are same states appearing in different positions in k-path $\overrightarrow{u}$. Formally,

$$\pi_{rs}^k(\overrightarrow{u}) := \bigvee_{x=0}^{k-1} \bigvee_{y=x+1}^{k} u_x = u_y$$

From the above definition, $\pi_{rs}^k(\overrightarrow{u}, n)$ is the same as $\pi_{rs}(k, n)$ $(n < k)$. Let $p \in AP$ be a proposition symbol and $p(v)$ be the propositional formula such that $p(v)$ is true whenever v is assigned the truth value representing a state s in which p holds.

Definition 8 *(Translation of PeCTL formulas). Let $k \geq 0$. Let v be a state variable and φ_0, φ_1 be state formulas and ψ_0, ψ_1 be path formulas. The encoding $[[\phi, v]]_k^{m,d}$ is defined as follows.*

$$
\begin{aligned}
&[[p, v]]_k && = p(v) \\
&[[\neg p, v]]_k && = \neg p(v) \\
&[[\varphi_0 \vee \varphi_1, v]]_k && = [[\varphi_0, v]]_k \vee [[\varphi_1, v]]_k \\
&[[\varphi_0 \wedge \varphi_1, v]]_k && = [[\varphi_0, v]]_k \wedge [[\varphi_1, v]]_k \\
&[[A\psi_0, v]]_k && = \forall \overrightarrow{u}.(P(\overrightarrow{u}) \wedge v = u_0 \wedge [[\psi_0, \overrightarrow{u}]]_k) \\
&[[E\psi_0, v]]_k && = \exists \overrightarrow{u}.(P(\overrightarrow{u}) \wedge v = u_0 \wedge [[\psi_0, \overrightarrow{u}]]_k) \\[4pt]
&[[X\varphi_0, \overrightarrow{u}]]_k^m && = ((m < k) \wedge [[\varphi_0, u_{m+1}]]_k) \vee (m = k \wedge \pi_{rs}^k(\overrightarrow{u}, n) \wedge [[\varphi_0, u_{n+1}]]_k)) \\
&[[F\psi_0, \overrightarrow{u}]]_k^m && = (\bigvee_{j=m}^k [[\psi_0, u_j]]_k) \vee ((n < m) \wedge \pi_{rs}^k(\overrightarrow{u}, n) \wedge (\bigvee_{j=n+1}^{m-1} [[\psi_0, u_j]]_k)) \\
&[[G\psi_0, \overrightarrow{u}]]_k^m && = (n < k) \wedge \pi_{rs}^k(\overrightarrow{u}, n) \wedge (\bigwedge_{j=min(m,n)}^k [[\psi_0, u_j]]_k) \\
&[[F^\infty\psi_0, \overrightarrow{u}]]_k^m && = \bigwedge_{i=m}^k \bigvee_{l=i}^k ((\bigvee_{j=l}^k [[\psi_0, u_j]]_k) \vee ((n < l) \wedge \pi_{rs}^k(\overrightarrow{u}, n) \\
& && \quad \wedge (\bigvee_{j=n+1}^{l-1} [[\psi_0, u_j]]_k))) \\
&[[G^\infty\psi_0, \overrightarrow{u}]]_k^m && = \bigvee_{i=m}^k \bigwedge_{l=i}^k ((n < k) \wedge \pi_{rs}^k(\overrightarrow{u}, n) \wedge (\bigwedge_{j=min(l,n)}^k [[\psi_0, u_j]]_k)) \\
&[[\psi_0 U\psi_1, \overrightarrow{u}]]_k^m && = (\bigvee_{j=m}^k [[\psi_1, u_j]]_k \wedge \bigwedge_{i=m}^{j-1} [[\psi_0, u_j]]_k) \vee ((n < m) \wedge \pi_{rs}^k(\overrightarrow{u}, n) \wedge \\
& && \quad (\bigvee_{j=l}^m [[\psi_1, u_j]]_k) \wedge (\bigwedge_{i=l+1}^{j-1} [[\psi_0, u_i]]_k) \wedge (\bigwedge_{i=m}^k [[\psi_0, u_i]]_k)) \\
&[[\psi_0 R\psi_1, \overrightarrow{u}]]_k^m && = (\bigvee_{j=m}^k [[\psi_0, u_j]]_k \wedge (\bigwedge_{i=m}^j [[\psi_1, u_j]]_k)) \vee ((n < m) \wedge \pi_{rs}^k(\overrightarrow{u}, n) \wedge \\
& && \quad (\bigvee_{j=l+1}^{m-1} [[\psi_0, u_j]]_i) \wedge (\bigwedge_{i=l+1}^j [[\psi_1, u_i]]_k) \wedge (\bigwedge_{i=m}^k [[\psi_1, u_i]]_k)) \\
& && \quad \vee ((n < k) \wedge \pi_{rs}^k(\overrightarrow{u}, n) \wedge (\bigwedge_{j=min(m,n)}^k [[\psi_1, u_j]]_k)) \\[4pt]
&[[Y\psi_0, \overrightarrow{u}]]_k^{m,d} && = ((d = 0) \wedge (1 \leq m \leq k) \wedge [[\psi_0, u_{m-1}]]_k) \vee ((1 \leq d \leq \delta(Y\psi_0) \wedge \\
& && \quad (1 \leq m \leq k) \wedge ((l_m \wedge [[\psi_0, u_k]]_k^{d-1}) \vee (\neg l_m \wedge [[\psi_0, u_{m-1}]]_k^d))) \\
&[[Z\psi_0, \overrightarrow{u}]]_k^{m,d} && = (m = 0) \vee (((d = 0) \wedge (1 \leq m \leq k) \wedge [[\psi_0, u_{m-1}]]_k) \vee \\
& && \quad (1 \leq d \leq \delta(Z\psi_0) \wedge (1 \leq m \leq k) \wedge ((l_m \wedge [[\psi_0, u_k]]_k^{d-1}) \vee \\
& && \quad (\neg l_m \wedge [[\psi_0, u_{m-1}]]_k^d)))) \\
&[[O\psi_0, \overrightarrow{u}]]_k^{m,d} && = ((d = 0) \wedge (1 \leq m \leq k) \wedge \bigvee_{j=1}^m [[\psi_0, u_j]]_k) \vee ((1 \leq d \leq \delta(O\psi_0) \\
& && \quad \wedge (1 \leq m \leq k) \wedge ((l_m \wedge \bigvee_{j=0}^k [[\psi_0, u_j]]_k^{d-1}) \vee (\neg l_m \wedge \\
& && \quad \bigvee_{j=0}^k [[\psi_0, u_j]]_k^d))) \\
&[[H\psi_0, \overrightarrow{u}]]_k^{m,d} && = ((d = 0) \wedge (1 \leq m \leq k) \wedge \bigwedge_{j=1}^m [[\psi_0, u_j]]_k) \vee ((1 \leq d \leq \delta(H\psi_0) \\
& && \quad \wedge (1 \leq m \leq k) \wedge ((l_m \wedge \bigwedge_{j=0}^k [[\psi_0, u_j]]_k^{d-1}) \vee (\neg l_m \wedge \\
& && \quad \bigwedge_{j=0}^k [[\psi_0, u_j]]_k^d))) \\
&[[\psi_0 S\psi_1, \overrightarrow{u}]]_k^{m,d} && = ((d = 0) \wedge \bigvee_{i=0}^m ([[\psi_1, u_i]]_k \wedge \bigwedge_{j>i}^m [[\psi_0, u_j]]_k)) \vee \\
& && \quad ((1 \leq d \leq \delta(\psi_0 S\psi_1) \wedge [[\psi_1, u_m]]_k^d \vee ([[\psi_0, u_m]]_k^d \wedge \\
& && \quad ((l_m \wedge [[\psi_0 S\psi_1, u_k]]_k^{d-1}) \vee (\neg l_m \wedge [[\psi_0 S\psi_1, u_{m-1}]]_k^d))) \\
&[[\psi_0 T\psi_1, \overrightarrow{u}]]_k^{m,d} && = ((d = 0) \wedge \bigwedge_{i=0}^m ([[\psi_1, u_i]]_k \vee \bigvee_{j>i}^m [[\psi_0, u_j]]_k)) \vee \\
& && \quad ((1 \leq d \leq \delta(\psi_0 T\psi_1) \wedge [[\psi_1, u_m]]_k^d \wedge ([[\psi_0, u_m]]_k^d \vee \\
& && \quad ((l_m \wedge [[\psi_0 T\psi_1, u_k]]_k^{d-1}) \vee (\neg l_m \wedge [[\psi_0 T\psi_1, u_{m-1}]]_k^d)))
\end{aligned}
$$

Theorem 3 *Let ϕ be an PeCTL formula. $M_k, s \models \phi$ iff there exists a $d \leq \delta(\phi)$ such that $[[\phi, v(s)]]_k^{0,d}$ holds.*

Remark. $v(s)$ denotes that the state variable v has been assigned a value corresponding to the state s.

Theorem 4 *Let ϕ be an PeCTL formula. $M, s \models \phi$ iff there exists a $d \leq \delta(\phi)$ such that $[[\phi, v(s)]]_k^{0,d}$ holds for some $k \geq 0$.*

6   Conclusions

There are only a few works to extend BMC to LTL with past operators, and how to extend BMC to past CTL remains a unsolved problem. In this paper, to tackle this problem, we present a bounded semantics for $PeCTL$ formulas and provide the corresponding QBF characterization of these properties. We establish a correct checking algorithm of $PeCTL$ properties based on solving QBF-formulas. Due to the more succinctness of an efficient QBF based decision procedure, QBF-based correct checking approaches for temporal logic specifications are most natural to encode symbolic model checking problems as QBF formulas [14]. Therefore, our QBF-based checking algorithm is more applicable.

The main contributions of the paper are: our translation from $PeCTL$ to QBF can reduce the size of the submodels submitted to the QBF solver while testing satisfiability of the formula to be verified. On the other hand, $PeCTL$ properties support some sort of fairness that are not handled by some well known model checkers such as Spin and NuSMV. Our bounded semantics based approach has advantage when a small k is sufficient for verification or error detection of given $PeCTL$ properties. To the best of our knowledge, our work is the first attempt to extend BMC to CTL with past operators. From the practical point of view, improving the efficiency by optimizing the QBF-based encoding techniques for $PeCTL$ formulas remains as future works.

Acknowledgements. This work is supported by Zhejiang Provincial Natural Science Foundation of China under Grant No. LY13F020009 and State Key Laboratory of Computer Science, Institute of Software, Chinese Academy of Sciences under Grant No. SYSKF1011.

References

1. Baier, C., Katoen, J.-P.: Principles of Model Checking. MIT Press, Cambridge (2008)
2. Dershowitz, N., Hanna, Z., Katz, J.: Bounded model checking with QBF. In: Bacchus, F., Walsh, T. (eds.) SAT 2005. LNCS, vol. 3569, pp. 408–414. Springer, Heidelberg (2005). https://doi.org/10.1007/11499107_32
3. Biere, A., Cimmatti, A., Clarke, E., Strichman, O., Zhu, Y.: Bounded model checking. Adv. Comput. **58**, 117–148 (2003)
4. Heljanko, K., Junttila, T., Latvala, T.: Incremental and Complete Bounded Model Checking for Full PLTL. In: Etessami, K., Rajamani, S.K. (eds.) CAV 2005. LNCS, vol. 3576, pp. 98–111. Springer, Heidelberg (2005). https://doi.org/10.1007/11513988_10
5. Penczek, W., Wozna, B., Zbrzezny, A.: Bounded model checking for the universal fragment of CTL. Fundam. Inform. **51**, 135–156 (2002)
6. Oshman, R., Grumberg, O.: A new approach to bounded model checking for branching time logics. In: Namjoshi, K.S., Yoneda, T., Higashino, T., Okamura, Y. (eds.) ATVA 2007. LNCS, vol. 4762, pp. 410–424. Springer, Heidelberg (2007). https://doi.org/10.1007/978-3-540-75596-8_29

7. Laroussinie, F., Schnoebelen, P.: Specification in CTL past for verification in CTL. Inf. Comput. **156**, 236–263 (2000)
8. Inverso, O., Tomasco, E., Fischer, B., La Torre, S., Parlato, G.: Bounded model checking of multi-threaded C programs via lazy sequentialization. In: Biere, A., Bloem, R. (eds.) CAV 2014. LNCS, vol. 8559, pp. 585–602. Springer, Cham (2014). https://doi.org/10.1007/978-3-319-08867-9_39
9. Benedetti, M., Cimatti, A.: Bounded Model checking for past LTL. In: Garavel, H., Hatcliff, J. (eds.) TACAS 2003. LNCS, vol. 2619, pp. 18–33. Springer, Heidelberg (2003). https://doi.org/10.1007/3-540-36577-X_3
10. Armando, A., Carbone, R., Compagna, L.: SATMC: A SAT-based model checker for security-critical systems. In: Ábrahám, E., Havelund, K. (eds.) TACAS 2014. LNCS, vol. 8413, pp. 31–45. Springer, Heidelberg (2014). https://doi.org/10.1007/978-3-642-54862-8_3
11. Kroening, D., Tautschnig, M.: CBMC – C bounded model checker. In: Ábrahám, E., Havelund, K. (eds.) TACAS 2014. LNCS, vol. 8413, pp. 389–391. Springer, Heidelberg (2014). https://doi.org/10.1007/978-3-642-54862-8_26
12. McMillan, K.L.: Symbolic Model Checking. Kluwer Academic Publisher, Dordrecht (1993)
13. Bryant, R.E.: Binary decision diagrams and beyond: enabling technologies for formal verification. In: ICCAD, pp. 236–243 (1995)
14. Jussila, T., Biere, A.: Compressing BMC encodings with QBF. Electron. Notes Theor. Comput. Sci. **174**, 45–56 (2006)
15. Allen, E.: Sometimes and not never revisited: on branching versus linear time temporal logic. J. ACM **33**(1), 151–178 (1986)
16. Zhang, W.: QBF encoding of temporal properties and QBF-based verification. In: Demri, S., Kapur, D., Weidenbach, C. (eds.) IJCAR 2014. LNCS (LNAI), vol. 8562, pp. 224–239. Springer, Cham (2014). https://doi.org/10.1007/978-3-319-08587-6_16
17. Zhang, W., Smentics, B.: Theor. Comput. Sci. **564**, 1–29 (2015)
18. Zhaowei, X., Zhang, W.: Linear templates of ACTL formulas with an application to SAT-based verification. Inf. Process. Lett. **127**, 6–16 (2017)
19. Zhang, W.: Bounded semantics of CTL and SAT-based verification. In: Breitman, K., Cavalcanti, A. (eds.) ICFEM 2009. LNCS, vol. 5885, pp. 286–305. Springer, Heidelberg (2009). https://doi.org/10.1007/978-3-642-10373-5_15
20. Clarke, E., Kroening, D., Ouaknine, J., Strichman, O.: Computational challenges in bounded model checking. Int. J. Softw. Tools Technol. Transfer **7**, 174–183 (2005)
21. Ganai, M.K., Gupta, A.: Accelerating high-level bounded model checking. In: ICCAD, pp. 794–801 (2006)
22. Wozna, B.: ATCL* properties and bounded model checking. Fundam. Inform. **63**, 65–87 (2004)
23. Cimatti, A., Roveri, M., Sheridan, D.: Bounded verification of past LTL. In: Hu, A.J., Martin, A.K. (eds.) FMCAD 2004. LNCS, vol. 3312, pp. 245–259. Springer, Heidelberg (2004). https://doi.org/10.1007/978-3-540-30494-4_18
24. Ji, K.: CTL model checking in deduction modulo. In: Felty, A.P., Middeldorp, A. (eds.) CADE 2015. LNCS (LNAI), vol. 9195, pp. 295–310. Springer, Cham (2015). https://doi.org/10.1007/978-3-319-21401-6_20
25. Kemper, S.: SAT-based verification for timed component connectors. Sci. Comput. Program. **77**(7–8), 779–798 (2012)

26. Wimmer, R., Braitling, B., Becker, B.: Counterexample generation for discrete-time markov chains using bounded model checking. In: Jones, N.D., Müller-Olm, M. (eds.) VMCAI 2009. LNCS, vol. 5403, pp. 366–380. Springer, Heidelberg (2008). https://doi.org/10.1007/978-3-540-93900-9_29

27. Gomes, C., Selman, B., Kautz, H.: SAT encodings of state-space reachability problems in numeric domains. In: IJCAI, pp. 1918–1923 (2007)

28. Navarro-Pérez, J.A., Voronkov, A.: Encodings of bounded LTL model checking in effectively propositional logic. In: Pfenning, F. (ed.) CADE 2007. LNCS (LNAI), vol. 4603, pp. 346–361. Springer, Heidelberg (2007). https://doi.org/10.1007/978-3-540-73595-3_24

A Cloud Based Three Layer Key Management Scheme for VANET

Wanan Xiong[(⊠)] and Bin Tang

School of Electronic Engineering, University of Electronic Science
and Technology of China (UESTC), No. 2006, Xiyuan Ave, West Hi-Tech Zone,
Cheng Du, Sichuan, People's Republic of China
18980802389@163.com, xwa985@163.com

Abstract. A Cloud Based VANET (Vehicular Ad hoc Network) is a convenient vehicular communication network which is commonly susceptible to
various attacks. Many key management schemes for VANETs are presented to
solve various security problems. Threshold secret sharing, ECC and Bilinear
Pairing computation is efficient approach for the key management design.
And PKI is also excellent key management method. In this paper, the above
approaches are adopted to construct three layer key management schemes for
VANET in order to realize secure communication. After constructing the
security structure, we carefully analyse the security performance and efficiency
of the scheme in detail. In the end, the conclusion is drawn.

Keywords: Three layer key management · Elliptic Curve Cryptography
Bilinear pairing computation · (n, t) Threshold key distribution
PKI (Public Key Infrastructrue)

1 Introduction

A Cloud Based VANET is a convenient communication network with high dynamic
topology, enough energy and storage space, moving track predictable and diversified
automotive network scenarios. It has many significant applications in transportation
and communication, such as vehicle safety, road traffic efficiency, and information and
entertainment [1].

VANET architecture consists of vehicles, Road Side Units (RSUs) and a Certificate
Authority. Each vehicle periodically broadcasts safety and traffic related messages such
as its speed, location, acceleration, etc. Vehicles also exchange life critical messages
that require real time response. RSUs are located at certain points on the road network
similar to access points in wireless networks to become the necessary infrastructure for
network setup and communications. Certificate Authority coordinates offering security
services to the whole network scale. So, communications in VANETs are classified into
three types which are vehicle to vehicle (V2V), vehicle to infrastructure (V2I) or hybrid
communication VANETs [2, 3].

So far, many key management schemes for VANETs are presented to solve various
security problems which mainly contain four security issues. (1) Message integrity
must be ensured to prevent changing messages contents. (2) Message senders must be

© Springer Nature Singapore Pte Ltd. 2018
H. Yuan et al. (Eds.): GSKI 2017, CCIS 849, pp. 574–587, 2018.
https://doi.org/10.1007/978-981-13-0896-3_57

authenticated to avoid counterfeit attack. (3) Privacy of the vehicle IDs may hide vehicles from tracking. (4) Real-time constraint should be important in order to deliver messages with acceptable delay time.

Li et al. [4] proposed a secure and efficient vehicle network communications scheme using asymmetric encryption to build authentication keys and protect privacy. De Fuentes et al. [5] presented an overview of security issues over VANETs. They focused on road safety communications. They also introduced several attacks. Then analyzed and described mechanisms to achieve the security goals. Finally, they stated that hardware implementation of efficient cryptographic primitives is required in vehicles in order to achieve easier computation availability. Singh and Singh [6] also reviewed different security schemes based on asymmetric cryptography, group based and symmetric schemes. They concluded that both asymmetric and group based adds computation and storage overhead because they depend on certificates and signatures.

In public key infrastructure (PKI), Certificate Authority (CA) is responsible for providing vehicles with a public/private key pair and a certificate [7]. This scheme doesn't support privacy. To support privacy issue using PKI, the vehicle should be preloaded with multiple public/private key pairs and their certificates [8]. In Symmetric key schemes, a shared symmetric is generated between the vehicle and RSU [9, 10]. Message verification at the sender side depends on a nonce of authenticity sent by RSUs.

In this paper, we present a cloud-based three layer key management scheme for VANET. This scheme has more advantages which will be discussed in the following.

The rest of of this paper is organized as follows: Sect. 2 introduces vehicles communication in VANETs and its Cloud-Based network architecture. Section 3 gives out the preliminaries knowledge of bilinear pairing and threshold technique. Section 4 describe the three layer key management scheme which includes the first layer (central cloud server), the second layer (road side unit) and the third layer (vehicle layer) key management scheme Sect. 5. Evaluate the scheme's secure performance based on all kinds of menaces of VANET. The paper is concluded in Sect. 6.

2 Vanet Communication and Its Cloud-Based Network Archi-Tecture

VANETs communication has three categories as follows:

- Vehicle-to-Vehicle Communication (V2V): Allows the direct vehicular communication (ad hoc mode), without support of fixed infrastructure.
- Vehicle-to-Road Communication (V2R): allows communication between vehicles and fixed road-side units, this is mainly for data gathering applications.
- Hybrid Communication: includes both Vehicle-to-Vehicle and Vehicle-to-road-side units (V2R). A vehicle can communicate with road-side units directly through single hop, or muti-hops, depending to the distance. It enables the long distance connection to infrastructure to connect to Internet.

Figure 1 illustrates a cloud-based network model that describes a typical VANET network:

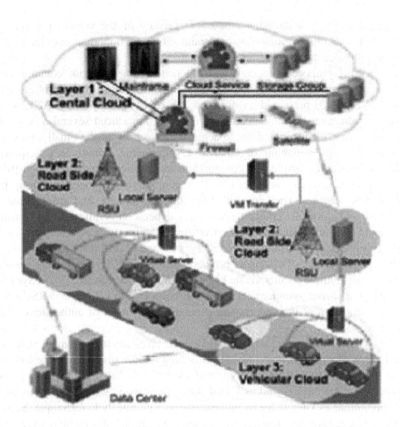

Fig. 1. Three-layer vehicular cloud network architecture with positioning for CCL, RSCL and VCL.

Three layer vehicular cloud network (VCN) architecture is designed to support deployment of the proposed VANET three layer key management frameworks. The VCN architecture, shown in Fig. 1, consists of three main layers: the central cloud layer (CCL), road-side cloud layer (RSCL) and vehicular cloud layer (VCL).

The CCL gathers a group of server clusters that have powerful computational abilities and massive storage capacities; furthermore, it provides services for road-side facilities and vehicles via V2R (vehicle-to-road-side units) communication. The CCL is designed to preserve some general information (e.g., a profile including vehicle's identity, certificate and pseudonyms identities) of authorized vehicles in VANET.

The RSCL is a set of road-side units, communication facilities and local servers are included. This layer plays the role of vehicles manager in a local area. It will create virtual environments for vehicles requesting security services and then undertake the calculation of security level as well as the communication with neighboring road-side units. As the RSCL is a root part of a VCL, it's also necessary layer of performance modeling and analysis, we will discuss it in detail in the following sections.

The VCL is a kind of local cloud on the road, which is built on a group of cooperating vehicles and managed by the RSCL. Vehicles share their resources (e.g., computation, storage and communication) in the cloud. Each vehicle is allowed to reserve cloud services by its demand. All physical resources can be scheduled dynamically based on the demands of vehicles. The VCL makes physical resources of vehicles virtual; however, virtual resources are managed by a component called the "cloud controller" embedded in the RSCL. A vehicle can choose a nearby road-side cloud to reserve a transient cloud service. Once the vehicle leaves the scope of the road-side cloud, its reservation will be transferred to the next road-side cloud through the RSCL. This short-lived cloud service is named the "Transient Cloud." The VCL provides physical resources (e.g., computing and storage) to support the RCL to complete the trust evaluation cooperatively. This layer improves the vehicle-resource utilization and QoS of VANET.

Overall, the three-layer VCN architecture supports the deployment of security communication framework which is applied to solve the key management issue in VCN. The following section will introduce details of key management framework and its implementation based on the architecture. Certainly, we first discuss the preliminaries.

3 Preliminaries

3.1 Bilinear Map and Pairing

The method of bilinear map and pairing should be adopted in practice for efficiency and security. Its basic theory in detail will be discussed.

Suppose p, q be two large primes. Literature [8, 9] gave the conditions that p, q must satisfy. E/Fp indicate an elliptic curve $y^2 = x^3 + ax + b$ over the finite field Fp. $G1$ denote a q-order subgroup of the additive group of points of E/Fp, and G2 denote a q-order subgroup of the multiplicative group of the finite field Fp. The Discrete Logarithm Problem (DLP) should be hard in both $G1$ and $G2$. For us, a pairing is a map $\hat{e} : G1 \times G1 \rightarrow G2$ with the following properties:

(1) Bilinear: V P, Q, R, S $\in$ $G1$,

$$\hat{e}(P + Q, R + S) = \hat{e}(P, R)\,\hat{e}(P, S)\,\hat{e}(Q, R)\,\hat{e}(Q, S) \qquad (1)$$

Consequently, for V a, b $\in$ $Z_q{}^*$, we have

$$\hat{e}(aP, Q)\,b = \hat{e}(P, bQ)\,a = \hat{e}(P, Q)\,ba \qquad (2)$$

(2) Non degenerate: there exists P, Q $\in$ G1, such that

$$\hat{e}(P, Q) \neq 1. \tag{3}$$

(3) Computable: There is an efficient algorithm to compute

$$\hat{e}(P, Q) \text{ for all } P, Q \in G1 \tag{4}$$

The Bilinear Diffe-Hellman Problem (BDHP) is hard. Examples of such bilinear maps include modified Weil [11] and Tate [12] pairings in which we can get more comprehensive description of how these pairing parameters should be selected in practice for efficiency and security.

3.2   Secret Sharing Technique

In order to share a secret among n users, we usually adopt secret sharing technique. Later, all the shareholders can get together and recover the secret. We cannot recover or reconstruct the secret for less than the needed number of users.

A (t,n) threshold secret sharing scheme based on polynomial interpolations has been proposed by Shamir in [13]. This scheme is described below:

(1) First, we select t points on the plane $(x_1, y1)$, (x_t, y_t), every xi is distinct, there exists an unique polynomial f of degree $t - 1$, such that f (xi) = yi for all i. After getting the t points, one can recover f by using the Lagrange interpolation formula.
(2) This also holds in the field Zp, p is prime. By doing the following steps, we can share a secret S among t parties:
(1) Let S be the secret chosen from Zp, p is prime.
(2) Select a random polynomial $f(x) = f_0 + f_1x + \dots + f_{t-1}x^{t-1}$, under the condition that $f_0 = S$ and $f_1, f_2, \dots, f_{t-1}$ are chosen randomly from Zp.
(3) For all $i \in [1,t]$, distribute the shares Si = (i, f(i)) to the i-th party.

If the secret has been shared, we can now reconstruct it from every subset of t shares by the Lagrange formula. When given t points (xi, yi), i = 1... t, we get

$$F(x) = \sum i = 1 \text{ tf(xi)} \prod j = 1, , j \neq \text{it}(x - xj)/(xi - xj) \text{ mod } p \tag{5}$$

In a word, Shamir's secret sharing scheme does not depend on the computational power of any party, and it is perfectly secure, flexible and efficient.

4   Three Layer Key Management Scheme

Our three level Key Management Scheme is based on cluster and tree structure which will be discussed in detail in the following.

4.1 Key Management Framework Based on the Three Layer Structure of VCN

Figure 1 point out the three layer structure of VCN. So, a nature key management mode that fit for this structure is three layer key management scheme. Their abstract topology structure is in Fig. 2.

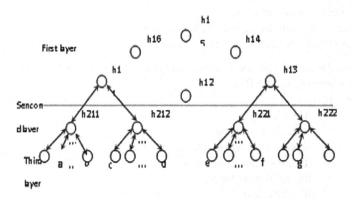

Fig. 2. Abstract fig of VCN's three level key management scheme

The CCL gathers a group of server clusters that have powerful computational abilities and massive storage capacities. So it has many peer nodes. PKI don't suit CCL nodes which have distributed structure. We are going to construct a new key management method which will be discussed in the following to solve the problem. Each CCL node is also the root of RCL nodes that is described in Fig. 2.

The RSCL is a set of road-side units, including communication facilities and local servers. Each node in RCL is also the root of RCL nodes that is described in Fig. 2. Obviously, in this kind of structure, we should adopt PKI as this layer's key management scheme.

The VCL is a kind of local cloud on the road. It is built on a group of cooperating vehicles and managed by the RCL. Vehicles share their resources (e.g., computation, storage and spectrum) in the cloud. It is convenient for us to adopt PKI as this layer's key management scheme. The detail will be discussed in the following.

Literature [14] indicates that in three layer network topology structure, if we adopt distributed structure as the first layer network, centralized structure as the second layer network and the third layer network (DCC), it costs less in communication to acquire the same security performance when compared with other network topology structure. Our key management framework based on the three layer structure of VCN is just DCC structure.

The following contents include equipment and notations applied in secure communication protocol equipment.

In our proposed Security protocol, we will apply the following equipment.

(1) Register Author that register information on all RCL node, vehicle node and driver node.
(2) Certificate Author which issue certificate on all RCL and VCL communication node. And it manages all PKI system parameters and keys.
(3) Road-side-cloud layer nodes are an entity that receives event information and distributes official vehicles.
(4) Vehicles represent the activity vehicles in service.
(5) Driver (Di) is an vehicle activities executor.

Then the Di gets access the Internet resources via RSCL, and obtains the services which are supported by the PKI.

. Notations

ID_X	X' s identity
$Cert_i$	node-i's certificate
SK_{X-Y}	session key between by X and Y
M_i	ith communication message
ΔT	the valid time length
C_i	ith ciphertext
$X\ ?= Y$	verify whether X is equal to Y
$X? \leq Y$	determine whether X is less than or equal to Y
$V_{Puk\ x}(M_i)$	verify message Mi with X's public key Puk_x
$S_{Pr\ kx}(M_{i)}$	sign message Mi with X's private key $Pr\ kx$
$E_{Puk\ x}(Mi)$	*encrypt message Mi with X's public key Puk$_x$*
$D_{Pr\ kx}(Mi)$	*decrypt message Mi with X's private key Pr kx*
$E_{SK\ X\ -Y}(Mi)$	encrypt message Mi with symmetric key SK_{X-Y}
$D_{SK\ X\ -Y}(Mi)$	decrypt message Mi with symmetric key $i\ SK_{X-Y}$
Ti	i th timestamp
T_x	the timestamp of X
‖:	connection symbol
$\oplus$	exclusive-or operation

4.2 CCL Key Management Scheme

4.2.1 Key System Parameters Generation

By literature [15], we known that user's public key is computed by using a one-way hash function and its own identity in identity-based public key cryptography. The key system parameters can be selected by trusted third party public key generation centre (PKGC). Usually the trusted third party is well-known company or government department. The PKGC runs the common parameter generation algorithm A. It works as follows:

(1) Suppose a security parameter k $\in$ Z+, runs A with input k to generate a prime q (q is large enough to make it infeasible to solve discrete logarithm problem in G1

and G2), G1, G2 are two cycle groups of order q, and P is the generator of G1, and an admissible bilinear map $e\hat{}$: G1 $\times$ G1 $\rightarrow$ G2.

(2) Select two hash functions h0: $\{0, 1\}^* \rightarrow$ G1, which maps arbitrary binary strings to nonzero elements in G1, h1: $\{0, 1\}^* \rightarrow$ ZP*, which maps arbitrary binary strings to integers in ZP*.

(3) PKGC chooses stochastic number SPKG $\in$ ZP* as its own private key, and the corresponding public key is QPKG = SPKGP $\in$ G1.

(4) Suppose (EK, DK) is a pair of symmetric encryption and decryption algorithm. For participator ui (i = 1, 2,...,n), its public parameter is Q_i = h0(IDi) and its public key is calculated by PKGC as S_i = SPKGQi.

(5) The system common parameters (P, q, e, h0, h1, G1, G2) are pre-distributed to each PKG node through TTP. Only SPKG keeps secret.

4.2.2 Key Management Scheme

The key management structure in Fig. 2 adopt DCC mode The first layer network CCN form the secure channel by means of the following:

Each cloud server node authenticates and communicates on the master public key and master private key. The node's identity-based public key system is constructed by master private key and node's identity.

Now we will discuss secure channel. If node ui wants to send message m to node uj securely, it will do the following things:

It randomly selects $x_j \in Z_P^*$,and calculate $k_j = (k_{j,1}, k_{j,2}) = h_1\left(\hat{e}(Q_j, Q_{PKG})^{xj}\right)$; ui calculates $r_j = m_j{}^{kj,2}$, $c_j = E_{kj,1}(m_j\|r_j)$, $R_j = r_jQ_i$ and $s_j = x_jQ_{PKG} - r_jS_i \in G_1$; ui sends (c_i, s_i, R_i) to the receiver uj.

After receiving the message (c_j, s_j, R_j), uj calculates $k_j = (k_{j,1}, k_{j,2}) = h_1\left(\hat{e}(Q_j, s_j)\,\hat{e}(S_j, R_j)\right)$. Then uj decrypts cj and gets $mj\|rj = D_{kj,1}(c_j)$, if $r_j = m_j{}^{kj,2}$ is correct, uj will think the secret is sent successfully.

After that, the secure channel is built. When some time passed, we can run Shamir (t,n) secret sharing scheme to produce a new S_{PKG} to update the private key.

4.3 RSCL Key Management Scheme

The RSCL node key management scheme is based on PKI (Public Key Infrastructure). Its RA (Register Author) and CA (Certificate Author) locate in CCL node. Each node should be registered and get the certificate signed by the CA.

The RSCL node should be regarded as a middle key management server and security level evaluate point for all vehicles passing by. After the vehicle proved to be security, the RSCL node can provide excellent server for the vehicle.

If a vehicle node (VN) is close to the RSCL node, the VN send itself certificate signed by the same CA, the RSCL node should verify it right now and send back the RSCL node's certificate signed by the same CA. etc.

Then, we will begin secure communication in the cloud-based VANET.

4.4 VCL Key Management Scheme

The VCL (vehicle cloud layer) node key management scheme includes these components: PKI RA which contains vehicle register, driver register and the association authentication of vehicle and its driver. Certificates are acquired. The pseudonym of the VCL node and the current communication time are get.

First, the driver of the vehicle should register himself/herself to the RA of the PKI and acquire himself/herself certificate which is signed by the CA. Each vehicle should register itself to the RA of the PKI and get the certificate which is signed by the CA. Each time when the vehicle is ready to go, the driver should associate his/her certificate with the vehicle by Biometric identification or password identification. This association relationship should report to the CA of the PKI. The CA should produce a new certificate on the association authentication, and the new certificate can represent the vehicle node to take part in the security communication.

Second, whenever a vehicle that is going in the road want to communicate with RCL node or the other VCL node, it broadcast the certificate signed by the CA and the current time Ts0 to all the nodes nearby. The other node receive the information, check the target address, if it is the communication target, it then check the current time, compare the time Ts0 with the receive time Tr0, if the difference is less than the ΔT, the secure communication will continue till the communication end.

We will adopt ECC (Elliptic Curve Cryptography) Algorithm realize our scheme. In the following, we will discuss the secure communication protocol.

Before the secure communication, we should have produced all nodes certificate with the signature of the corresponding CAi. Of course, all nodes include RCL nodes, drivers and VCL nodes must have registered. All nodes own itself signed certificate.

(1) VCL node-i communicate with VCL node-j

Step1, VCL node i have got the signed association authentication certificate as described above.

Node i send to node-j:

$$S1 = S \, Pr \, kCAi \, (Certi) \, \|IDi\| \, T1 \, \|target \, node-j \, address \tag{6}$$

Step2, node-j receive S1, and node-j verifies $T1$ as follows:

$$T \, node-j - T1 \, ? \leq \Delta T \tag{7}$$

If the verification holds, node-j decrypt S1:

$$Certi = V \, PukCA \, i \, (Certi) \tag{8}$$

After got $Cert_i$, node-j look for the certificate valid time in the $Cert_i$. if the time is in valid time, node-j will send the following messages to node-i:

$$S2 = E_{SKj-i}(\text{Nonce 1}) \| E_{Pukx}(SKj-i) \| S_{PrkCAi}(Cert_j) \| IDj \| T_2 \| \text{target node}-i\text{ address} \quad (9)$$

If one of the above conditions don't be satisfied, node-j will discard the received message and report an error to the CAi.

Step3, node-i receives the message S2 and node-i verifies $T2$ as follows:

$$T\text{ node}-i-T2\,? \leq \Delta T \quad (10)$$

If the verification holds, node-i verify $S_{Pr\,kCAi}$ *(Cert_j) with public key CAi*, get Certj, node-i look for the certificate valid time in the $Cert_j$. if the time is in valid time, node-i will receive the message and process as follows:

$$SK\ j-i = D\,Pr\,ki(E\ Pukx(SK\ j-i), \quad (11)$$

$$\text{Nonce 1} = D\,SK\ j-i(E\,SK\ j-i(\text{Nonce 1})) \quad (12)$$

Node-i send the following messages to node-j in order to build a secure channel:

$$S3 = E_{SK\,i-j}(Nonce2) \| E_{Pukx}(SK\,i-j) \| T_3 \| target\,node-j\,\text{address}$$

If one of the above conditions don't be satisfied, node-j will discard the received message and report an error to the CAi.

Step4, node-j receives S3, and node-j verifies $T3$ as follows:

$$T\text{ node}-j-T3\,? \leq \Delta T \quad (13)$$

If the verification holds, node-j decrypts the message and get Nonce2.
The last symmetric key

$$SK\,i-j = \text{Nonce1} \| \text{Nonce2} \quad (14)$$

Now, the secure channel between node-i and node-j has been built.
If one of the above conditions doesn't be satisfied, node-j will discard the received message and report an error to the CAi

(2) VCL node-i communicate with RCL node-j

In order to build a secure channel between VCL node-i and RCL node-j, we can adopt the same 6 steps as in situation (1).

(3) When VCL node-i pass through to the next RCL node-j

If VCL node-i passes through to the next RCL node-j, for the anonymous communication, we should change the pseudonym of the VCL node-i.

When the VCL node-i are communicating within one RCL node-j, the secure system CAi has selected a new random value ri, produce a new pseudonym of the VCL node-i as

$$Idi\,(new) \,=\, ri \,\oplus\, Idi\,(old) \tag{15}$$

And the CAi will store each value ri for the VCL node-i in order to restore the real identities of VCL node-i. Then CAi will produce a new pair of public/private key for the VCL node-i. Then it issues a new signed certificate for node-i and send the new signed certificate to node-i.

When node-i passes through the net RCL node-j, node-i can adopt the same method to build a secure channel with other node.

(4) When VCL node-i pass through to the next CCL security server node-k

When node-i passes through to the next CCL security server node-k, the Certi signed by CAi(old) will be changed to be signed by CAi(new). The real identity of node-i will be transferred to the new CAi. After that, we can process all the new situations as the same as in the old CCL security server node.

5 Annalysis on the Three Layer Key Management Scheme

The three layer key management scheme will be discussed in order to find out whether it is secure and reliable to be used in cloud based VANET environment.

5.1 The Character of Our Scheme

The scheme is about a cloud-based three layer key management construct. The first layer is a distributed network construct based a cluster which adopts many popular security methods. It brings us the following characters:

(1) In the forming phase of the first layer network, we present the secure channel which gives a security algorithm. It is right :

$$\hat{e}\,(Qj,\,sj)\,\hat{e}\,(Sj,\,Rj) \,=\, \hat{e}\,(Qj,\,QPKG)\,xj \tag{16}$$

Proof

$$\hat{e}\left(Q_j, s_j\right)\hat{e}\left(S_j, R_j\right) = \hat{e}\left(Q_j, x_jQ_{PKG} - r_jS_i\right)\hat{e}\left(S_j, r_jQ_i\right)$$
$$= \hat{e}\left(Q_j, x_jQ_{PKG} - r_jS_i\right)\hat{e}(S_j, Q_i)^{r_j}$$
$$= \hat{e}\left(Q_j, x_jQ_{PKG} - r_jS_i\right)\hat{e}\left(S_{PKG}Q_j, Q_i\right)^{r_j}$$
$$= \hat{e}\left(Q_j, x_jQ_{PKG} - r_jS_i\right)\hat{e}(Q_j, S_i)^{r_j} \qquad (17)$$
$$= \hat{e}\left(Q_j, x_jQ_{PKG} - r_jS_i\right)\hat{e}\left(Q_j, r_jS_i\right)$$
$$= \hat{e}\left(Q_j, x_jQ_{PKG} - r_jS_i + r_jS_i\right) = \hat{e}\left(Q_j, x_jQ_{PKG}\right)$$
$$= \hat{e}\left(Q_j, Q_{PKG}\right)^{x_j}$$

(2) We can realize secure communication by secure channel and this make us almost not need memory in symmetric key.

This scheme comes down to almost every aspect of key management in distributed network, including symmetric key communication, identity authentication, etc.

5.2 The Security and Efficiency of the Scheme

The proposed cloud-based three layer key management scheme has a low communication overhead and reduced computational consumption as the following causes.

(1) It adopts ECC (Elliptic Curve Cryptography), the scheme provides high security level with 160 bit keys and is equivalent in strength to RSA with 1024 bit. So, based on each node's identity, the public/private key can be much shorter compared with the public key in RSA cryptosystem.
(2) In order to ensure node identity is authenticated and secure communication is acquired, we preload the initial security parameters for each node.
(3) We construct the three level key management schemes which reduce the burden of network nodes and add the security of the network. Our scheme has DCC three layer structures, so it has less communication overhead.

5.3 This Scheme Can Against Replay Attack

The layer that applies PKI can count the time that send and receive message, and monitor the time. This character can against replay attack.

5.4 This Scheme Can Against Vehicle Tracking

The second layer and the third layer all adopt PKI construct. The vehicle's identity changes quickly, this action against vehicle tacking.

In a word, the cloud-based three level key management schemes for VANET should be an efficient and security scheme waiting to be applied.

6 Conclusion

In summary, the proposed scheme is cloud-based three layer key management scheme. In CCL key management scheme, we adopt Elliptic Curve Cryptography (ECC) algorithm in this paper to reduce the key length with the same security level environment. We apply (t, n) threshold secret sharing algorithm to update the secret value in first layer network key management. The pairing technology provides authentication and confidentiality with reduced communication overhead and computational cost. In RSCL key management, we adopt PKI scheme. Each RA node and CA node locates in CCL. The RSCL node can process messages from vehicles and CCL node. It can resist vehicle tracking attack when cooperate with CCL node and VCL node. In VCL key management, each vehicle can realize secure communication with other node. Our scheme which combined the distributed key management and PKI construct. That can satisfy the secure requirements of the cloud -based three layer key management.

References

1. Engoulou, R.G., Pierre, S.: VANET security surveys. Comput. Commun. **44**(15), 1–13 (2014)
2. Cunha, F., Boukerche, A., Viana, L.V.A., Loureiro, A.A.F.: Data communication in vanets: a survey, challenges and applications (2014)
3. Meshram, S.S., Golait, P.M., Ghodichor, P.M.: Inter-infrastructure and vehicle communication for traffic information sharing in vanet. IOSR J. Comput. Sci. (IOSR-JCE), 5–12 (2014). www.iosrjournals.org
4. Li, C.T., Hwang, M.S., Chu, Y.P.: A secure and efficient communication scheme with authenticated key establishment and privacy preserving for vehicular ad hoc networks. Comput. Commun. **31**(2), 2803–2814 (2008)
5. De Fuentes, J.M., Gonzlez-Tablas, A.I., Ribagorda, A.: Overview of security issues in vehicular ad-hoc Networks. In: Handbook of Research on Mobility and Computing. IGI Global, pp. 1–17 (2010). www.igi-global.com
6. Singh, U., Singh, P.: Review of solutions for securing the vehicular networks. Int. J. comput. Technol. Appl. **2**, 1652–1656 (2011)
7. Blum, J., Eskandarian, A.: The threat of intelligent collisions. IT Prof. **6**(1), 24–29 (2004)
8. Raya, M., Hubaux, J.P.: Securing vehicular ad hoc networks. J. Comput. Secur. **15**(1), 39–68 (2007)
9. Zhang, C., Lin, X., Lu, R., Ho, P.H.: Rise: an efficient Rsu-aided message authentication scheme in vehicular communication networks. In: ICC. Proceedings of IEEE International Conference on Communications, ICC 2008, Beijing, China, 19–23 May 2008, pp. 1451–1457 (2008)
10. Wu, H.T., Hsieh, W.S.: RSU-based message authentication for vehicular ad-hoc networks. Springer Multimed. Tools Appl. **35**, 1–13 (2011)
11. Frey, G., Muller, M., Riick, H.: The Tate pairing and the discrete logarithm applied to elliptic curve
12. Menezes, A., Okamoto, T., VanstoneL, S.: Reducing elliptic curve logarithms to logarithms in a finite field
13. Shamir, A.: How to share a secret. Commun. ACM **22**(11), 612–613 (1979)

14. Sun, B., Yu, B.: The three-layered group key management architecture for MANET. In: 11th International Conference on Advanced Communication Technology, ICACT 2009, 15–18 February 2009, vol. 2, pp. 1378–1381 (2009)
15. Xiong, W.A., Gong, Y.H.: Secure and highly efficient three level key management scheme for MANET. WSEAS Trans. Comput. **10**(1), 6–15 (2011)

An Evaluation Method Based on Co-word Clustering Analysis – Case Study of Internet + Innovation and Entrepreneurship Economy

Yunjie Ji[1], Yao Jiang[1], and Ling He[2(✉)]

[1] Human Resource Department, Wuhan University of Technology,
Luoshi Road, Wuhan, Hubei, China
[2] School of Management, Wuhan University of Technology,
Luoshi Road, Wuhan, Hubei, China
1586172144@qq.com

Abstract. Co-word clustering analysis can be used to discover new trends of socio-economic behavior. In this paper, several key words for youth innovation and entrepreneurship under the internet crowdfunding were extracted through literature search. Based on the Co-word clustering analysis, combining with the test of algorithm validation parameters, the results showed that market guidance, continuous innovation and profitability were the key factors for the success of the project.

Keywords: Co-word analysis · Cluster analysis · Internet economy
Innovation and entrepreneurship

1 Introduction

The effect of Internet thinking on the real economy is that "the product is no longer a mere product, but a multi-functional emotional expression medium." [1] Apple Inc, which built the APP Store over the Internet, built "places" that support iPhone's improvements to make the software fast update. The Internet has become a "place" for customers to enrich their lives and express their emotions. Internet crowdfunding products have become an "interface" to enhance customer communication and life improvement, connecting common feelings, functional preferences and spending habits of customers to achieve demand-side scope economic.

Asymmetry of information in the "Internet +" economy diminishes, while environmental uncertainty continues to increase. The boundary of innovation "core competitiveness" is more extensive and vague. "Xiaomi" interacts emotionally with consumers through the Internet to surpass the "Samsung" which is stronger than itself. The youth innovation and entrepreneurship under the internet crowdfunding rely more on the social mobility integration of complementary assets and the large-scale sharing of knowledge. While breaking through the economies of scale, the youth innovation and entrepreneurship also face a strong pressure of external innovation transform. Integration advantages become the traditional "core competitiveness" interpretation,

© Springer Nature Singapore Pte Ltd. 2018
H. Yuan et al. (Eds.): GSKI 2017, CCIS 849, pp. 588–595, 2018.
https://doi.org/10.1007/978-981-13-0896-3_58

but integrated capabilities often show in the "platform" model and it needs tremendous energy, Google through platform to involve a variety of business areas, but it integrates each business unit to make them orderly update, therefore liquidity competitive advantage is established [2].

"Scenario + Products" is a powerful and concise explanation of the youth innovation and entrepreneurship under the internet crowdfunding [3]. It brings the online (virtual scene) together with offline (product use) synergies, while breaking the traditional value chain; it reconstructs the new Internet value Chain and promote a highly modular division of labor. The liquidity and diversification of complementary assets have significantly increased. The youth innovation and entrepreneurship under the internet crowdfunding are often the source of a first-mover advantage. It is easier than pulling-driven innovation to get rid of the path dependence, implementing faster than pushing innovation and eventually evolving into a powerful integration advantage. The youth Innovation and Entrepreneurship under the internet crowdfunding is a structural convergence of multi-layered elements (Fig. 1).

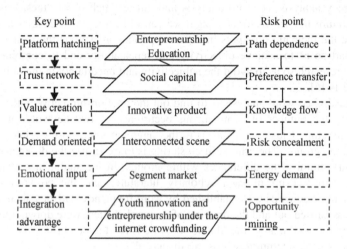

Fig. 1. Key points and risk points distribution

As shown in Fig. 1, the level of youth innovation and entrepreneurship under the internet crowdfunding can be attributed to the five-tier structure that is "entrepreneurship education - social capital - innovative products - Internet scene - market segments. The key point derivation is: platform incubation, trust network, creation, demand-oriented, emotional investment and they become the advantage of the youth innovation and entrepreneurship under internet crowdfunding. Correspondingly, each Level of prominent risks is: Path Dependence, Preference Transfer, Knowledge Flow, Risk Hidden and Energy Demand. Deviation at every level of risk points can easily lead to opportunities for youth innovation and entrepreneurship [4].

2 Model Building

2.1 Co-word analysis and clustering

In discipline of management, many concepts are not created by nature but by people. Many concepts cannot be observed directly. Instead, the concepts need to be manipulated. The concept of being transformed into an indicator or indicator system that can describe in quantity. Different scholars choose different indicators to observe and measure concepts for different reasons (sometimes based on the research questions and sometimes on the realistic conditions) [5]. Whatever how to select indicators, the process of operation is actually a concept of alternative process and this will bring more or less research errors. Therefore, that how to select the observation index is an important issue in empirical research.

The key words of the academic literature characterize the research topic of the essay, which is one of the basic elements of the academic literature. At the time of publication, the author independently establishes the core content of the essay. Through the frequency analysis, co-word analysis and cluster analysis of "thesaurus" of academic literature in each historical stage, we can objectively and clearly describe and summarize the thematic hot spots in different periods as well as the thematic change history chart so as to achieve objectivity and repeatability and to combine with the qualitative research so as to avoid the subjectivity and uncertainty in the policy change study defects [6].

Specifically, co-word analysis is to find out the relationship between the keywords by counting the number of simultaneous occurrence of two keywords in the same scholarly literature. Clustering analysis further aggregates the closely related keywords to form ethnic groups. The criteria of clustering is to maximize the difference between groups and minimize the differences within groups. In the study, first of all, 3 to 4 keywords were set up in each scholarly literature, and the co-word matrix of high-frequency keywords was established by word frequency statistics, then the cluster analysis was carried out and the drawing of co-word clusters were drawn. On the basis of the common word matrix, the Matlab software is used to do cluster analysis, and the word clusters of the common words are displayed.

2.2 Algorithm Performance Evaluation

Confidence intervals reflect the degree of confidence of diagnostic accuracy. In the same level of confidence, confidence intervals which are narrow indicate that the diagnostic results are highly reliable and have good robustness. Therefore, when the sample data is small, the improved confidence interval calculation method obtains more accurate diagnosis performance. Especially in practical systems, the confidence intervals when the diagnostic accuracy is close to 100% tend to be more concerned, in this case, the confidence intervals obtained by the traditional methods cannot be used to measure the system diagnostic capabilities. On the contrary, the confidence interval the improvement methods are not directly affected by the accuracy, but the accuracy estimates fall within the confidence interval. As the accuracy changes, the distribution of confidence intervals will change.

Different papers usually use a variety of evaluation indicators to compare the performance of different algorithms, such as CLL-loss [7], F-measure and so on. CLL-loss (conditional log likelihood loss) is a measure of probability method.

$$CLL - loss = \sum_{k=1}^{n} \log(\frac{1}{P(y^{(k)}|x^{(k)})}) \tag{1}$$

For the test data instance x(k), the CLL-loss value is small when the prediction probability of the correct category vector y(k) is close to 1; when the prediction probability of the correct category vector y(k) approaches 0, this means the CLL-loss value is large.

F-measure is an external evaluation method that combines the precision and recall of information retrieval to classify performance evaluation [8].

The definition of accuracy rate r is:

$$R = \frac{\sum_{i=1}^{k} a_i}{n} \tag{2}$$

Where: a_i denotes the number of samples that are finally correctly classified, k denotes the number of classes, and n denotes the number of samples in the data set. The higher the accuracy, the better the classification of the algorithm. When the value of r is 1, the classification result of the algorithm on the data set is completely correct.

Average classification purity:

$$P = \sum_{i=1}^{k} \frac{|C_i^d|}{|C_i|} / K \tag{3}$$

Where: K is the number of clusters, C_d is the number of data points in cluster i that has the most significant class number of the cluster, and C_i is the number of all data points contained in cluster i. The higher the average classification purity, the better the classification effect of the algorithm.

$$F = \frac{2 \times P \times R}{P + R} \tag{4}$$

Where F-measure can be seen as the classification of i's score.

3   Risk Indicators of Youth Entrepreneurship

Chinese Academy of Labour and Social Security (2014) has developed a set of "entrepreneurial quality assessment system", which selects eight necessary factors for ordinary entrepreneurs (such as responsibility, leadership, risk-taking, team integration, teamwork, Honesty, etc.) and seven distinctions (such as achievement orientation, innovation, self-confidence, decision making, setbacks, etc.) targeting at elite entrepreneurs, and formed 15 questionnaires with a total of 248 questions. Evaluators can choose their own scale according to the need for testing, but the model validity needs to be verified currently.

Most of the domestic entrepreneurship assessment model scales are developed by human resources experts, most of whom are good at researching the human resources selection of large and regular enterprise groups and multinational corporations, orientation and personality testing and the career planning. However, there is a lack of depth of personal quality research and intuitive feeling for the small and micro enterprises' entrepreneurship, especially the Self-employed and the entrepreneurial level of freelance entrepreneurs.so there are some theoretical deviations in the design of entrepreneurial evaluation mode [9].

Entrepreneurial potential is a dynamic concept which is the potential situation at some point. In the three dimensions, "entrepreneurial trait" is basically congenital, it is not easy to change, and the score of evaluation should be relatively stable. "Behavior" refers to habit formation, and changing the habit is to change some behavior patterns. Therefore, the "behavior pattern" will have some changes at different points in time. But the "personal background and resources "are less stable and involve family harmony, physical and mental health, and personal opportunities such as increased entrepreneurial skills, aging bodies and family failures.

The combination of Internet crowdfunding and innovation and entrepreneurship makes the entrepreneurs more diverse in personality and quality. It is more crucial for the operation of social relations and the improvement of external collaboration capabilities. Team-building and strategic planning can be assisted by more data support and consulting services currently [10]. Based on the above analysis, a set of index system of youth innovation and entrepreneurship evaluation and risk identification have been formed. As shown in Table 1.

Table 1. High frequency subject words of youth innovation and entrepreneurship under the internet

Number	Subject words	Frequency	Number	Subject words	Frequency
1	Market demand	16	6	Platform capital	16
2	Persistence ability of innovation	11	7	Project return rate	15
3	Partner industry influence	22	8	Financing amount	11
4	Industry fields	21	9	People concerned	18
5	Credit investigation	13			

The combination of Internet crowdfunding and innovation and entrepreneurship makes the entrepreneurs more diverse in personality and quality. It is more crucial for the operation of social relations and the improvement of external collaboration capabilities. Team building and strategic planning can be assisted by more data support and consulting services currently. According to the latest 100 Chinese 100 Chinese literatures in 2017, we extracted the high-frequency subject words and co-word matrices of youth innovation and entrepreneurship under the internet crowdfunding.

In this study, cluster analysis was carried out by using hierarchical clustering and DBSCAN [11] and contrastive analysis is carried out. Furthermore, CLL-loss and F-measure were calculated to measure the consistency of the two methods.

A distance matrix was obtained according to the common frequency of the nine keywords. As shown in Fig. 2.

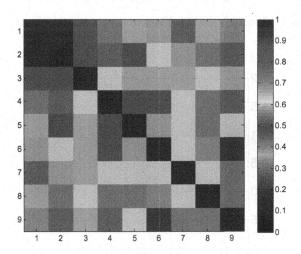

Fig. 2. Common distribution of subject

According to the common distribution of the keywords, we get the clustering results in Figs. 3 and 4.

Through hierarchical clustering, the topics are divided into three categories at the top of the hierarchy: profitability, innovation and market. Among them, the profitability involved most factors, innovation related to the ability to adhere to innovation, partner industry influence, industry, and market was a crucial factor.

According to the DBSCAN clustering, the topic is divided into three types of external environment and project features at the top of the hierarchy. The external environment includes market demand, platform capital, financing amount and number of people concerned. Under the current pattern of crowdfunding and entrepreneurship, the external environment plays a more prominent role and the role of project features is weaker.

Many samples are needed for tracking with regard to the calculation of CLL-loss value and F-measure value. However, there is still a lack of data in this field, which is the focus of future research. It is worth mentioning that this study is helpful for making decision reference.

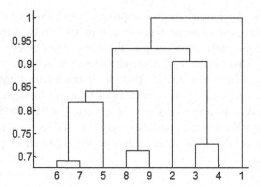

Fig. 3. Hierarchical clustering results of Internet crowdfunding youth innovation and entrepreneurship co-word

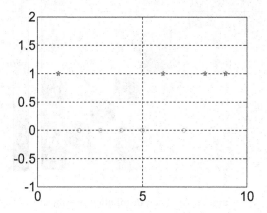

Fig. 4. DBSCAN clustering results of the Internet crowdfunding youth innovation co-word

4   Discussion and Conclusion

This paper aimed to verify the key points of youth Internet innovation and entrepreneurship under the Internet crowd raising by high frequency subject words clustering and algorithm classification testing, and it found that: (1) the role of market guidance was remarkable. In the Internet economy, the long tail market could be developed actively through the mobile Internet and the Internet of things to guide people's consumption behavior. (2) Profitability is still critical. Internet public funding actually played the role of angel investment. In the middle stage of entrepreneurship, it paid close attention to the profitability of the project, and even to the extent that it needed a considerable profitability in the early stage of crowd financing so as to achieve the expected amount of financing. (3) Innovation ability and connection network were important foundation for the development of the project. The duration of a crowd-funding project is often related to the R&D capabilities and the leader's personal connections of the team. Projects with high level of model innovation, strong R & D ability and wide contacts tend to persist for longer.

Acknowledgments. This paper was funded by the National Natural Science Foundation of China (No. 61402344) and supported by the Fundamental Research Funds for the Central Universities (WUT: 2017VI129, 2017-GL-A1-03). National Natural Science Foundation of China (Grant No. 71603197, 71371148), Junior Fellowships for CAST Advanced Innovation Think-tank Program (DXB-ZKQN-2016-013), Special Project of Technology Innovation of Hubei Province -Soft Science (No. 2016ADC094).

References

1. Bretschneider, U., Leimeister, J.M.: Not just an ego-trip: exploring backers motivation for funding in incentive-based crowdfunding. J. Strateg. Inf. Syst. (2017). http://dx.doi.org/10.1016/j.jsis.2017.02.002
2. Gamble, J.R., Brennan, M., Mcadam, R.: A rewarding experience? Exploring how crowdfunding is affecting music industry business models. J. Bus. Res. **70**, 25–36 (2016). https://doi.org/10.1016/j.jbusres.2016.07.009
3. Arenas, A., Goh, J.M., Podar, M.: A work-systems approach to classifying risks in crowdfunding platforms. Explor. Anal. Eng. Econ. **21**(2) 151–159 (2015). http://aisel.aisnet.org/amcis2015/e-Biz/GeneralPresentations/27/
4. Frydrych, D., Bock, A.J., Kinder, T., Koeck, B.: Exploring entrepreneurial legitimacy in reward-based crowdfunding. Ventur. Cap **16**(3), 247–269 (2014). https://doi.org/10.1080/13691066.2014.916512
5. Naghizadeh, R., Elahi, S., Manteghi, M., Ghazinoory, S., Ranga, M.: Through the magnifying glass: an analysis of regional innovation models based on co-word and meta-synthesis methods. Qual. Quant. **49**(6), 1–25 (2014). https://link.springer.com/article/10.1007%2Fs11135-014-0123-7
6. Huang, C., Su, J., Xie, X., et al.: A bibliometric study of China's science and technology policies: 1949–2010. Scientometrics **102**(2), 1521–1539 (2015). https://doi.org/10.1007/s11192-014-1406-4
7. So, B.S.: Maximized log-likelihood updating and model selection. Stat. Probab. Lett **64**(3), 293–303 (2003). https://doi.org/10.1016/S0167-7152(03)00174-3
8. Hripcsak, G., Rothschild, A.S.: Agreement the f-measure, and reliability in information retrieval. J. Am. Med. Inform. Assoc. **12**(3), 296–298 (2005). https://academic.oup.com/jamia
9. Kunz, M.M., Bretschneider, U., Erler, M., et al.: An empirical investigation of signaling in reward-based crowdfunding. Electron. Commer. Res. **17**(3), 425–461 (2017). https://doi.org/10.1007/s10660-016-9249-0
10. Jullien, C., Pignon, V., Robin, S., et al.: Coordinating cross-border congestion management through auctions: An experimental approach to European solutions. Energy Econ. **34**(1), 1–13 (2012). https://doi.org/10.1016/j.eneco.2011.08.017
11. Tran, T.N., Drab, K., Daszykowski, M.: Revised DBSCAN algorithm to cluster data with dense adjacent clusters. Chemometr. Intell. Lab. Syst. **120**(2), 92–96 (2013). https://doi.org/10.1016/j.chemolab.2012.11.006

An Empirical Case of Applying MFA on Company Level

Lina Wang[1(✉)] and Koen Milis[2]

[1] Department of Management, Liaoning University of Technology,
Jinzhou 121001, Liaoning, China
lina1976113@126.com
[2] Campus Vesta, Oostmalsestw 75, 2520 Ranst, Belgium
Koen.milis@campusvesta.be

Abstract. Material flows analysis (MFA) is used regularly in tracing and estimating domestic and international natural resource's usage. This article examines the use of MFA to model and manage the use of natural resources within a large Chinese chemical company. This company, situated within the China-ecology industry zone, provides an excellent case of how MFA can be used on the level of an individual company to analyze natural resources' flows for an improved understanding and management of the economical, environmental and socio-economic consequences of industrial production processes. Its deployment further supports efficient production investment policies. The case study supports the assumption that MFA is particularly suited on a company level because the required data can more easily by collected and the effect of an MFA application can easily be weighted and calculated. MFA can help a company to leverage its resources and its investment decisions. Due to the fact that the MFA method considers all possible materials related to the transformation processes, (including easy-omitted materials such as steam which has no direct monetary value), MFA offers data on environmental emission factors that can be incorporated into green GNP accounts.

Keywords: MFA · Ecology · Management · Metal industry

1 Introduction

The Material Flows Analysis (MFA) method is developed to trace and estimate natural resource usage within a domestic and international context and is perceived as an adequate instrument for countries to help them develop sustainable and ecologically sound ways to deal with the use of natural resources. MFA is characterized by the substitution of monetary units by weight units and tracks material migration from the point where they enter the human economic system through nature mining, move through economic activity and finally return to the natural environment [1].

MFA allows the monitoring of resources usage. It expresses and traces material migrations that are often non-monetary in nature but have great influence on the environment. Furthermore MFA also expresses dependency on import of nature resources and thus indirectly a country's ability for economic development by its home

© Springer Nature Singapore Pte Ltd. 2018
H. Yuan et al. (Eds.): GSKI 2017, CCIS 849, pp. 596–610, 2018.
https://doi.org/10.1007/978-981-13-0896-3_59

natural resource, including metals. There are two types of often used material flow analyses: One focuses on substance substitution (metabolism) flows and is called SFA; the other is referred to as bulk-MFA and mainly studies material's inflow and outflow of an economic system [2–4]. The latter emerged in the 1990s, along with sustainable development consciousness and intensified economical globalization. The bulk-MFA method gradually became the research and application mainstream method, due to its capabilities to examine material flows at state level [5]. Hence, the use of bulk-MFA became popular in a growing number of countries.

At the beginning of 90's, the MFA was applied in Austria, Japan, the US and Germany [7, 8]. More recently, many other EU countries engaged in MFA research such as Denmark [9], Finland [10], Sweden [11], the UK [12, 13], Czechoslovakia [14], Poland [16], Hungary [17], and so on. In the 1990's, the European Union and the European Free Trade Association (EFTA) collected and published material flows statistics of the member states as a part of an inter-state statistics system [6]. Australia applied MFA at the end of the '90 as well [15]. Along with economical development and growing environment distress, many developing nations engaged in MFA research as well. (Examples: Chile, Thailand, Laos, Vietnam and Philippines [18–28]). In addition, benefiting from the European Union Committee's subsidization and the efforts of some scientific research institutions, a number of South American country - Brazil, Venezuela, Bolivia and Colombia - performed an MFA analysis and published the results [20].

In China, Chen of the Beijing University used the MFA method to map and analyze the material input of the Chinese economic system from 1989 to 1996 [34–37]. Xu of the Qinghua University used MFA as a framework to analyze China's fossil fuel in- and output in the period 1990 to 2000 [38]. Liu of the Northeast University used the material flows account system as proposed by the German Wuppertal Climate Energy Environment Research institute as a foundation to calculated the Chinese economic system's direct material investment from 1990 through 2002 [39] and Ding performed an analysis of the ecology burden of iron ore [40].

MFA is not only popular at the level of individual countries. In 2001 for example, the European environment bureau (EEA) [44–47] used MFA to analyze the material input flows of the European Union. In 2002, the European Union Statistics bureau published material input flows and expense statistics of the member states as well as for the European Union area as a whole [33]. This was the first and only time, till now, that the MFA method was applied at a supra national level [29–32].

Although MFA is a generally accepted and mature instrument to perform input/output analyses at the national or supra-national level [42, 43], far less research has been done on the usability of MFA at company level. By applying MFA within a large Chinese chemical company the authors aim to demonstrate that: first, MFA is a powerful analysis and management tool at company level; MFA is equally valid as a management tool – but also complementary to - traditional monetary based management techniques; and MFA can help a company to achieve both economic and ecological goals. It can help detecting ways to achieve more efficient processes and reduce the ecological footprint of production processes, by reducing a production processes' waste.

2 MFA's Concepts

In this section a synopsis of the MFA method is presented [35, 36].

2.1 The Basic Concepts

The Metabolism main body:

When constructing an MFA account to map the metabolism (input – production – output) of an economic body, it is extremely important to be able to accurately differentiate between inputs, consumed goods and residue quantity. The so-called main body metabolism refers to the "intake", "digesting" and "excretion" of material in an economic cycle.

The metabolism main body in MFA expresses the quantity of material that stored to be used in the different stages of the economic cycle.

Hidden flows: refers to material acquired or generated but with no immediate economic use. For example, in order to mine iron ore, mining techniques are applied such as constructing tunnels or peeling surface soil and cap rock.

These mining processes result in iron ore, but also generate scarp materials such as soil and rock that do not enter the metabolism process. These are referred to as hidden flows.

The domestic material mining's hidden flows are called "Domestic Unused Extraction". These materials are considered an "investment". Indirect flows: refers to import and export of material. It includes both used and unused materials.

Used indirect flows are for example imported iron ore or iron product used in the metabolism process. The import or export flows of scrap material that occurs for mining iron ore is referred to as non-use indirect flows [42].

2.2 Rationale

MFA's rationale lies in the economy - environment interplay. The social-economic system is contained in a natural environment. The social-economic system exchanges material- and energy flows with its periphery natural environment systems.

In order to describe the relation between the systems, industrial metabolism and societal metabolism concepts are applied. The social/economy system is regarded as an organism that has a metabolism function in the natural environment. It consumes and digests and excretes material and energy. This organism may use its metabolism ability to weigh its influence on the natural environment.

According to the law of conservation of matter, the quantity of material entered in a system is equal to the sum of this system's reserves and material output. Regarding the above social/economy system, input by the natural environment enters this system (for example by mining). After processing, trading, using, recycling, abandoning and so on, one part results in finished goods produced by the system, the other part of the output material returns to the natural environment. Hence, the entire process input quantity is identical to the sum of the output- and reserve quantities.

2.3   System Boundary

MFA's focal point is the material metabolism of the social/economy system in its natural environment and the interplay with other environments and systems. Hence, MFA research needs to take into consideration following system boundaries (Huang) [45].

The boundary between the social/economy system and the natural environment system: Raw material that was mined from the natural environment enters the social/economy system for further processing.

Administrative boundaries between the domestic country and other nations: End products, half-finished products as well as raw material are imported and/or exported between the domestic country and other nations.

2.4   The MFA Analysis Frame

The MFA analysis frame is as follows.

One part of the material input into the economic system exists out of various raw materials that are mined in the home country. These materials are referred to as natural environment-domestic extraction (DE) (Fig. 1).

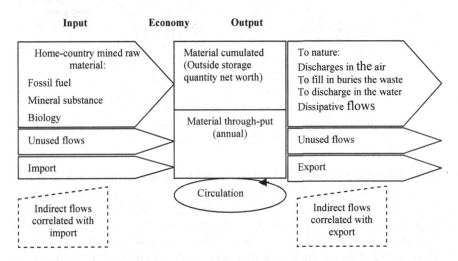

Fig. 1. Fundamental structure of MFA.

DE includes fossil fuel, mineral substance, and biological materials such as wood and so on. Unused domestic extraction (UDE) - a hidden flows resulting from the above domestic mining for raw material – does not enter the economic system and has not direct economic value. It is released in the form of emissions in the natural environment.

In addition, another source of material flow is the import of raw materials, half-finished products and end products - as well as the indirect flows related to the production of this material from other national and local entities.

Production transforms the accumulated input into goods, like infrastructure and durable products (referred to as internal material storage), export materials, rejected materials and emission that eventually return into the natural environment. Part of the rejected materials result in Dissipative Flows, namely rejections that are inevitably in product usage processes.

As an example, an MFA carried out in Austria in 1996, using officially published figures that express the volume of the materials involved is presented in Fig. 2. In order to construct a comprehensive MFA balance, this data was insufficient though. Some substances such as steam resulting from a combustion process need to be accounted for in an MFA, but are rarely considered in traditional output reports.

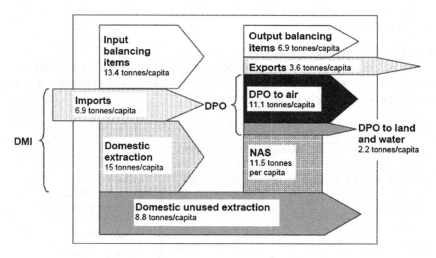

Fig. 2. Austria MFA balanced result in 1996.

DPO stands for domestic processed output; NAS is a measure for economic growth, expressed in physical units [3]. In a combustion process, fuel is blended with air and an oxidizing reaction (burning) is invoked, producing carbon dioxide which is discharged into air, steam and other residuum like ash and so on. 27% of the carbon dioxide emission is merely carbon, but 73% is oxygen, therefore the difference between the fuel weight (input) and the emission (output), can be big if elements such as oxygen are not considered. Based on the above considerations, a considerable revision of the available statistical data was needed to be able to compose a relatively complete picture of the overall system's material flows balance. A more detailed analysis can be found in [5].

3 MFA on a Company Level

3.1 The Company's Targets

The case study presented hereafter was conducted in a large petroleum chemical company located in an ecology industry zone in China. The company designed and carried out a

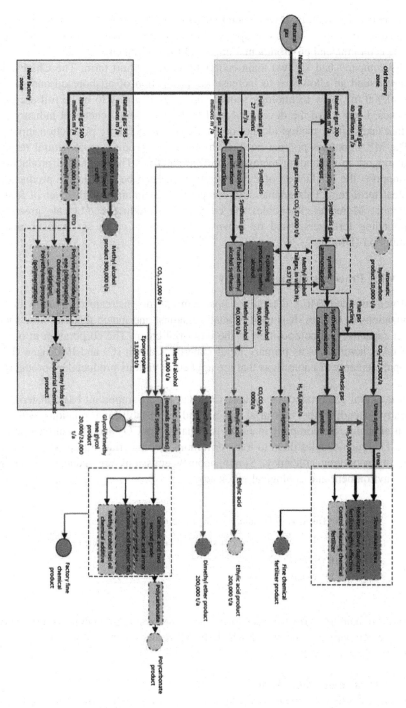

Fig. 3. Industrial chain MFA figure of the company in long term.

plan to reduce the quantity of waste and to improve its production processes by adopting advanced technologies. MFA was applied as technique to analyze, model and manage both the economic and environmental impact of the investments.

The company had set two main economic targets: Short term: The Chinese government issued an allowance to increase the production of offshore oil and gas with 400,000,000 m^3. New technology should allow the company to make full use of this allowance. Long term: the development of high value-added chemical industry products that takes either methyl alcohol or dimethyl ether as basic production input.

The MFA analysis pointed out that the increased production of natural resources could support an expanding methyl alcohol production. This expanded production in turn supports the production of dimethyl ether that can be used in the production of chemical fertilizers. This enables the company to maintain a high level of fertilizer production. Moreover, it enables the company to produce ecological "green" and compounding fertilizers, used by downstream industry chain as domestic material consumption (DMC).

3.2   MFA Processes of the Company

As aforementioned, MFA determines upstream and downstream relations with other organizations or entities. It is used to analyze, adjust and match material flow's route, current capacity, and composition of the industrial chain. The corporation in our case study takes natural gas as primary input material. Carbon (C) and Hydrogen (H) are principal elements of natural gas that are applied in various products, by-products and waste.

In a natural gas production system, CO_2 and H_2 are important basic materials. By gradually extending the industrial chains and by establishing relations with other industrial chains, the company manages to enhance the CO_2 and H_2's utilization ratios (Table 1), which enables them to transform more raw materials into products and thus increasing economic efficiency. Simultaneously emissions are reduced, resulting in better environment and ecological efficiency.

Table 1. CO_2 and H_2 usage rate changing situation

	Present stage	Short term	Long term
CO_2 usage rate	67%	67%	92%
H_2 usage rate	86%	88%	88%

In the remaining part of the section, we will focus on the analysis of CO_2 and H_2 within the company and the way in which the MFA analysis helped to optimize the use of those basic materials.

3.2.1 CO_2's Integration Analysis
In the present situation, the CO_2's originates from two different sources: the first part (640,800 t/a) comes from natural gas' burning and transformation; the second part (26,800 t/a) comes from a nearby refinery (Fig. 4).

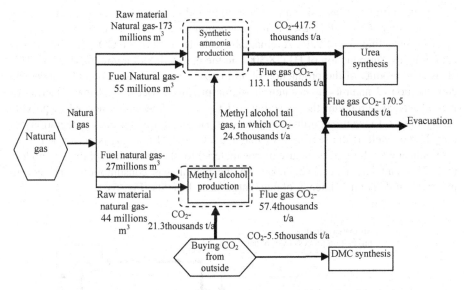

Fig. 4. CO_2 MFA figure of system in the current situation.

The production of CO_2 from natural gas happens in two different ways: one part of CO_2 (445,800 t/a) comes from the gasification, while another part (24,500 t/a) comes from the methyl alcohol tail gas. They are all used in urea products and are fixed in urea products (Fig. 2). The natural gas that is utilized in the production of synthetic ammonia and methyl alcohol is burned and offers heat to system. Part of the CO_2 (113,100 t) that results from this action is not utilized but emitted into the atmosphere. The CO_2 from the nearby refinery is used in the DMC and methyl alcohol production process. Hence, the MFA analysis points out that on the one hand CO_2 is emitted into the air while on the other hand, CO_2 is imported from another plant. This suggests that economic and ecologic optimization can be realized. The combination of the MFA analysis with more traditional investment appraisal techniques leads to the formulation of the short-term investment goals.

After realization of the short-term goals (see supra), the production of methyl alcohol expands from 60,000 t/a to 150,000 t/a due to the improved production processes and the enhanced efficiency of the use of CO_2. The comparisons between the current situation and the situation after realizing the short term goals show that the quantity of methyl alcohol production tail gas (CO_2 resulting from the production of a unit of methyl alcohol and used as input in the production of ammonia) per production unit of methyl alcohol reduces, but the total methyl alcohol production increases so that total quantity of tail gas remains invariable. Because the thermal efficiency of the improved production process is high, the fuel gas needed to produce methyl alcohol is not increasing. Therefore, after the realization of the short-term goals, CO_2 demand and output do no change remarkably, the quantity of CO_2 bought from outside is still limited. The majority of CO_2 in flue gas is still not used in a sustainable way; therefore it is unnecessary to construct a flue gas recycling installation in the short term. But in long term, through industrial chain construction and integration with other production processes, more CO_2 will be used in the production processes of the company, resulting in a CO_2 recycling rate of 92%. A remarkable enhancement of the CO_2 recycling rate is caused by the introduction of H_2 (18,300t) in the production of ammonia (Fig. 3). This H_2 is a by-product of the production of aromatization and acetic acid and reduces the consumption of natural gas per unit ammonia produced. Because of the reduction of natural gas consumption, the recycling of CO_2 out of flue gas is needed to provide sufficient CO_2 to the urea production processes. Hence, through process integration, H_2 recycling as well as the recycling of massive CO_2 out of flue gas is performed in an economical way. It reduces the use of raw material for the production of urea by no less than 27% and has a positive impact on the natural gas consumption. The system material's utilization efficiency obtains large-scale benefits (Fig. 5).

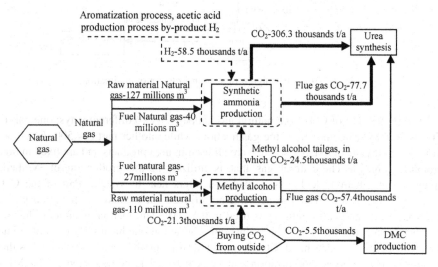

Fig. 5. CO_2 MFA figure of system in long term.

The MFA analysis provided the company with viable information on the input, use and output of CO_2 in their production processes, enabling them to pinpoint opportunities for optimization.

3.2.2 H_2 Integration Analysis

In the current situation, the use of H_2 in the production process is quite simple (Fig. 6). H_2 is a by-product of the production of synthetic ammonia and methyl alcohol. This H_2 is used in a next step to enrich and purify the ammonia and methyl alcohol (synthesis process). The total usage rate of H_2 is 85%.

After the realization of the short-term investment goals, the H_2 utilization augments mainly due to the expanding production of methyl alcohol. Because the higher efficiency of the new production processes, the quantity of hydrogen per synthesis of a unit methyl alcohol will be reduced slightly. Hence, the H_2 utilization rate enhances to 87.5%. In the long term, H_2 resulting from the production of methyl alcohol is used as

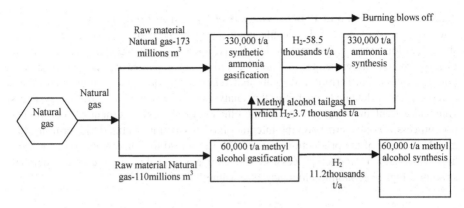

Fig. 6. H$_2$ MFA figure of system in the present situation.

feed gas for the synthetic ammonia production. In addition, enhanced new production of aromatization (10,000 t/a benzene) and acetic acids (200,000 t/a) result in the production of hydrogen as a by-product (resp. 2300 t/a and 16,000 t/a). Integration of the ammonia production processes with the processes that by-produce hydrogen saves a vast amount of natural gas (Fig. 7). Because of the short-term investment goals, the efficiency of H$_2$ will be quite high. Hence, the additional impact of the long-term investment projects on the H$_2$ utilization rate will be rather small. But through integration of processes, a bottleneck problem of using high amounts of natural gas is solved and the high emission of flue gasses is reduced (waste reduction). Again, the detailed analysis of input, use and output quantities of processes lead to the identification of opportunities which will eventually lead to a more efficient and more ecological production environment.

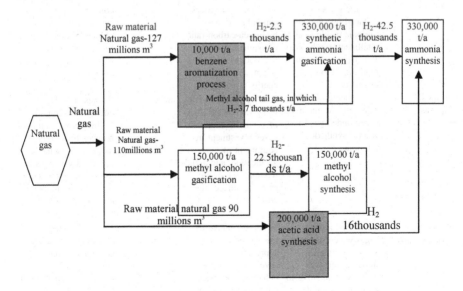

Fig. 7. H$_2$ MFA figure of system in long term.

3.2.3   Correlations and Benefit Analysis of System in Long Term

The MFA analysis provided valuable input, used by the company to determine their short- and long term investment policy. Based upon the goals set, an overview of the planned changes is presented in Tables 2 and 3, accompanied by the expected economic benefits. Furthermore, absolute and relative economic value indicators of the company are calculated, enabling the analyses of the company product system's value-added enhancement and economic efficiency. The enhancement of the production processes (short-term) and the integration of production chains (long term) lead to a scale increase of the production system. They also lead to a diversification as well as high value-added product processes. The company's profits are increased, demonstrating a higher economic efficiency (see Table 3).

Table 2. Economic indexes of system in different terms

	Total output value (hundred million Yuan/a)	Total profit (hundred million Yuan/a)
Present stage	13	4
Short term	31	19
Long term	89	54

Table 3. Correlations and benefit analysis of system in long term

Factors	Way	Description of economic benefit	Economic benefit (thousand/a)	Environmental benefit
Ammonia synthesis	Through the process of aromatization first, the synthetic gas which is produced by synthetic ammonia making-gas installment, synthesizes the benzene under the condition of low conversion-rate, to	The hydrogen that comes from the aromatization process can enhance the hydrogen-carbon ratio of synthetic gas, reduce the amount used of steam, and reduce energy consumption	4400	Reduces energy consumption during the conversion process of synthetic gas, namely reduces amount used of fuel CH_4, and thus reduces the CO_2 emissions
Aromatization process	by-producing the few hydrogen and massive un-responded gas to produce synthetic ammonia	Passing in one time by using raw material gas of synthetic ammonia, saves investment in equipment of gasification, and avoids reducing the cyclic process, reduces the cost	8000	Avoids reducing the energy consumption of cycling process, thus reduces fossil fuel usage and discharge of tailgas; The tailgas is used in the production of synthetic ammonia, no tailgas was produced
Ammonia synthesis urea	The methyl alcohol tailgas which passes over the synthetic ammonia into the second-section stove to be as raw material supplement; partial	Massively increases raw material supplemented that, saves raw material, enhances the material usage efficiency, and reduces production cost	36000	Reduces energy consumption during conversion process of synthetic gas, namely reduces amount used of fuel CH_4, and thus reduces CO_2 emissions

(continued)

Table 3. (*continued*)

Factors	Way	Description of economic benefit	Economic benefit (thousand/a)	Environmental benefit
Methyl alcohol	synthetic gas of making gas section supplies production of acetic acid: CO_2 produces acetic acid, H_2 produces synthetic ammonia; flue gas CO from processes of methyl alcohol and synthetic ammonia is recycled, being used in the urea synthesis, carbon-hydrogen ratio adjustment of synthesis gas of methyl alcohol, and acetic acid production	Avoids waste which is created by burning hydrogen or the tailgas blows off; The CO_2 which is recycled from flue gas is used in adjusting carbon-hydrogen ratio, saving CO_2's cost of making gas, enhancing material usage efficiency	14000	Avoids CO_2 emissions which tailgas burning blows off; Avoids massive CO_2 emissions from burning of fuel natural gas
Acetic acid		Has solved the problem of rich-of-hydrogen in synthesis route of acetic acid in method of carbonyl reduction	-	-
DMC	The CO_2 which obtained by recycling methyl alcohol and synthetic ammonia flue replaces CO_2 bought from outside to be as raw material gas of DMC synthesis	CO_2 synthesis raw material which recycled from methyl alcohol and synthetic ammonia flue gas, its cost is inexpensive, saving cost of gasification, enhancing efficiency of material usage	1600	-
Methyl alcohol ammonia synthesis		The flue gas which is recycled and used enters the product, to enhance material usage efficiency, and reduce greenhouse gas emissions	-	Avoids the massive CO_2 emissions from burning of fuel natural gas

4 Conclusions

The Material Flows Analysis method (MFA) is used regularly and typically as a method to trace and estimate domestic and international natural resources' usage. In this paper, MFA is used to analyze natural resources flows within a Chinese chemical company. The figures generated by the MFA analysis formed an important basis for the firm's short and long-term investment decisions. It helped identify ecologically and economically sound investments. In the long term, the company's main MFA figures show that the company can benefit from extending material flows across processes, (i.e. a growing intertwinement between processes in the industrial chain) and longitudinal material flows integration (i.e. further integration of the different steps in the industrial chains). By carrying out a profound analysis of CO_2 and the H_2 material integration, it was demonstrated that the MFA method could practically enhance the material flows utilization rate in a system. It helps to establish relations between different processes in the industrial chain and helps to pinpoint possible investments that cause a higher utilization rate of raw material, ultimately leading to a higher economic efficiency and to reduced emissions.

The case study supports the assumption that MFA is particularly suited on a company level because the required data can more easily by collected and the effect of an MFA application can easily be weighted and calculated. MFA can help a company to leverage its resources and its investment decisions. Due to the fact that the MFA method considers all possible materials related to the transformation processes, (including easy-omitted materials such as steam which has no direct monetary value), MFA offers data on environmental emission factors that can be incorporated into green GNP accounts.

Acknowledgments. This work was financially supported by the Science and Technology project of Liaoning Science and Technology Bureau of 2016; project (SY2016016); the project's name: The pollution controlling model system's construction based on middle-micro scale.

References

1. Reijnders, L.: The factor X debate: setting targets for eco-efficiency. J. IndEcol 2(1), 13–22 (1998)
2. Hashimoto, S., Moriguchi, Y.: Proposal of six indicators of material cycles for describing society's metabolism: from the viewpoint of material flow analysis. Resour. Conserv. Recycl. **40**, 185–200 (2004)
3. Hashimoto, S., Moriguchi, Y., Saito, A., Ono, T.: Six indicators of material cycles for describing society's metabolism: application to wood resources in Japan. Resour. Conserv. Recycl. **40**, 201–223 (2004)
4. Hubacek, K., Giljum, S.: Applying physical input-output analysis to estimate land appropriation (ecological footprints) of international trade activities. Ecol. Econ. **44**(1), 137–151 (2003)
5. Fischer, M., Hüttler, W.: Society's metabolism: the intellectual history of material flow analysis, part II, 1970–1998. J. Ind. Ecol. **2**(4), 107–136 (1999)
6. EUROSTAT: Materials flow accounting: experience of statistical offices in Europe. Directorate B: Economic Statistics and Economic and Monetary Convergence, Luxembourg (1997)
7. Rogich, D.G., et al.: Trends in material use: implications for sustainable development. In: Conference on Sustainable Development: Energy and Mineral Resources in the Circum-Pacific Region and the Environmental Impact of their Utilization, Bangkok, 9–12 March 1992 (1992)
8. Schütz, H., Bringezu, S.: Major material flows in Germany. Fresen. Environ. Bull. **2**, 443–448 (1993)
9. Gravgaard Pedersen, O.: Material flow accounts and analysis for Denmark. In: Meeting of the EUROSTAT Task Force on Material Flow Accounting, Luxembourg (2000)
10. Muukkonen, J.: TMR, DMI and material balances, Finland 1980–1997. EUROSTAT Working Paper No. 2/2000/B/1. EUROSTAT, Luxembourg (2000)

11. Isacsson, A., Jonsson, K., Linder, I., Palm, V., Wadeskog, A.: Material flow accounts, DMI and DMC for Sweden 1987–1997. EUROSTAT Working Papers No. 2/2000/B/2. Statistics Sweden (2000)
12. Bringezu, S., Schütz, H.: Total material resource flows of the United Kingdom, Final report. EPG 1/8/62. Wuppertal Institute, Wuppertal (2001)
13. Schandl, H., Schulz, N.: Using material flow accounting to operationalize the concept of society's metabolism: a preliminary MFA for the United Kingdom for the period of 1937–1997. ISER Working Paper No. 2000-3. University of Essex, Colchester (2000)
14. Scasny, M., Kovanda, J., Hak, T.: Material flow accounts, balances and derived indicators the Czech Republic during the 1990s: results and recommendations for methodological improvements. Ecol. Econ. **45**(1), 41–57 (2003)
15. Poldy, F., Foran, B.: Resource flows: the material basis of the Australian economy. Working Document, No. 99/16. CSIRO, Canberra (1999)
16. Mündl, A., Schütz, H., Stodulski, W., Sleszynski, J., Welfens, M.: Sustainable development by dematerialization in production and consumption: strategy for the new environmental policy in Poland. Report 3, Institute for Sustainable Development, Warsaw (1999)
17. Hammer, M., Hubacek, K.: Material flows and economic development: material flow analysis of the Hungarian economy. Interim Report, No. 02-057. International Institute for Applied Systems Analysis (IIASA), Laxenburg (2002)
18. Giljum, S.: Trade, material flows and economic development in the south: the example of Chile. Journal of Industrial Ecology
19. Gravgaard Pedersen, O.: Physical input-output tables for Denmark. Products and materials 1990. Air emissions 1990–92. Statistics Denmark, Kopenhagen (1999)
20. Machado, J.A.: Material flow analysis in Brazil. Internal Report, Manaus (2001)
21. Spangenberg, J., Bonnoit, O.: Sustainability indicators: a compass on the road towards sustainability. Wuppertal Paper No. 81, February 1998. A physical input-output table for Germany. StatistischesBundesamt, Wuppertal (2001)
22. Steurer, A.: StatistischesBundesamt Deutschland, Wiesbaden. Stoffstrombilanzösterreich, 1988. SchriftenreiheSozialeÖkologie, No. Band 26. IFF/AbteilungSozialeÖkologie, Wien (1992)
23. Sznopek, J., Goonan, T.: The materials flow of mercury in the economies of the United States and the world. U.S. Geological Survey Circular 1197. U.S. Department of the Interior, Washington, D.C. (2000)
24. United Nations: A system of national accounts (SNA), Series F, No. 2, Rev. 3, Studies in Method. United Nations, New York (1968)
25. United Nations: Draft guidelines for statistics on materials/energy balances. UN document E/CN.3/493. United Nations, New York (1976)
26. United Nations: Handbook of National Accounting: Integrated Environmental and Economic Accounting. Studies in Methods. United Nations, New York (1993)
27. United Nations: System of environmental and economic accounting. In: SEEA 2000 Revision. United Nations, New York (2001)
28. United Nations, European Commission, International Monetary Fund, Organization for Economic Co-operation and Development, World Bank: Handbook of national accounting: integrated environmental and economic accounting 2003. Studies in Methods. United Nations, New York (2003)
29. Kleijn, R., Bringezu, S., Fischer-Kowalski, M., Palm, V.: Ecologizing societal metabolism. Designing scenarios for sustainable materials management. CML report 148, Leiden (1999)
30. Korhonen, J., Wihersaari, M., Savolainen, I.: Industrial ecosystem in the Finnish forest industry: using the material and energy flow model of a forest ecosystem in a forest industry system. Ecol. Econ. **39**, 145–161 (2001)

31. Leontief, W.: Quantitative input-output relations in the economic system. Rev. Econ. Stat. **18**, 105–125 (1936)
32. Loebenstein, R.: The materials flow of arsenic in the United States. U.S. Bureau of Mines Information Circular 9382. U.S. Department of the Interior, Washington, D.C. (1994)
33. EUROSTAT: Material use in the European Union 1980–2000: indicators and analysis. Statistical Office of the European Union, Luxembourg (2002)
34. Chen, X., Qiao, L.: A preliminary material input analysis of China. Popul. Environ. **23**(1), 117–126 (2001)
35. Chen, X., Qiao, L.: Chinese economy - environment system's material flow analyzes. J. Nat. Resour. **15**(1), 17–23 (2000)
36. Chen, X., Zhao, T.T., et al.: Chinese economic system's material input-output analysis. J. Beijing Univ.: Nat. Sci. Edn. **39**(4), 538–547 (2003)
37. Chen, X., Guo, Y., et al.: Material energy metabolism and environmental effect analysis of cement line in Beijing area. In: Proceeding of Ecology Burden and Ecology Footprint Two Sides Across the Taiwan Strait Academic Exchanges, Shenyang (2004)
38. Xu, M., Zhang, T.: Material flow analyzes of fossil fuel in Chinese economic system. J. Tsinghua Univ. Nat. Sci. Edn. **44**(9), 1166–1170 (2004)
39. Liu, J., Wang, Q., et al.: Chinese material decrement analysis and international comparison about direct material input. In: Proceeding of Ecology Burden and Ecology Footprint Two Sides Across the Taiwan Strait Academic Exchanges, Shenyang (2004)
40. Ding, Y., Wang, Q., et al.: Ecology burden computation and analysis of Chinese iron ore. In: Proceeding of Ecology Burden and Ecology Footprint Two Sides Across the Taiwan Strait Academic Exchanges, Shenyang (2004)
41. Matthews, E., Bringezu, S., Fischer-Kowalski, M., Huetller, W., Kleijn, R., Moriguchi, Y., Ottke, C., Rodenburg, E., Rogich, D., Schandl, H., Schuetz, H., van der Voet, E., Weisz, H.: The Weight of Nations: Material Outflows from Industrial Economies. World Resources Institute, Washington (2000)
42. Palm, V., Jonsson, K.: Including chemical products in environmental accounts: the magnitude of chemical product use in different industries in Sweden 1996–1999. European Statistics, Luxembourg (2001)
43. Liu, T.: Ecology, vol. 7, pp. 85–116. China Environmental Science Press, Beijing (2004)
44. EUROSTAT: Economy-wide material flow accounts and derived indicators: a methodological guide. Statistical Office of the European Union, Luxembourg (2001)
45. Huang, X.: Circulation economy: industrial pattern and policy system. Nanjing University Press, Nanjing, vol. 12, pp. 35–86, 121–155, 217–259 (2004)
46. Qinghua University J company ecology industry zone construction topic-based group. Plan of J Company Ecology Industry Zone, 10 (2004)
47. Bertram, M., Martchek, K.J., Rombach, G.: Material flow analysis in the aluminum industry. J. IndEcol **13**(5), 650–654 (2009)

PAPR Reduction Using Interleavers with Downward Compatibility in OFDM Systems

Y. Aimer[1,2(✉)], B. S. Bouazza[2], S. Bachir[1], C. Duvanaud[1], K. Nouri[2], and C. Perrine[1]

[1] XLIM Laboratory, UMR-CNRS 7252, University of Poitiers,
11 Boulevard Marie et Pierre Curie,
86962 Futuroscope Chasseneuil Cedex, France
younes.aimer@univ-poitiers.fr
[2] Laboratory Technologies of Communications,
University of Dr. Tahar Moulay, BP 138 En-Nasr, 20000 Saida, Algeria

Abstract. In this paper, we propose a new PAPR reduction method using interleaving technique without data rate loss. The main idea is to set up all possibility of interleaving to get the best reduction of PAPR and to transmit the resulting information via null-subcarriers (NS) available in OFDM (Orthogonal Frequency Division Multiplexing) standards. Thus, we develop a new coding of interleaver key based on mapping symbols at the transmitter and a robust decoding procedure at the receiver. Simulation results in the context of WLAN IEEE 802.11a standard show an improvement of PAPR reduction about 5,2 dB, with the same performance in BER (Bit Error Rate), while respecting the communication criteria (Data Rate and spectrum specification).

Keywords: OFDM systems · PAPR reduction · Interleaving technique
Downward compatibility · Interleaver key

1 Introduction

Because of its high spectral efficiency, high quality of service and robustness against narrow band interference and frequency selective fading [1], OFDM technique is widely adopted in many recently standardized wireless communication systems. However, a major drawback of this technique is the high envelope fluctuations of the transmitted signal defined by the PAPR values [2]. These signals with high instantaneous power are affected by Radio-Frequency (RF) circuits, mainly the nonlinear RF-PA (Power Amplifier), which may severely impair system performance due to induced spectral regrowth and detection efficiency degradation [3]. The aim of PAPR reduction methods is to reduce these fluctuations to operate near the saturation region (high efficiency region) while respecting communication criteria like data-rate, BER, spectrum specifications and downward compatibility (i.e. additional signal processing at the transmitter don't need any change at the receiver).

PAPR reduction in OFDM systems has been a subject of intense research and a large number of methods have been proposed in the literature. Among them, methods

© Springer Nature Singapore Pte Ltd. 2018
H. Yuan et al. (Eds.): GSKI 2017, CCIS 849, pp. 611–621, 2018.
https://doi.org/10.1007/978-981-13-0896-3_60

like Clipping and filtering [4–6], Active Constellation Extension [7, 8], Tone Reservation [6, 9, 10], Selected Mapping [11, 12], subcarrier switching [13], Coding methods [14] and Partial Transmit Sequence [8, 15, 16] are popular. Authors in [17] proposed a PAPR reduction technique based on frequency interleaving of mapped symbols and the one that presents the lowest PAPR is selected. However, the problem of the SI (Side Information) transmission is not addressed. In [18], authors proposed to send the SI on the chosen interleaver via pilots symbols. This has the advantage of not affecting the data rate, but it influences the receiver. In this paper, we studied how to improve this technique and how to use the null-subcarriers available in each OFDM standard to transmit interleaver key-code (code of the used interleaver), thus answering the SI and the downward compatibility. The difficulty of the proposed method is to ensure a correct transmission of the key-code despite the degradation introduced by the transmission channel. To solve this problem, we propose a decoding process of the correct key-code based on the comparison of the one received with the different possibilities. The one presenting the minimum of error is selected. Preliminary evaluation of this method for WLAN 802.11a standard shows improvement on PAPR reduction while maintaining the same performance in terms of Quality-of-Service. Also, the decoding process presents a low complexity and a low probability of error even for AWGN and Rayleigh channel.

After a brief overview of the PAPR problem, we will describe the interleaving method in Sect. 3. We also describe the proposed scheme that uses the null-subcarriers for transmission of interleaver key. Finally, we will provide simulation results in Sect. 5 and we will conclude.

2 Problem Position

In discrete-time, the transmitted OFDM signals x_n which are obtained by taking IFFT (Inverse Fast Fourier Transform) can be expressed as:

$$x_n = \frac{1}{\sqrt{N}} \sum\nolimits_{k=0}^{N-1} X_k e^{\frac{j2\pi kn}{N}}, 0 \le n \le N - 1 \tag{1}$$

Where $X_k, k = 0, 1, \ldots, N-1$, are mapped symbols, usually modulated by a Quadrature Amplitude Modulation (QAM), and k is the discrete-time index.

OFDM modulator offers high spectral distribution and efficiency, high data rate, robustness to multi-path channel and easier implementation. However, as shown in relation (1), the resulting signal is the superposition of N independent narrowband channels that can generate high envelope fluctuations. These high instantaneous peaks limit the nonlinear RF-PA at lower average power efficiency, known as linear region. It degrades transmitter efficiency. Improving the power efficiency needs to deal with the reduction of fluctuations to maintain a higher average power without signal degradation. PAPR value quantifies this problem and defines the ratio of the maximum instantaneous power and its average power for each OFDM symbol, which can be written as:

$$PAPR(x) = 10.log_{10} \left(\frac{\underset{0 \le n \le N-1}{Max} |x_n|^2}{E\left[|x_n|^2\right]} \right) \quad (2)$$

Where $E\left[|.|^2\right]$ denotes the mathematical expectation function.

3 Interleaving Method

Coding and interleaving are commonly used in OFDM systems for transmission reliability. Channel Coding consists on adding redundancy on bit stream to improve immunity over a noisy channel. This operation is characterized by the code rate reflecting the introduced redundancy. To deal with channel fading which implies burst errors, add redundancy is not sufficient if all the redundant bits are transmitted on the same carrier. Thus, frequency interleaving is used to avoid these drawbacks where the redundant bits are spread over different carriers. As the fading channel depends on the frequency, some redundant information can pass without distortion. Interleaving is a simple breakdown of mapped symbols on more code words before transmission over the ODFM modulator. Thus, we define the number of code words M (also called the depth of the interleaver) and the number of symbols per code word, called the word-length, and noted K. Figure 2 shows an example of an interleaver with $N = 16$ subcarriers per OFDM symbol, $M = 4$ code words and $K = 4$ word-length. The mapped symbols are spread in serial on a matrix of 4×4 and send-out in parallel, i.e. column-by-column, to the OFDM modulator. Note that we choose $N = 16$ subcarriers to make easier the comprehension of interleaving method.

Let us define the vector of modulated symbols such as:

$$X_{1 \times N} = [X_0 X_1 \cdots X_{N-1}] \quad (3)$$

To split this vector into M code words, noted Y_m, we use here the modulus function. If we note b_m the remainder after division of the codeword position m by M, the code word Y_m contains the group of mapped symbols which have the same remainder. We can write the mathematical expression of the m_{th} codeword as follows:

$$Y_m^{k*1} = X_{M*0+b_m} X_{M*1+b_m} \cdots X_{M*(K-1)+b_m} \quad (4)$$

At the receiver, there is no additional complexity to system and only the inverse process is performed with the deinterleaver.

3.1 Interleaving for PAPR Reduction

With sufficient depth, the interleaving presented previously allows decor relation of transmitted symbols on the same carrier, reducing the risk to distort the successive symbols of the same code word. In practice, only one kind of interleaving is performed as function of the channel characteristics and the chosen Coding. For PAPR reduction, the idea is to perform several kinds of interleaving at the transmitter. After IFFT operation, the smallest PAPR among them is chosen to be transmitted (Fig. 1). The major advantage of this technique is that it is less complex than the Block Coding Techniques [14] or PTS method [8, 15, 16] and provides same performance. However, its major drawback is the need of SI concerning the chosen interleaving possibilities for decoding at the receiver, which degrades data rate. Also, to insure possibility to reduce significantly the PAPR, a large number of interleaving possibilities is needed. Unfortunately, this way increases the key length of interleaving possibilities, reducing more the useful data rate. Authors in [17] use only six possibilities to reduce PAPR in IEEE 802.11 g standard. Each symbol is permuted from original position and the specific block of data sequences are reversed. Here, we propose to deal with reducing PAPR using all possibilities of interleaving without useful data rate loss by:

- coding key-code in minimum of length,
- transmitting chosen key-code via null-subcarriers,
- and decoding the received key-code with robust process

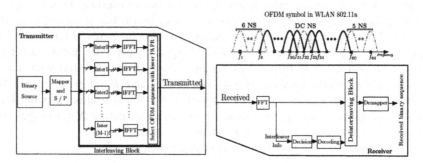

Fig. 1. Digital communication system with PAPR reduction based on frequency interleaving method

3.2   Transmitting the SI via Null-Subcarriers

To increase the probability to improve the PAPR reduction, it is important to use the maximum possibilities number of interleaving. By taking the previous example ($N = 16$ subcarriers, $M = 4$ code words and $K = 4$ word-length), we can generate $M! = 4! = 24$ possibilities of permutations, as shown in Fig. 3.

In communication systems, adding redundancy in Source Coding and FEC (Forward Error Correction) provides correlated data which influence the PAPR value. In [17], it is shown that sequence of highly correlated binary data in multicarrier systems is characterized by a large PAPR.

Thus, it is important to decompose a long correlation patterns to reduce high values of the complex envelope. In the proposed scheme (Fig. 3), after permuting new symbol OFDM, we reversed the last block of each permuted sequences as proposed in [17]. After IFFT block, the smallest PAPR pattern among all possibilities is chosen to be

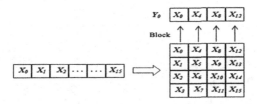

Fig. 2. Illustration of interleaving (N = 16, M = K = 4)

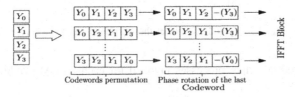

Fig. 3. Example of interleaving possibilities with M = 4 code words.

transmitted. Each possibility of interleaving has its key-code and the one chosen is transmitted to the receiver via null-subcarriers. Here, the rank of the possibility of interleaving is coded in binary and mapped using Binary Phase Shift Keying modulation (BPSK). Table 1 shows key-codes in binary words of 5 bits and their equivalent in mapped symbols, where (−3) and (+3) are the chosen BPSK constellation positions. In communication standards, one OFDM symbol is used to transmit user data, pilots and also some reserved subcarriers which are set to zero. For example, in a WLAN system with 64 IFFT/FFT size, 48 tones are data subcarriers, 4 tones are pilots subcarriers and 12 are null-subcarriers (NS) (see Fig. 1 on the top-right).

Table 1. Interleaver keys

Interleaver	Binary code	BPSK code
0	[0, 0, 0, 0, 0]	[−3, −3, −3, −3, −3]
⋮	⋮	⋮
23	[1, 0, 1, 1, 1]	[+3, −3, +3, +3, +3]

3.3 Decoding Process

Unfortunately and as for data subcarriers, PA nonlinearities and channel noises may affect transmitted key-code subcarriers, which will damage the decoding process at the receiver. To reduce the risk of error, we define a decoding process based on the comparison of the received key-code with all possibilities using xor gate on each BPSK position; the one which gives the maximum of zero is selected (see Fig. 4b).

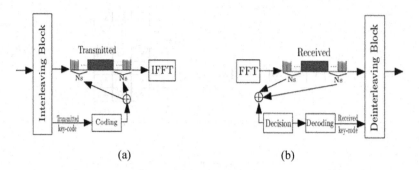

Fig. 4. Key-code on NS at the (a) transmitter (b) receiver

The proposed decoding processes invoked for each OFDM symbol with the following steps:

Variables:

$KC_r^{M \times 1}$: received key-code
$KC^{M \times k}$: Matrix of all key-codes at the transmitter
$KC_c^{M \times 1}$: The correct key-code
$R^{M \times k}$: Resulting xor operation matrix

> Step 1: Extract $KC_r^{M \times 1}$ from the received null-subcarriers and convert BPSK symbols to binary.
>
> Step 2: In k^{th} iteration, compare $KC_r^{M \times 1}$ to each key-code row of matrix KC according to $R[:,k] = KC_r \oplus KC[:,k]$.
> Where $R[:,k]$ denotes the kth row of matrix $R^{M \times k}$ and operation $\oplus$ is the binary xor gate.
>
> Step 3: Repeat step 2 for the chosen number M of interleaving possibility or stop when $R[:,k]$ is a vector of zeros.
>
> Step 4: KC_c corresponds to the line providing a maximum of zeros.
>
> Step 5: Select KC_c and deinterleaver.

4 Simulation Results

The proposed method is evaluated through simulations as shown in Fig. 5, for the WLAN 802.11a standard by using MATLAB^{TM} Mathworks platform. According to the parameters presented in Table 2. Three contexts are studied:

- Signals properties as function of the number of interleaving possibility.
- Communication criteria (CCDF, BER, PSD) using a Gaussian and Rayleigh channel.

Figure 6 shows, in the Time-Domain, the normalized envelope of OFDM signal with and without interleaving. We can see that the number and amplitude of the peaks are considerably reduced compared to the original signal.

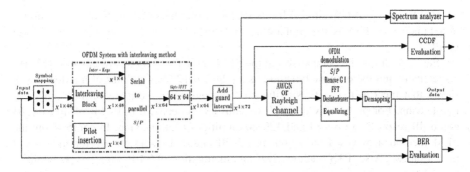

Fig. 5. Simulation block of WLAN 802.11a standard with interleaving method

Table 2. Simulation parameters

Parameter	Value
Num. of sub-carriers	64 (48 data, 4 pilots and12 NS)
Modulation	16-QAM
Num. of binary data	384000 bits
Num. of OFDM blocks	2000
Performance metrics	CCDF, BER, PSD
Num. of interleavers:	
Case 1	4! = 24 interleaving possibility coded on 5 NS
Case 2	5! = 120 interleaving possibility coded on 7 NS
Rayleigh channel:	
Sampling period	10^{-3}
Max doppler freq. shift	0
Path delays	[0, 10 −5, 3.5.10−5, 12. 10−5]
Average path power gains	[0, −1, −1, −3]

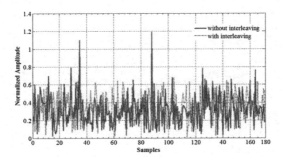

Fig. 6. Envelope amplitude in Time-Domain

PAPR can be also evaluated by its CCDF (Complementary Cumulative Distribution Function) which is the probability that PAPR is higher than a threshold level $PAPR_0$.

Figure 7 shows the comparison of the SLM and PTS methods presented in [17, 16] respectively and the proposed method using 24 and 120 possibilities of interleaving. It shows that the PAPR can be significantly reduced when we increase the number of interleaving. For probability of 10^{-3}, we illustrate a decrease in PAPR of up to 4 dB and 5 dB respectively for 24 and 120 possibilities of interleaving. In comparison, the SLM method achieves a reduction of 1.5 dB and 4 dB respectively for m = 4 and m = 5 blocks. Also, PTS method gives an amelioration of 3 dB with 256 possibilities (m = 4 blocks and v = 4 phases).

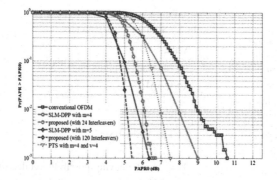

Fig. 7. Comparison of CCDF curve

Figure 8 presents the BER for the proposed system in Gaussian and Rayleigh channel contexts for different Signal to- Noise Ratio (SNR). From these results, we can observe that the obtained curves are almost the same with and without interleaving. In other words, there is no degradation of communication quality in term of error transmission when we used the interleaving method for PAPR reduction.

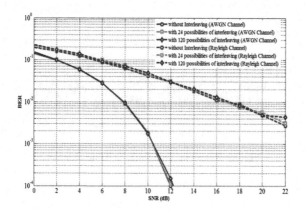

Fig. 8. BER with Gaussian and Rayleigh channel

In Sect. 3.3, we presented a decoding process of the interleaver. Therefore, it is necessary to explore what happens to this information as it pass through a noisy and/or a multipath channel. This is achieved by studying the probability of the correct decoding.

As shown in Fig. 9, we found that the correct key-codes are decoded with high probability for small SNR. For SNR greater than 10 dB, the probability is close to 1, which is a sign of a correct decoding in the case of 24 and 120 possibilities of interleaving. For Rayleigh channel, we see also that the probability is slightly affected for small values of SNR (about 0.96 of probability for 24 possibilities of interleaving and 0.987 for 120).

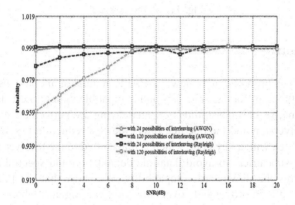

Fig. 9. Statistical study of correct decoding

To illustrate the impact of using some null subcarriers to send the key-code, we show in Fig. 10 the frequency response with and without interleaving.

Using null sub-carriers affects the spectrum by expanding the band, while still meeting the frequency specifications imposed by the standard (see the zoom view representing the band in Fig. 11).

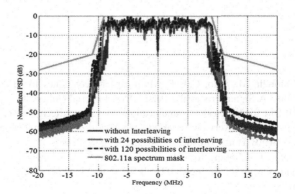

Fig. 10. Spectrum of WLAN signals with interleaving method

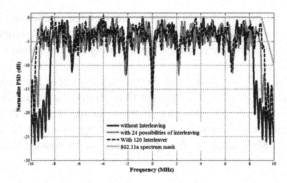

Fig. 11. Zoom in-band

5   Conclusion

In this paper, we proposed a review of PAPR reduction method using frequency interleaving without useful data-rate loss and compatible with OFDM standards. In the proposed scheme, several possibilities of interleaving are performed at the transmitter before time-conversion and the one that offers the best reduction is selected. The used interleaver is coded with a key-code which is transmitted to the receiver via a minimum number of null-subcarriers to avoid data-rate degradation and spectral regrowth. This technique ensures the downward compatibility. We show that the proposed scheme offers about 5 dB improvement over the original signal, which is also 1 dB improvement compared to the results given in [3] for the conventional methods. In order to find the correct possibility of interleaving at the receiver despite the errors of transmission, a decoding process has been proposed. Simulation results show a high decoding probability close to 1. The obtained results are promising and this work is continuing, but results in term of implementation and energy efficiency have to be confirmed taking in presence of the nonlinear RF-PA.

Acknowledgment. This work is the result of a scientific cooperation between France and Algeria and the authors wish to acknowledge the support of the Hubert Curien Partnership (PHC-TASSILI).

References

1. Pun, M.-O., Morelli, M., Kuo, C.-C.J.: Multi-carrier Techniques for Broadband Wireless Communications: A Signal Processing Perspective. Imperial College Press, London (2007)
2. Prasad, R.: OFDM for Wireless Communications Systems. Artech House, Boston (2004)
3. Jiang, T., Wu, Y.: An overview: peak-to-average power ratio reduction techniques for OFDM signals. IEEE Trans. Broadcast. **54**(2), 257–268 (2008)
4. Guel, D., Palicot, J.: Clipping formulated as an adding signal technique for OFDM peak power reduction. In: VTC Spring 2009 - IEEE 69th Vehicular Technology Conference, pp. 1–5, April 2009

5. Saroj, R.: A cooperative additional hybrid and clipping technique for PAPR reduction in OFDM system. In: 2016 Fifth International Conference on Eco-friendly Computing and Communication Systems (ICECCS), pp. 53–57, December 2016

6. Azizipour, M.J., Mohamed-pour, K.: Clipping noise estimation in uniform tone reservation scenario using OMP algorithm. In: 2016 8th International Symposium on Telecommunications (IST), pp. 500–505, September 2016

7. Zheng, Z., Li, G.: An efficient FPGA design and performance testing of the ACE algorithm for PAPR reduction in DVB-T2 systems. IEEE Trans. Broadcast. **63**(1), 134–143 (2017)

8. Youssef, M.I., Tarrad, I.F., Mounir, M.: Performance evaluation of hybrid ACE-PTS PAPR reduction techniques. In: 2016 11th International Conference on Computer Engineering Systems (ICCES), pp. 407–413, December 2016

9. Tellado-Mourelo, J.: Peak to average power ratio reduction for multicarrier modulation. Ph.D. dissertation, University of Stanford (1999)

10. Sohtsinda, H., Bachir, S., Perrine, C., Duvanaud, C.: An evaluation of hybrid tone reservation method for PAPR reduction using power amplifier with memory effects. In: 2016 IEEE International Conference on Electronics, Circuits and Systems (ICECS), pp. 676–679, December 2016

11. Bauml, R.W., Fischer, R.F.H., Huber, J.B.: Reducing the peak-to-average power ratio of multicarrier modulation by selected mapping. Electr. Lett. **32**(22), 2056–2057 (1996)

12. Ji, J., Ren, G., Zhang, H.: A semi-blind SLM scheme for PAPR reduction in OFDM systems with low-complexity transceiver. IEEE Trans. Veh. Technol. **64**(6), 2698–2703 (2015)

13. Hossain, M.S., Shimamura, T.: Low-complexity null subcarrier-assisted OFDM PAPR reduction with improved BER. IEEE Commun. Lett. **20**(11), 2249–2252 (2016)

14. Jones, A.E., Wilkinson, T.A., Barton, S.K.: Block coding scheme for reduction of peak to mean envelope power ratio of multicarrier transmission schemes. Electr. Lett. **30**(25), 2098–2099 (1994)

15. Muller, S.H., Huber, J.B.: OFDM with reduced peak-to-average power ratio by optimum combination of partial transmit sequences. Electr. Lett. **33**(5), 368–369 (1997)

16. Hanprasitkum, A., Numsomran, A., Boonsrimuang, P., Boonsrimuang, P.: Improved PTS method with new weighting factor technique for FBMC-OQAM systems. In: 2017 19th International Conference on Advanced Communication Technology (ICACT), pp. 143–147, February 2017

17. Wen, J.H., Lee, G.R., Kung, C.C., Yang, C.Y.: Coding schemes applied to peak-to-average power ratio (PAPR) reduction in OFDM systems. In: 2008 International Wireless Communications and Mobile Computing Conference, pp. 807–812, August 2008

18. Ryu, H.-G., Kim, S.-K., Ryu, S.-B.: Interleaving method without side information for the PAPR reduction of OFDM system. In: 2007 International Symposium on Communications and Information Technologies, pp. 72–76, October 2007

Design and Implementation of Wireless Invoice Intelligent Terminal Based on ARM

Yuexia Zhang[✉], Shuang Chen, and Yijun Jia

School of Information and Communication Engineering,
Beijing Information Science and Technology University, Beijing 100101, China
zhangyuexia@bistu.edu.cn

Abstract. In this paper, in order to solve the complexity and limitations of the current invoice issued, it designs and implements a wireless invoice intelligent terminal based on ARM [1]. The terminal is based on ARM embedded platform and the hardware part of the terminal is composed of main control module, memory module, LED liquid crystal display module and GPRS communication module. The software part of the terminal mainly includes the bottom driver design of Win CE system, the design of application software interface and the design of GPRS dial-up program. The invoice can be printed conveniently by using the wireless data interaction between software and tax administration information system. The system has been tested, which has the advantages of stable operation, friendly interface, convenient operation, low cost and easy popularization.

Keywords: Wireless billing · ARM · GPRS · Intelligent terminal

1 Introduction

With the growth of the total domestic and international trade and the level of personal consumption, the important role of invoice business in trade and consumption has been gradually highlighted [2, 3]. The amount and aggregate amount of invoice has become an increasingly important component of the government tax report to measure tax and economic growth. The traditional invoice issuing terminal uses the computer as the operating platform and uses the wired network to access the tax administration information system website to carry out the invoice business. This kind of wired, fixed type printing mode has greatly restricted the development of related industry. Therefore, it is of great significance to design and implement a wireless invoice intelligent terminal.

At present, the tax mechanism is very different between domestic and foreign governments. There is no uniform invoice system in foreign countries and the form of printing in those countries is limited to small ticket printing and receipt voucher printing. The existing invoice machine device on the domestic market can achieve relatively simple functions. The interface of it is not friendly enough. It does not support wireless interaction. There are many cases of ARM embedded technology applied to intelligent terminals, but there are few cases applied to the invoice industry.

In this paper, it designs and implements a wireless invoice intelligent terminal based on ARM.

© Springer Nature Singapore Pte Ltd. 2018
H. Yuan et al. (Eds.): GSKI 2017, CCIS 849, pp. 622–630, 2018.
https://doi.org/10.1007/978-981-13-0896-3_61

The terminal based on ARM embedded platform and the hardware part of the terminal is composed of main control module, memory module, LED liquid crystal display module and GPRS communication module. The software part of the terminal mainly includes the bottom driver design of Win CE system, the design of application software interface and the design of GPRS dial-up program. The invoice can be printed conveniently in the terminal by using the wireless data interaction between software and tax administration information system. The system has been tested, which has the advantages of stable operation, friendly interface, convenient operation, low cost and easy popularization.

2   The Overall Design of System

The overall design of the wireless invoice intelligent terminal based on ARM is shown in Fig. 1. It mainly includes LED liquid crystal display module, main control module, memory module, GPRS communication module and print output module.

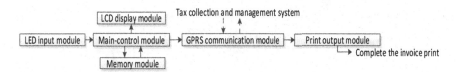

Fig. 1. The overall design of wireless invoice intelligent terminal based on ARM

The LED liquid crystal display module includes the LED input module and the LED liquid crystal display module [4]. The main function of LED input module is to provide the input of invoice or other information. The main function of LED liquid crystal display module is to demonstrate the man-machine interaction function of the terminal. The main control module is the core of the system. Its main function is to save the information of the LED input module to the memory module and call the information in the memory module and control the LED liquid crystal display module for functional demonstration and command GPRS communication module to complete the printing and output. The memory module can store the input information and its storage information can also be called by the main control module. When the GPRS communication module receives the command of the master module, it realizes the wireless data interaction and verification with the tax administration information system. The function of the print output module is to print the invoice.

When the invoice information is input through the LED input module, the main control module stores the input information into the memory module and sends the verification command to the GPRS communication module. When the GPRS communication module receives the command, it can realize the wireless interaction with the tax administration information system, and verify the invoice information. When the verification is completed, the GPRS communication module sends a print command to the print output module, which controls the printer to complete the invoice print [5].

3 The Design of Hardware

In order to reduce the cost of the overall design and ensure the normal operation of all functions, the wireless invoice intelligent terminal based on ARM should try to select low power, high-performance and cost-effective components and circuit design. The hardware circuit of the system is shown in Fig. 2.

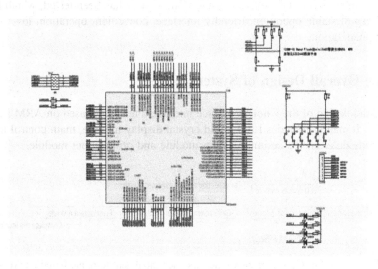

Fig. 2. System hardware circuit diagram

3.1 The Main Control Module

The main control module circuit is shown in Fig. 3. It adopts the Cortex-A53 (BCM2837) 64 bit 1.2 GHz central processor to improve the instability of the main frequency of the terminal. CPU adds Wi-Fi/Bluetooth module to meet the needs of wireless communication. The main control module also contains a BCM438 Wi-Fi/BLE chip, which solves the problem of incompatibility between complex USB and Wi-Fi and reduces the difficulty of development. The design of ceramic antenna type has a wide range of operating frequency and dielectric loss is small. In addition, it does not cause too much pressure on the main control module and is very suitable for exploitation and utilization [6].

3.2 The Memory Module

The memory module consists of two flash memory NAND Flash and two slice synchronous dynamic random access memory SDRAM, which consist of a 32-bit memory system.

The wireless invoice intelligent terminal needs bootloader, Win CE operating system, NAND Flash graphical interface library and application software programming, and the terminal has higher requirements for the FLASH chip. So flash memory selects the 256 M K9F2G08, which is an 8-bit data width range chip [7].

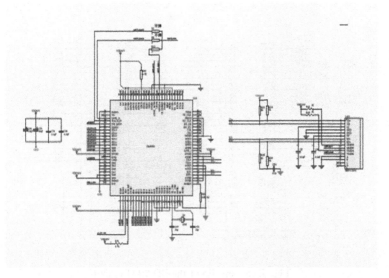

Fig. 3. The circuit diagram of main control module

The synchronous dynamic random access memory (SDRAM) is used as the main memory of the terminal, and it adopts the 4s561632c-tc75 (32 MB) SDRAM chip. The schematic diagram of the circuit is shown in Fig. 4. The external synchronous clock rate of the memory can be changed continuously in a certain frequency range. Each synchronous dynamic random access memory has five independent storage units, and the operation frequency is up to 124 MHz. The memory supports multiple reading and writing modes and its data control and address arrangement can be effectively scheduled, which greatly improves the operation efficiency.

3.3 The LED Liquid Crystal Display Module

The circuit diagram of the LED LCD module is shown in Fig. 5. The terminal uses the MP1541DJ regulator chip, which contains the HDMI high definition multimedia interface and the terminal does not require digital/analog or analog/digital conversion before signal transmission. The screen uses raspberry pie the 3 generation Raspberry Pi 3.5-in. LCD screen, and its refresh rate is 60 frames per second. The display supports adjusting the resolution between 480*320 and 1920*1080. It has various multimedia interface inputs and High fidelity audio input and output. It also has the custom driver installation and the body touch controls.

The GPRS communication module uses SIM900A chip to complete the wireless transmission function of the system. The SIM900A block diagram is shown in Fig. 6. The SIM900A operating frequency band is divided into GSM90 MHz and CS180 MHz, which supports multi slot function and its transcoding mode is CS1 ~ CS4. SIM900A uses power-saving technology and its minimum power consumption is only 10 mA in the sleep mode. It can be easily connected to the external hardware through the serial port, TTIL or RS2232 level signal control.

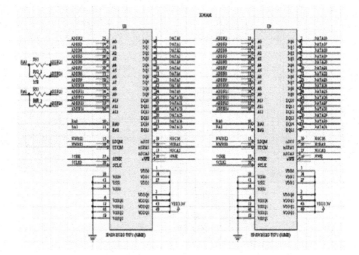

Fig. 4. Schematic of the SDARM circuit

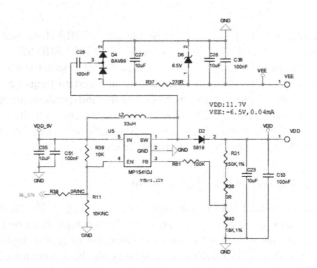

Fig. 5. The LED LCD module circuit diagram

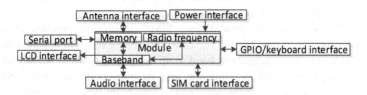

Fig. 6. SIM900A functional block diagram

4 The Design of Software

The software flow chart is shown in Fig. 7. When the user opens the terminal, the system will enter the invoice information input interface. When the invoice information is completed, the terminal will request the tax administration information system to verify the invoice information When the invoice information is accurate and meets the requirements, the terminal performs printing operations. If the system detects the incorrect entry of the invoice information, the system will display the information error on the LED LCD screen and return to the initial invoice information input interface and re-entered. If the re-creation fails, the system may have an error and the user can restart the operation.

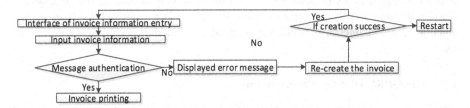

Fig. 7. Software flow chart

The software part mainly includes the bottom driver design of Win CE system, the design of application software interface and the design of GPRS dial-up program.

4.1 The Bottom Driver Design of Win CE System

All the drivers in the Win CE operating system are dynamic link libraries, which can improve the speed of the system. Win CE programs include stream drivers and local drivers. The local driver interface has no uniform standard and needs to be designed and developed according to the specific type of device. The structure of the stream driven interface is relatively basic, and its functional interface consists of some fixed stream interface functions. The source of the command is only the application and the resource manager. It converts the received command into the information required in the stream interface driver and calls it for the relevant device.

The printing area is 122 mm × 193 mm. The text should be justified to occupy the full line width, so that the right margin is not ragged, with words hyphenated as appropriate. Please fill pages so that the length of the text is no less than 180 mm, if possible.

The Win CE system driver is designed as follows:

(1) GWES will be loaded into the system display and input drivers, such as the screen, mouse driver, etc. These drivers are local drivers.
(2) The system loads the local driver and the stream driver module through the device processor, in which the local drivers are mainly bus type, such as memory card controller, USB driver and so on.

(3) When the system is turned on, it adopts dynamic loading method. When the external device is connected to the system, it allows the driver to be transferred to the kernel, so as to improve the operation efficiency.

4.2 The Design of Application Software Interface

The terminal uses the Win CE system, which uses graphical user interface (GUI) technology to provide interface design. GUI provides users with operation which is similar with Windows operation. The operation mode adopts the combination mode of mouse and keyboard, which makes the operation and use of the user more convenient and simple. The main interface is divided into invoice information input interface, query interface, system management interface and extension interface according to the functional requirements of software. Users can view system information and system settings through the system management interface. The extended interface is the function reserved interface, which can expand the function according to the actual need.

4.3 The GPRS Dial-Up Programming

GPRS wireless communication data interface is similar to the work of the modem and the terminal needs dial-up to access the Internet. The dialing process is as follows. First, the terminal performs dial-up operations by using the commands of the modem. Then, the terminal establishes PPP data link and password authentication protocol (PAP) or handshake protocol by the link control protocol (LCP) to authenticate Finally, the IP channel of the PPP connection is established according to the IPCP protocol. Terminal GPRS communication module used in the SIM900A chip is the use of serial communication between the master module. The user need to configure the serial port for the Win CE kernel without having to reset the serial port and finally add the appropriate components.

5 The System Test

When the software program is finished, the program is burned into the microcontroller by STC-ISP to check the operation of the MCU and test the running state of the system. The wireless invoice intelligent terminal based on ARM is shown in Fig. 8.

Fig. 8. Wireless invoice intelligent terminal based on ARM

When the user opens the software system, it enters the Win CE main interface, as shown in Fig. 9. The serial interface of the system is shown in Fig. 10.

When the serial port information is set up, the GPRS communication function test is carried out, and the GPRS communication debugging interface is shown in Fig. 11

When the GPRS wireless communication function is debugged and the invoice information is entered, invoice printing and invoice printing samples can be shown as shown in Fig. 12.

Fig. 9. Win CE main interface

Fig. 10. System serial information settings interface

Fig. 11. GPRS module debugging

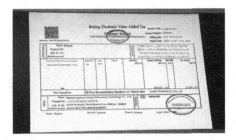

Fig. 12. Invoice printing example

6 Conclusion

In this paper, it designs and implements a wireless invoice intelligent terminal based on ARM. The invoice can be printed conveniently by using the wireless data interaction between software and tax administration information system. The terminal has broken through the traditional wired and fixed invoice printing mode, and has the advantages of simple operation, friendly interface and stable operation.

References

1. Shi, L.: Design and implementation of an invoice database grid based on OGSA. Comput. Eng. Appl. **57**(6), 134 (2005)
2. Yun Hong, L.I., Zhang, H., Zhang, Y., et al.: Design and implementation of Wi-Fi wireless terminal based on ARM. Comput. Digital Eng. **89**(8), 45–53 (2017)
3. Gao, M., Zhang, F., Tian, J.: Design and implementation of wireless sensor network data collection terminal based on ARM9. In: ISECS International Colloquium on Computing, Communication, Control, and Management, pp. 587–590. IEEE Computer Society (2015)
4. Jiang, D., Tian, M., Liu, W.C., et al.: Design and implementation of a novel wireless sensor network system terminal based on embedded web server and database. In: International Conference on Automatic Control and Artificial Intelligence, pp. 772–775. IET (2013)
5. Pang, Q., Gao, H., Xiang, M.: Design of intelligent terminal unit for smart distribution grid. In: China International Conference on Electricity Distribution, pp. 1–6. IEEE (2011)
6. Fan, P., Yebin, H.U., Sheng, L.U., et al.: An intelligent terminal device with high timing accuracy based on FPGA. Electr. Energy Manag. Technol. **89**(3), 233–243 (2015)
7. Wang, L., Yang, D., Kong, B., et al.: Modeling and implementation of intelligent terminal devices based on IEC 61850 protocol. Gaoya Dianqi/High Voltage Apparatus **51**(5), 89–94 (2015)

The Design and Implementation of Swarm-Robot Communication Analysis Tool

Yanqi Zhang[1](✉), Bo Zhang[1,2], and Xiaodong Yi[1,2]

[1] State Key Laboratory of High Performance Computing (HPCL),
College of Computer, National University of Defense Technology,
Changsha, China
{zhangyanqi15,zhangbo10,yixiaodong}@nudt.edu.cn
[2] Artificial Intelligence Research Center (AIRC),
National Innovation Institute of Defense Technology (NIIDT),
Beijing 100072, China

Abstract. With the rapid development of artificial intelligence and automation technology, robots have been widely applied in various fields. Compared with the single robot case, swarm robots have more strength in executing tasks by cooperation. However, multi-robot cooperation needs high-quality communication, which is also concentrated by this paper. In order to analyze the communication behavior of the swarm robots in the process of moving, this paper designs and implements a swarm-robot communication analysis (SRCA) tool in the Robot Operating System (ROS) software framework. This tool selects the packet error rate (PER) as the communication quality metric, simulates communication channels and packet loss, and provides visualization and playback capabilities, which are the functions that is not provided by existing ROS simulator. Then we simulate an outdoor formation application which involves 10 quadrotors, and verify the effectiveness of our tool in three different scenarios.

Keywords: Packet error rate · Multi-robot · ROS

1 Introduction

With the development of artificial intelligence and automation technology, robots are becoming more and more popular in life, the study on robots attracts more and more attention of academics and industry.

The Robot Operating System (ROS) is a flexible framework for robot software development. We can use a set of tools and libraries that offered by ROS to write applications across a wide variety of robotic platforms [1], [2]. ROS has become the de facto standard in robotics software.

Compared with the single robot case, the movement of the swarm has the unparalleled advantages of the monomer movement, especially with the development of robots, the cost of a single robot drops but the performance increases.

With the increase in the number of cooperating robots, many factors that affect swarms have been drawing attention. A very important factor is the communications

© Springer Nature Singapore Pte Ltd. 2018
H. Yuan et al. (Eds.): GSKI 2017, CCIS 849, pp. 631–640, 2018.
https://doi.org/10.1007/978-981-13-0896-3_62

limits faced by multi-robot [3, 4]. As for the coordination for swarms, it may be extremely complicated for inter-robot communication. The restricted communication environments faced by multi-robot that limit the development of synergistic behaviors [5, 13].

For existing communication network emulations, such as EMANE (Extendable Mobile Ad-hoc Network Emulator) [6] and OPENET [7], they don't support simulations of multiple robots tasks. And in ROS there is no software package which realizes the function of communication simulation.

In order to analyze the communication behavior of the moving robots in swarm, this paper designs and implements a swarm-robot communication analysis (SRCA) tool in the ROS software framework. This tool selects the packet error rate (PER) as the communication quality metric, simulates communication channels and packet loss, and provides visualization capability, which are the functions that is not provided by existing ROS software framework. Finally, we do experiment in three different scenarios which involves 10 quadrotors, and prove the effectiveness of the tool.

The PER model is described in the following Sect. 2. Section 3 provides an overview of the system architecture and the detail of design and implementation. The experiment results and analysis are presented in Sect. 4. Finally, conclusion is provided in Sect. 5.

2   Communication Quality Metric

In order to evaluate the communication quality at different locations in space, we should establish a reasonable wireless channel model. We select the point-to-point PER as a measure of communication connectivity to describe the channel quality between robots [12]. Then we analyze the point-to-point PER model.

The robot i as a transmitter, the robot j as a receiver, then the instantaneous point-to-point PER between robot i and robot j is given by Eq. (1).

$$
\text{PER}_n\left(\gamma_{i,j}\right) \approx
\begin{cases}
1, & 0 < \gamma_{i,j} < \gamma_{pn}, \\
a_n \exp\left(-g_n \gamma_{i,j}\right), & \gamma_{i,j} \geq \gamma_{pn}.
\end{cases}
\tag{1}
$$

In Eq. (1), n is the index of the transmission mode, which represents the different channel coding rate and modulation modes. γ_{pn}, a_n and g_n are constants related to the transmission mode index n. Their values depend on the choice of transmission mode, details shown in Table 2 of [8]. We can select different modes according to different scenes. $\gamma_{i,j}$ is the instantaneous received signal-to-noiseratio (SNR) of robot j, which can be calculated by Eq. (2).

$$
\gamma_{i,j} = \frac{P_i}{\left\|x_i - x_j\right\|^{\beta} N_0 B}.
\tag{2}
$$

In Eq. (2), P_i is the transmit power of the robot i, and β is the path loss exponent. B is the bandwidth of the communication system, and N_0 represents the power spectral density of the additive white Gaussian noise. x_i and x_j are the positions of robot i and robot j respectively. $d_{i,j} = \|x_i - x_j\|$ is the Euclidean distance between robot i and robot j. From the Eq. (2), we can know that the transmit power is greater, the sender and receiver become closer, then the instantaneous received SNR is greater.

3 System Design and Implementation

The SRCA system consists of three modules: swarm behavior control module, PER calculation module and packet loss simulation module.

Swarm behavior control module is mainly to control the movement of the robot. PER calculation module is mainly to simulate communication channels and get the PER. Packet loss simulation module is mainly to simulate the process of packet loss in communications. PER calculation module gets the positions of robots published by swarm behavior control module, then publishes the PER. The Packet loss simulation module gets the PER from PER calculation module, and then performs the simulation process. The structure of the system is shown in the Fig. 1.

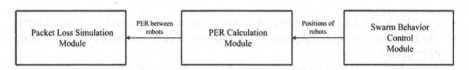

Fig. 1. The structure of the system.

3.1 Swarm Behavior Control Module

We use a group of nodes which called Node Group B to control swarm behavior, such as formation or other potential behaviors caused by different assignments. Node Group B contains a set of nodes, each node corresponding to a robot is used to control the movement of the corresponding robot by publishing velocity commands. The relationship of nodes and topics published or subscribed in this module are shown in Fig. 2.

We choose the Gazebo [9] as the simulation tool. We can use Gazebo to simulate robots behaviors accurately and efficiently in complex indoor and outdoor environments [10]. In the process of robot movement, Gazebo will publish a group of topics about the locations of all robots at each moment. Then we get the information about the locations of all robots. The location information will be used in the PER calculation module.

3.2 PER Calculation Module

We use a node called Node P to simulate communication channel and calculate PER between any two robots. The specific calculation of the PER and the choice of the channel model are described in detail in Sect. 2. The relationship of nodes and topics published or subscribed in this module are shown in Fig. 2. The processing flow in this module is as follows:

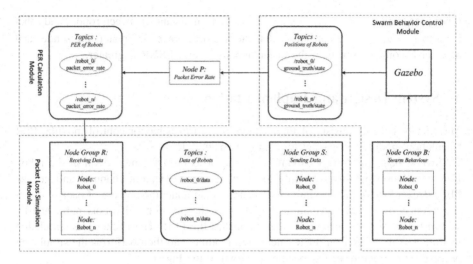

Fig. 2. The relationship between nodes in all module.

- First, Node P subscribes a group of topics about positions of robots from Gazebo.
- Then, we use the obtained position information to calculate the PER based on the PER model.
- Afterwards, Node P publishes a group of topics about PER between each robot and others. For instance, messages from topic i contain an array which represents the PER between robot i and any other robots.

3.3 Packet Loss Simulation Module

To simulate the process of packet loss when n robots send and receive messages each other, we need two groups of nodes to play the role of sending and receiving data. Each node group has a set of nodes that represent each robot. Node Group S is used for sending messages. Node Group R is used for receiving messages. And these messages can be commands used for controlling or useful information (e.g., information about locations of all robots when they are in a search area mission) in practical swarm coordinated operations. In order to simplify our experiment, messages published by Node Group S just contain the number of the robot that sent the message and the time when the message was sent. Node Group R also subscribes to PER topics in addition to message topics. The relationship of nodes and topics published or subscribed in this module are shown in Fig. 2.

In the process of simulating packet loss of a communication, supposing that we have n robots, the specific steps are as follows:

First, nodes in Node Group R subscribe to message topics from all other robots (each robot should get information from other n − 1 robots) and PER topic.

- Then, for each node in Node Group R, n random numbers in the range 0 to 1 are generated by a random number generator after a node receiving a PER message which contains n elements representing the PER between any two robots.

- Afterwards, comparing all PER and their corresponding random numbers, if the random number is less than the PER, we think the communication between these two robots should be lost, then the corresponding callback function of message topic has no action; on the contrary, if the random number is greater than the PER, we think the communication between these two robots is connected, then the corresponding callback function of message topic processes the received data. In our experiment, the callback function just prints the content of messages.

3.4 Visualization

Rviz is a 3D visualization tool for the ROS framework. We can use it to convert the robotic model into a visual 3D model for easy observation [11].

We divided the PER in the range of 0 to 100% into strong, medium and weak three levels. 0 to 20% is the strong level, which means strong connections between robots. 20% to 60% is the medium level, which means that the communication quality is normal. 60% to 100% is the weak level, which means poor communication quality.

In Rviz, we display all the robot models, and the lines between the robots indicate the quality of the communication. We use green lines to represent the strong level, blue lines to represent the medium level, and red lines to represent the weak level.

4 Experiments

During the experiment, we firstly set the parameters required to calculate PER, the specific settings, see Sect. 4.1. Then, we configure three different behaviors that may occur in the swarm collaboration. In the next step, we test the changes of PERs in three different motions of the swarm, and then analyze the communication behaviors to prove the effectiveness of our tool.

4.1 Experimental Setup

In the experiment, we choose 10 quad-rotor UAVs as a swarm to simulate.

The transmission mode that we choose according to the multi-UAV motion scene is the Mode 2 in Table 2 of [8]. So, the modulation is QPSK, coding rate R_c is 1/2, rate is 1.00 bits/sym, $\gamma_{pn} = 1.0942\,\mathrm{dB}$, $a_n = 90.2514$, and $g_n = 3.4998$. The bandwidth $B = 10^6\,\mathrm{Hz}$. The channel path loss exponent $\beta = 2.68$, and $N_0 = 10^{-12}\,\mathrm{dBm/Hz}$. All P_i is set to 0.05 dBm.

The three behaviors that we configured in the swarm behavior control module are flocking, leader-follower and a swarm separated into two sub-swarms.

4.2   Experimental Results and Analysis

The following is the results and analysis of the test in three different motion scenarios:

4.2.1   Flocking

Flocking is the group that is brought together by the separated state, moving together in a particular direction, and is able to maintain a particular rule during motion.

The instantaneous movement at a moment in Gazebo is shown in the Fig. 3(a), and the corresponding instantaneous communication quality in Rviz is shown in the Fig. 3(b). The relationship between PER and simulation time in the task is shown in Fig. 3(c).

Fig. 3(a). The movement in Gazebo.

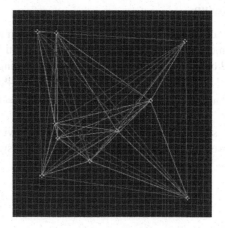

Fig. 3(b). The communication quality in Rviz.

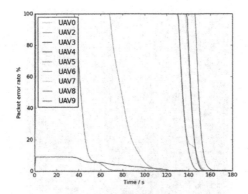

Fig. 3(c). The PER - time relationship diagram.

From Fig. 3(c), we can observe that the PERs between UAV1 and other UAVs decrease with time, and this change is consistent with the motion state of the swarm.

4.2.2   Leader-Follower

In the leader-follower formation, each robot (except for the leader) has only one leader. Here, we configure that 9 quadrotors have a common leader. The public leader is UAV0, and UAV1 to UAV9 are the followers. The scene is ten quadrotors from takeoff to follow the leader to perform the task.

The instantaneous movement at a moment in Gazebo is shown in the Fig. 4(a), and the corresponding instantaneous communication quality in Rviz is shown in the Fig. 4 (b). The PER changes over simulation time in the task is shown in Fig. 4(c).

From Fig. 4(c) we can observe that the PERs between UAV0 and other UAVs increase with time, but still remain in a relatively small range, because there is a need for good communication between followers and the leader. This change is consistent with the motion state of the swarm.

Fig. 4(a). The movement in Gazebo.

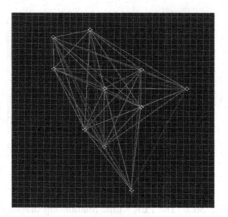

Fig. 4(b). The communication quality in Rviz.

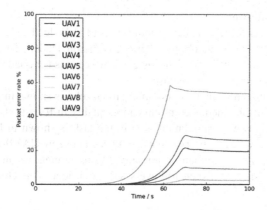

Fig. 4(c). The PER - time relationship diagram.

4.2.3 Separated into Two Swarms

We separate 10 quadrotors into two sub-swarms with 5 quadrotors to perform mission respectively. UAV0 to UAV4 is the first sub-swarm, and UAV5 to UAV9 is the second sub-swarm.

The instantaneous movement at a moment in Gazebo is shown in the Fig. 5(a) and the corresponding instantaneous communication quality in Rviz is shown in the Fig. 5 (b). The relationship between the PER versus simulation time is shown in Fig. 5(c).

From Fig. 5(c) we can observe that the PERs between UAV9 and UAVs in the first sub-swarm are growing with time, and the PERs between UAV9 and other UAVs in the second sub-swarm are changing in a small range. This change is consistent with the motion state of the swarm.

Fig. 5(a). The movement in Gazebo.

Fig. 5(b). The communication quality in Rviz.

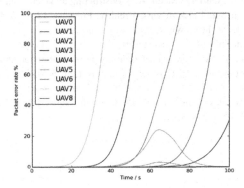

Fig. 5(c). The PER - time relationship diagram.

5   Conclusion

In this paper, we design and implement a swarm-robot communication analysis (SRCA) tool for analyzing the communication behavior of the swarm robots in the process of moving in ROS software framework. The SRCA tool selects the PER as the communication quality metric, simulates communication channels and packet loss, and provides visualization capability. By simulating an outdoor formation application which involves 10 quadrotors, we verify the effectiveness of our tool in three different scenarios.

Acknowledgement. This work is supported by the National Natural Science Foundation of China (No. 615307, No. 916484, No. 61601486), Research Programs of National University of Defense Technology (No. ZDYYJCYJ140601), and State Key Laboratory of High Performance Computing Project Fund (No. 1502-02).

References

1. Quigley, M., Conley, K., Gerkey, B.P., Faust, J., Foote, T., Leibs, J., et al.: ROS: an open-source Robot Operating System. In ICRA Workshop on Open Source Software (2009)
2. ROS official website. http://www.ros.org
3. Hauert, S., Leven, S., Varga, M., et al.: Reynolds flocking in reality with fixed-wing robots: communication range vs. maximum turning rate. In: International Conference on Intelligent Robots and Systems, pp. 5015–5020. IEEE Press (2011)
4. Bekmezci, İlker, Sahingoz, O.K., Temel, Şamil: Flying Ad-Hoc Networks (FANETs): a survey. Ad Hoc Netw. **11**(3), 1254–1270 (2013)
5. Davis, D.T., Chung, T.H., Clement, M.R., Day, M.A.: Consensus-based data sharing for large-scale aerial swarm coordination in lossy communications environments. In: International Conference on Intelligent Robots and Systems, pp. 3801–3808. IEEE Press (2016)
6. EMANE emulator official website. http://labs.cengen.com/emane/
7. OPNET modeler official website. http://www.opnet.com/products/modeler/home.html
8. Liu, Q., Zhou, S., Giannakis, G.B.: Cross-layer combining of adaptive Modulation and coding with truncated ARQ over wireless links. IEEE Trans. Wirel. Commun. **3**(5), 1746–1755 (2004)
9. Roberts, D., Wolff, R., Otto, O., Steed, A.: Constructing a Gazebo: supporting teamwork in a tightly coupled, distributed task in virtual reality. Presence **12**(6), 644–657 (2003)
10. Gazebo official website. http://www.gazebosim.org/
11. Rviz official website. http://wiki.ros.org/rviz
12. Wu, Y., Zhang, B., Yi, X., Tang, Y.: Communication-motion planning for wireless relay-assisted multi-robot system. IEEE Wirel. Commun. Lett. **5**(6), 568–571 (2016)
13. Shan, F., Liang, W., Luo, J., Shen, X.: Network lifetime maximization for time-sensitive data gathering in wireless sensor networks. Comput. Netw. Int. J. Comput. Telecommun. Netw. **57**(5), 1063–1077 (2013)

The Research and Implementation of the Fine-Grained Implicit Authentication Framework for Android

Hongbo Zhou[✉] and Yahui Yang

Peking University, Beijing, China
hongbozhou@pku.edu.cn, yhyang@ss.pku.edu.cn

Abstract. Nowadays, in order to protect sensitive information in Android apps, plenty of identity authentication techniques were developed, including the password, graphical-password, fingerprinting, etc. Unfortunately, these schemes have many disadvantages. For example, the graphical-password could be reproduced by the trace on the screen. Different from the explicit authentication above, the implicit authentication scheme silently collects user behavior patterns for authentication, without the actions like inputting password. In this paper, firstly, we realized a more fine-grained implicit authentication scheme for the first time, which has refined the unit for authentication from App-level to Activity-level. Secondly, we improved the feature extraction and applied the classification algorithm called SVDD. Thirdly, we developed a no-buried-point library to enhance the usability. Finally, we recruited 21 volunteers for experiments. The experimental results reveal that the accuracy of proposed scheme can double the previous work and the no-buried-point feature can greatly improve the efficiency of app development.

Keywords: Android security · Implicit identity authentication
Fine-grained

1 Introduction

With the growing popularity of the Android and Android app, in order to protect sensitive information and privacy information in mobile from accessing by unauthorized people, a variety of identity authentication technology is gradually developed, including the password, graphical password, fingerprint recognition, face recognition, iris recognition, voice print recognition and so on. But these authentication methods still have many disadvantages. For example, some biometric schemes require specific auxiliary equipment; the password may be stolen or forgotten [1]; the graphical-password may be reproduced by the trace on the screen [2].

Different from explicit authentication above, the implicit authentication mechanism silently collects various, measurable, user behavior patterns (without the specific action by user such as inputting password) to authenticate users. But the implicit authentication frameworks still exist many shortcomings by now, such as the coarse granularity (App-Level) of the analysis, leading to inaccurate results; such as the poor usability of the authentication library to be embedded in the app, which will do damage to the original program structure.

In this paper, firstly, we realized a more fine-grained implicit authentication scheme, which has refined the unit used in authentication from the App-level to the Activity-level, as the previous scheme trained all the touch features from all the activities of one app into one model. Our scheme separated the touch features of different activities and trained diverse classifiers for different activities.

Secondly, we enriched the feature extraction and applied the classification algorithm called SVDD.

Thirdly, through the analyzation of the Android source code, we have developed a no-buried-point scheme for our released authentication library, which is easier to use for developers, as they need to add only one line of code in order to embed the authentication module.

Finally, we recruited 21 volunteers for data collection and test work. The experimental results show that the proposed scheme can achieve up to 83% accuracy, and it allows the developers to embed our authentication framework almost without modifying the app code, which greatly improves the efficiency of their development.

2 Related Work

Murmuria et al. [3] presented an implicit authentication framework based on power consumption, touch gesture, physical movement and other factors. In this scheme, the researchers combined power consumption, touch gestures, physical movement and other biological factors to train a classifier so as to model a different user. The results show that the model is highly effective to identify different users.

Khan et al. [4] proposed an implicit identity authentication scheme with high usability, high flexibility and high scalability. The researchers were aimed at solving the following disadvantages: the current implicit authentication schemes for Android were difficult to be simply deployed and required the support at the framework level; the real-time training and classification operations took up too many resources considering the limited computing resources on Android mobile. So, some researchers have proposed "Itus", an implicit validation framework that allows developers to work together to improve the performance and the performance of authentication. Meanwhile, it also allowed app developers to apply this framework in their own app without having to modify the system framework.

Google published the biometric technology Project Abacus project at the I/O Developers Conference in 2016, which can use the "trust scores" to determine the legitimacy of the user. Here, the trust score will be calculated out from a variety of models together, including the click mode, voice and voice pattern, the location and face recognition [5].

3 Approach

3.1 Workflow

After a user has touched the screen for several times, our system will collect the touch data and do the preprocessing. Then our system will extract the features and then decide based on the number of features collected by the current Activity, whether to continue collection or stop to train the model and then classify the follow-up touch data. If the classification result is continuous negative, the system will force the user to re-enter the password (Fig. 1).

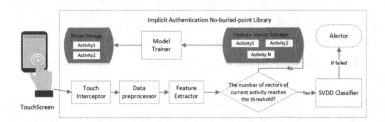

Fig. 1. The workflow of our framework.

3.2 Fine-Grained Model

In the past, the analysis of user behavior was aimed at the level of app, which will gather the touch behavior from different activities together and do the training. But different behaviors corresponding to the specific activities are also different, sometimes sliding, sometimes clicking and sometimes long-press and so on.

For example, as shown in Fig. 2, as we analyze a simple scatter diagram of some experimental data, we found that if the level of data collection is App-level, the touch pattern of the two users is similar. But if the level narrows to Activity-level, we will find that the touch points distributions are significantly different between two users on the same Activity, as the left-hand touch operations of user1 are significantly more than those of the user2.

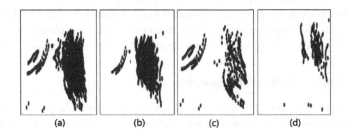

Fig. 2. Touch points with its true coordinates on the screen. (a), (b) represents the touch points from all activities by two different users, while (c), (d) are touch points from just only one Activity of the activities used in (a), (b) by the same users.

As the previous scheme trained all the touch features from all the activities of one app into one model, our scheme separated the touch features of different activities and trained diverse classifiers for different activities (Fig. 3).

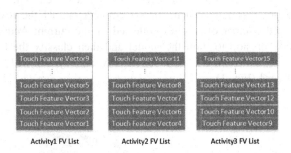

Activity1 FV List   Activity2 FV List   Activity3 FV List

Fig. 3. The touch feature vectors list separated according to Activity.

Therefore, after our framework captured a sequence of the touch action, the framework will first extract a feature vector and then insert this feature vector into different activities' feature vector lists. Once the number of the stored feature vectors of any Activity reaches a certain amount, the classifier of this Activity will be trained to classify the following captured touch feature vector.

3.3   Improved Feature Extraction

When each touch action triggers, the Android system will generate a Motion Event object for us, which contains the X coordinate, Y coordinate, action category (press/slide/lift), pressure, press area, timestamp, the direction of the finger, the number of active fingers at the same time.

Therefore, for the feature vector extraction of the touch sequence, the first step is to combine a number of continuous touch actions (Motion Event) into a complete touch action sequence. A complete touch sequence starts from the finger touching the screen, with multiple sliding operations in the middle (optional) and ends with the uplift action of the finger. So the system will divide the dataset into a complete touch sequence vector based on the action category of the Motion Event object.

Our framework not only retains the initial touch features provided by the Android system but will also extract a series of new features for each complete touch sequence. After a large number of experiments, we came to the following features in Table 1.

3.4   One-Class Classification Algorithm

Most of the previous authentication schemes used the 2-class classification algorithm [7], but the 2-class classification algorithm did not work well under this circumstance because of the fact that only legitimate user himself was using app at the initial stage, which means there were only positive samples at the initial stage. So in our framework, after the normalization and the string mapping step for the original data, we use the

Support Vector Domain Description (SVDD) algorithm for training and classification. SVDD is another type of one-class SVM proposed by Tax and Duin [6], in which the training only needs the positive samples.

Table 1. The list of extracted features vector

Feature ID	Feature description
1–2	Start X, Y
3–4	End X, Y
5	Duration time
6	Time between the end of two touch sequence
7	Direct distance from Start to End
8	Mean resultant length
9–11	30%, 50%, 70% velocity
12–14	30%, 50%, 70% acceleration
15	Direction of End-to-End line
16	Median velocity of the last three points
17	Length of trajectory
18	Average velocity
19	Average touching area
20	Average pressure
21	Direction flag
22	Ratio of direct distance
23	Average direction of Pairs
24	First touch area: touch area of the first touch
25	Average moving direction
26	Median acceleration of the first 5 points

4 No-Buried-Point Implementation

At present, in the industry, there are many products that provide users with the ability to collect click data, such as Heap analytics, Mixpanel, Talking Data and so on.

In Android, in order to capture the user's touch behavior, the developers need to re-write the dispatch Touch Event() method of Activity class and this common practice can be seen as a buried-point scheme. The industry usually uses such schemes. But with the continuous expansion of code scale, developers will suffer from the need to make more and more buried-point, which brings a lot of inconveniences.

4.1 No-Buried-Point Scheme

The Android system generates an instance of the Application class (singleton) after each app starts, and the lifecycle of the instance is equal to the lifecycle of the program. It starts before all the activities. So developers will also follow the various SDK requirements to initialize the SDK in the on Create() method of Application class.

Besides, Android has provided a method, register Activity Life-Cycle Callbacks(), in which we can insert custom functions in the callback functions of all activities to make the activities run our code after they begin.

So we only need to insert the touch-capture code in on Activity Resumed() or on Activity Created() method. The code example is shown below in Fig. 4.

```
registerActivityLifecycleCallbacks(new Application.ActivityLifecycleCallbacks() {
    @Override
    public void onActivityCreated(Activity activity, Bundle bundle) {
        Window window = activity.getWindow();
        final Window.Callback mCallback = window.getCallback();
        window.setCallback(new Window.Callback() {
            @Override
            public boolean dispatchTouchEvent(MotionEvent motionEvent) {
                //TODO: Here we can insert our code to capture the MotionEvent
                return mCallback.dispatchTouchEvent(motionEvent);
            }
```

Fig. 4. The example of no-buried-point scheme (without touch event capture)

4.2 Touch Event Capture Implementation Under No-Buried-Point Framework

We also need to capture the touch event in the above functions such as on Activity Resume().

As mentioned above, the industry often captures the touch event through the overriding of dispatch Touch Event() method which is cumbersome. In order to achieve our goal to allow the developers to apply our library with only one line of code, we have analyzed the Android source.

The reason why there is a callback method, "dispatch-Touch Event", is because the Activity class has implemented this callback interface and this callback instance can be obtained through get Window().get Callback() method. Meanwhile, this instance can also be modified through the set Callback() method. So we can use get Window().set Callback() to set the new callback. However, considering that many developers will override the dispatch Touch Event method of the Activity class, we need to call get Window().get Callback().dispatch Touch Event(event) to execute the original code before our code.

So that we can encapsulate all of our code into an SDK. Developers only need to call the initialization function provided by our SDK, such as init(), to transparently execute register Activity Life Cycle Callbacks() in our SDK in order to insert our own code in the on Activity Created() method of all activities and this is realized through the modification of Window. Callback interface. With the help of this scheme, developers no longer have to override the dispatchTouchEvent() function in each Activity. This only costs 2 ms extra time.

5 Experiment

5.1 Experiment Setup

5.1.1 Mobile Phone Models and Android System Versions

During this experiment, a total of 21 volunteers was recruited. After the simple statistics on the dataset, the main models of mobile phones are Huawei Honor Play, Huawei Honor, Huawei G9 Youth edition, Huawei P8/P9, XiaoMi 4/4C/5/5S, RedMi Note, as well as Vivo Y51, Meizu U20, and Moto X. As for the version of Android system, six of them are Android 7.0 (Nougat), four of them are 6.0.1 (Marshmallow) while the system versions of the rest of the phones are 5.0.1, 5.0.2, 5.1.1, etc.

5.1.2 App for Testing

Through the analysis of the common apps, we try to find an open source app among them. Ultimately we determine the experimental test app to be a recently popular app called geek news. The well-known information platform such as ZhiHu, WeChat News are the built-ins of this app.

5.1.3 Data Collection

In order to facilitate the model testing and algorithm testing, in the actual experiment, we have the app collect up to 10000 touch actions and send them to the cloud in CSV format. Then we will use the same program as expected to do the simulation experiments.

5.2 Performance Overhead

First of all, this paper assesses the CPU consumption of the system and the size of the heap memory of our framework.

The results show that the CPU and memory overhead will be relatively high in training, but such large overhead will only appear once. After the classifier is trained, it will take only ten milliseconds to do the classification each time (Table 2).

Table 2. CPU and memory overhead of different period

Initialization		Preprocessing		Training		Classification	
CPU	Heap	CPU	Heap	CPU	Heap	CPU	Heap
4 ms	16.7 kB	125 ms	92kB	6350 ms	3512 kB	13.3 ms	53.4 kB

5.3 Results

As shown in Fig. 5, with the same classification algorithm and the same granularity, the accuracy of our feature extraction scheme is obviously higher than the previous scheme. As shown in Fig. 6, with the better feature extraction scheme and the same classification algorithm, the result of fine-grained (Activity-Level) scheme is better than the coarse-grained one (App-Level).

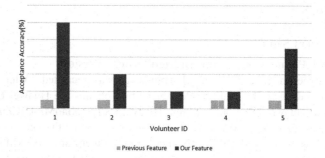

Fig. 5. The accuracy comparison of two feature selection schemes

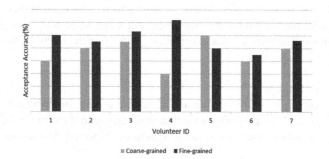

Fig. 6. The accuracy comparison of fine-grained scheme and coarse-grained scheme

6 Conclusion

In this paper, first of all, we realized a more fine-grained implicit authentication scheme, which has refined the unit used in authentication from the App-level to the Activity-level. Secondly, we improved the feature extraction and applied the classification algorithm called SVDD. Thirdly, we developed a no-buried-point library to enhance the usability. Finally, we recruited 21 volunteers for data collection and test work. The experimental results show that the accuracy of proposed scheme can double the previous work and the no-buried-point feature greatly improved the efficiency of app development.

In the future, we will enrich the touch data from the volunteers and seek more effective one-class classification algorithm.

References

1. Burnett, M., Kleiman, D.: Perfect Passwords. Syngress Publishing, Rockland (2006)
2. Aviv, A.J., Gibson, K.L., Mossop, E., Blaze, M., Smith, J.M.: Smudge attacks on smartphone touch screens. Woot **10**, 1–7 (2010). http://dl.acm.org/citation.cfm?id=1925004.1925009

3. Murmuria, R., Stavrou, A., Barbará, D., Fleck, D.: Continuous authentication on mobile devices using power consumption, touch gestures and physical movement of users. In: Bos, H., Monrose, F., Blanc, G. (eds.) RAID 2015. LNCS, vol. 9404, pp. 405–424. Springer, Cham (2015). https://doi.org/10.1007/978-3-319-26362-5_19

4. Khan, H., Atwater, A., Hengartner, U.: Itus: an implicit authentication framework for android. In: Proceedings of the 20th Annual International Conference on Mobile Computing and Networking, pp. 507–518. ACM (2014). http://doi.acm.org/10.1145/2639108.2639141

5. Google Project Abacus To Replace Android Passwords with Biometric and Environmental 'Trust Score'. http://hothardware.com/news/google-project-abacus-replace-passwords-trust-score

6. LIBSVM. http://www.csie.ntu.edu.tw/~cjlin/libsvm/

7. Frank, M., Biedert, R., Ma, E., Martinovic, I., Song, D.: Touchalytics: on the applicability of touchscreen input as a behavioral biometric for continuous authentication. IEEE Trans. Inf. Forensics Secur. 8(1), 136–148 (2013). https://doi.org/10.1109/TIFS.2012.2225048. Vancouver

8. Budulan, Ş., Burceanu, E., Rebedea, T., Chiru, C.: Continuous user authentication using machine learning on touch dynamics. In: Arik, S., Huang, T., Lai, W.K., Liu, Q. (eds.) ICONIP 2015. LNCS, vol. 9489, pp. 591–598. Springer, Cham (2015). https://doi.org/10.1007/978-3-319-26532-2_65

Fair Electronic Voting via Bitcoin Deposits

Xijuan Wu[1,2,3(✉)], Baodian Wei[1,2,3], Haibo Tian[1,2,3], Yusong Du[1,2,3], and Xiao Ma[1,2,3]

[1] School of Data and Computer Science,
Sun Yat-sen University, Guangzhou, China
wuxj5@mail2.sysu.edu.cn
[2] Guangdong Key Laboratory of Information Security Technology,
Guangzhou, China
[3] Chongqing Key Lab of Computer Network and Communication Technology,
Chongqing, China

Abstract. Bitcoin is the most popular decentralized digital currency now in use. Block chain is the basic technology of Bitcoin, providing a trustable ledger that can be publicly verified. Research on distributed applications based on block chain has become a new trend. We propose an electronic voting scheme based on block chain and prime numbers, which can support voting situations for multiple candidates. We design protocols for the Bitcoin voting situation, in which there are n voters and k candidates. Each voter will vote for one candidate. The proposed protocols could guarantee that the candidate who gets the majority voting wins the game and no individual voting information is disclosed. Due to the nature of the block chain, the voting results could not be tampered. It is transparent since the block chain is open to the public for verification.

Keywords: Bitcoin · Blockchain · Electronic voting · Deposit

1 Introduction

With the rapid development of the current communication network, a variety of network services have been widely used in our daily life and work. Electronic voting is a substitute for the traditional way of voting network services. The electronic voting system provides a more simple and efficient way for voting organizations and voters to participate in the voting process. There have been many electronic voting systems being used to meet diverse needs in real life. In this work, we describe how to use blockchain to implement an anonymous, secure electronic voting system.

1.1 Related Works

Neumann proposed the principle of electronic voting, including the following [1]:

- system integrity
- data integrity and reliability
- voter anonymity and data confidentiality
- operator authentication

© Springer Nature Singapore Pte Ltd. 2018
H. Yuan et al. (Eds.): GSKI 2017, CCIS 849, pp. 650–661, 2018.
https://doi.org/10.1007/978-981-13-0896-3_64

The blind signature [2, 3], Mixnet [4–6] and homomorphic encryption [7–9] are the mainstream building blocks for electronic voting. A blind signature is a cryptographic protocol used to verify the identity of a voter, without disclosing the voting content. Mixnets use encryption and replacement to disrupt the correspondence between voters and their ballots through anonymous channels to ensure the confidentiality of ballot information. The homomorphic encryption makes use of the homology of the public key cryptosystem. The voting results can be easily obtained without decrypting every single ballot to achieve the confidentiality of votes.

There have been new methods of e-voting using block chain, such as FollowMyVote [10] and TIVI [11]. They use the block chain as a ballot box to store voting data and a trusted third party to guarantee the privacy of voters. In FollowMyVote, the trusted third party blurs the correspondence between the voter's identity and the voting key. In TIVI, the encrypted votes must be shuffled before decrypting and counting through the trusted third party. Trusted third parties are most likely to be attacked and difficult to defend. In our work, we use Blockchain as a trustable global database to store voting data without a trusted third party.

The Bitcoin protocol has inspired many research topics since its launch in 2008 [12]. Fairness, validation and privacy are usually the most interesting issues in these studies. The Bitcoin system provides a natural way to implement the "fair compensation" concept. Bentov and Kumaresan formalize the "Claim-or-Refund" pattern in a universal composable model [13]. This mechanism allows the protocol parties to reveal their secrets one by one so that the first party who deviates from the protocol must compensate the parties who have honestly revealed their secrets. Andrychowicz et al. propose a new timed-commitment mechanism to achieve fairness, which is designed to enforce the commitment made by each party that he will pay other parties a certain amount, unless he (publicly) reveals a certain secret before a certain time [14]. The timed-commitment mechanism is extended for multiple-parties to reveal their secrets together in [15]. Andrychowicz et al. further give a "Simultaneous-Timed-Commitment" pattern to provide mutual fairness [16]. However, Bitcoin's scalability problem makes it temporarily unable to support large-scale voting data. Therefore, the scene we studied was some small-scale voting, like a boardroom voting.

Zhao et al. use both patterns to design voting protocols in [17]. They include two components. One is the vote commitment. The other is the vote casting. They use the "Simultaneous-Timed-Commitment" pattern as "Joint Transaction" and designed protocols for the Bitcoin-based voting. There are n voters in the voting scheme, each of which wishes to fund exactly one of two candidates A and B. The candidate who is funded more will win. The scheme is suitable for the situation when there are only two candidates. Following this framework, we propose a voting scheme based on block chain and prime numbers, which can support voting situations for more candidates.

2 Preliminaries

In this section, we introduce notation and cryptographic primitives used in subsequent sections, including Bitcoin & Blockchain, threshold signature scheme, commitment scheme and zero-knowledge proof. It should be noted that we only describe the necessary content, not a complete introduction.

2.1 Bitcoin and Blockchain

Bitcoin is a decentralized cryptocurrency and a payment system [12]. The concept of virtual currency Bitcoin was originally proposed by Satoshi Nakamoto in 2008, which is now also used to refer to Bitcoin's open source software on the P2P network. Blockchain is the basic technology of Bitcoin, providing a trustable ledger that can be publicly verified and could not be tampered. The money is transferred directly between two parties without a trusted third party. Bitcoin currency system consists of addresses and transactions between them.

Bitcoin Addresses. A Bitcoin address is simply a public key pk, technically the hash of pk. Bitcoin user is associated with the public-private key pairs (sk, pk). Then $\text{Sig}_{sk}(m)$ represents a signature on the message m computed with sk and $\text{Ver}_{pk}(m, \sigma)$ represents the result (true or false) of the verification of a signature σ on message m with respect to the public key pk.

Bitcoin Transactions. A Bitcoin transaction has some inputs, outputs and an optional locktime. We follow the work in [16] to denote a Bitcoin transaction in diagram notation. In Fig. 1, user A associated with key pair (pk_A, sk_A) wants to transfer 10 Bitcoin to user B associated with key pair (pk_B, sk_B). They generate two transactions T^A and T^B respectively. The transaction id TxID is the hash of the transaction's contents. Each input contains a reference to a previous transaction and an input-script. Each output contains a transferred value and an output-script. Input and output scripts are used to check the validity of the transactions. An output-script serves as a validation algorithm and input-script is a signature, serving as the parameter of the output script in the previous transaction. Figure 1 shows transactions between A and B. The output script $\text{Ver}_{pk_B}(\sigma)$ inside T^A transaction indicates that the money is given to user B. User B can create T^B transaction with input script $\text{Sig}_{sk_B}([T^B])$ to provide his own signature and if verified, user B can get 10 Bitcoin. A transaction can also have a locktime t, meaning that it is valid only if time t is reached.

2.2 Threshold Signature Scheme

As defined in the Encyclopedia of Cryptography and Security, a (t, n)-threshold signature scheme is a digital signature scheme where any t or more signers of a group of n signers can produce signature on behalf of the group [18]. No less than t group members can do so. In general, we generate a private signing key and a public verifying key for everyone, a private group key and a public group key for the trusted group authority. We have also an operation for signing messages and an operation for verifying signatures against a public group key. It is common to share a private group key

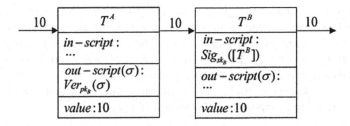

Fig. 1. Transactions TA and TB between A and B

among all the members, employing the technique of a secret sharing scheme. The private pairs are then used to produce partial signatures which are further combined by the trusted group center to get the threshold signature verifiable against the public verifying key of the group.

2.3 Commitment Scheme

Making a commitment simply means that the player in the agreement can choose a value from some (limited) set and promise his choice so that he can no longer change his mind. However, he does not have to reveal his choice - although he may later choose to do so.

The commitment scheme includes two phases, the committing phase and the opening phase. In the committing phase, the sender generates commitment $(c, k) \leftarrow$ Commit$(m)$for the secret value m, where k is the opening key. Commitment c is sent to the receiver, while m and k remain secret. In the opening phase, the sender reveals k to the receiver, so the receiver gets the original secret value $m \leftarrow$ Open(c, k). If the pair (c, k) is considered to be invalid, Open(c, k) will return $\perp$. There are two basic properties of this scheme, which are essential to any commitment scheme:

- binding property: After making a commitment, the sender can no longer change the content of the commitment. So, when the commitment is opened, we know that the revealed content is the original choice of the sender.
- hiding property: When the receiver gets a commitment, he could not tell what is inside before receiving the corresponding opening key.

2.4 Zero-Knowledge Proof

We use the definition for zk_SNARKS (zero-knowledge Succinct Non-Interactive Argument of Knowledge) from [19]. It proves a statement such as "there exists w such that $z = F(x, w)$" without revealing the corresponding witness w.

Consider a Boolean circuit $C: \{0,1\}^n \times \{0,1\}^h \rightarrow \{0,1\}$, a binary relation $R_C = \{(x, w) \in \{0,1\}^n \{0,1\}^h : C(x, w) = 1\}$, and its language $L_C = \{x \in \{0,1\}^n : \exists w, C(x, w) = 1\}$. For every $x \in L_C$, w is a witness for x such that $C(x, w) = 1$. Zero-knowledge proof allows a party to convince others that he knows a secret witness w such that $C(x, w) = 1$, where x is publicly known by all parties and w is remained secret. We can informally summarize zk_SNARKS as a triple (G, P, V):

- Generator G: $(1^{\lambda}, C) \rightarrow (pk, vk)$. The security parameter 1^{λ} and the Boolean circuit C are taken as inputs, and G outputs a proving key pk and a verification key vk. These two keys are publicly known and can be used any number of times.
- Prover P: $(pk, x, w) \rightarrow \eta$. The proving key pk, $x \in L_C$ and a corresponding witness w are taken as inputs, and P outputs a proof η.
- Verifier $V : (vk, x, \eta) \rightarrow \{0, 1\}$. The verification key vk, x and a corresponding proof η are taken as inputs, and V outputs 1 if $x \in L_C$.

In short, zero-knowledge-proofs is used to allow one party to prove the correctness of a statement to another party, without revealing additional information. Furthermore, the use of zk_SNARKS in this work is to guarantee that the votes and the random numbers that voters generate are valid, without revealing the specific voting information.

3 Models for Electronic Voting Schemes Based on Bitcoin System

The participants of the system are an organization Org, n voters $V_1, ..., V_n$, k candidates $C_1, ..., C_k$, and the public ledge blockchain. Voters vote for candidates through blockchain transactions. The model consists of the following four stages: Set-up, Vote-commitment, Vote-casting, Vote-auditing.

Set-Up. This stage declares the participants of the system and the resources they have, as well as the pre-interaction process between the participants. Each V_i registers his own ID to Org. Org verifies their identity and issue ballots, and then publish a list of valid voters and candidates.

Vote-Commitment. In this stage, each V_i makes a commitment to his ballot to ensure that the ballot is valid and lawful.

Vote-Casting. This stage is achieved through the Bitcoin transactions, including paying the deposit, claiming the votes, and finally redeeming the deposit. For each V_i that is dishonest, his deposit will be used for compensation.

Vote-Auditing. After every V_i has revealed his ballot, anyone can count the votes and get the winning candidate.

4 The Proposed Voting Scheme

We propose a voting scheme based on blockchain transactions and prime numbers, which can support voting situations for multiple candidates. It consists of four stages and will be described in detail as follow.

4.1   Set-Up

Suppose there are n voters $V_1, ..., V_n$, k candidates $C_1, ..., C_k$. At the registration stage, each voter is required to register at the organization, presenting proof of identity and providing its own voting address (the hash of Bitcoin public key). The organization maintains a list of valid voters and their corresponding voting addresses, as shown in Table 1.

Table 1. Voting addresses of voters

Voter	Voting address
Alice	1DSrfJdB2AnWaFNgSbv3MZC2m74996JafV
Bob	1Cdid9KFAaatwczBwBttQcwXYCpvK8h7FK
...	...

The organization publishes all valid voter polling addresses so that everyone can verify the validity of each vote. Then the organization assigns a different small odd prime number to each candidate from the set P, e.g. $\{3, 5, 7, 11,...\}$. Suppose m is the maximum number in P, we define a parameter M, which is the smallest number greater than m^n and is the power of 2. Then the list of the candidates with their corresponding prime numbers and Bitcoin addresses is published and the candidate is associated with the only prime number. In this way, voting for different candidates can be done by choosing different prime numbers, as shown in Table 2.

Table 2. Prime numbers and addresses of candidates

Candidate	Prime	Address
A	3	1GdK9UzpHBzqzX2A9JFP3Di4weBwqgmoQA
B	5	1hvzSofGwT8cjb8JU7nBsCSfEVQX5u9CL
...	...	...

4.2   Vote-Commitment

Each voter V_i has a private vote $O_i \in \{3, 5, 7, ...\}$, O_i is the prime number associated with the selected candidate. V_i and other voters apply the voting commitment protocol to generate R_i. He commits to R_i and mask the vote $\widehat{O}_i := R_i * O_i$. After all the voters revealing their $\widehat{O}_i$'s, the outcome could be calculated, and the winner is determined. Each voter has proving and verification keys for zk_SNARKS. For each $i \in \{1, ..., n\}$, the procedure for V_i is as follows.

1. Generate n secret random numbers $r_{ij} \in Z_M$, for $j \in \{1, ..., n\}$, such that their product equals 1 (mod M). This is done by generating $n-1$ random numbers and derives the last. Check the r_{ij} to ensure that the prime factor of the candidate is not included.
2. For $j \in \{1, ..., n\}$, commit $(c_{ij}, k_{ij}) \leftarrow \text{Commit}(r_{ij})$ where k_{ij} is the opening key to the commitment c_{ij}.

3. Generate zero-knowledge proofs that shows $\prod_j r_{ij} = 1 (\mathrm{mod}\, M)$ using the zk_SNARKS.
4. Broadcast the commitments and zero-knowledge proofs to all other voters.
5. Receive commitments and verify the zero-knowledge proofs from all other voters.
6. For all $j \in \{1, ..., n\}\backslash\{i\}$, send to V_j the opening key k_{ij} via the secret channel.
7. For all $j \in \{1, ..., n\}\backslash\{i\}$, on receiving the opening key k_{ji} from V_j, check that $r_{ji} =$ Open $(c_{ji}, k_{ji}) \neq \bot$.
8. Compute $R_i \leftarrow \prod_j r_{ji}$ and $\widehat{O}_i \leftarrow R_i * O_i$, and commit $(C_i, K_i) \leftarrow$ Commit(R_i) and $(\widehat{C}_i, \widehat{K}_i) \leftarrow$ Commit$(\widehat{O}_i)$, where K_i, $\widehat{K}_i$ are the corresponding opening keys respectively.
9. Broadcast the commitment C_i and $\widehat{C}_i$ publicly.
10. Generate and broadcast publicly the zero-knowledge proofs for the following statements using the zk_SNARKS:
    (a) $R_i := \prod_j r_{ji} (\mathrm{mod}\, M)$.
    (b) The quotient of the committed value in $\widehat{C}_i$ to that in C_i is a prime number that appears in the specified prime set.
11. Receive and verify all proofs from other voters.

4.3 Vote-Casting

Figure 2 shows the overall voting transaction scheme of the Vote-casting and Vote-auditing phase.

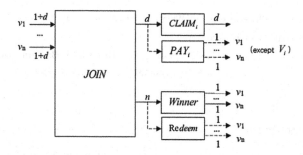

Fig. 2. The voting transaction scheme

Each voter V_i needs $(1 + d)$ Bitcoin, 1 Bitcoin is to be paid to the winning candidate; d Bitcoin is for deposit. We suppose $d := n - 1$ and if someone is dishonest, his deposit will be taken away by other $n - 1$ participants as compensation.

The timed-commitment technique can be used to handle the deposit and compensation. The protocol can guarantee that:

- If a voter reveals his masked vote, he can get back the deposit d Bitcoin.
- If every voter reveals his masked vote, the product $\prod_i \widehat{O}_i$ determines the winner who receives n Bitcoin.

– If at least one voter does not reveal his masked vote, the n Bitcoin originally intended for the winner will be redeemed by all voters. For each voter that does not reveal his masked vote, his deposit will be used for compensation.

The complete procedure for Vote-casting protocol is as follows.

1. **Key Setup.** In this phase a $(\lfloor\frac{n}{2}\rfloor + 1, n)$ threshold signature scheme is required. It is assumed that at least half of the voters are honest. The n voters jointly generate a group address such that voter V_i learns the group public key $\widehat{pk}$ and his share $\widehat{sk}_i$ of the private key. (pk_i, sk_i) denotes the address of V_i in the Bitcoin system.

2. **Check Input.** For each i, V_i broadcasts a transaction T^{Vi} with $(1 + d)$ Bitcoin. And V_i receives transactions of all other voters and checks whether each transaction has at least $(1 + d)$ Bitcoin unspent.

3. **JOIN Transaction.** Suppose t_1, t_2 are times far enough in the future and $t_1 < t_2$. Each voter runs the following protocol:

   (a) Each voter generates the same simplified transaction JOIN (as shown in Fig. 3) as follows. It has n inputs, each of which refers to $(1 + d)$Bitcoin from T^{Vi}. And it has $n + 1$ outputs:

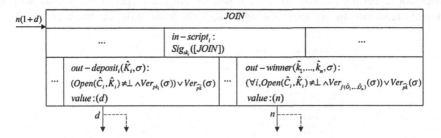

Fig. 3. JOIN transaction

   – *out-deposit$_i$*, $i\in\{1, ..., n\}$: each has value d Bitcoin, and requires either (1) the opening key $\widehat{K}_i$ and a signature verifiable with V_i's public key pk_i, or (2) a valid signature verifiable with the group's public key $\widehat{pk}$, to get the d Bitcoin deposit.
   – *out-winner:* has value n Bitcoin, and requires either (1) all opening keys $\widehat{K}_i$s and a signature verifiable with the winning candidate's public key pk_w, where the output script includes expressions to identify a winner, or (2) a valid signature verifiable with the group's public key $\widehat{pk}$.

   (b) The voters jointly sign JOIN using their own private key sk_is. There are n signatures to be created.

   (c) Each voter generates, for each $i\in\{1, ..., n\}$, the same simplified transaction PAY$_i$ with timelock t_2 whose input refers to *out-deposit$_i$*. The PAY$_i$ transaction is signed under their threshold signature scheme. The output script of PAY$_i$ could share V_i's deposit between other honest voters.

(d) Each voter V_i verifies that the above steps have been completed, and submit JOIN to the Bitcoin system.

(e) if JOIN has not appeared on the blockchain, say by time t_1, any voter V_i can terminate the whole protocol by submitting a transaction to get back $(1 + d)$ Bitcoin.

4.4   Vote-Auditing

As shown in Fig. 4, after JOIN appears on the blockchain, each voter V_i can collect his deposit d Bitcoin by submitting a CLAIM$_i$ transaction that provides the opening key $\widehat{K}_i$ to reveal his masked vote $\widehat{O}_i$ (If one voter V_j does not reveal his masked vote after timelock t_2, other voters can submit PAY$_j$ transaction to redeem his deposit for compensation). If all voters have submitted their transactions CLAIM$_i$s, $f(\widehat{O}_1,\ldots,\widehat{O}_n)$ in the output script can be computed. Divide the product of all $\widehat{O}_i$ by the unique prime number corresponds to each candidate until it could not be divisible, finally we can get the power which is the number of votes he wins. The function f returns the public key pk_w of the winner, so the winning candidate is determined and can redeem n Bitcoin from *out-winner* with his signature through a Winner transaction. If at least one voter does not reveal his masked vote, the n Bitcoin originally specify the winner will be directly redeemed by all voters through a Redeem transaction, as shown in Fig. 5.

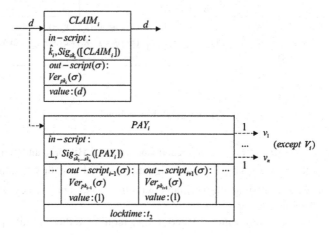

Fig. 4. CLAIM$_i$ and PAY$_i$ transactions

4.5   Security Analysis

Privacy. For each $i\in\{1,\ldots,n\}$, V_i reveal his masked vote $\widehat{O}_i \leftarrow R_i * O_i$, where O_i is the real vote. Since R_i is a distributed random value generated during the voting commitment process, and this random value is used only once, no one can easily guess O_i. As a result, individual votes remain private.

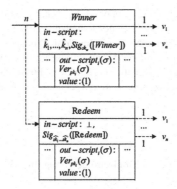

Fig. 5. Winner and Redeem transactions

Irrevocability. If all voters have revealed their votes, the winner is determined. Only the winner can spend the *out-winner* output inside JOIN transaction. Please note that when the JOIN transaction is confirmed, all voters' deposits and funds have been redeemed. As long as the Bitcoin blockchain can prevent double spending, no voter can withdraw his funds.

Verifiability. Each voter has only one chance to vote on the blockchain. In the vote commitment protocol, there are $n(n + 2)$ proofs of żk_SNARKS to ensure that each voter's behavior is correct. Specifically, the random number r_{ij} is generated correctly, the random number R_i is multiplied correctly, and the masked vote $\widehat{O}_i$ is formed correctly.

4.6 Secure Channel

In the vote commitment protocol, we mentioned a secure channel between any two voters. We can easily create a secure channel in the Bitcoin blockchain environment. It is now assumed that the "Check Input" step of the votecasting is performed before the vote commitment. And it is required that the exchanged transaction of V_i should be signed by himself. Then V_i can generate a dynamic shared secret key with V_j through the Diffie-Hellman protocol and the current block header hash. That is, V_i and V_j use the public key in the transaction they exchange to establish a fixed secret value, and update the secret by the current header hash value. As the block chain grows, the secrets are updated. This secret can be used as a symmetrical key to establish a secure channel between the two voters.

5 Conclusions

In this work, we describe how to use blockchain to implement an anonymous, secure electronic voting system. We propose a voting scheme based on blockchain and prime numbers. It can support voting situations for multiple candidates. And we modify the protocols to make it more reasonable and fair.

660   X. Wu et al.

Acknowledgments. This work was supported by National Key R&D Program of China (2017YFB0802500), National Natural Science Foundations of China (U1636118, 61472457 and 61309028), Natural Science Foundation of Guangdong Province (2016A030313298), Science and Technology Planning Project of Guangdong Province (2014A010103017), the Fundamental Research Funds for the Central Universities (17lgjc45) and the Opening fund of Qiongqing Key Lab of Computer Network and Communication Technology (CY-CNCL -2017-04).

References

1. Neumann, P.G.: Security criteria for electronic voting. In: 16th National Computer Security Conference, vol. 29 (1993)
2. Okamoto, T.: An electronic voting scheme. In: Terashima, N., Altman, E. (eds.) Advanced IT Tools, pp. 21–30. Springer, Boston (1996). https://doi.org/10.1007/978-0-387-34979-4_3
3. Fujioka, A., Okamoto, T., Ohta, K.: A practical secret voting scheme for large scale elections. In: Seberry, J., Zheng, Y. (eds.) AUSCRYPT 1992. LNCS, vol. 718, pp. 244–251. Springer, Heidelberg (1993). https://doi.org/10.1007/3-540-57220-1_66
4. Sako, K., Kilian, J.: Receipt-free mix-type voting scheme. In: Guillou, Louis C., Quisquater, J.-J. (eds.) EUROCRYPT 1995. LNCS, vol. 921, pp. 393–403. Springer, Heidelberg (1995). https://doi.org/10.1007/3-540-49264-X_32
5. Jakobsson, M., Juels, A., Rivest, R.L.: Making mix nets robust for electronic voting by randomized partial checking. In: USENIX Security Symposium, pp. 339–353, San Francisco (2002)
6. Neff, C.A.: A verifiable secret shuffle and its application to e-voting. In: The 8th ACM Conference on Computer and Communications Security, pp. 116–125. ACM (2001)
7. Baudron, O., Fouque, P.-A., Pointcheval, D., Stern, J., Poupard, G.: Practical multi-candidate election system. In: The Twentieth Annual ACM Symposium on Principles of Distributed Computing, pp. 274–283. ACM (2001)
8. Cramer, R., Gennaro, R., Schoenmakers, B.: A secure and optimally efficient multi-authority election scheme. Trans. Emerg. Telecommun. Technol. **8**(5), 481–490 (1997)
9. Benaloh, J., Tuinstra, D.: Receipt-free secret-ballot elections. In: The Twenty-Sixth Annual ACM Symposium on Theory of Computing, pp. 544–553. ACM (1994)
10. Aradhya, P.: Distributed Ledger Visible to All? Ready for Blockchain? Huffington Post (2016)
11. Business Wire: Now you can vote online with a selfie. Business Wire (2016). http://www.businesswire.com/news/home/20161017005354/en/Vote-Online-Selfie
12. Nakamoto, S.: Bitcoin: a peer-to-peer electronic cash system (2008). http://bitcoin.org/bitcoin.pdf
13. Bentov, I., Kumaresan, R.: How to use bitcoin to design fair protocols. In: Garay, Juan A., Gennaro, R. (eds.) CRYPTO 2014. LNCS, vol. 8617, pp. 421–439. Springer, Heidelberg (2014). https://doi.org/10.1007/978-3-662-44381-1_24
14. Andrychowicz, M., Dziembowski, S., Malinowski, D., Mazurek, L.: Secure multiparty computations on bitcoin. In: 2014 IEEE Symposium on Security and Privacy, pp. 443–458. IEEE (2014)
15. Kumaresan, R., Bentov, I.: How to use bitcoin to incentivize correct computations. In: 2014 ACM SIGSAC Conference on Computer and Communications Security, pp. 30–41. ACM (2014)

16. Andrychowicz, M., Dziembowski, S., Malinowski, D., Mazurek, Ł.: Fair two-party computations via bitcoin deposits. In: Böhme, R., Brenner, M., Moore, T., Smith, M. (eds.) FC 2014. LNCS, vol. 8438, pp. 105–121. Springer, Heidelberg (2014). https://doi.org/10. 1007/978-3-662-44774-1_8

17. Zhao, Z., Chan, T.-H.H.: How to vote privately using bitcoin. In: Qing, S., Okamoto, E., Kim, K., Liu, D. (eds.) ICICS 2015. LNCS, vol. 9543, pp. 82–96. Springer, Cham (2016). https://doi.org/10.1007/978-3-319-29814-6_8

18. Tilborg, V.H., Jajodia, S.: Encyclopedia of Cryptography and Security, 2nd edn. Springer, Cham (2011)

19. Ben-Sasson, E., Chiesa, A., Tromer, E., Virza, M.: Succinct non-interactive zero knowledge for a von Neumann architecture. In: USENIX Security, pp. 781–796 (2014)

Research and Development of Door Handle Test Equipment Electrical System Based on Automatic Control Technology

Kang Gao[1(✉)], Hangjian Guan[2], Chengyang Wei[1], Zhuang Ouyang[1], Zhijie Wang[1], and Xiaoping Huang[1]

[1] Guangdong Zhaoqing Supervision and Inspection Institute of Quality and Metrology, Zhaoqing 526000, China
gaokang2010@yeah.net
[2] Guangzhou Xiaowei Intelligent Technology Co., Ltd., Guangzhou 510641, China
cncsiah@126.com

Abstract. This paper presents an electrical control system that applied automatic control technology to the door handle test equipment. The system can realize the automation and intelligence of test process, which collect and process key data such as torque, angle, time and speed, as well as realize data input and output through friendly human-computer interaction interface. The system was able to adjust the speed of the power according to the test task, and when the door handle turns to the specified angle, it can be used to remove or reverse the power in time. This function, called delayed reset, ensured that all actions are performed in an orderly manner.

Keywords: Door handle · Test equipment · Automation technology

1 Introduction

Compared to the modern metrology industry, traditional contact detection has far can not meet the requirement of the test, the test link consists of a single testing data of the instrument, and need to invest a lot of manpower, which not fit for the rapid detection. Therefore, non-standard automatic test equipment is the development direction of the future metering test towards rapid, accurate, effective and intelligent detection, which adopts non-contact, light, mechanical, electrical, visual and other integrated detection technique [1]. Compared with the similar standard testing equipment, non-standard automation testing equipment is the special customized testing equipment, tailored for object detection, and it is characterized by advanced technology, complicated structure, high integration degree, which represents intelligent detection equipment.

Professionally, the automation test system based on sensor and optoelectronic technology is feasible, and it has been widely recognized [2–4]. Comprehensive performance test equipment for the door handle, the automatic test system not only need to take full account of the mechanism design scheme, measurement error due to objective factors such as transmission mode, it needs to be more fully consider the relationship

© Springer Nature Singapore Pte Ltd. 2018
H. Yuan et al. (Eds.): GSKI 2017, CCIS 849, pp. 662–669, 2018.
https://doi.org/10.1007/978-981-13-0896-3_65

between the mechanical properties of detection and handle life detection, sensor precision attenuation and site inspector convenient operation degree [5, 6]. We need full automation system development, which is from the installation to the output sample test report of the test process, the comprehensive performance of which is more convenient, accurate and reliable measurement of the door handle.

2 General

Test equipment needed to run the system, the test detection required for signal acquisition and communication systems, through the sensor signal acquisition and debugging system design, the main control board hardware and software design, drive device hardware and software design, control and data communication system design and integrated electromagnetic compatibility design and other aspects of the five aspects of automatic control equipment and computer communication functions.

3 System Structure Design

According to the measurement of the relationship between door handle driving torque and switch angle, operating force and torque, open/close cycle count, performance parameters of offset angle and deformation measurement requirements, determine the test equipment required to meet the design requirements of electrical structure as shown in Fig. 1.

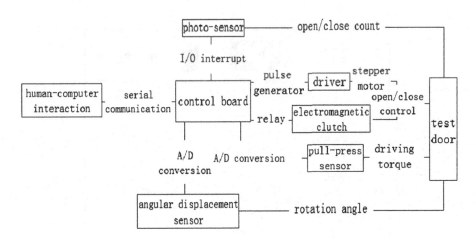

Fig. 1. Electrical control system structure design drawing.

3.1 Data Communication

We have considered the serial communication between the data, including the data between the main control board and the pull- press sensor, angular displacement sensor, photoelectric sensor contact with counting, motor speed sensor, torque sensor and so on, as well as the main control board and human-computer interaction interface. The control panel, as the control center of the whole system, is responsible for receiving command from PC start the test. The test results will be sent back to the host computer for further processing, the stepper motor driving/rotating speed, electromagnetic clutch control handle direction, through the angular displacement sensor measuring real-time handle rotation angle.

3.2 Interactive Design

The human-computer interaction interface, prepared using LabView, was designed as the control and data processing center of the whole system. Each test sends command from the human-computer interaction interface and receives the test data from the lower computer, further analyzes the test data and displays, and outputs the test report. The drive will be responsible for receiving the pulse and direction signals from the control panel, that driving the stepper motor to rotate. Each time, a pulse stepper motor rotates a step angle in the set direction to drive the test handle to turn the control pulse, and the frequency is to achieve the control handle of the rotation speed.

4 Main Control Board Design

4.1 Control Module

Test equipment main control board design block diagram was shown in Fig. 2.

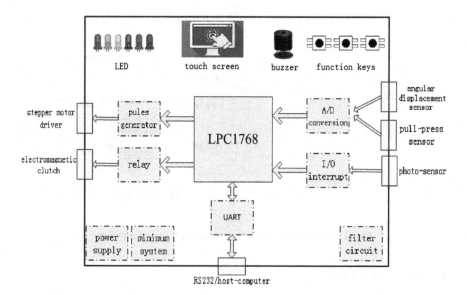

Fig. 2. Main control board design block diagram.

The system used ARM Cortex-M3 core microcontrollers for processing embedded applications that require a high degree of integration and low power consumption. The power module is responsible for providing a stable power supply for the system, including buck, rectification, filtering, etc., and power supply for both analog and digital circuits. The project was designed to the minimum system for the main control MCU, including crystal oscillator, reset circuit and so on, as well as the filter circuit including the IC power supply filter, reference power supply, A/D conversion. The system intends to RS232 serial port and the host computer communication, transmission control commands and test data. The control panel outputs the direction signal and pulse signal through the I/O port to the drive, which controls the rotation of the stepper motor.

4.2   Auxiliary Module

System designed a number of auxiliary devices, such as lights, touch screen, buzzer, common function keys. Indicators are mainly used to indicate the current working status of the system, such as power indicator, pulse light and so on. The touch screen is used to display numbers such as the number of fatigue tests, the real-time rotation angle of the handle, etc. The buzzer is used for sound prompts or alarms, such as when an error occurs in the system. Common function keys include emergency stop key, reset button, manual open, manual close and so on.

5   Software Development

The software is intended to contain four levels, namely, the hardware driver layer, the device driver layer, the protocol layer and the application layer, and use the bottom-up data transfer route to design the whole test software. The hardware driver layer is responsible for providing the set of peripheral register operations, such as A/D conversion, D/A conversion, I/O, timer, UART and other equipment driver, written as an interface function for the upper call.

The device driver layer is responsible for the operation of various external devices, such as stepper motor equipment, there will be start, stop, turn, acceleration, deceleration and other operations, these operations are packaged as a function for the protocol layer call. The protocol layer is responsible for the encapsulation of various test activities and other operations, including the measurement of the relationship between the self-positioning torque and the switching angle, the operating force and torque, the counting of the open/close cycle, the offset angle and the deformation.

A protocol command corresponds to a host computer command, and the command to the host computer is parsed and executed. The application layer will be responsible for communication with the host computer, and the host computer command analysis, and even call the protocol layer to perform the different functions, and then the results will be sent to the host computer. Test software flow chart was shown in Fig. 3.

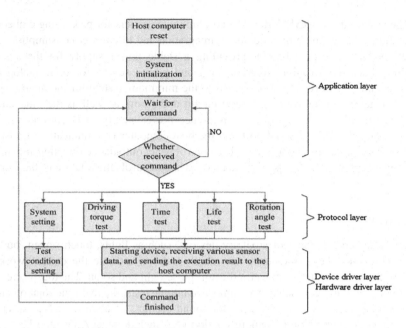

Fig. 3. Test software flow chart.

6 System Implementation

The system was conducted to demonstrate and validate the proposed strategy for testing door handle. We study the design life test interface as shown in Fig. 4. The system is to test the parameters required by the door handle, such as the number of times, speed and angle of the initial setting and monitoring.

We also carried out humanized design, developed the manual operation interface, as shown in Fig. 5, which can manually operate the opening and closing of the hand.

The operation torque test interface, as shown in Fig. 6, showed the operating torque and the corresponding opening angle in real time, and records the peak torque value in the opening process.

The system can realize the automation and intelligence of test process, which collect and process key data such as torque, angle, time and speed, as well as realize data input and output through friendly human-computer interaction interface. The system was able to adjust the speed of the power according to the test task, and when the door handle turns to the specified angle, it can be used to remove or reverse the power in time. This function, called delayed reset, ensured that all actions are performed in an orderly manner.

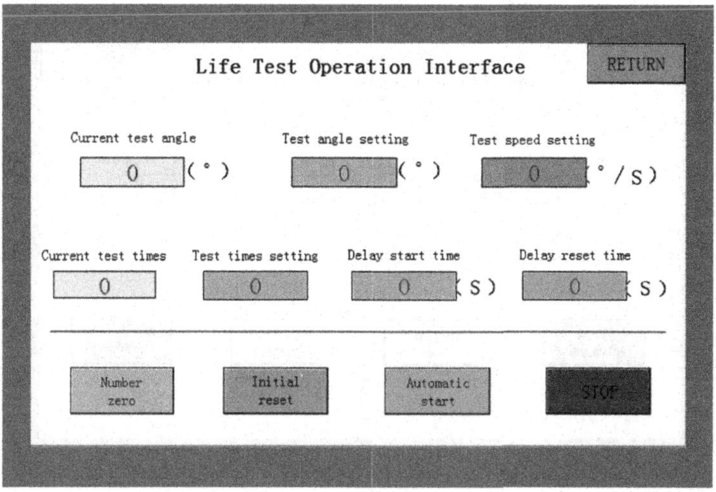

Fig. 4. Life test operation interface.

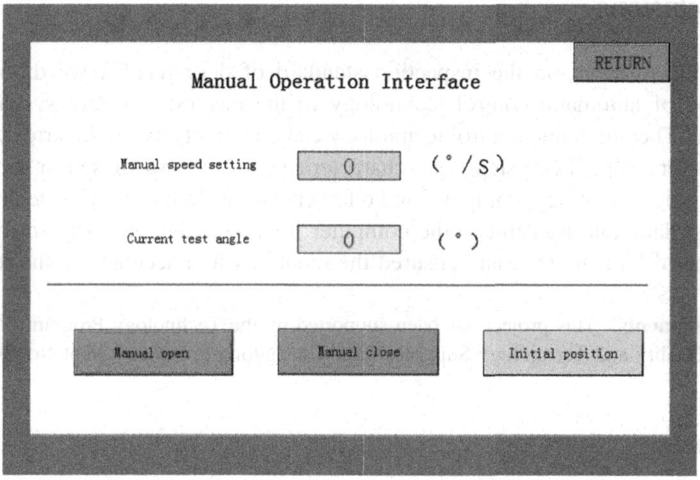

Fig. 5. Manual operation interface.

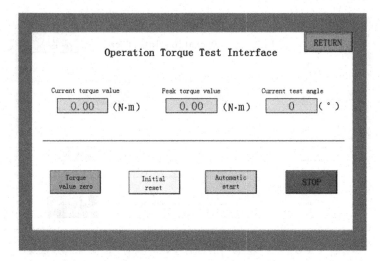

Fig. 6. Operation torque test interface.

7   Conclusions

Through the research on the inspection standard of door handle, we discussed the application of automatic control technology in the electrical control system of test equipment. The automatic control technology can effectively avoid the error caused by human factors [7]. The system was characterized by the use of sensor technology, optoelectronic technology, computer and other electronic communication technology to collect test data, and transmit to the computer for processing, so as to maximize the elimination of human error, and ensured the reliability and accuracy of the test result.

Acknowledgments. This project has been supported by the Technology Program of Administration of Quality and Technology Supervision of Guangdong Province (Grant No. 2015PZ01).

References

1. Wang, C.-L., Xu, B.L.: The development status, problems and countermeasures of the inspection and testing service industry in China. J. Technol. Market **5**(20), 297–300 (2013). (in Chinese)
2. Andreopoulos, A., Tsotsos, J.: Active vision for door localization and door opening using Playbot: a computer controlled wheelchair for people with mobility impairments. In: Computer and Robot Vision (CRV) (2008)
3. Klingbeil, E., Saxena, A., Ng, A.Y.: Learning to open new doors. In: IEEE International Conference on Intelligent Robots and Systems (IROS) (2010)
4. Scalise, L., Paone, N.: Pressure sensor matrix for indirect measurement of grip and push forces exerted on a handle. J. Elsevier **5**(44), 419–428 (2015)

5. Jain, A., Kemp, C.C.: Behaviors for robust door-opening and door-way traversal with a force-sensing mobile manipulator. In: RSS Workshop on Robotic Manipulation, Intelligence in Human Environments (2008)
6. Nagatani, K., Yuta, S.: Designing strategy and implementation of mobile manipulator control system for opening door. IEEE Int. Conf. Robot. Autom. (ICRA) **3**, 2828–2834 (1996)
7. Peterson, L., Austin, D., Kragic, D.: High-level control of a mobile manipulator for door opening. In: IEEE International Conference on Intelligent Robots and Systems (IROS) (2000)

Analysis and Solution of University Examination Arrangement Problems

Dengyuhui Li[(⊠)], Yiran Su, Huizhu Dong, Zhigang Zhang,
and Jiaji Shen

University of Science and Technology Beijing, Beijing, China
574666867@qq.com, 1114082953@qq.com, 476809697@qq.com

Abstract. In order to give the best examination arrangement, we first analyzed the relevant factors and set up the model. Meanwhile, we calculated the probability of conflict arising from the random arrangements. Later, in order to better select the time period of the subject arrangement and evaluate the results, we established the local conflict function and the global benefit function. In addition, we used the dye matching algorithm and the genetic algorithm to solve it. Finally, we provided ideas for solving this problem with other intelligent algorithms.

Keywords: Examination arrangement · Modeling · Benefit function
Dyeing matching algorithm · Genetic algorithm

1 Basic Description

In the academic administration of university, examinations usually take place during the exam week. Due to the number of subjects, limited time and classrooms, it is difficult to arrange examinations.

1.1 The Basic Principles

Combined with practical issues, there are some considerations:

a. Each student can only attend one exam at the same time
b. The examination time should be limited to a minimum period to complete the assessment of all courses;
c. All classes of the same course should be arranged at the same period;
d. Required course with a large number of candidates may be pre-arranged for a certain period of time;
e. The exam periods in each class should be as uniform and long as possible to ensure full review of candidates;
f. The last exam in each class should be arranged for as long as a day or two before the end of the exam week;
g. Courses with special requirements are arranged in special classroom exams;
h. Some courses needs longtime to assess, accounting for multiple time periods;
i. Some courses open the limitations of natural classes, and re-group classes, requiring special consideration.

© Springer Nature Singapore Pte Ltd. 2018
H. Yuan et al. (Eds.): GSKI 2017, CCIS 849, pp. 670–683, 2018.
https://doi.org/10.1007/978-981-13-0896-3_66

1.2   Instantiation Study

Take into account the arrangements for teaching week and curriculum areas to Beijing University of Science and Technology, for example. In our model, we set to complete the exam within two weeks; each working day is divided into 9: 00–11: 00,13: 30–15:30 and 16:00 to 18:00 three periods for arranging exams. If there is a holiday during the week, the available periods will be reduced. In the curriculum, the course type and credits together determine the importance of the course, and the more important course, the longer intervals for review are requested.

For this examination arrangement, the analysis is as follows: First, we hope to make full use of teaching resources, to achieve a uniform distribution of examination time with shorter test periods. Second, to the executive class as a unit for electives, re-students and cross-disciplinary candidates as long as conflict-free courses to meet, temporarily not consider the uniform degree of the examination time. Third, the factors involved in this issue are course credit, the number of classes for routine course, the type of course, the periods, the interval between the two time points, and so on. In the meantime, we need to use local functions to determine the advantages and disadvantages of different subjects can be placed in the specific position. In addition, a global benefit function needs to be used to judge the overall evaluation effect.

Based on the above analysis, we arrange them in descending order of importance, which is considered in class as a unit, that is, each class can have at most one exam at the same time. Based on the premise that there is no conflict between courses, the examination model is established in this paper, ensuring the uniform distribution of adjacent exams, assuring review time, fully embodies the human feelings. To this end, we have established local and global benefit function, which will help optimize the evaluation in a timely manner.

2   Factors and the Model

2.1   Factor Analysis

Exam arrangements involve a variety of objects, including student set A, course set C, time set T and course selection set S, which are the most basic but important parts. Based on the course selection, we establish a many-to-many relationship between students and courses set (Fig. 1).

Exam arrangements involve a variety of objects, including student set A, course set C, time set T and course selection set S, which are the most basic but important parts. Based on the course selection, we establish a many-to-many relationship between students and courses set.

Due to the large number of students, we think the class set B as a unit to consider the relationship between classes and courses. Each class has an additional attribute: the number of students 'p'. After that, we take the student as a unit and investigate the refreshed courses one by one to ensure that there is no conflict of time.

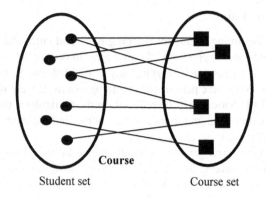

Fig. 1. The relationship between students and courses

Course set has the following properties:

(1) Course code u
(2) Credit g (ranging from 1 to 4)
(3) The degree of importance l (Considering the course's credit, class and total number of classes, course categories, give the degree of importance index, the index ranges from 1 to 5)
(4) Other marks (such as advanced mathematics or basic foreign languages, whose candidates are nearly thousand, and should be occupied for a period independently. Some of the lab exams need to occupy multiple time periods, etc.)

Time set T has the following properties:

(1) Time parameter t_{ijk}: where i indicates the order of the week (i = 1, 2), j indicates the order of the day (j = 1, 2, 3, 4, 5), and k indicates the order of the Time points (k = 1, 2, 3).
(2) Time number n: a total of 30 time periods, we can calculate the number based on time parameters, the formula is as follows:

$$n = 15 \times (i - 1) + 3 \times (j - 1) + k \qquad (1)$$

(3) Time interval T: The time interval between two time points can be calculated according to the time parameter, and the calculation formula is as follows:

$$T(2) = \begin{cases} 2 \times |n_1 - n_2| + 2 \times |j_1 - j_2| & i_1 = i_2, j_1 \neq j_2 \\ 2 \times |n_1 - n_2| i_1 = i_2, j_1 = j_2, k_1 \, or \, k_2 = 1 \\ 0 & i_1 = i_2, j_1 = j_2, k_1, k_2 \neq 1 \\ 2 \times |n_1 - n_2| + 2 \times (7 + j_2 - j_1) + 12 \times |i_1 - i_2| i_1 \neq i_2 \end{cases} \qquad (2)$$

The adjacency matrix can be used to describe the course selection S. Assume there are 'n' courses in 'm' classes, and the courses should be conducted at 't' (t ≤ n) periods. We use two matrices to store the correspondence between the class information and the course exam time. The values of the matrix elements are as follows:

$$s_{ij} = \begin{cases} 1, & \text{The } i - \text{th class needs to take the } j - \text{th course} \\ 0, & \text{otherwise} \end{cases} \tag{3}$$

$$i = 1, 2 \ldots m, \ j = 1, 2, \ldots n$$

$$y_{ij} = \begin{cases} 1, & \text{The } j - \text{th course is arranged at the } i - \text{th period} \\ 0, & \text{otherwise} \end{cases} \tag{4}$$

$$i, j = 1, 2, \ldots n$$

In order for each exam to be tested only once and all exams have been completed, there should be:

$$\sum_{i=1}^{n} y_{ij} = 1, \ j = 1, 2, \ldots n \tag{5}$$

In order for each class to choose the course exam time does not conflict, there should be:

$$\sum_{j=1}^{n} s_{kj} y_{ij} \leq 1, \ \begin{array}{l} k = 1, 2, \ldots m, \\ i = 1, 2, \ldots n, \end{array} \tag{6}$$

In order to meet the requirements of the examination field, there should be:

$$\sum_{i=t+1}^{n} y_{ij} = 0, \ j = 1, 2, \ldots n \tag{7}$$

2.2 Model Establishment

Among the questions we discussed, the number of exams has been determined. We hope that the schedule for the final exam can be as suitable and uniform as possible. However, the rigid constraints in the course of examinations and the formulas (5), (6) and (7) are consistent. Therefore, the problem will be properly transformed, satisfying the above two types of constraints, making the minimum number of exams. In this way, in the subsequent adjustment, each day can be adjusted as a whole, to avoid too concentrated examination day, after that, we will continue to make adjustments to different sessions on the same day. And in the adjustment process, alternative exam days and exams are not the only ones, so we give the local and global benefit functions to better choose where to adjust and to evaluate the results of the final adjustment.

Take the minimum number of exams as the goal and consider the optimization problem, and we have:

$$\min f(Y) = \sum_{i=1}^{t} \sum_{j=1}^{n} i \cdot y_{ij} \tag{8}$$

$$
\text{s.t.}\begin{cases}
\sum_{i=1}^{t} y_{ij} = 1, & j = 1, 2, \ldots n \\
& k = 1, 2, \ldots m, \\
\sum_{j=1}^{n} s_{kj} y_{ij} \leq 1, & i = 1, 2, \ldots n \\
y_{ij} = \{0, 1\}
\end{cases} \tag{9}
$$

Let $Y = \left(Y_1^T, Y_2^T, \ldots Y_n^T\right)^T$, $Y_i = \left(y_{i1}, y_{i2}, \ldots y_{in}\right)^T$. Well, the above planning problem can be expressed as:

$$
\min f(Y) = \sum_{i=1}^{t} i * \left(\sum_{j=1}^{n} y_{ij}\right) \tag{10}
$$

$$
\text{s.t.}\begin{cases}
EY_1 + EY_2 + \ldots + EY_t = I_n \\
SY_1 \leq I_m \\
SY_2 \leq I_m \\
\quad \ldots \\
SY_n \leq I_m \\
y_{ij} = \{0, 1\}
\end{cases} \tag{11}
$$

Where E is an n-th order identity matrix; I_n is an n-dimensional one-dimensional column vector whose elements are each 1, and I_m is an m-dimensional one-dimensional column vector whose elements are each 1.

3   Conflict Resolution

During the exam arrangements artificially, some students may have two or more exams in a certain period of time. We define the probability of conflict, that is, given the number of students, the number of exam periods, and the enrollment of each student, we can calculate the number of conflicting test plans among all the test plans.

3.1   Solutions

We use C# to simulate when the amount of data is small. First, given a random five classes, each class has 30 people; given 15 courses, each person up to choose five courses. The 15 classes are scheduled to be completed within a total of 30 sessions in two weeks (excluding weekends). We define that when more than 10% of the people have test conflicts, the corresponding test plan will be recorded as a conflict plan. Even with few data, there are still 30^{15} kinds of situation; we only choose 100,000 of them.

3.2   Conflict Function

For a randomly given test arrangements for each student to judge, if there is a student exam conflicting, then count, for each conflict, the count plus one. For each test plan, it is judged as a conflict plan if more than 10% of the total number of people in conflict.

3.3 Conflict Probability Calculation

According to the above description, we define p as the probability of conflict, count is the number of conflict test programs in the simulation process, and n is the number of simulations. We have:

$$p = \frac{count}{n} \tag{12}$$

3.4 Program Simulation

Of the 100,000 random scenarios given, more than 87% of the exam scheduling scenarios generated conflicts. In the figure, the abscissa indicates the number of simulations and the ordinate indicates the collision probability (Table 1). We find that when the number of simulations is small, the probability of conflict changes very rapidly. However, as the number of simulations increases, the conflict probability begins to stabilize and slowly approaches the theoretical value (Fig. 2).

Table 1. Conflict probability calculation

Classes	Periods	Courses	Selection	Students	Value
5	30	5	15	150	0.874
5	30	5	10	150	0.746
5	40	5	10	150	0.689
5	40	5	15	150	0.864

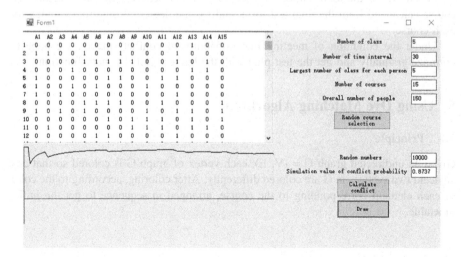

Fig. 2. The results of simulation

4 Benefit Functions

4.1 Local Benefit Function

Put a course into the test schedule, in general, there are multiple locations to choose, in order to choose a better location, we define a local benefit function to evaluate the pros and cons of each location

$$f = \frac{a}{T_{fro} \times l_{fro} + T_{be} \times l_{be}} + \left| T_{fro} \times l_{fro} - T_{be} \times l_{be} \right| \tag{13}$$

Among them, the smaller the value of f, the better this position, where T_{fro} represents the time interval between the current position and the point in time of the closest subject to it before, which we call it the closest previous lesson, and similarly, there is the closest following class. l_{fro} is said the importance index of the closest previous lesson, T_{be} and l_{be} are similar. And 'a' is a constant, owning different value during different situations.

4.2 Global Benefit Function

During the exam arrangement, we also need to make a comprehensive evaluation of the overall exam schedule.

Therefore, we define the global benefit function as follows:

$$Z = \sum_{i=1}^{m} f_i \times l_i \tag{14}$$

Where 'm' is the total number of courses, f is the local benefit function for each course calculated from the final test form, and l is the degree of importance index for each course.

Under the condition of meeting the probability of conflict smaller, we hope to optimize gradually and get the test plan with the highest global benefit function.

5 Using Dye Matching Algorithm

5.1 Principle

Given an undirected graph G = (V, E), each vertex of graph G is colored so that any adjacent two vertices in G are colored differently. After coloring, according to the color of each element corresponding to the course, arranged in sequence to get the initial timetable.

5.2   Procedure

First of all, suppose a total of 'm' classes to participate in the exam, a total of 'n' exams and 't' test exam time periods. There is a correspondence matrix $S = (s_{ij})_{m \times n}$ between classes and exams.

5.2.1   Pretreatment

Course corresponding to the label set is $I = \{1, 2, \ldots, n\}$, take the class as a unit, take the course-exam relationship $G = (V, E)$, V is the course set, the two ends v_i and v_j of the element e_{ij} in E are the commonly chosen courses, they cannot be put on the same time period. Adjacency matrix of G, $A = (a_{ij})_{n \times n}$ is 0–1 Symmetric matrix: when $i \neq j$ and there is edge e_{ij}, $a_{ij} = 1$; otherwise, $a_{ij} = 0$. Dye set $C = \{c_1, c_2, \ldots c_n\}$: $c_i \neq c_j (i \neq j, i, j \in I)$. According to the importance of the course, the elements in V are arranged in descending order.

5.2.2   Basic Algorithm

a. Let $C_i = C$ be the to-be-colorized set of v_i, and initialize $i = 1$.
b. Take the first element c_i^* of C_i to dye v_i, and let $V = V \backslash \{v_i\}$. Find the undyed point in V, if v_j is the neighbor of v_i, take $C_j = C_j \backslash \{c_i^*\}$, $i = i + 1$.
c. If $i < n$, go to b; if $i = n$, go to d.
d. Take the first element c_n^* of C_n to dye v_n. Assuming a total of p different colors are used, there must be $p \leq n$.
e. Output v-c corresponding set of relations and the corresponding color set $C^* = \{c_1, c_2, \ldots c_p | c_i \neq c_j (i \neq j)\} \subset C$.

5.2.3   Time Allocation Algorithm

a. Initialization data, let $i = 1$, $T = \{t_1, t_2, \ldots t_t\}$
b. Take the element c_i^* in C^*, and find the course 'v' corresponds to the curriculum concentrated courses. (may have more than one).
c. When $i = 1$, randomly select a time sequence t_i^* in T, put the corresponding course exam time of c_i^* to t_i^*. $T = T \backslash \{t_i^*\}$; When $i \neq 1$, select t_i^* satisfying the smallest value of f, and place the appropriate course.
d. The matrix will be updated to the column of the scheduled exam to 0. If $W = 0$, stop, otherwise, $i = i + 1$, go to b.

5.3   Evaluation

Using the algorithm of color matching to solve it, the non-conflicting courses can be arranged at the same time to the greatest extent. By this way, the number of the test sessions can be minimized, however, this will result in excessive number of courses in the same session and uneven distribution of the number of courses in different sessions, as a result, where the number of exams is limited, there may be situations where the number of exams taken is greater than the capacity of the exam room.

6 Using Genetic Algorithm

As a random search algorithm, genetic algorithm draws on a number of biological concepts, through optimization, coding, selection, crossover, mutation and other processes continue to find the best solution, commonly used to solve the NP problem.

6.1 Problem Setting

We first set up a global constant matrix according to the periods and courses set, and then establish a correlation matrix of course conflicts according to the course selection so as to facilitate the subsequent calculation (Tables 2 and 3).

Table 2. Periods setting

Number	Date	Time period	Review time
t_1	Friday	8:30–10:30	15
t_2	Friday	13:30–15:30	2
t_3	Friday	16:00–18:00	0
t_4	Monday	8:30–10:30	15
t_5	Monday	13:30–15:30	2
t_6	Monday	16:00–18:00	0
t_7	Tuesday	8:30–10:30	4
t_8	Tuesday	13:30–15:30	2
t_9	Tuesday	16:00–18:00	0

Table 3. Courses setting

	Degree of importance				Marks
	Credit	Number of students	Category	Index	
u_1	6	244	Professional course	5	Fixed at t_1
u_2	5	113	Professional course	4	
u_3	4	178	Professional course	4	
u_4	4	156	Compulsory course	3	
u_5	2	302	Compulsory course	2	
u_6	2	154	Compulsory course	2	
u_7	2	58	Elective courses	1	
u_8	2	63	Elective courses	1	
u_9	2	60	Elective courses	1	Non-participate

We first set up a global constant matrix according to the periods and courses set, and then establish a correlation matrix of course conflicts according to the course selection so as to facilitate the subsequent calculation (Table 4).

Table 4. Couse selection setting

	Courses									Number of students
	v_1	v_2	v_3	v_4	v_5	v_6	v_7	v_8	v_9	
u_1	✓		✓	✓	✓		✓		✓	30
u_2	✓		✓	✓	✓		✓			28
u_3	✓	✓			✓	✓				33
u_4		✓			✓	✓				28
u_5	✓	✓	✓		✓					25
u_6		✓			✓	✓				30
u_7	✓	✓	✓		✓					30
u_8	✓		✓	✓	✓					35
u_9	✓		✓	✓	✓		✓	✓		30
u_{10}	✓		✓	✓	✓		✓			33

6.2 Coding and Initialization

Rather than using conventional binary coding, we take a natural coding approach that treats each exam schedule as one chromosome, and the course scheduled for each period as a single gene. Each population contains several solutions, which are chromosomes (Fig. 3).

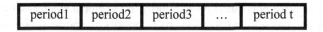

period1	period2	period3	...	period t

Fig. 3. The Structure of chromosomes

The initialization process has a great influence on the steps after the algorithm. Generally speaking, with the higher the fitness of the initial population, the faster the convergence speed of the corresponding algorithm is. For the initial test plan, we adopt a combination of the stained matching algorithm and random generation, resulting in 25 kinds of solutions, while the other 5 kinds of programs will be generated by randomly arranging the course to the time period. At the same time, when each program is given, the course should be judged whether there is a conflict.

6.3 Fitness Function and Conflict Function

Fitness function is used to determine whether the results meet the requirements of the basis. The more uniform the examination, the greater the fitness function is. In previous sections, we have defined a global benefit function that can be taken directly as a global fitness function. Unlike other problems, the local efficiency function we proposed earlier can be regarded as a local fitness function, that is said, be used as a reference for optimization in the subsequent process, which can effectively improve the efficiency of the algorithm.

The conflict function is used to determine whether the resulting test scheduling curriculum conflicts. During the initialization, crossover and mutation process, it should be considered and tested.

6.4 Selection, Crossover and Mutation

The selection process takes the roulette method, that is, according to the ratio of the local benefit function to the global benefit function, assign choose probability to each individual. It not only guarantees excellent individual retention, but also maintains the diversity of the population.

The crossover process adopts the method of adaptive crossover, that is, the crossover probability is not a constant, but changing with the fitness function. When the fitness is low, the crossover probability is large, which can guarantee the problem quickly converge to feasible solution in the early period. At the same time, the crossover probability will decrease when the fitness is high, so as not to undermine the structure of the solution.

Compared with the crossover probability, the mutation probability is very low, often taking 0.01 to 0.1. Because of less favorable mutation, the effect of the optimal solution convergence is weak. We take a single point mutation, then randomly select a course from a random chromosome and change the allocation of time periods. If the global benefit function is enhanced, the variant individuals are kept; otherwise, the next iteration is performed.

In the process of crossover and mutation, choose the better one based on the benefit function. The selected population gives priority to the global efficiency function of the low value, while the selected location gives priority to the lessons with low local benefit function value. Since MATLAB is superior to other programming language in the handling of arrays, we use MATLAB for major programming (Table 5).

6.5 Parameter Setting

Table 5. Parameters setting

Population size	30
Chromosome length	8
The maximum number of iterations	200
Cross probability	0.6
Mutation probability	0.01
benefit function parameters a	5

7 Other Algorithms to Solve

7.1 Ant Colony Algorithm

The basic idea of ant colony algorithm comes from the shortest path principle of ants seeking food in nature. When ants look for food sources, they release pheromones in the path they walk through so that other ants within a certain range can perceive them. The more pheromones there are, the higher the probability that an ant chooses this path is, resulting in an increase in the number of pheromones on this path and an increase in the probability that the ant will follow this path.

Specific steps are as follows:

(1) Simplify the initial alignment of the algorithm
First of all, we use greedy algorithm to divide the most important subjects into all periods, and the two subjects with the same class attribute are not adjacent.

(2) Pheromone initialization
The pheromone concentration Ω between the initial point and the point is the same as 1, and if there are two classes of class attribute conflicts, the pheromone between two points is 0.

(3) The first iteration
Each ant chooses the first iteration from the point that the initial greedy algorithm has assigned the test time attribute. The probability of each step is determined by the pheromone and roulette method is used for selection.

(4) Pheromone concentration adjustment
When performing the review time attribute between the subjects' exams for the same class attribute at each step of analysis, the increase in concentration is proportional to the length of review time and inversely proportional to the importance of both subjects.

(5) Multiple iterations
Iteration m times, when the objective evolutionary trend is not obvious, the optimal solution is output, otherwise m = m + 1, continue iteration.

7.2   Simulated Annealing Algorithm to Solve the Train of Thought

The simulated annealing algorithm is derived from the principle of solid annealing. According to the Metropolis criterion, the probability that the particle tends to be in equilibrium at temperature T is $e^{-\frac{\Delta E}{kT}}$, where E is the internal energy at temperature T, ΔE is its amount of changes and k is Boltzmann's constant. With solid annealing simulation combinatorial optimization problems, the internal energy E is simulated as the objective function value f, the temperature T evolves into the control parameters t, that is, use the simulated annealing algorithm for solving combinatorial optimization problems.

The main steps are as follows:

(1) The formation of the initial course schedule
According to a given time or computer-generated time, for each examination in a limited cycle to find the appropriate classroom, and each examination cannot be arranged twice a day, generating a viable initial solution. The initial solution does not require that all exams be ranked.

(2) Design the appropriate optimization function for optimization goals, the use of annealing process to achieve optimization goals.

The first objective function f_1 is equal to the total number of non-scheduled exams, the second objective function

$$f_2 = \sum\nolimits_{c_i \in C} K_i \tag{15}$$

Where $C = \{c_1, c_2, \ldots c_n\}$ the number of times an exam c_i was ranked in the adjacent day in a week is K_i, the third objective function

$$f_3 = \sum\nolimits_{c_i \in C} (A_i - a_i) * \omega_3 + (B_i - b_i) * \omega_4 \tag{16}$$

Among them, a_i and A_i are respectively for exam c_i's demand and actual allocation of classroom capacity.

So, the total objective function is expressed as:

$$f = f_1 * \omega_1 + f_2 * \omega_2 + f_3 \tag{17}$$

Among them, $\omega_1, \omega_2, \omega_3, \omega_4$ are the weights. In practice, we will choose the appropriate weights according to the actual needs of the specific examination.

Acknowledgments. In the process of research, we should especially thank Mr. Zhang for his guidance and supervision. Without his help, we can't understand the pattern of the exam arrangement in our school. It will be hard for us to stick, and apply our model to reality. At the same time, we are grateful to become each other's partners. We read the related literature or books together, and discuss for the model and algorithms. Besides, thank you to our school for providing us with a good learning environment.

References

1. Shasha, Y.: Research on resource conflict optimization algorithm for college examination system. Wirel. Internet Technol. **03**, 66–68 (2016). (in Chinese)
2. Li, C.: An improved graph algorithm for the examination of college entrance examination under the credit system environment. Appl. Comput. **24**(03), 220–225 (2015). (in Chinese)
3. Long, H., Tan, C.: Requisition system based on genetic algorithm. Appl. Comput. Syst. **23** (01), 184–187 (2014). (in Chinese)
4. Deyan, W.: Optimization of dynamic test arrangements algorithm. Wuxi Voc. Tech. Coll. **12** (06), 14–16 (2013). (in Chinese)
5. Deyan, W.: Study on dynamic test arrangement based on particle swarm optimization. Digit. Commun. **40**(05), 11–13 (2013). (in Chinese)
6. Wen, L.: Design and implementation of college course arranging system based on genetic algorithm. University of Electronic Science and Technology of China (2012)
7. Niu, Y., Yan, G., Xie, G., Xie, K.: Research on genetic algorithms based on knowledge. J. Taiyuan Univ. Technol. **42**(02), 121–125 (2011). (in Chinese)
8. Cai, M.: Design and implementation of automatic college test-taking algorithm. Comput. Eng. Appl. **46**(24), 69–72 (2010). (in Chinese)
9. Yong, O., Tao, L.: Design and implementation of college automatic examination system. J. Hubei Univ. Technol. **24**(04), 67–70 (2009). (in Chinese)

10. Ling, T.: Design and implementation of university automatic test engine. Comput. Eng. Des. **10**, 2443–2445 (2007). (in Chinese)
11. Qing, W., Yawen, Z., Wei, Z.: Staining-matching algorithm for college examination papers. J. Univ. Shanghai Sci. Technol. **02**, 157–161 (2005). (in Chinese)
12. Zhu, S., Cao, S., Zou, X.: Mathematical model and its algorithm for scheduling problems. Syst. Eng. **02**, 62–65 (1999). (in Chinese)
13. Wang, T., Su, Z., Xia, Y., Qin, B., Hamdi, M.: Towards cost-effective and low latency data center network architecture. J. Comput. Commun. **82**, 1–12 (2016)
14. Wang, T., Xia, Y., Muppala, J., Hamdi, M.: Achieving energy efficiency in data centers using an artificial intelligence abstraction model. IEEE Trans. Cloud Comput. (2015)

Analyzing the Information Behavior Under the Complexity Science Management Theory

Rongying Zhao[1,2(✉)], Mingkun Wei[1,2(✉)], and Danyang Li[1,2]

[1] Research Center for Chinese Science Evaluation, Wuhan University,
Wuhan 430072, China
zhaorongying@126.com,
weimingkun24@163.com, whusimldy@163.com
[2] School of Information Management, Wuhan University,
Wuhan 430072, China

Abstract. Information behavior is a complicated process. Using the method of complexity science management to study the information behavior has important theoretical significance and practical guiding value. This paper provides a new perspective for information behavior, and introduces the theory of complexity science management, method, and the basic thoughts to solve the problems. The application of complexity science management in the research of information behavior was expounded from three aspects that includes theoretical system, research methods, research process to analyze the transformation of information behavior paradigm based on complexity science management.

Keywords: Information behavior · Complexity science management
Complex network

Classification code: G350

1 Introduction

General systems theory was proposed by Ludwig von Bertalanffy who is the Austrian biologist, to provide alternatives for conventional models of organization. H.S. Tsien, a Chinese scholar, put forward the giant system to open the door for the problem of complexity and complex system research, which had contributed to study complexity for scholars from the perspective of science. In 1980s, the complexity science was proposed in the world, and soon it became the hot spot and front of the world's scientific development. There were many scholars who discuss the complexity science will bring new challenge to the development of management. Cheng Siwei discussed the relationship between complexity science and management, analyzed the application

Rongying Zhao, PhD, is a professor at the School of Information Management, Wuhan University. Her research interests focus on knowledge management and competitive intelligence, Informetrics and scientific evaluation.

prospect of complexity science in management, which included group decision, technology innovation, economic development, etc. [1].

With the development of information science, it is inevitable requirement of management theory and practice to introduce the complexity science to management. The integration of complexity science and management science has led to the birth of complexity science management. Complexity Science Management (CSM) is a new management thoughts put forward by Professor Xu Xusong according to the time feature of the 21st Century following the thoughts of scientific management, humanistic management, strategic competition, Japanese management skills and learning organization [2]. She pointed out that the complexity science management made the split mode of thinking into the system mode of thinking from simplification to diversification based on the new mode of thinking, new observation point of view, to study the ideas of management, theory and methods of management. The complex scientific management highlights the systematic thinking pattern, whose way of thinking is centered with holistic view as the core, combining and integrating various resources both within and out of the system in order to change the existing resources and ability of conversing resources to fortune as well as changing the output of resources aiming to make the system a competitive one. During the whole procedure, integration and collocation are of great significance, which will make a great difference when the differences lie in the aforesaid two aspects. Complexity science management put forward the holistic view from the perspective of system thinking. The holistic view of complexity science management mainly refers to the organization when thinking about the problems should stand at the height of the overall system to analyze the problem of the starting point and destination. The holistic view shows a new perspective of dealing with problems. All the elements in the system should not be split, but a complex interaction of various elements. We should stand at a higher level to understand the question from the perspective of the holistic system to solve and analyze them when we considering the problems. Based on CSM to research information user behavior, the paper proposed information behavior as a complicated process and pointed out that it provided a new perspective for researchers.

Over the past decades complexity science management has evolved from purely theoretical contributions towards applications with information behavior. Complexity science management is based on classical theory, experience theory and the pure science which is absorption and integration of systems theory, rational theory and latest development of humanities, with the complexity of the nature and society as the new science that studies the complexity and complex systems. Complexity science management studies the complex problems in the real world by integration methods, in order to reveal the structure of complex system, understand the subsystem, the characteristics and mechanism of the system. The object of the complex scientific management is the complex systems on the social level, such as social and economic systems, financial systems, enterprise organization and managerial system and so on, whose basic theories include the holistic view, the outlook on new resource concept, integration theory, interactive theory, theories of disorder - order theory, the thinking mode of which is the systematic thinking. The complexity science management has been paid attention to by the scholars because of the new way of thinking and analysis.

The theoretical study on information behavior can be traced back to the beginning of the 20th century, and has a history of roughly one hundred years so far. The information sources at the early stage were so limited, and the researches on the users' information behavior put emphasis on the studies of how the literature has been utilized. As the object of information service, information users' are simply the recipients as well as the receivers of information, whose purpose is doing something related with information activities by making use of information to satisfy the information demands from individuals. Wison mentioned in his research about the information user behavior research development and stage division that the information user was the focus of some attention, but the attention was directed towards the systems used, most of the reports and papers related to the documentation of science and to technical methods of handling the documents, when the Royal Society Scientific Information Conference was held in 1948 [3]. The outstanding exception to the general run of papers was that by Professor J. D Bernal on Preliminary analysis of pilot questionnaire on the use of scientific literature [4]. Information user behavior research in this period was also carried out by the Aslib Research Group, which included Margaret Slater and John Martyn that undertook a number of projects from the mid-1960s onwards, for example, Martyn's investigation into literature searching by scientists [5] and Slater's study of social scientists [6]. The principal research methods employed were questionnaire-based surveys and interviews and, in large part, there was little or no attention to theoretical conceptualization: the focus was on the discovery and description of aspects of library and document usage [3]. The situation began to change in the late 1970s and early1980s, through the example of the INISS Project [7] and Wilson's advocacy in 'on user studies and information needs' [8]. When reorganizing research results of 85 scholars form 10 different countries, Karen E. Fisher and others found that most of them are construction of theoretical model and researches and introduced 70 structural models for information search, management, sharing and usage [10]. "Knowledge" shows information activity has obvious attribute of knowledge and the acquirement, sharing and innovation of knowledge are also closely connected with user's information activity. With the occurrence of "performance" and "design", paying attention to the user perception and experience to the system design is becoming increasingly important and gradually changes the design concept into user demand oriented. "Context" is also a popular keyword of oversea researches which distinguishes specific situations, such as daily living environment, complex multi task environment, network environment, etc. After 2000, the network user's information behavior has become a new hotspot of the research and network users' information behavior continue to emerge, reveals the impact factors of network user's information behavior, and to improve the efficiency of network user's information behavior is very important. In the past 10 years, the customer's information demand on medical field has become the center of researches. For example, Leydon, GM and others analyzed characteristics of the information needs of cancer patients and their psychological impact through interview while Gonzalez, Al and others analyzed the information requirements, contents and characteristics of primary care physicians with survey [11, 12]. In this paper, we study on information user behavior from the perspective of complexity science management.

2 Data Collection and Mythology

We have collected research output data for "complexity science management" theme from Web of Science (WOS) for the period of 25 years i.e., 1992–2016. In WOS, we found a total of 1908 records as a result of the search query [TS = Complexity Science Management, Timespan = 1992–2016, Indexes = SCI-EXPANED, SSCI, A&HCI]. The data collection comprises of records of the type article, review. These papers can easily be located in Fig. 1.

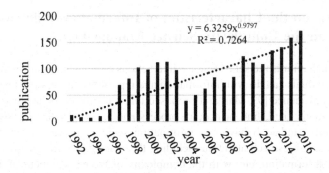

Fig. 1. Annual statistical literature documents related CSM (for the papers from 1992 to 2016)

Complexity science management is composed of complex phenomena, complex problems, complex systems and complex environment. It is necessary for the development of the theory and practice of information behavior to introduce the complexity science management. In this paper, we use the knowledge domain visualization software CiteSpace to depict the evolution of complexity science management research by analyzing the key-words (see Fig. 2). In CiteSpace network mapping, a landmark node was defined as the main field which can be identified by different size.

Fig. 2. A time-zone view of complexity science management, showing the prominent lines of research.

From the Fig. 2, the research scope of complexity science management is more and more extensive, especially including mode of science, decision making, strategy, information behavior, information system and etc. in the era of big data, the use of complexity science method to study is very common. It is helpful to understand the development trend of information behavior from the perspective of complexity science management. Information behavior is an important part of the information science. The research on information behavior is conductive to the further development of information science.

3 Analysis on the Characteristics of Information Behavior Based on the Complexity Science Management

Information behavior is the set of actions, interactions or behaviors that an individual or group of individuals can do with information and represents an important research area for information science [9]. Margaret proposed that information behavior is concerned with how humans need, find or acquire process and eventually use information. The most frequently studied behavior is information seeking, however, other behaviors have also received research attention including the sharing, avoiding, organization and re-finding of information, etc. with the complexity of the environment of information dissemination and exchange of information system, the complexity of internal system and interactions, the user information behavior had changed greatly in research object, the research subject, research process and research content. From the perspective of theory of complexity science management, it has mainly the following characteristics for user information behavior as a theory of complex system.

(1) The Complex Diversity of Information Behavior Research Object
    The objects of information behavior include information seeking behavior, information retrieval, information communication and etc. the study of modern information behavior presents unprecedented complexity and diversity accompanied with the production of information and knowledge, dissemination and use of change. At present, more and more kinds of individuals and organizations involved in the information activities, the scope and depth of the information behavior's activities continue to expand. To take advantage of advanced technology, methods and means to satisfy the demand of user's knowledge and improve the user's personalized information service. The current hot research focuses on information behavior model, information requirements, information retrieval, information systems and design, etc. These researches focus on information query behavior, consumer behavior, information needs, information retrieval systems, information services, information resources, youth groups, information retrieval, and theoretical framework and so on.

(2) The Complexity of Information Behavior Research Subject
    The enrichment and complicated phenomenon of information behavior under the environment of big data requires the researchers attach importance to the thinking of their own information philosophy, philosophy thinking and logic analysis based on information facts. It should actively participate in information activities

to analyze the role and impact of exploration and study user information behavior process. Thus, in the study of information behavior, user is both research subject and object, which has double status. Information behavior begin to change from passive to active under the environment of complexity science management. The status of users has changed, to be part of main body of information behavior. The relationship between users and information behavior is becoming more and more complicated with the development of information science. The users' knowledge structure, cognitive ability, cognitive style and judgment directly affect the methods and research ideas of information behavior.

More and more users involved in researching information behavior with emerging information technology is widely used in information science. Although information behavior is a component of information science, technology and users have been closely together in the information science research organic system, which plays the better function in cooperation, harmonization, exploration. Therefore, information behavior become the main component of information science.

(3) The Dynamic Complexity of Information Behavior Research

Information behavior is changed from linear to nonlinear, multipath and interactive motion mode. It is difficult to grasp the rules and characteristics of information behavior phenomenon under the environment of complexity, which needs to research from the perspective of complexity science management. For example, researching on information seeking and searching for specific theoretical framework (social network theory, actor network theory, cultural historical activity theory, type theory etc.), and information seeking, search, use and sharing under specific context (health, education, business, public service and emergency services), the network virtual society study on information seeking and search; researching information system designed to meet the needs of users of information sharing, social media and collaborative behavior (CIB); the course of study gradually from system centered over the "user centric" to "knowledge centric" that are presented to the user perspective the trend of population subdivision, but tools is slightly different with the development of intelligent and interactive information. Information science is to study the process of acquisition and utilization of information for users. In the process of information behavior, it is an integration for information awareness, recognition, exchange, analysis, storage, processing, regeneration, etc. and it is influenced by the values, culture, society, economy, technology and other factors. The whole research process is complex, difficult to predict, and full of uncertainty.

(4) The Multi Discipline Integration of Information Behavior

In the development of information science, the compatibility and interdisciplinary of information science is the essential feature of information behavior. Information behavior has developed at an unprecedented rapid in human society, closely related to information theory. Under this condition, information behavior continues to absorb and learn from other disciplines, which involves specialized types of applications, different structure areas. The research content of information behavior presents metrology, psychology, sociology, science and technology, etc.

with the development and changes of information subject, information object, information process, and the complex problems cannot be solved by a single discipline. It requires extensive absorb and draw the theory and method from other disciplines, in order to effectively solve the problems of information science under the condition of complexity. Thus, it is very necessary to study information behavior by using the method of complexity science management.

(5) Feedback of Information Behavior Research

The complex scientific theory deems that the complex system always includes the dynamic mechanism of positive feedback and negative feedback, and conversely the two kinds of feedback will influence behaviors of the complex system. The traits of feedback require the system to relentlessly offer the information feedback and correct the errors in accordance with the actual situations. Under general circumstances, negative feedback is the stable support for the continuous research and efficiently enables the information behavior research to be orderly conducted in virtue of negative feedback and possibly makes the group behavior get the comprehensive and justified assessment, which benefits the holistic work of the information behavior research and accelerates the evolution level of research from lower to higher.

(6) Openness of Information Behavior Research

In view of the complex scientific theory, all things are not existing in isolation, and are always getting contact with surroundings by positive interrelations and interactions, in which, the exchanges of information and energy are ongoing without any stops. Openness acts as the base of the system evolution, only when all things are open, and then experience the fluctuation and steer away for the balance status can they come to be well-aligned and prosperous. This kind of openness refers to two facets, namely, the functional opening as the first and structural opening as the second. The opening of group structure gives permission to the intervention of factors related with information behavior away from the group, thus leaving sufficient space for thinking and expanding together, which realizes the internalized development of information behavior in order to achieve the goal of horizontal development and expansion.

4 New Paradigm of Information Behavior Research Based on Complexity Science Management

Complexity science management not only provides a new theoretical tools and methods for information behavior, but also directly affect the transformation and development of information behavior paradigm.

(1) The Dynamic Development of Information Behavior

In the process of development of the humanities paradigm, it expressed as the changing of information behavior, more often intertwined between information behaviors. The external environment promotes the development of information behavior in research object, content and process of information science. Information behavior pays more attention to user values and dignity in addition to rational thinking, and the emotion, will, value and belief of the users in the process of information behavior. The old paradigm of information science has been difficult to study the complexity of subject, content, objects and procedures about the information behavior. It cannot conduct research practice scientifically and objectively. The development characteristics of information behavior and its postmodernism position needs a new paradigm to lead, which is the complexity science management. The method of complexity science is a complex thinking to study as the leading paradigm of diversification.

Information behavior is regarded as a complex system which is closely related to other disciplines. After the development of nearly a hundred years, information research has formed an important research field of information science, and gradually integrated with other disciplines, which is glowing with a new glory. It reveals the intrinsic regularity of the information behavior process in the chaotic region and unstable region by using the theory and method of complexity science management. Complexity science management is not a negation of the existing paradigm, but the eclectic and integration of the advantages of existing paradigm. The paradigm of complexity science management is highly generation of research logic of information behavior. It not only embodies the information behavior research to 'user' as focus, with 'nature' as main research of quantitative paradigm of method, which is the 'interaction' as the focus of the information behavior. Thus, the paradigm of complexity science management is the dominant paradigm of information behavior, as to conform to the characteristics and trends of information science.

(2) Introducing Classic Theories from Other Disciplines and More and More Cross-disciplinary Researches Occur

The theoretically basic system of any subjects has the process of gradually accruing and completing, the interaction between different disciplines might give birth to more creations, and so is the information behavior research. No matter it is the historical process of exploring information behavior of mankind as the combination of information behavior and theory of evolution or is the research on information foraging behavior combined with ecology, or the research on information retrieval system for system retrieval, information, as well as the multiple cognitive relations among information users, every time the combination between different disciplines all drives the development of information behavior research and enriches the research view of other disciplines, whose developing tendency undoubtedly will be further enhanced.

(3) Collaborative Information Behavior Research Becomes More Pervasive

Collaborative information behavior signifies as an important development direction in the field of information behavior. Although collaboration refers to an important part of other forms of working, however, most of the researches stress on the personal information behavior other than collaborative aspect of information behavior. Therefore, to know the concept and technical methods of this kind of behavior is necessary. At present, the domestic relevant researches are in a small number, researchers might positively probe into this field, where it can offer them great development and innovative space.

(4) Be Bold to Absorb the Nutrition from Other Disciplines and Enabling Continuous Innovation of the Theory

There's one module, as one of the hot spots of foreign information behavior researches, is named animal foraging mechanism. The researches put forward the optimal feeding theory through their observation of animal foraging rules. P. Pirolli and S. K. learns and adopts some relevant contents of optimization of foraging theory and combines the related features of information behavior, and puts forward Information Foraging theory. It is for the analysis of behavioral strategies and techniques such as information search, information collection, and information acquisition and information usage to help understand how people can quickly adapt to the constantly changing information environment.

(5) Taking the Behaviour of Library Users as the Basis and Continuously Expanding to Other Areas

Information behavior research in China starts with the researches on the library users. At the beginning period, it is the educational circumstances of research on library users, and then conducting the research on the information needs and intelligence behavior of the library users. With the popularization of computer retrieval tools in the library, the rise of emerging concepts such as "digital library", information service personnel in order to better grasp the users' information needs along with the use of tools, they conducted a theoretical and practical in-depth discussion. We should pay attention to the use of mass data generated by user information behavior. For example, libraries can analyze actual problems in the field of user information behavior based on the objective data of user borrowing and database access. We should pay more attention to the comparative analysis of the information behaviors of users at different levels and countries, and help the information service institutions to improve the service quality accordingly. The focus of research will be extended to the development of network retrieval system, use, strategy and technology, users' searching needs and behavioral research, information behavior mode as well as other aspects, for instance, researches on the user's information behavior in society.

(6) Information Behavior Research Method to Complex Method

In research methods, quantitative research is based on data, and qualitative research is based on the value of the standard. In the ideological trend of emphasizing the relationship between diversity and pluralism, information behavior has become a hot topic of cross disciplinary and paradigm. We can find its development from qualitative research to quantitative research, and then to complexity science throughout the development of information science research. Compatibility and interdisciplinary is obvious with the development of information behavior, which indicates the multiple structure and numerous branches of complexity science theoretical system become more and more mature. It needs a complex and comprehensive research method, which is the combination of quantity and quantity research. We can use mature research methods named questionnaires and observation. In addition, some new methods under the network environment are available, such as video capture method, eye tracking method, log analysis and so on. They are applied to the study of user information behavior, while paying attention to the normative method.

Under the environment of big data, the research content of information behavior is more and more abundant, and the research subject is becoming more and more complex. The research paradigm of information science, which is dominated by the complexity paradigm, will be studied as a dynamic complex system. In the process of studying, it is not only need the scientific and positive attitude, but also needs the humanistic spirit. It can learn about the complex phenomenon of information behavior and the basic characteristics of information systems by using the method of complexity science management to analyze the characteristic of the complex information behavior deeply. It is helpful to reveal the relationship between the information behavior and the potential value of the user, in order to know well the basic laws of information behavior.

5 Summary

This paper analyzes the development of information behavior base on the CSM theory and method, introduces the development trend of information behavior, and then puts forward that information behavior is the carrier of complexity science management. Acting as CSM carrier, bid data offer space for information behavior theories and methods to further expand. At the same time, CSM theories, methods and thinking modes can be applied extensively to research of information behavior. Acting as CSM carrier, information behavior has a broad application prospects. The research of information behavior still needs further improvement, nonetheless, information behavior drives the development of CSM.

Acknowledgments. This paper is supported by National Social Science Foundation in China (Grant No. 16BTQ055).

References

1. Chen, S.: Complexity science and management. J. Nanchang Univ. **31**(3), 1–6 (2000)
2. Zheng, Z., et al.: Complexity science management and big data. In: IEEE International Conference on Granular Computing (2014)
3. Wilson, T.: The information user: past, present and future. J. Inf. Sci. **34**(34), 457–464 (2008)
4. Bernal, J.D.: Preliminary Analysis of Pilot Questionnaire on the use of Scientific Literature (1948)
5. Aslib: Report of an investigation on literature searching by research scientists. Aslib Research Department (1964)
6. Slater, M.: Social scientists' information needs in the 1980s. J. Documentation **44**(3), 226–237 (1988)
7. Wilson, T.D.: Information needs in local authority social services departments: an interim report on project Iniss. J. Documentation **35**(2), 120–136 (2013)

8. Wilson, T.D.: On user studies and information needs. J. Documentation **62**(6), 658–670 (2006)
9. Schamber, L.: Relevance and information behavior. Ann. Rev. Inf. Sci. Technol. **29**(1), 3–48 (1994)
10. Case, D.O.: Looking for Information: A Survey of Research on Information Seeking, Needs, and Behavior. Academic Press, San Diego (2016). 002: 138–139
11. Leydon, G.M., Boulton, M., Moynihan, C., et al.: Cancer patients' information needs and information seeking behaviour: in depth interview study. BMJ **320**(7239), 909–913 (2000)
12. Gonzalez-Gonzalez, A.I., Martin, D., Jose, S.-M., et al.: Information needs and information-seeking behavior of primary care physicians. Ann. Fam. Med. **5**(4), 345–352 (2007)

Risk Explicit Interval Linear Programming Model for CCHP System Optimization Under Uncertainties

Ling Ji[1(✉)], Lucheng Huang[1], and Xiaomin Xu[2]

[1] Research Base of Beijing Modern Manufacturing Development,
College of Economics and Management, Beijing University of Technology,
Pingleyuan Road 100, Beijing, China
hdjiling@126.com, hlch@bjut.edu.cn
[2] College of Economics and Management,
North China Electric Power University, Beinong Road 2, Beijing, China
Xuxiaomin0701@126.com

Abstract. A risk explicit interval linear programming model for CCHP system optimization was proposed to provide better system cost-risk tradeoff for decision making. This method is an improved interval parameter programming, which can overcome the shortages of traditional interval parameter programming. The proposed approach can provide explicit system cost-risk tradeoff information by introducing aspiration level and system risk metric objective function. The explicit optimal strategies for decision maker with certain risk tolerance degree is more executable than the interval solutions in practice. The developed approach was applied to the CCHP system for a residential area. The results indicated that the aspiration level would have great effects on the system investment and operation decision making. For the pessimistic decision maker, the total cost would be higher with less system risk and safer system operation. For the optimistic decision maker, the total cost would be lower with higher system risk.

Keywords: CCHP · Risk explicit · Interval programming
Energy management optimization

Classified Index: C931.6

1 Introduction

Combined cooling, heating and power generation (CCHP) system is a novel and high efficient way to satisfy multiple energy demands simultaneously. Since it can realize cascade utilization of energy, improve primary energy utilization efficiency, and reduce

L. Ji—Research field in energy system optimization.
This study is financial supported by National Natural Science Foundation of China (No. 71603016) and Natural Science Foundation of Beijing Municipality (No. 9174028).

H. Yuan et al. (Eds.): GSKI 2017, CCIS 849, pp. 695–708, 2018.
https://doi.org/10.1007/978-981-13-0896-3_68

environmental pollution, CCHP system has gain great concern in recent decades and was widely employed in commercial and industrial applications [1]. Reasonable design and optimal operation are key factors to achieve the advantages of CCHP system.

So far, great efforts have been carried out to address the design and operation problems of CCHP system. Dedicated models were developed for technology selection, unit sizing, and operation optimization of CCHP system with single objective or multiple objectives. Ref [2] developed a mixed integer nonlinear programming model for the design and operation of CCHP system with the purpose of minimizing the total annual cost and CO2 emission. Ref [3] formulated a profit-oriented mixed integer linear programming model for the optimal plant design and operation of CCHP system. Ref [4] proposed a mixed integer nonlinear programming model for the design and optimum scheduling of a solar CCHP system with the aim of minimizing total energy procurement cost.

In fact, many uncertainties, such as fluctuate electricity price, random energy demand, and unpredictable market, have great impact on the design and operation of CCHP system [5]. However, in these deterministic models, parameters are the estimated expected value, which may lead to infeasible or sub-optimal. Therefore, inexact programming methods like stochastic programming, fuzzy programming and interval parameter programming were developed to tackle the complex uncertainties in CCHP system [6–8]. In general, scenario-based or probability-based stochastic programming methods require accurate probability distribution information to formulate the uncertainties. However, increasing the number of scenarios can improve the quality of the solution, but it also introduces a much heavier computational burden in practice. It is impossible to examine all the uncertainty realizations [9]. In the framework of fuzzy programming, membership functions are usually employed to deal with the uncertain parameters and the decision maker's satisfaction in multi-objective programming [10, 11]. By contrast, in the interval parameter programming method, uncertainties expressed as interval value with lower and upper bounds require less probability distribution information and computational efforts. Due to these advantages, interval parameter programming has become popular and gained widely applications in many fields [12, 13]. Ref [14] proposed an interval two-stage stochastic robust programming for the energy management in the residential microgrid system with CCHP. Under the framework of interval linear programming, Ref [15] developed a multi objective mixed-integer linear programming model for microgrid planning with the consideration of uncertain renewable energy generation.

However, the obtained interval solution cannot provide effective and direct suggestions in real world decision making. In addition, it fails to provide tradeoff information of system cost and risk under uncertainties [16]. To overcome the limitations of ILP, a risk explicit interval linear programming (REILP) method was proposed. So far, it has been successfully applied in many complex and uncertain system optimization problems [17–19], but its application in CCHP system is still few. Therefore, in this paper, a risk explicit interval linear programming model for the optimal design and operational schedule of CCHP system under uncertainties was developed. It can provide optimal solutions with minimizing system cost and risk simultaneously, and present better tradeoff between system cost and decision risk, which is more close to practice.

2 Methodology

A general interval linear programming model is usually expressed as [20, 21]:

$$\min \ f^{\pm} = \sum_j c_j^{\pm} x_j^{\pm} \tag{1}$$

Subject to

$$\sum_j a_{ij}^{\pm} x_j^{\pm} \geq b_i^{\pm}, \ \forall i \tag{2}$$

$$x_j^{\pm} \geq 0, \ \forall j \tag{3}$$

where, $\pm$ represents the interval numbers with lower and upper bounds; $x_j^{\pm}$ denotes the decision variables; $a_{ij}^{\pm}$ and $c_j^{\pm}$ are coefficients; and $b_i^{\pm}$ is the right-hand constraints. The interval parameter programming model can be solved by interactive algorithm proposed by Huang et al. [22]. The above model can be decomposed into two sub-models corresponding to the lower and upper bounds of the objective function, f^- and f^+ respectively, and the optimal objective function value can be obtained as $\left[f_{opt}^-, f_{opt}^+\right]$.

Since the obtained solutions of ILP model are expressed as interval number, they are ambiguous and less efficient for decision making in practice. The risk explicit interval linear programming was original proposed to overcome the defects of the traditional ILP method by introducing risk function and risk aspiration level. The REILP model can be formulated as follows [23]:

$$\min \ \zeta = \oplus_i \left[\sum_j \lambda_{ij} \left(a_{ij}^+ - a_{ij}^- \right) x_j + \eta_i \left(b_i^+ - b_i^- \right) \right] \tag{4}$$

Subject to

$$\sum_j c_j^+ x_j - \lambda_0 \left(c_j^+ - c_j^- \right) x_j \leq f_{opt}^+ - \lambda_0 \left(f_{opt}^+ - f_{opt}^- \right) \tag{5}$$

$$b_i^+ - \sum_j a_{ij}^- x_j \leq \xi_i, \forall i \tag{6}$$

$$\lambda_0 = \lambda_{pre} \tag{7}$$

$$x_j \geq 0, \forall j \tag{8}$$

where, ζ represents the risk metric of the entire system, which evaluates the total risk of violating system constraints under the uncertainties. λ_0 is the system risk aspiration level, ranging from 0 to 1, which represents the decision maker's risk attitude. Higher risk aspiration level indicates that the decision maker expect lower system cost with more risk tolerance, in other word, the decision maker is aggressive. While, lower risk aspiration level means that the decision maker prefer bear higher system cost with less risk tolerance, and the decision maker is conservative. f_{opt}^{+} and f_{opt}^{-} are the upper and lower bounds of the optimal solutions for the objective function of the ILP model. λ_{ij} and η_i are real numbers between 0 to 1. $\oplus_i$ represents general arithmetic operation which can be a simple addition, a weighted addition, simple arithmetic mean, weighted arithmetic mean, or a maximum operator.

3   System Description

In this study, a smart building with multiple smart homes is considered, where a microgrid system is available as local energy supplier to meet its electricity, heating, and cooling demands. The microgrid system with CCHP is consisted of gas engine, boil, absorption chiller, and electricity chiller, seen in Fig. 1. It is connected to the main grid, so as to sell the surplus electricity for extra revenue or purchase electricity for the shortage. The microgrid system manager should identify the installed capacity of each device and make operation schedule for the typical day with the main of minimizing total cost. The uncertainties in the complicated energy system include the future energy demands, the fluctuant real-time electricity price, the variable energy price, the capital cost and operation cost. Based on some existing researches [24, 25], the key economic and technical parameters of various elements in microgrid system are summarized in Table 1. The forecasted energy demands are profiled in Fig. 2.

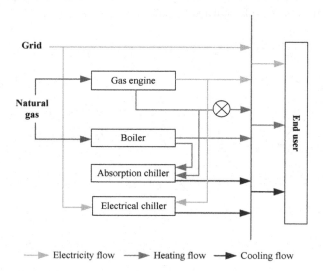

Fig. 1. Structure of CCHP system operation

Table 1. Key economic and technical parameters of the elements in CCHP system

Index	Value
Capital cost of gas engine	[800, 850] \$/kW
Capital cost of boil	[700, 720] \$/kW
Capital cost of absorption chiller	[380, 400] \$/kW
Capital cost of electricity chiller	[350, 400] \$/kW
Gas price	[0.687, 0.712] \$/m^3
Emission penalty	[0.020, 0.025] \$/kg
Low heat value of natural gas	10.72 kWh/m^3
Emission factor of gas engine	0.2 kg/kWh
Emission factor of boil	0.2 kg/kWh
Emission factor of main grid	0.6 kg/kWh

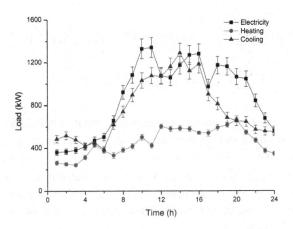

Fig. 2. Forecasted energy demand profiles

4 Model Formulation

4.1 Model Formulation

(1) *Interval Linear Programming for CCHP System*

$$Min \ f^{\pm} = (1) + (2) + (3) + (4) \tag{9}$$

The initial investment of the micro-grid with CCHP is the purchased cost of all equipment. Here we split it into the equipment's lifetime which is set at the same for simplicity.

$$(1) = CRF \times (IC_{GE}^{\pm} \cdot CAP_{GE}^{\pm} + IC_{B}^{\pm} \cdot CAP_{B}^{\pm} \\ + IC_{AC}^{\pm} \cdot CAP_{AC}^{\pm} + IC_{EC}^{\pm} \cdot CAP_{EC}^{\pm}) \tag{10}$$

$$CRF = \frac{i}{1 - (1+i)^{-L}} \tag{11}$$

where, $IC_{GE}^{\pm}$, $IC_{B}^{\pm}$, $IC_{AC}^{\pm}$ and $IC_{EC}^{\pm}$ represent the capital investment cost for gas engine, gas boiler, absorption chiller and electric chiller ($/kW); CAP_{GE}, CAP_{B}, CAP_{AC} and CAP_{EC} are the installed capacity of various equipment (kW); L is the total years of simulation (year); and i denotes the discount rate.

Annual energy consumption cost includes the gas cost of gas engine and boil and the electricity purchased from the grid. The operation cost of all the technologies can be expressed as:

$$(2) = \sum_{t=1}^{T} P_{gas}^{\pm} \cdot \left(P_{B,t}^{\pm} / \eta_B \times HV + P_{GE,t}^{\pm} / \eta_{GE} \times HV \right) \\ + \sum_{t=1}^{T} P_{elec,t}^{\pm} \cdot \left(IP_{GRID,t}^{\pm} - EP_{GRID,t}^{\pm} \right) \tag{12}$$

where, $P_{B,t}^{\pm}$, $P_{GE,t}^{\pm}$ and $P_{GRID,t}^{\pm}$ are the pre-regulated output of boiler and gas engine and electricity purchase from main grid in the first stage, respectively; η_B and η_{GE} are the thermal efficiency of gas boiler and gas engine respectively; $P_{gas}^{\pm}$ is price of gas ($/m^3$); $P_{elec,t}^{\pm}$ is price of electric ($/kWh); and HV is the heat value of natural gas (kWh/m^3).

The energy conversation cost include the operation cost of pre-regulated energy generation in the first stage, and excess generation cost under the generation targets failed meet the demand.

$$(3) = \sum_{t=1}^{T} OC_{B}^{\pm} \cdot P_{B,t}^{\pm} + \sum_{t=1}^{T} OC_{GE}^{\pm} \cdot P_{GE,t}^{\pm} \tag{13}$$

where, $OC_{B}^{\pm}$ and $OC_{GE}^{\pm}$ represent the operating cost of boiler and gas engine for pre-regulated energy generation.

$$(4) = \sum_{t=1}^{T} EP^{\pm} \cdot \left(\zeta_B \cdot P_{B,t}^{\pm} + \zeta_{GE} \cdot P_{GE,t}^{\pm} + \zeta_{GRID} \cdot IP_{GRID,t}^{\pm} \right) \tag{14}$$

(2) **Constraints** *Description*
(1) Energy mass balance

$$P_{GE,t}^{\pm} + IP_{GRID,t}^{\pm} - EP_{GRID,t}^{\pm} \geq P_{EC,t}^{\pm} \Big/ COP_{EC} + ED_t^{\pm} \qquad (15)$$

$$Q_{R,t}^{\pm} + P_{B,t}^{\pm} \geq P_{AC,t}^{\pm} \Big/ COP_{AC} + HD_t^{\pm} \qquad (16)$$

$$Q_{R,t}^{\pm} = P_{GE,t}^{\pm}(1 - \eta_{GE})\eta_{rec} \Big/ \eta_{GE} \qquad (17)$$

$$P_{AC,t}^{\pm} + P_{EC,t}^{\pm} \geq CD_t^{\pm} \qquad (18)$$

where, $Q_{R,t}^{\pm}$ is the recovered waste heat from gas engine; COP_{AC} and COP_{EC} are the coefficient of performance of absorption chiller and electric chiller; η_{rec} is the heat recovery system efficiency; $HD_t^{\pm}$, $CD_t^{\pm}$ and $ED_t^{\pm}$ are the load of heating, cooling and electricity demand respectively at time t (kWh).

(2) Emission constraints

$$\sum_{t=1}^{T} \left(\xi_B \cdot P_{B,t}^{\pm} + \xi_{GE} \cdot P_{GE,t}^{\pm} + \xi_{GRID} \cdot IP_{GRID,t}^{\pm} \right) \leq ECAP^{\pm} \qquad (19)$$

(3) Operation constraints

$$0 \leq P_{B,t}^{\pm} \leq CAP_B^{\pm}, \forall t \qquad (20)$$

$$0 \leq P_{GE,t}^{\pm} \leq CAP_{GE}^{\pm}, \forall t \qquad (21)$$

$$0 \leq P_{AC,t}^{\pm} \leq CAP_{AC}^{\pm}, \forall t \qquad (22)$$

$$0 \leq P_{EC,t}^{\pm} \leq CAP_{EC}^{\pm}, \forall t \qquad (23)$$

(4) Transmission line constraints

$$EP_{GRID,t}^{\pm} \leq eu_t^{\pm} LP^{\max}, \ \forall t \qquad (24)$$

$$IP_{GRID,t}^{\pm} \leq iu_t^{\pm} LP^{\max}, \ \forall t \qquad (25)$$

$$iu_t^{\pm} + eu_t^{\pm} \leq 1, \forall t \qquad (26)$$

where, $LP^{\max}$ is the limited transmission power between main grid and micro-grid (kW).

B Risk explicit interval linear programming for CCHP system

$$Min \ \xi = 2\lambda_0 \cdot [CRF \cdot (IC_{GE}^+ - IC_{GE}^-) \cdot CAP_{GE} + CRF \cdot (IC_B^+ - IC_B^-) \cdot CAP_B + CRF \cdot (IC_{AC}^+ - IC_{AC}^-) \cdot CAP_{AC}$$

$$+ CRF \cdot (IC_{EC}^+ - IC_{EC}^-) \cdot CAP_{EC} + \sum_{t=1}^{T} (P_{gas}^+ - P_{gas}^-) \cdot (P_{B,t}/\eta_B \times HV + P_{GE,t}/\eta_{GE} \times HV) + \sum_{t=1}^{T} (P_{elec,t}^+ - P_{elec,t}^-) \cdot IP_{GRID,t}$$

$$+ \sum_{t=1}^{T} (P_{elec,t}^+ - P_{elec,t}^-) \cdot EP_{GRID,t} + \sum_{t=1}^{T} (OC_B^+ - OC_B^-) \cdot P_{B,t} + \sum_{t=1}^{T} (OC_{GE}^+ - OC_{GE}^-) \cdot P_{GE,t}$$

$$+ \sum_{t=1}^{T} (EP^+ - EP^-) \cdot (\xi_B P_{B,t} + \xi_{GE} \cdot P_{GE,t} + \xi_{GRID} \cdot IP_{GRID,t}) + (f_{opt}^+ - f_{opt}^-)]/(f_{opt}^+ + f_{opt}^-) + 2 \sum_t \lambda_{1t}(ED_t^+ - ED_t^-)/(ED_t^+ + ED_t^-)$$

$$+ 2 \sum_t \lambda_{2t}(HD_t^+ - HD_t^-)/(HD_t^+ + HD_t^-) + 2 \sum_t \lambda_{3t}(CD_t^+ - CD_t^-)/(CD_t^+ + CD_t^-) + 2\lambda_4(ECAP^+ - ECAP^-)/(ECAP^+ + ECAP^-)$$

$$\tag{27}$$

Subject to

$$CRF \cdot [IC_{GE}^+ - \lambda_0(IC_{GE}^+ - IC_{GE}^-)] \cdot CAP_{GE} + CRF \cdot [IC_B^+ - \lambda_0(IC_B^+ - IC_B^-)] \cdot CAP_B$$

$$+ CRF \cdot [IC_{AC}^+ - \lambda_0(IC_{AC}^+ - IC_{AC}^-)] \cdot CAP_{AC} + CRF \cdot [IC_{EC}^+ - \lambda_0(IC_{EC}^+ - IC_{EC}^-)] \cdot CAP_{EC}$$

$$+ \sum_{t=1}^{T} [P_{gas}^+ - \lambda_0(P_{gas}^+ - P_{gas}^-)] \cdot (P_{B,t}/\eta_B \times HV + P_{GE,t}/\eta_{GE} \times HV) + \sum_{t=1}^{T} [P_{elec,t}^+ - \lambda_0(P_{elec,t}^+ - P_{elec,t}^-)] \cdot \left(IP_{GRID,t} - EP_{GRID,t}\right)$$

$$+ \sum_{t=1}^{T} [OC_B^+ - \lambda_0(OC_B^+ - OC_B^-)] \cdot P_{B,t} + \sum_{t=1}^{T} [OC_{GE}^+ - \lambda_0(OC_{GE}^+ - OC_{GE}^-)] \cdot P_{GE,t}$$

$$+ \sum_{t=1}^{T} [EP^+ - \lambda_0(EP^+ - EP^-)] \cdot (\xi_B P_{B,t} + \xi_{GE} \cdot P_{GE,t} + \xi_{GRID} \cdot IP_{GRID,t}) \le f_{opt}^+ - \lambda_0\left(f_{opt}^+ - f_{opt}^-\right)$$

$$\tag{28}$$

$$CRF = \frac{i}{1 - (1+i)^{-L}} \tag{29}$$

$$ED_t^+ + P_{EC,t}\Big/COP_{EC} - P_{GE,t} - IP_{GRID,t}$$
$$+ EP_{GRID,t} \le \lambda_{1t}\left(ED_t^+ - ED_t^-\right), \forall t \tag{30}$$

$$HD_t^+ + P_{AC,t}\Big/COP_{AC} - Q_{R,t} - P_{B,t}$$
$$\le \lambda_{2t}\left(HD_t^+ - HD_t^-\right), \forall t \tag{31}$$

$$Q_{R,t} = P_{GE,t}(1 - \eta_{GE})\eta_{rec}\Big/\eta_{GE}, \forall t \tag{32}$$

$$CD_t^+ - P_{AC,t} - P_{EC,t} \le \lambda_{3t}\left(CD_t^+ - CD_t^-\right), \forall t \tag{33}$$

$$\sum_{t=1}^{T} \left(\xi_B \cdot P_{B,t} + \xi_{GE} \cdot P_{GE,t} + \xi_{GRID} \cdot IP_{GRID,t}\right)$$
$$- ECAP^- \le \eta_4(ECAP^+ - ECAP^-), \forall t \tag{34}$$

$$0 \le P_{B,t} \le CAP_B, \forall t \tag{35}$$

$$0 \le P_{GE,t} \le CAP_{GE}, \forall t \tag{36}$$

$$0 \le P_{AC,t} \le CAP_{AC}, \forall t \tag{37}$$

$$0 \le P_{EC,t} \le CAP_{EC}, \forall t \tag{38}$$

$$EP_{GRID,t} \le eu_t LP^{\max}, \ \forall t \tag{39}$$

$$IP_{GRID,t} \le iu_t LP^{\max}, \ \forall t \tag{40}$$

$$iu_t + eu_t \le 1, \forall t \tag{41}$$

$$0 \le \lambda_{1t}, \lambda_{2t}, \lambda_{3t}, \lambda_4 \le 1 \tag{42}$$

The developed REILP model is implemented through LINGO on a PC with an Intel Core i5-4590 CPU and 8.00 GB of RAM.

5   Results Analysis and Discussion

REILP model provide sufficient insight into the tradeoff information between total cost and risk value. It can provide decision maker the explicit optimal solutions according to his/her risk aspiration level. Figure 3 illustrates the detail risk-cost tradeoff curve with aspiration level from 0 to 1. It implicates that the pessimistic decision maker with lower aspiration level would bear higher total cost but face less risk value. By contrast, the optimistic decision maker with higher aspiration level would like bear greater risk value but achieve lower total cost. Besides, there would be a linear relationship between aspiration level and total cost, which implicates that the total cost would increase $ 2.89 × 103 with the decision maker's risk aspiration decreasing 0.1. However, the relationship between system risk and aspiration level would be nonlinear, and the curve's slope would increase with the increment of aspiration level. This indicates that when the decision maker become more aggressive, he/she would bear more total

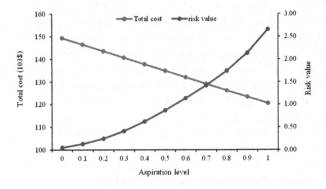

Fig. 3. Relationship between aspiration level, risk level and total cost

system risk. In other word, the decision maker would bear more risk to reduce the extra total cost. For example, when the aspiration level of decision maker increases from 0 to 0.1, the decreased total cost would be $ 2.89 × 103, and the increased system risk value would be 0.08; when the aspiration level of decision maker increases from 0.9 to 1.0, the reduced total cost would still be $ 2.89 × 103, while the increased risk value would be 0.53.

The REILP model can also provide the explicit and executable solutions for installed capacity and units schedule strategies under certain aspiration level. Table 2 presents the installed capacity of various devices under different aspiration levels. In general, with the decreasing aspiration level, the installed capacity of gas engine and electricity chiller would increase accordingly. For example, when λ is 0.9, 0.5 and 0.1, the installed capacity of gas engine would be 1163, 1300, and 1371 kW; and the required capacity of electricity chiller would be 1130, 1139, and 1184 kW, respectively. For the investment of boil and absorption chiller, when the aspiration level increase from 0 to 0.1, the installed capacity of boil and absorption chiller would decrease. However, when the aspiration level increase from 0.2 to 1, the installed capacity of boil and absorption chiller would increase accordingly. This may indicate that the risk attitude would affect the technology selection. When the risk attitude of decision maker is more optimistic, he/she would invest less capacity of electricity chiller and gas engine, but still higher capacity of boil and absorption chiller.

Table 2. Installed capacity of various devices

Devices	Aspiration level										
	0	0.1	0.2	0.3	0.4	0.5	0.6	0.7	0.8	0.9	1
Gas engine	1371	1371	1378	1366	1333	1300	1267	1233	1198	1163	1126
Boil	642	634	602	602	602	604	605	606	607	608	610
Absorption chiller	135	120	62	61	61	61	61	61	70	70	114
Electricity chiller	1184	1146	1181	1139	1139	1139	1139	1139	1130	1130	1086

Figure 4 presents the purchased electricity from main grid under different aspiration levels. It can be found that there would be no spare electricity from microgrid sold to main grid. Purchasing electricity from the main grid would be a better choice for decision maker to support the daily operation while not more capital investment. The purchased electricity would satisfy the electricity consumption from 8:00 to 22:00, and no purchased electricity would be required during the night and early morning. Besides, with more optimistic risk attitude, the decision maker would like to purchase more electricity from main grid. For example, at time 12:00, when aspiration level λ is 1, 0.7, 0.3 and 0, the purchased electricity would be 266.62, 215.88, 133.35, 105.42 kW, respectively.

Figure 5 illustrates the performance of gas engine and boil during planning horizon under different aspiration levels. From 9:00 to 22:00, the gas engine would work at its maximum capacity to satisfy the local base load, and the rest would be satisfied by purchased electricity. Due to the low load demand at night and early morning, the

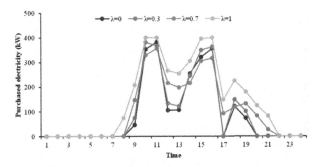

Fig. 4. Purchased electricity from main grid under different aspiration levels

electricity from the gas engine would guarantee the local load demand. Besides, for the optimistic decision maker with higher aspiration level, the electricity output from gas engine would decrease. For example, at time 11:00, when the aspiration level is set as 1, 0.7, 0.3 and 0, the electricity output of gas engine would be 1125.55, 1232.70, 1365.79 and 1370.82 kW, respectively. Accordingly, since the heating output of gas engine has the positive relationship with its electricity output, the heating output of gas engine would be stable from 9:00 to 22:00, and it would also decrease under higher aspiration level. The rest heating requirement would be satisfied by traditional boil device. The boil would mainly work at its maximum capacity from 12:00 to 20:00. Similarly, under lower aspiration level, the heating output of boil would be greater. For example, at time 11:00, when the aspiration level is set as 1, 0.7, 0.3 and 0, the heating output of boil would be 435.80, 440.17, 473.43, and 476.32 kW.

Figure 6 presents the performance of cooling devices during the planning 24 h under different aspiration levels. The performance of absorption chiller is mainly limited by the available waste heat from gas engine. Therefore, it would mainly work from 8:00 to 21:00 when the gas engine work at its maximum capacity. During the night and early morning, the absorption chiller could not provide any cooling load. When the aspiration level of decision maker is low, the output of absorption would be high to guarantee system safety. For example, at time 11:00, when the aspiration level is 0, 0.3, 0.7 and 1, the cooling load of absorption chiller would be 134.60, 113.83, 61.35 and 60.77 kW, respectively. While, in fact, the cooling load provided by absorption chiller is as supplement, and the main cooling load would be satisfied by electricity chiller. The aspiration level would affect the cooling output of electricity chiller from 8:00–22:00, while the cooling output of electricity chiller during night and early morning would still keep the same. For example, at time 11:00, when the aspiration level is 0, 0.3, 0.7 and 1, the cooling load of absorption chiller would be 1091.53, 1090.95, 1017.70, and 888.17 kW. While at time 4:00, the cooling load of absorption chiller would be 448.50 kW under any aspiration level.

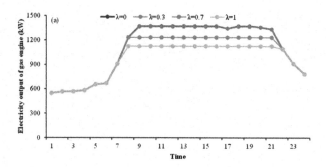

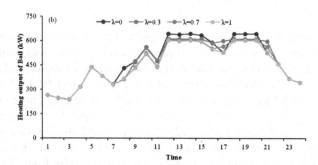

Fig. 5. The performance of boil and gas engine under different aspiration levels

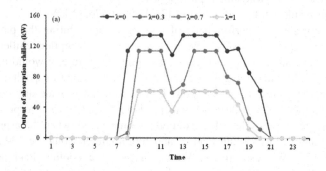

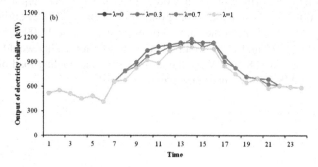

Fig. 6. Electricity output of electricity chiller and absorption chiller under different aspiration levels

6 Conclusions

This paper developed an explicit interval linear programming model for supporting the investment and operation decision of microgrid system with CCHP under multiple uncertainties. The proposed method can effectively tackle uncertainties expressed as interval values with less history information and computational efforts. The obvious advantage of the proposed method is that it can provide more detail information on system cost and decision risk, which can suggest more explicit and executable strategy for decision maker according to his/her risk preference. The developed approach was applied in the investment and operation decision of microgrid system with CCHP. The results revealed that the risk attitude of decision maker would affect the installed capacity investment and the operation strategy of microgrid system. The optimistic decision maker would bear more system risk to reduce the total cost as his/her aspiration level increasing. According to the detail cost-risk information, the decision maker can identify the optimal investment and operation strategies for the microgrid system.

Acknowledgement. The authors gratefully acknowledge the financial support from National Natural Science Foundation of China (No. 71603016) and Natural Science Foundation of Beijing Municipality (No. 9174028).

References

1. Kim, I., James, J., Critternden, J.: The case study of combined cooling heating and power and photovoltaic systems for building customers using HOMER software. Electr. Power Syst. Res. **143**, 490–502 (2017)
2. Zhu, Q., Luo, X., Zhang, B., Chen, Y.: Mathematical modelling and optimization of a large-scale combined cooling, heat, and power system that incorporates unit changeover and time-of-use electricity price. Energy Convers. Manag. **133**, 385–398 (2017)
3. Piacentino, A., Gallea, R., Catrini, P., Cardona, F., Panno, D.: On the reliability of optimization results for trigeneration systems in buildings, in the presence of price uncertainties and erroneous load estimation. Energies **9** (2016). https://doi.org/10.3390/en9121049
4. Jabari, F., Nojavan, S., Ivatloo, B.M.: Designing and optimizing a novel advanced adiabatic compressed air energy storage and air source heat pump based μ-Combined Cooling, heating and power system. Energy **116**, 64–77 (2016)
5. Akbari, K., Jolai, F., Ghaderi, S.F.: Optimal design of distributed energy system in a neighborhood under uncertainty. Energy **116**, 567–582 (2016)
6. Ünal, A.N., Ersöz, I., Kayakutlu, G.: Operational optimization in simple tri-generation systems. Appl. Therm. Eng. **107**, 175–183 (2016)
7. Sheng, W., Peang, S., Tang, Y., Meng, X., Wang, D., Wu, Z., Gu, W.: Stochastic multi-objective scheduling of a cooling, heating and power microgrid containing a fuel cell. J. Renew. Sustain. Energy **7** (2015). https://doi.org/10.1063/1.4937471
8. Hu, M., Cho, H.: A probability constrained multi-objective optimization model for CCHP system operation decision support. Appl. Energy **116**, 230–242 (2014)
9. McLean, K., Li, X.: Robust scenario formulations for strategic supply chain optimization under uncertainty. Ind. Eng. Chem. Res. **52**, 5721–5734 (2013)

10. Jing, Y.Y., Bai, H., Wang, J.J.: A fuzzy multi-criteria decision-making model for CCHP systems driven by different energy sources. Energy Policy **42**, 286–296 (2012)

11. Nieto-Morote, A., Ruz-Vila, F.: A fuzzy AHP multi-criteria decision making approach applied to combined cooling, heating, and power production systems. Int. J. Inf. Technol. Decis. Mak. **10**(3), 497–517 (2011)

12. Xie, Y.L., Xia, D.H., Ji, L., Zhou, W.N., Huang, G.H.: An inexact cost-risk balanced model for regional energy structure adjustment management and resources environmental effect analysis – a case study of Shandong province, China. Energy **126**, 374–391 (2017)

13. Ji, L., Huang, G.H., Huang, L.C., Xie, Y.L., Niu, D.X.: Inexact stochastic risk-aversion optimal day-ahead dispatch model for electricity system management with wind power under uncertainty. Energy **109**, 920–932 (2016)

14. Ji, L., Niu, D.X., Huang, G.H.: An inexact two-stage stochastic robust programming for residential micro-grid management-based on random demand. Energy **67**, 186–199 (2014)

15. Boloukat, M.H.S., Foroud, A.A.: Stochastic-based resource expansion planning for a grid-connected microgrid using interval linear programming. Energy **113**, 776–787 (2016)

16. Yang, P., Dong, F., Liu, Y., Zou, R., Chen, X., Guo, H.: A refined risk explicit interval linear programming approach for optimal watershed load reduction with objective-constraint uncertainty tradeoff analysis. Front. Environ. Sci. Eng. **10**(1), 129–140 (2016)

17. Simic, V., Dimitrijevic, B.: Risk explicit interval linear programming model for long-term planning of vehicle recycling in the EU legislative context under uncertainty. Resour. Conserv. Recycl. **73**, 197–210 (2017)

18. Zhang, X., Huang, K., Zou, R., Liu, Y., Yu, Y.: A risk explicit interval linear programing model for uncertainty-based environmental economic optimization in the Lake Fuxian watershed, China. Sci. World J. (2013). Article ID 824078. https://doi.org/10.1155/2013/824078

19. Liu, Y., Zou, R., Guo, H.C.: Risk explicit interval linear programming model for uncertainty-based nutrient-reduction optimization for the Lake Qionghai watershed. J. Water Resour. Planning Manag. **137**(1), 83–91 (2011)

20. Tong, S.C.: Interval number, fuzzy number linear programming. Fuzzy Sets Syst. **66**, 301–306 (1994)

21. Huang, G.H., Baetz, B.W., Patry, G.G.: A grey fuzzy linear programming approach for waste management and planning under uncertainty. Civ. Eng. Syst. **10**, 123–146 (1993)

22. Huang, G.H., Loucks, D.P.: An inexact two-stage stochastic programming model for water resources management under uncertainty. Civ. Eng. Environ. Syst. **2**(17), 95–118 (2000)

23. Zou, R., Liu, Y., Liu, L., Guo, H.C.: A risk explicit interval linear programming approach for uncertainty based decision making. J. Comput. Civ. Eng. **24**(4), 357–364 (2010)

24. Farzan, F., Farzan, F., Jafari, M.A.: Integration of demand dynamics and investment decisions on distributed energy resources. IEEE Trans. Smart Grid **7**(4), 1886–1895 (2016)

25. Suchitra, D., Jegatheesan, R., Deepika, T.J.: Optimal design of hybrid power generation system and its integration in the distribution network. Electr. Power Energy Syst. **82**, 136–149 (2016)

Wireless Sensor Network Localization Approach Based on Bayesian MDS

Zhongmin Pei[✉]

Science and Technology on Complex Electronic System Simulation Laboratory,
Space Engineering University, Beijing 101416, People's Republic of China
xiaopeizx@163.com

Abstract. The aim of wireless sensor networks (WSNs) are to perceive, collect and process the information of sensor nodes within the coverage of the network. As a bridge between the physical world and the digital one, WSNs have widely been applied in many fields. One of the key issues for most applications is to know the location of sensor nodes. Though localization algorithms based on multidimensional scaling (MDS), which only need several anchor nodes, have been proven to be robust with respect to range-based implementations, these methods are sensitive inaccuracy range measure. This article proposes a novel localization algorithm based on Bayesian MDS, named as MDS-MAP(P, B), where P and B denote the use of patching of local maps and Bayesian MDS, respectively. Experimental results in real-world systems show that our method is more robust and efficient.

Keywords: Wireless sensor network (SNS) · Multidimensional scaling (MDS)
Bayesian MDS (BMDS) · Received signal strength

1 Introduction

A wireless sensor network (WSN) is a wireless network consisting of spatially distributed autonomous devices using sensors to monitor physical or environmental conditions. The aim of WSN is to perceive, collect and process the information of sensor nodes within the coverage of the network [1]. As a bridge between the physical world and the digital world, WSNs are widely used to deal with sensitive information in many fields, ranging from military surveillance [2], search-and-rescue [3], environmental monitoring [4] to underground mines [5], auction [6], supermarket guiding [7].

In above-mentioned applications, it is essential to know where all collected information is sensed, that is, the location of sensor nodes. In most cases, sensors are not equipped with any Global Positioning System (GPS), since it is a costly solution in terms of volume, money and power consumption. Therefore, the localization is an inevitable problem in the WSNs. This problem attracted significant research interest [5, 7–9], and the interest is expected to grow further with the proliferation of the Internet of Thing (IoT) [10] applications.

Various localization approaches have been proposed in the literature. The most existing localization approaches of WSNs can be classified into two groups [9, 11]:

© Springer Nature Singapore Pte Ltd. 2018
H. Yuan et al. (Eds.): GSKI 2017, CCIS 849, pp. 709–716, 2018.
https://doi.org/10.1007/978-981-13-0896-3_69

range-based and range-free. Range-based methods utilize distance information between unknown nodes and anchor nodes to determine the absolute position of each unknown node, while range-free techniques only use connectivity information. This article mainly focuses on the range-based localization techniques. The typical distance measurement techniques include Received Signal Strength Indicator (RSSI) [12], Time of Arrival (TOA) [13], Time Difference of Arrival (TDoA) [14], Angle of Arrival (AoA) [15] and so on.

Localization algorithms based on multidimensional scaling (MDS) [16, 17], such as MDS-MAP(C) [8, 18], MDS-MAP(P, C) [7, 19] and MDS-MAP(P, O) [5, 20], have been proven to be robust with respect to range-based implementations. Furthermore, only several anchor nodes are necessary to determine the absolute locations of unknown nodes in 2D or 3D space. These MDS-based localization algorithms [7, 18–20] achieve a higher accuracy than some others. In this work, we propose the implementation of Bayesian MDS [21] for localization in WSNs. By using the similar terminology in [18, 20], our proposed approach is named as MDS-MAP(P, B), where P and B denote the use of patching of local maps and Bayesian MDS, respectively.

The rest of the paper is organized as follows. After MDS-MAP(P, B) localization approach is described in detail in Sect. 2, Sect. 3 conducts extensive performance comparisons with MDS-MAP(P,C) [7, 19], and MDS-MAP(P,O) [5, 20]. And then Sect. 4 concludes this work.

2 MDS-MAP(P, B) Localization Approach

In this section, we describe our proposed MDS-MAP(P, B) localization algorithm. Similar to MDS-MAP(P, C) and MDS-MAP(P, O), MDS-MAP(P, B) is also distributed and can be considered as an generalization of MDS-MAP(P, C) and MDS-MAP(P, O). The modification is the use of the Bayesian MDS (instead of classical MDS and ordinal MDS) during the estimation phase. Main reason for the modification is that it is difficult to obtain accuracy range measure due to complex environmental conditions. The major steps of the MDS-MAP(P, B) are summarized as follows.

Step 1.   Each node first gathers the distance information (such as RSSI, TOA, TDoA, AoA and so on) within its two-hop neighborhood.

Step 2.   In each node, the Dijkstra's algorithm [23] is invoked to determine the shortest path between each pair of nodes within the two-hop neighborhoods. For convenience, let $\Delta = [\delta i,j]$ denote the distance matrix containing pairwise shortest path distance between nodes $i \in N$ and $j \in N$, where N includes all the nodes within the two-hop neighborhood, which is the input to the Bayesian MDS. Due to range measure inaccuracy, the matrix Δ is usually asymmetric.

Step 3.   The Bayesian MDS algorithm [21] is applied to create the relative local map for each node.

Step 4.   The local maps are then patched (or merged) into a global map by using a predetermined initial starting node's local map and sequentially adding each neighbor that has the largest number of common nodes to the starting node. This map then grows until all nodes have been included.

Step 5.   The global absolute map is created by using the anchor nodes' positions and the global relative map with the procrustes procedure [16, 17].

The Bayesian MDS algorithm [21] in Step 3 above use a Euclidean distance model and assume a Gaussian measurement error within a Bayesian framework. The graphical model representation for the Bayesian MDS is shown in Fig. 1. The Bayesian MDS can be viewed as a generative process, which can be described as follows.

1. Draw σ^2 from the inverse Gamma distribution Inverse Gamma (a, b);
2. For each dimension $k \in \{1, \cdots, p\}$ (often $p = 2$ or $p = 3$)

   – Draw each element λ_k in diagonal covariance matrix Λ from the inverse Gamma distribution IG(α, β_k);

3. For each $i \in N$

   – Draw the coordinate x_i of the node i from the Gaussian distribution N$(0, \Lambda)$;

4. For each $i \in N$ and each $j \in N\backslash i$

   – Let $\delta_{i,j} = \sqrt{\sum_{k=1}^{p} \left(x_{i,k} - x_{j,k}\right)^2}$
   – Draw the Euclidean distance $d_{i,j}$ from the Gaussian distribution N$\left(\delta_{i,j}, \sigma^2\right) I\left(d_{i,j} > 0\right)$;

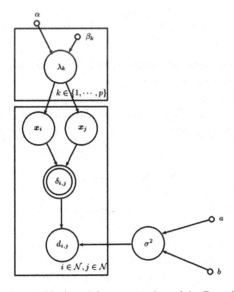

Fig. 1. The graphical model representation of the Bayesian MDS

From the above generative process, one can see that BayesianMDS is parametrized as follows:

$$\lambda_k \sim IG(\alpha, \beta_k)$$
$$\sigma^2 \sim IG(a, b)$$
$$x_i \sim N(0, \Lambda)$$
$$\delta_{i,j} = \sqrt{\sum_{k=1}^{p} (x_{i,k} - x_{j,k})^2}$$
$$d_{i,j} \sim N(\delta_{i,j}, \sigma^2) I(d_{i,j} > 0)$$

where the indicator function $I(x) = 1$ if x is true and 0 otherwise.

In order to estimate $\{x_i\}, \sigma_2$, and $\{\lambda_k\}$, Markov chain Monte Carlo (MCMC) simulation technique [24] is utilized. For more elaborate and detailed introduction we refer the readers to [21].

3 Experimental Results and Discussions

The performance of MDS-MAP(P, B) in real-world systems is studied through two experiments, one from [22] and one from our previous work [5]. The first experiment was conducted in a parking lot, and the second experiment was conducted in a grass lawn. For comparison, the locations of the unknown nodes were also estimated using the three localization techniques: MDS-MAP(P, C) [7, 19] and MDS-MAP(P, O) [5, 20]. The quality of the methods is measured by average location error, defined formally as follows.

$$\varepsilon = \frac{1}{n} \sqrt{\sum_{i=1}^{n} \sum_{k=1}^{p} (x_{i,k} - \hat{x}_{i,k})^2} \qquad (1)$$

where n is the number of unknown nodes, $x_i = (x_i, 1, \cdots, x_{i,p})$ and $\hat{x}_i = (\hat{x}_{i,1}, \ldots, \hat{x}_{i,p})$ are the true and estimated locations, respectively.

In all of the experiments, the hyperprior $\alpha = 5$, β is set to 0.5 times the column variance of $X = [x1; x2; \cdots; x|N|]$ obtained from classical MDS or ordinal MDS, a = 5, and b is chose to match the prior mean of $\sigma2$ with $\frac{SSR}{m}$ obtained from classical MDS or ordinal MDS, where

$$SSR = \sum_{i > j} (d_{i,j} - \delta_{i,j})^2 \qquad (2)$$

$$m = \frac{|N|(|N| - 1)}{2} \qquad (3)$$

And the number of iterations in the MCMC simulation is set to 25,000. The number of MCMC iterations that are discarded as burn-ins is set to 5000. Here we focus on the 2D space, i.e., $p = 2$.

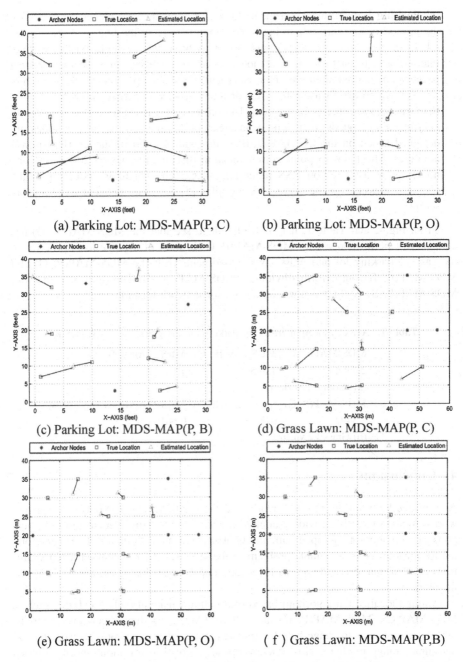

Fig. 2. Comparisons between true locations and estimated locations. (a)–(c) are for parking lot experiment, and others are for grass lawn experiment

(a) Parking Lot. In this experiment, 11 MICA 2 motes were placed randomly on the ground of an outdoor parking lot. All motes were in the line of sight of each other, and all of them were programmed to broadcast a single packet without interfering with each other. The motes recorded the RSS values of the received packets and stored them in their electrically erasable programmable read-only memory (Eeprom). Please refer [22] for more detailed experimental setting.

(b) Grass Lawn. In this experiment, 15 nodes of the Cicada series were randomly distributed in a grass lawn within an arean of 60 m × 60 m. Cicada nodes are designed based on the CC2430 ZigBee chip with a radio frequency (RF) power amplifier. The point to point communication distance reaches to 200 m. All the nodes broadcast one-hop RSS request message. The neighbor nodes report the response message to the server. Please refer [5] for more detailed experimental setting.

From Fig. 2 and Table 1, it is not difficult to see that the MDS-MAP(P, B) has comparative performance with MDS-MAP(P, O) in term of average location error in the case of parking lot and grass lawn experiments. But the MDS-MAP(P, O) and MDS-MAP(P, B) outperform obviously MDS-MAP(P, C). This indicates that our MDS-MAP(P, B) is efficient for wireless sensor network location.

Table 1. Average location errors for parking lot and grass lawn experiments.

MDS-MAP(P, C)	MDS-MAP(P, O)	MDS-MAP(P, B)
2.7994	1.8857	1.2484
(a) Parking Lot (feet)		
MDS-MAP(P, C)	MDS-MAP(P, O)	MDS-MAP(P, B)
1.5492	0.7903	0.6016
(b) Grass Lawn (m)		

4   Conclusions

As a bridge between the physical world and the digital one, the wireless sensor networks (WSNs) have been widely applied in many fields. However, in most applications, sensors are not equipped with any Global Positioning System (GPS). Therefore, the localization is an inevitable problem in the WSNs. This problem attracted significant research interest, and various localization approaches have been proposed in the literature.

Though localization algorithm based on multidimensional scaling (MDS), such as MDS-MAP(C), MDS-MAP(P, C) and MDS-MAP(P, O), have been proven to be robust with respect to range-based implementations, these methods are sensitive to inaccuracy range measure. This article proposes a novel localization algorithm based on Bayesian MDS, named as MDS-MAP(P, B), where P and B denote the use of patching of local maps and Bayesian MDS, respectively. Experimental results in two real-world systems, parking lot and grass lawn, show that our approach is more robust and efficient.

Acknowledgments. This work was supported partially by the National Social Science Foundation of China [grant number 15GJ003-180].

References

1. Akyildiz, I.F., Su, W., Sankarasubramaniam, Y., Cayirci, E.: Wireless sensor networks: a survey. Comput. Netw. **38**(4), 393–422 (2002)
2. Onur, E., Ersoy, C., Delic, H., Akarun, L.: Surveillance wireless sensor networks: deployment quality analysis. IEEE Netw. **21**(6), 48–53 (2007)
3. Wu, H., Zhang, Q., Nie, S., Sun, W., Guan, X.: An energy distribution and optimization algorithm in wireless sensor networks for maritime search and rescue. Int. J. Distrib. Sens. Netw. **2013**, 1–8 (2013)
4. Oliveira, L.M.L., Rodrigues, J.J.P.C.: Wireless sensor networks: a survey on en environment monitoring. J. Commun. **6**(2), 143–151 (2011)
5. Pei, Z., Deng, Z., Xu, S., Xu, X.: Archor-free localization method for mobile target sin coal mine wireless sensor networks. Sensors **9**(4), 2836–2850 (2009)
6. An, X., Xu, S., Chen, J., Zhang, Y.: Distributed risk aversion parameter estimation for first-price auction in sensor networks. Int. J. Distrib. Sens. Netw. **2013**, 1–9 (2013)
7. Pei, Z., Yibin, L., Xu, S.: A fast localization algorithm for large-scale wireless sensor networks. J. China Univ. Min. Technol. **42**(2), 314–319 (2013)
8. Xu, S., Qiao, X., Zhu, L., Zhang, Y., Li, L.: Fast but not bad initial configuration for metric multidimensional scaling. J. Inf. Comput. Sci. **9**(2), 257–265 (2012)
9. Han, G., Xu, H., Duong, T.Q., Jiang, J., Hara, T.: Localization algorithms of wireless sensor networks: a survey. Telecommun. Syst. **52**(4), 2419–2436 (2013)
10. Uckelmann, D., Harrison, M., Michahelles, F. (eds.): Architecting the Internet of Things. Springer, New York (2011)
11. Pei, Z., Deng, Z., Xu, S., Xu, X.: A new localization method for wireless sensor network n-node based on n-best rank sequence. ACTA Automatica China **36**(2), 119–207 (2010)
12. Girod, L., Bychkovskiy, V., Elson, J., Estrin, D.: Locating tiny sensor in time and space: a case study. In: Proceedings of the 2002 IEEE International Conference on Computer Design: VLSI in Computers and Processors, Los Alamitos, CA, USA, pp. 214–219. IEEE Computer Society (2002)
13. Harter, A., Hopper, A., Steggles, P., Ward, A., Webster, P.: The anatomy of a context-aware application. In: Proceedings of the 5th Annual ACM/IEEE International Conference on Mobile Computing and Networking, New York, NY, USA, pp. 59–68. ACM (1999)
14. Girod, L., Estrin, D.: Robust range estimation using acoustic and multimodal sensing. In: Proceedings of the 2001 IEEE/RSJ International Conference on Intelligent Robots and Systems, vol. 3, Los Alamitos, CA, USA, pp. 1312–1320. IEEE Computer Society (2001)
15. Niculescu, D., Nath, B.: Ad hoc positioning system (APS) using AOA. In: Proceedings of the 22nd Annual Joint Conference of the IEEE Computer and Communications, vol. 3, Los Alamitos, CA, USA, pp. 1734–1743. IEEE Computer Society (2003)
16. Cox, T.F., Cox, M.A.A. (eds.): Multidimensional Scaling, 2nd edn. Chapman & Hall/CRC, Boca Raton (2001)
17. Borg, I., Groenen, P.J.F. (eds.): Modern Multidimensional Scaling: Theory and Application, 2nd edn. Spinger, New York (2005)
18. Shang, Y., Ruml, W., Zhang, Y., Fromherz, M.P.J.: Localization from mere connectivity. In: Proceedings of the 4th ACM International Symposium on Mobile Ad Hoc Networking & Computing, New York, NY, USA, pp. 201–212. ACM (2003)

19. Shang, Y., Ruml, W.: Improved MDS-based localization. In: Proceedings of the 23rd Annual Joint Conference of the IEEE Computer and Communications Societies, vol. 4, Los Alamitos, CA, USA, pp. 2640– 2651. IEEE Computer Society (2004)

20. Vivekanandan, V., Wong, V.W.S.: Ordinal MDS-based localization for wireless sensor networks. Int. J. Sens. Netw. **1**(3/4), 169–178 (2006)

21. Oh, M.S., Raftery, A.E.: Bayesian multidimensional scaling and choice of dimension. J. Am. Stat. Assoc. **96**(455), 1031–1044 (2001)

22. Yedavalli, K., Krishnamachari, B.: Sequence-based localization in wireless sensor networks. IEEE Trans. Mob. Comput. **7**(1), 81–94 (2008)

23. Dijkstra, E.W.: A note on two problems in connexion with graphs. Numer. Math. **1**(1), 269–271 (1959)

24. Andrieu, C., de Freitas, N., Doucet, A., Jordan, M.I.: An introduction to MCMC for machine learning. Mach. Learn. **50**(1–2), 5–43 (2003)

Empirical Study on Social Media Information Influencing Traveling Intention

Chunhui Huang[(✉)]

Birmingham Institute of Fashion and Creative Art,
Wuhan Textile University, Wuhan, China
hchui2000@163.com

Abstract. Through the data and path coefficient analysis on the 509 valid samples. We develop a conceptual model to investigate the factors that may influence tourists' travelling intention. The results show that these factors, such as perceived novelty, perceived reliability and perceived interest have an obviously positive impact on perceived enjoyment; however, perceived understand-ability has little impact on perceived enjoyment. On the other hand, perceived enjoyment, perceived trustworthiness and perceived similarity have obviously positive impacts on travelling intention.

Keywords: Information technology · Mobile navigation
Technology acceptance model

CLC Number: G206 · F592

1 Introduction

In recent years, tourism has been highly competitive from offline to internet-based online competition [1]. It is difficult to attract and retain visitors for travel companies [2]. Consumers become accustomed to collecting information about travel destinations through social media [3], and they can share their travel experience anytime and anywhere on social medias [4]. Many tourists read and publish the corresponding comments on the social media, and form the tourist destination "reputation" and "experience" from which tourism practitioners obtain the information about the feelings of tourists travel to the market share of tourism products. Academia and industry are very concerned about the influence mechanism of social media information on travel decisions, and the characteristics of these information.

Empirical studies show tourists are reluctant to read these information which is less relevant to themselves, however, they usually trust such information on micro-blog and we-chat published by those who are close to them. Research on social media trust is a hot topic in recent years [5]. For example, Huang Yinghua (2014) studies the social media behavior of tourists [6], and Shao Jun studied the influence of social media marketing on the choice of travel destination [7].

This work had been supported by Humanities and Social Sciences Project of Department of Education, Hubei Province (16D048).

© Springer Nature Singapore Pte Ltd. 2018
H. Yuan et al. (Eds.): GSKI 2017, CCIS 849, pp. 717–724, 2018.
https://doi.org/10.1007/978-981-13-0896-3_70

Based on the empirical analysis of regression and path, we construct a conceptual model of tourists' intention to travel, moreover, the variables and factors are from the perceived entertainment theory and the information relevance theory, which are proved to have a good explanation in the research of the predecessors [8].

2 Literature Review and Hypotheses

A. *Perceived Entertainment Theory*
The concept of entertainment was first proposed by Lieberman in 1977 [9]. Barnett defined entertainment from two different angles [10]. Moon and Kim (2011) argued that entertainment was an intrinsic belief or motive which was formed by individual experience in some environment. Perceived entertainment is defined as the strength that internets satisfied his internal motives. Perceived entertainment is divided into three dimensions: focus, perceived novelty perception and perceived enjoyment.

B. *Information Relevance Theory*
The information relevance once has been used as a criterion to determine whether the retrieved information meets consumers' needs since 1970s. Because these researches about information can serve consumers and satisfy their specific purposes, they can objectively measure from the effectiveness of the service. Sigala suggested that the perception of emotion or social values were derived from information search on travel planning [12].

Consumers' impression of destination has an impact on their future travel destination decisions, although some new factors reinvent this kind of impression. Consumers are exceptionally impressed with their associated destination [14].

(1) *Perceived novelty*
The irrelevant information usually has nothing to do with tourists' travel planning, however, they tend to focus their attention on social media information which maybe much more useful for their planning. Therefore, probing novelty is one of the main motivations for tourists to travel [15]. In this case, tourists may have not novel experience, on the contrary, they may feel a little boring, and the desire to browse social media may absolutely decline, however, if the information about traveling destination is novel, tourists can be easily absorbed and they have a good impression [13]. Therefore, the following assumptions are made: H1: Perception of novelty Perceptions novelty has a positively impact on social media usage enjoyment.

(2) *Perceived reliability*
Because most of information on social media is anonymous, tourists' perceived reliability of content and source is very important. Tourists suspecting the reliability of the information content is understandable, however, if tourists who publish the information use their real-name (such as real-name microblogging), the information reliability will increase a lot [16]. Therefore, the following hypothesis is proposed: H2: Perceived reliability has a positive impact on the social media usage enjoyment.

(3) *Perceived understandability*

If the information posted on social media is easy to understand, tourists are likely to create some good impression of the destination after reading the information. However if the information is vague, or vague, tourists may think it is a waste of time to read it. Thus, difficult-to-understand information may make tourists confusion. The more understandable the social media, the more pleasant it is for tourists to experience it. Therefore, the following hypothesis is proposed: H3: Perceived understandability of content positively influences social media usage.

(4) *Perceived interest*

When interacting with social media, tourists can easily find posts or tweets which are interesting or not, in addition, the uninteresting information will be filtered out. Interesting things usually can easily stimulate the passion of exploration. If the information is very interesting, tourists tend to spend more time reading it, however, it takes time to form a good impression of some destination, and tourists usually enjoy social media usage and acquiring information during the process. Therefore, the following hypothesis is proposed: H4: Perceived interest in the content has a positive impact on social media usage enjoyment.

(5) *Perceived enjoyment*

When tourists browse social media, they may not have some specific purpose, just for leisure and entertainment only. Tourists usually perceive some enjoyment when reading travel blogs or articles in WeChat friends' circles, and they are more likely to read such social media, moreover, they may focus their attention on in this type of media. Therefore, the following hypothesis is proposed: H5: Perceived enjoyment has a positive impact on the intention to visit some destination.

(6) *Perceived similarity*

One of the most fundamental principles of communication relates to the belief that source receiver similarity promotes communication effectiveness. As defined by Rogers (1983), perceived similarity denotes the extent to which individuals are similar in terms of certain attributes, such as age, gender, education, or lifestyle. While traditional notions of perceived similarity described similarity in terms of demographic characteristics and lifestyle, recent conceptualizations of perceived similarity in the online environment refer more particularly to shared interest and shared mind-set, thus the hypotheses: H6: Perceived similarity positively influences the intention to visit a destination.

Based on above literature and hypotheses, the theoretical model is constructed (shown in Fig. 1).

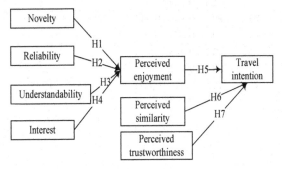

Fig. 1. The research model.

3 Research Design

A. *Measurement*

Based on above hypotheses, we use a questionnaire survey to measure all research constructs and validate the concept model. Items used for measuring the constructs are adapted from existing scales in the extant literature which have good validity and reliability. After the drafts of the questionnaire are prepared, they are sent to users and experts who are familiar with social media and have much traveling experience for their suggestions.

Table 1. Scale properties

Factor	Item	STD	Cronbach's α	C.R	AVE
PN	PN1	0.583	0.762	0.861	0.516
	PN2	0.532			
	PN3	0.681			
	PN4	0.821			
	PN5	0.877			
	PN6	0.753			
PR	PR1	0.789	0.896	0.887	0.725
	PR2	0.902			
	PR3	0.859			
PU	PU1	0.910	0.877	0.853	0.660
	PU2	0.773			
	PU3	0.745			
PI	PI1	0.872	0.921	0.913	0.778
	PI2	0.903			
	PI3	0.870			
PE	PE1	0.854	0.938	0.938	0.790
	PE2	0.897			
	PE3	0.912			
	PE4	0.891			
PS	PS1	0.812	0.894	0.875	0.637
	PS2	0.791			
	PS3	0.804			
	PS4	0.784			
PT	PT1	0.886	0.943	0.947	0.817
	PT2	0.873			
	PT3	0.943			
	PT4	0.911			
TI	TI1	0.872	0.802	0.881	0.788
	TI2	0.903			

B. *Sample*

First, a principle components factor analysis with varimax rotation is used to test the convergent validity; furthermore, exploratory factor analysis is conducted. The Kaiser-Meyer-Olkin (KMO) values are used to determine whether the collected data can be used for factor analysis. The KMO measure of sampling adequacy is 0.935. Bartlett spherical test results at the level of p = 0.000 are very significant, indicating that the maximum variance of rotation can be used for the principal component analysis. The result of analysis is: eight factors with eigenvalues greater than 1.0 were extracted. The total percentage of variance explains by all factors was 77.697%. The average variance extracted (AVE) of each factor is above 0.50, furthermore, the factor loading value of all the measures is greater than 0.5 on all the variables, however, it is larger than that on other factors. The scale has a good convergence efficiency, as shown in Table 1.

According to the observed AVE values, we find that the square root of AVE is greater than the correlation coefficient of other factors, which show that the difference validity of the measurement model is better. As shown in Table 2, the black-body number is the square root of the corresponding factor AVE, which is larger than the corresponding correlation coefficient, moreover, the difference validity of the measurement model is ensured. There might exist the common method bias, it is found that the explanatory variance of each factor is no more than 15% with the Harmon single factor test, therefore, the common method bias is not significant.

Table 2. Factors correlation coefficients and square roots of the AVE

	PN	PR	PU	PI	PE	PS	PT	TI
PN	**0.718**							
PR	.404	**0.851**						
PU	.491	.405	**0.812**					
PI	.457	.410	.620	**0.882**				
PE	.504	.368	.477	.601	**0.889**			
PS	.482	.423	.487	.607	.634	**0.798**		
PT	.397	.611	.434	.469	.440	.612	**0.904**	
TI	.415	.368	.503	.503	.470	.547	.529	**0.888**

4   Hypothesis Validation

Structural equation modeling method is used to analyze and validate the sample with AMOS; furthermore, the test includes the fit goodness of those hypotheses. Table 3 is the model of the indicators of fit. From the analysis results, the absolute fitting index (GFI), adjusted fit goodness index (AGFI), comparison of fitting index (CFI), incremental fitting index (IFI) and Root Mean Square Error of Approximation (RMSEA), all of which reach the standard. The results show that the model fits very well.

Table 3. Fit induces and recommended values

Fit index	Fit value	Recommended value
x^2/df	2.662	<3
		>0.8
		>0.8
		>0.9
		>0.9
		<0.06
GFI	0.879	<3
		>0.8
		>0.8
		>0.9
		>0.9
		<0.06
AGFI	0.851	<3
		>0.8
		>0.8
		>0.9
		>0.9
		<0.06
CFI	0.944	<3
		>0.8
		>0.8
		>0.9
		>0.9
		<0.06
IFI	0.945	<3
		>0.8
		>0.8
		>0.9
		>0.9
		<0.06
RMSEA	0.059	<3
		>0.8
		>0.8
		>0.9
		>0.9
		<0.06

To analyze and detect the relationship between variables, various factors in the theoretical model constitute the eight important factors, furthermore, according to the verification of each variable, each factor is measured with some observed variables, and finally, the normalization coefficient between the factors is obtained, as shown in Fig. 2.

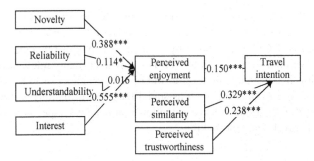

Fig. 2. Test results of the research model *p <0.05; **p <0.01; ***p <0.001

The standardized path coefficients reflect the influencing degree between variables. The standardized path coefficients, standard errors, T values and P values between the variables were clear. It is easy to find that the significance test of the path between perceived understandability and perceived entertainment has not passed, P value is 0.826, which is above 0.1, therefore, H3 was not supported. The other six hypothesis, whose P values are less than 0.05, thus they pass the verification, furthermore, these hypothesis get support

5   Discussion and Conclusion

Hypothesizes such as H1, H2, and H4 are established, perceived novelty, perceived reliability, and perceived interest have a significant positive effect on perceived enjoyment, indicating that tourists are curious about social media information about travel destinations, especially those from friends Circulation, for example, the Consumer Generated Media, CGM. This information, which seems relatively high reliability, its form and language are diverse. A variety of experiences, which are emerged on the social media, it is very reading interesting to read it, when tourists read this information, you maybe feel you are just in that place, therefore, mood is also pleasant. Hypothesis three is not established, perceived understandability has less effect on perceived enjoyment, indicating that there is not any obstacle for young people to understand the network language. More and more people are accustomed to the expression of the network; such various CGM is mainly from the tourists, thus, it easy to understand perceived understandability has no effect on perceived.

Hypothesizes such as H5, H6 and H7 are established, perceived enjoyment, perceived similarity and perceived trustworthiness will have a significant positive influence on tourists' travel intent. Indicating that the social media information about traveling, is highly accepted with pleasant mood. Although many people express themselves in their travel diary or road books with some kind of subjective color, however, many people read and enjoy happily, therefore, more people are willing to travel. In social media, those, who are similar age, familiar people, or background similar, spread the information of the tourist destination, when people are concerned about the information, their emotions easily can be excited, furthermore, travel intention maybe increased. There is a higher trust in social media information, there must be a greater intention to travel.

Combined the social media and people's traveling intention, this paper analyzes and explores the law of action which the social media information has an influence on traveling intention. UGC is generated by interactive behavior on social media, which are the subjective information from the tourists, however, many relevant researches on tourism decision-making pay attention to the objective factors of tourism destination, however subjective information (such as social media information) is considered less, therefore, analyzing the issue of travel intention from a new perspective, will contribute to the study of travel decision-making.

References

1. Horng, J.S., Liu, C.H., Chou, H.Y., et al.: Understanding the impact of culinary brand equity and destination familiarity on travel intentions. Tour. Manage. 33(4), 815–824 (2012)
2. Ho, C.I., Lee, Y.L.: The development of an e-travel service quality scale. Tour. Manage. 28(6), 1434–1449 (2007)
3. Grant, R., Clarke, R.J., Kyriazis, E.: A review of factors affecting online consumer search behavior from an information value perspective. J. Market. Manage. 23(5–6), 519–533 (2007)
4. Yoo, K.H., Gretzel, U.: Use and creation of social media by travelers. In: Social Media in Travel, Tourism and Hospitality: Theory, Practice and Cases, p. 189 (2012)
5. Zafiropoulos, K.: Wine blogs influence and blogs' community connectivity: a social network analysis. Eur. J. Tour. Hospitality Recreation 3(1), 135–156 (2012)
6. Huang, Y.H.: A study on the social network behavior of tourists in postmodern perspective. Tour. Tribune 29(8), 9–11 (2014)
7. Jun, S.: Chinese tourists exit destination selection and social media marketing. Tour. Tribune 26(8), 7–8 (2011)
8. Lieberman, J.N.: Playfulness. Academic Press, New York (1977)
9. Barnett, L.A.: The playful child: measurement of a disposition to play. Play Cult. 4, 51–74 (1991)
10. Moon, J.W., Kim, Y.G.: Extending the TAM for a world-wide-web context. Inf. Manage. 38, 217–230 (2001)
11. Sigala, M.: The impact of geo-collaborative portals on group decision making for trip planning. Eur. J. Inf. Syst. 21(4), 404–426 (2012)
12. Xu, Y.C., Chen, Z.: Relevance judgment: what do information users consider beyond topicality? J. Am. Soc. Inf. Sci. Technol. 57(7), 961–973 (2006)
13. Vogt, C.A., Fesenmaier, D.R.: Expanding the functional information search model. Ann. Tour. Res. 25(3), 551–578 (1998)
14. Jang, S.C.S., Feng, R.: Temporal destination revisit intention: the effects of novelty seeking and satisfaction. Tour. Manage. 28(2), 580–590 (2007)
15. Chesney, T., Su, D.K.S.: The impact of anonymity on we-blog credibility. Int. J. Hum. Comput. Stud. 68(10), 710–718 (2010)
16. Shang, R.A., Chen, Y.C., Chen, C.J.: The social and objective value of information in virtual investment communities. Online Inf. Rev. 37(4), 498–517 (2013)

Evolution of Online Community Opinion Based on Opinion Dynamics

Liang Yu[1], Donglin Chen[1], and Bin Hu[2(✉)]

[1] College of Economy, Wuhan University of Technology, Wuhan, China
[2] Huazhong Science and Technology University, Wuhan, China
bin_hu@hust.edu.cn

Abstract. Collective opinion of online community with different age structure obviously have different mechanisms of evolution, especially for different types of opinion events. For exploring the mechanIsms and providing management strategies for government, the bounded confidence model of individual opinion is constructed according to the related research on opinion dynamics. Chinese netizens psychology-behavior characteristics are considered in simulation modeling for presenting the relation of different types of opinion events to different types of age structure of communities. Simulation results show how three types of people (i.e., young, middle-age and old people) influence the evolution of two different collective opinion (i.e., society and low, and livelihood events). The corresponding management strategies for government are then given.

Keywords: Opinion · Bounded confidence model · Simulation
Society and low · Livelihood

Chinese Library Classification: C936 · TP39

1 Introduction

Network public opinion is the process of collection which makes network as the carrier, thus the broad netizens can express opinions, and make it possible for communication, interaction, and subsequent influence. But when people have sudden changes in attitudes for a certain event, it will accelerate a vicious development of mass incidents [1]. For example, the two types of opinion events on society and law, and livelihood, are the hot topics of netizens in recent years [13]. Prediction before the outbreak of network public opinion and taking corresponding measures are the hot point on which Chinese government focuses.

L. Yu and D. Chen—Supported by National Natural Science Foundation of China "Modelling, Behavioral Analysis and Optimized Design for Organizational System Structure under IoT environment" (Grant No. 71531009).
Senior engineering, Master degree of Computer science, Center for supervisionand command of urban management, Shenzhen City. Research field: Supervision andManagement of public sentiment and opinion.

Now there are a lot of researches about network public opinion prediction. Hui used discrete time model for opinion propagation and public opinion formation based on the node influence [2]. Wei et al., proposed a dynamic network public opinion to realize prediction for information database mined by individual sentiment [3]. Chen and Gao proposed chaos theory to analyze and predict risk of network public opinion [4]. Galam proposed a diffusion reaction model to analyze the dynamics of spreading of the minority opinion in public, which can apply to rumor and fear propagation [5]. Cheng et al., modeled the process of adopting new opinions and found opinion diffusion depends on the DMGs' proportion, the opinion's acceptability and the tolerance threshold of society [6]. Dong et al., based on the concept leadership, developed a consensus building process in opinion dynamics, and proposed a strategy adding a minimum number of interactions in the social network [7]. Most studies above are focused on individual behavior studies, Gabbay established the opinion evolution model for groups opinion interaction [8]. Although studies have begun to focus on the group, but there is still no study on classification for specific age structure.

To study how age structure of the community influence network public opinion, and put forward effective suggestions for the government to manage online opinion evolution, we use opinion dynamics model proposed by Weisbuch et al. [9]. In the domain of opinion dynamics, the main method is based on agent and rules [10], i.e., so called multi-agent modeling and simulation. Individual is seen as agent, every one influence other one's opinion by interaction between each other. The interaction follows the rules and happens randomly or in a specific pattern. The collective opinion evolution, i.e., the collective behavior in macro-level, can be formed over time. This modeling just imitates the real life of evolution of social opinion. Thus, opinion dynamics have been broadly accepted as the methodology in the domain of social computing.

Dynamic model can be divided into discrete model and continuous model. Discrete model refers to using binary values or other discrete integral numerical to model the opinions, including Ising model, Sznajd model, Voter model, Majority Rule model and its extended model. Continuous model describes the individual's opinion by using continuous real value in an interval, mainly including DW model based on bounded confidence hypothesis [11], HK model and its extended model [12].

Opinion dynamic model introduced in this work is bounded confidence model (BC model) proposed by Weisbuch, Deffaunt, Amblard in 2002 [9]. BC model of individual opinion in this work is introduced next section.

2 Organization Behavior Prediction Modeling of Network Community Based on Opinion Dynamics

In BC model, the characteristics of each individual are decided by two continuous variables: the opinion values and uncertainty value.

Let x_i and x_j be opinion value of individual i and j, respectively, and u_i and u_j uncertainty value of individual i and j, respectively. h_{ij} represents opinion repeat part of individual i and j, μ represents a amplitude parameters which controls the whole group interaction speed. The functions of our model are written as follows:

$$h_{ij} = \min\left(x_i + u_i, x_j + u_j\right) - \max\left(x_i - u_i, x_j - u_j\right) \tag{1}$$

$$x_{j+1} = x_j + \mu\left(\frac{h_{ij}}{u_i} - 1\right)\left(x_i - x_j\right) \tag{2}$$

$$u_{j+1} = u_j + \mu\left(\frac{h_{ij}}{u_i} - 1\right)\left(u_i - u_j\right) \tag{3}$$

Bounded confidence model makes individual point value become real number between 0 and 1, and every individual chooses a neighbor randomly in each step length, if it is within the scope of threshold value, then individual interacts with the neighbor according to the established rules; if the neighbor's opinion difference is greater than the threshold, interaction will not occur. Individuals select a neighbor randomly to interact at any time, and use above expression to update opinion value after the completion of the interaction.

We make individual i as example, $x_i = 0.5$ represents that i holds a neutral opinion; $0 \leq x_i < 0.5$ represents i holds an opposite opinion, and the smaller the value, greater the degree of opposition; $0.5 < x_i \leq 1$ represents i holds a supportive opinion, and the greater the value, greater the degree of approval.

In order to differentiate the relation of two types of opinion event (i.e., society and low, and livelihood) to three types of people (i.e., young, middle-age and old people), we specify the scopes of initial opinion vale x and uncertainty value u. Thus, the features of two types of opinion for three types of communities can be identified clearly in simulation experiments. The detailed specifications of x and u are given in Sect. 3.

3 Experimental Results and Analysis

Community size: Total population $N = 2000$ (young people are between 14 and 44 years old, middle-aged people are between 45 and 59 years old, old people are over 60 years old).

Youth Community: young people account for 60%, middle-age people account for 35%, old people account for 5%; middle-age community: young people account for 35%, middle-aged people account for 60%, old people account for 5%; old community: young people account for 45%, middle-age people account for 45%, old people account for 10%.

Interaction rules: Individuals have the priority of the interaction with the same age range. An individual can only communicate with one individual at the same time, interaction process uses the Eqs. 1, 2 and 3 to evolve.

The prediction model uses Any logic to implement, and uses Matlab 2012 to do a numerical analysis. From 2015 public opinion pressure index [13], we can find that social and law events and livelihood events are hot topics in public opinion field, so our research focuses on two kinds of events: social and law events and livelihood events.

3.1 Simulation Results for Network Public Opinion Event of Society and Law

Initial state values of different age structure groups:

(1) In the face of social injustice, inequality, corruption and moral anomie, young people are easy to show the strong moral indignation. We set initial value x_y in [0.1, 0.3] or [0.7, 0.9] randomly, which shows opinion value of young people is extreme. We set uncertainty value u_y as 0.8, which shows that they are easy to be influenced by others.

(2) Middle-age people are the salt of the earth that could control their attitude and mood according to the objective situation. We set initial value x_m in [0.4, 0.6] randomly, which shows their own opinions tend to be neutral. We set uncertainty value u_m as 0.2, which shows that they are difficult to be influenced by others.

(3) Old people's life experience make them counter society and law with a "cooling" thought, and they are not easy to be influenced by others. We set initial value x_o in [0.45, 0.55] randomly. We set uncertainty value u_o as 0.1.

Simulation results are shown in Fig. 1.

Simulation results show that the patterns of three communities are almost similar between each other. The main reason is that the middle-age and old people have almost the same opinion on the event of society and law in the real world. This can be confirmed in Sect. 3, we set initial value x_m in [0.4, 0.6] randomly and uncertainty value u_m as 0.2 for middle-age people, while we set initial value x_o in [0.45, 0.55] randomly and uncertainty value u_o as 0.1 for old people. But we can still draw some distinct conclusions among three simulation results as follows:

(1) The red curved lines, i.e., young people's opinion, converge faster than the other two types of lines in all three simulation experiments. It means young people in youth community have the fastest convergence of opinion values. It is consistent with the current situation of young people's strong learning ability. The more young population, the much fully interactive information, the faster they learn, the faster to reach a consensus.

(2) In middle-age community opinion converge faster than the other two communities. See Fig. 1c and d, the time of convergence is before 100. See the other 4 figures, the convergence times are after 100. Meanwhile, the evolution trend of the overall average opinion values in the three different communities are the most close to the evolution trend of middle-age group's opinion values in each community. These results mean middle-age people guide the core opinion direction of the community.

(3) Concentration degree in all three communities is always densest. It indicates that old group has stable effect on opinion evolution tendency for community and can control suddenly changing situation such as a few young people' extreme opinion values.

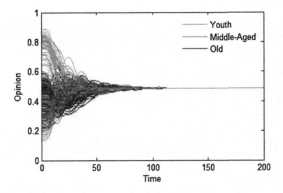

(a)Opinion evolution of youth community

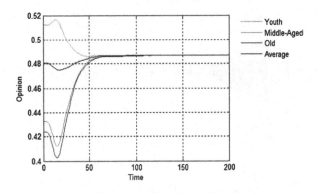

(b)Overall average opinion of youth community

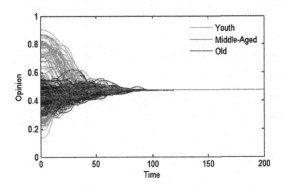

(c) Opinion evolution of middle-age community

Fig. 1. Simulation results for opinion on society and law (Color figure online)

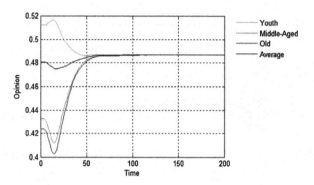

(d) Overall average opinion of middle-age community

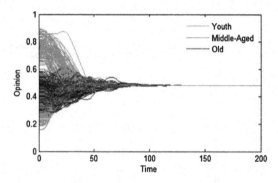

(e) Opinion evolution of old community

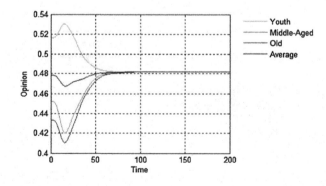

(f) Overall average opinion of old community

Fig. 1. (*continued*)

3.2 Simulation Results for Network Public Opinion Event of Livelihood

Initial state values of different age structure groups:

(1) Young people accept quickly for this kind of information, and their updating frequency is high. They tend to have a certain value for such events, and are not easy to be affected, we set initial value x_y in [0.1, 0.4] or [0.6, 0.9] randomly, which shows part of young people's opinion value will be extreme. We set uncertainty value u_y as 0.1, which shows that they are not easy to be influenced by others.

(2) Middle-age people will still have the most rational judgment. We get initial value x_m in [0.4, 0.6] randomly, which shows their own opinion tends to be neutral. We get uncertainty value u_m as 0.1, which shows that they are a little difficult to be influenced by others, but easier than young people.

(3) Such events are so up-to-date that old people can't understand very well or have enough experience, they are easily affected by the people around them. We set initial value x_y in [0, 1] randomly, which shows the initial opinion values of old people will be very random. We set uncertainty value u_y as 0.8, which shows that they are easy to be influenced by others.

Simulation results are shown in Fig. 2.

Youth group is the most difficult to reach a consensus in three kinds of community groups, because young people have a relatively strong personal will for the livelihood event. Although a few of young people will form a neutral opinion as time goes by, most of them will eventually evolve into extreme opinion values. Middle-age group is the most stable group, and their views' changing trends are basically same in the three kinds of communities, but different from public opinion events of society and law, for event of livelihood they don't always keep a neutral opinion. In three kinds of communities of different age structure, the middle-age group is the only one which is close to the neutral opinion in the evolution process. When the proportion of the old people is equal to aging rate 10%, all the old people reached a neutral consensus and they have a convergence acceleration for young people's opinion, and could lead some young people evolve into neutral opinion value; When the proportion is less than 10%, as shown in youth community (Fig. 2a and b) and middle-age community (Fig. 2c and d), the old group could turn into a very extreme opinion value, and reaches consensus of extreme opinion value, that is easy to lead a group polarization phenomenon, and they hold the opposing opinions with youth groups, which caused great negative impact on the stability of society.

In summary, young people still prone to the extreme opinion eventually, which is influenced by evolution trend of old people; the middle-age group is relatively stable; although old group accounts for a small proportion, on the basis of previous research group, they have no big impact on the whole community, but play an important guiding role in the community, which has a very important influence on the stability and evolution trend of the whole community public opinion.

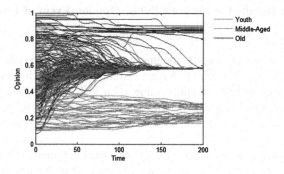

(a)Opinion evolution of youth community

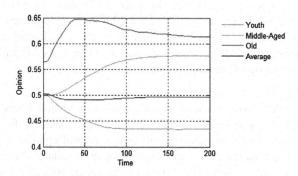

(b)Overall average opinion of youth community

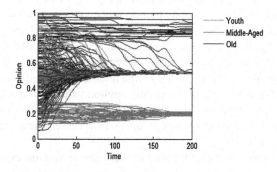

(c)Opinion evolution of middle-age community

Fig. 2. Simulation results for opinion on livelihood

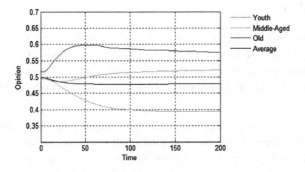

(d)Overall average opinion of middle-age community

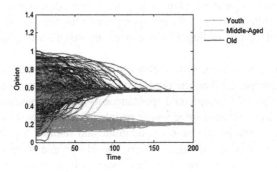

(e)Opinion evolution of old community

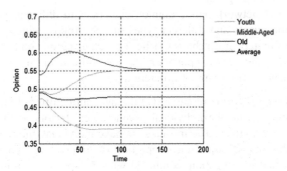

(f) Overall average opinion of old community

Fig. 2. (*continued*)

4 Conclusion

Two hot Internet public opinion events, i.e., social and law, and livelihood are considered in this work. We build a dynamic prediction model under different age structure to explore evolution mechanisms of three community with different age structure (i.e., young, middle-age, and old community). Contributes of this work are summarized as follows:

(1) In network public opinion of social and law, proper guide for youth group is the key for controlling all society's opinion evolution. The reason is that collective opinion of youth group always shows sudden change, and maybe lead to unstability of opinion of whole community. But this phenomena can be aligned by middle-age group. Meanwhile, the old group can control the sudden changes of young people's opinion, which can effectively reduce the mutation phenomenon of young individual opinions. Thus, our government should focus on stabilizing opinion of middle-age group. At the appropriate time the old ones, e.g., expert in the domain of corresponding event, can be invited to talk about the event by government.

(2) In the network public opinion of livelihood, opinions of all individuals are difficult to reach a consensus. When the proportion of old people meets the proportion of the aging society, old group could spontaneously reach a consensus on the neutral opinion, and they will lead some young people to reach a consensus on the neutral opinion, thus the old people have a good guide and stability for young people. But when our country is not in aging society, the old people is easy to reach a consensus on the extreme opinions, and then forms polarization of collective opinion. Thus, our government should make effective strategies to keep old people remain stable in the network public opinion. It can be beneficial for social public opinion situation of other age groups.

(3) This research of network public opinion elaborates to different types of network public opinion events and different types of age groups, which assists the government to accurately grasp characteristics of each age group on the network public opinion. It also provides supports for the government to take more appropriate measures for network groups of different age.

The future direction of the research: (1) the age can be divided into more precise levels, and combined with the individual psychological factors, such as personality, emotion or cognitive abilities. The mental state have individual differences even in the same age. (2) We should adjust the proportion of different age groups in network community by actual investigation, combined with the specific data for more simulation experiments.

References

1. Zhao, Y.: Public opinion evolution based on complex networks. Cybern. Inf. Technol. **15**(1), 55–68 (2015)
2. Hui, J., Xu, U., Xi, A.: Opinion propagation and public opinion formation model for forum networks. Comput. Sci. **5**, 150–152 (2013)
3. Wei, W., Gao, H., She, L.: Opinion mining for web public sentiment based on dynamic knowledge base. In: International Symposium on Emergency Management, pp. 199–203 (2009)
4. Chen, X., Gao, H., Fu, Y.: Situation analysis and prediction of web public sentiment. In: 2008 International Symposium on Information Science and Engineering, pp. 707–710 (2008)
5. Galam, S.: Minority opinion spreading in random geometry. Eur. Phys. J. B Condens. Matter Complex Syst. **25**(4), 403–406 (2002)
6. Cheng, Z., Xiong, Y., Xu, Y.: An opinion diffusion model with decision-making groups: the influence of the opinion's acceptability. Physica A **461**, 429–438 (2016)
7. Dong, Y., Ding, Z., Martínez, L., et al.: Managing consensus based on leadership in opinion dynamics. Inf. Sci. **397–398**, 187–205 (2017)
8. Gabbay, M.: The effects of nonlinear interactions and network structure in small group opinion dynamics. Physica A **378**(1), 118–126 (2007)
9. Weisbuch, G., Deffaunt, G., Amblard, F., Faure, T.: How can extremism prevail? A study based on the relative agreement model. J. Artif. Soc. Soc. Simul. **5**(4), 1 (2002)
10. Van Gerven, M., Farquhar, J., Schaefer, R., et al.: The braincomputer interface cycle. J. Neural Eng. **6**(4), 1–10 (2009)
11. Deffuant, G., Neau, D., Amblard, F., et al.: Mixing beliefs among interacting agents. Adv. Complex Syst. **3**(1–4), 87–98 (2000)
12. Hegselmann, R., Krause, U.: Opinion dynamics and bounded confidence models, analysis, and simulation. J. Artif. Soc. Soc. Simul. **5**(3), 1–8 (2002)
13. Report of hot Internet public opinion [OL]. http://yuqing.people.com.cn/GB/401915/408999/index.html

Research on the Growth of Engineering Science and Technology Talents from the Perspective of Complex Science

Haifeng Zhao$^{(\boxtimes)}$ and Weijia Jiang$^{(\boxtimes)}$

School of Economics and Management, Tongji University, No1. Rd Zhangwu,
Shanghai, China
{hfzhao,1631071}@tongji.edu.cn

Abstract. With the rapid development of information technology and the strategy of "Made in China 2025", the state has met new requirement for talents training. Under the background of "made in China 2025", based on complex science theory, this paper established the model of "Gong" model of engineering talents. The growth of engineering talents can be divided into three stages, that is, the basic and higher education stage, the social stage and the continuing education stage. Based on the phased characteristics of talent growth, this paper studied the law of the growth of engineering talents and the path of the road and summed up the law of phased growth of engineering talent in "Gong" type, and proposed deepening the reform of continuing education to improve the training mechanism for engineering talents.

Keywords: Engineering talents · Growth law · Made in China 2025
Complex science

CLC Number: G642

1 Introduction

Complex science is an interdisciplinary field dealing with various complex phenomena in natural and social systems, which was born in 1980s. It is one of the frontier fields of modern natural science, and it has penetrated into the fields of philosophy, humanity, social science and education [1]. Complex adaptive system is one of the main theories of complexity science. It mainly studies the interaction between the main body of self-organizing behavior, and explores the complexity and mechanism of the system. To some extent, the process of talent training can be regarded as the process of adapting individual talents to social environment and satisfying social needs [2]. Uncertainty is the main characteristic of complex science, and it also has strong uncertainty, that is, it can not be fully predicted. Because there are multiple positive and negative feedback between the main body, the system and the environment of the training system, some initial factors or minor events may cause wider changes [3].

With the rapid development of information technology and the "Made in China 2025" strategy, the state put forward basic policy, "innovation-driven, quality first,

© Springer Nature Singapore Pte Ltd. 2018
H. Yuan et al. (Eds.): GSKI 2017, CCIS 849, pp. 736–745, 2018.
https://doi.org/10.1007/978-981-13-0896-3_72

green development, structural optimization, talent-based". With the complexity of personnel training and the change of demand, we should reexamine our talent training system. China's talent researchers divided the type of talent according to the knowledge structure, from the width and depth of the knowledge and proposed "T-type talent" concept. According to the concept of "T-type talent", this paper puts forward the law of the growth of "engineering" talents for the cultivation of high-tech scientific and technological talents based on the background of "Made in China 2025", hoping to make some reference for the cultivation of higher engineering science and technology talents in China.

2   "Gong" Type Engineering and Technology Talent Training Mode

A. The basic concept of "Gong" type engineering and technology talent

At the beginning of the 20th century, domestic scholars put forward the concept of T-type talent [4] which is a new type of talent training model with the focus on continuing learning ability training professional practice ability. The letter 'T' of T-type talent show the knowledge structure and basic quality that talent needed to master [5].

Based on the T - type talent, we put forward a new model of "Gong" engineering science and technology talent, and explores the optimal growth path of engineering talents from the beginning of basic education to continuing education. This model is taken from Chinese character "工", which takes the characteristics of career development into consideration and commits to cultivate a "broad and solid theoretical basis +professional technical skills in depth+centralized management skills" talent. The longer horizontal lines represent the basic general ability to support the development of engineering and technology talent, which are usually obtained in the basic education and higher education stages and are the cornerstone part of the professional development of engineering and t professional ability can be called "Gong" engineering a technology talent. Vertical lines indicate the depth of engineering and technology talent to master the professional knowledge. The shorter horizontal line indicates the comprehensive development ability of engineering and technology talent, such as the ability to manage coordination and the ability to engage in large and complex projects. This combination of ability and nd technology talents. "Gong" type of talent as shown in Fig. 1.

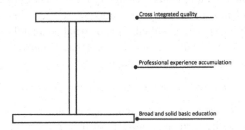

Fig. 1. Sketch map of "Gong" type talent

B. *"Gong" type engineering and technology talent under "China-made 2025"*

The proposition of "made in China 2025" puts forward new capacity requirements for engineering and technology talents, which is the opportunity and challenge for the training of engineering talents in China. Facing the transformation and upgrading of the manufacturing industry, there is an urgent need for high-quality personnel to provide support, fundamentally solve the bottleneck of manufacturing development [6]. We must rely on talent to promote the development of the way to develop, suitable for "Made in China 2025" under the background of engineering and technology talents.

Accordingly, we propose engineering and technology talent growth model adapting to the background of "China made 2025", as shown in Fig. 2 [7, 8].

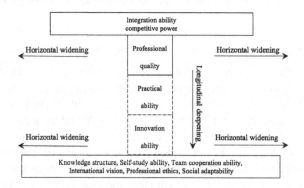

Fig. 2. Engineering and technology talent model under "China made 2025"

In the next five to fifteen years, the traditional industrialization and emerging industrialization are alternated, the era of industrialization and information epoch-making intertwined, industrialization and information technology in-depth integration of the "three superposition" period. China's "Made in China 2025" is also to meet the challenges of this new industrial revolution, trying to seize the opportunities for manufacturing development and the commanding heights. China is a big manufacturing country, but the independent research and development level is weak, lack of independent intellectual property rights of high technology, as well as the lack of world-class research resources and technology knowledge, so the current situation of Chinese culture "manufacturing project 2025" science and technology talents under the background of the new requirements. "Gong" type engineering and technology talent need to have a complete knowledge system structure, self-learning ability, international vision, teamwork ability, professional ethics and social adaptability. They also need to deepen their professional quality, practical ability and innovation ability, and then acquired the ability to integrate and competitive.

C. *Characteristics of phased development of engineering and technology talent*

The growth of talent is both a continuous process and a phased process. With the time T as the abscissa, the vertical coordinate of the upper curve of Fig. 3 shows the engineering talents Output capacity growth rate, Fig. 3, the vertical curve of the lower part of the curve shows the degree of creativity of engineering and technology talent.

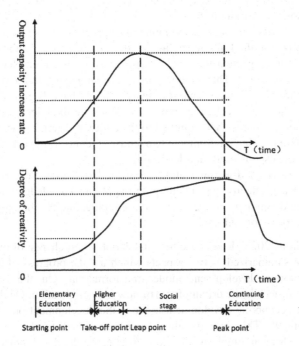

Fig. 3. Growth curve of engineering and technology talents

Figure 3, the starting point for the innovative engineering and technology talent began to grow point of time to take off for the growth of engineering and technology talent to maximize the acceleration; leap point is the fastest time point, The output capacity growth rate reached the maximum, and from this point, the output capacity growth rate began to decline gradually, but the output capacity of engineering and technology talent is still increasing the leap soon, engineering and technology talent to play the bottleneck, Growth is slow, the peak speed when the acceleration achieve the smallest and maximize the degree of creativity. Output capacity growth rate of zero means that since that point, its output capacity began to decline, while, Engineering and technology talent growth rate slowed down, the degree of creativity also began to decline until the stagnation.

3 The Law of Talent Growth in the Basic and Higher Education Stages

A. *Basic education stage*
The basic education in the modern sense belongs to the foundation stage of the national education system. Overall, the direct mission of elementary education is to

cultivate citizen society in the future, lay the foundation for the talents of lifelong learning, to master basic learning skills, survival skills and survival ability, so the basic education during the key personnel training is also focused on the general ability of horizontal training base.

(1) *Team work ability:* In large-scale engineering projects, the success of the whole project depends on the full cooperation of the sub projects and subsystems. Partial success does not represent the whole. Sometimes too much emphasis on the part will hurt the whole job. That's the importance of teamwork. In the basic education stage, the domestic primary and secondary schools have begun to try to group activities as the main teaching activities, emphasizing the interaction between the team members, students are committed to the ability to learn, and trying to provide a collaborative learning environment to exercise students teamwork ability, training team sense of responsibility and leadership.

(2) *Self-study ability:* Self-learning ability is a kind of ability that an individual is independent and effective in obtaining and applying knowledge and skills under the guidance of any person. His core lies in thinking, and the thought runs through the whole process of self study.

"Made in China 2025" lead to the new industrialization change of our country. Its meaning can be summarized as two aspects which are the progress of high-tech progress and economic development mode transformation. On the one hand, the advancement of hi-tech is the driving force of new industrialization. On the other hand, the upgrading of economic development mode is the development orientation of new industrialization [9]. This requires those who can adapt to the development of high-level technology and high-quality skills to upgrade the development of technical personnel or technical personnel, because they will be at the core of the manufacturing sector. In addition, engineering and technology talent even need to engage in service work, to efficient handle of customer needs and gradually based on the emerging service career. All of these need our engineering and technology talent to master self-learning ability.

In general, this stage of personnel training because it is the basic stage. In contrast to the professional knowledge of the professor, the basic education stage is more inclined to grant the basic disciplines of knowledge, as the future of professional knowledge to learn the cornerstone. What's more, this stage focuses on the cultivation and excavation of students' comprehensive ability and special potential, so the stage of personnel training mainly cultivates part of the horizontal general ability, for the professional ability part has not been involved. Because of this part of the basic, this stage of the quality of education has become one of the key factors to open the gap between the quality of talent.

A. *Higher education stage*

Higher education stage is the stage that engineering and technology talents understand the world and to inheritance, learning, accumulation of previous results. In terms of physiological characteristics, the ability of memory, judgment and reaction has reached the peak of life that they can learn a lot and study a wide range of knowledge. They have great enthusiasm and technological potential and a strong plasticity. This stage is the accumulation phrase for scientific and technological talents' quality. It is insurmountable and extremely important stage.

The key to the growth of talent in higher education is to understand the inherent laws of things, to develop the system (dialectical) to think of habits; to cultivate the quality of independent thinking; to establish business goals, to establish the basis of social work; to develop curiosity and interest, to establish the correct outlook on life, values, world view. Therefore, although this stage is also focused on cultivating students' horizontal general ability, but the focus of its training and basic education stage is not the same.

(1) *Knowledge structure:* Knowledge structure refers to the large system of knowledge that the knowledge subsystem of engineering science and technology talent has the interrelations and interaction of various concepts, methods, experience and other knowledge. Its most important feature is the integrity and adaptability. The knowledge structure of innovative engineering science and technology talent emphasizes "thick foundation, wide caliber". As the last stage of education before the entry of engineering talents into the workplace, the stage of higher education is bound to take on the role of the transitional leader of the student's identity to the worker's identity. Therefore, the construction of relatively complete knowledge structure system will be carried out mainly in the higher education stage.

(2) *International vision:* At present, a new round of scientific and technological revolution, industrial transformation and China to accelerate the transformation of economic development mode to form a historical intersection. We urgently need to cultivate international engineering science and technology talents who are familiar with international rules, international standards, international technical level and adapt to cross-cultural mobility. Today, China has developed into the world's second largest economy. The state requires college students must have international knowledge and skills, which is the responsibility of the times to give colleges and universities, but also the mission of the university [10].

(3) *Professional ethics:* Professional ethics education is the process of students' moral cognition, so that students can change their professional ethics into their own qualities. It is difficult for the students themselves to have a relatively clear concept of engineering ethics. Each industry has the need to strictly abide by the ethics and norms, different industries have different characteristics. The main responsibility for cultivating engineering science and technology talents lie in colleges and universities. Colleges and universities not only is to impart professional knowledge of the institutions, also they are the institutions of enlightening quality, the primary responsibility of professional ethics education.

(4) *Social adaptability:* Social adaptability is the individual in the process of interaction with the environment, through the continuous adjustment of self-physical and mental state, so that the physical and mental and consistent with the real environment, and thus to develop self-ability. The ability of society to adapt to innovative engineering and scientific and technological talent should be unified with the community itself, through contacting with the community continue to develop their resilience to a proactive attitude to adapt to society to speed up its socialization process [11].

4   The Law of Talent Growth in the Social Stages

The growth of engineering and technology talents is inseparable from the environment where they transform knowledge into practical. Engineering discipline is the formation and development of practical guidance theory. Engineering and technology talent who has been into social career improve their professional quality and technical capacity through practice. the development of the potential and creativity of talent. In the field of engineering, generally set 5 years of work experience as a watershed for engineering talent, according to which social education can be divided into social adaptation stage and innovation and creative stage.

A. *Social adaptation stage*

As the current high education stage group is mainly the implementation of general education, so the professional knowledge and the transformation from knowledge into practical experience is not perfect. Talent in the pre-entry must have a training process to adapt to the professional role of engineering and technology talent. The work of the engineering and technology talent at this stage is mostly related to the background of their education and training, combined with some scientific simplification methods to solve the problem. The difference is that the application of these theoretical knowledge is usually confined to a very professional field. These tasks are usually done under the guidance of experienced engineering and technology talent, which is a stage of rapid progress for new engineering and technology talent. The most important feature of this stage is the starting point of the engineering and technology talent career, belonging to the pure technical stage.

During this period engineering science and technology personnel think about the correlation between theory, practice. In the course of social experience, they make adjustments in knowledge, beliefs, attitudes and behaviour to overcome the incompatibility of social work, resulting in a desire to deepen professional competence and demand.

The career orientation of engineering and technology talents is clear. They follow the experienced master to learn engineering experience according to "master effect". They participate in the project team to be familiar with the cork environment.

Talent deepen the purpose of professional depth through the training of organization or to participate in the professional institutions of higher education and then further educated in order to achieve the updated knowledge. To enhance professional quality and practical ability is the focus of this stage [12]. Through the work practice, the professional knowledge of engineering talents can be expanded, and the framework of stable knowledge can be set up in an all-round way.

B. *Innovation creation stage*

Then, engineers and technicians entered the period of creation, and they have been able to create, transform and develop new human knowledge with the accumulated cognitive abilities and knowledge. From a psychological point of view, the 30 year old is the most creative individual talent period [13]. The characteristics of talent creation is the basic structure of intelligent structure, talent development is the golden age, the prime of life, practical experience, social background. The general characteristics of the psychological career of talent creation for the pursuit of maturity and prestige, quick thinking and rich willpower. The key to the success of creation is: First, the courage to make original exploration, into the cross-disciplinary areas, no man's land, quickly into the frontier positions; Second, pay attention to the art of research, methods and scientific; perseverance. From the research and application of various technical methods to solve the problem, the process of solving the problem of participation management needs holistic, global perspective and related knowledge. This requires a holistic, holistic perspective and related knowledge. For many engineers and technicians, this is a difficult change, but most people will find that after the painful process of transformation success, there will be a lot of unexpected results. To achieve sustained development at this stage, you must master such basic skills as project management, interpersonal processing, communication and coordination, and other disciplines, such as finance and marketing.

This stage focuses on training innovative ability. The ability to innovate is a basic characteristic of an excellent engineering and technology talent, and an important symbol of the excellence of an excellent engineer [14]. After 5 years of production practice, the individual has the necessary expertise to complete the job and the qualification for professional work. Engineering talents find new engineering problems in a large number of Engineering practices. According to the needs of economic and social development, they find new demands of society for products, technologies, industries and equipment, as well as the engineering goals formed by their own ideals and aspirations. The ability to solve these engineering problems through creative engineering practices, research, design, and develop new products to achieve new engineering goals.

5 Growth Pattern of Scientific and Technological Talents in Continuing Education Stage

When engineers and technicians have a large amount of professional knowledge and experience and have enough creative ability, they usually go through middle or senior management positions through job promotion. The higher level engineers and technicians have higher demand for their management skills. At the same time, the vertical expertise and the general ability of the engineering and technology talent are not enough to meet their job demands. With the rapid development of modern science and technology, many disciplines of the original industrial sector have been reorganized and eliminated, and new industrial and interdisciplinary disciplines, interdisciplinary and comprehensive disciplines have been springing up. Engineers and technicians at the higher education stage were unable to meet the needs of the present work. Based on the concept of lifelong learning, through continuing education, updating professional knowledge, mastering management skills, training integration ability and competitive ability, this is the focus of this stage. In combination with the establishment of the position of engineers and technicians in this stage, the integration ability and competitive ability of engineering and technology talents are usually emphasized, and the management knowledge of them is understood and mastered.

Enterprises are also places where scientific research results are transformed into productive forces. The continuous growth of engineering talents in the enterprise is the key to their creativity. Nowadays, the research of training talents in higher education has become more and more mature. The field of engineering is the discipline that guides the development of experience, and it is important to train the talents of Engineering Science and technology with the stage of higher engineering education through continuing education. However, as the continuing education phase is divorced from the full-time education environment in Institutions of higher learning, it is difficult to guarantee the educational universality and the quality of education. Therefore, the reform of continuing education system is of great importance to the training of engineering talents of science and technology, especially those of Engineering Science and technology under the background of "2025 made in China".

6 Conclusion

Under the background of "made in China 2025", we analyse the law of phased growth of engineering scientific and technological talents, and put forward a model of "Gong". The development of Engineering Science and technology talents is divided into basic education and higher education, social training and continuing education. According to the emergence of talents in Engineering Science and technology, the social training stage is divided into the social adaptation stage and the creation innovation stage. Combined with the characteristics of engineering development and the particularity of engineering discipline, we believe that Team, work, ability and self-learning ability should be cultivated in the basic education stage. The higher education stage focuses on improving the knowledge structure, international outlook, professional ethics and social adaptability. The social adaptation stage emphasizes on improving the professional quality and practical ability. The creative stage is mainly based on the ability of innovation. While entering the continuing education stage, we should focus on training the ability of integration and competition. Twenty-first Century is a rapidly changing, complex and diverse era, complex systems problems emerge in an endless stream. Based on the analysis of the law of the growth of engineering scientific and technological talents, this paper holds that efforts should be made to break through the bottleneck of continuing education and improve the engineering training mechanism so as to cope with the challenges of informatization and globalization.

Acknowledgment. This research was supported by MOE (Ministry of Education in China) Project of Humanities and Social Sciences (Project No. 14JDGC016) and the NSFC General Program (Grants nos. 71272045).

References

1. Zhou, K., Zeng, Y.: A new talents training mode of undergraduate education from the perspective of complexity science-taking the talents training of engineer education as an example. Chongqing High. Educ. Res. **5**(2), 91–100 (2017)
2. Noor, A.K.: Envisioning engineering education and practice in the coming intelligence convergence era - a complex adaptive systems approach. Open Eng. **3**(4), 606–619 (2013)
3. Gattie, D.K., Kellam, N.N., Schramski, J.R., et al.: Engineering education as a complex system. Eur. J. Eng. Educ. **36**(6), 521–535 (2011)
4. Lin, C., Hu, W.: Growth rules and cultivation models of creative talents. J. Beijing Normal Univ. **1**, 36–42 (2012)
5. Tan, J.: On the construction of training mode of T-type in higher vocational and technological college. J. High. Educ. **10**, 68–72 (2005)
6. Zhang, Y., Zhang, Y.: Guided by third industrial revolution: the strategic choice of transformation of higher engineering education in China. Educ. Res. **5**, 37–42 (2014)
7. Bai, C., Chen, Q., Zhang, H.: A review of the research on the growth pattern and training mode of top-notch innovative talents. Educ. Res. **12**, 147–151 (2012)
8. Li, T., Li, F., Lu, G.: On improving the quality of engineering technology talents cultivation in terms of the "Made in China 2025" plan. Res. High. Educ. Eng. **6**,17–23 (2015)
9. Zhang, L., Zhang, C.: The career flow and professional ability framework of skilled personnel in the perspective of "made in China 2025". Voc. Educ. Forum **10**, 17–21 (2016)
10. Du, W., Guo, S.: A probe into the cultivation of College Students' international vision in the global environment. Educ. Asia Pac. **6**, 222 (2015)
11. Sun, L., Zeng, F., Wang, S.: A study o the model of social adaptation of college students-taking students born after 1995 as an example. J. Sichuan Univ. Sci. Eng. **31**(1), 20–29 (2016)
12. Hu, Z., Liu, Y.: Searching for the origin: three regressions to raise college students' engineering practice ability. Res. High. Educ. Eng. **1** (2015)
13. Li, S.: The best age and the law of success – on the law of becoming a useful person. Talent Dev. **8**, 21 (1994)
14. Jian, L.: On outstanding engineers' innovation ability training. Res. High. Educ. Eng. **5**, 1–17 (2012)

Research on the Relationship Between Entrepreneurship Learning and Entrepreneurship Ability Based on Social Network

Gang Hao[1], Qing Sun[1], and Yingying Ding[2(✉)]

[1] School of Economics, Harbin University of Commerce,
No. 138 tongda street, daoli district, Harbin, China
Haogang131@126.com, 13895730129@163.com
[2] Innovation and Entrepreneurship College, Harbin University of Commerce,
No. 138 tongda street, daoli district, Harbin, China
18714509769@163.com

Abstract. The entrepreneurship ability determines whether the entrepreneurship will be successful, the entrepreneurial learning (Project Support: Philosophy and Social Sciences Project of Heilongjiang Province (17JYC146), Heilongjiang Province Postdoctoral Fund (LBH-Z15114).) is the key element to enhance the entrepreneurial capacity, while the social network provides a lot of knowledge resources to enhance the entrepreneurial capacity, but few researches explore the action mechanism between the social network, entrepreneurial learning and entrepreneurial capacity from the entrepreneurial point of view. Based on the social network. This paper establishes the theoretical relationship model between the three aspects, and uses the structural equation analysis method to validate the theoretical hypothesis. The empirical results show that the entrepreneur can make the social network as an important platform for entrepreneurial learning, both the formal network and the informal network have a significant positive impact on the implementation of entrepreneurial learning. The entrepreneurial learning mode under the social network can be divided into three types: imitation learning, exchange learning and guidance learning, which will play a positive role in promoting the entrepreneurial capacity; entrepreneurs can choose the right way to learn entrepreneurship, and effectively enhance the entrepreneurial capacity.

Keywords: Social network · Entrepreneurial learning
Entrepreneurial capacity

CLC Number: F204

1 Introduction

Entrepreneurship learning has become a new hotspot in entrepreneurial research. Entrepreneurs' learning ability plays an important role in entrepreneurial activities and has an impact on all aspects of entrepreneurship. Social network is an important platform for entrepreneurs to pursue entrepreneurial learning, and entrepreneurs can acquire others' previous experiences through social networks and integrate them into the upcoming entrepreneurial practices. In other words, entrepreneurs can gain resources and information related to their own business on a social networking platform and build their own learning networks, improve their entrepreneurial knowledge and skills, and eventually learn or create new knowledge, skills, or learning behavior. How to enhance the entrepreneurial ability is the urgent problem in the current business practice, the promotion of entrepreneurial ability is essentially a learning process [1]. Most of the relevant research on entrepreneurial ability explain the formation process of entrepreneurial ability from the empirical point of view, but put too much emphasis on the important role of previous experience learning on the entrepreneurial ability, but there are many entrepreneurs in reality who obtain the success in the absence of previous or related. More and more scholars began to emphasize the importance of social networks, and social network-related business learning begins to be concerned about, which is considered an important platform for entrepreneurs to learn, and has also become an important factor affecting entrepreneurial ability [2, 3].

However, everyone has their own network of social relations more or less, why some people can get valuable knowledge, while some people can't? What kind of social network and what kind of network relationship structure are conducive to entrepreneurs to start business learning? What aspects of entrepreneurial learning can improve the ability of entrepreneurs? In order to better understand the relationship between social network, entrepreneurial learning and entrepreneurial ability, this paper, based on the research results of domestic and foreign scholars, defines the relevant concepts and establishes the research framework, so as to reveal the action mechanism of entrepreneurial learning on entrepreneurial ability from the perspective of social network.

2 Theoretical Basis and Research Hypothesis

2.1 Concept Definition

Entrepreneurial Network. Social network refers to the social relations, business contacts, or the unique relationship between individuals in social groups created in carrying out the entrepreneurial activities and in the process of business operations [4]. Social networks can provide entrepreneurs with a variety of resources, and create the opportunities of low-cost learning, which is a key platform for business learning.

The existing research shows that the entrepreneurial ability is accessible, the openness, diversity and inclusiveness featured by social network make it increasingly become an important platform for entrepreneurial learning, entrepreneurs choose the appropriate learning method to access to knowledge, and then internalize and integrate the knowledge into entrepreneurial ability, so as to achieve the changes of entrepreneurial awareness or entrepreneurial behavior. Mulder et al. argues that observational learning and exchange learning are significantly relevant to the three abilities of and entrepreneurs: strategic competencies, organizational skills and opportunity abilities [5, 6]. The studies of Radu et al. have proved that the guidance learning has a significant positive impact on the entrepreneurial commitment and endurance.

Entrepreneurial Learning. The importance of entrepreneurial learning has been widely recognized by academia, but different scholars have different ideas on the concept definition of entrepreneurial learning. Some scholars explained the connotation of entrepreneurial learning from the perspective of knowledge management, thinking that entrepreneurial learning is the process of knowledge creation [7]. Deakins and Free who first put forward entrepreneurial learning pointed out that the entrepreneurial learning is the process that the entrepreneurs are constantly acquiring new knowledge and combining and assimilating knowledge to influence entrepreneurial behavior. Rae and Carswell defined the entrepreneurial learning as a process of restructuring the methods by the individuals in organizing and managing new businesses by identifying and creating opportunities. Atuahene-Gima and Murry argued that entrepreneurial learning is the learning of entrepreneurs, which is the process of absorbing and accumulating the information and knowledge [8]. Another part of the scholars argued to explain the concept of entrepreneurial learning from the perspective of knowledge acquisition. Holcomb and Ireland argued that entrepreneurial learning is the process of acquiring new knowledge from direct experience or observing others' behavior, actions and structures. The studies of Petkova and Crick et al. argued that the observation of others's behavior, the transformation of previous experience and trial and error are the methods to obtain and master the knowledge for entrepreneurs [9, 10]. Although there is disagreement about the connotation of entrepreneurial learning, scholars have reached a consensus on the concept that entrepreneurial knowledge is the process of entrepreneurial learning.

With regard to the division of entrepreneurial learning dimensions, scholars have differentiated from different perspectives. Chandler and Lyon used organizational learning theory to classify entrepreneurial learning into five learning methods: initiation, experience, imitation, search, insight and grafting. Slater and Narver divided entrepreneurial learning into two dimensions: adaptive learning and creative learning [11]. Cope argued that entrepreneurial learning can be divided into adaptive creative learning and expected creative learning. Since the unified and mature concept on the measurement scale has not yet been formed in the field of entrepreneurial learning, it is less involved in the entrepreneurial network. Therefore, this paper divides the entrepreneurial learning into the three methods of imitation, exchange and guidance based on the study classification of Radu and Xie Yaping et al. as shown in Table 1 [12–14].

Entrepreneurial Ability. Entrepreneurial ability is the collection of a series of knowledge, skills and attitudes for the entrepreneurial success, which is the internal driving force of the entrepreneurial activities, and significant to the success of entrepreneurial practices and activities. Bird is a scholar who put forward the concept of entrepreneurial ability earlier, and defined the connotation of entrepreneurial ability from the perspective of trait, and thought that entrepreneurial ability is the innate ability of entrepreneur, including motive and character [15]. Many subsequent scholars tended to examine the role of entrepreneurs and their tasks in analyzing the entrepreneurial ability, thinking that entrepreneurial ability is the necessary knowledge and skill of the entrepreneurs to implement entrepreneurial tasks and achieve the ultimate success.

Table 1. Classification and connotation of entrepreneurial learning

Learning type	Concept connotation	Concept source
Imitation learning	It's the process "knowledge transfer", and an important learning method to observe and follow the behavior, actions and results of others, which can be said to be a "model" learning	Ozgen et al.; Xie Yaping
Exchange learning	It's the learning behavior that the entrepreneurs who communicate and cooperate with the network members to acquire skills, knowledge, or cognitive changes	Taylor et al.; Xie Yaping
Guidance learning	It's the learning behavior that the entrepreneurs realize knowledge creation or cognitive change through the guidance of others in the process of entrepreneurial activities	Jones et al.; Xie Yaping

Entrepreneurial ability is a multi-dimensional concept, for the division of dimension, different scholars put forward different basis and contents of the division. Man's six-dimensional concept is most representative, which is opportunity ability, relationship ability, conceptual ability, organizational ability, strategic ability and commitment ability. Tang Jing et al. divided the entrepreneurial ability into a second-order six-dimensional concept, namely the opportunity ability (opportunity development ability, opportunity recognition ability) and operation and management ability (organization and management ability, strategic ability, relationship ability and commitment ability) [16, 17]. Xia et al. thought that the entrepreneurial ability is owned by the entrepreneur, which is an integration of knowledge, skills, personality and ability that is conducive to the success of entrepreneurial activities and promotes the growth of entrepreneurship [18]. It is not difficult to see that, for the division of entrepreneurial ability dimension, domestic and foreign scholars mainly explained it from the entrepreneur's characteristics, opportunities, relationships and other aspects. The improved entrepreneurial ability of entrepreneurs can be attributed to that the entrepreneurial activity is embedded into the entrepreneur's social network, so it needs to consider its social network situation in the study of entrepreneurial ability.

2.2   Proposal of Research Hypothesis

Entrepreneurial Network and Entrepreneurial Ability. Entrepreneurial ability is the key to the success of entrepreneurs, social networks provide an important learning platform for entrepreneurs, which can provide entrepreneurs with entrepreneurial resources. Research showed that the entrepreneur's social network contains a complex information network and commercial network, the personal network can provide moral support for entrepreneurs, entrepreneurs can also access to the path and platform with the help of the communication between the network members, so as to complete the sharing and circulation of knowledge, and improve their entrepreneurial abilities. Accordingly, this paper proposes that:

H1: Entrepreneurial network has a significant positive impact on entrepreneurial ability

The role of entrepreneurial networks in entrepreneurial ability varies with the nature of the network. Generally speaking, the entrepreneurial network can be divided into two categories: formal and informal, in which the formal network is based on business contacts and interests, which is mainly composed by the suppliers, competitors and industry associations and other members; informal network, linked by the blood and trust, is mainly the association between friends, family members and colleagues [19]. Although it is difficult to form a highly trust relationship between formal network members due to the existence of background differences, it also creates the opportunity for the entrepreneurs to access to heterogeneous information, and the communication with the formal network members let the entrepreneurs obtain more valuable commercial information intangibly, thus reducing the risk and uncertainties of entrepreneurial activity; the communication and information sharing among informal network members have higher reliability, and the close links between them make the members become more familiar and trustful, providing more emotional support for the entrepreneurs. Accordingly, this paper proposes the following hypothesis:

H1a: Formal network has a significant positive impact on entrepreneurial ability
H1b: Informal network has a significant positive impact on entrepreneurial ability

Entrepreneurial Network and Entrepreneurial Learning. Social network learning is an important method of entrepreneurial learning, which takes place in the relationship network of the entrepreneurs. It's a learning activity that obtains the support and guidance from the social network members through the observation and imitation of others' entrepreneurial activities and entrepreneurial behavior, so as to help the entrepreneurs to master the knowledge and information related to the entrepreneurship and business operations, and better promote the success of entrepreneurship. St-Jean et al. divided into the learning outcomes into three categories through the analysis of guidance learning between teachers and pupils, namely, skills to identify opportunities and management skills, related management knowledge and self-positioning, self-efficacy and toughness and other cognitive factors [20]. In general, the formal network has larger relationship scale than informal network. Different forms of business relationship and political relations will provide entrepreneurs with more opportunities of imitation learning and guidance learning. The emotional and trust features in the informal network will enhance the willingness of entrepreneurs to communicate and share knowledge. Therefore, this paper proposes the following hypothesis:

H2: Formal network has a significant positive impact on business learning
H2a: Formal network has a significant positive impact on imitation learning
H2b: Formal network has a significant positive impact on exchange learning
H2c: Formal network has a significant positive impact on guidance learning
H3: Informal network has a significant positive impact on entrepreneurial learning
H3a: Informal network has a significant positive impact on imitation learning
H3b: Informal network has a significant positive impact on the exchange learning
H3c: Informal network has a significant positive impact on guidance learning

Entrepreneurial Network Learning and Entrepreneurial Ability. Entrepreneurial ability is accessible, the openness, diversity and inclusiveness featured by the social network provide the entrepreneur the opportunity to choose the right way to learn, access to knowledge, internalize knowledge, integrate knowledge, and ultimately achieve the changes of entrepreneurs or entrepreneurial behavior. Mulder et al. believed that observational and exchange learning will have a positive impact on the strategic competencies, opportunity ability and organizational skills needed by the entrepreneur. Radu et al. proved that the guidance learning has an important impact on the commitment ability of entrepreneurs [21]. Accordingly, this paper proposes the following hypothesis as shown in Fig. 1:

H4: Entrepreneurial learning has a significant positive impact on entrepreneurial ability
H4a: Imitation learning has a significant positive impact on entrepreneurial ability
H4b: Exchange learning has a significant positive impact on entrepreneurial ability
H4c: Guidance learning has a significant positive impact on entrepreneurial ability

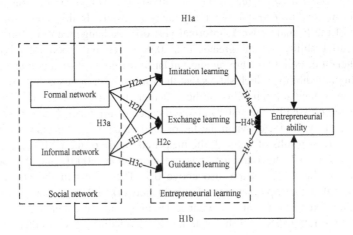

Fig. 1. Conceptual model of the relationship between entrepreneurial learning and entrepreneurial competence based on social network

3 Research Methods

(1) *Entrepreneurial network.* This study defines the entrepreneurial network as a formal network and an informal network, based on the related research from Johannisson (1995), Littunen (2000), Hansen (2005), Watson (2007), Cai Li and Shan Bian'an (2010), it formed the final questionnaires of the entrepreneurial network [22–24]. Entrepreneurship learning. This study divides the entrepreneurship learning into imitation learning, exchange learning and guidance

learning, with the reference to the studies on the connotation of entrepreneurial learning by Taylor et al. (2004), Rae (2005), Jones et al. (2007), Ozgen et al. (2007), Xie Yaping et al. (2014) and Xie Yaping et al. (2016), it formed the final questionnaires of the entrepreneurial learning [25–27]. Entrepreneurial ability. Based on the studies of De Noble (1999), Ahmad (2010), Man (2012) and He Xiaogang et al. (2005), with the reference to the existing mature scale and combined with the design of the entrepreneurial ability scale [28]. It formed the final measurement scale of this study shown in Table 2.

(2) *Data requirements.* In this study, take entrepreneurs and potential entrepreneurs as the respondents. 512 valid questionnaires were collected through the maximum likelihood method, which was in accordance with the requirements of the structural equation model, so the AMOS17.0 software can be used to further analyze the data.

(3) *Reliability and validity test.* This study does not require the subject to repeat the measurement, so it's required to test the data reliability by testing the heterogeneity. First, use the SPSS17.0 software to carry out reliability analysis to 25 items of 512 samples. The results are shown in Table 3. In general, the reliability value *Cronbach's* α is greater than or equal to 0.7, which can be considered as a sufficient condition for the reliability analysis results. In this study, the α coefficient of the formal network, informal network, exchange learning and the entrepreneurial ability are all greater than 0.9, which has good reliability, the α coefficient of imitation learning and guidance learning are greater than 0.8, which has high credibility, which shows that the variables set in this article are related to the consistency and reliability of the indicators in a high degree. The validity test can be expressed by the statistical significance of the factor load value, it can be explained by the factor when the factor load value is greater than 0.5. From the data analysis results of Table 3, the measured values of the KMO samples are all greater than 0.7, the Bartlett test is not more than 0.0001, and the factor load values of the 25 items are also above 0.7. The results of the above analysis showed that the topic settings of formal network, informal network, imitation learning, exchange learning, guidance learning and entrepreneurial ability scale has strong rationality, and the scale has good reliability and validity.

Table 2. Variable measurement scale

Variable		Code	Measuring item
Social network	Formal network A1	V1	Maintain close communication and cooperation with customers
		V2	Maintain close communication and cooperation with suppliers
		V3	Maintain close communication and cooperation with relevant government departments
		V4	Maintain close communication and cooperation with the tax department
		V5	Maintain close communication and cooperation with intermediaries and trade associations

(continued)

Table 2. (*continued*)

Variable		Code	Measuring item
	Informal network B1	V6	Maintain close contact and communication with relatives and friends
		V7	Maintain close contact and communication with colleagues
		V8	Maintain close contact and communication with other personal relationships
Entrepreneurial learning	Imitation learning C1	V9	Take the observation of the behavior, actions and results of the network members as important learning method
		V10	Take the imitation of the behavior, actions and results of the network members as important learning method
		V11	Take the observation and imitation of the behavior, actions and results of the network members as important learning methods
	Exchange learning D1	V12	The entrepreneurs often get the guidance from the members in the social network
		V13	The guidance social network members can help entrepreneurs solve entrepreneurial activity problems
		V14	The guidance social network members can help entrepreneurs obtain emotional support
	Guidance learning E1	V15	Entrepreneurs often learn from social network members through formal cooperation or exchange
		V16	Entrepreneurs often learn from informal cooperation or exchange with social network members
		V17	The formal exchange or cooperation and informal communication between the entrepreneurs and social network members are conducive to the success of entrepreneurial tasks
		V18	The formal exchange or cooperation and informal communication between the entrepreneurs and social network members facilitate the access to relevant emotional support
Entrepreneurial ability F1		V19	Accurate knowledge of customer needs
		V20	More time and efforts spent on the products and services required by the clients
		V21	Accurate knowledge of the products and services required by the clients
		V22	Cooperate with the staff to predict the prospects of the company investment

(*continued*)

Table 2. (*continued*)

Variable	Code	Measuring item
	V23	Maximize your interest in making resource allocation decisions
	V24	Effectively organize and encourage employees to achieve business goals
	V25	Carry out effective organization and coordination for different tasks

Table 3. Reliability and validity of each variable

Variable	Corresponding item	Factor load value	Cronbach's α coefficient
Formal network A1	V1	0.762	0.956
	V2	0.816	
	V3	0.810	
	V4	0.735	
	V5	0.732	
Informal network B1	V6	0.726	0.914
	V7	0.781	
	V8	0.802	
Imitation learning C1	V9	0.860	0.852
	V10	0.848	
	V11	0.870	
Exchange learning D1	V12	0.827	0.932
	V13	0.706	
	V14	0.885	
Guidance learning E1	V15	0.830	0.855
	V16	0.918	
	V17	0.902	
	V18	0.763	
Entrepreneurial ability F1	V19	0.848	0.918
	V20	0.870	
	V21	0.865	
	V22	0.865	
	V23	0.824	
	V24	0.731	
	V25	0.736	

4 Analysis of Model Results

4.1 Model Test

Based on the test results of the validity and reliability test of the variables formal network, informal network, imitation learning, exchange learning, guidance learning and entrepreneurial ability, and supported by the concept model of the relationship between the entrepreneurial learning and the entrepreneurial ability based on the social network, use the AMOS7.0 software, and apply the structural equation model to test the relationship between the various variables. The indicators are as follows:

$$\chi^2/df = 2.114,\ RMR = 0.046,\ RMSEA = 0.015,\ GFI = 0.949,\ AGFI = 0.911,$$
$$NFI = 0.927,\ CFI = 0.911.$$

From the above indicators, the fitting degree of the SEM model is good, and the fitting index values fall within the acceptable range. Therefore, the test results of this theory are credible.

4.2 Analysis of Hypothesis Test

The path coefficients and the hypothesis test results of the theoretical model constructed in this study are shown in Table 4.

Assuming that the path coefficient of H1 is 0.160, it is statistically significant at $p\langle 0.001$, which is consistent with the theoretical hypothesis, showing that the entrepreneurial network can actively promote the formation of entrepreneurial ability. Assuming that the path coefficient of is 0.704, it is also statistically significant at $p\langle 0.001$, showing that the formal network also has a significant positive impact on the entrepreneurial network. Assuming that the path coefficient of H1b is 0.652, it is also statistically significant at $p\langle 0.001$, showing that the informal network has a significant positive impact on the entrepreneurial ability.

Assuming that the path coefficient of H2 is 0.540, it is statistically significant at $p\langle 0.001$, which supports that the formal network of the entrepreneur has a significant positive effect on entrepreneurial learning. Corresponding to the different dimensions of entrepreneurial learning, the impact path coefficient of the formal network is 0.306, 0.588 and 0.809 respectively, the relationship between formal network and imitation learning is not very significant, indicating that the formal network does not have a strong impact on imitation learning, it may be because that the simple imitation may not bring positive impact on the entrepreneurship in the eyes of most entrepreneurs. Therefore, it hopes to create a unique entrepreneurial behavior, the formal network has strong influence on the exchange learning and guidance learning of entrepreneurs.

Assuming that the path coefficient of H3 is 0.366, it is statistically significant at $p\langle 0.001$, indicating that the informal network of the entrepreneur has a positive impact on entrepreneurial learning, thus the assumption of H3 is validated. Corresponding to the different dimensions of entrepreneurial learning, the path coefficients of the informal network are -0.322, 0.145 and -0.014 respectively, only the assumption of H3b is validated, the assumptions of H3a and H3b are not validated. This showed that the informal network characterized by emotion and trust has a stronger effect on the exchange learning of entrepreneurs, and that the learning that is generated in the informal communication process is "interactive", except that it involves the flow or transfer of entrepreneurial knowledge, it will involve a certain degree of emotional communication or interaction, and have a greater impact on the entrepreneur's cognitive model, entrepreneurial attitude and other inner experience. But because it's composed by the entrepreneurs or start-up enterprises and friends and family members or colleagues, the education, life and work background have a large degree of similarity, which is difficult to provide effective guidance and imitation learning models for entrepreneurs.

Table 4. Path coefficient and hypothesis test

Corresponding hypothesis	Relationship between the variables	P	Path coefficient	Test results
H1	Entrepreneurial network → Entrepreneurial ability	***	0.160	Support
H1a	Formal network → Entrepreneurial ability	***	0.704	Support
H1b	Informal network → Entrepreneurial ability	***	0.652	Support
H2	Formal network → Entrepreneurial learning	***	0.540	Support
H2a	Formal network → Imitation learning	*	0.306	Partially support
H2b	Formal network → Exchange learning	***	0.588	Support
H2c	Formal network → Guidance learning	***	0.809	Support
H3	Informal network → Entrepreneurial ability	***	0.366	Support
H3a	Informal network → Imitation learning	0.142	−0.322	Not support
H3b	Informal network → Exchange learning	***	0.145	Support
H3c	Informal network → Guidance learning	0.232	−0.014	Not support
H4	Entrepreneurial learning → Entrepreneurial ability	***	0.256	Support
H4a	Imitation learning → Entrepreneurial ability	*	0.104	Partially support
H4b	Exchange learning → Entrepreneurial ability	***	0.259	Support
H4c	Guidance learning → Entrepreneurial ability	***	0.652	Support

Assuming that the path coefficient of H4 is 0.256, it is statistically significant at $p\langle 0.001$, indicating that entrepreneurial learning will positively affect the entrepreneurial ability, assuming that H4 is validated. The influence factors of entrepreneurial learning on the entrepreneurial ability of different dimensions are 0.104, 0.259 and 0.622 respectively, which are in the significant level, assuming that H4a, H4b and H4c are validated, it also shows that the entrepreneurial ability is indeed accessible, there are some differences in the impact of different learning styles on entrepreneurial ability. Therefore, entrepreneurs need to choose the right way to learn and break through their own shortage in the entrepreneurial ability through corresponding learning, so as to achieve an effective upgrade of the entrepreneurship level.

5 Conclusion

Based on the research perspective of the relationship between entrepreneurial learning and entrepreneurial ability of social network, this paper constructs the relationship mechanism model between the three aspects, and uses the structural equation to carry on the empirical analysis and the test hypothesis to the research data, and analyzes action mechanism between the three aspects from the theory and the empirical levels, and get the following conclusions according to the test results:

First, the entrepreneurial network has a positive impact on entrepreneurial ability. Whether it is an informal network based on emotion and trust, or a formal network linked by interest and cooperation, it will have a positive impact on the entrepreneurial ability of entrepreneurs, among which the role of formal network is stronger. Therefore, the entrepreneur should expand the size of the social network of individuals and organizations to a certain extent, strengthen the contact and exchange with the members, play their own subjective initiatives, and actively promote the relationship management ability through active planning, operation and mobilization, and deepen the utilization degree of social network, so as to ensure the sustainability and stability of resources.

Second, the entrepreneurial network can promote entrepreneurial learning. The study found that the formal network is more conducive to the exchange learning and guidance learning, informal network is more conducive to exchange learning. The business relationship and the political relationship in the formal network are complex, which contain a lot of business information, industry knowledge and even policy information that can be utilized by the entrepreneurs in the process of entrepreneurship. Especially the communication and experience sharing between the entrepreneurs and their business relationship network, it can bring different skills and methods to entrepreneurs and help them better grasp the new knowledge. Informal network will promote the willingness of entrepreneurial learning and exchange and sharing of ideas and knowledge, which is an exchange learning in terms of emotion and trust to the entrepreneurs, the communication and trust brought from this learning can become an important driving force for the entrepreneurs to carry out entrepreneurial learning, and the knowledge and information contained can also be an important source of entrepreneurial learning. In short, entrepreneurs should recognize the importance of entrepreneurial network as a business learning platform. For different types of entrepreneurial networks, entrepreneurs should choose appropriate online learning methods, focus on learning behavior and improve their entrepreneurial learning efficiency.

Third, entrepreneurial learning has a positive impact on entrepreneurial ability. The empirical results showed that the different dimensions of entrepreneurial learning have a significant impact on entrepreneurial ability, the imitation learning, exchange learning and guidance learning have a positive role in promoting entrepreneurship. Among which the guidance learning has the biggest impact on entrepreneurial ability (path coefficient is 0.652), followed by the impact of exchange learning on entrepreneurial ability (path coefficient is 0.259). The effect of imitation learning on entrepreneurial ability is relatively small (path coefficient is 0.104), The Entrepreneurial ability can be learned, entrepreneurs should first assess their own entrepreneurial abilities, and take a different way of learning, so as to carry out efficient entrepreneurial learning, which is conducive to help entrepreneurs overcome shortages as soon as possible and ultimately achieve the success of entrepreneurial activity.

Acknowledgment. The authors gratefully acknowledge the contributions of the Heilongjiang Province Postdoctoral Fund (LBH-Z15114).

References

1. Cope, J.: Toward a dynamic learning perspective of entrepreneurship. Entrepreneurship Theory Pract. **29**(4), 373–397 (2005)
2. Xie, Y., Huang, M.: Social network, entrepreneurial learning and entrepreneurial ability - an empirical study based on small business entrepreneurs. Stud. Sci. Sci. **32**(3), 400–409 (2014)
3. Qin, S., Li, S.: Relationship between entrepreneurial experience and entrepreneurial ability - role of learning ability and network technology. Technol. Econ. **6**, 48–54 (2015)
4. Zhang, Y., Wang, X.: Empirical study of previous experience, learning style and entrepreneurial ability. Manage. Sci. **24**(3), 1–12 (2011)
5. Man, T.W.Y.: Developing a behavior-centred model of entrepreneurial learning. J. Small Bus. Enterpr. Dev. **19**(3), 549–566 (2012)
6. Belteki, G., Kempster, S.L., Forhead, A.J., et al.: Paraoxonase-3, a putative circulating antioxidant, is systemically up-regulated in late gestation in the fetal rat, sheep, and human. J. Clinical Endocrinol. Metab. **95**(8), 3798–3805 (2010)
7. Ahuja, G.: Collaboration networks, structural holes, and innovation: a longitudinal study. Adm. Sci. Q. **45**(3), 425–455 (2000)
8. Rae, D.: Entrepreneurial learning: a narrative-based conceptual model. J. Small Bus. Enterpr. Dev. **12**(3), 323–335 (2005)
9. Verstegen, J., Meijer, Y., Mulder, M., et al.: Competence development of entrepreneurs in innovative horticulture. J. Workplace Learn. **19**(1), 32–44 (2007)
10. Redien-Collot, R., Radu, M.: How to do things with words: the discursive dimension of experiential learning in entrepreneurial mentoring dyads. J. Small Bus. Enterpr. Dev. (JSBM) **51**(3), 370–393 (2013)
11. Deakins, D., Freel, M.: Entrepreneurial learning and the growth process in SMEs. Learn. Organ. **5**(3), 144–155 (1998)
12. Rae, D., Carswell, M.: Towards a conceptual understanding of entrepreneurial learning. J. Small Bus. Enterpr. Dev. **8**(2), 150–158 (2001)

13. Atuahene-Gima, K., Murray, J.Y.: Exploratory and exploitative learning in new product development: a social capital perspective on new technology ventures in China. J. Int. Market. **15**(2), 1–29 (2013)
14. Cai, L., Tang, S., Ma, Y., et al.: Research on the relationship among entrepreneurial learning, entrepreneurial ability and new enterprise performance. Stud. Sci. Sci. **32**(8), 1189–1197 (2014)
15. Holcomb, T.R., Ireland, R.D., Holmes, R.M., et al.: Architecture of entrepreneurial learning: exploring the link among heuristics, knowledge, and action. Entrepreneurship Theory Pract. **33**(1), 167–192 (2009)
16. Petkova, A.P.: A theory of entrepreneurial learning from performance errors. Int. Entrepreneurship Manage. J. **5**(4), 345–367 (2008)
17. Crick, D.: Enterprising individuals and entrepreneurial learning: a longitudinal case history in the UK tourism sector. Int. J. Entrepreneurial Behav. Res. **17**(2), 203–218 (2011)
18. Politis, D.: The process of entrepreneurial learning: a conceptual framework. Entrepreneurship Theory Pract. **29**(4), 399–424 (2005)
19. Chandler, G.N., Lyon, D.W.: Involvement in knowledge-acquisition activities by venture team members and venture performance. Entrepreneurship Theory Pract. **33**(3), 571–592 (2009)
20. Slater, S.F., Narver, J.C.: Market orientation and the learning organization. J. Market. **59**(3), 63–74 (1995)
21. Xie, Y., Huang, M.: Entrepreneurial learning, entrepreneurial ability and entrepreneurial performance - social network research perspective. Econ. Surv. **33**(1), 101–106 (2016)
22. Ozgen, E., Baron, R.A.: Social sources of information in opportunity recognition: effects of mentors, industry networks, and professional forums. J. Bus. Ventur. **22**(2), 174–192 (2007)
23. Taylor, D.W., Thorpe, R.: Entrepreneurial learning: a process of co-participation. J. Small Bus. Enterp. Dev. **11**(2), 203–211 (2004)
24. Jones, O., Macpherson, A., Thorpe, R., et al.: The evolution of business knowledge in SMEs: conceptualizing strategic space. Strateg. Change **16**(6), 281–294 (2007)
25. Lans, T., Biemans, H., Mulder, M., et al.: Self-awareness of mastery and improvability of entrepreneurial competence in small businesses in the agri food sector. Hum. Resour. Dev. Q. **21**(2), 147–168 (2010)
26. Bird, B.: Towards a theory of entrepreneurial competency. Adv. Entrepreneurship Firm Emerg. Growth **2**(1), 51–72 (1995)
27. Jing, T., Yanfu, J.: The theory construction and empirical test of concept of entrepreneurial ability. Sci. Sci. Manage. S. .T. **29**(8), 52–57 (2008)
28. Zhang, X., Wang, L., Zeng, X.: Study on the transformation mechanism of entrepreneurial ability based on the growth of entrepreneurial enterprises. Sci. Technol. Progress Countermeasures **28**(11), 77–80 (2011)

Using C Programming in Analytic Hierarchy Process and Its Application in Decision-Making

Gebin Zhang[1] and Jianmin Zhang[2(✉)]

[1] School of Economics, Yunnan University, Kunming, China
318629689@qq.com
[2] School of Business and Tourism Management,
Yunnan University, Kunming, China
Jmzhang16@qq.com

Abstract. AHP (Analytic Hierarchy Process) is one of the common methods used to deal with complex decision problems. On the basis of introducing AHP, this paper focuses on the difference of programming between C language and Matlab. According to the characteristics of open library Eigen in C language matrix programming, C language is used to realize AHP, and meanwhile the scale and complexity are greatly reduced.

Keywords: AHP analytic hierarchy process · C language · Eigen

CLC Number: TP311.1

1 Preface

1.1 Research Background

Analytic Hierarchy Process (AHP) is an important method used to deal with multi-objective decision-making problems, whose basic ideas are basically identical to people's thinking on some complex decision-making problems. First of all, it stratifies and serializes the problem which is needed to be solved, i.e. according to the nature and the goal of the problem, divides the problem into different components, and according to the factors between the interaction and affiliation of its hierarchical clustering, constructs an ordered hierarchical model. Then, for the relative importance of a factor in each layer of the model, according to the judgment of the objective reality, it gives a quantitative representation and determines the weight of the relative importance order of all the factors in each layer by mathematical method. Finally, by calculating the weights of the relative importance in each layer, it obtains the combination weights of the relative importance order of the lowest layer (scheme layer) which is relative to the highest layer (general objective) as the basis for evaluation and selection [1–3].

Fund Project: Yunnan Province Philosophy and Social Science Planning Project (YB2017018).

H. Yuan et al. (Eds.): GSKI 2017, CCIS 849, pp. 760–768, 2018.
https://doi.org/10.1007/978-981-13-0896-3_74

After deep and careful study of AHP, it is not difficult to find that in the process of using mathematical models to solve the problem, the auxiliary tools are almost all Matlab. However, Matlab has two weaknesses: First, the use of Matlab is not simple for a general user to grasp; Moreover, Matlab programming needs to build a special compilation environment. Therefore, this paper believes that the use of a very simple way to deal with more complex decision-making issues is a worthy discussion. Secondly, during the realization of the original intention of the process, the author found that for the simplest programming language C, there is an open source library Eigen, so that C language can be used to achieves to some extents application in the matrix-related computing functions and then, it can reduce the algorithm complexity and space.

1.2   A Cited Example

A college freshman has just entered the university and he has decided to buy a smart phone. According to his budget, there are three options: iPhone7, Samsung S7edge and MEIZU Pro6. The main factors that affect the purchase are: price, configuration, system, design and workmanship. How does he make a decision?

According to the above factors that affect the choice of smart phones, we can build the following hierarchical model as shown below (Fig. 1):

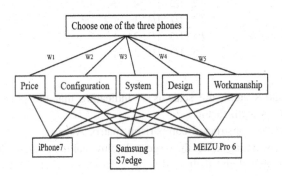

Fig. 1. The smart phone purchase model

2   The Basic Steps of AHP and the Realization of C Language

2.1   The Principal Steps of AHP

In the process of applying AHP, firstly a hierarchical model including the target layer, the system layer and the strategy layer is established [3]; then the comparison matrix that reflects the relative importance of all the factors related to the factors in the upper layer is constructed. The assignment of the comparison matrix is often preceded by the nine-scale method (i.e. the relative importance is shown between the numbers 1 to 9 and its reciprocals), the scale method is shown in Table 1:

Table 1. Nine-scale method

Scale	Definitions and descriptions
1	For a property, the two factors are of the same importance
3	For a property, a factor is slightly more important than the other
5	For a property, a factor is more important than the other
7	For a property, one factor is much more important than the other
9	For a property, a factor is more important than the other
2, 4, 6, 8	To represent a scale that requires a compromise between the two criteria
$1/b_{ij}$	The inverse comparison of two elements

According to the previous example, by investigating the needs and considerations of the freshmen, we integrated and objectively analyzed the relationships among all the factors to get a comparison matrix A (Using P1, P2, P3, P4, P5 respectively to represent the five factors: price, configuration, system, design and workmanship), see Table 2:

Table 2. The comparison matrix A of the factors

A	P1	P2	P3	P4	P5
P1	1	2	7	5	5
P2	1/2	1	4	3	3
P3	1/7	1/4	1	1/2	1/3
P4	1/5	1/3	2	1	1
P5	1/5	1/3	3	1	1

With price and system, the scale is 7, indicating that the price factor is more important than the system factor.

Theoretically, the constructed comparison matrix A $\left(a_{ij}a_{ji} = a_{ik}\right)$ is a completely consistent comparison matrix, i.e. the largest absolute value of eigenvalue of the matrix equals the dimension of the matrix. But in real life, to meet the above equation is impossible; we can only search the second best, as it allows that the matrix has a certain degree of inconsistency. So, it needs to do a test of consistency for the matrix. The specific steps are as follows:

(a)
$$CI = \frac{\lambda_{\max}(A) - n}{n - 1},\tag{1}$$

Where CI represents the degree of inconsistency of the comparison matrix A, $\lambda_{\max}$ is the largest eigenvalue of the matrix.

(b) Calculating the random conformance rate of the comparison matrix A:

$$CR = \frac{CI}{RI}, \tag{2}$$

Where RI is called the mean random consistency index, which is only related to the matrix dimension, see Table 3:

Table 3. Mean random consistency index

n	1	2	3	4	5	6	7	8
RI	0	0	0.58	0.90	1.12	1.24	1.32	1.41
n	9	10	11	12	13	14	15	
RI	1.46	1.49	1.52	1.54	1.56	1.58	1.59	

(c) When RI < 0.1, it means that the degree of consistency of the comparison matrix A is acceptable for example, the maximum eigenvector of matrix A in the example is 5.07005 and the CR value is 0.01564, this degree of consistency is acceptable in this case, the eigenvector corresponding to the largest eigenvalue of matrix A is:

$$U = (U_1, U_2, U_3, U_4, U_5)^T = (0.840898, 0.465862, 0.0949439, 0.17326, 0.191986).$$

Then we need to normalize the vector (the sum of each component is 1):

$$U = (U_1, U_2, U_3, U_4, U_5)^T$$
$$= (0.475912, 0.263641, 0.0537342, 0.0980574, 0.108656).$$

The normalized vector is called the weight vector, which reflects the relative importance of the five considerations from high to low: price, configuration, workmanship, design, and system (The implementation of results by program will be given in the content below).

After obtaining the weight vector among the various factors in the system layer, it is necessary to consider the performance of each candidate in the strategy layer relative to each factor in the system layer.

In this case, we need to consider the scores of the three candidates on five factors (price ($x1$), configuration ($x2$), system ($x3$), design ($x4$) and workmanship ($x5$)). Firstly, we compare the price of the three candidates and get the comparison matrix B1, see Table 4:

Table 4. Comparison matrix B1

B1	iphone7	Samsung 7edge	MEIZU Pro6
iphone7	1	3	2
Samsung S7edge	1/3	1	½
MEIZU Pro6	1/2	2	1

After calculated, the weight vector of B1 is:

$$\omega_{x1}(Y) = (\omega_1^1, \omega_2^1, \omega_3^1) = (0.539651, 0.163374, 0.296975),$$
$$\lambda_{\max}(B1) = 3.00884, CI = 0.00442, CR = 0.00762 < 0.1.$$

So, the degree of inconsistency of B1 is acceptable $\omega_{x1}(Y)$ can be intuitively seen as the score of each candidate in price.

Similarly, compare the configuration, system, design and workmanship of the three candidates in order to form a comparison matrix, see Tables 5, 6, 7 and 8:

Table 5. Comparison matrix B2

B2	iphone7	Samsung 7edge	MEIZU Pro6
iphone7	1	3	1/2
Samsung S7edge	1/3	1	1/6
MEIZU Pro6	1/2	1/6	1

Table 6. Comparison matrix B3

B3	iphone7	Samsung 7edge	MEIZU Pro6
iphone7	1	3	5
Samsung S7edge	1/3	1	3
MEIZU Pro6	1/5	1/3	1

Table 7. Comparison matrix B4

B4	iphone7	Samsung 7edge	MEIZU Pro6
iphone7	1	1/3	2
Samsung S7edge	3	1	6
MEIZU Pro6	1/2	1/6	1

Table 8. Comparison matrix B5

B1	iphone7	Samsung 7edge	MEIZU Pro6
iphone7	1	1/2	3
Samsung S7edge	2	1	6
MEIZU Pro6	1/3	1/6	1

According to the programming related to the AHP steps, we calculated the following results (The implementation of results by program will be given in the content below):

$$\omega_{x2}(Y) = (\omega_1^2, \omega_2^2, \omega_3^2) = (0.385463, 0.128316, 0.486221),$$

$$\omega_{x3}(Y) = (\omega_1^3, \omega_2^3, \omega_3^3) = (0.637049, 0.258238, 0.104714),$$

$$\omega_{x4}(Y) = (\omega_1^4, \omega_2^4, \omega_3^4) = (0.222168, 0.666726, 0.111106),$$

$$\omega_{x5}(Y) = (\omega_1^5, \omega_2^5, \omega_3^5) = (0.300014, 0.600028, 0.099958).$$

They can be respectively treated as the score of candidates in configuration, system, design, workmanship, and the degree of inconsistency of the four matrices is acceptable the final score is:

iPhone7: $\sum\limits_{i=1}^{5} U_i \times \omega_1^i = 0.447085,$

Samsung S7edge: $\sum\limits_{i=1}^{5} U_i \times \omega_2^i = 0.256033,$

MEIZU Pro6: $\sum\limits_{i=1}^{5} U_i \times \omega_3^i = 0.296905.$

The highest score is the best program, so the freshman should buy the iPhone7.

2.2   The Realization of C Language

2.2.1   The C++ Library Eigen
The use of C language to realize AHP is a noticeable feature of this research and the difficulties lie in the calculation of the matrix. Eigen is a high level open source library of C++, which effectively supports linear algebra, numerical analysis and related algorithms. Especially in the matrix and vector calculation, it can almost achieve the same function as Matlab, which will greatly reduce the total length of the C language programming of AHP.

2.2.2   The Construction of Comparison Matrix
The core of AHP is to construct the comparison matrix by scoring of experts. Input and store the data in a two-dimensional array and convert to a previously defined matrix:

$$tmp\_A(i, j) = psrc[i][j];$$
$$A = tmp\_A;$$

Here, the related problems of matrix element access in the Eigen library are involved, where tmp_A is used as an intermediate matrix to input carrier of the data at first. When the data input is completed, the complete data is assigned to the matrix A.

2.2.3   Conducting Consistency Test

For the consistency test of a matrix, it is necessary to judge whether the final CR value is less than 0.1 according to the formulas (1) and (2). Among them, the difficulty lies with how to calculate the maximum eigenvector of a given matrix:

$$\text{Eigen::VectorXf v1(N)};$$

$$\text{v1} = \text{EigenSolver.Eigenvalues().real()};$$

We declare the variable of type vector v1, which is used to store all the eigenvalues of the given matrix. After using the function Eigenvalues(), we can directly calculate the eigenvalues of the given matrix. The function Eigenvalues() will return a variable of type vector (the function real() represents the real part of the variable), that is the reason why we need to declare a variable of type vector to store it. Next, we traverse the eigenvalues of the given matrix, find the largest eigenvalues, and record the subscript j of the largest eigenvalue in vector v1. Finally, according to the formula, we calculate the consistency coefficient and compare it with the mean consistency index:

```
Float RI[16]={0,0,0,0.58,0.9,1.12,1.24,1.32,1.41,1.45,1.49,1.52,1.54,1.56,1.58,1.59};
   float CI,CR;
CI=(m-N)/(N-1); CR=CI/RI[N];
            if(CR<=0.1) return true;
            else return false;
```

Among them, RI is the mean consistency index.

2.2.4   Weight Vector

When the comparison matrix satisfies the consistency test, the AHP needs to calculate the Normalized eigenvector corresponding to the maximum eigenvalue:

```
Eigen::MatrixXf B(N,N);
B = EigenSolver.Eigenvectors().real();
Eigen::VeCtorXf v2(N);
v2 = EigenSolver.Eigenvectors().col(j).real();
```

As the way of finding the eigenvalues, a variable of vector v2 is defined to store the eigenvectors corresponding to the largest eigenvalues. Where the matrix B is a matrix to store the eigenvectors corresponding to the eigenvalues, I think the function Eigenvectors() in the Eigen library will return a matrix of the eigenvectors corresponding to the eigenvalues in column vectors. Using the previously recorded j, retrieve the jth vector of the matrix by function col(j), which is the eigenvector corresponding to the largest eigenvalue. Finally, execute the process of normalization and the results reflect the degree of importance.

2.2.5   Total Taxis of Hierarchy and Decision Making

Repeatedly constructing the comparison matrix of each candidate relative to each influencing factor, and using the program 1 of the weight vector calculating, we can get the description of the importance of each candidate related to each influencing factor. Finally, we get the final "scoring" of each candidate which will provide the basis for decision-making. Firstly, the number of attributes and the number of schemes is closely relating to the calculation, so the beginning of the program requires the user input data. Secondly, the weight vector is directly needed to calculate the data. Finally, according to the formula $\left(\sum U_i \times \omega_j^i \right)$ for the level of the total row, we can obtain the one of the scheme's score:

$$sum = sum + (project[j] * target[j][i]);$$

2.2.6   The Example of AHP

Program 1 (Fig. 2): Calculating the maximum eigenvalue of the comparison matrix corresponding to the eigenvector and doing a test of consistency.

Program 2 (Fig. 3): After getting the weight vector of the system layer and the policy layer, the total taxis of hierarchy and the final decision reference is obtained.

```
input dimension of matrix:
5
input matrix
1 2 7 5 5
0.5 1 4 3 3
0.142 0.25 1 0.5 0.333
0.2 0.333 2 1 1
0.2 0.333 3 1 1
initial matrix A:
     1      2       7       5       5
    0.5     1       4       3       3
  0.142   0.25      1     0.5   0.333
   0.2   0.333      2       1       1
   0.2   0.333      3       1       1
the largest eigenvalue of matrix A:
5.07005
the largest eigenvalue of matrix A coresponding to the largest eigenvector

 0.840898
 0.465832
0.0949439
 0.17326
 0.191986
matrix A passed the consistency check!
after normalization, the largest eigenvalue of matrix A coresponding to th
largest eigenvector:
0.475912
0.263641
0.0537342
0.0980574
 0.108656
```

Fig. 2. Screenshot of program, finding the weight vector of comparison matrix

```
input the property number of subtarget layer :5
input the number of project:3
input procedure AHP calculated weight of property of subtarget layer:
0.475912 0.263641 0.0537342 0.0980574 0.108659
input, subtarget layer property Num 1 ,3 projects mark:
0.539651 0.163374 0.296975
input, subtarget layer property Num 2 ,3 projects mark:
0.385463 0.128316 0.486221
input, subtarget layer property Num 3 ,3 projects mark:
0.6374049 0.258238 0.104714
input, subtarget layer property Num 4 ,3 projects mark:
0.222168 0.666726 0.111106
input, subtarget layer property Num 5 ,3 projects mark:
0.300014 0.600028 0.099958
project 1 final grade is: 0.447085
project 2 final grade is: 0.256033
project 3 final grade is: 0.296905
```

Fig. 3. Screenshot of program of total taxis of hierarchy

3 Conclusions

Based on open library Eigen's characteristics of matrix in C language programming, this paper makes an implementation of AHP (analytic hierarchy process) in C language.

The final results of this paper (two small programs) can make it more convenient for decision-makers to use and get the final result, which means that more efforts can be done in the future, such as packaging the programs, presenting visually, doing time complexity analysis and optimizing etc. And, finally, a very practical large-scale application software will be gained, which is the revelation that the author obtained during the process of programming.

However, in the process of programming, there is still some room for improvement. For example, combining the two programs will save much more time and bring convenience for users, who do not need to constantly switch programs. We can further develop the programs into an open source tool, or more practical application software. Furthermore, if the structure of the comparison matrix tends to exceed the range of inconsistency, then the program can help decision-makers to correct the comparison matrix. After all, if we overthrow the comparison matrix and re-build it artificially, that will be an extremely arduous work.

References

1. Xu, X.M.: Application of analytic hierarchy process. Stat. Decis. **2008**(01), 131–278 (2008)
2. Li, Y., Hu, X.H., Qiao, J.: Improved fuzzy analytic hierarchy process. J. Northwest Univ. (Nat. Sci. Edn.) **2005**(01), 11–12, 16 (2005)
3. Tan, H.Q.: C Programming, 3rd edn. Tsinghua University Press, Beijing (2008)

Author Index

Printed in the United States
By Bookmasters